Marketing strategy and management

Marketing strategy and management

JAMES A. CONSTANTIN

RODNEY E. EVANS

MALCOLM L. MORRIS

All of the
College of Business Administration
University of Oklahoma

 1976

Business Publications, Inc. Dallas, Texas 75231
Irwin-Dorsey International Arundel, Sussex BN18 9AB
Irwin-Dorsey Limited Georgetown, Ontario L7G 4B3

© BUSINESS PUBLICATIONS, INC., 1976

First Printing, April 1976

ISBN 0-256-01694-1
Library of Congress Catalog Card No. 75–39471
Printed in United States of America

Preface

This is a book on marketing management. It is a different book from the many now available, in a number of ways—and those differences are its reason for being. While the differences are mostly subtle ones, they are very profound. Because our concept of what a marketing book should be is different from the apparent concepts underlying the other marketing books, we use this preface to point out those differences. Marketing managers and marketing management books should *focus* on marketing: its principals, its principles, its concepts, notions, and ideas; its problems and their solutions; and on decision making in the marketing context. This focus on marketing is what we refer to as management *of* the marketing function and is what so many books do so well. But without *emphasis* on the firm to accompany the focus on marketing, the result is only half an understanding of marketing management. To supply the missing ingredient, we have placed great emphasis on the firm and the role of the marketing manager in planning the overall strategy of the firm and in providing for the integration of the marketing and other functional activities into a working system. In short our first objective was to take a systems view of the firm as well as a systems view of marketing. This emphasis on the firm is what we refer to as management *and* the marketing function. Accordingly our concept of the book is based upon those two parts. First, we *emphasize* the firm and the marketing manager's role in *strategy* formulation. Second, we *focus* on marketing and the marketing manager's role in marketing management and decision making.

The second objective is practically inseparable from the first and flows from it: to integrate the basic concepts of corporate planning into the study of marketing. Strategy and management are the two key descriptive words in the title of the book and are crucial to the application of the systems approach and to the dual role of the marketing manager. Again, our dichotomy of managerial roles is significant. The marketing manager is concerned with management *and* the marketing function when objectives are being set for the firm, in developing plans and strategies to attain those objectives, and in determining policies and

v

guidelines. In this sense the marketing manager is looking to the future, helping determine what the company wants to have happen, and developing programs to make it happen. The major concern at this point is with *effectiveness*. As before, the implementation of tactical planning and action takes place in the framework of management *of* the marketing function when the major concern is with *efficiency*. The emphasis on planning is directed not only toward the ongoing management of the marketing function but also toward the marketing oriented organization as a whole.

Our third objective centers upon the importance of change and the management of change. One facet of this theme is the emphasis on the development of the discovery process: not only the discovery of problems but also the discovery of new opportunities that sometimes are lurking about in the disguise of old problems. Colleges of business administration typically do a very good job in teaching students the solutions process in dealing with problems. The discovery process is another matter. One reason for the emphasis on planning and the analyses underlying it is to help inculcate in the student the notion of discovery of opportunities and problems. Even if it is true (as some claim) that the discovery process cannot be taught, we believe that a climate can be created whereby the seeds of the discovery process can be planted and allowed to germinate.

A fourth objective was to design a book that is a challenge to both the teacher and the student. This one should challenge the teacher because we have designed a framework and put the basic appurtenances on it. However we have left the rounding out of the design to the teacher. Thus, the teacher has an opportunity to teach. As for the student, we provide clues to things, give directions through illustrations, and leave to him the excitement of discovering that he can go on from there and apply things he knows but does not realize he knows. Both the teacher and the student have an active role to play.

In recapitulation, this book is different in several ways:

1. The firm is emphasized in order to integrate the systems concept but focus is on marketing to present its concepts.
2. The concepts of objectives and planning are handled in a marketing context at both the corporate and the functional levels to help implement the systems concept and to serve as foundations for the discovery and solutions processes.
3. The analysis of environments is emphasized as necessary ingredients—not only as ingredients of the systems approach and planning, but also of the management of change and the discovery of opportunities and problems and their solution.
4. Overall, we make more visible the importance of the strategy of the firm in relation to the strategy and decision making of marketing.

The entire firm is viewed as a resource system. Strategic decisions that are often thought of as "marketing" decisions and which have impact throughout the firm are viewed in a different context. They are viewed as marketing decisions to be made by the top executives of the marketing-oriented firm. They are not viewed as marketing decisions to be made by the marketing manager in managing the marketing function. To this extent, the role of marketing managers has been enlarged to recognize the emergence of the marketing-oriented firms. The function of marketing has been placed in perspective as a function of the firm rather than just a function of a more or less autonomous division of the firm. The marketing-oriented firm cannot effectively operate unless marketing managers are concerned not only with management *of* the marketing function but also with management *and* the marketing function. If the marketing manager either does not like planning or cannot plan, he lacks the qualifications for being a manager of the future.

The book has four parts. Part I, Marketing, Marketing Management, and Marketing Planning, has four chapters. The purposes of this part are to explain the concepts of marketing and marketing management, to analyze the foundation upon which the marketing system rests, to help position the marketing manager in the hierarchical structure of the firm, and to present some basic techniques and concepts of planning for the marketing-oriented firm. Chapters 3 and 4, dealing with marketing in the managerial hierarchy and planning in the market-oriented firm, either do not usually appear in basic marketing books or the material is treated very differently. As presented here, the material in these chapters is important—even essential—in understanding both the role of the marketing manager and the managerial performance of that role. In these respects they are very important to our dichotomy of management *and* the marketing function and management *of* the marketing function.

Part II, Analysis for Marketing Strategy and Management, consists of five chapters. The rationale for positioning this part here is that analysis is one of the two principal processes underlying decision making of all kinds. Analysis is a necessary prerequisite to the development of strategy and is a foundation for managerial decisions, so a logical place for its discussion is just before the strategic and managerial section. A second rationale for positioning it there is that it is something of a bridge in the framework of the book. The material builds upon that of Part I and provides an enlarged foundation for what is to come.

The subjects of four of the five chapters are usually found in basic marketing books (marketing research, opportunities and innovations, external environment, and consumer behavior). The fifth, on strategic planning and objectives, is not usually found in those books. In keeping with our concern with concepts and the analysis function, we have concentrated on concepts of information for planning, decision making for marketing managers, and marketing information flows in the chapter on marketing research. It is also heavily influenced by our concern with the discovery process. Information is presented partially as a tool for discovery of opportunities and problems. In addition, some aspects of the traditional market research approach are included.

The opportunities and innovation chapter also represents a departure from the usual. One thrust of this chapter is the role of the satisfaction process (consumer and producer satisfactions) in discovering marketing opportunities and making consumer-satisfying innovations. A part of this chapter later becomes a part of the framework of the consumer behavior chapter. The other thrust is directed toward kinds of opportunities and the role of the marketing manager in exploiting them.

The approach to the external environment also differs, but is in keeping with the basic framework of the book. We examine each of ten segments of the environment with which the marketing manager must cope—among them consumers, competitors, suppliers, channel members, and society in general. Certain roles of governments are also analyzed including their activities in curtailment of abuses, protection from abusive practices, and in prevention of further concentration of eonomic power.

Our approach to consumer behavior is also different. First, the basic premises and concepts of consumer behavior are considered. Then the marketing activities of the firm are linked to the behavior processes. Finally the strategic aspects of consumer behavior are linked to the process of discovering consumer aspirations. In this portion the elements of the consumer satisfaction process are related to the several stages of the consumer's process of problem solving. Also a matrix is developed in which a chain of strategic and tactical programs are identified for the several stages in the consumer satisfaction process.

The final chapter in Part II analyzes the concepts of strategic, managerial, and operational planning and objective setting in a marketing context. This chapter draws on material from earlier chapters to illustrate the planning concepts in a marketing context. Also it introduces the important concepts that are at the heart of the chapters which follow in Part III.

Product, channels of distribution, logistics, promotion, and price as elements of the marketing mix are covered in Part III, Strategic and Managerial Functions of Marketing Management. Two chapters are devoted to each of the five elements. One of the two chapters covers marketing strategies and policies which emphasize the firm, while the other focuses on marketing in its coverage of implementation and decision making. For example, Chapter 10, Product Strategies and Policies, ties directly to management *and* the marketing function. Management *of* the marketing function is tied to Chapter 11, Product Management.

There are two ways in which these chapters can be handled in the classroom. One approach is to take the chapters in the order they appear in the book. An equally acceptable way is to deal first with strategic and policy matters for each of the elements of the marketing mix (Chapters 10, 12, 14, 16, and 18) and then cover the management chapters (Chapters 11, 13, 15, 17, and 19). The logic of this approach is, of course, that it makes sense to follow analyses for objective setting and formulation of plans and strategies with the discussion of strategies of all elements of the mix. Then, after strategies are developed, the implementation program and decision making and management of the elements begins.

Finally, Part IV, Management of the Marketing System, has two chapters. The first is Control of Marketing Strategy and Management. Again in this chapter the book departs in several ways from the usual handling of this subject. First, a program for a control system which involves several key concepts is identified. Second, in addition to showing the typical cost breakouts into functional accounts and the separation into fixed and variable components, several dimensions are added to the analysis. Many text illustrations of the importance of control systems use volume of sales in connection with a sales analysis in order to isolate trouble spots. One of the dimensions added was that of *quality* of sales volume by examining not just volume but also cost associated with volume, income associated with price, and net income reflecting cost at various rates of output. This approach recognized not only short run and long run aspects of revenue and profit but also the *quality* of revenue and profit as distinct from their *quantity*. Other portions of the chapter deal with systems of control of productivity and profitability such as the sales analysis and the marketing audit. Finally the concept of the marketing controller is introduced.

The final chapter is The Components of Marketing Management: Linkage and Change. In a very real way, it might be said that the title of this chapter should be "This is What We Did." While it was not designed as a summary, it does summarize; while it was not designed as an overview, it does present an overview. It was designed to help the student see the whole thing in one chapter instead of a series of parts strung out over 20 chapters. We linked the central parts of the whole to provide a miniature entity. To use an analogy: each of 20 chapters was devoted to the characteristics of 20 different parts of the forest. Chapter 21 describes the forest in terms of its parts.

Norman, Oklahoma
March 1976

JAMES A. CONSTANTIN
RODNEY E. EVANS
MALCOLM L. MORRIS

Acknowledgments

When the concepts underlying this book were a collection of vagrant thoughts seeking to become solid citizens, Dennis M. Crites helped sort them out. He served passively as a sounding board for sometimes random and oftentimes inarticulate statements. Also, he served actively as a constructive critic, and even we do not know the full extent of his contribution. James M. Kenderdine, another of our colleagues at the University of Oklahoma, gave us the benefit of his rare insights into some of our conceptual problems. His comments on all chapters were a great help to us, but we are especially indebted to him for his contributions to Chapter 8. Eugene C. Bell gave us the benefit of his wide business experience in criticizing portions of the manuscript.

E. Grosvenor Plowman of the University of Maine shared with us his wisdom and expertise as an academic, author, and top business executive. We are grateful for the constructive and analytical comments of R. Clifton Anderson of The University of Southern Illinois and Thomas V. Greer of The University of Maryland. They read and criticized the manuscript at several stages. Raymond L. Smith of Texas A&I at Laredo is another of our creditors. At both the conceptual premanuscript stage and in manuscript form his criticisms, additions, and comments were helpful.

Roger E. Jerman of Indiana University at Indianapolis and Roy K. Teas of The University of Wisconsin at Oshkosh were also multiple contributors. They read, criticized, and improved the manuscript. In addition they prepared the teachers' manual. Our students who used the manuscript in several classes made a number of suggestions. Some of them we took. Because the book is now in print, it is obvious that we ignored one or two of their suggestions.

In this joint venture each of the three of us took primary responsibility for certain chapters because of our areas of expertise. However, the mark of each of us is on all chapters because of the way we worked together. The synergy of coauthorship is evident to us even though it may not be apparent to others. As coauthors we agree that the book is better for that synergy. As for responsibility, each of us also agrees that the other two would be responsible for all errors if there were any.

J. A. C.
R. E. E.
M. L. M.

Contents

List of figures . . . . **xix**

List of tables . . . . **xxiii**

**PART ONE: MARKETING, MARKETING MANAGEMENT, AND
MARKETING PLANNING**

1 Marketing and marketing management 3

What is marketing? *Exciting aspects of marketing; Marketing defined.* The marketing concept: *Elements of the concept; Evolution
of the concept; Implications of the marketing concept and the
marketing company.* The marketing concept in a shortage economy. An approach to marketing management: *Systems approach; Systems approach and planning.*

2 Foundations of the marketing system 16

The business firm: A system of relations: *Responsibilities of
marketing management; Environmental conditions affecting marketing management; The external system; The internal system;
Environmental problems: A summary of managerial decision
problems.* Putting the parts together.

3 Marketing in the managerial hierarchy 34

Management and the organization: *The nature of business; The
function of business; The definition of management; The function
of management; The nature of managerial activities.* Management
as a network of hierarchies: *The hierarchy of aims; The hierarchy of satisfactions; The hierarchy of objectives; Development
of objectives.*

4 Planning in the marketing-oriented firm 52

Planning in perspective: *An ancient art modernized.* Managing
and planning: *Traditional and modern approaches; Planning
premises; Types of premises.* Managers and planning: *Man-*

agerial participation. Management of planning. Planning and plans. Philosophies of planning: *Satisficing; Optimizing; Adaptivizing; Satisficing, optimizing, adaptivizing [contrasted and compared].* Approaches to planning: *Outside-in approach; Inside-out approach.* Steps in planning.

PART TWO: ANALYSIS FOR MARKETING STRATEGY AND MANAGEMENT

5 Marketing research and information 79

Information for planning: *Organization of the company; Information for the organization as a whole.* Information for managing: *What is information?* Marketing research and management: *Uncertainty and risk; The scientific method; A definition of research; Research in everyday life; Basic and applied research; Objectives of research.* Marketing research procedure: *Research process.* Marketing information flows: *A route of information flows; The consumer; Channel members; Manufacturers; Suppliers; Coordinating flows; Environmental flows.* Marketing information systems . . . and computers: *Information system characteristics; And now . . . computers.*

6 Marketing opportunity and innovation 111

The satisfaction process: *Recognition of consumer aspirations; Creation of selective dissatisfaction; Anticipated satisfaction; Realized satisfaction; Antidissatisfaction inoculation.* Consumer and producer satisfactions: *Sources of opportunities; Consumers; Producers.* Marketing, opportunities, and innovations: *Marketing; Kinds of opportunities; Innovation objectives.* Management, marketing, and innovations: *Management and successful innovations; Venture management.*

7 The external environment of marketing 137

One way: *The social environment; The economic environment; The political-governmental environment.* Our way: *Consumers and the consumption process; Prospective consumers; Employees; Community; Competition; Suppliers; Owners; Creditors; Channel members; Society.* Governments: *Introduction; Curtailment of abuses; Protection from abusive marketing practices; Preventing further concentration of economic power.* Marketing management and the external environment: *Planning, strategy, and the external environment; Managing and the external environment.*

8 Consumer behavior 159

Introduction. Basic premises of consumer behavior: *Consumer behavior as a subset of human behavior; The problem-solving nature of consumer behavior; The rationality of behavior.* The marketing activities of the firm and the behavior process of consumers: *Consumer problem solving and the consumer satisfaction process.* The strategic aspects of consumer behavior: The discovery of consumer aspirations: *Planning, consumer satisfaction, and the marketing mix.*

9 Strategic planning and objectives **182**

Strategic, managerial, and operational planning: *Introduction; Strategic planning; Management control; Operational control; A final point concerning the planning hierarchy.* Objectives: *Hierarchical interaction: Setting objectives; A final point concerning objectives and plans.*

PART THREE: STRATEGIC AND MANAGERIAL FUNCTIONS OF MARKETING MANAGEMENT

10 Product strategies and policies **203**

The product and the future: *Marketing, the firm, and the product; Product planning and corporate planning; Coordination with research and development; New organizations for new products; Shortened product life cycles.* Product planning: *Management concerns; Planning and organization; Features of product policy.* Product life cycles and marketing strategy: *The nature of product life cycles; Life cycles and profit objectives; Life cycles and the marketing mix; A different perspective.* Other product strategies: *The product line and the product mix; Product elimination; Product diversification.* Kinds of products: *Consumers' goods; Industrial goods.*

11 Product management **229**

Definitions. The product manager's job: *Hierarchical relationships; The position of product manager; The reporting hierarchy; Standards of performance.* Functions of the product manager: *The discovery and filtering of new products; Preventing product failures (why products fail).* Managing the marketing mix.

12 Distribution channel strategies and policies **251**

Marketing and the channels of distribution: *Environmental conditions; The external system.* The function of channels of distribution. The traditional view of channels: *An illustration; The traditional channel concept.* The channel as a support system for the marketing effort: *Support of marketing or performance of tasks? An illustration; One channel component's record: Some insights; How a channel component supports the marketing system; How to effect coordination to support the marketing system.* The strategy of channel design: *Make or buy strategies; Channel length and width.* Marketing management and channel strategy.

13   Distribution channel management **274**

Objectives of channel management derived from channel theory: *Improve efficiency of marketing program; Improve effectiveness of channel; Control inventory for customer service, corporate cost; Improve service to middlemen; Maximize efficiency; Other objectives.* Channel management and marketing satisfactions: *Product and patronage satisfactions; Variables in the satisfaction process.* The retailing system: *Retail operations; The wholesaling system; Size and efficiency: Channel implications.* Types of channel decisions: *Sell direct or use a middleman? Selection of channel components; Selective or intensive channels; Multiple channels; Other decision areas.*

14   Logistics strategies and policies **295**

Environmental conditions affecting logistics management: *First-order conditions; Second- and third-order conditions; Fourth-order conditions; Other strategic considerations.* Relation of logistics to marketing: *Some aspects of customer service; Small firms.* Some problem-causing characteristics: *Nature of logistics problems; "Natural" problems; Conceptual problems; Organizational problems.*

15   Logistics management and operations **322**

Logistics decisions: *Customer service and environmental conditions.* The transportation environment: *Types of carriers; Transportation rate structures; Other transportation rates and services.* Managerial decisions on carriers and rates: *Carrier decisions; Decisions pertaining to rates.* The warehousing environment: *Types of warehouses; Storage and warehousing; Functions of warehouses.* Managerial decisions on warehousing: *Direct service; Indirect service; Good service at low cost; Changes in managerial policies.*

16   Promotion strategies and policies **359**

The communication process: *The theoretical communication process; The adapted communication process.* Communication strategy decision process. The components of promotion: *Personal selling; Advertising; Sales promotion; Other forms of promotion.* Organization and institutions of promotion: *The sales force; Sales agents; Advertising and sales promotion; The advertising agency.* Role variation. Planning promotion strategy: *Corporate level planning and decision areas; Positioning of product; Dimensions of promotion strategy; Specific target audiences; Messages and communications tasks; Assignment of tasks to promotion instruments; Magnitude of the promotion effort; Promotion budget allocation.*

17   Promotion management **383**

Personal selling: *Selling functions; Selling tasks; Sales organizations; Sales force size; Sales territories; Developing a sales force; Motivation and supervision; Evaluation and control.* Advertising: *Advertising objectives; The advertising message; Advertising media decisions; Measurement and evaluation.*

18 Price strategies and policies **407**

Theoretical aspects of price determination: *Elasticity of demand; Pure competition; Monopoly; Oligopoly.* Factors affecting price strategy: *Objectives; The internal environment; The external environment.* Some representative price strategies: *Skimming pricing; Penetration pricing.* Methods of price determination: *Cost-oriented approaches; Market test approaches; Break-even analysis; Modified break-even; In practice; Transfer pricing.*

19 Managing pricing decisions **436**

General price policies: *Single-price policy; Semivariable-price policy; Variable-price policy.* Methods of pricing: *Complete pricing methods; Other pricing methods; Limitations; Multistage pricing.* Managed price adjustments: *Discounts; Geographic adjustments; Other trade adjustments.* Legal issues in price management: *Robinson-Patman Act; Resale price maintenance; Sales below cost.* Price versus non-price competition.

PART FOUR: MANAGEMENT OF THE MARKETING SYSTEM

20 Control of marketing strategy and management ... **469**

The nature and purpose of control: *The purpose of controls; Control systems.* Control of marketing operations: *Steps in the control of operations; Cost-price-volume relationships; Control of productivity and profitability; Other aspects of control systems.*

21 The components of marketing management: Linkage and change **491**

Central features of marketing management: *Management defined; Approach to marketing management; Concern of marketing management.* Functional integration of the marketing-oriented firm: *As things often are: Problems; As things should be: A starting point; Integration through objectives.* Planning and planning effort: *Establishing responsibility; Dimensions of planning; Planning philosophies; Approaches to planning; Types of planning.* Developing planning premises: *Premises; Information; Opportunities; Environments; Consumer behavior.* Developing strategies and policies: The discovery process: *Product; Channels of distribution; Logistics; Promotion; Pricing.* Developing managerial and operational control: Problem solving and decision making: *Strategic-managerial gray areas; Prior arrangements for integration; Concepts of decision points; Decision orientation.* Controlling the planning effort.

INDEX **515**

List of figures

2–1   Roles and Responsibilities of Marketing Management   19

2–2   A Channel of Distribution   27

2–3   Planning and Managing Marketing   32

3–1   Organization Responsibility for Level 1 and Level 2
        Decisions   38

4–1   Planning and Control Model   75

5–1   Sequence of Information Characteristics   85

5–2   The Research Management Process   88

5–3   The Relationship of Research and Testing and Theory
        Development   93

5–4   Marketing Information Flows   100

6–1   Scales of Consumer and Producer Satisfactions   116

6–2   More Scales of Consumer and Producer Satisfactions   120

7–1   Areas of External Relationship of Marketing Management   142

8–1   A Generalized Consumer Problem-Solving Process   168

8–2   Relationship Between the Problem-Solving Behavior of
        Consumers and the Customer Satisfaction Process of the
        Business Firm   174

8–3   Strategic and Tactical Aspects of the Consumer
        Satisfaction Process   178

9–1   Overlap of Types of Planning   190

9–2   An Example of the Planning Hierarchy   191

9–3   Areas of Objectives   193

10–1   Life Cycle of a Product.   211

10–2   New Product Introductions to Meet Sales Objectives   216

10–3   The Significance of the Marketing Mix in the Stages of the
        Life Cycle   218

10–4   Relative Degree of Impact of Elements of the Marketing
        Mix in Various Stages of the Life Cycle   221

11–1   New Product Evaluation Check List   242

11–2   New Product Evaluation Chart—Preliminary   243

11–3   New Product Evaluation Chart—An Alternative 244

11–4   Flow Chart for New Product Planning 246

11–5   The Marketing Mix in Life Cycle Stages 249

12–1   Public Warehouse and Distribution Center Concepts
        Compared 264

12–2   Attitudes of Users and Public Warehousemen Toward
        Warehouse Services 266

12–3   Make or Buy Strategy 269

12–4   Consumer Goods Distribution Alternatives 271

12–5   Hierarchy of Marketing Channel Policies 272

13–1   A Network of Channel Satisfactions 280

14–1   The Cost-Performance Trade-off 300

15–1   A Format for Analyses Underlying Managerial Decisions 333

15–2   Division of Territories of Distribution Points 344

15–3   Relation of Number of Distribution Points to Percentage of
        U.S. Market Served 347

15–4   Variation of Cost Elements with Number of Distribution
        Points 348

15–5   Variation of Total Cost with Number of Distribution Points 349

15–6   Cost of Providing Levels of Customer Service Related to
        Number of Distribution Points 352

15–7   A Decision Tree: Logistics Activities 355

16–1   The Theoretical Communication Process 360

16–2   The Adapted Communication Process 362

16–3   An Application of the Communication Process Using a
        Salesperson as the Communicator 363

16–4   An Application of the Communication Process Using an
        Advertising Medium as the Communicator 363

16–5   Push and Pull Promotional Strategies 371

16–6   The Flow of Decisions and Processes in Planning a
        Promotion Strategy 374

16–7   Hypothetical Examples of Promotion Objectives 378

17–1   The Workload Method of Computing Sales Force Size ... 387

18–1   The Firm under Conditions of Pure Competition 413

18–2   The Firm under Conditions of Monopoly 414

18–3   The Firm under Conditions of Oligopoly 416

18–4   Break-even Points and Profit Opportunities for Two
        Different Cost Structures 422

18–5   Linear Break-even Analysis 431

18–6   A Family of Break-even Points 432

18–7   Curvilinear Break-even Analysis 432

19–1   Unit Costs in Two Plant Sizes at Various Rates of Output 440

19–2   Demand, Revenue, and Cost Data for Price Analysis   444
19–3   Uniform Delivered Price Zones   455
19–4   The Corn Products Basing Point System   456
19–5   An Example of a Multiple Basing Point System   457

List of tables

10–1   New Product Introductions to Meet Sales Objectives   215
14–1   Increase in Profit from Logistics Cost Reduction or
       Increase in Sales   310
14–2   Percent Distribution Costs Are of Net Sales   311
15–1   Format for Determining the Least Cost Distribution Point
       for a Territory   342
15–2   Cost and Percentage of Total Cost for Each Logistics Cost
       Component Related to Number of Distribution Points . . .   350
15–3   Variation in Cost of Transportation and Maintenance of
       Inventory with Number of Distribution Points   350
15–4   Cost of Providing Levels of Customer Service Related to
       Number of Distribution Points   351
15–5   Improvement of Service and Increase in Cost with Increase
       in Number of Distribution Points   353
15–6   Time Required for Delivery under Different Options   356
17–1   Advertising Volume by Media: 1973 and 1974   400
19–1   Expected Value Approach to Pricing Decisions   442
19–2   Effect on Profit of Alternative Price Methods   443
20–1   Classification of Cost on a Functional Basis   479
20–2   Unit Cost Modules   480
20–3   Cost of Operations at Various Rates of Output   481
20–4   Revenue and Cost of Operations at Various Rates of Output   482
20–5   Revenue, Cost, Net Income at Various Rates of Output   483
20–6   The Profitability Report   486

Marketing, marketing management, and marketing planning

chapter 1

Marketing and marketing management

What is marketing?
  The exciting aspects of marketing
    Assembling parts into a whole
    Marketing efficiency and the firm
    Marketing effectiveness and the firm
  Marketing defined
    Implications of the definition
    Marketing and the transaction
The marketing concept
  Elements of the concept
  Evolution of the concept
  Implications of the marketing concept
    Effectiveness
    Efficiency
    Managerial decisions
  The marketing concept in a shortage economy
An approach to marketing management
  Marketing and managers
  Systems approach
  Systems approach and planning

WHAT IS MARKETING?

Exciting aspects of marketing

Marketing is exciting. It is also challenging and rewarding to study and practice. There is a series of concepts of marketing which may be used to satisfy the wants and needs of potential customers. One set of these concepts pertains to the identification of customers the marketer wants to reach. Marketers call this customer identification process the selection of the target market or markets. Another set of these concepts is involved with the product itself; the wholesale, retail, or other

3

channels through which the product is distributed; the promotion of the product; and finally setting a price on the product. Marketing people refer to these activities as the marketing mix.

Assembling parts into a whole. The thing that is exciting about these concepts—which are used to satisfy consumer wants and needs—is the putting together of a group of ideas relating to the marketing mix to create a marketing program. Assembling the parts of a marketing program into an effective whole is roughly like assembling the parts of an automobile to make an effective auto. Let's draw an analogy. Say that you have separate bins in which engines, wheels, carburetors, and other parts are stored. All engines, of all sizes and horsepower, are stored together. The assembler takes the first one from each bin. Imagine the result: a diesel engine, a four-barrel carburetor, 20-inch truck wheels, and so on. The parts will not fit into a workable whole. Engines, wheels, and the like are designed for specific products, and if they are mixed the wrong way you will have an ineffective and/or an inefficient automobile.

The same holds for marketing. You don't design a product just on the basis of its function. If you were in the wastebasket business you wouldn't design a single wastebasket to be used everywhere—in the living room, children's room, office, and shop. You would design it to meet the wants and needs of the target market. Imagine an animal-decorated wastebasket designed for a child's room sitting in the executive suite! Likewise, you do not use the same channels of distribution, or the same promotion program, or the same price policy for every product.

To find the right combination of the elements of the marketing mix to meet the needs of the target market is a complex job. It requires knowledge of concepts of each of the elements of the mix and the ability to put the parts together into a workable whole. This is one reason marketing is exciting.

Marketing efficiency and the firm. A second reason is to be found in the task of relating the marketing function to the firm as a whole. This requires using the concepts and tools of business to accomplish the job efficiently and to integrate the marketing activities with other activities of the firm such as production, finance, and accounting. This is not an easy task, yet some efficiency must be attained—enough at least to enable the firm to make a profit. So now we have two things about marketing that both make it exciting and serve to define what marketing is all about:

1. The elements of the mix must be put together is such a way that the target market is satisfied.
2. They must be put together efficiently so that the firm can make a profit.

Marketing effectiveness and the firm. The third exciting part of marketing is related to the second one: marketing must be integrated with other activities so that the performance is effective. Effectiveness relates to the objectives of the firm and the degree to which they are attained.

Marketing defined

So what is marketing? If we put together all three of these reasons why marketing can be exciting and rewarding both to study and practice, we can derive a working definition. Marketing is the exchange process between seller and buyer. It involves a number of interrelated business activities designed to promote, distribute, and price a product or service in order to meet the wants and needs of both consumers and producers.

The words *product* and *service* in the foregoing definition must be taken in the broadest sense. Insurance programs, medical care, and educational systems use concepts of marketing as do religious organizations, universities, and professional football teams. Politicians have discovered marketing concepts and techniques. Candidates and platforms are designed to meet target markets; the promotion programs are worked out to market the product; the candidate is "distributed" through carefully selected channels; and the "price" is carefully worked out—programs designed to appeal to selected groups.

We fully explain what is meant by "product" in the appropriate chapters. For now, let us say that the word refers not only to the physical thing being sold but all of its want-need satisfying characteristics such as guarantees and service after the sale is made.

In your economics classes you have heard of the concepts of form, time, and place utility. Marketing brings these concepts to life. Marketing is also a people-oriented discipline because it is directed to the satisfaction of people.

Implications of the definition. There are several noteworthy aspects of this definition. *First,* it refers to the total system of the firm. *Second,* it implies that all of these activities are or should be directed toward the consumer. *Third,* it suggests that there is a total corporate planning program which integrates these activities. From this we can infer logically that the plan is designed around a program of marketing-oriented objectives. All of these can be said to be concerned with management *and* the marketing function from the standpoint of the organization.

At the same time the definition recognizes the other side of the marketing manager's responsibility—management *of* the marketing function where the focus is on the function itself. In this context a *fourth* significant feature of the definition is the emphasis on a product or service designed to satisfy wants of the customer, present and potential. *Fifth,* it refers not only to the product as an important element of the marketing mix, but also to the other elements of that mix: price, promotion, and the channels of distribution. *Sixth,* while no specific objectives such as profit levels are mentioned, one can again logically infer that all this effort is toward the achievement of the firm's objectives which include some kind of profit.

Marketing and the transaction. This is such a critical point in your study of marketing that we want to reflect on the impact of the transaction on the operation of a firm that markets its product. The most efficient producer, the most astute financial manager, the most skilled manager of any kind accomplishes nothing unless a transaction occurs between a seller and a customer. Such transactions are very complex. Producers and consumers are often great distances from one another. We rarely find an individual who has chosen to provide totally for himself; even Robinson Crusoe eventually discovered the value of the division of labor. Thus, most of us must go into the market place to satisfy our needs. These trips into the market place set the stage for the transaction.

Marketing's job is to make the transaction or the exchange process as efficient as possible consistent with the objectives of the parties to the transaction. In effect, marketing has the task of using as few resources in its work as possible—again *consistent with the objectives of all parties in the exchange process.* Further, it may be said that before any transaction takes place both parties must *anticipate* some satisfaction or gain. And for transactions to continue between the same two parties, such satisfaction or gain must have occurred.

Certain other terms are sometimes used interchangeably, but erroneously, with marketing. Merchandising and selling are narrower concepts than marketing. They are only portions of the marketing program. The term *distribution* is closer in meaning, but because of the significance of physical distribution some confusion arises when "distribution" is used to mean marketing.

THE MARKETING CONCEPT

Elements of the concept

Marketing is a function or a set of activities. A number of institutions are used in its accomplishment, and both products and services are involved. The marketing concept is the philosophic base from which the function gains direction. It is constructed of three interrelated elements: (1) a consumer orientation, (2) attention to objectives, including profit, and (3) integrated marketing activities throughout the firm.

The dominant element in the concept is the centrality of the consumer. If the consumer must make a purchase or engage in exchange for the firm to survive, then it is logical that the firm be particularly attentive to the consumer's satisfaction. In today's changing competitive environment, no firm can expect to maintain a self-serving posture and continue to satisfy the customer. The market place is "where the action is," and the firm's posture must be oriented toward it.

The second element, attention to objectives, is the completion of the thought begun in the previous paragraph. A consumer orientation implies attention to the objectives of the consumer. But since both parties must gain from the transaction, it follows that the firm must also satisfy its own objectives by the transaction. Thus, the focus now must be on these corporate objectives.

Corporate objectives are defined typically in terms of profit, growth, and survival. We all know, however, that just to say that the firm must make a profit is not sufficient to guide the management. Management requires more specific, concrete objectives with which to operate. Profit may be stated as return on invested capital or stockholders' equity, or return on sales, or gross dollar profits. You will find, however, that firms have many other kinds of objectives, such as:

To be the largest firm in the industry.

To be regarded as a "good corporate citizen."

To be the most progressive firm.

To provide stable employment for workers and managers.

The point is, of course, that not only the profit objective must be satisfied by the transaction, but also all others objectives. The significance of including attention to objectives in the marketing concept is to establish the importance of clear, concise, communicable objectives to the firm and to emphasize the transaction as the means of satisfying *all* of these objectives.

Integration of marketing effort is the third member of the triumvirate of marketing concept elements, and it is drawn from the need to make the exchange process more efficient. Since most marketing managers have working for them a number of specialists, each of whom has some responsibility for marketing actions, the only sure way to make these specialists operate efficiently is to integrate or focus their activities on a common point. That point should be the customer. A lack of integration of corporate activities is inefficient and leaves the achievement of both customer and corporate objectives to chance.

Evolution of the concept

Even though the marketing concept makes a lot of sense and has been enunciated for 200 years, it still is not as widely used as logic suggests it should be. In the 1770s Adam Smith wrote words very similar to those now being written about the concept. He said:

> Consumption is the sole end and purpose of all production; and the interest of the producer ought to be attended to, only so far as it may be necessary for promoting that of the consumer. . . . But in the mercantile system the interest of the consumer is almost constantly sacrificed to that of the producer; and it seems to consider production, and not consumption, as the ultimate end and object of all industry and commerce.[1]

In saying that the organization considered production as the ultimate end of industry and commerce, Smith was describing the situation in the era of the Industrial Revolution. In the early years of this period production was more or less geared to consumer demand—since apparently little need was felt for a function to market the output of the factory. In later years of the period, mass production began to develop. This required mass distribution. It was at this point that the salesman and the sales manager began to "market" (in this instance, *sell*) the output. Product planning was still the function of the production people. Consumers were still the "they" who bought what production people wanted to produce. Thus, the *first* stage of the marketing concept focused on production. The thought was that whatever was produced would be sold.

Henry Ford often has been quoted as saying that he would give the people whatever color of car they wanted as long as it was black. It really doesn't matter if he actually said it or not; perhaps he should have, for that statement fairly well represented a widely held attitude toward consumers. It has been said, on the other hand, that Ford was one of the first great marketers. He found what the consumer wanted and set out to make it: a cheap car. To make it cheap, he had to devise a suitable production system. Thus, his statement about color may have been made within a marketing context and with a lack of judgment of what the consumer wanted or what the producer tried to force him to take. In short, he may have done the wrong thing for the right reasons.

It is difficult to specify a time when one era closed and another began, but many believe that this production-sales era ended about the time of World War II.

The *second* stage more or less equated sales with marketing. This era was characterized by bringing together all of the sales-related activities under one executive. Sales training was moved from the personnel department, advertising and sales promotion from the advertising department, product servicing from the production department, and so on.

---

[1] Adam Smith, *The Wealth of Nations* (New York: Random House, Inc., The Modern Library, 1937), book 4, p. 625.

Product planning, however, remained with the production department. The primary emphasis on sales in this stage continued into the 1950s.

The *third* stage is underway now, but some experts think we are evolving into a fourth stage. In many respects it might be said we are evolving from the second stage through the third stage and into the fourth one. A number of companies have adopted the marketing concept which is considered the hallmark of the third stage. In this stage, the marketing manager is in charge of a fully integrated marketing department.

Product planning becomes one of the major cornerstones of the marketing manager. This includes decisions on product development, design, packaging, and so on. Under the marketing concept, the marketing manager comes on the scene at the beginning of the production program, even to the point of determining what is to be produced. This approach is distinguished from the former situation where he was faced with goods already produced and told to sell them.

The *fourth* stage that we appear to be moving toward is subtly different from the third. This is the stage of the marketing company. It represents mostly an attitudinal change in which the entire company becomes a marketing organization.

In short, this means that we have made something less than rapid strides in recognizing the maxim Adam Smith wrote of 200 years ago.

Implications of the marketing concept and the marketing company

Both this chapter and the book are devoted to the implications of the marketing concept. Accordingly, in discussing those implications, two things are done at the same time: a summary of what has been said so far, and a preview of the remainder of the book. This will be done in three stages. First, we refer again to effectiveness of marketing management, or management *and* the marketing function. Second, we comment on efficiency of marketing management, or management *of* the marketing function. Third, we comment on the nature and broader aspects of managerial decisions.

Effectiveness: Management <u>and</u> the marketing function. Analysis. Before a firm can be effective in doing something, it must decide what to do. This involves analyses of all relevant environments. One can hardly set useful and potentially attainable objectives without knowing what is desirable from the consumers' point of view. Also, these objectives cannot be set without an indication of the feasibility of their attainment. Accordingly, analyses must first be made to decide *what to do.*

In addition, a different set of analyses must be made to determine the *best way to do it.* The strategic planning to attain the objectives cannot take place in a vacuum either. The development of strategy includes not only the setting of objectives but also the methods of acquisition of resources needed to attain those objectives. Also, it includes the development of broad policies for use of the resources.

In short, a situation analysis must be made of the environment to (1) discover opportunities and problems, (2) set objectives related to exploiting and/or solving them, (3) develop plans to attain those objectives, and (4) design policies as a framework to guide managers of functional areas.

Organization. However large or small an organization may be, however complex or simple its organization chart may be, for the firm to be effective it must have some means of developing policies on an integrated basis. All departments of the firm which are affected significantly by a particular proposed policy must have interface to provide inputs into whatever policy is developed. We do *not* imply putting these matters to a vote. We only say that at whatever point the buck stops, it is *at* that point the decisions should be made. That "point" may be a committee, a group vice president, a president, or a board of directors.

To this extent the organization must be structured in such a manner that marketing policies and problems affecting the effectiveness of the organization are considered by the organization. This means that marketing and other executives become in effect a planning and policy-making body which works with the planning department if the firm has one. If it does not have a separate planning department, this group of executives becomes that department. It further means that duties of such functional executives as the marketing and production managers are extended to include some functions ordinarily thought of as staff functions. This is to assure emphasis on the organization.

Efficiency: Management of the marketing function. After the two basic decisions to do something and the strategy of doing it have been made, the marketing manager is charged with the responsibility of actually doing it. At this point one focuses attention on the marketing function. The manager's concern is to carry out the marketing activities and assignments efficiently. The marketing manager's decisions fall into two major categories: those stemming from external and internal analyses, and those related to the evaluation of opportunities.

Analysis. We have discussed analyses required to set objectives and plan for the organization. Similar analyses are necessary to manage the marketing function. Some of these analyses are directed toward the discovery of opportunities both in the external environment and in the internal environment. In many respects this is the most difficult of the marketing tasks. It involves a total analysis of the marketing situation, including attempts to determine actual and potential consumer wants, sources of consumer satisfaction and dissatisfaction, and methods of serving those wants and needs profitably.

Evaluation of alternatives. Equally important are analyses leading toward the solution of problems and the exploitation of opportunities. Here the ground rules are much clearer. The first step in this process is to define the problem. This is probably both the most difficult and the most important step in the whole process. Sometimes what we think is the problem is only a peripheral issue, and when we seek a solution we go to the periphery of the problem instead of to its heart.

Other steps include the identification of alternative solutions, isolating and analyzing the several aspects of the problem, and selecting and developing what appears to be the best of the alternatives.

THE MARKETING CONCEPT IN A SHORTAGE ECONOMY

In the first half of the 1970s, the marketing concept as a principle faced substantial reevaluation. Shortages of many things, especially money, credit, and raw materials, brought pressures on businesses to switch from *marketing* their goods to *allocating* them to buyers. When goods are in short supply, there is a tendency to make that subtle shift in concept from finding out what the consumer wants and providing it at a profit, to taking orders for some future delivery of what the seller wants to produce.

It is still too early to generalize on what is happening to the marketing concept and the attitude of the producer in making the allocations of scarce items. Note, for example, the actions of some gasoline service station operators during the fuel shortages of 1974. They often displayed disregard for the consumer in both service and price, while at the same time still others continued showing concern for the consumer. Many banks did not lose their marketing approach although money was in short supply. Yet, human nature being what it is, many bankers behaved toward their customers as did many service station operators. Again, in this sense it is difficult to generalize on what happened to the marketing concept.

In another sense, some good things did happen. Some companies had gone overboard in developing extensive product lines to meet wants and needs of customers. With shortages of material, however, they cut many of those lines back. As is shown in Chapter 10, one company cut 50 percent of its color television models and 40 percent of its refrigerator models. Another cut 60 percent of its paper product lines while auto companies cut 20 percent of their models from 1970 to 1974. Necessity forced many companies to eliminate the "fat" from their product lines.

The shortages of the mid-1970s were only part of a confusing and complex economic situation which plagued marketing managers. The economy was characterized by both recession and inflation. By the winter of 1975 there were signs that both were beginning to "bottom out." Also shortages of many items had become less visible. Even so, shortages and inflationary pressure seemed almost certain to be a part of the marketing manager's environment both in the short run and in the long run. Many experts predicted a return of high interest rates in 1976, which would cause marketing managers short-run problems.

These problems affect strategic policies of the firm in various ways. For example, there may be additional pressures to reduce the number of different models in the product line. As the number of models decreases, the need for working capital to maintain inventories and spare parts also decreases. Thus, there is pressure on the marketing manager to determine which consumer wants will not be satisfied in the short run.

In addition to this type of strategic decision of the firm, the marketing manager is pressured by shortages of money to become more efficient in managing the marketing function. In the name of efficiency, there is a tendency to look at transactions which have been only marginally profitable with the thought of reducing the quality of service to those customers involved and again leave some wants and needs unsatisfied. This is not necessarily bad; it is merely a change in application of the marketing concept. In fact, it may very well be a good change because marketing-oriented firms cannot economically satisfy *all* consumer wants and needs.

Shortages of money and materials may have an even more profound effect on marketing priorities in the long run than in the short run. In an ad in *Business Week* of April 14, 1975, the Chase Manhattan Bank estimated that in the 1980s there would be a deficit of $2.5 trillion in capital needed for business unless something is done. Over a ten-year period $2.5 trillion reduces to $677,000,000 per day, or $28,000,000 per hour. The shortage of oil and natural gas for energy is also receiving a great deal of attention. The U.S. supply of other basic resources for the metals industries is also diminishing, making the availability of those resources more subject to problems of balance of payments, international exchange rates, and higher prices.

The consideration of scarcity and the marketing manager should be done in the context of the two major marketing functions—the selection of target markets and the design of a marketing program to serve those markets. The product, channels of distribution, promotion, and price as elements of the marketing mix are the basic building blocks of the marketing program. In the context of the selection of target markets and the marketing mix, certain types of decisions are implied by long-term shortages of money and materials.

The outline below gives some commonly practiced marketing tactics during a shortage economy. It should serve as a springboard from which the student may think of some alternative tactics, decisions, and implications. First, with the list serving as a stimulus, write down other implications or alternative decisions for each point listed. Second, give a little thought to each point listed and ask yourself if the implication of the decision stated is good, bad, or neutral in terms of your personal value system. Finally, challenge the validity of the statements as generalizations based upon your own reasonable assumptions.

I. Target Market
    A. The firm: only the most profitable and easiest-to-attract segments will be served.
    B. The marketing activity: less attention to post-sale service because of seller's market.
II. The Marketing Mix
    A. Product
        1. The firm: design for durability and long life to conserve materials.
        2. The marketing activity: reduce post-sale service; shift function to retailer and customer.
    B. Channels of Distribution: Institutions
        1. The firm: bypass wholesaler and sell direct to retailer.
        2. The marketing activity: concentrate sales with large retailers.
    C. Channels of Distribution: Logistics
        1. The firm: reduce both the amount of goods held in inventory and the number of warehouse locations.
        2. The marketing activity: switch to a slower and cheaper form of transportation with a lower quality of service.
    D. Promotion
        1. The firm: reduce the size of the sales force and the advertising and sales promotion budget.
        2. The marketing activity: have sales people substitute telephone calls for personal calls on customers; reduce expenses where possible.
    E. Price
        1. The firm: increase the amount required to be bought to qualify for quantity discounts.
        2. The marketing activity: reduce promotional allowances to retailers and wholesalers; avoid competitive price-cutting.

On their face, several of the points listed above appear at best to be stupid decisions. You probably, and correctly, reached this conclusion as you challenged the validity based upon the assumptions you made. Yet, given another set of assumptions in a different context, each of the decisions could be good marketing strategy—not only for the producer, but also for the consumer or middleman.

Scarcity of goods and the ability of a firm to sell everything it produces will and does provide incentives and subtle pressures on a marketing manager to abandon thinking in terms of the marketing concept. Those who succumb to the pressures will have reverted to the production-centered stage of selling. There is no way of presuming what most firms wll do and whether the marketing concept will survive on as broad a basis under conditions of relative scarcity as under conditions of plenty.

One thing is sure: those firms which abandon the marketing concept and its consumer orientation will create tremendous opportunities for other marketing-oriented firms which are concerned with consumer satisfaction. Also, scarcity is often temporary. Sometimes acceptable substitutes surface during periods of scarity. Under such conditions customers will long remember and reward those suppliers who retained a concern for their interests. Marketing managers under conditions of relative scarcity will have to evaluate priorities more carefully in the future than they ever have in the past.

In short, it is imperative that managers manage change rather than react to change and thus become managed by it.

AN APPROACH TO MARKETING MANAGEMENT

Systems approach

The systems approach recognizes that it may not be in the best interests of the firm to have each part work at optimum efficiency; that one part may operate inefficiently in order for the efficiency of the firm to be systemized and its effectiveness realized. "Systems" has become a watchword in the lexicon of those who concern themselves with business. This new attention to systems was a stimulus for a number of excellent books on planning. Also, many large organizations have given planning a prominent place in the list of managerial activities. The books on managerial marketing, managerial finance, and so on, generally speak of the importance of planning as part of the foundation of managerial decisions in the functional area. Where planning is emphasized in managerially oriented books, it is usually done in the context of the functional area and with the tacit assumption that corporate-level planning has taken place. In this context the planning emphasis is directed more toward the ongoing management *of* the functional area, with relatively little emphasis on management *and* the functional area.

This preoccupation with the functional area to the virtual exclusion of the firm is in direct opposition to the systems approach and to the basic concepts of planning. When coupled with certain methods of administration, control, and managerial reward there is a tendency to create a series of feudal baronies which are detrimental to the wellbeing of the organization. Further, there is a tendency to create bureaucratic organizations more concerned with the comforts of the status quo than with the risks involved in the management of change.

Systems approach and planning

In this book we view the systems approach and the planning concepts as operating in tandem. Together they can further an understanding of the role of the functional areas in the organizational scheme of things, create a climate for management of change, and improve the efficiency and effectiveness of functional performance. Whatever the system is— economic, social, antisocial, religious, business—and however systematically it may function, there is a hierarchical relationship within each component and perhaps among the components. In business there is an organizational hierarchy: corporate level and functional area. There is a hierarchy of plans: strategic, tactical, and operational. There is a hierarchy of objectives: effectiveness in meeting objectives and efficiency in use of resources. And so on through a wide range and a long list of hierarchies.

Planning is not feasible without information. Also a complex network of hierarchies of planning, managing, and so on are a fact of environmental life with which the modern marketing manager must cope. The framework of this book is designed in such a manner that *planning* and *information flows* are the common factors which link the functions of marketing to create a marketing system. They also link the marketing system to other functional areas to create a system of the firm.

The modern marketing manager must be a planner at one level of the managerial hierarchy and a doer at another. At one level the manager is involved with other functional area managers in strategic planning for the development of corporate objectives, plans, and broad policies for guidance of the functional areas. At this level managers should participate in all aspects of analysis required for the development of these objectives, plans, and policies. For example, they may be involved in decisions relating to the development of foreign subsidiaries, investment in new plant facilities, or major expansion of trade areas.

Also, at this level they participate in developing overall strategies of the firm and particularly those directly related to marketing: product, channels of distribution, logistics, promotion, and price. This may involve such things as the development of new product lines, alteration of distribution systems, or deciding upon an appropriate promotional pattern.

In addition, the manager must function at another hierarchical level: the traditional managerial and operational level involving decision making for the marketing system. Here the marketing manager makes packaging decisions, selects modes of transportation, approves a media schedule for advertising, or initiates a new bonus plan for the sales force.

chapter 2 | # Foundations of the marketing system

The business firm: A system of relations
　Responsibilities of marketing management
　　Philosophical
　　Functional
　　Activities
　　Environmental conditions affecting marketing management
　　First-order conditions
　　Second- and third-order conditions
　　Fourth-order conditions
　The external system
　　Suppliers, customers, intermediaries
　　Competitors
　The internal system
　　The resource management system
　　The information system
　　The resource conversion system
　　The product distribution system
　Environmental problems: A summary of managerial decision
　　Problems
Putting the parts together

Marketing is broadly familiar to practically everyone, and for this reason it is easy for people to relate to. Examples of the marketing effort are all around. The objective of this chapter is to help you integrate what you know about marketing with some things you don't know about it, and weave them into a framework for an orderly and disciplined study of the subject. This framework will give you a preview of things to come. It will also serve as something of a map of a strange territory, and help you to keep a perspective of the whole as you study specific aspects of the parts.

One part of the framework consists of the responsibilities of the marketing manager to the organization and to the marketing function. A second part consists of the environmental conditions affecting marketing management. The third and fourth elements of the framework are the external and internal systems. The chapter concludes with a discussion of how the parts fit together.

THE BUSINESS FIRM: A SYSTEM OF RELATIONS

Responsibilities of marketing management

The executive in charge of the marketing function of the firm has two areas of responsibility. The first responsibility is to the firm as a whole. In discharging this area of responsibility, there should be involvement with the managers of other functional and service divisions of the firm, including the planning manager if the firm has a separate planning department. In this role the marketing executive is working on behalf of the firm as a whole in the design of a framework of objectives and policies which will guide the managers of the several functional departments.

The executive's second responsibility is to marketing as a functional area. In discharging this area of responsibility the manager should work primarily with members of the marketing department to see that resources are used efficiently in attaining the objectives of the organization. In this role, the manager is focusing on the marketing department.

Unfortunately, there is a vast difference between what *should* be done and what *is* done in many firms. Too often, one might think that the managers of the several divisions were not working for the same firm. Each appears to think only of his own division. Logically, if each manager were to "optimize" his function as a separate function, then the firm as an entity would also be optimized. But the logical course of action turns out to be expensive in practice. The "optimization" of a function by each manager almost always produces a situation in which the overall operations of the firm are actually impaired.

For example, one company president had four profit center heads who worked toward optimization of their respective areas. He could not get them to collaborate as a corporate group on the exploration of new markets, the development of new product lines, and the improvement of managerial manpower policies. "He finally started getting results when he told his four top executives that henceforth, although they would still be fully accountable for short-term profits, only 60 percent of their annual bonuses would be based on profit performance, while 20 percent would be based on their contributions to the development of their subordinates."[1] In the spring of 1974, stockholders of Manufacturers Hanover Corporation, the fifth largest bank in the United States, approved a new executive bonus plan that "will for the first time relate the compensation of its top executives both to corporate performance and to their own performance on the job."[2] These types of bonus programs should go a long way toward encouraging managers to be at least as interested in the effectiveness of the organization as they are in the efficiency of their functional areas.

There are many reasons for this phenomenon. At the risk of oversimplification, let us say that it stems from a lack of coordination and communication among the several divisions of the firm. It is aggravated by a system of rewards to executives which measures departmental effectiveness according to the volume of sales, or by the return on investment earned on resources assigned to the department, or by the reduction of costs. The problem has been overcome in many firms by an integrated planning program in which the several functional and service managers participate.

It was stated above that the marketing manager should work in two capacities: for the firm and for the marketing function. These dual capacities are shown in Figure 2-1. That schematic diagram and the comments which follow illustrate the basic responsibilities of the marketing manager. They also illustrate the philosophy underlying the design of this book.

The division of the responsibilities of the marketing manager as shown in Figure 2-1 suggests a further blurring of the already-blurred distinctions between staff and line functions of managers. It implies that line managers should be more involved in some of the activities traditionally thought of as staff functions of planning, or chief executive functions of policy making, or directors' functions of setting objectives.

Also, it implies the sharing of jurisdictions which have been traditionally—and feudalistically—guarded as belonging to a particular division. Probably the most important operational implication is that all of the division managers are working for the same firm. Probably the most important conceptual implication is that of a change in emphasis in education, management development programs, management selection procedures, and managerial outlook.

For convenience in discussion, the several overlapping roles of the manager shown in Figure 2-1 are grouped into three broad groups: Philosophical, Functional, and Activities.

Philosophical. Since the firm's reason for being is to market its output, the development of marketing policies is too important a factor

---

[1] Richard Beckhard, "The Executive You're Counting on May Be Ready to Mutiny," *Innovation*, May 1972, p. 9. Emphasis supplied.

[2] "Payoff in 'Performance' Bonuses," *Dun's*, May 1974, p. 51.

FIGURE 2–1
Roles and Responsibilities of the Marketing Manager

Roles of the marketing manager	Responsibilities of the marketing manager					
	Philosophical			Functional		Activities
	Mission	*Focus*	*Concern*	*Approach*	*Purpose*	
In the firm	Management *and* the marketing function	Marketing in the organization	Effectiveness	Analysis of environments	Development of strategy	Setting of objectives Discovery of opportunities Discovery of problems
In the functional activity	Management *of* the marketing function	Marketing as a function	Efficiency	Rationalization	Management of marketing	Exploitation of opportunities Decision making (control) Problem solutions

to be placed under the sole jurisdiction of the marketing manager. Management cannot effectively be conducted in a vacuum. If the firm is to operate as a system and to reap the synergistic benefits of its parts working together, the managers of particular functions must be concerned with the effects of their decisions upon all significant segments of the firm.

It is for this reason that special reference is made to management *and* the marketing function, since all members of the management of the firm should be concerned with the marketing function. Conversely, the marketing manager should be concerned with management of the firm as a whole. In addition, the marketing manager must be concerned with the management of the marketing function.

This duality of responsibilities is necessary to the optimal functioning of the firm. The *emphasis* of the marketing manager should be on the role of marketing in the organization; the *focus,* however, should be on marketing as a specific function. The manager's concern should also be a dual one: *effectiveness* in helping to meet the objectives of the firm; *efficiency* in the use of resources allocated to the marketing activity.

As has been implied, the marketing manager can be very efficient in meeting sales goals but not very effective in meeting corporate objectives. Conversely, the firm may be effective, but the marketing department may be very inefficient. The situation faced by a firm and its own philosophical orientation will fairly well dictate what constitutes the "best" balance between efficiency and effectiveness of individual departments. Some firms will choose to "maximize" effectiveness of one department subject to some minimum level of efficiency. For another department they will choose to "maximize" efficiency, subject to some minimum level of effectiveness. In their own way, both approaches are correct, and each approach will in turn dictate an internal structure of operations: which departments are to be run at some "maximum" or "optimum" level and which are to be run at some "minimum" or "suboptimum" level.

In fact, to assure effectiveness, two or more departments may each have to operate at less than optimum efficiency. Imagine the marketing department working toward increased volume by promising earlier delivery dates in smaller quantities with more liberal credit terms. Meanwhile, production is working overtime, logistics costs are rising, and finance is pulling its hair. Customer service decisions of this kind should obviously not be marketing department decisions; they are properly decisions of the organization as a whole.

Functional. The marketing manager functions in two different ways, corresponding to the dual responsibilities we have already described. On the one hand, the manager is vitally concerned with what the firm decides to do. On the other, the manager is concerned with doing the job well. Again, we have the relationship between effectiveness and efficiency; between the development of objectives and the efficient use of resources.

Figure 2–1 shows that in performing a function in the firm, the marketing manager is concerned with the *analysis of environments*. These analyses lead to decisions to do something: open a new plant; improve customer service; add or drop a product; increase volume of sales. After taking part in this decision, the manager then must do efficiently whatever the group has decided upon. This is the *rationalization* process which the dictionary defines as the use of modern methods of efficiency to achieve an objective. In short, the manager must do it, and do it well.

Before the manager can do whatever is decided on effectively as well as efficiently, guiding objectives and policies must be established. The manager should participate in the development of those objectives and policies. Then he can get down to the business of managing the marketing function.

Activities. The tasks of the marketing manager are also shown in Figure 2–1. As in performing broader duties in the firm, the manager's thinking is oriented to setting objectives and developing strategy. Also, the manager is oriented to the discovery process: the discovery of opportunities and problems. In managing the marketing function on the other hand, the manager is oriented toward controlling that function and making decisions affecting it as well as toward the exploitation of opportunities and the solution of problems.

It should not be inferred from these discussions of the dual responsibilities of the marketing manager that they are discrete responsibilities. Many marketing managers now make decisions affecting the firm as a whole, but they make them within the context of managing the marketing function. That is the problem discussed earlier. Because of the overall impact of these decisions, they should be made in the context of *corporate* decisions, not *marketing* decisions.

In this sense, the dual responsibilities of the marketing manager are greater. Also, these responsibilities are in a continuum rather than in two discrete boxes. The roles overlap, are mutually interdependent, and are mutually supportive. These interrelationships will become more pronounced as the nature of the environmental conditions with which the marketing manager must cope are examined.

Environmental conditions affecting marketing management

Sorting out the responsibilities of the marketing manager is only one step in the construction of a framework for the study and practice of the broad area of marketing management. A second component of that framework consists of the environmental conditions with which the marketing manager is confronted. The marketing manager must examine, from at least four points of view, the environmental conditions which have an impact upon the system. These we will call the first-, second-, third-, and fourth-order conditions of the environment which affect marketing planning and decisions. Even though we label some parts of the environment uncontrollable, the wise manager should consider all aspects of the environment to be variable and subject to change. In discussing these environmental conditions, the several responsibilities of the marketing manager are merely put into more homogeneous categories. These categories then become a part of the framework for the orderly study of marketing management.

First-order conditions. We define the first-order conditions as those which exist outside the firm. They are uncontrollable but some may be influenced by the firm. These aspects of the environment include such things as:

The market—its size, geographic distribution, facilitating agencies, customers, competitors, supporters.

The state of the economy—growing, stagnating, declining, inflation, deflation, potential changes.

Political and legal—attitudes of political parties, laws affecting the firm, possible future laws.

Cultural and social—attitudes, preferences, customers, mores of the public, trends in aspirations.

These aspects of the environment become more significant when examined in the context of the responsibilities of marketing management. Some are clearly associated with the organization and others with the marketing function.

At least one aspect of the external environment lends itself to an approach by the marketing manager in managing the marketing function: size of market. The manager can attempt to enlarge the total market and/or gain a larger share of the present market. for example, while it may not be possible to do much in the short run about increasing the male population and thus the number of men who buy electric razors, the manager can try to enlarge the total market for the razors. By both a product development and a promotional campaign, women may be encouraged to use electric razors. Similar examples might be the development of markets for second cars and second homes, and efforts to encourage women to smoke cigars. In the mid-1970s the maker of Arm & Hammer baking soda was pushing the product as an odor-absorbing agent for refrigerators and cat boxes.

The share of the market may also be enlarged. The marketing manager may adapt the environment by judicious use of the marketing mix; product design; a promotion program; channels of distribution; or price adjustments. It may also be possible to influence certain cultural changes by marketing department action. For example, many years ago a lady would not smoke a cigarette, but if she did, she smoked it away from the public view. The tobacco companies worked on that!

The other aspects of the external environment do not lend themselves readily to simple action within the marketing function. There is not much the marketing department can do on its own to change a law it considers repressive. It can lay the groundwork for change by a promotion program to sway public opinion. However, for the most part, the actual lobbying at the legislature or Congress would probably require a more concerted effort of the firm. Some aspects of the external environment seem to be out of the reach of any individual firm, such as the state of the economy and the geographic distribution of the market. Accordingly, the firm has to adapt to those segments of the environment.

Efforts to deal with these first-order environmental conditions are thus largely beyond the scope of the marketing function as such and are a responsibility of the whole firm. Of course, that responsibility may ultimately be assigned, with guidelines, to the marketing manager.

Second- and third-order conditions. Second-order conditions are those (1) which are external to the marketing function but internal to the firm, and (2) which when dealt with have an impact on marketing and/or require a reaction from it. Third-order conditions are the obverse side of the second order: (1) they are internal to the marketing function, but (2) actions taken to deal with them may have an impact on other

parts of the firm and/or a reaction may be required from other departments. Because the second-order and third-order conditions are so similar, we discuss them in the same context.

The financial manager, operating unilaterally to reduce cost, can have
a profound effect on the marketing function. Reflect, for a moment,
on the effect of a decision to reduce investment in inventory by a given
amount. What effect will this have on the ability of the firm to meet
customer demand? Will it increase the time required to make deliveries,
or decrease the ability of the field salespeople to keep their customers
happy?

Turning to third-order conditions for a moment, what would be the
effect on logistics if the marketing manager reduced the purchase volume
needed to qualify for a price discount from 40,000 pounds to 20,000
pounds? What would be the impact on finance and on lengthening of
payment terms?

Because of the impacts of actions taken in the area of second- and
third-order conditions, decisions concerning them should be made in
conjunction with the affected departments. This is the type of situation
we considered when the role of the marketing manager *in* the organization was discussed, and special reference was made to management
and the marketing function.

Fourth-order conditions. Because much more will be said about them
later, only a brief statement on fourth-order conditions will be made
here. These are conditions which exist within the marketing department;
actions taken concerning them have little or no direct impact on other
parts of the firm. For example, the marketing manager may reduce overhead by rearranging work schedules. Or, by putting his money in bill-
board advertising instead of bus placard advertising, he may increase
sales. He may switch advertising agencies, or he may develop a better
way of measuring the results of promotion efforts. None of these actions
directly affects other functional areas of the firm. Naturally, improvements
in efficiency have their effect on profit, but other departments are not
required to react.

The external system

So far we have examined two components of the framework for the
study and practice of marketing management: the two broad sets of
responsibilities of the marketing manager and the environmental conditions affecting marketing management. The discussion of the environmental conditions emphasized the manager's roles with respect to the
organization and to the marketing function under different sets of
conditions.

Having recognized that division of responsibility, we will look at the external environmental system from a less constrained point of view. The legal-political and the cultural-social aspects need no further comment at this time. The primary concern in this section is with suppliers, customers, and intermediaries. To a lesser extent we are concerned with the competitive relationships experienced by the firm.

Suppliers, customers, intermediaries.   Until now emphasis has been on the functioning of the organization as a system and on the importance of all of its parts being in balance, even at the expense of one or more parts being suboptimized. But this is only a part of the story. The firm as an entity is only a part of a larger system also consisting of several parts. Each firm has at least four roles: it is a customer of some suppliers; it uses some intermediary agency as a link to suppliers; it is a supplier of some customers; and it uses some intermediary agency as a link to customers. These four roles involve the firm in *channels of distribution.*

In this respect the managers of the firm have two major systems to bring into balance: the firm on the one hand and its channels of distribution on the other. Actually, the channel system is itself a composite of three subsystems: the supplier system; the intermediary system; and the customer system. This implies that the managers of the firm will have the task of bringing all four systems (the firm; the supplier system; the intermediary system, and the customer system) into balance if the marketing goals set by the managers are to be achieved.

The subsystems of the channels of distribution may be defined as follows:

1.   The existing supplier system of the firm is only one of several possible systems that might supply the firm with its requisite materials. Thus, the supplier system is only part of a larger supply system.

2.   The intermediary system includes the transportation system with its subsystems, the materials handling and warehousing system, and the multiple systems of wholesalers, retailers, and other middlemen.

3.   The customer system has two broad divisions: final users of a product, and those who will process it further and then sell it. Within these broad divisions, the customer system can be further divided according to the patterns of needs, wants, expectations, and desires of different groups of customers.

These systems will be discussed in greater detail later. They are mentioned now to emphasize the complex interrelationships faced by the firm in distributing its product.

From the point of view of the individual firm, the ideal working relationship in the channel of distribution is one in which each segment of the channel is brought into balance with the others. The criteria for what constitutes "balance" are the marketing objectives the firm wants to achieve. Because many firms with many different marketing objectives have similar channels of distribution, the channel members are subjected to an incredibly large number of diverse pressures.

Other authors have expressed the notion that the several members of the channel system and the companies they serve should act as if they were unofficial parts of each other in the following manner:

> From this viewpoint, the complex of external relationships may be regarded as merely an extension of the marketing organization of the firm. When we look at the problem in this way, we are much less likely to lose sight of the interdependence of the two structures and more likely to be constantly aware that they are closely related parts of the marketing machine. The fact that the internal organization structure is knit together by a system of employment contracts, while the external one is set up and maintained by a series of transaction contracts of purchase and sale, tends to obscure their common purpose and close relationship.[3]

An example may help to clarify the essence of the relationship between the firm and its channels of distribution. A large Midwestern manufacturer of heavy duty trucks purchases diesel engines from a supplier located in a nearby town. Because of limited storage space at the plant, a large supply of truck engines cannot be kept on hand. Accordingly, the truck manufacturer, his supplier of engines, and a local hauling company have developed a channel to meet this particular set of circumstances. The system is fairly complex, and it calls for a high degree of cooperation and coordination between the firms involved. But it is a good example of how this external system, called a channel of distribution, can be brought into balance.

The question may well be asked: "Can this type of distribution system, including cooperation and coordination, be achieved by a large firm marketing a number of products to consumers—particularly since demand for consumer products is not nearly as predictable as was the demand of the truck manufacturer for diesel engines?" The answer is yes!

> This was proved more than a generation ago by the automobile industry and especially by General Motors. Henry Ford, in building River Rouge, had had the premature but great vision of the manufacturing plant as the central switchboard in a flow of physical matter from mine to customer (and from there to scrap heap and back into the furnace as raw material). With this as its starting point General Motors, in the middle and late Twenties, built its business around the economic characteristics of the distributive process—beginning with the customer's buying habits, proceeding thence to the structure and characteristics of dealer finance, dealer inventories, and dealer compensation, going back further

[3] Richard M. Hill, Ralph S. Alexander, and James S. Cross, *Industrial Marketing*, 4th. ed. (Homewood, Ill.: Richard D. Irwin, Inc., 1975).

to the design, location, size, product mix, and scheduling of assembly plants, and finally all the way back to corporate organization. For well over three decades General Motors' distribution system has made the automobile the highly engineered mass-consumption product with the lowest total distribution costs.[4]

These illustrations have been presented to show several points previously made: (1) from an overall point of view, they show that a system can be created out of the several elements of the external system of supplier, customers, and intermediaries; (2) they show that the marketing manager's responsibility transcends the management of the marketing function, that it embraces the entire firm; (3) they show the significance of the discovery process in arriving at innovative solutions to environmental problems facing the firm; and (4) they show the significance of the marketing concept and the importance of a firm becoming a part of the distribution systems of its suppliers, intermediary agencies, and customers.

Too often in the past, marketing people have considered the components of the channels of distribution in a detached sort of way as being more or less "there." This has been, and still is, true of the transportation and warehousing intermediaries as well as some others such as banks, insurance companies, and advertising agencies. These intermediaries are often called *facilitating agencies.* Over the years firms have felt that they needed to direct their channel-building efforts only at their suppliers and customers. It was assumed that other intermediaries or facilitating agencies would always be there when needed. As will be seen in Chapter 12, this myopic approach has probably been due to the way in which business has defined channels. The results are all too predictable: the facilitating agencies have not been used as creatively as they might have been, and the channels of distribution that have been constructed as a result are not nearly as well adapted or suited to the environments in which they must operate as they might have been.

Part A of Figure 2–2 illustrates the traditional view of the relationship among suppliers, customers, and intermediary or facilitating agencies. The attitude seems to be that the goods are at one place in the channel at one point in time; later they need to be somewhere else, so facilitating agencies are called into play. One has the impression of a series of stops and starts—discrete steps in the process of distribution. Notice too that this traditional concept allows for no feedback along the channel for all the movement from left to right. Should there be some delay at a point along the channel, one is struck with the notion that it would be impossible to stop the distribution process, and that at some location along the line a monumental traffic jam of unwanted boxes, bales, and

---

[4] Peter F. Drucker, "The Economy's Dark Continent," *Fortune,* April 1962, p. 103.

FIGURE 2–2
A Channel of Distribution (symbolized)

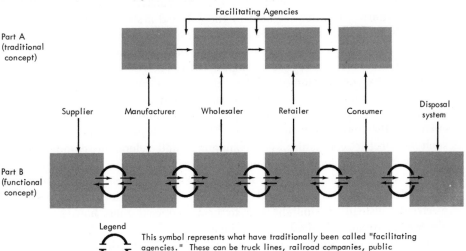

Legend

⌒⌣ This symbol represents what have traditionally been called "facilitating agencies." These can be truck lines, railroad companies, public warehouses, banks, insurance companies, or similar types of institutions.

barrels would accumulate. People would be scurrying around trying to solve the problem that created the stoppage to begin with, and also trying to cope with the problem of what to do with all the material that was continuing to arrive.

Part B of the diagram recognizes the supply function of logistics in getting goods to the manufacturer. Instead of relegating facilitating agencies to a peripheral position, it brings them into the mainstream of the channel's activity where they have functioned all along. The linkages between the participants in the channel are bidirectional, indicating that communication is two-way and that feedback is an equally important part of a channel of distribution. This view dramatizes the notion that in a channel the participants become extensions of each other.

In Part B each participant in the channel of distribution is depicted as being open to the other members of the channel. This emphasizes two points: (1) that channel relationships are designed to bring into the internal system of the firm parts of what would otherwise be the external system faced by the firm; and (2) that the relationships in a channel of distribution are mutually interdependent relationships: all parties are equally dependent upon one another for their effective operation. Many firms such as grocers have integrated the activities of channel members by creating wholesaling, warehousing, and transportation systems as parts of their systems. A disposal system is included to recognize the fact that product recycling, which has always occurred in our economy to some degree, is becoming an increasingly important activity.

Witness, for example, the activity of beer manufacturers in repurchasing from consumers the aluminum cans used to package their product.

Competitors. Another segment of the external system worthy of discussion is the competition faced by the firm. One reason to be nice to your customers is that you are not the only company in town. (In fact, even if you were the only company in town, you would still have to be nice to your customers. There are at least two reasons for this. First, even a monopolist faces some sort of indirect competition; and second, even a portion of a monoplist's marketing effort is aimed at enlarging the market for his product. Why else would public utilities, such as electric companies, gas companies, and telephone companies advertise? Even if you were a monopolist you would be trying to get people who have never used your product to try it, or to use more of it. Electric utilities consistently try to get people to dry clothes with electricity instead of sunlight and to heat and cool their houses with electricity instead of fuel oil or natural gas or a cool breeze.)

Thus the marketing manager has several reasons to think about the competition. One reason is the price elasticity of demand, because price is one of the competitive tools. The manager is also concerned with service and with the functional and aesthetic design of the product—for the same reason. There is also the promotion program to consider, designed to attract and retain customers—again for the same reason. And the manager is concerned with the cross elasticity of demand, important to the objective of enlarging the market. Equally important in this respect is that the manager does not want some other company's market to be enlarged at the expense of the shrinking of the company's market, or the slowing of its growth.

The presence of competitors in the external system gives an added dimension to the marketing program. What a competitor does may affect the demand for one's own products. For example, a customer may be perfectly happy with four product models and a three-day delivery schedule. But if a competitor provides six product models and a two-day delivery schedule, your firm may have to do the same thing.

The program of the marketing manager, therefore, has at least two dimensions: (1) a marketing program designed for customer satisfaction and corporate profit reasons, but (2) modified because there are competitors lurking about in the system. You should never forget that you are another company's competitor as well, ever on the lookout for opportunities.

The internal system

The internal system is the fourth portion of our framework for the practice and study of marketing management. Because so much has already been said about the internal system, we shall here be concerned to reemphasize the role of mangement *and* the marketing function. This is done in two ways: first, the several subsystems of the firm are grouped in several very broad categories; and second, the nature of some of the system's components is outlined.

The resource management system. The firm has at least three major categories of resources:

1. People resources, including janitors, craftsmen, supervisors, vice presidents, and directors.
2. Tangible resources, including money, inventory, machinery, and buildings.
3. Intangible resources, including credit, goodwill, quality of management, and image.

We do not know of any major firm which is organized in such a manner that one resource manager will be in charge of people, buildings, and corporate image. The responsibility for management of resources is, of course, widely diffused among many different managers. This makes it necessary for the several resource managers to integrate their activities, or, as was stated earlier, to remember that they all work for the same firm; they must place their emphasis on management *and* the organization while focusing on management *of* their respective functions.

In the discussion of second- and third-order environmental conditions, we noted that the actions of one department can affect another. This point can be illustrated in the management of resources. A decision of the marketing manager to build goodwill (intangible) by a change in customer service may require more money for inventory and buildings (tangible) and more people to act on the decision (people). Certainly, customers can be recognized as a resource; but since they are the means to whatever end the firm has in mind, we can take them for granted at this time. Another facet of the resource system also may be taken for granted at this time: the need to overcome resistances in order to exploit resources. Furthermore, the market has wants and needs; there are many resistances to the satisfaction of those wants and needs; resources are created and used to overcome those resistances in order that the wants and needs may be satisfied.

The information system. Information is a second system which pervades the entire firm. Information is important at all levels. It is a necessary ingredient to the management of the organization in the development of strategy for the firm, in analyzing environments to determine what it wants to do, in setting objectives, in discovering opportunities and problems, in the selection of alternatives, and in determining the effectiveness of operations.

Information of a different kind is necessary to the management of the several functions. The marketing manager must have information in order to control the marketing function, to use as a basis for decision making, to help identify problems and opportunities, to use in the development of alternatives and in the solution of problems, and to determine the efficiency of operations.

The foregoing illustrate several significant features about the information system from the marketing manager's viewpoint. One of the first things required is an analysis of the nature of marketing decision making and the existing information system. Second, for the information to fit the requirements of the marketing manager, the economic aspects of the marketing function must be analyzed in detail. Third, the system can then be used as a part of the discovery process for the identification of opportunities and problems.

The resource conversion system.   This is the production function of the firm. The system consists of all those resources necessary to convert raw materials and supplies into the product: expertise, people, machines, and money.

The product distribution system.   This is the marketing and logistics system. It performs all those functions required to move goods through the channels of distribution. It is also composed of all of those components of marketing which center on performing the marketing function well. Because both the production and distribution systems have been previously discussed, there is little need to say more about them at this time.

Environmental problems: A summary of managerial decision problems

Four elements of a framework for the study and practice of marketing management have been discussed, centering upon the system of relationships of which the firm is a part. First, we looked at the responsibilities of the marketing manager to the firm and to the functional area. Second, we examined the environmental conditions with which the manager must cope in carrying out these responsibilities. Third, the discussion of the environmental conditions led to a discussion of some aspects of the external system with particular emphasis on the "cooperative" segments of that system: suppliers, customers, and intermediaries in the channels of distribution. Also, we discussed competitors in that system. Fourth, again leading from environmental conditions, we commented very briefly on each of several systems of the firm.

Several problem areas have been emphasized. First, the marketing manager is concerned with operating problems in managing the function, yet he must also be concerned with nonoperating or staff decisions in acting as a planner and objective setter for the firm. This type of executive role requires a different breed of cat—one who is equally at home both in planning and in managing. Second, the marketing manager is accustomed to making decisions internal to the department and accepting trade-offs internally which suboptimize one facet of the marketing operating to the benefit of another facet of that operation. However, he is not generally accustomed to accepting trade-offs which suboptimize the marketing activity in order to benefit another department.

A third complex decision area involves that centering on extending the arms of the firm through the channels of distribution to customers and suppliers. The melding of these groups into a workable system is complex but exceedingly fruitful, as many firms are discovering. One thing which makes this a problem is the need for the marketing manager to rely upon outsiders whom he cannot control. A fourth problem is finding a base for appraising alternatives. As our information systems improve and as we accept some of the techniques of management science, this becomes less and less of a problem. In addition, there is a group of problems centering on such things as the size, location, geographic distribution, and volatility of the market. Others center on competitors, government, and labor.

PUTTING THE PARTS TOGETHER

There is a network of environmental forces and conditions with which the marketing manager must cope. We have tried to sort out these forces and partially extricate the parts from the whole in order to examine them separately in context of the whole. They are now put back together again so that the whole may be examined in context of the parts. Figure 2–3 will help us look at the whole system so far as marketing management is involved.

Let us take one of the boxes through the entire process. The market is a logical place to start. The first step is to analyze the market from the point of view of its characteristics, the opportunities it presents, and the problems it poses. The analysis would consider such things as the present and projected size, the geographical distribution, the characteristics of the buyers, the nature of the competition, and, to determine opportunities, the aspirations of the buyers. Tentative alternatives would be identified.

Second, still focusing on the market, the analysis would shift to an analysis of the organization to determine whether the organization had or could acquire the resources to make the tentative alternatives feasible. Also, analyses would be made of actual and potential resistances to pursuing the alternatives identified. These resistances may be in the form of availability of resources or attitudes of management. For exam-

FIGURE 2–3
Planning and Managing Marketing

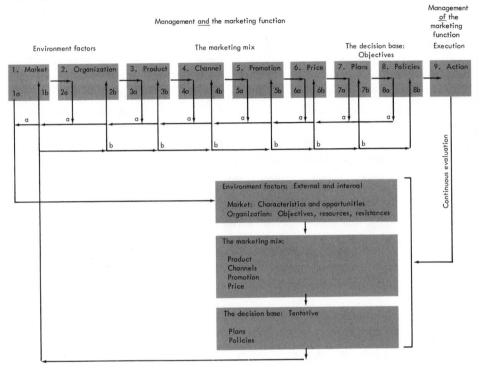

ple, a company may have had no experience with anything resembling some of the alternatives. Or, it may have had a bad experience and not want to get into the field again. Or, one alternative may be too volatile. Or, a powerful individual or group may just be opposed to it. After these analyses, alternatives may be narrowed or opportunities may come into focus more clearly so that a tentative set of conclusions and objectives can be reached.

Third, still from the point of view of the market, analyses would be made to determine whether the alternative products are suitable for the market and/or the nature of any changes required. In addition, the suitability of channels of distribution would be determined. Also, the implications surrounding promotion and pricing—including credit, discounts, and other policies—would be considered. Fourth, on the basis of all of these analyses, some tentative plans and policies would be developed.

At this point, the first of several "recycling" or iterative processes would start. The conclusions would be examined much more carefully in light of their impact on the organization than they could have been the first time around, when emphasis was on the market. Initially, there was only a relatively vague notion to be considered. But now a fairly concrete proposal must be analyzed and perhaps modified as it goes through the cycle, this time with organizational capability being the focal point of attention; and so on through the entire process until a complete program emerges.

At this level all of the affected executives would be in on the analyses. They would necessarily have to furnish information from their areas as to costs and effects. Once more, we point out that, in the large organization, the planning department may "shepherd" the whole project. It would also do some of the analyses and furnish information the functional departments could not. However, the planning department would not make the decisions; they would be made by the executives or by the board of directors.

We cite the experience of one large company in using this process. Until it started the analysis, the company thought it was in the abrasives manufacturing business. An examination of the market made it realize it should be in the "excess materials removal business," because the scope of that market was broader than the abrasives market. An internal analysis disclosed that it did not have the technological expertise to participate in a growing segment of the excess materials removal market. However, the company decided to acquire the expertise. This decision introduced other alternatives to be considered. Should it hire the necessary people, train workers, buy machinery, and in general start from scratch and develop a total marketing program? The alternative eventually chosen was to acquire a company already in the business.

In a small company the procedures discussed would be followed without the help of a planning department. The "shepherd" may be any one of the managers involved in the procedure. Also, in small companies the analyses may not be on as sophisticated a level because fewer resources are available. The point of emphasis is that *any* company should go through this procedure. The purpose is to provide for the altogetherness of things.

chapter 3 | # Marketing in the managerial hierarchy

Management and the organization
  The nature of business
  The function of business
  The definition of management
  The function of management
  The nature of managerial activities
    Innovation
    Adaptation and the external environment
    Adaptation and the internal environment
Management as a network of hierarchies
  The hierarchy of aims
    Purpose or mission
    Objectives and goals
  The hierarchy of satisfactions
    Chief executive
    Employees and other managers
    Owners and creditors
    Public
    Consumers
  The hierarchy of objectives
    Focus of objectives
  Development of objectives
Summary and conclusions

MANAGEMENT AND THE ORGANIZATION

The nature of business

In this book we define a business as an organization of human, material, and intangible resources created to afford satisfaction to its owners and maintained so as to afford satisfaction to its managers. The fundamental purpose of a business is considered to be the achievement of maximum satisfaction for its owner-managers (in a closely held busi-

34

ness) or its managers (in a widely held business). It is true that in many instances, perhaps even in a vast majority, the way to maximize managerial satisfaction is to maximize corporate profits. However, we do not believe business can be defined solely in terms of the dollar-profit motive, nor can its purpose be stated only in these terms. Other types of profit can accrue to the owners and managers of businesses,[1] and the motives for creating, managing, and expanding businesses are so numerous, complex, and diverse that they cannot be explained in dollar-profit terms alone. Such profit is only one of the devices by which satisfaction to owners and managers can be measured. Thus maximization of profits can be seen as one goal of business, and the creation and retention of profitable customers as one means to earn dollar profit.

A number of things about business which cannot be explained if dollar profit is regarded as the only method of keeping score on success become clear when the purpose of business is defined in terms of satisfaction. Factors other than profit are significant in explaining the motives behind many ventures. Some examples:

1. Universities start nonsubsidized book stores.
2. Retired wealthy executives start new careers and in some cases create new empires.
3. The heir of a large fortune subsidizes, year in and year out, a magazine devoted to the arts.
4. A major conglomerate locates a new plant in a high-cost ghetto area.
5. Small businessmen stay in business when total return on investment and salary are less than social security benefits or less than they could earn in wages.
6. Businessmen continue enterprises even though, if their investments were liquidated, they could earn more from certificates of deposit.
7. Division managers of large firms refuse new-product ideas with great potential but some risk.
8. A businessman continues acquisition and expansion programs after having created a foundation to give money away because it keeps piling up so fast.

---

[1] The broadest possible definition of profit is "a receipt in excess of expenditure." Under this definition, a firm that desires to be a champion of environmental causes, and which expends corporate resources to enhance the environment or to support such activities will earn a profit if the returns—either in the form of a better environment or in terms of public recognition of its activities—are greater than the resources the firm uses in the processes. Thus, when speaking of "profits" we can mean something far broader than the traditional accounting concept of "an excess of income over expenses."

Although we recognize this broader implication inherent in the word profit, our use of it in this text will be in the context of the more traditional accounting or economic meaning of the word.

We define business and express its purpose in terms of satisfaction for several reasons. Rarely is a chief executive of a company established in office for being a good housekeeper who will keep the company on its course, straight and true. The executive is expected to put his own stamp on the company and lead it toward its basic purpose or to shape a new purpose through the objectives he brings with him—those of the new employer, and those of his new associates. The basic sources of the objectives that the executive eventually synthesizes and causes to be adopted by the company are the several sets of values held by him and his senior executives as modified by the values of others in the organization: owners, directors, and workers.

A second reason for emphasizing satisfaction is that there may be several routes to the same objective. One executive may get satisfaction from very high volume and low margin because of a desire to be among the top ten producers in the industry. A second prefers low volume, high quality, and high price in order to develop a reputation for quality of product. A third may choose to be dominant in a region even though small nationally.

For example, one entrepreneur whose sales doubled every year for five years and whose profits kept pace believed he could better that record and could continue to do so for some time in the future if he had more capital. With little difficulty he could have raised what he needed by selling about 30 percent of his stock to the public, but he resisted going public because he would rather have 100 percent of a company whose worth may be measured by an index of 100 than 70 percent of a company worth 300 or more. His independence was a major source of satisfaction. Dollar profit played two roles in his business. First, some minimum profit was necessary for the growth he sought—another source of satisfaction. Second, it was a valuable score-keeping system against which to measure his managerial performance, innovations, and so on.

A third reason for emphasis on satisfaction is that it is the central feature of the consumer orientation. Customer satisfaction achieved through the actions of the firm must be the basis for managerial satisfaction. That is, managers cannot expect to achieve satisfaction independent of the corporate structure they have designed for the purpose of assuring the satisfaction which is essential to the success of the enterprise. They adjust their values and satisfactions so as to be consistent with the greater demands of customer satisfaction.

The function of business

Marketing is not only a function of business, but, from the consumer's point of view, it *is* the business. We conclude, therefore, that the function of business is to create, retain, and satisfy a profitable customer as a means of reaching the desired ends of corporate success.[2] Corporate success generally is synonymous with marketing success.[3] Further, for the chief executive to carry out the marketing plans successfully, he must "recognize the lead position of marketing, recognize in fact that his own position is fundamentally a marketing function, and so must be his objectives and planning."[4]

The definition of management

Management is the *analysis* and *rationalization* of all environments, functions, components, and activities of the organization for the purposes of establishing aims, plans, and policies at all levels and using resources effectively and efficiently. This definition states what managers do or should do, and it serves as a basis for a hierarchical framework of analysis. The definition implies a hierarchical relationship because it distinguishes between two different sets of management activities: the decision to do something, and the art and science of doing it. The decisions to do something may relate to the management of the organization as a whole (Level 1 decisions) or they may relate either to a functional division such as marketing or to a support division such as accounting (Level 2 decisions). Rationalization means "to apply modern methods of efficiency to an industry," among other things.[5]

Figure 3–1 shows the organization responsibility for the two levels of decisions. The group that makes the Level 1 decisions is led by the chief executive and consists of functional and support group executives, including the marketing manager. This group is often assisted by a formal planning department. Generally the decisions of this group will be concerned with strategic matters such as the objectives of the organization, plans and policies, and the acquisition of resources.

The Level 2 decisions are the responsibility of the several managers of departments and their staffs. One set of these decisions concerns operations of the marketing department and the development of plans and policies to reach marketing objectives. This set of decisions is made within the guidelines set by Level 1 objectives, plans, and policies. The

---

[2] See Peter Drucker, *The Practice of Management* (New York: Harper & Row, 1954), p. 37.

[3] George A. Steiner, *Top Management Planning* (New York: The Macmillan Company, 1969), p. 520.

[4] John M. Brion, *Corporate Marketing Planning* (New York: John Wiley and Sons, Inc., 1967), p. 1.

[5] *Webster's New Twentieth Century Dictionary*, 2d ed., unabridged (Cleveland: The World Publishing Company, 1962), p. 1496.

FIGURE 3–1
Organization Responsibility for Level 1 and Level 2 Decisions

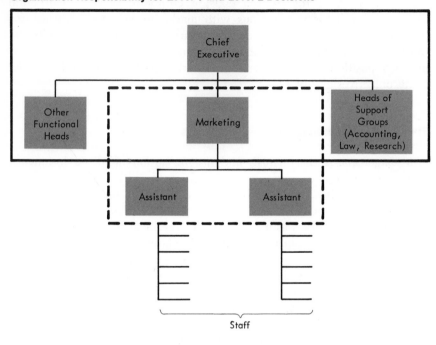

Level 1 ▬ Analysis: As a basis for strategic decisions, the setting of objectives, acquisition of resources, and establishing policies and guidelines for implementation.

Level 2 ▬▬ Rationalization: The application of modern methods of efficiency to acquire, manage, and operate the resources to attain objectives.

other set of Level 2 decisions relates to the effective and efficient use of resources to reach the objectives.

In dividing the activities of management into those that are concerned with the management of the firm and those that are concerned with management of the functional area or division, we do not imply two different and discrete sets of activities. To do so would destroy the systems approach we have adopted. Rather, we see the one as taking place within the framework of the other and existing only because the other exists. Recognizing the hierarchy of management activities, we have applied the hierarchical concept to designate those factors that impinge upon certain activities.

The hierarchical relationship implied between analysis and rationalization and between Level 1 and Level 2 can be extended to a number of other concepts. The application of the hierarchical approach to the analysis of aims, satisfactions, and plans provides a way to draw a line between objective setting and planning for the firm as a whole and for the marketing division. In this book the hierarchical approach is taken to place emphasis on the firm and to focus on the marketing function. This approach also makes it easier to separate the processes involved in planning and doing, or between analysis and rationalization. In addition, it is a convenient means to explain and provide for the division of labor in planning and, more important, to assure that the proper people at the proper level are involved in planning for the proper things. In short, the hierarchical framework is a device for breaking a problem into its several components for analysis and for restructuring the parts into a system that is both coherent and workable.

The function of management

The function of management arises from the environments within which the firm exists. From an environmental point of view, consumers and organizations have much in common: they both have wants and needs which they seek to satisfy; they both face resistances which must be overcome before satisfaction can be attained; and they both have resources they can use to overcome these resistances. Another point in common is that the consumer, as the source of profit and sustenance, is the sole means by which the ends of the organization can be reached, and the organization is one important means through which the consumer can obtain satisfaction.

The organization cannot exist without the customer. Partially because of this primacy of the consumer, we can state that *the function of management is to acquire and manage resources effectively and efficiently in finding opportunities and in overcoming resistances in order to maximize the satisfactions of consumers and management.*

Management operates in both external and internal environments in order to fulfill its function of maximizing organization and consumer satisfactions. Opportunities for satisfaction, as well as resistances to be overcome, are found in both these environments. In fact, in many instances the opportunities exist because the resistances are present. There are opportunities to innovate (design a new product or develop a new order-processing system), opportunities to change or influence the external environment and adapt it to the objectives of the firm (e.g., promote revision of federal financing rules on mobile homes to facilitate participation in the low-cost housing market), and opportunities to adapt the firm and its resources to the requirements of the external environment (any market-oriented action).

The nature of managerial activities

The discovery and exploitation of the opportunities provided by the firm's environments constitute the challenge to management. From the marketing perspective the activities of innovation, adaptation of the environment, and adaptation to the environment are reflected in the marketing-related objectives of the firm and its marketing-related plans, strategies, programs, and projects. While these three aspects of the managerial function of maximizing satisfactions are separately identifiable, they are not mutually exclusive. To the contrary, they are so interwoven in concept that it is difficult to separate them.

Innovation. Managerial activities related to innovation are of two types: product innovation and managerial innovation. Product innovation is the most spectacular of these, since it directly affects all those involved in marketing. Also, it has the greatest potential for making an impact on both the market and the income statement, as well as on all the types of managerial satisfaction.

It is important to identify two types of *product innovation:* breakthrough innovations, and routine "suggestion box" innovations which are essentially product improvements. This classification suffers from problems of definition, such as whether the addition of a self-cleaning apparatus to an oven is a breakthrough or merely a product improvement. There is also the question of whether a product change is really an improvement or merely a change.

Managerial innovation refers to types of innovation that are not directly concerned with the product but are directed toward improving both the quality of service to the market and the methods of serving and dealing with the external environment. In addition, these types of innovation have to do with the effectiveness and efficiency with which the resources of the firm are used to reach objectives.

In an organization that has conceptually converted itself to a marketing-oriented company and has been structured organizationally to that end, a substantial amount of effort will be directed to finding methods of improving the satisfactions the product brings to the consumer. These satisfactions have many dimensions other than absolute usefulness, including all those things referred to as the marketing mix. Of prime importance are the nature and utility of the product—including price, service and guarantee policies, and method of packaging. The channels of distribution present many possibilities for management innovation; whether the purchaser is a reseller or ultimate user, the product's availability and ease of acquisition in time and place, as well as quantity, are also sources of satisfaction. For example, L'Eggs women's hosiery products are distributed in part through consignment racks in supermarkets, historically an unlikely place for pantyhose. These products have, however, had success there because both the ultimate consumer and the distribution channel have derived satisfaction from such unusual and innovative distribution. The promotional element of the marketing mix is also a fruitful area for innovation in attracting the potential customer's attention and convincing him of the virtues of the product or the marketing agent.

Such managerial innovations are directed toward the external environment to attract, satisfy, and retain customers. In the internal environment there are many opportunities for both conceptual and operating innovations in all areas of the firm. Conceptually, there are possibilities for improving order processing time, using analytical methods to improve the effectiveness of the advertising dollar, devising more effective methods of physical distribution, or improving the quality of market information and communication. From an operational point of view, innovative efforts can be directed toward reducing the costs involved in transportation, selling, packaging, promotion, and other areas.

Adaptation and the external environment. The three managerial activities of innovation and adaptation to and adaptation of the internal and external environments are related to one another by their common basis in the environments, the purposes of business, and the function of management. Together they point up the need for a system of environmental analysis to enable managers to function and fulfill their purposes.

While the external environment cannot be controlled by the managers of an organization, this does not imply that they must passively accept it. Managers may actively seek to influence the external environment and to adapt those of its features that are incompatible with their desired firm-environment relationship. Management likewise can adapt the firm to those environmental features it cannot change.

Environment has been used as a collective term to refer to such specific environments as: the market and competitive environment, including competitors, customers, suppliers, and creditors; the legal environment, including antitrust laws, pure food and drug laws, import duties, and labor laws; the social and cultural environment, including the political party in power, preferences of customers rooted in religious, ethnic, and geographic forces, and concerns of the public over such matters as poverty, pollution, and education; and the economic conditions prevailing at a given time, such as employment, interest rates, and inflation.

Through the various elements of the marketing mix, managers are able to influence some of the elements of the market and competitive environments. As Part three, on the uses of the elements of the marketing mix, will point out, policies for product design, price structure, channels of distribution, and promotional programs are designed to influence the customer to move away from competing products and to consume more of the products of the firm.

To influence other segments of the external environment, other approaches are used. Managers must cope with a number of legal situations, which they may feel are unduly restrictive or do not provide the desired protection. Some managers may consider antitrust laws to be too restrictive and the lack of certain import duties to be too lenient. In dealing with these types of situations, management has several options. It can violate the laws and, if successfully prosecuted, pay the fines or go to jail. Generally, this is considered to be an untenable option. A second option is to seek to bring about changes in laws considered to be either incomplete or repressive by making the appropriate overtures directly to legislative bodies and indirectly through public appeals. A third option is to influence commissions to change regulations by the systematic presentation of evidence supporting a particular viewpoint. And finally, recourse to the courts may or may not influence the environment.

If the external environment cannot be influenced and changed to meet the desires of management, perhaps the firm can be *adapted to* the environment. In dealing with consumers and competitors, failure to influence can lead to insolvency. The company may also shift its sights to another target; for example, failure to capture a national market could result in turning to an international or a regional one. Or, of course, resources can be withdrawn completely from one endeavor and shifted to another.

Adaptation to the environment may be the way to deal with laws considered to be either too open or too restrictive. If foreign competition erodes a domestic market and management cannot convince Congress of the wisdom of raising import duties, it can set up a foreign subsidiary. Alternatively, it can shift its own business from manufacturing to become an importer-distributor. When competition created a cost-prize squeeze for one company, an analysis of the situation revealed it could manufacture its very lightweight components in this country, air freight them abroad for assembly, and then ship the assembled product back. This plan works both ways; in 1972, some Japanese manufacturers of calculators considered opening assembly plants in the United States in order to reduce costs and compete in the U.S. market.

Adaptation and the internal environment. In innovation and the external environment, the emphasis is primarily on objectives and the effectiveness of managerial policies and actions in overcoming environmental resistances in order to reach those objectives. Adaptation of or to the internal environment is concerned primarily with the *efficiency* of managerial actions. The concept of efficiency in reaching goals is based upon the idea of cost *management* rather than cost *reduction*. If management is preoccupied with cost reduction, its horizons are lower and its options are fewer. While cost reduction has only one goal, cost management has at least two: cost reduction when the interests of the firm are thus best served, and selected cost increases to bring about greater profit. Thus, cost management is oriented toward profit rather than toward cost.

Any manager with authority can reduce costs merely by ordering a 10 percent cut across the board, which may reduce costs immediately but is almost guaranteed to increase them eventually. A 100 percent increase in advertising cost, however, can result in lower overall sales costs to such an extent that total marketing costs are decreased substantially. But even this extreme example does not illustrate the full power of a cost management program.

An organization that typically spends large sums on advertising does so to attract and retain customers. The company may decide to increase expenditures on product design in order to provide better customer appeal and to reduce those on advertising. Or it may decide that the opposite course would be more rewarding. This type of trade-off relationship is often considered.

The internal environment of the firm and the possibility of adapting it to changing conditions depends upon the attitudes of the managers, their aspirations as expressed in the firm's objectives, and to some extent the organizational structure within which the firm's objectives are bred, plans made, and tasks performed. Cost management decisions and trade-offs must be the result of careful analysis of the effects on *the firm as a whole*.

A great amount of analysis of the total environment, internal and external, must underlie almost any business decision. In the areas of innovation and adaptation of or to the external environment, the management functions are strategic in nature: the purpose of the firm is defined, objectives are set forth, environments are analyzed, resources are acquired, policies are determined, communication systems are established, and methods of testing and appraising effectiveness are designed.

In adaptation of or to the internal environment, the concern is with the efficiency with which the firm's resources are used. Thus, as was stated above, managers are concerned with both analysis and rationalization: they decide what to do (plan), and they do it (implement). In dealing with innovations and the external environment, management decisions are made on what to do. In doing, it is implied, the managers will do it well. Internal environmental adaptation involves doing it efficiently. Of course, analysis and planning also underlie these implementing types of activities, but here the emphasis is on the rationalization process of applying modern methods of efficiency to the resources of the firm to assure their best use.

MANAGEMENT AS A NETWORK OF HIERARCHIES

The systems approach to management involves the bringing together of a number of different parts to form a coherent entity. The two central features of the systems approach are the determination of objectives toward which these diverse parts will be directed and the development of plans by which the objectives can be reached. The statement of objectives is complicated by the fact that there are at least two levels of objectives: corporate and marketing. Objectives emerged from the concept of satisfaction, which also has two levels: managerial and consumer. The development of plans similarly involves corporate and marketing plans. These multilevel and multidimensional situations characterize the whole process of creation of a managerial system.

One of management's tasks is to sort out certain of the marketing and managerial concepts in order to identify and analyze the relationships at the several levels of the managerial hierarchy. For example, consider the following situation, which starts at a point close to the customer. A manager is told to operate an efficient physical distribution system. The physical distribution system is an integral part of the company's efforts to develop a marketing policy of good service at low cost, which, in turn, is part of a marketing plan to capture a larger percentage of the market. The plan was derived from the strategy of the firm to increase sales by a given amount in order to reach the corporate objective of a certain return on investment. This objective was set for any combination of reasons.

Somehow there must be a traceable relationship to link the objective of the firm with the project of the physical distribution manager. Management must first be able to transform that objective from a series of motives, through a series of strategies, programs, and alternative projects, to a set of procedures and rules as bases for action. Also, it must be able to establish tests of performance or audit procedures to determine the effectiveness of the project in satisfying not only corporate objectives but also consumer needs.

To build a framework for sorting out and analyzing such relationships, the concept of the hierarchy is used in the dictionary sense of a group of persons or things arranged in order of rank, grade, or class. Thus the managerial framework consists of a network of hierarchies, each of which represents one of the major components of the management process. These are the hierarchies of:

1. Aims—purpose, mission, objectives and goals.
2. Satisfactions—chief executive, employees, owners, public, consumers.
3. Objectives—corporate, functional area, individual.

4. Plans—strategic and operational, corporate and functional area.
5. Strategies—corporate and marketing.

Points 1–3 are discussed below. Discussions of points 4 and 5 are delayed until Chapter 9 when they are considered in depth.

The hierarchy of aims

An aim, a goal, or an objective is something that somebody wants to accomplish. A utility worker leaves his truck with the aim of installing a telephone. A salesman starts the year with the aim of adding 25 new customers by year's end. A manager aims to improve the effectiveness and efficiency of the sales force. A company aims to increase profits by 25 percent in the next five years. While all of these are *aims*, they differ from one another in numerous ways: degree of complexity, difficulty of formulation or attainment, effect on the organization of their attainment, the hierarchical level where they are held, and time spectrum involved, among others. Some words commonly used to identify aims are purposes, missions, objectives, and goals.

Purpose or mission. The *purpose* of the organization is at the top of the hierarchy of aims. Underlying the purposes is a set of beliefs or a creed which, for practical purposes, is a reflection of the values and attitudes of the management. It is a guide for all of the other aims at the several levels of the hierarchy because it represents not only the philosophy of the firm which will influence relationships with the public, owners, creditors, employees, and customers, but also the direction that the firm will take. The creed, or set of beliefs, serves as a basis for identifying the purpose of the organization.[6]

Some refer to the purpose of the organization as the *grand design*. Charles H. Granger referred to the grand design as "a visionary, but conscientiously-pursued, long-range concept of the enterprise." As a specific example of the grand design, he cited the philosophy attributed to Theodore Vail of A.T.&T.: "We will build a telephone system so that anybody, anywhere, can talk with anyone else, any place in the world, quickly, cheaply, and satisfactorily."[7]

The purposes of the firm blend into the *mission* in such a way that the two may be indistinguishable from one another. In fact, the purpose may be so stated that it becomes the mission. Whether the mission is separately stated is for practical purposes a matter of indifference,

---

[6] For a complete discussion of company creeds, including many illustrations of those creeds, see Stewart Thompson, *Management Creeds and Philosophies* (New York: American Management Association, 1958).

[7] Charles H. Granger, "The Hierarchy of Objectives," *Harvard Business Review*, May–June 1964, p. 66.

but it should be understood to be the means of fulfilling the firm's purpose. George Steiner said:

> Companies more and more are thinking seriously about basic mission statements because they do, in fact, direct a company's efforts. A company that says its mission is automobile production is in a much different business than one that says its business is ground transportation.[8]

One company which prefers to be unidentified and which separated its purpose and mission states its purpose as:

> To support the marketing effort of our customers everywhere through innovative strategic, managerial, and operational leadership in all facets of our industry; to improve the effectiveness of the distribution system and the efficiency of the several distribution processes.

Its mission is:

> To be in all facets of the industry necessary to fulfill our purpose and meet market requirements.

Objectives and goals. Next on the hierarchical ladder are the objectives and the goals of the firm. These two words are often used interchangeably by both businessmen and students of management, so any distinction between them is arbitrary. However, like some authors, we find it convenient to distinguish between them on the basis of the time they involve. According to Steiner, "The time dimension of an objective is long-range, as distinguished from short-range targets and goals."[9] By defining objectives as long-range concepts, we give them a higher rank in the hierarchy of aims. Mark Stern refers to the long-range concepts as goals which are attained through the objectives of marketing.[10]

The company whose purpose and mission are cited above also distinguishes between beliefs and objectives. Its objectives are based upon certain of the beliefs of company management and designed within the framework of the purposes and mission. The following are among its beliefs and objectives:

1. Belief: Our country in the future must be more involved in international intercourse than at any time in the past.

   Objective: To provide leadership in improving the effectiveness and efficiency of the international flow of goods, services, and ideas.

---

[8] Steiner, *Top Management Planning*, p. 143.

[9] Ibid., p. 150.

[10] Mark E. Stern, *Marketing Planning: A Systems Approach* (New York: McGraw-Hill Book Company, Inc., 1966), p. xi.

2. Belief: Companies in our industry have not been as diligent in supporting the marketing effort of their customers as we think is desirable and profitable.

   Objective: To be a marketing support system and consider ourselves as extensions of our customers' managerial group.

3. Belief: Change is the only constant in the economic environment.

   Objective: To be an agent of effective change in our sphere of operations.

These and another dozen objectives are followed by statements discussing their implications to managers, other employees, customers, and the company. The implications are designed to serve as bases for making some of the philosophical objectives operational.

The hierarchy of satisfactions

The hierarchy of satisfactions is concerned with forces which cause a set of objectives to be articulated. We leave to the psychologist the task of analyzing those forces that drive people to do certain things and content ourselves with saying that people have needs they seek to satisfy.[11]

Chief executive. Objectives of an organization do not just materialize; they are the reflection of somebody's wants or needs. Since the chief executive of a firm is responsible for the direction the firm takes, both his mark and his seal of approval are on the firm's objectives. The objectives are a reflection of the executive's needs and wants, but it is neither fair nor accurate to consider them a perfect reflection. Compromises of all sorts have to be made with reality, and his final objectives reflect these compromises. While attainment of these objectives will not bring him the perfect satisfaction he might like, it will bring him as much as he can reasonably expect.

Employees and other managers. A second group of satisfactions in the hierarchy serves the needs of other managers and employees. The objectives of the firm as ultimately stated reflect compromises with this group, which has its own aspirations. The compromise may be necessary because of either covert or overt situations. Covert situations may arise from such things as executive or employee morale, and overt situations may involve the demands of influential vice presidents or employee representatives. Both types can result in modification of objectives.

---

[11] See for example Abraham H. Maslow, "A Dynamic Theory of Human Motivation," *Psychological Review*, March 1943, pp. 370–96. See also Douglas M. McGregor, "The Human Side of Enterprise," in Douglas M. McGregor, ed., *The Essays of Douglas McGregor* (Cambridge, Mass.: MIT Press, 1966).

Owners and creditors.   The stockholders and creditors are a third group whose interests must be satisfied and therefore become a part of the hierarchy of satisfactions. Their wants and needs may suggest another compromise with the basic objectives of the chief executive. For example, while one of his objectives might be a given growth rate financed by retained earnings, equity, and debt, he may have to settle for a slower growth rate, and pay dividends and establish sinking funds in order to satisfy owners.

Public.   Another group of satisfactions in the hierarchy are those sought by the public. The public can require a "good citizen" type of objective to take certain directions, or it can otherwise restrict the freedom of action of management in setting its objectives. An example of the good citizen situation is the expected contributions of executive time and corporate resources in such public endeavors as charity drives or community task forces.

Consumers.   Perhaps the most important component of the hierarchy of satisfactions concerns the consumer. While the wants and needs and satisfactions required by other groups may modify the major objectives of the chief executive, they nevertheless are cast in terms of consumer satisfaction. Attending to the many dimensions of consumer satisfaction is probably the most difficult task management has. Chapter 8 provides detailed consideration of the multistep consumer satisfaction process.

The hierarchy of objectives

To evaluate specific decisions of management properly, it is necessary to know the context within which they are made. A pricing policy, a promotion policy, or any other policy may be good under one set of circumstances and bad under another. Generally, the decision must be evaluated in light of the objective sought. This is one reason so much attention is focused in this book on objectives and the planning of how to reach them.

Focus of objectives.   The definition of management above differentiated two sets of activities requiring decisions: Level 1, concerned with management of the entire organization and largely devoted to analysis, and Level 2, concerned with management of a functional or support group and largely devoted to rationalization. Similarly, there are two levels of objectives: Level 1 for the firm as a whole, and Level 2 for the functional area—marketing. (Further levels of objectives such as Level 3, promotion, a subset of marketing, and Level 4, advertising copy, a subset of promotion, will not be discussed here.) Thus, objectives are stated at several levels in the organization.

While the major activities of Level 1 involve analysis and those of Level 2 involve different types of analyses which lead to rationalization, analysis or rationalization is not the exclusive property of either, for both steps are involved at both levels. In the first stages of the development of objectives all appropriate aspects of the environment—external and internal—must be considered in arriving at tentatively feasible objectives. In Level 1, a given opportunity is analyzed in light of the present and future economic, social, technological, and political environments. If the objective passes these analyses, the Level 2 group tests alternative means of feasibly attaining it. The thrust of Level 1 environmental analysis is environmental compatibility between the objective and the environment. The double thrust of Level 2 analysis is the feasibility of the objective and the best or alternative means of reaching it.

Development of objectives

We have noted that the basic objectives reflect the chief executive's search for satisfaction and self-fulfillment within the constraints of consumer satisfaction. There may be a number of motives underlying his objectives: to earn a larger bonus, to show up his predecessor, to get written up in *Fortune,* or to make a personal fortune. He may also be motivated to enhance either the value of the company as an acquisition or the value of the stock in acquiring other companies. All of these may be regarded as ends to be attained by objectives or as motives for setting objectives. But they do not give direction to the firm or serve as guidelines for managers in integrating the several parts of the firm into a system.

Most of the basic objectives of the firm will originate at Level 1, because at this level the managers are concerned with the purpose of the firm and its long-run future. However, managers at Level 2 may discover opportunities for the firm and transmit them upward, where they may be transformed into objectives. Wherever objectives originate, before they are made final there is a substantial amount of analysis at both levels. There are a number of reasons for this interaction between levels, which will be discussed later. For now, we will merely say that they include the need for determining whether objectives are feasible and whether they are in conflict with one another.

SUMMARY AND CONCLUSIONS

In order to sharpen your perspective of what business is all about, the first part of this chapter was devoted to an analysis of some fundamental concepts of management. The rather offbeat statement that a business is created to bring satisfaction to its owners or managers was used for two very fundamental reasons. First, to say that profit is *the* reason people start or manage businesses is not only wrong, it also reflects a view so narrow that it does not accommodate the many reasons people are in business. Second, the concept of satisfaction as we have used it demonstrates the importance of objectives of different kinds in the managerial process.

Marketing was established as the function of business because it is through the creation and retention of satisfied customers that the firm can exist and managerial satisfactions can be realized. Recognition of the primacy of marketing as a vehicle for attainment of these satisfactions points up the significance of marketing-oriented objectives.

We do not believe that traditional definitions of management provide an adequate foundation for the management of change, or allow for its primary ingredient: the discovery of problems and opportunities. In our concept, management first decides that something must be done—a recognition of the importance of change. Then management decides what to do—a recognition of the importance of setting objectives to attain the desired satisfactions. Whatever management decides to do is followed by the doing of it, and doing it well. Thus (1) attainment of objectives is another of the managerial roles and (2) systems are necessary to control and measure the efficiency of work performed to attain the objectives are established.

Our definition of management embraces these three steps. Dale D. McConkey points out that the Association of Consulting Management Engineers concluded in 1968 that management is comprised of three steps: (1) establishing objectives, (2) directing the attainment of them, and (3) measuring results.[12] McConkey feels this approach renders obsolete definitions of management which include such phrases as "getting things done through people by planning, organizing, directing, and controlling." He further states that these functions are properly considered as subfunctions of the three larger steps.

The hierarchical relationship among aims, satisfactions, and objectives illustrates several points. First, it emphasizes the setting of objectives, their attainment, and their measurement as the things managers do. Second, it emphasizes that these things are done through people and that the processes are planning, organizing, directing, and controlling, which are subfunctions of the things managers do. Third, it emphasizes that the hierarchy of objectives is derived from the managerial drive for personal satisfactions, which, in turn, is modified by the realities of marketing and the need to satisfy the consumer.

There are several identifiable conclusions resulting from this hierarchical arrangement. One is that the desires of managers form the basis for the creed of the firm, or those things the firm believes in. In turn,

---

[12] Dale D. McConkey, "MBO—Twenty Years Later, Where Do We Stand?" *Business Horizons*, August 1973, p. 27. The following discussion is based in part upon Professor McConkey's comments.

the creed establishes the character of the firm. Third, the purpose or mission establishes where the firm is going. Fourth, the objectives identify the direction the firm will take or the means to be used to accomplish the end, and the direction the several departments will take. Fifth, policies provide guidelines for managers in establishing programs and projects to attain the objectives.

The interrelations of the managerial hierarchy can be compared to the operation of an automobile. Remove a spark plug lead, give an improper mixture to the fuel, let air out of a tire, distort the linkage in the steering, or remove the brake fluid, and the car will continue to function, although inefficiently. The firm can continue to function even if certain of its parts are out of balance. But the car can be brought to a stop by removing the oil, the carburetor, or the left front wheel. In the same way, the whole hierarchy can be made to tumble by getting certain parts out of balance such as sales and costs, cash receipts, and cash payments.

chapter 4 | # Planning in the marketing-oriented firm

Planning in perspective
   An ancient art modernized
Managing and planning
   Traditional and modern approach
   Planning premises
   Types of premises
Managers and planning
   Managerial participation
Management of planning
Planning and plans
Philosophies of planning
   Satisficing
   Optimizing
   Adaptivizing
Approaches to planning
   Outside-in approach
   Inside-out approach
Steps in planning
Conclusion

This section is concerned with the nature of planning and introduces the first step in the planning process. First we take a look at planning in perspective. Then we examine the general relationship between the acts of managing and planning, and between managers and planning. After a brief look at the management of planning, we go on to discuss some philosophies of planning and approaches to planning.

PLANNING IN PERSPECTIVE

One constant that has been with us since the beginning of time is change. One certainty that we can *always* count on is the uncertainty surrounding change, and risk is one element that is *never* absent from change. The impact of change can be managed better if it is anticipated.

There are two basic aspects of planning, and both are related to the inevitability of change. In the first place, since marketing managers know that there will be changes in such things as, technology, advertising media, and the like, they also know that these changes will affect their decisions. Such knowledge should trigger a strong effort on the part of the manager to anticipate the kinds of changes, to estimate the effects of change on his ability to achieve his objectives, and to make preliminary plans of action should particular changes take place. This is the kind of planning with which we are most familiar. And it is essential that you study very carefully the logic of anticipating change and preparing for it in advance.

A second aspect of planning is innovation. A firm can influence the direction of change. It has been suggested by marketing executives that one facet of their firms' planning is directed toward determining what they want to happen and setting about to make it happen. In this sense planning is the key to the discovery of opportunities and problems. When a firm decides to alter traditional distribution channels and sets down an orderly process to alter the channel, it is planning for and managing change.

In both cases planning is an active process. In short, much change is predictable if one will "read the signs," and anticipation of change can influence the impact of it by putting the manager in position to react appropriately. Reacting to change is not inherently bad. In fact, it may be good. The only time we would call it bad is when managers who could have seen the change coming didn't even bother to look for it.

An ancient art modernized

Planning has always existed in one form or another, going under various names. If the good guys did it in history, they were great planners; if the bad guys did it they were engaging in intrigue or plotting; if the good-bad guys did it (con men, defalcators, embezzlers) they were scheming. It is all planning.

David Ewing has several interesting things to say about the development of planning, from the days when it was an individual or small group matter through the point when it became a device for leadership and management of organized society, until today.[1] Not only has the concept changed by assuming complexities and subleties it never had before, but, equally important, its connotations as a management tool have changed. Once it was a "useful extra" for leaders wanting to bring about change. Ewing states:

---

[1] David W. Ewing, *The Human Side of Planning* (London: The Macmillan Company, 1969), p. 3.

More often than not, organizations succeeded without it. Today this is no longer so. We seem to be fast approaching a point at which the very fate of corporations, cities . . . will depend upon their leaders' willingness and ability to plan.[2]

This greatly expanded role of planning is attributed to the fact that big organizations such as governments, labor, business, and agriculture have become externally interdependent, while their parts have become internally interdependent.

Another new thing about planning is that more and more companies and other organizations are doing it. Ewing reports the results of several studies made in 1967. For example, a *Business Week* study showed that 71 percent of respondents did long-range planning, many having established their systems during the preceding few years. A National Planning Association study showed 85 percent of the respondents were preparing long-term plans. However, well over half of them started work about 1960.[3] So while planning is an ancient art, its widespread use as a tool to assist in creating operational and organizational change is fairly new. This is of such significance that several managerial approaches to change and planning bear summing up:

1. *Let change take place and then plan to react to it.* This cannot even be called planning. It is oriented to the solution of problems after they have arrived or have become evident. This is the "putting out the fire" approach in which managers are in effect managed by change.

2. *Identify possible or probable changes and prepare plans to avoid, hasten, adapt, or live with them.* This type of planning is designed to recognize potential problems and head them off. It is acceptable as a passive adaptation to change, though it is largely oriented to the solution of problems after they become apparent. This is the "fire-prevention" approach and is one facet of managing change.

3. *Identify those changes that are wanted and plan to make them happen.* This is the other facet of management of change, and it involves an active, creative approach to environmental analysis and adjustment. The first two approaches are solution-oriented, while this approach is oriented first toward the discovery process and then to the solution process. In contrast to the military search and destroy mission, the mission of this approach is to "search and create."

MANAGING AND PLANNING

Traditional and modern approaches

One executive illustrated in a single sentence both the traditional and modern bases for marketing planning when he said that his company

---

[2] Ibid., p. 4.

[3] Ibid., p. 5.

had shifted its emphasis from the traditional approach of planning for "what should happen" to planning "what do we do to make happen those things we want to have happen?"[4] In the broader context of management as a whole, Peter Drucker has said: ". . . and managing is not just passive, adaptive behavior; it means taking action to make the *desired* results come to pass."[5] Both of these observations illustrate a way of looking at the future and planning for it. Both in effect say that managers should *design* the future of their companies and develop a program consistent with that design. The antithesis of that modern context is the traditional approach by which managers seek to *predict* what the future holds and develop programs to accommodate the expected future. In the one case, managers take an active role in attempting to adjust their environments in order to make happen what they want to have happen. In the other case, they passively react to what appears to be "in the cards" and adjust their firms to the expected environments.

Planning premises

One part of our definition of management emphasized a two-stage notion of management: (1) deciding to do something; and (2) doing it. The first stage rests on analysis, and is or should be carried on at Level 1 in the organizational hierarchy. The second stage is implementation which involves the action or implementation arts and skills of managers at Level 2. This phase also rests upon an analytical base.

Whether the specific decisions of the marketing manager and the staff concern such complex subjects as pricing and new product strategy or whether they concern such subjects as recruiting of college graduates and frequency of sales calls, they are made within a broad framework established by the corporate planning process. The action or implementation programs are derived from the analytical phase. In this sense, the entire process is a continuum beginning with analysis for planning and ending with evaluation of results. For example, as was discussed in Chapter 3, planning is based upon a number of interactions between Level 1 and Level 2 managers, staff, and operating personnel.

Basic to the planning process is the development of a set of planning premises, or assumptions concerning what is expected to happen in the company's internal and external environments—"other things remaining the same." These premises are derived from an estimate of the impact on the firm of expected future occurrences in the economic, social, and

[4] Norman Judelson, manager of sales and distribution planning of American Standard, as quoted in Ernest C. Miller, *Marketing Planning* (New York: American Management Association, Inc., 1967), p. 89.

[5] Peter Drucker, *The Practice of Management* (New York: Harper and Row, 1954), p. 11. Emphasis added.

political environments. The direction, magnitude, scope, and impact of the projected future occurrences are made in a variety of ways ranging from economic and technological forecasts to educated guesses. The planning premises based upon these estimates may also be the result of careful analyses which compare alternatives. Right or wrong, non-quantifiable subjective forces often enter the picture such as: "I've got a 'gut-feeling' about that"; "History repeats itself"; "We've always done it this way"; "This is what the boss wants to do."

There is more seriousness than frivolity underlying these statements. Management is very much an art, and the "gut-feeling" is an expressive way of saying that the sum total of a manager's experience leads him to a given conclusion. It should also be remembered that some of our more esoteric forms of mathematical analysis are based upon assumptions which may be derived from the analyst's own gut-feeling for the proper equation to use.

Writing in a similar vein, David Ewing said:

> One of the most tragic illusions in planning is that "hard facts" alone can determine what goals and courses of action should be taken. Again and again we hear statements such as "The company's peculiar strengths and weaknesses determine its optimum strategy." This is nonsense.[6]

There are two reasons for calling the notion nonsense. First, an analysis does not decide a strategy, people do. Second, people's values and attitudes influence their interpretation of information.

We can cite a classic example of management based on "gut-feeling" and on the notion that history repeats itself. After World War II many people predicted a new depression. The head of Montgomery Ward expected it annually for a number of years; so he caused his company to hold cash waiting for a time when prices would fall to a "sensible" level, at which time the company would embark on a major building program.

This set of premises—that is, of assumptions about future economic, social, political, and other environmental influences—is the take-off point for the development of objectives and plans to reach those objectives. While we have said that developing premises is the first step in planning, it should be recognized that it is a continuing step, as are almost all other steps in planning. In developing the planning premises, it may become necessary to choose among alternative premises. Further, after initial premises are made and work begins on objectives designed to make happen what the firm wants to have happen, additional premises may be necessary.

---

[6] David W. Ewing, *The Practice of Planning* (New York: Harper and Row, 1968), p. 81.

Types of premises

George Steiner says that there are many ways of classifying premises: environmental versus internal,[7] important versus unimportant, certainty versus uncertainty, procedural versus substantive, personal versus impersonal, and so on. He has developed a fivefold classification of premises to illustrate their purposes and to define what he calls the network of premises.

Implied premises are present in probably every planning process. Some of them were mentioned above in connection with the gut-feeling or the powerful boss syndromes. *High-impact premises* are those which have a major effect on planning. They can arise from almost any source and take a variety of shapes. The government may offer inducements to, or propose restrictions on, a firm regarding its location. The boss may set constraints. The marketing manager may also have a set of biases. *Low impact premises,* on the other hand, are those which should be recognized as a potential force. Steiner illustrates this by reference to a candy manufacturer who may recognize long-term GNP growth but not accord it more than a possible low impact. *Analytical premises* refer to those made as a result of either superficial or penetrating analyses. They may be the results of comparisons of alternatives, or perhaps of cause-and-effect relationships. *Procedural premises* may establish constraints which are fundamental to both the planning process and to the end result. One type of procedural premise may relate to company policies, such as: no dilution of owner's equity, or marketing only through established wholesalers. Another type may be to facilitate the planning process, such as: growth of the market will be at 10 percent per year, or wages will rise at 15 percent per year.

MANAGERS AND PLANNING

Managerial participation

Probably the most important requisite of strategic planning is that it have the participating support of the managerial hierarchy. However good or bad the premises of planning may be, however complete the necessary information, however competent the technical planning staff, a well-thought-out program cannot be developed without the active participation of the heads of important areas of the firm. Further, without their belief in the values of not only the actual process of planning but also of the objectives and programs growing out of the process,

---

[7] George A. Steiner, *Top Management Planning* (London: The Macmillan Company, 1969), pp. 199–200. We have used environment in both the external and internal senses. Steiner, among others, generally uses the word to refer to external influences.

the whole thing can become an exercise in futility. "At many companies, almost every executive—from staff to line operating head—is expected to get involved in the planning action."[8]

We have never seen a list of the duties of managers that did not include planning as one of the major categories. By the same token we have never seen a book or article on planning which did not state in one way or another that one of the serious problems surrounding the activity is the neutral, negative, or mistaken attitudes of managers. Also, experienced planners who are recognized authorities place the burden of planning on the chief executive. Steiner, for example, has said:

> I have clearly identified the overriding responsibility of the chief executive for corporate planning. But surveys of planning problems that I have seen, as well as my own observations, point to the fact that an insufficient commitment to planning by top management is far too prevalent.[9]

The major functions which demand his involvement are the establishing of objectives and the provision of overall leadership in the planning process. Even so, the literature is full of illustrations which show that many chief executives believe that corporate planning is not a function with which they should be directly concerned. They feel that it is a function to be delegated to subordinates. Worse yet, some even act as if planning and policymaking are functions of *ad hoc* committees of managers.

As for the subordinate heads of the functional areas, many of them take a dim view of the planning process for several reasons. First, it takes them away from their duties of managing the day-to-day activities of the firm. Second, many of them got where they are because they were good in their fields; the good sales manager who becomes a marketing manager may be very good in the decision-making aspect of management *of* the marketing function but be disinterested in planning. Also, the farther away his activities take him from management *of* the function and the closer to management *and* the marketing function, the less interested in planning he may become. And then third, there may be very little in their backgrounds which prepared them for the very different types of thinking required for planning and for decision making.

In short, the distinction between line and staff activities inhibits thinking about planning. The performance of these planning activities and the general change in the scope of overall managerial functions at least

---

[8] "The Return of the Long-Range Planner," *Dun's*, July 1974, p. 87.

[9] Steiner, *Top Management Planning*, p. 90.

partially explain why Ewing says: ". . . in modern organizations it is often difficult to make neat distinctions between 'line' and 'staff.' "[10]

MANAGEMENT OF PLANNING

Like any other efficiently managed function, the planning function must be organized. In a growing number of firms central planning units have been organized to *manage* the planning process. Referring to the rapid growth of planning departments as a new sort of population explosion, one writer in 1967 reported that the number of these departments had been doubling every three years over the previous decade, ". . . and the end is nowhere in sight."[11]

What does a planning department do if it doesn't do planning? It sees that the planning process proceeds in an orderly way and it helps management shape objectives and derive strategies. It is ordinarily a part of top management, often with the title of vice president for its head, and reports to the chief executive. The planning department also makes economic forecasts, analyses of markets, and in general provides technical support and analytical services to line executives functioning in their planning capacity. The planning staff may consist of a variety of professional types, depending upon the nature of the company and the role of the planning department, but they will include economists, management theorists, management scientists, and other technical support people as needed. Finally, the planning department helps sell the planning concept and process to the other managers of the firm. In short, it makes analyses to assist line managers in planning and smooths the way for the process to take place. It also suggests areas of planning.

What does the planning department *not* do? We've already said that it doesn't do planning. Ackoff said that if the planning unit prepares plans and submits them for approval, in most cases this is the kiss of death. He added:

> The probability of success of a planning effort decreases as the organizational autonomy of the planning activity increases. Such autonomy ensures the noninvolvement of line managers and often of executives as well.[12]

What about the future of planning departments? The inevitability of change applies to the planning function as well as to any other function. As instruments of change—if not architects of change—planning

---

[10] Ewing, *The Human Side of Planning*, p. 176.

[11] Richard F. Vancil, "—So You're Going To Have a Planning Department," *Harvard Business Review*, May–June 1967, p. 88.

[12] Russell L. Ackoff, *A Concept of Corporate Planning* (New York: Wiley Interscience, 1970), p. 129.

groups should be concerned with the management of change. George Steiner has suggested that several notable changes will occur in the role of the planner by 1980.[13] The areas in which change is predicted to take place are:

1. The planner will have more of a role in decision making. Since the chief executive and other top managers spend such a great amount of their time planning, it is almost inevitable that the planning function and the top planner will have a greater influence on decisions. In many instances this is already the case.

2. Greater emphasis will be placed on environmental matters. In this context the total environment includes such matters as competitive relations, international affairs, and technological developments. In short, any aspect of the external environment which will have an impact upon the management of change will be of concern, because the major opportunities and threats both lie in that portion of the environment.

3. Splitting of the functions of planning. As the role of planning in decision making expands, the line-staff relationship in planning may emerge from the one large function. In the functional areas the distinct line-staff activities are becoming blurred. In the planning function they will probably emerge and develop into something of a blurred form. In other words, the line-staff relationship of the planning function and the other functions appear to be moving toward one another from opposite poles. The function splitting will probably center on (1) strategic planning, and (2) operational planning. It may even extend to a third area of task planning.

4. Planners will be more concerned with guiding change. Like the function splitting, this is clearly predictable from present trends. A large part of our previous discussion of the management of change was centered on this subject.

While Steiner was writing in 1970 about the planner of the 1980s, planning was already in an evolutionary stage. The focus of long-range planners is on 5, 10, 15 years into the future. Many were considered expendable when the recession hit. In 1975 firms began hiring planners again, but assigning them different functions. "Only this time around the much sought-after planner is being asked to turn his sights from the long range to the near term."[14]

The disenchantment of business with planning and planners was probably caused in part by the *bad management of planning*. First the planner was concerned too much with the *process* of planning instead of the results. Second, too many planners and their superiors apparently misconstrued their role. They apparently *made* plans instead of *facilitat-*

---

[13] Steiner, "Rise of the Corporate Planner," *Harvard Business Review*, September–October 1970, pp. 136–39.

[14] "The Return of the Long-Range Planner," p. 87.

ing the making of plans by the responsible executives. There is more than a bit of irony in the new short-term assignment of planners. There is even a great amount of incongruity involved. The previously cited *Dun's* article says,

> Ironically, what has brought the planners back are the crunching corporate problems that many long-range planners could not foresee as little as five years ago: the energy crisis, the raw-material shortage, even gold price fluctuations and 12 percent money.[15]

The irony and incongruity is that planners are being assigned "company problems right around the corner" instead of the "crunching" problems down the next block. If it is a fact that many did not foresee the energy problems, raw material shortages, gold price fluctuations, and 12 percent prime interest rates, it was because the planners were blind and were bad planners. It was not the fault of planning, for even the most superficial 1970 analysis of the future would have disclosed impending shortages. The timing may not have been predictable, but the fact of shortage was. We cannot argue with the statement that many did not foresee the problems cited. We can say that if they didn't they were not reading popular magazines, business magazines, reports from university research projects, government bulletins, and newspapers which expressed great concern for those very things. Even in the summer of 1975 these same types of shortages, but substantially more severe ones, seem a serious threat for the 1975–1985 decade unless we take drastic action to counter them. Yet with planners being assigned problems "right around the corner" business will not be prepared to counter them or to face up to them. Then the pendulum will swing again.

PLANNING AND PLANS

Wine, meat, vegetables, salad, dessert; silver, linens, crystal; background music, dim light, atmosphere—all are brought together for an assembled group. The setting may be for a meeting of the gourmet society; on the other hand it may be in an alley behind a restaurant awaiting the arrival of the sanitation truck. It all depends on how the contents were assembled.

Because the meeting is called a Planning Meeting, that does not mean it will produce anything other than garbage. The process of planning has to be an orderly process. The mere process itself can produce favorable results by causing managers to think in a reasonably orderly fashion about the business, its future, and its problems. In addition, overall managerial quality will be improved, partly because the participants

---

[15] Ibid.

have worked together in a common cause. Both the conflict and the cooperation involved in the process can have a salutary effect on the participants.

If the process of planning is well designed, it will result in plans, even though they may not be written. The process implies a "rigorous obligation to come to a specific action to be taken today. Planning without plans is a waste of time. Some managers who reject the value of planning have been guilty of precisely this sin."[16] They have produced garbage because the meeting was a brawl instead of an orderly process.

It should be emphasized that there may be more than one type of process of planning. In the early 60s Stewart Thompson reported an interview with the chief executive of a fast-growing company who was asked if he did planning:

> If you are asking me, "Do you do a lot of planning?" my answer is "yes." If you are asking me whether we print a number of papers about it, headed Planning, the answer is "no."
>
> I am engaged in planning, 12 hours a day, every day. . . . We do not have a formal ritual for planning. But, believe me, our planning gets an enormous amount of attention, continuous attention, even though it is not formalized.[17]

Apparently the unstructured process used in this case was different from other processes. Approaches to the process may also be different. Perhaps it is more appropriate to say that different processes have different phases. For example, one phase of the process may be completely unstructured "brainstorming" sessions where the subject may be problems, opportunities, objectives, or any other subject reasonably relevant.

Still another approach or phase of the process may consist of a series of meetings held to identify problems, not to answer questions or solve problems. Ewing reports one such situation where weekly meetings of the chief and five subordinates were held. Brief oral reports were expected to identify problems with efforts to solve them deferred for other meetings. The executives were asked to go through the same process with their subordinates.[18]

Finally, the existence of written plans does not mean that the plans are good. They may be well thought out, but so vaguely written that they lack the necessary precision and mean different things to various people. Written plans are not necessarily good if they are poorly written or if they are well written but with a poor underlying foundation.

[16] Steiner, *Top Management Planning*, p. 8.

[17] Stewart Thompson, *How Companies Plan* (New York: American Management Association, 1962), p. 49. Quoted in David W. Ewing, "Corporate Planning at a Crossroads," *Harvard Business Review*, July–August 1967, p. 79.

[18] Ewing, *The Human Side of Planning*, pp. 185–86.

PHILOSOPHIES OF PLANNING

The following discussion of the philosophies of planning uses both a framework designed by Russell L. Ackoff and his nomenclature.[19] His framework consists of three points of view which he calls *satisficing, optimizing,* and *adaptivizing.* Also, the framework and nomenclature of David Ewing are used.[20] Ewing refers to the approaches to choosing goals as the *outside-in* and *inside-out* approaches. Both the Ackoff and Ewing frameworks have significant implications for the marketing manager in search of new marketing opportunities.

Satisficing

The term satisficing was coined by Herbert A. Simon to designate efforts to attain some level of satisfaction, but not necessarily to exceed it. In other words, it is the level of attainment one is willing to settle for. Ackoff says that this is the most prevalent type of planning.

Apparent characteristics of the satisficer. By and large the satisficing type of planner appears to be a don't-rock-the-boat type who applies the art of the possible to planning. If changes are minor and if they don't make waves, they are more feasible than the other type. Of course, feasibility in this sense refers to acceptance by the group.

The correction of generally accepted deficiencies of the present situation is of greater concern to the satisficer than searching out opportunities for the future. Satisficing planners tend to avoid the future, except to accommodate those things which are going to happen. Since their forecasts are usually limited, they deal with expansions or contractions of the market and thus are concerned with money. They avoid organizational changes because of the effects of such changes. Also, because of their *now* orientation, satisficers don't realize such changes may be desirable; so they seldom have to avoid them.

Characteristics of satisficing plans. The objectives set in a satisficing plan are usually those considered attainable, without too much boat-rocking, and desirable. They are formulated in terms that are easily understood because they are quantitative—a percentage increase in earnings or in return on investment. Alternatively, meaningless or harmless qualitative terms are frequently used—such phrases as "good service at low cost," "good employee relations," or "a day's pay for a day's work." It is quite common for satisficers to set simple goals and to give no thought to whether conflict among them exists or to the resolution of such conflict.[21]

---

[19] Ackoff, *A Concept of Corporate Planning,* pp. 6–22.
[20] Ewing, *The Practice of Planning,* pp. 32–75.
[21] Ackoff, *A Concept of Corporate Planning,* p. 7.

Evaluation. A deficiency of satisficing is that it seldom adds anything to the understanding of the system or of the planning process. Only available knowledge is used, and accordingly it requires less time, money, and brains. It is hard to refute the argument that "profits are increasing each year, so we must be doing something right." Also, it is hard to object to the logic that it is better to produce a feasible plan that is not optimal than an optimal plan that is not feasible.

There are several possible explanations for the satisficing type of planning and its apparent prevalence. First, most companies are accustomed to the budgeting process. Accordingly, they attempt to develop a planning program out of the familiar budgeting process. We can't be too critical of using a familiar concept as a vehicle to pierce the unknown. The first locomotives and automobiles were wagons and carriages with engines replacing animals. The first airplanes were motorcycles and autos with a few adjustments. Since technological innovations frequently begin with modification of the old, perhaps we should expect conceptual innovations to have similar antecedents.

The second reason why satisficing planning is so frequently used is that the resources available to the firm may make unfeasible any other approach at a given time. It is easy for the critic to say that the company can't afford *not* to plan the way it *should*. Some students reading this book know they are "wasting" their time working at more or less menial jobs and going to school part-time. They should quit work and increase their academic load in order to get out of school faster and increase their earning power. They will make more money in two months after graduation than they now make in a year of part-time work. There is only one "minor" problem: they can't afford this neat solution, so they do what is *feasible* rather than what is best. In this case what is feasible is also best.

Optimizing

Where satisficing planning is based on the idea of doing well enough to be satisfied, the idea underlying optimizing is that one should be satisfied only when the job is done as well as possible. The development of the expanding concept of management science is what has made optimizing planning at least partially possible. Optimizing cannot become *fully* possible until methods are developed for optimizing nonquantifiable variables.

Characteristics of the optimizer. While the satisficer primarily emphasizes financial resources, the optimizer tries to consider all resources in an attempt to rationalize the system or that part of the quantifiable system with which he can deal. In this context the optimizer has three basic alternatives: (1) to seek the best balance between costs and benefits; (2) to attain a target performance level with minimum resources; or (3) to maximize performance with available resources.

These alternatives tell us something about the approach of the optimizers. For one thing, as already implied, they attempt to transform objectives into quantifiable terms and ignore those they cannot quantify. One can imagine the frustrations in trying to quantify the early mission of A.T.&T.: "We will build a telephone system so that anybody, anywhere, can talk with anyone else, any place in the world, quickly, cheaply, and satisfactorily."

Second, they approach their work mathematically, and try to develop the best programs possible as well as the best policies underlying those programs and the procedures for program implementation. Third, they go further than just to design the program; they also design systems to control programs.

Characteristics of optimizing plans.   The output of the planning process is likely to be a set of resource allocation programs which are developed and portrayed with mathematical precision, subject, of course, to the availability of information. They are also likely to be stated in very definite terms, appraising alternative decisions affecting such things as advertising media schedules, size of sales force, design of distribution systems, location of fixed facilities, make or buy decisions, and the timing of replacement of equipment.

Evaluation.   The optimizing process can be a very positive force with positive results in areas where information is available and lends itself to mathematical analysis. On the other hand, there is a gray area where the process cannot be used definitively, but where it can be used helpfully. For example, one can definitively establish a "best" location for a warehouse, but in dealing with the term "good service at low cost," the optimizers can only be helpful. They can identify the cost of providing service of different quality standards. They can even help identify the effects of varying qualities of service. But their tools cannot say which quality of service is the *best* for the firm.

One of the difficult things about the optimizing function is the perversity of problems. Very often, they will not fit the techniques available to solve them. Ackoff says that the best that can be done is to optimize complex structures relative to very simple problems or simple structures relative to complex problems, but we can't optimize complex structures relative to complex problems.[22]

The optimization techniques are useful in the tactical aspects of planning—that is, in the rationalizing activities of management. They are very good at the solution of problems that fit the techniques available, but they do very little to assist in the processes of discovering problems

---

[22] Ibid, p. 13.

and opportunities. In this sense their usefulness in the management of change is somewhat limited to improving the use of resources.

However, the act of improving the allocation of resources or of quantifying their present productivity may stimulate the discovery process by pointing the way toward new opportunities or toward the discovery of otherwise hidden problems. One of the failures of the optimizers is that while they can design systems to establish expectations and set up controls to monitor their attainment, they cannot determine when the system has failed to exploit the unexpected.

In summary, optimizing planning can deal effectively only with those parts of the system which lend themselves to quantification. The development of the strategic plan that requires handling of *qualitative* variables must meld the quantitative with the qualitative, which is one of the many facets of the art of management.

Adaptivizing

Ackoff reports that adaptivizing planning is often referred to as innovative planning.[23] It is an approach which attempts to place the organization in a better position to deal with the future. Those features of the environment which are almost certain to develop can be dealt with by *commitment* planning. When we cannot pinpoint the characteristics of the future environment, but can identify possible and even probable directions it will take, the appropriate step is to develop *contingency* plans. Finally, *responsiveness* planning is called for when there are aspects of the future which cannot be anticipated either as to their nature, their direction, or their timing.

Commitment planning. There are some things about the future that one just "knows" will develop. Forces have been set in motion, and barring a cataclysm, certain things will result. Counterforces may be developed which will neutralize those forces to prevent the same result from continuously recurring. For example, if the gates of a dam are opened, forces have been set in motion, the results of which will have to be coped with downstream for an extended period. The people downstream know the water is coming, unless something very unexpected happens. The water will continue to flow for a time after the original forces have dissipated—after the gates are closed. These are the "inevitable" developments about which we can be virtually certain.

One of these inevitable developments that was accurately predicted dealt with the population structure following World War II, specifically, the 1946 and subsequent baby crops. A whole chain of marketers has for about 30 years reaped benefits from the inevitable arrival of a huge market. And that chain continues down the road for another 50 or more

---
[23] Ibid., p. 15.

years. The first marketers of nurseries, diapers, and baby food may have been caught off guard, but those producing schoolrooms, station wagons, and yard swings were ready. On down the road the chain of marketers anticipated the arrival of the teenagers, college students, and young marrieds. That group is still being eyed for its impact on the nursing home market several decades away; so the chain extends from nurseries to nursing homes.

A bit of imagination is all that is needed to see the inevitability of demand and the need for commitment planning to accommodate that demand as it arrives. Whatever forces we may have set in action or which may be set in action will not stop that flow. Figuratively speaking, we may close the gates of the dam, but that won't stop the water already flowing.

There are a number of other forces visible today which are going to bring about certain "inevitable" results which commitment planning can accommodate. We need not look beyond population-related phenomena to see some of their inevitabilities. For example, the rate of increase in new home construction for new families will diminish because of fewer family formations. Also, the rate of increase for replacement homes will rise because of changing life styles demanding different kinds of housing (such as apartment and permanently located mobile homes), destruction of substandard housing for the poor, and upgrading of living quarters as affluence improves. There will be increased demand for leisure time and leisure-time activities and associated products (such as vacation resorts, campers, fishing poles, and mosquito spray). Demand for cleaner air, water, and land will rise, which, in turn, opens new markets for pollution control units, waste disposal facilities, and recycling equipment.

These and other visible things show the inevitability of certain types of events and indicate the role of commitment planning. While we *know* these things are going to take place and we know the general direction in which they will move, there is uncertainty as to the specific characteristics which lead to contingency planning and even to responsiveness planning.

Contingency planning. While new housing for new families may slow down, it is virtually certain that new housing for the replacement market will increase. But we are not sure of the nature of that housing. The marketing program of the manufacturer of building materials such as bathtubs, molding, and windows becomes a case in point. Does he assume that housing of the future will follow the patterns of the past? If so, perhaps his channels of distribution are adequate to deal with the marketing of the future. There is more than just good reason to believe that housing of the future will require a substantially different approach.

For example, while perhaps statistically unimportant in 1973, modular houses built in a factory and transported to the development area are becoming well established. They are conceptually important as a potential threat to established housing marketing practices. A new group of home builders is being created for these products, and if they survive, existing marketing practices may be inadequate. Mobile homes as a form of modular housing are not only statistically important today, but certainly are conceptually important for the future. They too will change the nature of building-materials marketing. The mobile home marketer's product and distribution channels are based upon market conditions today. But if we were to consider the additional market for modular housing, his marketing program would certainly change.

Thus, contingency planning is to provide for the future when we can see the direction of change but not its form. Again, with a bit of imagination we can predict the direction that numerous changes will take, even though we can't predict either the timing or the form of the change. For example, consider the rash of contingency plans which should now be underway to reduce air pollution from traffic congestion in downtown areas. What does this mean for the auto maker, the pollution control maker, or the law enforcement agency? How does it affect the demand for automobiles? What about the trucking companies and other haulers that block traffic, merchants who receive deliveries from the traffic blockers, parking lot operators, and auto commuters? What role should be played by the manufacturers of "people conveyers" (escalators, horizontal as well as vertical elevators, moving sidewalks, trams), the contractors for apartment houses, homes, and office buildings, and so on?

While we are fairly certain that pollution will diminish in the downtown area and that one of the ways it will diminish is through less traffic congestion, we don't know for sure about other facets of the future of this problem. We may just build more streets and have cleaner auto engine exhaust. As Ackoff puts it, we should plan for each reasonable eventuality so that oportunities can be explored when "the future makes up its mind."[24] We add to this that the opportunities or problems may be *discovered* when the future makes up its mind.

To illustrate the point further, let us look backward at some well-known events which have transpired with rather volatile results. Turn the calendar back months, years, and decades and ask what happens if peace breaks out; if money is not further increased for space exploration; if Congress restores the supersonic transport project; if a technological breakthrough comes (diesel locomotive); if foreign competition gets tougher (autos, textiles, shoes); if assets in a foreign country are acquired by that government.

---

[24] Ibid., p. 17.

In every case cited the fact that the event could take place was very well known. The probabilities may have been very slim or they may have been almost certain. Whether these contingencies were planned for, we do not know. If they were, and steps were taken to reduce the impact, we wonder how serious the events would have been if such plans had not been made. In both commitment and contingency planning we can do something to prepare for the future and to discover and anticipate some of the problems it will bring. The reasonably unexpected or the totally unexpected future is another matter. The organization can only be prepared to respond to the unexpected, and this is primarily an organizational matter.

Responsiveness planning.   Some things just can't be anticipated by reasonable persons. An earthquake in California, a hurricane along the gulf coast, or floods in certain areas can be anticipated. But earthquakes or dam breakings where they are not supposed to occur are different matters. Some technological breakthroughs are sudden; some are long anticipated.

Responsiveness planning is oriented toward the organization as an entity and the management as a group. A structure for rapid reaction to the unexpected should be designed. Building flexibility and the capacity to respond into an organization is responsiveness planning.

Satisficing, optimizing, adaptivizing

We have discussed the approaches to planning by drawing neat distinctions among them and labeling them satisficing, optimizing, or adaptivizing. Furthermore, we neatly subdivided the latter approach by spelling out three subtypes of planning: commitment, contingency, and responsive. An illustration of the way in which an admixture of approaches works may be provided by citing a real-life illustration.[25]

A company distributed its products directly to retail stores. It found that its profitable customers accounted for:

53 percent of all customers.
89 percent of sales volume.
55 percent of marketing costs.
144 percent of marketing profit.

Some of the principal alternatives considered were:

1. To shift some selling effort from the unprofitable accounts.
2. To adjust price structures for unprofitable customers.

---

[25] Charles H. Sevin, *Marketing Productivity Analysis* (New York: McGraw-Hill Book Co., 1965), pp. 72–75.

3. To adjust channels of distribution to include mail order or wholesale distribution.
4. To eliminate unprofitable customers.

We do not know what aspects of satisficing were involved, for complete information is not available. Optimizing was involved in several ways. About half the selling time was devoted to unprofitable accounts, so finding optimum use of that time by redirecting the efforts of sales personnel was one alternative. Further, overhead time in order filling and billing would be used elsewhere if unprofitable accounts were dropped.

Measures to adapt to the environment were also considered, so an experiment was run. In one group of territories unprofitable customers were served by mail order. Sales went up 11 percent and net profit contribution was up almost the same amount. In other territories wholesale distributors were used, and sales rose 13 percent while net profit contribution rose 20 percent.

Management's decision was adaptivizing. All unprofitable accounts were turned over to wholesale distributors. All data of the case are not available, but one can infer that there were probably some decisions made of a satisficing nature. And it is reasonable to infer that after having gone to the trouble to experiment, the company would surely attempt to optimize its new system. Further, after learning more about the operation, it is likely that controls were established to warn of potential repetition of the situation.

None of these approaches is really concerned with creating a desired future. They are concerned with restrospective planning in that they attempt to undo deficiencies in the system. They really involve planning either for when "the future makes up its mind" or because the future had been ignored or badly anticipated. In this sense crisis prevention is the underlying philosophy.

APPROACHES TO PLANNING

Outside-in approach

From a conceptual point of view, the outside-in approach to planning implies an analysis of the external environment, discovering both potential opportunities and problems for the future, determining the desired future, and developing plans to attain that desired future. It is the very heart of the concept of management of change, for the attention of management is centered on discovery of opportunities and problems that the future creates rather than on just the solution of problems created by the past.

If the focus of the outside-in approach is discovery and innovation, its major tool is the forecast. Here we use forecast in a variety of ways with a variety of meanings, ranging from economic forecasts and technological forecasts to educated guesses and gut feelings. When we say the forecast is the beginning point, we are tacitly assuming that proper managerial attitudes and adequate resources are present or attainable.

Why outside-in? One reason for analysis of the external environment as a philosophy for strategic planning is that it is consonant with the marketing concept. Before managers and owners can derive their satisfactions, the customer must be satisfied—profitably. This approach is dedicated to finding opportunities for satisfying customers and finding problems which may interfere with that satisfying process.

A second reason for the outside-in approach is, as Ewing says, an antidote to the temptation to stay with a good thing too long.[26] This is what can be labeled the you-don't-argue-with-success syndrome, and is illustrated by Ewing's account of the fall of the Underwood Corporation, which in 1937 had sales of $30 million—equal to the sales of IBM.

A third and powerful argument for the outside-in approach pertains to the orientation of many of the production-, process-, and scientific-minded people who can't understand why the public would prefer a purple and gold 17-ounce widget at $9.95 when a functionally comparable black 11-ounce one could be provided at $1.98. The catch is that marketing people don't always know *why* such a preference exists, but they know *of* the preference. The "engineering mind" is concerned with technical perfection while the "marketing mind" is concerned with perfection of consumer satisfaction—at a profit. If emphasis is put on the product rather than on the customer, disaster may result—as was nearly the case with Henry Ford. The outside-in approach to planning attempts to identify needs and wants of which even the customer is unaware. Before the famous English sanitary engineer, Thomas Crapper, identified a need, the world got along very well without an adequate flush mechanism for the indoor flush toilet.[27] He saw an opportunity.

Evaluation. By taking the outside-in approach to planning, the marketing manager is constantly analyzing the external environment for the discovery of both opportunities and problems. It also encourages the manager to behave more as an active leader in the management of change than as either an administrator of the status quo or a passive reactor waiting for the future to make up its mind. One of the greatest advantages lies in the second phase of the outside-in approach. Once an opportunity or problem has been identified (the first phase), focus must then shift to the internal environment to determine if resources

---

[26] Ewing, *The Practice of Planning*, p. 35.

[27] Yes, he did. Yes, that is probably the reason it is called that. See *Newsweek*, December 1, 1969, p. 63.

are available to cope with the situation. Thoroughgoing internal analyses and action made with such a motivation can't help but have salutory effects upon the strength of the organization. Another advantage of the outside-in approach is that most inventions are demand-induced and are stimulated by a market opportunity.[28]

The major negative aspects of the approach have to do with forecasting the future, and forecasting is one foundation of strategic planning. The prediction of markets for established goods and their characteristics is risky enough, but isolating an opportunity for something that doesn't exist and then identifying the nature of a market for it is risk compounded. Other disadvantages also concern the uncertainty of the future. Management of change often involves timing. While the producer may be committed to the management of change, his customers may not be so committed. Or the customer may not have the same view of the value of the innovation as the producer.

Steiner reported a study of 19 inventions introduced before 1913 and concluded that there was a time interval of 24 years between the date of the first patent and the first practical use of the invention; 14 more years to commercial services; and 12 more years to important use.[29] To reverse an old saying: there is no force so weak as an idea whose time has not come. Other negative features of this approach include the difficulty of coordinating new product development and marketing planning, choosing the proper projects for development, and development of an organizational structure.

Inside-out approach

One basic difference between this approach and the outside-in lies in the order in which environmental analyses are made. Another difference probably lies in the type of results obtained. This concept involves an analysis of the internal environment first in order to develop clues which may lead to the discovery of opportunities and potential problems around which the desired future would be built. It too is (1) at the heart of the concept of the management of change and (2) consonant with the marketing concept.

Why inside-out? The foundation of this approach consists of the organization itself: the attitudes of its managers and the availability of resources. The thrust is the *ability* of the firm to deliver satisfactions to the customer. With ability as the focal point, the firm moves forward to the market in several stages of analysis. First, it concerns itself with

---

[28] Steiner, *Top Management Planning* p. 665. Also see Chapter 6 for additional discussion.

[29] Ibid., p. 688.

the external environments in those areas it has staked out by virtue of its abilities. The second step is the creation of the goods or services to deliver satisfactions. This approach provides a focus for the analyses of the external environment and thus may avoid much wasted effort. While the focus may limit the scope of the external search for opportunities, it also reduces the chasing of rainbows.

Closely related is another reason for the use of this approach. It helps managers identify the business they are in and encourages them to concentrate on improving performance in that area. Conversely, it discourages the diffusion of effort for the investigation and exploitation of opportunities only distantly related to the major thrust of the firm. In this sense, emphasis is placed upon doing better those types of things the firm has been able to do well.

Evaluation.   All of these reasons can be shown as limitations to the horizons of the organization. Also, the outside-in advantages may be turned into disadvantages, or may be applied to support the inside-out approach. For example, there is nothing in the inside-out approach which necessarily limits the horizons of a company just because it first analyzes itself and then the environment. It may find, as did the Carborundum Company, that its weaknesses or total lack of resources are no bar to opportunity exploitation. That company had long considered itself in the abrasives business. After self-analysis it decided it was not in the abrasives business but in the material-removing business. With the extended horizons, it discovered that there was another materials removal method with which it had no experience. The result was a decision to enter that business via the acquisition route.

Critics say that the inside-out approach ignores the marketing concept but the charge cannot be made to stick. It merely postpones the marketing viewpoint until later in the analytical process. While there is nothing inherent in the approach that makes the company stick to the status quo, there is probably a very strong tendency to do so—again the "don't argue with success" syndrome.

It is interesting to note that many innovations have come from outside the basic industry involved. For example, Henry Kaiser, who was not a shipbuilder until World War II, brought mass production and prefabrication techniques to that industry. Aerospace companies, not shipbuilders, developed hovercraft and hydrofoil vessels; razor companies did not develop the electric razor; the airplane was not designed by auto companies; and the successful small cars were introduced in the United States from abroad. Some steam locomotive makers fought the diesel, and water transport companies fought the railroads, which in turn fought the truckers rather than discover and exploit these opportunities themselves. Whether these were the results of the inside-out approach or no approach by the "inside" companies concerned we cannot say. It is fairly certain, however, that for the outsiders who brought about the innovations, they were the result of an outside-in approach.

The fact that a number of companies are setting up venture teams and venture divisions to house the efforts of entrepreneurial oriented managers suggests the difficulty of overcoming the lethargy inspired by an inside-out approach.[30] On balance, it is probably fair to say that the inside-out approach taken by itself encourages an evolutionary walking away from the past and makes it harder for the organization to make leaps into the future.

STEPS IN PLANNING

The steps to be taken in developing a planning program fall into two broad groups. The first four preliminary steps are essential to the actual planning process.

The preliminaries.

1. Establish the concept of the organization in order to identify the basic purpose for its existence.
2. Determine the mission of the organization to further refine the purpose. Sometimes the purpose and mission are the same.
3. Set the objectives of the organization at appropriate managerial levels in order to give a more precise direction than given by the purpose and mission. These objectives are sometimes partially philosophical and partially operational.
4. Plan the planning effort.

The planning process.

5. Develop planning premises.
6. Develop plans, strategies, and policies to attain the objectives.
7. Develop implementation plans at the functional level.
8. Develop systems for evaluation, integration, and control.
9. Design a system for review and modernization of purpose, mission, objectives, plans, and policies.

These steps in planning may be illustrated by Figure 4–1. It presumes that the preliminaries of establishing the concept and mission have been taken care of and starts with setting objectives. Notice how the model provides for the continuous review of results, execution of plans, strategies, and objectives.

---

[30] The role of venture management as a device to overcome the difficulties of the inside-out approach is discussed by Frederic Cook, "Venture Management As a New Way to Grow," *Innovation,* October 1971, pp. 28–37. See also almost any article in almost any issue of *Innovation* for examples of the management of change and the use of the outside-in approach in bringing about change.

FIGURE 4–1
Planning and Control Model

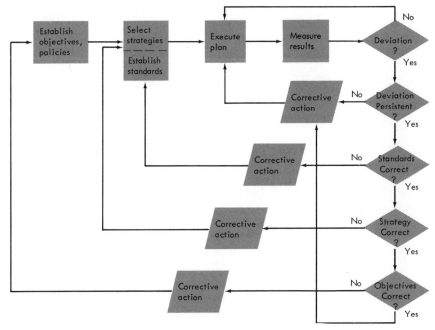

Source: Lt. Col F. D. Roberts. Reproduced with permission.

CONCLUSION

We have discussed what planning is in this chapter, and have only mentioned at times what planning is not. To conclude the chapter we list Ewing's seven things that planning is not.[31]

1. Planning is not words, communication, and public relations.
2. Planning and budgeting are not the same.
3. Planning and forecasting are not the same.
4. Planning and report writing are not the same.
5. Planning is not the maintenance of a formal organization.
6. Planning is not designed to avoid risk.
7. Planning is not even necessarily an attempt to improve efficiency.

Further analyses will be made of strategic, managerial, and operational aspects of planning in Chapter 9.

---

[31] Ewing, *The Practice of Planning*, pp. 14–17.

PART TWO

Analysis for marketing strategy and management

chapter 5 | Marketing research and information

Introduction
Information for planning
    Organization of the company
    Information for the organization as a whole
Information for managing
    What is information?
        Data versus information
        Characteristics of information
    Sequence of information characteristics
    Transforming data to information
Marketing research and management
    Uncertainty and risk
    The scientific method
    A definition of research
    Research in everyday life
    Basic and applied research
    Objectives of research
Marketing research procedure
Marketing information flows
Marketing information systems . . . and computers
Conclusion

Information is a critical factor in the *effective* and *efficient* management of an organization. Many firms, ranging from the mom-and-pop outfits to *Fortune's* 500, seem to survive and grow even though they do not have adequate information. For example, some startling facts were turned up by Richard T. Hise almost a decade ago in a study which included responses of 131 of *Fortune* magazine's list of 500 largest manufacturing firms. Companies were asked if they examined the profitability of the four key areas: products, customers, salespeople, and territories. Only 43 percent indicated that they examined *only* one of the areas. Only 19 percent indicated that they examined all four.[1]

---

[1] Richard T. Hise "Have Manufacturing Firms Adopted the Marketing Concept?" *Journal of Marketing*, July 1965, p. 11.

Despite these rather appalling statistics showing successful operation of very large organizations without adequate information, we repeat our opening sentence: information is a critical factor in the *effective* and *efficient* management of an organization. Because the subject is so critical, it is discussed in each of the other chapters as appropriate. Therefore, in this chapter we discuss some general aspects of information in planning and management in general and in the decision process in particular. Then we look at the concepts of research as an information base as a prelude to a discussion of marketing information flows and systems. In short, we introduce the subject of information in the context of management *and* the marketing function and management *of* the marketing function: the requirements of information for strategic purposes and for managerial-operational purposes.

INFORMATION FOR PLANNING

Chapter 4 was concerned with planning concepts in general and accordingly took for granted some of the information concepts underlying planning and the control of the planning process. In this section, we very briefly, and mostly in outline form, touch upon the areas where information is critical for the effective management of the organization. Information's role in *efficient* management is discussed in another section.

Organization of the company

To a considerable extent, the information required to deal with the organization scheme of the company is of a philosophical nature in the sense of designing the organization. However, in managing the organization, a different picture emerges. For example, the organizational decision resulting in a centralized or decentralized organization depends upon the philosophy of the organizers, which in turn should depend upon information concerning strengths and weaknesses of different organizational schemes related to objectives of the company.

However, once the scheme is established, information of various kinds must flow among the branches. One useful way of examining information needs is on the basis of areas of responsibility such as profit centers, cost centers, and investment centers.

Information for the organization as a whole

Our definition of strategic planning indicated that it was concerned with the setting of objectives, with the resources used to attain them, and with policies to govern acquisition and use of resources. The elements of the marketing mix provide a convenient vehicle to use in relating information in planning directly to strategic planning for marketing. The central points in marketing strategy for which information is required concern (1) product development, (2) promotion, (3) channels of distribution including both the wholesaling and retailing institutions and the facilitating agencies such as transportation and warehouse companies, and (4) price policies. In addition, information for sales forecasting is essential.

Other areas for which information is necessary for planning purposes include production, research and development, finance, accounting, personnel, and the like. When you reflect upon the information needed just for planning alone, the task of providing it appears almost overwhelming. Just remember that one aspect of management really is the process of acting on information to set objectives and attain them. That is why we have established one part of our framework for this chapter from the planning area. Information is what is analysed when we say that management's activities included *analysis* as a foundation for a decision to do something and to do it effectively. Now, let us turn to a discussion of the other aspect of management which is the process of acting on information to the end of improving efficiency.

INFORMATION FOR MANAGING

Chapter 2 pointed out that the business firm is a system of relations, a set of interrelated elements organized to achieve a particular set of objectives. There is a tendency for the elements to be managed as if they were entities unto themselves, or what we have labeled a series of feudal baronies. When this occurs the attainment of the objectives of the firm becomes a matter of chance, a condition under which a business can rarely expect to be both effective and efficient. There are many examples of elements of the firm working at cross purposes to one another. The key connector of system elements is information communicated through the organization. A "horror story" illustrating the effect of a failure to communicate information involves a major airline organized on a regional basis. The seasonal peaks in traffic came at different times for two of the regions. Yet, each region had enough airplanes to meet its peak demands. If both had been managed as parts of a system instead of independent companies, the surplus of one region would have met the peak demands of the other. Yet the two divisions acted as if they did not work for the same firm.

We have also suggested that the system of relations includes not only elements within the organization, the internal subsystem, but also many outside environments and the external subsystem. Because of this, the task of management is made more difficult since it must plan for and adjust to conditions which are not readily at hand. In order for management to operate it must have information about the remaining elements in the system.

The need to understand and appreciate the role of information is even more evident when you reflect on the basic planning orientation taken in Chapter 4. Planning does not and cannot take place in a vacuum. It requires vast quantities of information about available resources within the firm, available resources outside the firm, such as distribution channels, and, perhaps most important, opportunities in the market. Remember that these opportunities are the basis for the firm's effort. All planners, especially marketing planners, must search for information upon which to develop objectives and plan strategies for the future.

In this chapter we shall discover that marketing information includes much more than information *for* marketing managers. Equal in emphasis is the information provided *by* marketing managers to other functional specialists within the firm, to members of the channel of distribution, and to consumers and prospective consumers.

What is information?

Sometimes we use the term "information" without being precise about the meaning of the word. Managers communicate for the purpose of achieving the firm's objectives. That is the transfer of information. It takes place because of the existence of the firm's objectives. Similarly, the transfer of information in a classroom is related to the objectives of both student and instructor. Such objective-oriented transfers do not characterize all communication, however, and we need to make this distinction. Keep in mind that the business is often a complex set of relationships and that the amount of possible communication of information is enormous. Thus, to be effective managers require some stringent limitations on the kinds and amounts of information they get.

Data versus information. One of the confusions which must be resolved is that between "data" and "information." They are not the same. Data are facts or assumptions to be treated as facts. Marketing managers require information for planning and decision-making. This information is derived from data which are put together in a unique combination appropriate for the particular planning task or decision under consideration. It is during this combining process that data become information.

Consider: if a patient has a headache that fact or datum itself is useless to the physician. The doctor cannot formulate a treatment plan unless that single datum is evaluated, synthesized, classified, and combined with other data about the patient's situation to provide an informative picture of the total condition. The same is true of other kinds of information: data are information because they relate to the issue at hand, and even then are a combination of a series of facts.

Characteristics of information. Many experts on information and information management describe it in terms of a series of characteristics.[2]

Accuracy is the characteristic of information which allows it to provide a true, valid, and precise representation of a set of facts as a foundation for sound decision making. Because some decisions do not require as high a degree of accuracy as others and because some facts can be described more accurately than others, the degree of accuracy should be consistent both with the nature of the decision and the nature of the information. By its nature some information must be of the "best guess" type—what will our competitors do if we do "this" or "that"?

Volume refers to the amount of information available to describe a specific situation, and can be described as adequate if it provides the marketing manager with all the information required to make good decisions. This does not mean that all managers at all levels within the organization require or receive the same quantity of information. Nor does it mean that managers will have or could reasonably expect perfect or complete information about any given issue. Assuming that all collected information can be made available, the volume of information necessary depends upon the predictability and uncertainty of events and the degree of detail desired. The detail of specific information requirements varies greatly from the lowest-level manager to the highest-level manager.

Relevance is defined as the characteristic of information which associates specific information with a specific situation. Information is relevant if it is necessary or desirable for the particular decision being considered. A manager may be provided with adequate quantities of information, but of marginal relevance to the decision problem at hand.

Simplicity is defined as the characteristic of information which allows it to be easily understood. Simplicity in the design of reports and in the symbolism used to present the information is very important to the manager. If the information is not simple, the manager must take time from other tasks to try to understand its meaning. Worse yet, the manager may ignore it and base decisions on guesses.

Information is *timely* if it is available when needed for the purpose it is supposed to serve. If a customer asks when to expect delivery of ordered goods, information on inventories must be available immediately. On the other hand, annual information on population changes in a given market area may suffice.

---

[2] See for example, Peter P. Schoderbak, *Management Systems* (New York: John Wiley and Sons Book Company, 1968); Donald H. Sanders, *Computers in Business* (New York: McGraw-Hill, 1968); or Donald E. Walker, ed., *Information System Science and Technology* (Washington: Thompson Book Co., 1967).

Compatibility is defined as the characteristic of information which allows information to be communicated and transferred. Among the things done to insure compatibility is to use a common language and common terminology. To say that an advertisement in one magazine costs more dollars than in another is not enough. The marketing manager needs to know the cost per reader or the results per dollar spent. Further, when we discuss information systems, it will become clear that this compatibility feature is essential if we expect to transfer information from one system to another to be used by different managers.

The *quality* of information is the composite of accuracy, quantity, relevance, timeliness, simplicity, and compatibility. The authors know an engineer in charge of a number of producing oil leases. Every morning he got a computer printout of everything that happened on each lease the previous day in exactly the form he requested. It was complete, relevant, timely, simple, and compatible. Also it was useless because it was unreliable. A typical report would show one lease producing more than all others combined, a second lease producing negative barrels of oil, and more money spent on a third lease than the company grossed in a year. He obtained his own information until the problem was eliminated.

Sequence of information characteristics. Figure 5–1 shows a view of the logical sequence in which to consider the information characteristics. The volume of information should be considered first. The manager's decision-making process will likely be hindered if either too much or too little information is available. Notice how the volume of data is reduced as it is tested by each characteristic.

The second characteristic to be considered is accuracy. Even if an adequate amount of data is present, the resulting information will not be accurate unless the data truly represent a specific situation. If the degree of accuracy required is greater than the accuracy present, then the probability of bad decisions is increased.

The third characteristic for consideration is relevance. A vast amount of accurate data may be available, but the information is of no value unless it provides information that relates to the impending decisions. If the data concern the decisions to be made, the manager has information relevant to his decisions. But data that are generally relevant but of no value to a particular decision should be filtered out. If either quantity or accuracy are not present in the desired degree, the relevancy of the information is immaterial. Even though the available information is relevant, the decision maker may not have enough accurate information for a decision.

Next in line is timeliness. Even if the desired amount of accurate data is available in the system and it is relevant to the decision being considered, the information has no value to the manager unless it is

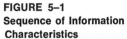

FIGURE 5–1
Sequence of Information
Characteristics

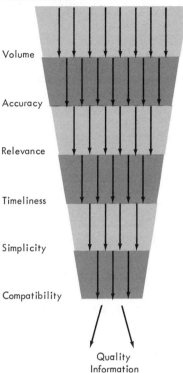

Volume

Accuracy

Relevance

Timeliness

Simplicity

Compatibility

Quality
Information

received before the decision is required. The efforts to produce vast amounts of accurate, relevant information must be balanced against the ability to deliver information in a timely manner.

The fifth characteristic for consideration is simplicity. This is an often overlooked but extremely important characteristic. It represents the ease with which the information is understood by the decision maker. Reports in an easily understood form reduce the time required by the decision maker to evaluate the information, thereby, allowing that person to devote more time in consideration of the decision.

Transforming data to information. Irwin Bross suggests a procedure for converting data to information. What we have called information he calls "good data." He said, "The price of good data is eternal vigilance."[3] The transformation of data to information proceeds according to the following outline:

---

[3] Irwin D. J. Bross, *Design for Decision* (New York: The Macmillan Company, 1953), p. 146.

1. Raw data is evaluated for:
   a. Relevance to the problem.
   b. Reliability, particularly concerning the source.
   c. Repeatability.
2. Tested data is classified.
   a. Operational terms are defined.
   b. Numerical measures are established.
3. Data collection.
   a. Controls on the collection process insure that what we want collected is in fact being collected.
   b. We want comparability in the collected data. The old apples and oranges example is appropriate.
4. Recording of collected data.
   a. We need to insure as high an accuracy as possible.
5. Summarizing the data.
   a. This completes the transformation.
   b. Some of the useful summarizing devices are ratios, averages, and index numbers.
   c. You will find another use for that statistics book here.

MARKETING RESEARCH AND MANAGEMENT

Everything that has been said so far in this book can be described as an admonishment to be systematic and rigorous in the marketing management effort. At this juncture, we find ourselves with an interesting choice.

We have said that information is critical to effective planning and to the discovery of opportunity. If this is so, then it follows that we must make a conscious effort to acquire information. This is part of the manager's job. We could, therefore, at this time devote our complete attention to developing a framework into which managers can fit their information and which will offer a systematic technique for subsequent action after it has been acquired. The interesting thing is that the systematic technique for handling acquired information is almost identical to the technique used by those specialists whose function includes the acquisition of information in the first place—the market researchers. In effect, we could outline a series of steps describing the management decision process here, and then at the time we deal with the identification of marketing opportunities we could detail almost identical series of steps which would be appropriate for the market researcher to use. Traditionally this is the way this material is handled. But we choose to alter our treatment to reflect the similarities between research and management. Thus we have chosen to combine into one section a systematic process which both (1) guides the acquisition of information *and* (2) guides its use in solving marketing management problems. Accordingly, when you encounter the word "researcher" you can replace it with "marketing manager."

Uncertainty and risk

Uncertainty is present in virtually all business decision situations.[4] Managers must make decisions when they do not know what the outcomes will be, or even, in many cases, whether all the relevant possible courses of action have been considered. You can appreciate by now the multiplicity of factors involved. Even though things seldom, if ever, happen the same way twice, they often fluctuate around some average. Probability and statistical mathematics help the marketing manager cope with uncertainty.[5] The risk accompanying uncertainty may be reduced when the manager can reasonably assign a probability of outcome to a decision. Of course, all of us are constantly assigning probabilities in our everyday life. We look at the weather in the morning to determine the need for a raincoat. We know that it might rain, but if it is a clear sunshiny day we consider the probability low. The same kind of behavior characterizes the marketing manager in making decisions. For example, if price is changed, will the competition follow us exactly, go us one better, or do nothing? If no judgment can be made about the probabilities of each possible competitive reaction, then the decision might as well be made by a roll of the dice, which figuratively speaking is sometimes done. But rolling the dice makes us uncomfortable, so we try to relate the uncertainty to *risk*. In risk analysis the manager assigns probabilities to several possible uncertain outcomes to gain a better understanding of the degree of risk incurred by choosing a particular alternative.[6] The reduction of uncertainty is by and large accomplished by acquiring and processing information. And acquiring and processing information are based on applying of the scientific method to the use of information.

The scientific method

The scientific method is nothing more than an objective, systematic way of looking at problems that provides a framework for finding an-

---

[4] A particularly good treatment of uncertainty, its implications, and techniques for handling it is found in Robert Schlaifer, *Analysis of Decisions Under Uncertainty* (New York: McGraw-Hill Book Company, 1969).

[5] David B. Hertz, *New Power for Management* (New York: McGraw-Hill Book Company, 1969), p. 8.

[6] Hertz, *New Power for Management*, p. 58.

swers. It may not necessarily give better, more accurate, or quicker solutions than common sense or executive judgment, but it does enable marketing managers to avoid skipping logical steps in the problem-solving process. Also, it provides a framework which will accept the known aspects of a situation while systematically and clearly identifying the unknown.

There are two separate but related facets of the relationship between marketing research and scientific method. First, the marketing researcher must look at the research problem as a whole, approaching it in a step-like fashion. The following sequence is helpful in approaching a problem and is diagrammed in Figure 5–2.

FIGURE 5–2
The Research Management Process

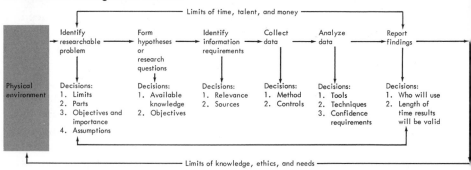

1. Identify a problem area.
2. Specify a researchable problem.
3. Formulate hypotheses or research questions.
4. Identify the information required to answer the research questions or accept or reject the hypotheses.
5. Collect the data needed to provide this information.
6. Analyze the information.
7. Report the findings.

Second, and equally important, the marketing researcher is involved in the decision process. In each of the seven steps in the study of a problem, decisions are required of the researcher. This means, for example, that it is not sufficient to say that data need to be collected. Decisions concerning the types of data, the method of collection, the techniques of analyses, and so on, must be made. This means that alternatives must be analyzed and that the researcher must choose from among those alternatives that particular method which best satisfies the research objectives. Therefore, marketing research and research management are similar to other types of management in their perspectives as well as in their decision-making process. Each step of the research process requires decisions that will establish the character of the complete study.

A definition of research

There are many definitions of research. The one we shall use is a composite. *Research is a rigorous, empirical inquiry into some phenomenon.* *Rigorous* implies that the research is thoroughly accurate or exact; so the researcher must be exhaustive and systematic. The inquiry must ultimately enter the "real" world, as implied in *empirical.* As you can see, this definition allows considerable latitude. But this is desirable; it reflects the pervasive nature of research. Moreover, it allows the researcher to investigate and to inquire into phenomena about which he has little prior knowledge. Some would argue that the researcher must have sufficient knowledge about the problem to formulate hypothetical propositions. At least two possible consequences can result from this view: (1) It may encourage the generation of spurious propositions to legitimize the research, (2) It may prevent a researcher without broad knowledge from investigating all the relevant variables around a specific issue about which he may have considerable knowledge. Neither of these consequences is functional; neither will appreciably enhance our state of knowledge.

Life is replete with problem situations requiring data collection and analysis. The difference between research and these day-to-day situations is probably no more than advance planning, some techniques, and most importantly, the rigor with which one goes about the task.

Research in everyday life

Research is involved in the fabric of our daily living as we cope with day-to-day problems. Certainly, there are differences between daily problems and the types of managerial problems we are talking about. However, the differences are probably a matter of degree rather than of kind. Nonetheless, it is useful to point out some of those differences.

First, scientific researchers tend to reject superficial or mystical explanations for situations. They do not accept the propositions that rain dances cause rain; instead they examine atmospheric conditions and their changes to explain the occurrence of rain. Presumably, they would not address themselves to the subject of the efficacy of the rain dance in causing atmospheric conditions to be just right. Statements such as "That's just the way it is," unverified by research, become unacceptable as data to solve a problem or as problem solutions themselves. While we may be comfortable with mystical explanations in everyday life, in research the probe must be deeper.

Second, in daily life we frequently introduce a bias into our problem-solving activity. This bias can take at least two forms: (1) assuming away or failing to recognize important related issues, and (2) settling on an answer and proceeding to find evidence supporting that answer. As an example of the first form of bias, suppose you are concerned about the stock levels of certain items in a warehouse. You are able to identify the individual item managers within the warehouse. These individuals have been presumed to have complete control of the stock levels. It would be absurd to research thoroughly the way these individuals perform their jobs without considering, in a systematic fashion, such things as the demand rates, the inventory control methods, stocking conditions, and incoming flow rates. To assume away these conditions or to treat them a priori as fixed may lead to useless or even detrimental conclusions. In like manner, in the second form of bias, everyday life permits us the luxury of forming an opinion and holding on despite any evidence to the contrary. "I have the answer. You get the evidence to back it up."

Third, and related to the above, an unsystematic approach to problem solution can lead to snap judgments and misinterpretations. For example, how many times in the course of a football game have you concluded that the defensive linemen are going to smother the quarterback only to discover moments later that the play is a "screen" pass? The same kind of situation can occur in the collection of information about a problem. This is the reason so much emphasis is placed on sampling. If you are inattentive to sample selection and size, you may well find yourself drawing conclusions about a large group based on information about a small group that is in no way representative of the large one. Some time ago a study to determine the status of an academic discipline was completed. The "sample" according to the authors was composed of schools in the American Association of Collegiate Schools of Business. The conclusions were generalized across all schools of business. But the schools in the sample were larger and better known than the average school, and probably more influential in getting massive educational change started. In this case, therefore, a specific level of development can be ascribed only to schools similar to those responding, not to all schools of business.

Fourth, it is common in daily life to accept as fact the opinion of persons in high positions. Parents are frequently accorded this status by children. College professors are sometimes (not nearly as often as we sometimes think) accorded this status. Neither group necessarily should be so regarded. The scientific investigator will require more evidence than the stature of the speaker or writer. Some of the things said in this book may seem to be out of line to you. There is nothing especially wrong with our writing them down. But neither is there anything wrong with your inquiring "Why?" "How do you know?"

Fifth and finally, we sometimes ascribe too much credence to our own experiences. Since each of us is physically and emotionally unique, each person's experiences are unique. We cannot say that all students respond to in-class questioning with excitement just because that is the way our own students respond. Similarly, all doctors are not quacks just because you have visited one who could not bandage a hangnail, and so forth.

As Tyrus Hillway succinctly records,

> No longer does man ascribe natural phenomena to supernatural influences, and no longer does he rely blindly upon accepted authority. He has developed an orderly system of searching for truth which, by basing conclusions upon factual evidence, and by using logic as a means of showing relationships between related ideas, has given him better and more accurate answers to his many questions. . . .[7]

Thus, while everyday problems could be subjected to scientific thinking, they frequently are not. Research problems cannot be confidently solved by the use of methods which are routinely acceptable for everyday problems. Of course, it is probable that many errors in daily decision making would be eliminated if these routine methods were not quite so acceptable.

Basic and applied research

The general orientation in this chapter is toward applied research rather than basic research. Applied research is undertaken for immediate use; that is, its purpose is to answer questions which have immediate applicability. Basic research, on the other hand, is more long-term in purpose. It is typically designed to add to our store of general knowledge. It is clear, however, that a dichotomous distinction is neither accurate or desirable. We need basic research in the growth of human cells so that we may ultimately discover the cause and treatment of cancer. At the same time we need to perform applied research in the area of retail store location using the knowledge and tools available to determine, for example, either an optimum or satisfactory location for a new restaurant. Basic research in marketing is often slighted because of the wealth of immediate problems requiring solutions. The development of guiding propositions in consumer behavior will be considerably enhanced as the amount of basic research increases. To distinguish rigidly

---

[7] Tyrus Hillway, *Introduction to Research,* 2d ed. (Boston: Houghton-Mifflin, 1964), p. 18.

between basic and applied research may prevent findings of applied research from being added to our store of knowledge. So the distinction is based upon the objectives of the particular research rather than the results.

Objectives of research

Earlier in this chapter, research objectives were stressed as part of the criteria for making research decisions. It is unlikely that research can be performed without objectives. These objectives take two general forms, both of which should be clearly and explicitly specified by the researcher before beginning the project in earnest.

The first form of objective is an overall one. What kinds of results do you require? What shape must they take? The second form of objective is specific to your individual problem. You must answer the question, "What am I trying to do?" In both cases, specifying objectives enhances the probability of successful completion because clear objectives prevent wasted motion. For example, if you wish only to describe a phenomenon, you need not use tools which are designed to predict the future behavior of that phenomenon.

The usual form of overall objectives contains one or more of the words: *describe, explain,* or *predict.* Indeed, one of these can be stated as the general objective for most, if not all, research regardless of subject or researcher. It is vital to think of these objectives as interrelated and as different only in degree. *The ultimate goal of the researcher in most instances is to predict the behavior of some phenomenon in the future.* To do so, he must have the capability to explain past and present behavior with sufficient validity and precision that a prediction will have some recognized value. It is clear, however, that explanation cannot occur unless we can precisely describe the phenomenon and those factors which influence it. Consequently, it is reasonable to suggest that there are three levels of research objectives, and the only things preventing achievement of the ultimate objective are the constraints of time, talent, and money which will govern the size and scope of the research project.

Probably the least highly regarded of the objectives—description—is nonetheless an essential prelude to any higher order objective. The determination that a research project shall be only descriptive is based upon the implicit judgment that insufficient descriptive material now exists to allow explanation or prediction, and the research limitations prohibit going beyond description. Suppose you were interested in the effect of the introduction of an automated system on supervisory personnel. As initially conceived, this system would reduce the number of workers reporting to each supervisor and eliminate most of the routine activities each supervisor now performs. It is clear that your task is one of prediction. But in order to predict, you must explain the behavior patterns now characteristic of the supervisor and you must explain the changes the new system would produce. In order to explain the patterns of the current job, you must describe the current environment: what the person does, how it is done, what factors in the environment are present, and other issues. If your limitations are such that only this description is possible, then you must start there. It is not possible to predict the effect of the new system without going through these steps.

In the foregoing case, the literature on the effect of automated systems on human behavior is sparse. Were this not so, it might be possible to proceed with a minimum of description and explanation to the prediction stage. This is true because other researchers would have performed much of the description and explanation required.

Theory and research

Much has been said and written about theory and its use in research. At the risk of oversimplification and misunderstanding, we can make the following statements about theory and research.

1. There is no such thing as "too theoretical." If we accept the proposition that theory contains predictions of practice, then there is an inseparable line between practice and theory. Moreover research has as its ultimate goal-prediction and it also, therefore, is linked to practice and theory. The better the theory we have developed and established, the less time and resources we must take to do more research. A way of looking at theory and its links in the environment is depicted in Figure 5–3.

FIGURE 5–3
The Relationship of Research and Testing to Theory Development

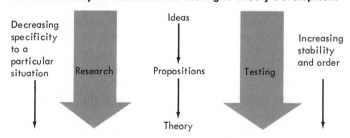

2. Theory provides a good starting point for additional research. It establishes a base from which reasonable hypotheses can be generated. It provides relationships and understanding which have been established by other research.

3. Theory encourages a broad perspective. Properly used, it promotes the inclusion of all relationships which are important to the new research study.

4. The use of theory helps prevent the fighting of old battles and the reinvention of the wheel because theory itself is based on research that usually has been duplicated under many different conditions. We know, for example, that hydrogen gas and oxygen gas combined in a container at room temperature will produce very little water. We have discovered that, by increasing the temperature, the rate of reaction rises rapidly. But at about 700°C we have found (probably by accident) that the mixture becomes explosive. So we can use the theory developed by research in the combination of oxygen and hydrogen to prevent the demise of more researchers.

The use of theory need not promote rigidity. Should additional research under new conditions not agree with theoretical predictions, then the theory may need changing. But nonetheless the theory provided the starting point.

Research enhances the individual researcher's capability for decision making. In the usual sense, the results of research are used to limit decision alternatives and to provide some direction to marketing. In addition, the individual researcher is faced with many decisions throughout the research process. The methods used in and the confidence developed through these decisions make positive contributions to one's decision-making capability and to one's ability to sell the results of research to other decision makers.

Although sometimes disconcerting because of it, research frequently generates more questions than it answers. Each time we discover an answer to a question, a whole new level of the unknown is displayed. The research in the various space problems certainly is an example of this. And while the value of all this question-generation is, like beauty, in the eye of the beholder, it clearly sensitizes the researcher to questions. The subsequent development of the inquiring mind is a necessary antecedent to progress.

Research is consumer-oriented. As noted in the earlier discussion, research objectives are the fundamental starting point for any study. The consumer may or may not be the researcher (it makes little difference) but if he is not, the objectives of the research must reflect those of both consumer and researcher.[8]

But industry has found that marketing research is an increasingly important means of acquiring information about its external environment.

---

[8] Russell Ackoff, *The Design of Social Research* (Chicago: The University of Chicago Press, 1953), pp. 21–22.

MARKETING RESEARCH PROCEDURE

Marketing managers are required to make a large number of decisions in their roles as functional managers and are also required to contribute to decisions which must be made by other managers in the firm. To make or contribute to these decisions requires information, but managers rarely have all the necessary information at their finger tips. Consequently, we need to return to Figure 5–2 (on page 88) and examine in somewhat more detail some of the key steps of that process which produces marketing information.

Most marketing research is done on a project basis. That is, it is designed to develop information which managers can use to solve a *particular* marketing problem.

Research process

Problem definition. In order to find a solution to a problem, the problem must first be defined. Problems are often identified during routine (but extremely important) studies of present operations of the firm. Sales managers may discover wide variations in selling performance not explained by differences in the people themselves. Competitors may be growing more rapidly than the firm. A previously successful product may fail to meet its profit objective. These examples will qualify as indications that a problem exists. They are *not*, however, statements of a problem; they are only *symptoms* of a problem. A decline in sales is never a problem; rather, it is symptomatic of a problem. The marketing researcher must examine the symptoms in order to accurately define the problem to be investigated.

Data collection. Data are described earlier in this chapter as the raw materials from which useful information is produced. The data collection process is particularly important because of the often large commitment of funds as well as time and effort required to accomplish it.

Data may be divided into two categories: secondary data and primary data. Most research projects require some of each. Secondary data are sometimes called available data. This means that someone else has already collected these data, normally for another reason, and that they can be examined without further collection activity. Primary data, on the other hand, must be collected by the marketing researcher to solve the problem at hand. As a general rule it is almost always less expensive and faster to use secondary rather than primary data. Further, it is sometimes possible to draw reasonable conclusions from secondary data alone. For example, if the marketing problem is to determine the feasibility of entering a new market, and the key to success is finding a sufficient number of households with incomes above $15,000 per year, then the sensible researcher would consult the Bureau of the Census before going directly to the market to count the number of such households.

Secondary data. Probably the best source of secondary data is the library. Good libraries often have data from many sources. Marketing researchers are major users of government publications and statistics. The Bureau of the Census and the Departments of Transportation, Labor, and Agriculture are the leading agencies providing marketing data. Industry trade associations often have detailed data on those firms in a particular industry. The publishers of magazines and newspapers frequently provide marketing data to potential advertisers. Universities through their research organizations are fruitful sources of data, particularly in limited geographical areas. Company records often are a source of very useful data which are not immediately available elsewhere. Marketing researchers should investigate their own companies before going outside.

Primary data. In spite of the wealth of data available from secondary sources, marketing researchers often find these data insufficient to solve a particular problem. When such a situation exists, researchers must collect their own data.

Primary data are collected from both internal and external sources. Internal data collection is frequently accomplished by interviews with company sales representatives or other employees. Such collection is often less structured, less formal, and less costly than external data collection.

External primary data collection can be accomplished through the use of surveys, observation, and experimentation. Of these, experimentation is the most rigorous but also the least used in marketing research. The experiment seeks to isolate the cause of change. It is possible, for example, to experiment with various price levels of a new product to determine which is most acceptable to the target consumers. Observation, such as taking traffic counts in front of a potential retail location or physically watching customers in a supermarket's produce department, frequently give insights into consumer behavior. Some observation should be included in most marketing research projects. But it is important to note that observation lacks the precision and accuracy to stand alone as the only source of data.

Survey method. A widely used and accepted method of collecting primary data is the survey method. The following questions commonly arise in a survey research effort.

Who should be questioned? Here the marketing researcher must decide whether to use a census (question every person concerned) or a sample (a small group which is representative of a larger group).

If sampling is to be used, marketing researchers must be very cautious in determining sample size and in locating specific persons to be questioned.

How should questions be asked? The principal choice here is whether questions will be structured or unstructured. An example of a structured question is a multiple-choice question such as you might see on an examination. Similarly, examples of unstructured questions are "essay" or "short answer" questions.

How should answers be obtained? The researcher has a basic choice of three methods of obtaining answers: personal interviews, telephone interviews, and mail questionnaires. The major advantages of the personal interview are: (1) it is possible to probe more deeply by asking additional questions after a respondent has already answered one; (2) it is easier to control the exact respondent—say the store manager rather than the assistant manager; (3) responses are likely to be higher since the interviewer is able to provide some motivation; (4) personal interviews are often most effective for a large number of questions. The major disadvantages of personal interviewing are its high cost and the possibility of bias being introduced by the interviewer.

The telephone interview is increasingly used by marketing researchers. Its main advantages are (1) low cost per contact, (2) speed of receiving answers, and (3) substantial elimination of interviewer bias. The disadvantages include (1) some reluctance on the part of respondents to answer highly confidential questions, (2) the difficulty of asking large numbers of questions, and (3) the possible bias introduced by the fact that not all people have telephones (although most do) and by the increasing number of unlisted telephones.

Mail surveys are a widely used tool for acquiring data. Their advantages include (1) the ability to cover a wide geographic area at relatively low cost per contact, (2) the ability to ask questions which require the respondent to look for answers or to give the answer some added thought, and (3) their use with large groups of people. The disadvantages are many: (1) since it is very rare that *all* mail questionnaires will be returned, it must be determined whether those people responding are approximately the same as those who did not respond; (2) mail surveys take considerable time, often four to six weeks, and therefore are not suitable when immediate responses are desired; and (3) it is impossible to control who actually fills out the questionnaire.

Every method has strong pluses and strong minuses. The researcher must pay careful attention to both when selecting a method.

What must be done to the data to make them useful information? This is commonly called analysis and often requires the use of both simple and sophisticated statistical tools. It may be possible to achieve the research objectives by simply producing a frequency distribution of the responses. Conversely, it may be necessary to use complex statistics to describe relationships and influences among different variables.

Data presentation.   Once useful information is obtained, it must be communicated. Strangely enough, this is the point where much marketing research effort fails. Research information must be communicated to managers who must make decisions to solve the original problem. Researchers must be careful not to be more concerned about the technical process of research than about the information the process produces. Conversely, marketing researchers must consistently guard against assuming that the manager who needs the information understands fully and accepts the techniques used. The manner in which results are communicated will strongly influence the acceptance of research results. Generally, this requires a short synopsis of the major research findings followed by full details of the study and its findings. Research techniques are often included as an appendix.

MARKETING INFORMATION FLOWS

A route of information flows

From the foregoing discussion it is apparent that marketing management, research, information, and everyday life have a great many common bonds. We have suggested almost incidentally that everyone practices a part of the management task in that information is collected through a kind of research and decisions are made based on that information. For most, the collection of information for personal decisions is a lifetime process beginning in early childhood. It is acquired from experience, education, parents, peers, and other sources. Sometimes the collection process is a systematic one. Sometimes it is done in a haphazard manner, but it is collected for many of the same reasons that a manager collects it in his job.

Research and management have been matched because research is a rigorous, systematic inquiry and requires many decisions in the process. Management also inquires rigorously and systematically and makes decisions. Thus researcher and manager perform many of the same kinds of activities. Both should recognize the similarities of their activities and embrace each other's techniques in the constant effort to be more efficient and effective in their individual endeavors. Information is the heart of both marketing research and marketing management. Consumers, as managers of their own resources, have similar needs.

The need for marketing information arises when one party in the exchange process cannot make a decision comfortably, that is, when sufficient uncertainty exists to make a decision not much more than a random action. Such a situation may exist for consumers, wholesalers, retailers, and suppliers as well as marketing managers in manufacturing firms.

For example, the concept of a shopping good is fundamentally based on consumers' search for information upon which to make buying decisions. They go to various stores, talk to numerous sales people, examine a variety of models and brands, and maybe read test results. They look at their needs, which are complex, and match available resources against alternative ways of satisfying their needs. *And then* they decide. You may have gone through something like this process yourself. Go back to the most recent such action on your own part and see if you can, in detail, *write down* the places you visited, the people you talked with, and the information you gained. It is useful to contrast this process with the last time you purchased what has been called a convenience good. We suspect you will find that, among other things, you had sufficient knowledge about the convenience good to make the collection of additional information prior to purchase unnecessary.

Members of the channel of distribution also require large quantities of information from many sources. Of course, channel members need market information. We know from our own experience that differing market conditions alter the mix of goods found in essentially similar establishments.

In some parts of the Southwest, supermarkets carry a wide range of prepared and do-it-yourself Mexican-style foods, but in other regions such goods are virtually impossible to buy, except in widely separated specialty stores. Weather factors influence the kinds of clothing available, and so on. Channel members cannot rely solely on their intuition or experience to tell them what kinds of goods the consumer expects to find in their establishments. They require sound market information. But they also need information about available goods and services as well as alternative sources of supply. This translates into information from suppliers, manufacturers, other channel members, and consumers.

Competition is nearly always present within these four information source/receiver groups. It appears only when we break down the information flow process into much smaller units than those of our current level of analysis. The emphasis often placed on manufacturing and its role in information should be joined by similar emphasis on the information needs and responsibilities of others in the exchange process. Thus, if we were to package information flows, we would need to consider all flows, not just some of them. Figure 5–4 depicts these flows.

At this point we have a choice of directions in which to proceed. We could take each flow, dissect it, and attempt to be exhaustive in describing the kinds of information available, methods of collection and transmission, and the values of the information to the recipient. Such a task would be monumental, and useful only for some generalized

FIGURE 5–4
Marketing Information Flows

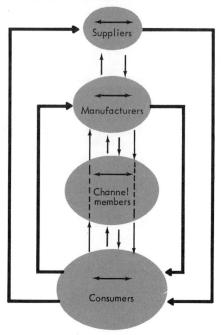

channel of distribution which might be said to be ideal and which probably does not exist in identical form in the market place.

A second possibility is to stop at this point, using the figure in conjunction with our earlier discussion of information flows. This course has the advantage of being sufficiently general to be applied to virtually any distribution structure encountered. But it has the distinct disadvantage of not carrying through the information theme and relating it to the material which follows in this book. Remember, we have said that information flow is essential to marketing management; since this is a marketing management book, and since this isn't the last chapter, it seems inappropriate to ask you to do all of the relating of information flows to specific marketing management areas yourself without further assistance. We have chosen a middle ground. We cannot realistically consider everything, but Figure 5–4 deserves some elaboration. In the process we will introduce some ideas about traditional marketing functions to which the reader should be particularly attentive.[9]

---

[9] In all three cases, we would construct a model of what actually occurs, i.e., the description will not contain all variables and relationships that actually exist. The difference between good models and bad ones is that the good ones contain the most influential and meaningful variables and relationships while bad models contain spurious, inconsequential, or inaccurate variables and relationships.

By now it should be clear that the reasons given for rejection of alternative one above are very strong indeed. Because man is a social animal and has large numbers of social interactions, each of which involves some transfer of information, it would be improbable at best that we could get all meaningful interactions into Figure 5–4. What the figure does show are those flows which are controlled to some degree by one or more of the parties to the exchange process: supplier, manufacturer, or channel member. It is the consumer's flows which are minimized. The following discussion is centered on the user of the information, and we consider only *inbound* information. Outbound information is considered under its destination.

The consumer[10]

As we have said a number of times, the consumer ultimately decides whether the firm will survive or fail. It is fitting therefore that we consider consumer information activities first. Looking at Figure 5–4, you will see five defined flows of information which the consumer may use in his decision making. First, note that consumers look to each other for information about what products and services to buy, and from which establishment, as well as other factors. This kind of information typically is classified in terms of social pressures, social class, informal conversation, values, mores, group behavior, and so forth. But, in effect, this information, sometimes solicited sometimes not, affects our own personal buying decisions.

Second and third, note the two flows which come to the consumer *through* the channel of distribution. In practice the consumer will have a difficult time distinguishing accurately between these flows, but as a student of marketing you need to know that some of the information available to the consumer through the channel originates with channel members and the rest originates with the manufacturer and is simply funnelled through the channel.

The reader has seen much retail advertising. This advertising offers the consumer vast quantities of information about the goods and services available at a particular retail store. This information need not be concerned only with technical product characteristics. It is also useful to the consumer decision-making process when the social and psychological benefits of purchase are indicated. This advertising when provided solely by the retailer constitutes one flow. We always hope that these messages are so constructed as to be of greatest value to the unique market the particular retailer serves. Included in retail advertising is information

---

[10] With the assistance of our social science colleagues, we can categorize the influences of others on individuals in terms of the disciplines of psychology, social psychology, sociology, and anthropology. See Chapter 8 on consumer behavior for a more detailed discussion.

which the manufacturer desires to make available to consumer. This is often in the form of cooperative advertising; where the costs are shared by both manufacturer and retailer.

Lest we become too oriented to advertising, do not forget that channel members employ hundreds of thousands of clerks, representatives, and salesmen whose primary responsibilities are to assist the consumer in personal decision making by providing information about products and services. Personal selling is a crucial tool for the seller and the buyer in the informing process. In addition to advertising and personal selling, information comes through the channel by other forms of sales promotion. Displays and point-of-purchase promotion provide valuable opportunities for informing consumers and prospective consumers. As is the case with retail advertising, these sales promotion tools are used by both manufacturer and channel members. But all are used in conjunction with the channel of distribution.

Fourth, probably the best known, most criticized, and most visible information flows to the consumer are those which come directly to the consumer from manufacturers. Considerable resources are devoted to this process. Both personal selling and advertising are used here. They are direct to the consumer without action of the channel of distribution. In those cases where the manufacturer has chosen to bypass existing channel members in favor of contacting the consumer directly, the information made available must be complete and meaningful since the consumer cannot directly fall back on the retailer for additional or clarified information. The reasons for these multiple information flows directed at the consumer supplier, manufacturer, or channel member can be classified in terms of differences in the consumer decision-making process, the need or desire for control over the message, distribution practices, competition, and available resources. By way of an exercise the reader should formulate examples of the effect of each of these variables on information flows directed to the consumer.

Fifth and finally, suppliers of raw materials and productive resources also communicate with the ultimate consumer. Companies such as U.S. Steel and Alcoa frequently inform consumers of the differential advantage of steel or aluminum in consumer products. Of course, some of this information also describes activities of the corporation which make it a good "corporate citizen." An example of this is the present series of Phillips Petroleum advertisements which describe other products, related to highway safety and surgical techniques, developed by the company.

Channel members

Channel members are, as you might suspect, in a particularly difficult position. They are the recipients of four major flows of information and transmitters of two. They are typically independent businessmen who, while serving the needs of both manufacturers and consumers, have their own objectives to satisfy. It is this triumvirate of masters that precipitates the greatest number of difficulties.

The different views of channel members. Distribution channels have a history of entrepreneurship. Their membership originated when adventuresome individuals found new markets for raw materials and processed goods. In the beginning these markets were small, and often geographically dispersed, and served by some very famous names in distribution annals including Marco Polo and Christopher Columbus. There is no immediately available evidence to our knowledge that Marco Polo ever set up a retail store when he tired of world travel, but he well could have. The Hudson's Bay Company is very good contemporary example of how a firm of itinerant traders developed into a major Canadian department store chain as its stores have begun to serve more concentrated and more stable markets.

Against this backdrop, you can see two roles for intermediaries. First, many channel members are independent structures; they continue to have objectives which we expect businesses in general to have. They cannot, however, continue to attain those objectives unles their mix of products and services is of sufficient value to their customers and prospective customers so that exchange takes place. Of course in order to sell their products and services, channel members must supply customers with information—information which establishes not only that their products and services are worthy of purchase but also that their establishment is a good place from which to acquire these products and services. In many cases the channel member is dependent on the manufacturer for information about the product. The channel expects this information to be communicated both to the customer directly and to the channel for internal decision making. The role the channel member plays in this case is one of seller, and consequently all the difficult market assessment and satisfaction issues prevail.

Second, the channel plays the role of buyers. Many manufacturers depend exclusively on independent channel members for distribution and sale of their products. Members play as vital a role as customers for manufactured products as the members' own customers play for them. Without the customer in either case the seller is in deep trouble. The consequence of this buyer relationship in information terms is that the channel must assess its customers' needs and search for products and services which will satisfy those needs from among the enormous number of manufactured products available. The manufacturers' dependence on channels also encourages them to seek those members whose customers may be satisfied by the products. So while the manufacturers communicate in many cases directly with the ultimate consumers, they recognize that they must also communicate with intermediate customers who deal directly with the ultimate consumer. Because they depend so heavily on channel members to relate to the market and because the ultimate consumer is the final judge of any product or service, the manufacturers must depend on information supplied by the channel to formulate strategic marketing plans and to develop managerial action programs.

All of this may seem to you to be quite abstract and stylized—a perfectly natural reaction. Since most of us are basically ultimate consumers, we rarely see much of the behavior we are talking about here.

Manufacturers and channel members handle these flows of information between them in a variety of ways. To get information to consumers while recognizing the important link the channel member has with the ultimate consumer, the manufacturer may agree to share promotional costs of informing the customer about his products. In many cases this amounts to paying certain costs, such as media costs, while leaving layout, timing, and, to an extent, content decisions to the channel member. The same job can be done in a different way by providing instruction booklets or informative brochures to channel members for distribution to ultimate consumers.

The manufacturer also recognizes that it must compete with other manufacturers for channel resources and attention. It will thus attempt to provide informative tools that are most effective to the channel. For example, point-of-purchase display materials often perform a number of information-related jobs:

1. They inform the ultimate consumers.
2. High-quality materials can give an advantage over competitors in that they more effectively inform the ultimate consumer.
3. They inform indirectly the channel member of the commitment the manufacturer has to both the products and to the channel member.
4. They provide, in many cases, an easy method for channel members to inform the manufacturer of the success (or failure) of its product.

Transmission of information by channel members takes a variety of forms. They employ thousands of sales representatives. Distributor salespeople call on prospective retail customers. Retail clerks perform roughly the same function in addition to their many other duties. There is a large body of magazines and trade journals sometimes called the "trade press" which has the general purpose of strengthening channel businesses. Channel members then find themselves in a unique position, playing the roles of both buyer and seller, and therefore having the complex requirement of being source, receiver, and conduit for information all at the same time.

Manufacturers

In our society the manufacturer's major role is that of seller, although from Figure 5–4 you can quickly see that the manufacturer also has an important buying role. Note that the manufacturer originates three flows of information and is the recipient of another three. In keeping with our original thought of dealing with the recipient flows more closely, we will discuss the originated flows only in passing.

The most visible of information flows originated by manufacturers are those directed at ultimate consumers via personal selling, advertising, and sales promotional efforts. We have just seen the importance of flows directed toward the channel members by manufacturers. But these flows cannot occur in a vacuum. The manufacturer cannot hope to satisfy constantly changing channel and consumer needs without monitoring these changes.

The relationship of the manufacturer to other groups in the information flow model exists because of the manufacturer's need to adjust its offering to constant change. Its products must be accepted by ultimate consumers in the face of competitive products which are exact substitutes—for example, those making men's shirts compete with all others who also make men's shirts; the local United Fund competes with churches and other charities as well as with the shirtmaker. The shirtmaker also competes with the brewer of beer. In addition, the shirtmaker's products must be accepted by channel members who directly serve the ultimate consumer. Ideally we prefer and expect that these several institutions will operate as a system and that these information requirements will be complementary. In practice, however, each institution has its own goals and, faced with the varying degrees of perceptiveness and the costs of information processing, often cannot accept the same kinds or quantities of information. We will see later that many firms have responded to this and related difficulties by taking over control of more than one set of institutions; this is called vertical integration. Sears, Safeway, and Ford Motor Company are among the prominent firms which have taken this route. The independent businessmen can also use advantageously a similar perspective without undergoing vertical integration.

Manufacturers acquire information about ultimate consumers in a variety of ways. They may create marketing research departments to acquire information directly. They may purchase information and data from a number of ongoing independent research and data-gathering firms whose very existence demonstrates the need for economical information. Moreover we expect field personnel, particularly salespeople, to be sensitive to their firms' need for market information and to communicate their knowledge through established communication channels of this information is derived from relationships with channel members.

As you might expect, manufacturers have an on-going relationship with suppliers of raw materials, parts, and other materials used in the manufacturer of their products. Changes also occur in this area, and manufacturers must be sensitive to information which will or could alter the resource mix with which we must work.

Suppliers

The major information relationship which suppliers have is that with their customers, the manufacturers. Suppliers require information about their customers' needs for the same reasons that others require information about their customers. Markets channge. If you supply a market, you need to keep tabs on it. In the other direction, customers need information about the products and services suppliers have available.

While some advertising is used in this information process, salespeople are major transmitters of customer information and major acquirers of market information. Enlightened suppliers recognize, however, that even at their position often distant from the final consumers of their products, they can profitably maintain contact with these final consumers. The purposes of such information flows are on the one hand to advise consumers of the qualities of products made from the materials, as in the case of U.S. Steel or Kaiser Aluminum, and on the other hand to be directly in touch with changing market patterns as the same U.S. Steel must, what with increasing use of glass and prestressed concrete for structural purposes.

Coordinating flows

Within each represented level of information flows (in Figure 5–4), the reader will see an arrow. This arrow represents coordinating flows of information. For suppliers, manufacturers, and channel members, these flows have two general characteristics. First, there are flows of information among firms at the various levels. Each is a competitor and, when abiding by the law, these competitors engage in a noncollusive exchange of information. Sometimes such information is funneled through another agency but it is still useful information for competitive purposes. The automobile manufacturers, for example, report not only production data but also anticipated policy changes through the publication *Ward's Automotive Reports*. The "trade press" provides these kinds of information as a part of its services. Of course, other less formal flows also occur in the form of social conversation and rumor.

Second, our presentation thus far has, in a way, ignored the complexity of internal marketing organizations. Just as specialization has taken place in other facets of life so too have the departments of the firm responsible for implementing marketing decisions become specialized. It is quite common, for example, to find product planning, advertising, sales, sales promotion, public relations, and customer services in separate, widely-dispersed departments. Yet each, while requiring specialized talents and resources, works toward achieving the same marketing objectives. It is an unfortunate circumstance, however, that the separation of these departments can create an environment in which the department loses sight of the overall goals or fails to evaluate the effect of its actions on other parts of the marketing organization. When such situations arise, the achievement of marketing and corporate objectives is in jeopardy. To overcome these potential problems we must allow for coordinative flows within the organization itself. We must provide for communication between sales and advertising; between logistics and production.

Consumers, conversely, have not had highly organized coordinating flows but there are influential and broad-based flows of information that affect consumer behavior. Decisions are assisted and altered by word-of-mouth personal communication, by rumor, and by consumer information publications. The effect is the same.

Environmental flows

We have deliberately constricted our model to exclude the influential information flows which occur external to the institutions in Figure 5–4. These flows are very important, however, and we have reserved Chapter 7 for a detailed discussion of the external environment. The reader should consider the effects on these information flows of the issues raised at that time.

MARKETING INFORMATION SYSTEMS . . . AND COMPUTERS

A great deal has been said and written about both information systems and computers.[11] This chapter has been developed around the concept of information; we have said that information is vital to the operation of the marketing system and we have outlined a portion of the flows of information. A marketing and information system should contain all of these elements. It seems unrealistic to suggest that any one system could contain so much information and still be responsive. But it is not unrealistic to consider that a manufacturer, for example, who sets up a marketing information system would have elements in the system which

---

[11] A good representative article on this subject is Donald F. Cox and Robert E. Good. "How to Build a Marketing Information System," *Harvard Business Review*, May–June 1967, pp. 145–154. A great deal more has been written in the subject of management information systems.

would formalize the relationship among inbound information, coordinating and control information, and outbound customer information.

A marketing information system is not just an automated marketing research department nor is it just a control system nor a system for massaging internal data for marketing decision making. Marketing information system thinking must proceed to the point where it is recognized that suppliers, channel members, and consumers make decisions which require information and which are equally as important to the firm's welfare as are internal management decisions. We are reluctant to suggest suboptimization just because the whole job looks difficult.

Information system characteristics

Some general characteristics of an information system should be considered. A good system is:

1. *Efficient.* Efficiency is the relationship between a given input and output.

2. *Responsive.* Information for decision making should be available as needed; so information systems should be designed to cope with a wide range of demands.

3. *Flexible.* Flexibility is of particular importance in marketing information systems. Since change occurs in both the market and the managerial environment, information systems should be easily and efficiently adaptable to change.

4. *Compatible.* Not all decisions made in the firm are strictly marketing decisions. Of course we realize that few decisions at Level 1 have no effect on marketing decisions. Consequently any marketing information system must be compatible with information systems set up to service other corporate decision areas.

In summary, the marketing information system should be so designed that the acquisition, recording, processing, retrieval, and communication of information is both effective and efficient. Clearly, system design is a complex, time-consuming, and frustrating process. Data are transformed and communicated to appropriate managers to be useful for decision making.

And now . . . computers

Computing equipment has developed at an extraordinary rate since the early 1950s when it was first used commercially on a large-scale basis. For a considerable period computers were capable of doing much more than they were being called on to do.[12] Marketing applications

---

[12] John Diebold, "ADP—The Still Sleeping Giant," *Harvard Business Review,* September–October 1964.

seem to be lagging behind. It is, however, likely that marketing will increase its usage in both "scope and rigor."[13]

Computers are a powerful and valuable tool in information system management. But we emphasize that a computer is a tool which can:

Add and subtract numbers.

Multiply and divide numbers.

Perform some logic operations.

Choose among stated alternatives when rules of choice are given.

Remember and recall.

Communicate with operators and other machines.

Direct itself in a predetermined manner.

Check its own accuracy.

and cannot:

Do anything without preprogramming.

Make nonpredetermined decisions.

Efficiently do nonrecurring tasks.

The most effective marketing information system will begin with a determination of information needs; of the decision task; of time, personnel, and money constraints; of data sources; and of communication (transmission) requirements. Only then will selection of the computer as a tool of implementation be appropriate. We end, rather than start, with the computer; we decide to use the computer just as we decide to use statistical or mathematical tools.

CONCLUSION

Information is a key, perhaps *the* key, to effective decision making whether that decision making be by consumers or by marketers. A recent study by Arthur D. Little and the Industrial Research Institute highlighted the importance of information and the lack thereof in marketing and especially in the innovativeness of managers.[14] The study found that the lack of market information was a significant barrier to marketing manager innovativeness.

We have reviewed the decision-making process and have emphasized the integral place of research in marketing management and research

---

[13] Robert J. Keggerreis, "Marketing Management and the Computer: An Overview of Conflict and Contrast," *Journal of Marketing*, vol. 35, January 1971, pp. 3–12. For a more generalized view, see Tom Alexander, "Computers Can't Solve Everything," *Fortune*, October 1969, pp. 126 ff.

[14] Ernest D. Phelps "'Study Finds Unavailability of Market Information and Executives' Fear of Failure Bar Innovations" *Marketing News*, May 1, 1974, p. 1.

and decision making. Thus, conceptually, the reader should have made the connection between these various terms before passing on to marketing information flows. The latter parts of the chapter included discussions of the information flows between suppliers, manufacturers, channel members, and consumers. Each receives and transmits information and marketing information; so systems must be designed to accommodate these flows. Finally, we have emphasized the strength of the computer as a tool in information system development, with the admonition that starting with the computer rather than with the information required will likely result in an unsatisfactory system.

chapter 6 | # Marketing opportunity and innovation

Introduction
The satisfaction process
    Recognition of consumer aspirations
    Creation of selective dissatisfaction
    Anticipated satisfaction
    Realized satisfaction
    Anti-dissatisfaction inoculation
Consumer and producer satisfaction
    Sources of opportunities
    Consumers
    Producers
Marketing, opportunities, and innovations
    Marketing
    Kinds of opportunities
        What are opportunities?
        Market segmentation as an opportunity
        The marketing concept as an opportunity
        Other kinds of opportunities
            Ecology
            Demography
            Miscellaneous
            Groups of opportunities
        Resistances to opportunity exploitation
    Innovation Objectives
Management, marketing, and innovations
    Management and successful innovations
        Top management commitment
        Involvement of scientists and program selection
        Organizing manpower resources
        Application of R&D results
    Venture management
Conclusion

Marketing managers have two very basic tasks to perform from the point of view of time. First, they must be concerned with today, which is yesterday's future. If they don't keep an eye on ongoing events, their companies won't be around for today's future. At the same time they have to keep an eye on the future. If they don't, when the future arrives they will be unprepared for it and will not last long. They must be prepared for the management of change. In fact, they must manage change. As one author put it, the manager "has to create tomorrow."[1]

In order to live well today and survive in the tomorrow they create, marketing managers must be concerned with marketing opportunities and innovations. The discussion in this chapter is centered on (1) the broad aspects of opportunities and innovations and (2) the managerial structures for exploiting these marketing opportunities. In many respects the management of change with which we are so vitally concerned involves the management of marketing opportunities which are inextricably linked with the innovation process. The analysis of environments for the discovery of opportunities and their exploitation is a part of the planning process in which resources are matched with opportunities.

The marketing concept and the marketing philosophy are intimately related to marketing opportunities. Lazer makes this point in the following manner:

> . . . the assessment of market opportunity focuses on the identification of company goals and their attainment through action in the marketplace. It considers the environmental factors necessary for implementing the marketing concept, perceives the business of business as creating customers, and so provides a perspective for present and future operations.[2]

Thus, business must be geared philosophically and organizationally to innovation—from planning and plans, through objectives and policies, to organization and management of marketing opportunities. The opportunities and innovations are not confined to products, but also include services, processes, and concepts, such as organizational structure of the firm (venture management), concepts of distribution (vending machines and discount houses), and concepts of pricing structure. Furthermore, as we shall see, the discovery process reaches far into the channels of distribution in search of opportunities. While most of our illustrations are product-oriented we have not lost sight of non-product-oriented opportunities.

The National Science Foundation commissioned a study on barriers to innovation. In Chapter 5 we pointed out that four of the nine barriers

---

[1] Peter F. Drucker, *Management* (New York: Harper & Row, 1974), p. 45.

[2] William Lazer, *Marketing Management* (New York: John Wiley & Sons, Inc., 1971), p. 44.

mentioned were related to information. Information problems can be more easily overcome than behavioral problems concerned with executive fear of failure, a condition we have mentioned before and will mention again. Even with information and other barriers to innovation in corporations in mind, "probably the most important is the reluctance of executives, of whatever level, to take the risk of being blamed for failure."[3] Accordingly, one of the managerial innovations being rapidly adapted by large companies is the venture management concept mentioned above. Of course, many marketing opportunities exist in trying to discover new ways of satisfying consumer wants and needs. With this in mind we turn to an analysis of the satisfaction process.

THE SATISFACTION PROCESS

Consumer satisfaction is absolutely essential to the accomplishment of most corporate objectives. In the hierarchy of satisfactions the consumer plays a key role, but to satisfy him is a complex process. A firm finds opportunity both by the analysis of this process and in its several steps toward carrying the process through. These steps in the satisfaction process are a part of the framework of this chapter and of Chapter 8.

Recognition of consumer aspirations

The first step in the process is the identification of the wants and needs or aspirations of the consumer which are not being satisfactorily served. The ordinary difficulties of market research are compounded in this case because consumers may not really know either what their wants are or what it will take to satisfy them. Furthermore, even if their wants can be pinned down at any one time, they may change rather drastically even as a marketing program is being designed to serve them. Despite these and other pitfalls of want identification, it remains the cornerstone of a marketing program.

Creation of selective dissatisfaction

The second step is the subtle creation of selective dissatisfaction with the present state of affairs by convincing consumers that their needs will be satisfied by only one brand or by one product. There are two types of dissatisfaction to be created in two different kinds of situations. One type stems from the desire of the firm to switch the consumer

---

[3] Ernest D. Phelps, "Study Finds Unavailability of Market Information and Executives' Fear of Failure Bar Innovation," *Marketing News*, May 1, 1974, p. 1.

of competing brands to its own brand. There are complications and hazards to a brand-switching strategy. Not only is it necessary to encourage disloyalty to a competing brand, but the firm must simultaneously establish a base for new customer loyalty to its brand and keep the loyalty of its old customers.

The other type of dissatisfaction to be created is more intangible and complex than that associated with brand-switching. It requires, among other things, that consumers be convinced that they should change the vague order of priority they have for the satisfaction of their overall wants and needs. Their needs are nearly insatiable and are as *they* see them. Their resources are limited, and the vague order in which they plan to satisfy their needs is constantly shifting. The firm is not only competing with every other producer of the same type of product or service, but also with producers of completely dissimilar products. In addition, it is trying to gain a solid place at or near the top of the shifting order of priorities of the consumer.

Even though we do not fully understand the catalytic action involved, we are all familiar with the result of that mysterious process of transforming wants to needs. The firm is faced with helping the consumer establish priorities of needs for such things as a first trip abroad, a second home for vacations, a third color television set, or a fourth car for the new 16-year-old. Before a brand can be switched, or a new product displace an old one, or an alternative product receive a higher priority in the needs hierarchy, selective disatisfaction with present consumption patterns must be created. Both subtlety and selectivity are important or the strategy may backfire.

Anticipated satisfaction

After having created dissatisfaction with the present state of affairs, the third step in the consumer satisfaction process is to create a state of anticipated satisfaction to be derived from the new brand, the new product, or the new order of priority of needs. At this point customers are created. They have been convinced that a change in their consumption patterns and priorities is desirable. From the point of view of the firm, they have been convinced that the product they have either bought or desire to buy will satisfy their needs. In short, they are anticipating satisfaction. There is evidence that leads us to believe that customers are determined to be satisfied if for no other reason than to prove the wisdom of their decision to buy.

Unfortunately, many managements stop here and consider that they have fulfilled the requirements of the marketing concept. They have won all the battles. Customers have not only bought, but are determined to be even more satisfied with their purchases than they expected to be. But through an incredible lack of foresight, planning, or control, or through massive doses of bad luck, competitive reactions, environmental changes, managerial ignorance, or stupidity, some of them are turned off. There are other steps to be taken before the firm can be said to have fulfilled the requirements of the marketing concept and the marketing-oriented company.

Realized satisfaction

The fourth step implies that the firm helps consumers feel that the satisfaction they anticipated has been realized. Basically, a state of realized satisfaction involves such things as feeling that they bought what they thought they were buying, that they bought what the seller told them they were buying, and that the product does what is claimed for it. In short, after using the product, customers must feel as satisfied as they anticipated they would be. The Sears Roebuck approach of "satisfaction guaranteed or your money back" is one facet of assuring that a customer, while dissatisfied with a *product,* remains a satisfied *customer.* The other facet, of course, is to correct the causes of the dissatisfaction.

Antidissatisfaction inoculation

The fifth step is the inoculation of consumers against dissatisfaction with the new patterns of consumption the marketing program helped create. The inoculation should serve to prevent a competitor from doing what you did and creating dissatisfaction among your customers. Of course, this step is closely related to the preceding one. It implies that the firm will not merely react to dissatisfaction, but will work as actively and assiduously to determine the degree of consumer satisfaction as it did initially in learning the consumers' wants and needs. Naturally the purpose of this step is to create loyal customers for repeat purchases.

CONSUMER AND PRODUCER SATISFACTIONS

Sources of opportunities

In a very real sense consumers and producers occupy polar positions when it comes to the process of maximizing satisfactions. Consumers want as much satisfaction from their purchases as they can get at the lowest possible outlay of money and effort; producers want the same thing. Probably more than any other one factor, the trade-offs inherent in these polar positions present the greatest number of opportunities to the innovative marketing manager. Also, even though the majority of consumers are reasonably satisfied, those still unsatisfied remain a pool of opportunity.

The two parts of Figure 6–1 depict consumers and a producer existing

FIGURE 6–1
Scales of Consumer and Producer Satisfactions

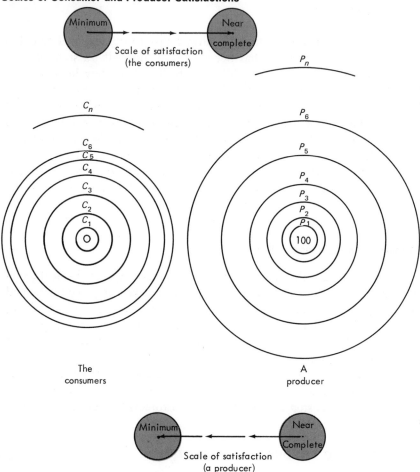

without any relationship to each other. We make this temporary separation to simplify certain explanations. We start with points showing zero satisfaction for consumers and 100 percent satisfaction for the producer—making the unrealistic assumption that satisfactions can be measured with such precision. Our awareness of the spurious precision we imply is illustrated on the two scales of satisfaction, where, instead of points showing zero and 100 percent satisfaction of the parties, we have zones of "minimum" and "near complete" satisfaction.

Consumers

The several rings around the point of zero satisfaction (C_1 to C_6) for consumers indicate additional increments of satisfaction. The arc C_n implies that we do not know the outer limits of satisfaction. What do these increments imply? How are they added? What do they mean to both consumers and producers? Obviously, they imply that somehow something has happened to the wants and needs of consumers, and they are willing to acquire more of the product than indicated by point zero and circle C_1.

What could have happened? Any number of things, but we will discuss possibilities in terms of the elements of the marketing mix.

1. Product. A new product may have come on the market, or an old one may have been redesigned to make it more wanted or needed and thus more satisfying. For example, a radio may have been redesigned to make it portable and capable of being moved from room to room in the home. Eventually it is redesigned again so that a student can put it in his pocket and take it to class and listen to the World Series through his ear plug during an interesting lecture on consumer satisfactions by the professor.

2. Promotion. More consumers may become aware of a product through a promotional campaign—or perhaps they are persuaded that the product is not only what they have always wanted, but that they *need* it. For example, while the professor is giving that interesting lecture on promotion, the student may be hearing on his pocket radio of great things that will happen to him if he buys a Honda.

3. Channels of distribution. The availability of the product will also affect the degree to which consumers will be satisfied. By coincidence the professor, in his interesting lecture, is talking about the same thing as the announcer. Of course, the student is unaware of the professor for he has just heard the announcer say that right down the street from the campus is the finest Honda sales and service organization in America—with mechanics factory-trained in Japan.

4. Price. Obviously, there is some relation between price and the number of people who can afford to buy. More people may become effective demanders of a product as the price is adjusted. So price may be a source of increased satisfaction to the consumer in meeting his wants and needs, and thus enlarging them. After the announcer finishes telling about a Price To Fit Every Pocketbook—while the professor is discussing Price Elasticity of Demand—there is time for one more commercial. This time a friendly banker tells the student how he can solve his no-Honda problem.

Things other than the elements of the marketing mix may bring added increments to consumer satisfaction. A consumer's income may go up, enabling him to enter a market otherwise closed to him. The product or service may become almost "indispensable" to the culture, as have air conditioned automobiles in some areas. Consumers may feel a need for the product to enhance their self-images. They may want it because their friends have it. And so on.

Producers

Producers, like consumers, have many opportunities. There are many things other than a minimum amount of profit that will satisfy a manager. Also, we can't measure satisfaction precisely, and there are different degrees of satisfaction—which also give rise to many opportunities. In Figure 6–1 we show the center of the producer's satisfaction at 100 and the center of consumers' satisfaction at zero, placing the two at opposite poles. The diagram indicates that the producer must accept less and less satisfaction in order to bring his satisfaction level in line with that of the consumers.

What does this imply for opportunities? Figure 6–1 suggests that the producer can give up satisfaction in a series of steps, or decrements, in order to provide more consumer satisfaction. He may have given up plenty by the time he arrives at P_5. Yet another producer may find that at the same level his satisfaction is "Near Complete." Why? To lay a foundation for answering this question, let us look at what the producer is giving up in the way of satisfaction. Further, consider that 100 percent satisfaction for the producer consists of a mish-mash of things: profit; volume of sales; quality of product; and the like. Since we used the marketing mix to illustrate increasing consumer satisfaction, we will use it to illustrate decreasing producer satisfaction.

1. Product. The producer likes the present product design; it appeals to him personally, and he does not want to change. To do so would mean an additional investment in new machinery, teaching everyone new things about a redesigned product. Nevertheless, his cabinet radio standing four or five feet high and weighing 150 pounds gives way to a portable one. He is serving more consumer wants and enjoying it less.

2. Promotion. To tell the public about the new product, to inform salesmen, to train dealers—all this is going to take more money. In addition, he is going to have to spend time of his own on the promotion program. Furthermore, he dislikes wasting money on advertising. Years before in one of his classes he heard his professor say, "Half of all advertising is wasted; we just don't know which half." But he goes ahead with the promotion program.

3. Channels of distribution. To establish appropriate channels takes not only money but also managerial time, neither of which the producer wants to spend. But he does it in order to make the product conveniently available to the consumer he is courting.

4. Price. This is the last thing he wants to touch. His feasibility studies show great profits if the product can be sold at the initial price. But he reduces the price and becomes reconciled to a less satisfactory profit level.

What the producer has done is to begin to market the product by seeking to satisfy the consumer. The tools have been the several elements of the marketing mix. The producer has examined the "behavioral" elasticity of demand and recognized the "behavioral" elasticity of supply. The producer traded what seemed to be perfect satisfaction for a lesser amount in order to satisfy consumers in sufficient quantities. Note that the producer can get no satisfaction without seeking and arranging for these trade-offs with consumer satisfaction.

Figure 6–2 takes the previously isolated consumers and the producer from their isolation. Join us in making some reasonable assumptions in order to explain the significant aspects of these trade-offs. The first assumption is a carryover from the prior illustration: we know what perfect and zero satisfactions are. Further, the figures indicate that we know (a) the magnitude of the satisfactions given up by the producer (P_1 to P_2) and (b) that consumer satisfaction rises in known increments (C_1 to C_2). Also, we imply that the producer reduces his satisfaction an increment and awaits the consumers' reaction.

Note on Figure 6–2 that at increments C_3 and P_3—as well as earlier ones—the producer and the consumers are still worlds apart. Increments C_4 and P_4 overlap and create a zone where the satisfactions of both are met. That group of consumers satisfied with the producer's efforts at P_4 is shown by the shaded zone. It would be exciting if we could identify this market as an absolute volume, but there are too many variables involved to do anything other than call it a zone of an approximate magnitude.

Now we assume that the producer gives up even more satisfaction in order to increase consumer satisfaction. The enlarged market zones are outlined by the heavy solid lines and the dashed line.

One of our implicit assumptions, not previously stated, is that the producer must give up some satisfaction in order to increase consumer satisfaction. This is not necessarily so. The producer may redesign the product at little or no loss in satisfaction, and substantially increase consumer satisfaction. For example, years and years ago a no-suds detergent for automatic washing machines was introduced. Consumers seemed

FIGURE 6–2
More Scales of Consumer and Producer Satisfactions

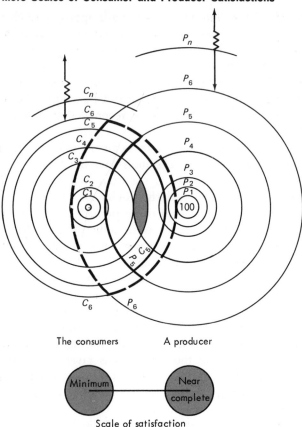

The consumers   A producer

Scale of satisfaction

to think that a sudsless detergent couldn't get clothes clean; so they refused to buy the product. A sudsing agent was added; and consumer satisfaction went, figuratively speaking, from C_1 to C_6 without reducing the producer's satisfaction any. A similar result—but better—was obtained by a cigarette company. Again referring to Figure 6–2, the zone of satisfaction was about where C_4 and P_4 overlap. Not very many men smoked Marlboro, for it was considered a woman's cigarette. By changing the package to a box and shifting to promoting featuring real he-men situations, the market was enlarged. Consumer satisfaction went from C_4 to C_6. Producer satisfaction also increased from P_4 to P_1.

Johnson and Johnson developed a program to increase consumer and producer satisfaction with their baby shampoo and powder. The company began telling us that Mommy was using her baby's shampoo on her own hair. Also, they let us peek in on Grandmother telling the child that, of course, she too uses Johnson's Baby Powder. Later that advertising program began to include men as targets of the message. Pause a minute to reflect upon the situation and reconstruct what may have happened to cause the company to develop this new campaign. Obviously, it had enlarged its target market to include adults as well as babies as ultimate users. What aspects of the environment may have caused the company to want to enlarge its target market? You know that birth rates are declining. For a company that sells baby powder there are at least three alternative courses of action in response to this fact. One is to plan a program to get a larger share of the future baby market—a viable approach but difficult to accomplish. A second alternative is to recognize the inevitable decline in the market and plan to accommodate to the smaller market. If this is done the future has grasped control of the company, and change has begun to manage it. A third alternative is the one apparently chosen by the company. It enlarged its concept of the target market from one consisting of babies to one consisting of people.

In terms of the discussions in previous chapters, what has the company done in this case to find new opportunities? Note that the company converted a serious problem into a great opportunity.

1. It determined what it wanted to have happen and set out to make it happen.
2. It decided to manage change instead of being managed by it.
3. It adapted the environment to the company by including other segments in the target market.
4. Of course, it also partially adapted the company to the environment.

These types of opportunities reflect shifting emphases, and added emphases, on product design and/or promotion to convert more potential consumers into actual consumers without diminishing producer satisfaction.

Within the framework provided by Figures 6–1 and 6–2 let us look at another facet of opportunities. One of the functions of what we have referred to as the discovery process is to discover new opportunities and problems. One of the characteristics of this discovery process is to examine the situation within a framework different from the "usual" one.

After the Second World War someone noted that housing options for the traveler were limited: hotels; a few tourist homes which were merely rooming houses with a sign saying "Tourist Home"; and a few tourist courts. Consumers were *apparently* well satisfied with the hotels.

Looking outside that framework, someone decided to change the often unsavory image of the tourist court. The motel industry was created. The mobile home industry is another case in point. There were a few house trailers around, but the market to be served was limited. The mobile home became a new addition to the housing industry. Someone discovered or "guessed" that consumers might be out there at Arc n on Figure 6–1.

Earlier we said that one producer may have to give up plenty of satisfaction to arrive at P_5 on Figure 6–2, while another producer may find near complete satisfaction at the same level. Many firms aim at the mass market. For example, a couple of decades or so ago most of the large record player companies aimed at that mass market. To get to C_6 on the figure, they had to design and market extremely high-quality sets. For their own satisfaction, primarily related to profits, they were unwilling to try for the small market consisting of people who wanted high quality and were willing to pay high prices. Of course, companies were serving that market and others came into existence to serve it. Presumably their satisfactions are as great as the other companies who serve only the mass market.

In concluding this section, we emphasize three points. First, we have put the consumer in a passive role ready to be courted by the producer: "If you satisfy me, I'll buy." Thus, the burden of marketing is upon the producer. He must subordinate his notion of his own satisfaction to that of satisfying the consumer. Second, since the reader has probably had a course in economics, he will be aware of the concept of price elasticity of demand. We are emphasizing additional dimensions and in effect are speaking of the behavioral elasticity of demand and supply where consumer behavior is the key factor in the elasticity concept rather than price or income. Price and profit are only one dimension of satisfaction of consumer and producer, respectively. We have added several other dimensions.

Third, the reader is accustomed to finding an equilibrium point at which demand and supply curves intersect. We prefer to think of a zone where the satisfactions of a portion of the market are more or less in balance with the expected satisfactions of the producer. In the latter case, the average cost curve, marginal cost, and marginal revenue may or may not be relevant. If a survival profit is earned in one case, the producer may be satisfied. If less than maximum profit is earned in another case, the producer may be dissatisfied. In short, satisfaction of consumer and producer are in balance in a zone, not at a point; there are other dimensions to demand and supply elasticity than price; change in demand and change in supply are extremely qualitative factors; and, finally, the precise limits of satisfaction of producer and consumer are not known and probably cannot be known.

MARKETING, OPPORTUNITIES, AND INNOVATIONS

Marketing

In a discussion of several aspects of inventions, innovations, and the timing of their introduction, George Steiner reported on a study of important inventions from 1800 to 1957 in agriculture, petroleum refining, papermaking, and railroading. He concluded that "in no single instance is a scientific discovery specified as the factor initiating an important invention in any of these four industries."[4] He added that inventions are mainly induced by demand or market considerations rather than knowledge; most are stimulated by a present or potential market opportunity. Another researcher concluded that, "Recognition of demand is a more frequent factor in successful innovation than recognition of technical potential."[5] Donald G. Marquis and Sumner Myers studied 567 product or process innovations made over a 5- to 10-year period by 121 companies in five manufacturing industries. They found that 45 percent were made in response to a perceived market demand or need. Another 30 percent were developed as a result of a production need. Thus, the external and internal needs or demands accounted for the development of three quarters of the innovations. Only about one fifth were "knowledge induced" in the sense of "maybe we can find a use for this technical idea."

It is interesting to note that innovations often do not come from the industries that use them. Synthetic fibers came from the chemical industry rather than the textile industry; synthetic industrial diamonds come from General Electric and not the machine tool industry. The fact that this seems to be an important characteristic illustrates the many opportunities for developing a market for innovations.

There are at least three morals that can be drawn from the foregoing. First, the constant searching for marketing opportunities through the analysis of demand should be an important area for management attention, as it is in many companies. Also, there should be more attention given to establishing closer communication among marketing, production, and R&D people. There seems to be a very effective communications barrier among these three groups, which leads to our third moral. A more effective organizational scheme needs to be adopted by more firms to facilitate the innovation process. We will discuss this point more fully later in the chapter.

---

[4] George A. Steiner, *Top Management Planning* (New York: The Macmillan Company, 1969), pp. 664 and 665.

[5] Donald G. Marquis, "The Anatomy of Successful Innovations," in *Managing Advancing Technology* vol. 1 (New York: American Management Association, 1972), p. 37.

These morals and the conditions from which they are drawn also underscore the importance of the firm developing a unity of purpose and action through the recognition that marketing managers perform in two worlds; they have two major areas of responsibility. The firm and the system it exists in is one of these worlds, while the marketing department and its system is the second. There again we refer to management *and* the marketing function, and management *of* the marketing function.

But the development of unity of purpose and action begins on an even higher plane than the two worlds of the marketing manager. The manager cannot function effectively in those two worlds if they have not been recognized in a planning program complete with objectives and policies that the manager has had a part in making.

Again, note the role of *analysis* in the functioning of the discovery process. Before the marketing manager can even begin to function as a manager of the marketing function, the corporate strategy must be determined. One fact of this strategy pertains, of course, to opportunity strategy.

Several sets of marketing analyses are necessary for the development of opportunity strategy: those made to discover the present and possible future demands of the market for want and need satisfaction; those made to relate the demands of the marketplace to the mission, objectives, and resources of the firm; those made to modify objectives and acquire resources if necessary; those made to segment the market; and those made to estimate the reaction of competitors to alternative marketing programs. Strategies growing out of these analyses will be discussed in the chapter on the external environment.

Kinds of Opportunities

What are opportunities? One dictionary defines opportunity as "a combination of circumstances favorable for the purpose"; "fit time"; "good chance or occasion." It is up to the marketing manager to do several things in the context of this definition. One of the things the manager should do is to identify *what* the purpose is that this "combination of circumstances" is favorable for. Another is to determine *which* circumstances must be combined to make the opportunity favorable for the purpose. A third marketing job is to determine *how* the circumstances should be combined to create or exploit a perceived opportunity.

The other definitions also provide a clue to the task of the marketing manager: "fit time;" "good chance or occasion." Sometimes opportunities are more apparent than real. One reason may be that the market is not actually ready for a perceived opportunity. On the other hand, the opportunity may be fading away just as the firm is ready to capitalize on it.

Market segmentation as an opportunity. We have discussed and defined opportunities for marketing oriented companies; so now we discuss market segmentation as one aspect of markets in general as an opportunity. However, before we discuss segmentation, let us put it into the market perspective. It is one of three major concepts related to markets. Another of the three concepts concerns the nature of markets. Using the hierarchical basis of classification we have employed with other concepts, we can start with the broad aspects of markets and successively narrow them down.

The geographic market. We have previously referred to the market as being "out there somewhere." Markets are generally considered to be places or locations. At the top of the hierarchy there is the world market followed by other geographic markets such as the Latin American, North American, and United States markets. We can work our way down through the southwestern market to that of a state, of a city, and finally to the ultimate market location: 1313 East 13th Street.

Opportunities are present in the geographic aspects of the market as a place or location. For example, in the context of the marketing mix, geographic aspects of the market may affect the design of the product since there are regional preferences. Or they may affect promotion programs. Most of our national publications have regional editions in which a national advertiser can place regional messages. The channels of distribution may vary from the use of the company sales force in densely populated regions to the use of distributors in others. Certainly, logistics strategy will vary from one region to another. Perhaps in one place company owned warehouses and transportation networks may be used, while public warehousemen and for-hire carriers are used elsewhere. Finally, many companies have regional difference in prices.

There are significant opportunities to improve effectiveness of the firm by developing marketing strategy based upon location of markets. Similar significant opportunities exist for the improvement of efficiency. Again, within the context of the marketing mix, we can see some examples of opportunities. We have identified the product as not just a physical collection of materials but as a concept including design, post-sale service, guarantees, and the like. In one location it may be more practical to offer a higher level of service than in another: the consumer may have to wait one day for the repairman in one area and ten days in another. The promotion mix may be more heavily weighted with personal sales calls and heavy doses of advertising here than it is there because of characteristics of location. Or the sales force may use the telephone here, and have the customer mail in his orders from there. The logistics consideration of routing salesmen, the direct delivery of goods to store door or indirect delivery through warehouses, may be viable alternatives.

The people market.   Since we do it ourselves in this book and elsewhere, we have no particular objection to looking at the market in general terms such as "the market" or 200 million mouths to feed, or ten million auto buyers. However, for marketing purposes we must be more specific than that, for there are not 200 million potential mouths to consume smoked oysters or ten million purchasers of Rolls Royces. Millions of infants can't eat smoked oysters and millions of drivers would prefer something other than a Rolls. Of course, there are other millions who can't afford either of the two products.

Moving from the consumer market to the industrial and institutional markets we run into the same type of situation. Corporations, governments, and institutions do not buy goods and services. They only pay for them and use them. People buy. The corporation, government, or institution may be the market, but people are the contact. It is the behavioral pattern of the buyer and his view of the commodity that is important. Neither the university nor the book store bought this book. In fact, you only paid for it; you didn't buy it. Your professor bought it for a combination of reasons. But you will have a powerful influence on whether he buys it again.

Our points are simple. People with known or latent demands and the ability to convert those demands to consumption are the market. But there are hierarchies there too. College teachers are not the market for books on marketing; college teachers who teach marketing courses are the market. Even they are intermediaries in the market, for, in the final analysis, college students who take courses in marketing have to be satisfied or the professor will switch books.

Market segmentation.   The discussion of the geographic and people aspects of "the market" has given us some insights into market segmentation. But geography and age groups and the like do not constitute segmentation. They are *one* aspect of it only. Marketing people at one time did think of segmentation primarily in geographic, social, cultural, and economic terms. As we learned more about markets, however, we recognized that segmentation as a strategic marketing concept has almost nothing to do with geography, and only a little more to do with demographic characteristics.

Market segmentation is a concept based upon the characteristics of the product and the benefits they provide to the user. The basis of segmentation is what behavioral characteristics consumers have in common and not what demographic characteristics they share. College students are not just college students. They form a homogeneous group in some respects; in others, they have little in common.

In an entirely different context for an entirely different purpose, Herman

Kahn made the point of dissimilarities within a demographic group. Referring to college students at Berkeley, he said,

> . . . you can almost tell what school the students are in by the way they dress. Roughly, engineering and business dress "square," physicists dress in half shirt-sleeves, half dress-half work pants; math students . . . tend to dress like "Hell's angels"; psychology and sociology students are often hippie. . . . I suspect Berkeley is a microcosm of part of our future.[6]

The point is that no longer do we view segmentation on the basis of similarities such as young marrieds, college students, blacks, women, or old people. Nor do we view it on the basis of location. Rather, we view *market segments* as groups who have behavioral characteristics in common and expect similar benefits from products or services. Then *market segmentation* is a marketing strategy designed to serve a group with similar characteristics. Of course, it is true that many young marrieds have things in common as do blacks, women, and old people; westerners, miners, and professional athletes. Even so, you don't market to westerners, miners, and athletes. You market to people who expect certain characteristics. Some of those people are young, black, married athletes; some are old, single, white miners.

Several points emerge from this discussion. They relate to the steps in segmentation, requirements for segmentation, and alternative segmentation strategies.

The steps in segmentation are:

1. Define the basis for segmentation you are going to use. This requires knowledge of consumer behavior of the segments.
2. Collect data on each segment. How many young, black, married athletes and old, single, white miners are in it? Where is each located?
3. See if they meet the requirements for a segmented group. (See below.)
4. Select the segments to be your target market.
5. Develop the marketing mix to deliver the benefits hoped for.

The requirements for segmentation are:

1. Identify according to the demographic characteristics to facilitate measurement and location.
2. Determine if there is an effective demand as well as actual or latent demand.
3. Determine if they can be economically served.

---

[6] Herman Kahn, ed., *The Future of the Corporation* (New York: Mason & Lipscomb Publisher, 1974), p. 138.

We have not said or implied much about segmentation strategies, but we now list two such strategies.

1. For products with more or less universal appeal and for which segments are not readily identified, there is an undifferentiated approach.

2. Differentiated strategies are adjusted to appeal to the demand of the segments. In one case the segments may be very broad; in another, very narrow. If the segment is concentrated, the strategy may be designed for that group. For example, people who have great knowledge of stereo sound equipment and want and can pay for "the best" may constitute one such segment.

Before turning to other kinds of marketing opportunities, we make one final point: like everything else, market segments are always changing. What a group looks for in benefits today may be much different from what it looks for tomorrow.

The marketing concept as an opportunity. There is an old saying which is relevant to the timing of opportunities. It goes something like this: "There is no force as powerful as an idea whose time has come." In Chapter 1 we did two things relevant to this discussion. We cited Adam Smith as an early proponent of the marketing concept. Also, we said that the adoption of the marketing concept was new, having come into existence in the 1950s, and that it is rapidly leading to the marketing company.

We have already seen the force exerted by this idea whose time has come. We can't really say why it wasn't adopted earlier, except in terms of our earlier discussion: it was an opportunity more apparent than real, for it was out of phase with time. The circumstances present in the environment apparently could not be combined favorably. Managers were production-oriented; they produced what they wanted to and somehow it got sold. This "proved" that they were following the right path. The fact that the path was destined to peter out into a dead end was apparently not even considered as a possibility, for one does not argue with success! With the marketing concept itself as the fountainhead of opportunity, let us examine some other kinds of opportunities.

Other kinds of opportunities. The marketing opportunities are in the environments as they exist at any one time and as they are projected to be. Because environments are changing, opportunities are multiplying disproportionately faster. We are all aware of the elements of the external environment and the fact that they are changing. However, it appears desirable to list some of these elements, some of the changes, and think of some possible opportunities these changes present.

Ecology. The world we live in and the way we live in it: ecology, the relation between organisms and their environment. There is probably no single area of human concern that presents as many opportunities for the marketing activities of the firm than the broad area we refer to as ecology. Before proceeding with this discussion, a note on perspective may be in order. The authors are not oblivious to social, spiritual, and humane aspects of improving the lot of our people and the condition of our environment. This chapter is not the place to express our concern for these matters. We view these situations of poverty, peace, ignorance, pollution, greed, corruption, permissiveness, irresponsibility, and repressiveness as opportunities. In some cases, as opportunities to make a buck; in others, as opportunities to do good; in still others as opportunities to do good *and* make a buck. One can "do good" and at the same time "do well." We view the marketing concept as a useful device for these purposes. Having recognized the other side of marketing, the social side, we will go on with our discussion of the economic side. Our discussion will center on opportunities for doing well for the company while doing good for the public.

What are some of the opportunities for marketing activities in the area of ecology? Start your thinking with the basics: food, clothing, health, shelter. The size of the potential market for good is almost staggering if all of the three billion or so people in the world were to be as well nourished as most of us in this country are.

What about the devices for preparing the land, storing and processing the crops, and so on? After sizing up opportunities for the basic things, shift your thinking to the opportunities in physical, visual, and audio communication. It is clear that there is money to be made out of misery if only the opportunities for doing good can be seen and capitalized on. Once this vast market is removed from misery, think of the market for the trappings of affluence: reducing machines, diet foods, water purifiers, litter baskets, solid waste reduction machinery, and so on!

Demography. The size of our population, the composition of it, and its health. Can you think of any new opportunities created by size and composition of the population of our country since the big spurt following World War II? What about new schools and portable school buildings? Birth control devices? Nursing homes? Hospitals with rising costs?

Miscellaneous. Here are a number of things:

1. The changing workweek. What opportunities has it created? What has it done to the leisure industry?
2. The increase in disposable income.
3. The explosion in knowledge.
4. The information industry.
5. Shortages of resources.

In addition to these rather basic things, opportunities have been and are being created by changes in technology, behavior of buyers, the characteristics of the market. Changes in the structure of the channels of distribution and our understanding of marketing in general present many opportunities.

Groups of opportunities. Perhaps we can group all of these opportunities into five small groups.

1. Opportunities to improve effectiveness in attaining the objectives of the firm.
2. Opportunities to improve efficiency both within the firm and in serving customers.
3. Opportunities for innovation through development of new concepts and things as well as by adapting concepts useful in one place to make them useful in another.
4. Opportunities for product differentiation to make the product more competitive.
5. Opportunities for market segmentation.

This last subject of market segmentation presents some very interesting challenges to marketing managers. Theodore Levitt has written, "The traditional idea of the mass market . . . is dying a gradual death."[7] He goes on to say that the mass market is being replaced by a new type of consumer who is more discriminating than the old. Instead of thinking of the market as being homogeneous, marketing managers are going to have to think selectively and think small. They must start thinking of smaller, more heterogeneous markets, each of which requires its own unique strategies.

Along the same line, Ralph Sorenson has written that European businessmen have had to work with small markets so they have been forced to develop skills in identifying their particular market niche and in developing new specialty products to meet the needs of that segment. He added that since the United States is retreating from the idea of huge mass markets and going toward greater segmentation, our marketing managers can take a leaf from "the segmentation book of their European counterparts."[8]

Resistances to opportunity exploitation. While man is the central force behind resource creation and the discovery of opportunities, he is also the central resistance to the exploitation of resources. The late Dr. E. E. Dale, a noted historian of the Southwest who helped to make its history, wrote it, and taught it, had an especially colorful method of expressing this point. He said that the problem with the West was

---

[7] Theodore Levitt, *The Marketing Mode* (New York: McGraw-Hill Book Company, 1969), p. 104.

[8] Ralph Z. Sorenson II, "U.S. Marketers Can Learn from European Innovators," *Harvard Business Review*, September–October 1972, p. 91.

that it had .45 calibre opportunities exploited by .22 calibre minds.[9]
"We have always done it this way." "We have never done it that way."
"We tried it 30 years ago." "Our situation is different."

Theodore Levitt variously refers to the human factor as "Management Myopia" and "Marketing Myopia."[10] Levitt seems to be more concerned with inability to see the forest for the trees than he is with the pettiness Dale was concerned with. In between, Erich W. Zimmermann speaks of resistances of this type as, "Human failings such as 'cussedness,' lack of foresight, mismanagement, . . . ignorance, stupidity, and greed."[11] Herman Kahn and B. Bruce-Briggs of The Hudson Institute wrote of *educated incapacity* as "an acquired or learned incapacity to understand or see a problem, much less a solution."[12] Educated incapacity is an affliction from which we all suffer at times and is responsible for the notions behind Levitt's "Marketing Myopia." They say that the more expert and more educated we are the more likely we are to be affected. The symptoms of educated incapacity: (1) if a problem or solution—or an opportunity—lies outside an accustomed framework, we may not see it, and (2) a reluctance to accept new methods.

There are other resistances to exploitation of opportunities, but compared with the human resistances they are minor. They include such things as:

1. Forces in the technological environment—physical capacity of resources, managerial abilities, information, and so on.
2. Forces in the economic environment—competitors, channels of distribution, the limit of the market.
3. Forces in the spatial and temporal environments—the ability of the logistics system to perform.

To relate the parts of this discussion on opportunities to each other, we return to the definition: a combination of circumstances favorable for the purpose; fit time. Opportunities of many types are "there" lying around waiting to be discovered. The greatest resistance to their discovery and exploitation lies in the nature of man himself, especially in his educated incapacity. The "circumstances" to be combined lie in the

---

[9] This statement appeared in some of Dr. Dale's writing, but we do not know where. Also, he used the phrase in private conversations. It is inaccurate to apply his comment to Westerners in general for the context in which it was used was in comparing the bigness of many of the early leaders of the West with the littleness of some of the petty politicians.

[10] Theodore Levitt, "Marketing Myopia," *Harvard Business Review*, July–August 1960, among other places.

[11] W. N. Peach and James A. Constantin, *Zimmerman's World Resources and Industries*, 3d ed. (New York: Harper & Row, 1972), p. 18.

[12] Herman Kahn and B. Bruce-Briggs, *Things To Come* (New York: The Macmillan Co., 1972), p. 80.

internal and external environments. The job of the marketing manager is to identify the circumstances and combine them in proper proportions when the time is right. Very simple.

One of the characteristics of one of the circumstances is that most of the opportunities are apparently demand-pull as distinct from technology-push. Most opportunities appear to arise in the market as a result of some need or want. The other side of that coin, technology-push, is also a marketing-oriented concept. How can we use what we have invented? General Electric has established a separate department to market those technological developments flowing from GE labs which it cannot immediately use. Also, NASA—the space agency—has established a program to transfer technology developed in the space program to other uses.

We now turn to a discussion of innovations.

Innovation objectives

Peter Drucker lists several innovation goals for a typical business. Notice how the first four relate to (1) marketing, and (2) the firm as a whole. In addition, notice that he includes *services* and *processes* as well as products; and that he is concerned with improvements on the old products and services as well as introduction of the new. Also notice how all of them imply a need for analyses of environments as a prelude to setting objectives. Further, notice how he refers both to the present and the future. Finally, note how they imply the collaboration of several people. These points specifically called to your attention relate to the marketing manager functioning on behalf of the firm as a whole: management *and* the marketing function. Drucker's list (with emphasis supplied):

1. *New* products or services that *are* needed to attain marketing objectives.
2. *New* products or services that *will be* needed because of technological changes that may make present products obsolete.
3. Product *improvements* needed both to attain market objectives and to anticipate expected technological changes.
4. New processes and improvements in old ones which are needed to satisfy market goals—manufacturing improvements to make possible the attainment of pricing objectives.
5. Innovations and improvements in all major areas of activity—accounting, design, office management, labor relations.[13]

---

[13] Peter F. Drucker, *The Practice of Management* (New York: Harper & Row, 1954) p. 69.

MANAGEMENT, MARKETING, AND INNOVATIONS

Management and successful innovations[14]

David Hertz examined a number of companies that have successfully explored new concepts through technical research and development. While we are already familiar with the ideas, we will repeat them for emphasis and to establish a basis for some of what follows. He said there were two basic assumptions that inhibit innovation. There seems to be a widespread notion that nothing can be done about resistance to change in an organization. Also, there is a communications barrier between scientist and management that must be forever unbreakable.

We have seen that these are problems in innovation, but to accept them as insuperable is to commit the organization to defeat. We will now look at some of the characteristics of successful innovators. Our approach will be to use the criteria for successful innovators that Hertz distilled from his study. As we go through these criteria, we will from time to time refer to our discussions in earlier chapters that seem to fit the criteria Hertz outlined.

Top management commitment. In the first several chapters we consistently emphasized the commitment that top managers must make not only to the process of planning and objective setting, but also to the objectives themselves. Hertz found that in the successful innovative companies, top management was not only committed to the research objectives, it was the source of many of the ideas. For example, in the chemical, petroleum, aerospace, and electronics industries, close to half of the productive research ideas were suggested by that group.

Involvement of scientists and program selection. The programs for research are tied to long-range planning for the business as a whole, and they are developed after consideration of the entire economic and other environment the company is in. The projects are selected in light of three questions related to the environment: the technical obstacles in the way; the economic factors influencing profitability; and how soon the problem must be solved to make the project technologically or economically feasible—that is, timing.

Again we refer to our analysis of the planning programs and the involvement of affected departments in setting objectives based upon analyses of environments. The Hertz study showed that communications between marketing and R&D people were successful when they dealt with the long-range objectives which were formulated in terms of trends in technical and socioeconomic matters. Hertz also found that the mar-

---

[14] The basic source of data in this section is David B. Hertz, "The Successful Innovators," in Roland Mann, ed., *The Arts of Top Management* (New York: McGraw-Hill Book Company, 1971), pp. 308–16.

keting-R&D communications were "often clogged with irrelevancies." Instead of focusing on opportunities, the meetings devolved to minor technical and procedural problems.

Organizing manpower resources. Hertz found that the functional organization is giving ground to "a combination of project and functional organization—often called 'matrix management.'" This sort of structural arrangement serves to keep R&D goals and personnel in balance. Also, it provides flexibility and mobility in assignment. We will comment more on this structure in the next section of this chapter.[15]

Application of R&D results. The successful innovators have often been able to apply the findings of one project to other projects. From an organizational point of view a problem has existed in persuading marketing and production to make the innovations because new things often have more opponents than proponents. One approach used to solve this problem was to bring the production and process engineers into the picture early. When this was done as soon as possible after the exploratory phase, the use of the innovation was spread. Also, because the users were a part of its development, their resistance was lowered. Further, in the initial operating and production stages, the researchers from R&D were used. They were also teamed with marketing people in the field trials. Since the marketing people had been involved from the beginning, communication difficulties and problems of resistance were minimized.

Venture management[16]

The most successful application of results of innovation has apparently been in those companies which have set up special structures such as commercial development departments, venture teams, or matrix organizations. Such structures facilitate the transfer of innovations from laboratory to production and marketing. Transfer is facilitated because the team is led by the idea that the marketing, production, and R&D people all have a commitment to the venture itself. The not-invented-here syndrome and resistance to change are broken down. One of the significant objectives of this venture team approach is the creation of new businesses under the umbrella of the organization. This results in new sales

[15] *Business Week*, June 9, 1975, pp. 50–8, shows how Hewlett-Packard Co. integrates these matters. See especially page 53, "Keeping close to the market."

[16] The literature on venture management is growing rapidly. An early article related the concept to marketing. See Richard M. Hill and James D. Hlavacek, "The Venture Team: A New Concept in Marketing Organization," *Journal of Marketing*, July 1972, pp. 44–50. For a broader role of venture management see David L. Wilemon and Gary R. Gemmill, "The Venture Manager as a Corporate Innovator," *California Management Review*, Fall 1973, pp. 49–56.

dollars instead of the replacement of sales of one product by sales of another.

These venture teams are handled in various ways. A common practice is for the venture team to present a proposal to the top management of the company and get it financed—in much the same way a banker finances an entrepreneur. The team then has a budget separate from the manufacturing and technical budgets with which it can "buy" plant time. The team consists of marketing, production, and R&D personnel, among others. If the project is a success, the venture may become a separate part of the firm or it may be assigned as a going concern to one of the divisions.

Some companies, such as 3M, Du Pont, and General Mills, have operated on the venture management basis for years, even decades. The idea is rapidly being adopted by other firms. Frederic Cook reports that in 1969–1970 his consulting company approached the 100 largest industrial corporations on the *Fortune* "500" list, plus a few others they knew were applying the technique. Of those contacted, 36 were using it.[17]

The venture team or matrix management approach promises to be one of the most significant management innovations of this century. In addition to the advantages of integration of effort and activities, and its use as a vehicle for innovation and opportunity exploitation, there is another advantage. It provides an outlet for the creative and entrepreneurial spirit of many executives, both young and middle-aged. Furthermore, it provides an excellent training ground for executives. In the venture teams, the young managers can get experience in responsibility, in finance, operations, marketing, etc., that they would never get in the ordinary manner.

An interesting approach to exploiting opportunities has been adopted by a number of companies. They have developed their expertise in certain areas for "in-house" purposes and have found marketing opportunities for that expertise, just as if it were an addition to their product line. Mack Hanan describes the marketing potentials of existing service functions, such as purchasing, personnel, and sales management, if they are spun off into subsidiary profit centers.[18] A number of companies have done this.

> Sony ran a full-page ad in *The Wall Street Journal* offering the use of its sales force to market in Japan the products of American manufacturers.

---

[17] Frederic Cook. "Venture Management As a New Way To Grow," *Innovation*, October 1971, p. 28.

[18] Mack Hanan, "Corporate Growth Through Internal Spin-outs," *Harvard Business Review*, November–December 1969, p. 55.

Alcoa sold its technical expertise by building a smelter for Anaconda, a competitor.

U.S. Steel provides engineering and consulting services for the steel industry.

Sun Oil sells consulting services in operations research and decision analysis.

Banks sell data processing services.[19]

CONCLUSION

Innovation and opportunity finding are the heart and soul of what we have called the discovery process. Our emphasis has been partially on the fact that there is no one single action involved in translating opportunities into innovations into satisfied customers into attained corporate objectives. Partially our emphasis has been on the fact that all departments must work for the same firm—a central theme of this book.

That is one reason we liked a definition of innovation as "a connected process in which many acts couple together for a common goal." These many acts coupled together include a series of logical steps.

First is the recognition of actual or potential demand—a marketing act—and of technical feasibility—an R&D act. But don't separate them!

Second is the development of a concept of a product or service and a tentative evaluation of its technological feasibility and marketability.

Third is the solving of any technical or economic problems that may arise. Notice the priority given to the discovery process; after discovery, solution is easy.

Fourth is the solution of the problem either by inventing what is needed or by adopting or adapting from another industry.

Fifth is the development of the product or service by creating and serving the market through the production process—use and diffusion.

---

[19] See *The Wall Street Journal*, May 31, 1972, p. 7, for the Sony ad; and the June 12, 1972 issue, p. 1, for a discussion of "Expertise for Sale."

chapter 7 | # The external environment of marketing

One way
    The social environment
    The economic environment
    The political-governmental environment
Our way
    Consumers and the consumption process
    Prospective consumers
    Employees
    Community
    Competition
    Suppliers
    Owners
    Creditors
    Channel members
    Society
Governments
    Introduction
    Curtailment of abuses
    Protection from abusive marketing practices
    Preventing further concentration of economic power
Marketing management and the external environment
    Planning, strategy, and the external environment
    Managing and the external environment
Summary

It should be clear by this time that marketing management does not operate in a vacuum and that planning and the search for opportunities in terms of "the market" are almost indispensable features of a marketing program. Neglect of an outside orientation on the part of marketing management is a luxury that cannot be afforded for the long term. For a time, some managers can orient themselves inside the firm, but ultimately the market will change in some unanticipated direction and these same managers will find they can no longer market their products because the products no longer meet consumer needs. There are, of course, many alternative explanations for this divergence between what the firm provides and what the market wants. It could be that the firm was market- oriented but misread the information it received. Or possibly the firm was so inefficient in production that too much management attention was required just to stay in business. It is also possible that management is inept.

But it is more likely that managers have chosen to deal with those parts of marketing management that require direct action and yield directly observable results, rather than engaging in the more difficult and less predictable relationships with vital external environments.

Our purpose in this chapter is to demonstrate that the marketing manager cannot ignore or even slight the firm's external relationships, since each of these relationships makes a substantial contribution to the firm's success—or failure. Further, we wish to dissect the generalized term "market" into a series of components. Each component impinges on the transaction process although some are more directly related to it than others. In this chapter we are first going to show you the broad outlines of one way of looking at the market. Then we are going to show you our way, which is an expansion of the first way.

ONE WAY

As you proceed through this chapter, you will see that we have chosen a particular line of reasoning in dealing with the external environment. In this section we point out one way of looking at these relationships and our reasons for using an alternative approach. It is possible to categorize marketing's relationships to the external environment in three groups: the Social, the Economic, and the Political-Governmental. These very broad categories offer one way of compartmentalizing the plethora of variable situations the marketer faces.

The social environment

If you were going to do a paper on the social environment, you would probably want to start by assembling all of those variables which describe "people" situations. It is not so much that people do not influence the other two categories, but rather that people are the core of the social environment. The social context provides the best opportunity to measure changes in relationships among people. If you were to trace the development of social environment, say from 1900, you would include a consideration of such things as:

1. The composition of the labor force, defined basically as those working or looking for work, and how its age, sex, and occupational characteristics have changed. You would note, among other things, that

the proportion of workers in agriculture decreased, while those employed in white-collar jobs increased proportionately.

2. The rise of industrial labor unions which contributed to the demise of the "toiling masses" and helped to bring increased consumption by a large segment of the population.

3. The effect of increased mobility on the traditional family organism. More recently, as the energy shortage tightens, you would wonder what long-term effects it will cause.

4. The fact that fewer and fewer instances occur of multiple generations of a family living in the same place.

5. A change in consumer attitudes toward the use of credit. Many readers will have grown up in a time in which credit is an accepted part of life. The judicious use of credit is now considered "sound household financial management," yet that attitude is relatively new. It may be that our society will never return to its historical position on credit, but the savvy marketing manager needs to know that what exists today did not always exist, if only to recognize that tomorrow will undoubtedly be different from today.

6. The changing societal view of physical factors around us. Air, once considered a free and unlimited commodity, now has become the subject of considerable discussion as pollution becomes a more visible fact to larger proportions of the population.

7. The changing composition of the general population. Death rates have been going down, life expectancy rising, and birth rates, until very recently, also rising. This condition has produced bulges in the number of babies and children and at the same time an increasing number of elderly. The most recent statistics indicate that the birth rate is now barely sufficient to replenish our population. Assuming that these figures have no particular significance except to show gross numbers of potential consumers, which probably is not a good assumption, you can clearly see the impact of such information on a marketing company. As you study consumer behavior, you will see that there are great differences in consumption patterns among these groups, and hence this kind of analysis takes on greater importance.

8. The attitudes of people toward the consumption behavior of others and, further, the patterns of consumption in terms of the kinds of products and services. If conspicuous consumption is not a viable phenomenon, then some manufacturers are likely to find their markets changing or perhaps disappearing.

The economic environment

In tracing the social environment, you will have brushed against the economic environment. If the social environment concerns the characteristics of people, the economic environment concerns what people do, such as the number of people employed in retailing, and the results of what people do, like the volume of retail sales. Various magazines, government agencies, and industry trade associations publish data on almost any type of economic activity you can think of. Keep in mind that people are inevitably related to economic activity, so the social and economic environments are closely allied. Still, the economy is influenced to a large extent by technology and science; these, as well as attitude changes, help to determine economic trends. If you were to do a paper on the economic environment, you would surely consider:

1.   The increased productivity of the labor force resulting in shorter workweeks and, therefore, increased leisure time and higher wages.[1]

2.   The effect of increased productivity in the production of essential goods and services, such as food and clothing. The result of this is that prospective consumers spend a decreasing proportion of their income on these essentials and have more income available for discretionary purchases. You would also see that periodic inflationary conditions alter this trend.

3.   The reliance of the economy on industrial production, but with increasing emphasis on services.

4.   The long-term relationship between supply and demand, which affects inflation.

5.   The shrinking of the world of business as firms become increasingly multinational in their operations.

6.   The rising role of government as a consumer of goods and services.

7.   The overall strength of the economy, based primarily on consumption rather than production. The increased consumption pressure has generated, along with science and technology, more opportunity for other producers. This is competition. Attention to it is marketing.

The political-governmental environment

We shall make only passing reference to this particular facet of the environment at this time because we want to consider it in another context. However, note that this portion of the environment is concerned with how the people govern themselves. Or, more clearly, the concern is for people—what people do; and how people live together.

With the external marketing environment divided into these three broad subgroups, the reader will find it helpful to return to the beginning of this chapter and take particular note of the subjects suggested as areas of consideration under the social and economic environment head-

---

[1] For an excellent review of the particular issue of leisure see Gilbert Burck, "There'll Be Less Leisure Than You Think," *Fortune*, March 1970, pp. 87–89 ff.

ings. Discover some things for yourself by performing two exercises. First, take our lists and expand them. Try to include as many other areas as you think appropriate while being certain that you understand why you have included them. Second, look carefully at the combined new list and determine why each is important to marketing managers. Make use of other chapters in this text, outside sources, and your professor if you have difficulty seeing the relationships.

Now let us consider another way of looking at the external environment of marketing.

OUR WAY

We believe the preceding three ways of looking at the environments of marketing have value, in that the approach is broad and inclusive. It is a kind of "first cut" at external relationships, and very useful for students of the marketing process, industry associations, or perhaps the very large firm. For these, the "big picture" is essential and the three categories do a very good job of providing it.

But we have earlier said two things that imply we ought to consider an alternative grouping. First, it has been suggested that marketing thought and techniques are as useful for nonbusiness organizations as they are for businesses. People consume the products and services produced by hospitals, charities, governmental agencies, lawyers, and others not typically categorized as businesses. It seems useful, therefore, to define the external environmental relationships in such a way that they are applicable to these other organizations. Second, on the business side, we have said that marketing management is firm-related, that it is an active ongoing process which, when done well, insures the success of an *individual* firm and when done poorly, may well insure the *individual* firm's doom. With an emphasis on the individual firm, the external relationships need to be defined in such a way that the firm may analyze its own unique relationships and plan its unique responses.

Thus, we have categorized the external relationships in the way shown in Figure 7-1. Before proceeding, note that the figure is drawn with the impact areas or sectors of the environment overlapping. This is a simplified graphic representation of reality. An employee may well be a stockholder, a member of the community in which the firm operates, and a consumer of the firm's products. Suppliers are often creditors as well. And so forth. The net result of this overlapping is that separating the firm's relationships from other sectors becomes more difficult and confusing. Nonetheless, it is essential that the major flows of influence be identified if only to demonstrate the complexity of the relationships. With these cautions in mind, we can proceed to consider each sector in turn.

FIGURE 7–1
Areas of External Environmental Relationships of Marketing Management

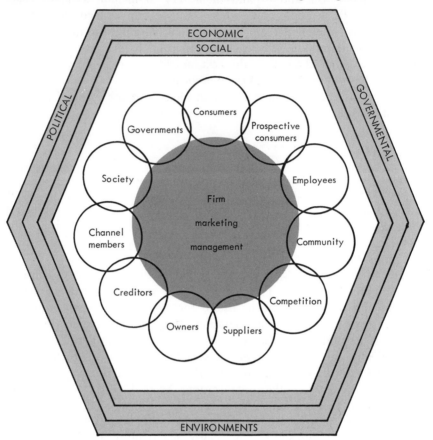

Consumers and the consumption process

Let's take another brief look at the relationships of processes and systems and at marketing and consumption. One way to differentiate between the former is to use an example: the digestive system aids the digestive process. In the same manner, marketing is one system which aids the consumption process. Also, just as ingesting—eating—is a step in using the digestive system to facilitate the digestive process, consuming is a step in using the marketing system to aid the consumption process. There are many steps in the consumption process before the act of consuming is complete—meaning that the consumer is satisfied.

In Chapter 6 on Opportunity and Innovation, we pointed out that both marketing and consumers are active partners in the consumption process. We especially emphasized that marketing has to be the more aggressive of the two for a very simple reason. Consumers do not have to understand (1) why they chose a particular product or service, (2) why they were pleased or displeased, or (3) why they did or did not choose it again. To them the answers are straightforward: (1) I wanted it; (2) I liked/disliked it; (3) I wanted to. Why did they want it, like it, and choose it again? Because! A gutsy and perfectly rational answer—to them.

It would be nice if, instead of answering "Because," consumers would say something like:

> While my basic needs for existence in the form of food, clothing, and shelter and my needs for security are all fairly well satisfied, I do feel the need for enhancing my image with myself and extending my prestige among my peer group. This product makes me feel like royalty, and when I use it my friends butter up to me and call me "Your Honorificship." That's why I buy your product.

But, they answer "Because!"—a totally unacceptable answer to marketing people who want to know why consumers buy and why they buy *what* they buy and why they are or are not satisfied after completing the consumption process.

This is why we say that consumers are at the heart of any business or nonbusiness organization. Unless the consumption process takes place, there is no need for the organization to exist. This seems to us to be true of *all* organizations, since it can be presumed that they are purposive to at least some extent.[2] Hence, consumers must make a decision to consume a particular product or service to insure the ongoing operation of a firm. Marketing's role is to help improve the quality of that decision before, during, and at the end of the act of consuming. Furthermore, to complete the consumption process, consumers must be glad they consumed. Again, marketing enters the picture to help assure that consumers will be satisfied.

We are directing our attention mostly to commercial business, but it will be useful to transpose what is said about commercial business to some kind of organization—say a local government. The kind of actions consumers take may be different, the time period over which the actions take place may be different, or the transactions may be different, but consumption occurs nevertheless. The relationships be-

---

[2] This is an important notion not fully developed here. Close consideration of the material in Chapter 8 on consumer behavior will show a view of human behavior that says "people do things for a reason." It may be that the reasons are obscure to you and/or us, or we may not believe the reason good or sufficient to justify a particular action, but there is, nonetheless, a reason. This notion reoccurs repeatedly in the study of marketing. Much criticism of marketing techniques, e.g., advertising, if examined closely, will be seen as criticism of the reasons people do what they do.

tween consumers and the firm follow a two-way street. The most fundamental of them are satisfaction, value, and price.

Satisfaction. As discussed in Chapters 2 and 6, the basis for a transaction is satisfaction for both parties. Consumers expect and demand
satisfaction from the goods or services they buy. In order for the firm
to have continued transactions with them, it must provide that satisfaction. Embodied in this requirement is the need to recognize the complexities of consumer satisfaction and the multitude of ways in which it
is achieved. For example, we do not normally get all our satisfactions
from actual consumption of a particular physical product. If we did,
the firm's interaction with us would be much simpler. But we value
our time, so where and when we obtain the goods is important as well
as the consumption of them. The development of different means of
distributing products demonstrates the time utility clearly.[3]

Value. Our society is one of scarcity. This does not mean that we
have extreme difficulty in finding particular goods and services. It does
mean that, as consumers, we are unable to satisfy all of our needs and
wants. Consequently, we must allocate our limited resources among those
products and services which will provide the greatest amount of satisfaction. Consumers translate this into the concept of value. Value flows
from the firm to consumers and is embodied in all actions of the firm
which affect its relationship to consumers. As durable goods become
increasingly complex and consumers become potentially less able to correct minor difficulties themselves, then service facilities and competent service technicians acquire greater value. Consider, for example, the earliest
model automobile you can remember; compare it with the most current
model you are familiar with. We are tempted (again) at this point
to compare Henry Ford's Model T with his company's current products.
The differences are, as some of you know, stark. The Model T was said
to be repairable with "a pair of pliers and some baling wire." Pliers
and baling wire would undoubtedly be useless in repairing a current
model Ford.

Similar analyses can be made of such common household products
as washing machines, refrigerators, and dishwashers. In the dishwasher
case, the method for 95 percent of American households in 1960 was
a sink of soapy water and a cloth. Now, about 20 percent have a machine
that loads water, dispenses soap, water softener, and a no-spotting agent,
washes, rinses, sanitizes, and dries. An oven was, in the very recent
past, a metal box with a thermostat and a heating element. Many of

---

[3] Economists customarily describe satisfactions in terms of utility. Typical categories of utility include time, place, form, and possession. This is to say that we
get something, a kind of satisfaction, from being able to get products at the *right*
place, at the *right* time, and in the *right* form; right being defined by the individual
consumer.

today's ovens will do nearly everything but put the meat in. The increase in the amount of services results in greater mechanical and electronic complexity, and thus the possibility of greater pleasure and pain in consuming.

Value, therefore, transcends the physical product itself and accrues to the consumer through a variety of avenues, each of which the firm ultimately has responsibility for. It is the firm which produces this value, and the consumer evaluates the amount of value in the market. Insufficient value in a product or service will result eventually in reduced or terminated consumption. This is the essence of what we call a "consumer boycott," a term which has come into use in recent years. In these cases, the consumer says, "value received does not justify the resources which must be given up to acquire the product or service," meaning the price is too high. The long-term success of such a boycott is really determined by the amount of *permanent* change that takes place in consumption. Note the success of fast-food companies, such as McDonald's, Kentucky Fried Chicken, and others in the past decade, and the corresponding difficulties which many full-service restaurants have encountered. Similar patterns can also be discerned in industries where self-service has become more important. In the end, value is related to price, which is the next topic of consideration.

Price. Price is clearly the most visible part of the firm-consumer interaction next to the products and services themselves. Price is one measure of satisfaction for both parties in the transaction. For the consumer, price is weighed against value and, where the value of the product or service is high enough, the consumer will exchange for it. For the firm, price determines revenue and profit, and while these may not provide all the firm's satisfactions, they do represent the opportunity the firm has to achieve other satisfactions.

Prospective consumers

Very few firms can expect to serve all those consumers who could derive satisfactions from their products or services. The dynamic nature of the market makes this virtually impossible. It is important, consequently, that the firm explicitly define its relationship to those it does not now serve and those it wishes to serve.[4] The same kinds of relationships are potentially present with prospective consumers. Satisfaction, price, and value are potential flows between prospective consumers and the firm.

The same kind of analysis can be made with respect to the firm's present customers, for their needs are also changing. When it finds itself

---

[4] On this point see Phillip Kotler and Sidney J. Levy, "Demarketing, Yes, Demarketing," *Harvard Business Review*, November–December, 1971, pp. 74–80.

unable or unwilling to adjust its products and services to some of these changes, the firm must replenish its supply of customers in much the same way that it replenishes stocks of raw materials. The absence of planning for raw material purchases often results in higher costs than necessary. The absence of planning for new customers produces the same result.

Employees

The firm's relationship to its employees is one in which the flows are concerned with work, pay, working conditions, and opportunity—the whole mixed bag of employee satisfactions. It is clear that employee performance affects the ability of the firm to satisfy customers. At the same time, management must realize that employees by and large work as a means to an end. In effect, employees gain a satisfaction from their work which comes partly from the wages they earn, partly from the positions they hold, and partly from the opportunity they have to upgrade and improve themselves.

The employee-firm relationship is a complex one, since employee satisfactions come from areas other than just wages. Thus, the firm, in return for a fair day's work, provides fringe benefits to supplement wages earned; it probably provides or could provide training and educational opportunities. Advancement with new titles and responsibilities is very important to some. Marketing management needs to be particularly attentive to this employee relationship because marketing employees are sometimes wrongly thought to obtain more simplistic satisfactions from the job. Salespeople, for example, are sometimes thought to work only for money. In years past, sales compensation systems were nearly exclusively oriented toward money income. We now provide a more meaningful opportunity for salespeople just as for other employees.[5] This employee-firm relationship includes the impact of unions or other kinds of employee organizations. These organizations influence the content of the flows between the two.

Community

We conceive of the community as essentially the immediate area surrounding the firm and leave to another section the wider issue of the firm-society relationship. This relationship of the community and the firm is a complex one, but we only consider some of its more important parts.

---

[5] For an interesting discussion of the "carrot and stick" approach to compensation and punishment, see Harry Levinson, *The Great Jackass Fallacy* (Boston: Division of Research, Harvard University, 1973).

The firm has a clear economic impact on the community. Employees customarily come from the surrounding area and customarily do the bulk of their purchasing in the same area. Consequently, the community must have prospective employees with the skills and talents required. The wages and salaries paid by the firm ripple throughout the economy of the area. It is unlikely that the firm performs all of the work on its products and services itself. It finds it advantageous to purchase much of this work from local business, and thus the economic impact on the private sector of the community is pervasive. Perhaps one of the most visible demonstrations of this occurs when a firm leaves the community. Of course, the total impact is larger and easier to see if the firm is very large. The closing of a large firm brings economic pressure on a wide range of community institutions, such as restaurants, clothiers, and realtors. Further, there is economic impact in the public sector for the firm pays local taxes which in many communities constitute a significant portion of revenues. Changes in these tax revenues produce changes in the levels of service which the community can provide. Sewage and water treatment facilities, roads, highways, mass transit systems, and protection departments are geared to the existing situation. A change in the size of the firm will increase or decrease the burden on these various departments.

The firm is really a member of the community, with the responsibility of being a good corporate citizen. Providing support for the community by making executives available to assist in community projects and give leadership in programs for the public good are ways in which the firm can demonstrate its commitment to the community.

Competition

Like it or not, in an economy of scarcity, competition exists. It may be argued that the firm makes every attempt to insulate itself and its customers from competition, but such efforts are rarely totally successful.

Competition is important to the marketing manager because the firm derives benefit from interaction with competitors. Let us consider the character of some of these interactions, keeping in mind that in the United States the law prohibits competitive interaction which is collusive. Competition is believed to result in higher living standards and more satisfied customers, because each competitor constantly searches for new and better ways to serve customers. Such a search begets new kinds of products and services: it fosters innovation in both production and marketing; it hones managements and sensitizes employees.

The efficiency and effectiveness of serving the customer is enhanced by competition in the same way as innovation. The natural consequence of competition is, of course, that somebody else wants to serve your customer. To this end he will be looking for those areas of your service that do not precisely meet the customer's requirements; he will be trying to create dissatisfaction in your customers. This is opportunity. If a firm faced with this situation makes no effort either (1) to anticipate competitive onslaughts by having substantive knowledge of customers' changing needs (antidissatisfaction innoculation), or (2) to react promptly and positively, it is very likely that the customer will leave. If that happens often enough, the firm will be out of business.

Competition influences the price a firm may charge. It is unlikely, for example, that Chevrolet would or could price its Chevette at $10,000 and still maintain its current sales volume. The same comments apply to product quality and post-sale service.

Suppliers

Sometimes the suppliers of materials and parts are not considered in planning a marketing program. This is a serious oversight because the quality of the parts bought and the reliability of delivery schedules must be as good as if the company made them itself. The outside supplier is in effect replacing the firm's own production department in the manufacturing process. Accordingly, suppliers should be considered in the planning process in the same way the production department is considered.

Owners

One of the phenomena that has characterized the development of U.S. business has been the increasing separation of those who own the assets of the firm and those who manage those assets. In your study of financial management, you will discover that the relationship between owners and managers can have a profound effect on the manager's freedom to manage. An adversary relationship can make the raising of added capital difficult or economically impossible. Owners, having invested time, credit, and/or dollars, expect an adequate return on their investment. Inadequate returns cause that capital to move to greener pastures. Inadequate capital, the final result, is a significant cause of business failure. Furthermore, ownership in our society is widely disseminated throughout the general public. An unhappy set of owners may well influence market performance insofar as owners form a part of the core of customers the firm serves.

Creditors

Banks and other financial institutions are not the only creditors of a firm. Suppliers, channel members, and sometimes customers often extend credit, which is an important resource as well as a significant tool of management. Without minimizing the rate of interest as a cost of doing business, it is relatively unimportant when compared with the resource it buys: money. If the predicted short-fall of funds for capital expansion which we discussed in Chapter 1 should materialize, credit may well become an even more important asset of the firm than it now is.

Channel members

It is easy to overlook in the environmental context the relationships the firm has with its channels of distribution and take them for granted just because they are there. As with suppliers, they should be viewed as extensions of the firm, to be managed as if the firm owned the assets. When they are viewed as agencies which support the marketing effort of the firm, as we view them in this book, their importance to the firm's marketing program is immediately evident.

In Chapter 5 the role of channels in communicating information was pointed out. We showed that information flowed both from the firm to the customer and from the customer to the firm. Inattention to even this phase of channel relationships eliminates an important connection with the firm's market. Channel relationships need to be considered actively, not passively. For many firms the channel members determine the firm's success or failure. This relationship is examined in greater detail in later chapters.

Society

This is a particularly difficult part of the external environment to define, let alone describe fully. Lately, it has become quite fashionable to talk of social responsibility: to assign to the firm the responsibility of instituting societal programs and making decisions which are good for society. It is important to come to grips with the question of the firm's responsibility to society. To this end, we believe it would be useful to again look at Figure 7–1 and the discussion accompanying it on the preceding pages. Try to establish a framework for determining whether a well-managed firm is not in fact socially responsible *given its prescribed role in society.* If you disagree with the role, then you must redefine the role precisely before you can determine what actions are or are not responsible. Further, you need to consider carefully whether the motivation behind a particular action is important, or whether the action is all that counts.[6]

---

[6] For an interesting view of this subject, see Gaylord A. Freeman, Jr., "For Business, a Call to Commitment," *The Wall Street Journal*, January 22, 1970; and Gilbert Burck, "The Hazards of Corporate Responsibility," *Fortune*, June 1973, p. 114 ff.

GOVERNMENTS

Introduction

To underscore the pervasiveness of government as an element of the environment and therefore as an element of the marketing decision, the subject is given a major topic head of its own. Almost any work on government-business relationships is bound to be incomplete. To provide some order to our own incompleteness, the discussion is divided into three parts. It will be clear that there is considerable overlap among the parts.

There are two major directions of government action that impinge upon the environment with which marketing managers are concerned. One is preventive or *regulatory;* the other is *promotional.* In what follows we will emphasize the regulatory actions. The promotional activities are so pervasive that the reader will be fairly familiar with them: highway construction to improve communications; statistical services to improve understanding of environments; direct subsidies of various sorts; and so on.

There are three sources of U.S. governmental forces which have an environmental influence: congressional, judicial, and executive. Since we cannot be complete anyway, we direct our discussion to the congressional forces. Also, we confine our discussion to the federal government.

The pendulum of government's role in business has swung through its arcs in at least three broad periods. The first began in 1887 when there was intense demand for legislative regulatory action. The pendulum swung toward enforced competition. This first period, lasting nearly 50 years, was characterized by legislative attempts (1) to correct the abuses and excesses that characterized so much of business activity, and (2) to enforce what amounted to free and unrestrained competition. This period is one of the elements in our framework of discussing government and the environment. We call it "Curtailment of Abuses."

Before the pendulum had swung to the other direction 50 years later, many laws were passed to attain the ends mentioned. We discuss the general nature and objectives of some of these laws, leaving the details of some of them for consideration elsewhere in this book. In the 1930s legislative efforts changed direction completely. The pendulum swung in a different time back *toward*—but not *to*—monopoly. No longer was there the great fear of business and the abuse of monopoly power. To the contrary, there was (1) fear of the results of unrestrained competition coupled with (2) a desire to continue protecting the public from some business practices, and (3) a desire to protect business from some business practices. This is the second element in our framework. We call it "Protection From Abusive Marketing Practices."

This time, it took the pendulum about 20 years to create a new period. During the period some laws were passed to attain the desired ends. Also, the courts threw out some of them. A new era began in the 1950s and the pendulum set to swing in still a different direction. This time there was a different sort of fear of a different set of potential abuses of bigness. This period is the third element of our framework. We call it "Preventing Further Concentration of Economic Power."

Before we discuss this role of government in the environment, we remind you that our purpose here is to help you develop a perspective of the *nature* of what one branch of the United States government was doing. At the end of your study of this section you should understand just that—the nature of what went on and why. You will not know the detailed provisions and application of the laws. You will know the nature of the environments within which managerial decisions have been made. You will also see in these laws the results of managerial efforts to change environments, for many of these laws were passed at the request of business. This is especially true of those in the middle period.

Curtailment of abuses

In order to put our discussion of the government environment in perspective, it is necessary to look back in history to the time when the initial legislation designed to control and regulate business was being passed. In other parts of this book, we label the external environment as uncontrollable but emphasize that it can be influenced. In all of the legislation to be discussed, you will note the impact of somebody doing something about a situation considered undesirable. Specifically, note how this legislation reflects, at least in part, the attitude of many people in the society: many businessmen themselves; farmers; workers; and most importantly for this section, the attitude of the members of the government and the president. Inherent in the discussion is the somewhat implicit attitude of government to business, but where this implicit attitude was accompanied by strong social feeling, strong political pressure, depressed economic conditions, or strong presidential leadership, much reaction in the form of legislation resulted.

The right of government to regulate business has been firmly rooted in the common law of England for centuries. The commerce clause of our Constitution established the right of Congress to regulate commerce among the states. That right was strengthened when the Supreme Court declared that the power of Congress to regulate interstate business is complete and absolute, in *Gibbons* v. *Ogden* (1824). There was, however, little action on the part of Congress or state governments in spite

of this—largely because of the view which developed that it was polit-
ically important that the government should exercise a minimal amount
of interference in business and economic affairs. This represents the
American version of the "laissez faire" doctrine. This doctrine has traditionally been attributed to the 18th-century economist Adam Smith and
has been interpreted as "government leave business alone." This, however, was not Smith's philosophy. Instead he advocated government in-
tervention in business when necessary to protect the public interest.

The original concept of *laissez faire* did not prevail in this country.
It has been suggested that the American version of the concept is the
result of the efforts of the American Bar Association and corporate lawyers who convinced the Supreme Court that "competition was an unregu-
lated process conducted without public rules or penalties, which should
not be restricted as long as it is carried on in good faith to make a
profit."[7]

This view prevailed through the era following the Civil War, which
saw the rise of industrial power, financial concentration, and expansion
of the railroad system. Under the pressures from farmers, shippers, and
small businessmen who were protesting discriminatory practices of the
railroads, the first major legislative act controlling business, The Interstate Commerce Act, was passed in 1887. The purpose of the act was
to correct abuses and excesses of the railroads and to enforce competition. The act prohibited rebates, discriminatory rate agreements, and
rate-fixing agreements, and required rate scale publication. The passage
of this act represented a substantial alteration of the American *laissez
faire* philosophy. However, a series of court decisions deprived the Interstate Commerce Commission, created to administer the act's provisions,
of much of its authority.[8] Consequently, the changed relationship seemed
to be limited to the fact that Congress had moved to attempt to regulate
business and that, in spite of the adverse court decisions, none had
resulted in the Interstate Commerce Commission being declared
unconstitutional.

In 1890, the Sherman Anti-Trust Act was passed. This Act prohibited
mergers and combinations in restraint of commerce and held individuals
who attempted to monopolize in violation of the law. Again, the influence
of court interpretation is not without impact. In fact, the law specifically
gives jurisdiction to the federal courts. The Supreme Court held, in
1895, in the "Sugar Trust" case, that monopolies of manufacturing were,
in effect, legal, since the combination of manufacturing plants was not
in direct relationship to commerce between the states. Thus, at the close
of the 19th century, there still was no effective government regulation

---

[7] Vernon A. Mund, *Government and Business,* 4th ed. (New York: Harper & Row,
1965), p. 16.

[8] Ibid., p. 316.

of business in general, even though some federal effort in this direction was apparent. But the situation was to change soon, for in the early years of the 20th century considerably more effort was exerted to regulate some of the practices of business.

Theodore Roosevelt, president of the United States from 1901–1909, seemed to express the philosophy that the government had an obligation to protect the general public. Roosevelt became known as a "trust buster," trusts being a kind of confederation of a number of companies administered by a single group of trustees. These trustees could dictate prices and other business decisions. In addition, this period produced the forerunner of today's Anti-Trust Division of the Department of Justice, the Bureau of Corporations; the Pure Food and Drug Act which attempted to insure that commercially grown and sold medicines and foods were safe for human consumption; and several pieces of legislation which gave the Interstate Commerce Commission the power to do what Congress originally intended. The government was becoming a more powerful force in relation to business.

This conclusion appears warranted when we consider that in 1914 the Clayton Act was passed. This law was an attempt to eliminate the vagueness in and facilitate enforcement of the Sherman Act. Among other things, it prohibited price discrimination in general, interlocking directorates, and exclusive selling or leasing agreements, subject to the clause that the result must tend to limit competition or create a monopoly. Significantly, the Clayton Act also served to provide exemption from antitrust laws of legal, agricultural, and horticultural associations.

In an attempt to create a concrete method of enforcement, also in 1914, Congress passed the Federal Trade Commission Act, which established a commission to prevent unfair methods of competition tending to create monopoly or lessen competition. The law gave the Federal Trade Commission the power to investigate practices considered suspect, publish its findings, and issue cease and desist orders. Again, however, the courts limited to a great degree the actions of the Federal Trade Commission.

Protection from abusive marketing practices

Most of the laws so far discussed were designed to eliminate the flagrant abuses of economic power and to try to implement a philosophy of competition. After correcting some of the more flagrant abuses, Congress began to give its attention to protecting business and the public from some abuses centering on marketing practices. These abuses will be dealt with next. Note that there really isn't too much difference in these two categories.

During the depression of the 1930s a rather peculiar turn of events took place. From the first law regulating business, the tendency of Congress had been to enforce competition and break up monopoly power. (An exception was the Transportation Act of 1920, which would have tended to restrain competition if it had been effective. But this is a special case, since the rail industry was subject to the Interstate Commerce Commission.) However, it was apparently the conclusion of Congress that the drastic measures were necessary to cope with the terrible times.

The pendulum began to swing away from free and enforced competition toward a less free and controlled competitive system. The National Industrial Recovery Act set up the National Recovery Administration (NRA) in 1933 and provided for the establishment of fair-practices codes by trade associations. These codes, when approved by the NRA, provided the ground rules for the industry to work under. Antitrust legislation was suspended as a regulator of those firms adhering to an approved code. The primary rationale was that the threat of antitrust prosecution caused ruthless competition, which was giving the consumer a bargain at the expense of labor and capital. Prices immediately rose, while insignificant gains were made in economic activity.

Another illustration of the swing of the pendulum away from unrestrained competition came during the same period. There was much concern among retailers over price cutting; so they set out to establish— through Congress—some means of control of prices. Resale price control was advocated. This action also was precipitated by the depression and by the presence of chain and "cut-rate" retailers offering reduced services and prices. The primary effort was brought to bear by trade associations of wholesale and retail outlets.

Under pressure from these same groups the Miller-Tydings Act was passed in late 1937 to enable the states to pass resale price maintenance laws applicable to goods in *interstate* commerce as well as in *intrastate* commerce. These laws enabled manufacturers to set a price on their goods and force retailers to honor that price.[9]

In this same vein, the trade associations, having not received the complete protection under resale price maintenance, turned their efforts to the passage of "unfair practices" acts which essentially prohibited the sale of goods below cost. Enactment of these started about 1935 and continued for some time.

During this same period concern was expressed by retailer and wholesaler trade associations, as well as the Federal Trade Commission, about the price policies of the increasingly important chain stores. Many states introduced bills to curtail chains. Anti-chain-store taxes were enacted.

---

[9] In late 1975, Congress repealed the Miller-Tydings Act removing the anti-trust exemption on resale price maintenance agreements for goods in interstate commerce. Most observers now believe that this was the final blow to such agreements.

The structure of these taxes was designed to allow small local chains of a handful of stores to survive. If a chain owned, say, a dozen stores, an astronomical tax per store in the chain would be levied regardless of where the stores were located. In other words, a 600-store chain with one store in a state with this type of tax was taxed on all 600. That tax didn't last long.

During the early 1930s there was considerable concern over the effect of a seller's price discrimination on the customers of the seller. It was assumed that chains were driving small retail stores out of business because sellers gave price concessions to the chains. Subsequently, in 1936, the Robinson-Patman Act was passed as an amendment to the price discrimination clause (Section 2) of the Clayton Act of 1914. The Robinson-Patman Act made it illegal to discriminate in price between different purchasers of commodities of like grade and quality, except where the difference could be justified on the basis of (1) cost differences or (2) because of competitive conditions or changes in the products being sold, e.g., perishability.

In addition, the Robinson-Patman Act prohibits brokerage fees except where services are rendered. It prohibits the paying of brokerage fees by a seller to a buyer where the buyer is subject to direct or indirect control of the consignee of the goods. It prohibits discrimination in the merchandising services or facilities which a seller may furnish a buyer, as well as discriminatory payment by the seller for services rendered by the buyer. The act also empowered the Federal Trade Commission to order the cessation of practices which it considered discriminatory. The act also prohibits discriminatory discounts, rebates, allowances, and advertising allowances, and makes provision for the prosecution of the buyer in some cases.[10]

Note that in all the above cases the restriction is applicable when the practice is held to have the effect of substantially lessening competition or tending to create a monopoly. Several judicial decisions have clarified the Federal Trade Commission's position on the matter of enforcement.

Pursuing the concept of protecting the public from injury by business, Congress passed the Wheeler-Lea Amendment to the Federal Trade Commission Act in 1938. This amendment prohibits unfair, deceptive, or false advertising to induce purchase of foods, drugs, or cosmetics. Advertising was defined in the amendment to include all advertising except labeling. Essentially, this legislation gave a consumer and a rival competitor injured by an unfair trade practice within the scope of this amendment equal standing in the eyes of the law.

These laws all extended the influence of government in the affairs

---

[10] Lawrence X. Tarpey, "Buyer Liability Under the Robinson-Patman Act: A Current Appraisal," *Journal of Marketing,* January, 1972, pp. 38–42.

of business. For a time they were designed to enforce competition, but in the 1930s the approach seemed to be one of regulating competition in the interests of business. Court decisions both strengthened and destroyed some of these laws.

Preventing further concentration of economic power

In 1950 the Celler-Kefauver Amendment to the Clayton Act (sometimes called the Antimerger Act of 1950) was passed. It prohibited the acquisition by one company of stock and assets of another where the effect would be to limit competition in *any section* of the country or sector of the economy. Integration, both horizontal and vertical, became more difficult and the Act provided that companies found in violation could be required to divest themselves of portions of their business. This law has been widely used in the past two decades.

Although there have been a number of new laws since the early 1950s, many dealing with consumer protection, the most significant trend to be observed is the increasing administrative power of governmental bodies, particularly the federal government. Terms like "guidelines" (set by a government department to suggest acceptable limits of price or wage change) and "jawboning" (high officials suggesting that companies which exceeded the guidelines should alter their decisions) are in common use. They represent a power position, rather than a strictly legislative one. They are indicative of the government's increasing ability to demand, sometimes through the use of governmental purchasing power, that certain actions be taken. The result of this is a much more vigorous interaction between firms and governments. Note that many of the smaller governmental units have also pursued an active regulation program, often including taxation. We are apparently still in this period.

MARKETING MANAGEMENT AND THE EXTERNAL ENVIRONMENT

We have looked at various segments of the environment to try to give the reader a feel for the complex relationships which the marketing manager must understand, sort out, and cope with. In the opening paragraphs of this chapter we said that one of our aims was to demonstrate that the marketing manager cannot slight external relationships. The purpose of this section is to discuss some of the managerial decision points related to some segments of the external environment. We intend to show how managers cope with some special problems. This will be done using the basic framework of the book. First, we will look at those things of strategic concern to the marketing manager in his role of planning and managing for the firm and then at those operational things he is concerned with in managing the marketing function. This is the familiar dual approach we have based our book on: management *and* the marketing function and management *of* the marketing function. To avoid going over the same grounds, our approach will be primarily to use examples.

Planning, strategy, and the external environment

A success. In an earlier chapter we alluded to the experience of Theodore Vail around the turn of the century. As head of AT&T he helped articulate the purpose of the firm. He wanted to make it possible for anyone to be able to talk with any one else anywhere in the world, rapidly, conveniently, and economically. There were several "minor" obstacles in his way. A federal law prohibited a telephone company from buying a competitor; the technology to accomplish what was needed was unavailable and not visible on the horizon; existing manufacturers did not have the expertise or the interest to supply needed equipment. There were other obstacles, but these are enough to suggest the magnitude of the obstacles he faced in dealing with government, competition, and suppliers—all segments of the external environment.

Vail lobbied for and got the law changed to enable his company to buy competing companies. He created Bell Laboratories to do research and develop the needed technology. He created the Western Electric Company to manufacture equipment and to assure its quality and availability. It takes a handful of lines to say what was accomplished; it took years of planning, scheming, and plotting to develop the strategy and tactics required.

Managing and the external environment

We attributed the success of AT&T to strategic matters and the effectiveness of strategy in dealing with the elements of the environment. From the point of view of implementing strategy we can credit good marketing management for any number of successes. But, a rather troublesome question arises: Are all of the successes we see the result of (1) good planning and strategy, and (2) good implementation by the marketing manager?

For example, did Edsel fail because of poor strategy or poor implementation? Did the Mustang succeed despite poor strategy and implementation? We are pretty sure of one thing: a portion of the Mustang strategy was wrong. The Mustang was designed for one age group, but it really succeeded with an older group apparently not originally considered to be the target market. In short, the "prospective customers" in the external environment were not fully identified. Happily, the only failure here was that the ultimate market proved to be much greater than had been identified. Most firms would probably be very well pleased to have many such "failures."

What caused the success? Strategy and planning? Implementation? We don't know. Maybe the marketing manager designed a promotional program which developed not only the target market, but also other segments of the market. If so, marketing is responsible.

SUMMARY

The intent of this chapter is to demonstrate the complexity of the external relationships which the firm must keep healthy. By doing so, the firm and its manager have a better chance of achieving their objectives and consumers are likely to get greater satisfaction from forays into the market place. If the firm chooses to emphasize its internal relations to the exclusion of external relationships, it runs a serious risk of losing the markets for its products.

chapter 8

Consumer behavior

Introduction
Basic premises of consumer behavior
    Consumer behavior as a subset of human behavior
    The problem-solving nature of consumer behavior
    The rationality of behavior
The marketing activities of the firm and the behavior
    process of consumers
    Consumer problem solving and the consumer satis-
        faction process
    The link between the consumer's process and the
        firm's process
The strategic aspects of consumer behavior: The dis-
    covery of consumer aspirations
    Planning, consumer satisfaction, and the marketing
        mix
    Recognition of consumer aspirations
    Creation of selective dissatisfaction
    Anticipated satisfaction
    Realized satisfaction
    Antidissatisfaction inoculation
Summary

INTRODUCTION

At this point it should be clear that consumer desires are the center of attention of the marketing manager and the business firm. Since consumer satisfactions are the most important component of the hierarchy of satisfactions presented earlier, an understanding of consumer behavior is an indispensable managerial tool. This chapter is designed to introduce you to the study of consumers and give you an appreciation of how an understanding of consumer behavior is used in making marketing decisions.

To an extent, all of us think we understand the behavior of at least a limited number of consumers. We all believe we understand why *we* consume the way we do. We may also feel that we understand why our spouses or friends bought a particular product or a particular brand over another. Usually we think this way until we are pressed for a specific explanation of a specific act of consumption. After several minutes of generalizations, qualifications, and platitudes, we are likely to be reduced to saying, "It seemed like a good idea at the time!" or some equivalent of that statement. The fact is, that when pressed to explain our own consumption behavior, frequently we cannot come up with an explanation. Not because there is no logical explanation, but simply because we don't understand the processes that direct our behavior as consumers. And if we have trouble understanding why we consume the way we do, how can we expect to understand how and why other consumers behave as they do, and then use this insight in making decisions? The simple answer is that we can't. Unlike a psychoanalyst, we need not totally understand ourselves before we attempt to understand others and use that information to make more effective marketing decisions.

Rather than segregate consumer behavior from marketing action, and present it as a subject unto itself, we shall try to present it within the same "strategic" and "managerial" decisions framework that we have developed earlier. In doing so, we are consciously sacrificing some of what might be called the "fine detail" in order to give you a better overall (or "big picture") perspective of the role of an understanding of consumer behavior within the business and marketing decision making of the firm.

To achieve this objective, we shall first discuss some basic premises upon which our study of consumer behavior rests. Then, using the five stages of consumer satisfaction developed in Chapter 6 as our framework, we shall discuss the role of consumer behavior information in both the strategic and the operational decision making of the firm. Information about consumers and their behavior processes will appear, then, in a context dictated by the decision-making requirements of the firm, not in a context dictated by academic research or study.

BASIC PREMISES OF CONSUMER BEHAVIOR

Before we begin an extensive discussion of consumer behavior, we need some place to start: we need a foundation on which we can build and from which we can develop an understanding of how consumers behave that will be useful to the manager. To provide this foundation, we are offering three sets of premises about the behavior of consumers. In themselves they are simple notions, yet in terms of what they portend they are complex. They are not premises newly developed by us in the course of preparing this book; rather they are taken from the work of researchers in the areas of human and consumer behavior during the past 30 years. They are not irrefutable propositions or "iron laws" but rather premises, and as such they may possibly prove to be invalid at some point in the future. As premises they are continually being investigated, at least implicitly, and they are constantly being refined. In spite of this potential drawback, we are of the opinion that these sets of premises have been sufficiently tested to insure that they are not too far wrong in substance, even if they may prove to be wrong in detail. And, they offer us an excellent starting point for our discussion.

Consumer behavior as a subset of human behavior

We start with the premise that *consumer behavior is merely one facet of human behavior.* Human behavior encompasses all of our behavior, including that portion specifically involved with consuming goods and services. Viewed in this context, it is obvious that consumer behavior study cannot proceed independently of a broader study of human behavior.

As human beings we do many things in the course of a day. Many of the things we do are the result of the human society or culture to which we belong and within which we function.[1] Much of our consumption is for goods and services designed to implement or facilitate our performing activities that are not primarily economic in nature—recreation, child rearing, and courtship, for example. Some consumption is directly related to economic activities—job-related consumption; and some of our consumption is related to both categories—clothing or a car would serve in either purpose.

If we know, for instance, a person's age and sex, occupation, family status, educational level and background, and location, it is possible to predict, with a fairly high degree of accuracy, the social and cultural activities in which the person will be engaged. From that, we can predict the types of goods and services that the person will be most likely to consume.

The first point to be considered is: *The kinds of goods and services this person is likely to consume are not so much a matter of individual choice as they are a cultural/societal necessity.* Consumption to a large degree may depend on the social roles that an individual takes at any given point in time. Understand those roles, the activities that are required to fulfill them, and the goods and services that would facilitate the performance of those activities, and you will understand, in large measure, the consumption behavior of the individual.[2] An individual

---

[1] Marvin Harris, *Culture, Man and Nature* (New York: Thomas Y. Crowell, 1971).

[2] See for example, "The Nature of Consumption Choices" in James S. Duesenberry, *Income, Saving and the Theory of Consumer Behavior* (Cambridge: The Harvard University Press: 1949), pages 19–22.

does not act in a social vacuum, but rather in concert with other individuals; so if you understand the social group (or groups) within which an individual is performing his set of roles, you will be able to understand even more of the individual's consumption behavior.

One objection to this premise is that it ignores the individual's needs, wants, desires, and motivations. To an extent, this is a valid objection. But one does not develop in isolation. One grows up in a given cultural environment interacting with other individuals. One is thus, in every sense, a product of a social environment. One's understanding of the role of "husband" or "mother" or "employee" is basically determined by what has been absorbed from the social environment in which one developed. Since every person is unique, each person's understanding of these roles will also be unique. And each person's performance of the activities associated with those roles will also be unique, in at least the fine details.

Further, in our society and culture the individual is not a passive creature, reacting only to actions initiated by others. Each is an active participant possessing an amazing degree of freedom of action. As we noted earlier, it is the recognition of problems by the consumer that commences the behavior process that may eventually end in consumption behavior. Thus the consumer has at least some degree of initiative. We do not ignore this aspect of behavior, but rather we choose to treat it within the larger social and cultural context of human behavior.

The problem-solving nature of consumer behavior

Our second premise is that *consumer behavior is a form of problem-solving behavior.* Generally, problem-solving behavior is characterized by at least the stages of (1) problem identification; (2) situational evaluation; (3) identification and evaluation of alternative actions; (4) selection of a course of action from among the available alternatives; and (5) post-event evaluation of the decision. This assumes that the individual engaged in problem-solving behavior has (1) a goal or set of goals and (2) some general plan or scheme for achieving these goals. Note that it is unimportant *where* the problem that precipitates this behavior originates: it may come from within the individual or it may come as the result of something outside. Note also the implicit assumption that prior to the recognition of a problem, the individual is assumed to be in a state of equilibrium. The critical point with regard to this last assumption is the fact that this pre-problem state of equilibrium may exist only in the individual's mind. An objective observer looking at him and his situation just prior to his recognition of the fact that he has a problem, and looking at him at the moment he recognizes the problem, might not notice any difference: the only difference would be that at some point the individual suddenly recognizes a problem. In problem-solving behavior, then, the problem may exist solely (or primarily) in the mind of the person involved.

One aspect of this premise that has troubled behavioral researchers is that problem-solving behavior is an "expensive" type of behavior for the individual involved. It is expensive in the sense that it takes a great deal of time and mental energy to frame and solve even quite simple problems. Placed in the context of consumer behavior and particularly within the context of daily consumption, the amount of mental effort and time that would have to be spent to frame and solve all of the consumption problems faced by an average American in an average day would leave little time for anything else. In light of this, some researchers have argued that most consumer behavior is *habitual behavior*—not problem-solving behavior—and that the consumer only engages in problem-solving behavior on rare occasions.[3]

Habitual behavior, or the repeating of a course of action that proved to deal successfully with a problem in the past, however, is merely a shortened form of problem-solving behavior.[4] It in no way violates our premise to classify much of an individual's consumption behavior as "habitual behavior." Why should a consumer go through an extensive mental exercise to solve a problem today that he or she has already solved in the past in a way that is satisfactory? Why, for example, should a homemaker agonize over which brand of coffee to buy if the usual purchase is entirely satisfactory? If the problem that the consumer faces today is in its key aspects identical with the problem solved last week, it makes very good sense simply to repeat the solution that worked so well before. Only when there is a change in the nature of the problem, the situation it relates to, or in the alternative solutions available is it necessary for the consumer to "re-solve" the problem in an extended process. Looking at the purchase behavior of consumers seems to lend credence to this explanation of the difference between habitual and problem-solving behavior.

The critical point regarding this premise is that we are assuming only that consumer behavior is some *form* of problem-solving behavior: we do not specify whether it will be an extended form of problem-solving or a shortened form. That will be determined by the kind of problem being dealt with, the situation within which it is being dealt, and by the nature of the person who is dealing with the particular problem.

---

[3] A good summary of this debate can be found in George Katona, "Rational Behavior and Economic Behavior," *Psychological Review*, September 1953, vol. 60.

[4] James F. Engel, David T. Kollat, and Roger D. Blackwell, *Consumer Behavior*, 2d ed. (New York: Holt, Rinehart and Winston, 1973), chap. 3.

The rationality of behavior

The final premise we start with is that *consumer behavior is rational behavior*. Economists have long started with this same premise. As they have traditionally used the term "rational behavior," it has meant behavior typified by the following example:

> The consumer is assumed to choose among the alternatives available to him in such a manner that the satisfaction derived from consuming commodities (in the broadest sense) is as large as possible. This implies that he is aware of the alternatives facing him and is capable of evaluating them.[5]

The almost mechanistic view of consumers postulated by microeconomists, coupled with the results of research that seem to indicate varying degrees of "impulsive" purchase behavior by consumers, has lead to widespread criticism of this notion of behavior rationality. Some critics might describe how marketing and advertising executives, seated around their conference tables high above Madison Avenue, burn aromatic herbs, drink ritual liquids, and smoke imported mixtures in their pipes to cast spells that cause innocent housewives and factory workers in Kansas City to rush out and buy new Edsels, Muntz Television sets, and Emerson transistor radios. The consumer, in their view, is a helpless creature in the clutches of these sinister men of business, totally without a will of his or her own, a vague blob of potential desire, awaiting only skillful manipulation and spell-casting to transform it into a consumer eager to buy.

As is often the case, the truth lies somewhere between the logical paragon postulated by economists and the other extreme proposed by the critics of business and marketing. The truth probably lies somewhere near a consumer who is not the analytical ideal, but is subject to social influences, shaped by background and environment, and equipped with all of the petty and grand desires and illusions to which human beings are subject in varying degrees. Despite these handicaps, our "typical" consumer *approaches* the ideal postulated by economists in that he tries to weigh these factors, along with the more analytical ones, and to arrive at the most rational decisions possible, under the particular set of circumstances he alone faces. And this is the essence of the premise with which we are starting—that *the rationality of any decision is relevant only in the context of the particular consumer making the decision and only at the point in time at which the decision is made.*

Our premise about rationality, then, focuses on the individual state

---

[5] James Henderson and Richard Quant, *Microeconomic Theory* (New York: McGraw Hill, 1958) p. 6.

of the consumer. We do not establish any criteria about what does or does not constitute rationality or rational behavior on the part of the consumer and then judge the actions of a consumer or a group of consumers based on these criteria. Rather we recognize that individual consumers and groups of consumers establish criteria for themselves as to what is rational and what is not. What may be rational behavior to a consumer may appear to be irrational to a researcher studying his behavior. For the researcher to label the behavior as "irrational" and then dismiss the behavior from his thinking is foolish. It may be irrational to him, but if it was rational to the consumer, then the consumer is likely to act, if not in the same manner, at least in a similar pattern, in the future. Hence, the researcher, by dismissing the behavior from consideration, is missing the opportunity to use the behavior pattern he has detected as inputs to decisions in the future. *Our function, in marketing, is not to judge people's behavior, but to understand it and to use that understanding in making better business decisions.*

Finally, perhaps one additional comment about our rationality premise is in order at this point: if we do not start with this premise, why bother to study consumer behavior at all? After all, if consumer behavior is not rational behavior, there is no point in trying to understand it because an understanding of it would be of no use in business decision making.

In summary, we are starting with three basic premises about consumer behavior: Consumer behavior is only one facet of the larger area of human behavior. Consumer behavior is a form or problem-solving behavior. And consumer behavior is rational behavior. And we are starting with the stages of consumer satisfaction that were developed in Chapter 6. From these we hope to develop an understanding of consumer behavior that will in turn be useful in understanding the decision-making processes.

THE MARKETING ACTIVITIES OF THE FIRM AND THE BEHAVIOR PROCESS OF CONSUMERS

In Chapter 6 we outlined the five stages of the consumer satisfaction process through which the firm goes in attracting and retaining profitable customers. We identified those stages as:

1. Recognizing consumer aspirations and desires
2. Creating selective dissatisfaction among consumers regarding how they are now realizing those aspirations and desires
3. Creating in consumers a sense of anticipated satisfaction with the offering of the firm

4. Helping the consumer to realize the satisfactions he anticipated receiving from the firm's offering
5. Innoculating the consumer against future dissatisfaction created by competitors.

The point of view here is that of the business firm operating in the market place, detailing what it must do in order to. attract and retain profitable customers. Presented as we have it here, this process probably evokes a response in most readers similar to, "Hey, wait a minute! You're talking about manipulating people. I thought business was supposed to follow consumer desires, not create artificial ones. The way you guys tell it is exactly the way the critics of business have been arguing for years!"

This response is understandable. You would probably be equally upset if you were told that a local hospital was taking internal human organs that were in perfectly good condition from one person, without paying that person for them, and installing them in another person who needed the new organ in order to be able to function normally, and that they were only doing this for people who could afford the price the hospital was charging. Yet when you investigate the matter, most people in our society not only condone what the hospital is doing, they applaud it! The difference in reactions lies not in what is actually being done, but in the objective that action is trying to achieve.

Most people in our society approve of the objective of prolonging life, and if organ transplants will help achieve that objective, they approve of them. Likewise, most people in our society disapprove of the notion of manipulating the behavior of others (particularly if they are the ones whose behavior is being manipulated), and if something seems to be aimed at this end, they disapprove of it heartily. If you *objectively* reread both the five stages of the consumer satisfaction process outlined above and the material that introduced this process in Chapter 6, you will notice that nothing in those stages *requires* the firm to manipulate people, and that nothing in those stages precludes the process from being one of *adaptation* to consumer desires. In fact the entire process starts with requiring the firm to recognize consumer aspirations and desires. Likewise, nothing in our description of an organ transplant requires that the donor be willing to give-up his healthy organ so that another person may have a better chance to live a normal life, and nothing in that description prevents the hospital from simply taking an organ from one person and selling it to the highest bidder. The key lies not in the description of the process, but in how it is applied and what it is trying to achieve.

In our view, the consumer satisfaction process is trying to achieve just that: better satisfaction of the consumer by the firm. If the process that the firm goes through in reaching that objective involves the firm learning a great deal about how and why people behave the way they do, it may be because the societal context in which the firm and the consumers are both operating is a bit more complex and involved than the one envisioned by Adam Smith and presented to you in a basic economics course. When society and human activity are simple, consumers' desires are also simple and easily identified. As society and human activity become more complex, consumer desires become more complex, and correspondingly more difficult to identify. And as it becomes more difficult to identify consumer desires, it is logical that the business firm find itself spending more time trying to figure out what it is that the consumer wants and how it can provide satisfaction for those wants. The marketing activities of the firm are not aimed at manipulating consumers: they are aimed at discovering consumers and what it is that consumers want.

Consumer problem solving and the consumer satisfaction process

The zone of congruence. In Figure 8–1 we have diagrammed a very general consumer problem-solving process. Reduced to its simplest elements, this is how we think people deal with problems—particularly the consumption-related problems—they face.[6] At the top of the diagram we have two circles, representing the *ideal state* and the *actual state* of the consumer. Where these two circles overlap the ideal state and the actual state are identical, and we have a "zone of congruence."

The ideal state of the consumer is a complex situation. Basically it encompasses his goals and objectives and his program for achieving them. One might characterize this state as being the consumer's conception of his life as he would like to live it, in all its facets: psychological, social, and economic. This ideal state is not a fixed concept for the consumer. It is constantly changing over time. What was an ideal state for the consumer yesterday will not necessarily be one today, and what is one today may not be ideal tomorrow. It changes for at least two basic reasons: the consumer himself changes, and the world in which the consumer operates changes.

The actual state of the consumer is no less complex. Basically it is the consumer's life as he is now living it. More specifically, it is his

---

[6] Our perspective here is similar to decision-process approaches suggested by other authors—or example, that of Engle, Kollat and Blackwell, *Consumer Behavior,* pp. 46 ff. One critical difference is our addition to this approach of the concepts of the "ideal state," the "actual state" and the "zone of congruence." These additions were suggested by the work of, among others, Alfred Emerson ("Dynamic Homeostasis: A Unifying Principle in Organic, Social and Ethical Evolution," *Scientific Monthly,* vol. 78, February 1954) and particularly Kenneth Boulding, *The Image* (Ann Arbor: The University of Michigan Press, 1956), especially pages 3–32.

FIGURE 8–1
A Generalized Consumer Problem-Solving
Process

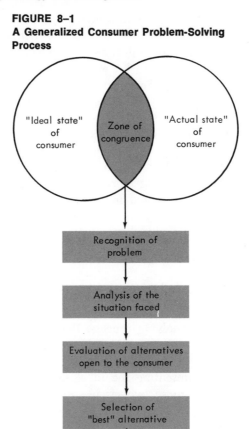

life *as he thinks he is living it.*[7] It represents what he thinks he is accomplishing in terms of the psychological, social, and economic facets of his life. To some extent this actual state of things overlaps with the consumer's ideal conception of how things should be. Since the consumer's concept of what is ideal is changing through time, the degree of overlap—or the degree of congruence—between his actual and his ideal states also changes over time. Grossly simplified, "problems" arise for the consumer when his actual and his ideal states are less than totally congruent.

---

[7] Fritz Heider, "Perceiving The Other Person," in E. P. Hollander and R. G. Hunt, ed. *Current Perspectives in Social Psychology* (New York: Oxford University Press, 1967), pp. 305–17.

Since the likelihood of total congruence is small for most consumers, this would imply a very unhappy and very active, problem solving consumer population. The fact that we don't find this suggests that there are some other factors at work in defining what is and what is not a problem. In operation, the lack of congruence is a source of potential problems for the consumer. Incongruence may not generate a problem for a number of reasons:

1. The consumer does not recognize the incongruence. He thinks that his actual state and his ideal state are in agreement in a particular area, and is thus unconcerned. This lack of recognition can come from two basic sources: ignorance of the situation or an inability (or an unconscious refusal)[8] to recognize that a given situation means that a lack of congruence exists.

2. The consumer may recognize that a lack of congruence exists, but he may feel that he can do nothing to remedy the situation; so, for the moment at least, he ignores the incongruence.[9] When the situation changes sufficiently to allow him to do something about it, then he may suddenly "recognize" the incongruence and move to correct it. The consumer's inability to do something about existing incongruence in any situation may be real or it may be imagined. In fact he may not be able to do anything about the situation that has created the incongruence he is facing. On the other hand, there may be actions which he is not aware of and thus he only thinks or imagines that he can do nothing about the incongruence that exists.

3. The consumer may recognize that a lack of congruence exists. Also, he may be aware of one or more things he could do to correct the situation, but he may feel that the benefit he would receive from the removal of the incongruence is not worth the effort it would take to accomplish it. In other words, he may regard the incongruence as being inconsequential in his scheme of things. Alternatively, the consumer may feel that acting to remove a minor incongruence would create a more severe state of incongruence in the future. The long-run benefits of acting to remove the state of incongruence may in fact be negative to the consumer. Finally, the consumer may feel that future events may, of themselves, create a situation that will remove the incongruence without the consumer having to do anything.

4. The third point above raises, by implication, another qualification to our basic assertion about incongruence: a consumer may feel that future events are going to be such that they will create a state of incongruence between his actual and his ideal state which does not now

---

[8] See Calvin S. Hall, *A Primer of Freudian Psychology* (New York: Mentor Books, 1954) for an excellent summary of Freud's basic theory of unconscious motivation.

[9] Leon Festinger, *A Theory of Cognitive Dissonance* (Evanston, Illinois: Row, Peterson, 1957).

exist. If the anticipatory action required to forestall this occurrence is easy, or if the state of incongruence that may be created is large, it is conceivable that the consumer may act at a time when he is faced with *no visible problem.* Stated differently, he may engage in problem-solving behavior when there is no visible state of incongruence.

With these qualifications, then, we suggest that the problems faced by the consumer are generated by situations where his actual state and his ideal state are not congruent.

Recognition of a problem.[10]   The next stage diagrammed in Figure 8–1 is problem recognition. It refers to the realization by the consumer that he is faced with what we have termed here a problem—a state of incongruence. For reasons detailed earlier, we are concerned only with his behavior after he realizes that he is faced with a state of incongruence. Recognition implies that the problem could have existed for some time and that the consumer has only just become aware of it, or it could imply that he has known of it but felt himself unable (or unwilling) to recognize it as a problem capable of solution until this moment. Problem-solving behavior, on the part of the consumer, really begins when the consumer feels that he is presented with a problem that can be solved, or that he feels must be solved, or that he wants very much to solve.

Recognition of a problem by the consumer does not necessarily imply its definition. Recognition may be no more than a feeling on the part of the consumer that all is not the way it should be and that something ought to be done about the situation. The consumer may not be specifically aware of what is wrong, what can be done, or what should be done about it at this point. On the other hand, for some consumers, problem recognition may also include a fairly precise definition of what the problem is and what sorts of action are required to alleviate the situation. Generally speaking, however, problem definition involves something more than simple problem recognition. It usually involves at least the stage we have labeled in Figure 8–1 as "Analysis of the Situation Faced," and sometimes it also extends into the "Evaluation of the Alternatives Open to the Consumer" stage.

Analysis of the situation.   In evaluating the situation with which he is faced, the consumer generally defines fairly well the nature of the problem with which he is confronted. At the same time, he generally fairly well defines both the outcome he desires from any action he may

---

[10] This and the remaining sections regarding the problem-solving process draw liberally from consumer behavior literature over the past decade, particularly F. Nicosia, *Consumer Decision Processes: Marketing and Advertising Implications* (Englewood Cliffs, N.J.: Prentice-Hall, Inc., 1966), J. A. Howard and J. Sheth, *The Theory of Buyer Behavior* (New York: John Wiley and Sons, 1969), and Engle, Kollat and Blackwell, *Consumer Behavior.*

take and the things which may limit the way in which he can react to solve the problem. Thus there are two aspects to problem definition: defining the nature of the problem itself and defining the constraints within which it must be solved.

Evaluation begins with the consumer attempting to determine as exactly as possible the degree of incongruence between his present ideal and his actual state. Implicit in this is an analysis by the consumer to determine whether his concept of his ideal state is still valid. In other words, can the problem be corrected by changing the ideal state so that it conforms to the actual state? We often speak of someone "resigning himself to the inevitable," and what we may be saying is that this individual has finally decided that the rational thing for him to do is to change what was apparently an unrealistic ideal state to one that is more realistic.

Should the consumer decide that the problem lies not in his concept of what is ideal, then this evaluation process focuses on where the incongruences arise between the ideal and actual states. At the same time, the consumer must also evaluate the resources he has or can acquire to bring his actual state into alignment with his ideal. It is this evaluation of resources that serves to set the constraints on what he will do. It does not tell him exactly what he will do, but it does tell him the general area within which he will be able to act in correcting his problem. And it may well be the case that in evaluating the situation he faces, the consumer will find that he has no available resources to use in solving his problem. This may cause him either to set aside the problem as temporarily insoluble or it may serve as a stimulus for him to look for a way to improvise a solution.

Evaluation of alternatives. The next stage and the prior one are closely linked; at times it is difficult to tell where one stops and the other begins. Basically, this stage is concerned with examining those courses of action that lie within the realm of action that the consumer has determined is open to him. The purpose of this examination is to determine what effect each course of action will have on the problem faced by the consumer, what expenditure of resources each alternative will require of him, and where each will leave him relative to problems that may occur in the future. The last purpose is analogous to that of the decision maker in a firm examining a course of action to see what it will do to his "freedom of action" at some point in the future. The result of this evaluation of alternatives is to create a basis for comparing disparate things. It is something like trying to compare apples and oranges objectively. Until you convert both to some sort of common evaluation unit—say sugar content per ounce or calories per ounce—it is an almost impossible task. Once they have been converted to a common base, it then becomes possible to compare them objectively. The common base of evaluation for a decision will be different for each consumer—and it may even be different in different situations for the same consumer.

Selection of "best" alternative.   Once the alternatives open to him have been evaluated and reduced to some common basis of comparison, it is possible for the consumer to select the one which seems "best" suited to his needs. That is the next stage in our process. How the consumer determines which of the alternatives is the best one depends on what is important to him, and on what he is trying to achieve by taking any action at a given time. Obviously, what is best is closely linked to the contents of the consumer's ideal state—the goals and objectives and plans that he has for himself. In those plans will be the various priorities that he has established among the things he wishes to do, and these priorities will be reflected in the comparison bases which he creates to assist him in evaluating alternatives.

Sometimes this selection process will be as simple and as "mechanical" as it appears to be when it is described. But what of situations when different alternatives offer different expectations about satisfying different goals: goals to which the consumer may have assigned equal priorities? Or suppose that different alternatives offer different expectations of satisfying different goals, and that one alternative offers a chance of satisfying to a very great extent a goal that, let's say, is ranked number 2; while another alternative offers a chance to satisfy to a lesser extent another goal ranked number 1. Does the fact that one goal is ranked higher than another mean that the consumer will act to satisfy it, when he could do something else and get more satisfaction of a lesser ranked goal?

The simplest answer is to say that he will select the alternative that yields the greatest possible utility to him. That which yields the greatest utility for one consumer will not necessarily yield the same utility for any other consumer. So we have a simple answer that is probably correct, but which raises a great deal of doubt and uncertainty.

Post-event evaluation.   The final stage in our diagram concerns what happens after the consumer chooses an alternative and acts upon it. After he has acted, and after he has a chance to see what has occurred because of his action, he evaluates what he did, what he expected his action to accomplish, and what it actually accomplished. The consumer is, in effect, evaluating his judgment and his decision-making ability at this stage. From this evaluation he will gain information and insight that should help him when he has to make similar decisions in the future. This feedback process may induce the consumer to take additional action to modify, or even reverse, what he did earlier. Or it may simply be stored as information for the future that does not require any immediate action on his part. What happens here will depend on how well the consumer solved his problem and on how good his performance at each stage in the problem-solving process was.

This discussion of the consumer problem-solving process is, admittedly, both general and cursory. It is intended to provide a framework to help you visualize how consumers deal with the consumption problems they face. The number of consumption situations in which a consumer goes through the entire process, starting with problem recognition and ending with post-event evaluation, is probably only a small portion of the total number of consumption situations in which he is involved. In many instances, the problems are insignificant enough or they are routine enough so that the consumer engages in what might be called a shortened version of this process: he does what he always does in that situation. Only when "what he always does" cannot be done would he then go through a longer version of this process. A consumer discovering that he is about out of cigarettes provides a good example of a routine consumption problem that is simply solved by doing what has been done before. In this case, the consumer simply buys the kind of cigarettes he always has, unless something is unusual. For example, he may be in a place that does not stock his brand, or he may realize that he hasn't really enjoyed the last few packs of cigarettes he has smoked and decide that maybe it's time to do something different such as changing brands or stopping smoking.

This type of habitual behavior, such as the loyalty to a particular brand of cigarettes, is simply the repetition of a solution which the consumer knows from experience (several post-event evaluations) is going to satisfy the objective in question. While it is not in itself an example of extensive problem-solving behavior, it is the product of that type of behavior at some point in the past. And if the objective of our firm is to get the consumer to use our product, and if the consumer is now habitually using the product of our competitor, then we must understand this problem-solving process well enough so that we may induce him to stop his habitual behavior and re-engage in extensive problem-solving behavior. Only then can we present our product to him as an alternative to what he is doing now. For it is only when he has considered our alternative and compared it along with the others open to him that we have a chance of getting him as a customer. A consumer is not going to stop doing something that is providing him satisfaction and start doing something else unless the new alternative promises to be more satisfying.

The link between the consumer's process and the firm's process. We have discussed the five stages that the firm goes through in attracting and keeping customers. Further, we have discussed in some detail the process consumers go through in selecting the products they are going to consume. In Figure 8-2 we have combined these two processes to get a view of the interaction that must occur between the customer satisfaction activities of the firm and the consumption decision processes

FIGURE 8–2
Relationship between the Problem-Solving Behavior of Consumers and the Customer Satisfaction Process of the Business Firm

The firm's viewpoint: Stages of the consumer satisfaction process	The consumer's viewpoint: Stages in a generalized problem-solving process					
	Consumer's desired ("ideal") state	Recognition of a problem by the consumer	Analysis of the situation by the consumer	Evaluation of available alternatives by consumer	Selection of one "best" alternative by consumer	Post-event evaluation by consumer
Recognition of the consumers' aspirations	*	*	*			
Creation of selective consumer dissatisfaction		*	*	*		
Creation of anticipated consumer satisfactions			*	*	*	
Realization of satisfactions by the consumer				*	*	
Antidissatisfaction innoculation of consumer by firm						*

of the consumer if a given consumer is to buy the products of a given firm.

Across the top of the diagram we show the consumer's view of what is going on in the marketplace. Down the side of the diagram we show the firm's view. In effect, this diagram presents a simplified, conceptual view of the interaction of the consumer and the business firm in the marketplace. The cells represent the points of interaction between the two processes.

Implied in this visual presentation is the idea that the consumer's problem-solving process and the firm's customer satisfaction process interlock at all stages. Yet this interlocking is not uniform; some aspects of the consumer's process interlock to a greater degree with some aspects of the firm's process than they do with others. The asterisks are placed in some cells to show the stages where the greatest degree of interaction occurs between the two processes. As you will notice, there is little evidence of a simple, one-to-one correlation between the stages of the consumer's problem-solving process and specific stages in the firm's customer satisfaction process. Rather, the processes appear to overlap, with a single stage in one process interlocking with two or three stages in the other process. At the same time, each stage in each of the processes interlocks and interacts to some extent with each stage in the other process. The asterisks are not the only points of interaction; they are only what appear to be the major points at which corresponding stages interact. Thus, while attempting to discover the aspirations and preferences of consumers, the firm is most interested in what consumers consider to be their ideal state, in how they recognize the existence of problems, and how they analyze and define those problem situations. It is also interested in how evaluation and selection of alternative courses of action are conducted by consumers and how they conduct post-event evaluation. But the firm is less interested, at this stage, in the last three steps in the consumer's decision process than in the first three steps.

Let us return to our example of the cigarette smoker who finds himself out of cigarettes. If he currently smokes Brand X and we produce Brand Y, our concern would seem to be with (1) creating some selective dissatisfaction and (2) altering an existing pattern of behavior (his walking up to the tobacco counter and asking for a package of Brand X). To accomplish this alteration in behavior, we have to understand what is necessary to cause him to recognize that he has a problem. We also have to understand how he analyzes this type of problem, how he evaluates alternative solutions to his problem, and how he reduces these alternatives to a common basis. These are our primary concerns at this stage. Because this consumer is already a smoker, we know that in some way smoking fits into what we have called his ideal state. At this point we are not certain *how* it fits in, even though that information would be very useful to us. We could take as given that he smokes for some reason that is good to him, and we could concentrate our attention on what action is needed to get him to reconsider his habitual behavior and to engage in a more extensive form of problem-solving activity.

Without a doubt, knowing how and why smoking fits into his ideal state would help in getting him to alter an existing pattern of behavior, but that knowledge is not necessarily required in order to induce a more extensive form of problem-solving behavior. Normally, in approaching the problem, the firm starts with trying to assess what the smoker's aspirations are and to discover as much as possible about his ideal state and the relationship between that state and smoking. Then it proceeds to the stage of attempting to create selective dissatisfaction. However, the many examples of firms that merely follow the lead of their competitor and enjoy some success in doing so would seem to support the notion that the firm may be able to "short-cut" its side of the process, too.

To view the job of the firm as beginning with what the competition is doing and trying to win customers away from competitors is somewhat like starting on a trip without a road map. In either case, you will eventually get somewhere—in one case by following your competitors, in the other by following the road. But in both cases, once you get to the end of the line, you may realize that you really don't want to be where you are.

Turning back once more to our cigarette smoker, it seems far more logical to start with trying to understand what his aspirations are and what his ideal state really contains. We may find, to our surprise, that he really doesn't want to smoke at all, but that it is simply a bad (from his point of view) habit to which he has been addicted for a number of years. He may well be concerned that smoking is shortening his life span, contributing to his run-down feeling, and keeping him from being attractive to members of the opposite sex. Discovering this, it may well be that we would now want to design our product, Brand Y, so that it would offer the consumer a chance to realize these goals. We may be able to design a cigarette that is much less harmful to the body and which reduces the individual's physical dependence on smoking. Or we may decide that the thing to do is to get out of the cigarette business altogether and produce another product.

The example brings out the point that we want to make here: unless the firm understands its customers at the most basic level possible, it is not as much of a master of its own destiny as it might otherwise be. If the firm depends on its competitors to show it the way, the day may come when the firm finds itself in a peculiar position—unaware of how it really got there, unsure of really where it is, and not having the slightest idea how to get out of wherever it is. The firm that short-cuts the customer satisfaction process is surrendering most of its chances for creative marketing activity and is resigning itself to a future of tactically trying to keep up with its competitors.

THE STRATEGIC ASPECTS OF CONSUMER BEHAVIOR: THE DISCOVERY OF CONSUMER ASPIRATIONS

Take another look at Figure 8–2. It is apparent that the movement in that figure is from the upper left-hand to the lower right-hand corner. From both points of view, the consumer's and the firm's, the beginnings are in the cell where the consumer's ideal state and the firm's attempts to recognize and discover the aspirations of consumers interlock. It is from this interaction that all the joint behavior of the firm and the consumer in the marketplace follows. The extent to which the firm is successful in uncovering the aspirations of the consumers it wishes to serve will control the degree of its later success in attracting and retaining those consumers as customers.

Figure 8–3 amplifies this notion by illustrating the degree to which the various stages of the firm's consumer satisfaction process are linked together: the strategy which the firm follows with regard to creating selective dissatisfactions in consumers directly depends on the tactics it has adopted for serving the consumer aspirations it has discovered. In a similar manner, the strategy that the firm will use to create antici- pated *satisfaction* on the part of consumers depends directly on the tactics it used in creating *dissatisfaction* earlier. Thus each stage in the consumer satisfaction process has both a strategic and a tactical aspect, and the strategic aspect of the third stage develops from the tactics used in the second stage, just as the strategic aspects of the fourth stage evolve from the tactics used in the third.

Given this relationship, it is apparent that a miscalculation on strategy in the first stage is likely to be more damaging to the firm than a similar miscalculation later in the process, for everything else descends from this first, strategic evaluation. An error made here will be amplified by subsequent decisions that are based upon and derived from previous decisions. Similarly, accurate evaluation and decisions from the start set patterns for successful tactics and strategies throughout the process.

Planning, consumer satisfaction, and the marketing mix

The importance of understanding consumer behavior has been empha- sized and illustrated throughout this chapter. The real importance, how- ever, relates to the firm's planning of the marketing variables in the development of the total marketing program. In the discussion that follows, each of the five stages of the consumer satisfaction process will be related to the planning and decision areas of the marketing mix.

Recognition of consumer aspirations. Consumer aspirations are key sources of opportunity for the firm. For that reason, a great deal of the firm's marketing research activity should be devoted to the discovery, recognition, and analysis of consumer aspirations. These opportunities can affect planning and decision making across all elements of the mar- keting mix. This stage is the one where needs and desires for new pro- ducts or modifications of old ones are discovered. Consumer aspirations and problems can often be translated directly into new product and new service ideas. Also, the need for product availability creates the need for new and different types of distribution channels and outlets. Consumer needs may dictate more, less, or even different distribution outlets in order to provide convenience, speed, shopping ease and assis- tance, or even prestige to the consumer.

The identification of needs and wants pertains to industrial customers and channel members (retailers, wholesalers, etc.) as well as the ultimate

FIGURE 8–3
Strategic and Tactical Aspects of the Consumer Satisfaction Process

Stages in the consumer satisfaction process		Strategic and tactical aspects of the process
I. The discovery and recognition of consumer aspirations	—yields→	A strategy based on discovered opportunity —yields→ A tactical approach to satisfy the discovered aspirations for satisfaction generation
		—— dictates ——
II. Creation of selective consumer dissatisfactions		A strategy of dissatisfaction —yields→ The tactics of dissatisfaction creation creation
		—— dictates ——
III. Creation of anticipated consumer satisfactions		The strategy of satisfactions to —yields→ The tactics of satisfaction be created creation
		—— dictates ——
IV. Realization of the satisfactions by the consumer		The strategy of satisfaction —yields→ The tactics to help the consumer realization realize them
		—— dictates ——
V. Anti-dissatisfaction innoculation of the consumer		The strategy of satisfaction —yields→ The tactics of protection anti-dissatisfaction innoculation

consumer. In these cases logistics could be a major factor in satisfying needs related to speed of delivery, reliability, storage, and similar requirements. The source of consumer needs may result from budget constraints. This would result in opportunities for price reductions or adjustments and creative credit arrangements. Since promotion is the communicative variable, it has fewer opportunities at this stage than any of the other elements. If it is recognized that the consumer needs information, a promotional opportunity exists and should be exploited.

On numerous occasions General Motors has modified its automobiles in response to consumer needs. Several years ago Johnson Wax changed the emphasis of its distribution from hardware stores to supermarkets in recognition of the need of the housewife to do one-stop shopping. It is not uncommon for Ely Lilly to make shipments of drugs by airfreight in order to maintain critical supply levels at its wholesalers. Levitz Furniture successfully adopted a pricing arrangement which separates delivery and set-up costs from the basic price of the furniture in order to meet the needs of budget-minded customers. And even though there have been a number of small economy cars on the market for many years, the energy shortage and the accompanying needs of consumers provided the opportunity for many foreign and domestic car makers to promote the gas-saving features of their automobiles.

Creation of selective dissatisfaction. The critical element of the marketing mix used in the creation of selective dissatisfaction is promotion. Assuming that your product has unique features that can better satisfy the consumer, these features need only to be communicated to the consumer in order for him to realize his untenable current situation. The same is true for price; assuming your price is lower or in some way meets consumer needs better than competitive prices, dissatisfaction may occur after this fact has been communicated to the consumer. The announcement of product availability in certain distribution outlets may cause consumers to reevaluate their current purchasing patterns. A salesman's presentation of speed and reliability of delivery may cause industrial customers or intermediaries some dissatisfaction with their current buying. The want-satisfying features of all the marketing elements can create selective dissatisfaction among consumers if effective communication is used.

Anticipated satisfaction. For the same reasons cited above, promotion is the critical element in the creation of a sense of anticipated satisfaction by consumers. Promotion is the vehicle used to expose the sources of anticipated satisfaction to consumers. This is done by emphasizing both the information and persuasion aspects of promotion. The other elements of the marketing mix, however, play a vital supportive role in the creation of anticipated satisfaction. For example, products and prices are highly visible. An advertisement emphasizing low prices and high quality will be very ineffective unless the actual price and product support the message.

Realized satisfaction. The product is the most important element in helping the consumer realize the satisfaction he anticipated. This is because the product is the primary delivery mechanism of satisfaction or dissatisfaction. If the product is what the consumer expected, he enjoys pride of ownership, prestige, comfort of warranty service, expected level of quality, and all of the other satisfactions gained by the use or consumption of the product. Distribution channels can also give satisfaction through realized convenience, availability, exclusiveness, shopping assistance, and similar attributes. Satisfaction can be gained from pricing through realized savings and credit arrangements. Even promotion can give satisfaction by assuring the customer that he made the right purchase decision.

Antidissatisfaction inoculation. The consumer is inoculated against future dissatisfaction created by competitors by developing brand loyalty to the largest degree possible. All of the marketing mix elements are critical at this stage by continuing to generate realized satisfaction and reassurance. The consumer has to remain satisfied with his current purchasing patterns and have his purchasing decision reinforced frequently if he is to withstand all of the actions of competitors attempting to create dissatisfaction.

If marketing research is generating a continuous flow of information relating to consumer aspirations and desires, the firm will also be changing and adjusting all of the elements of the marketing mix to match the changes in the consumer. In fact, the more successful firms will generate change that may even cause them to be forced into creating dissatisfaction among their present consumers in order to bring about the change. Polaroid has done this with its advanced technology. Automobile companies do this through style changes and are accused of planned obsolescence. The major soap companies created low-suds detergents and liquid detergents, and then had to convince the housewife that conventional soaps and detergents were inferior.

SUMMARY

This chapter provides an overview of consumer behavior, with emphasis on the problem-solving process. The subject of human behavior would fill many volumes and still leave great voids. In the few pages allowed here, we can only approach the subject in a simplified manner and hope to relate behavior to the area of marketing decision making.

It is important that all students of marketing gain an appreciation for and a knowledge of consumer behavior. For all decision making in marketing begins with the consumer and an understanding of what he wants to buy—when, where, how, and why. No matter how creative or technically ingenious a marketing decision may be, if it does not match consumer needs, wants, and desires, it is almost certainly doomed to failure. On the other hand, the firm that recognizes and understands consumer aspirations and desires and makes its marketing decisions accordingly is well on the road to success.

| # Strategic planning and objectives

Strategic, managerial, and operational planning
Introduction
Strategic planning
Management control
Overlap with strategic planning
Operational control
A final point concerning the planning hierarchy
Objectives
Hierarchical interaction: Setting objectives
A final point concerning objectives and plans

STRATEGIC, MANAGERIAL, AND OPERATIONAL PLANNiNG

Introduction

There are three types of planning for any organization. The first type involves planning which will provide the basic direction for the firm. The second type is concerned with the planning for the management of the functional areas such as marketing and for the implementation of plans. The third type involves the more routine features of operations. Planning experts have designed a variety of frameworks for these three types of planning and have applied different names to them. Some have made no differentiation between the two bottom levels because of their similarities and because they both deal with implementation in the functional area of plans developed for the organization as a whole. The terms, concepts, and definitions used here are those developed by Robert N. Anthony.[1]

Strategic planning is the term applied to the first type of planning. *Management control* and *operational control* refer to the second and

---

[1] Robert N. Anthony, *Planning and Control Systems: A Framework for Analysis* (Boston: Division of Research, Harvard Business School, 1965).

third types of planning. Two somewhat bothersome situations arise. The first small troublesome area arises from the overlap between the concepts of strategic planning and management control as well as between those of management control and operational control. The conceptual overlap is explained by the fact that planning constitutes something of a continuum which defies a neat slicing of the whole into separate parts. The three parts do not just "join" at some point where one abruptly leaves off and the other starts. The juncture is more like the mixing of water where a river and the sea come together.

The second minor problem may arise from the terminology used: management control and operational control. We hope that the reader will not let semantics cause too much trouble and obscure the meaning of the concepts. The absence of the word planning from these two concepts should pose no difficulties; nor should the distinction between management control and operational control.[2]

Strategic planning

Strategic planning defined. This aspect of planning has been variously termed and referred to as "comprehensive planning," development of the "grand design," long range planning, and others. It is concerned with such things as the development of objectives and policies to guide management. Anthony defines it as follows:

> *Strategic planning* is the process of deciding on objectives of the organization, on changes in these objectives, on the resources used to attain these objectives, and on the policies that are to govern the acquisition, use, and disposition of these resources.[3]

As stated above, strategic planning gives direction to the firm. In addition, it determines the character of the firm by virtue of the objectives it identifies and the policies developed to reach those objectives. While many tend to equate strategic planning with long-range planning, no such equation is made here. The automobile provides an excellent illustration for this point. The planning underlying the decision to introduce such *new automobiles* as the small car, the Mustang, and the Edsel several years down the road necessarily involved *strategic* decisions, because such introductions indicated a change in direction for the firm. On the other hand, the planning for *new models* of old automobiles several years from now is not strategic. Both involve long time

---

[2] For a complete explanation of the terms used here and for a comparison with comparable terms used by planning experts, see Anthony, Ibid. While we credit Professor Anthony with the framework we use, he is not responsible for our interpretations and modifications of it.

[3] Ibid., p. 16.

periods, but the planning activities and processes are entirely different. Also their effects are different.

Strategic activities. The types of activities envisioned by the definition of strategic planning include such things as:

1. Choosing objectives relating to profitability, products, sales, and markets, among others.
2. Assembling resources required to attain the objectives.
    a. Developing managerial skills (tangible: people).
    b. Raising money (tangible: money).
    c. Enhancing reputation (intangible: image).
3. Setting policies governing acquisition, use, and disposition of resources.
    a. Increasing profitability.
        1. Phasing out unprofitable lines.
        2. Mechanizing to improve productivity.
    b. Improving products.
        1. Developing a pollution-free engine.
        2. Enlarging the product line.
    c. Enlarging sales and markets.
        1. Decreasing reliance on the defense market.
        2. Developing the poverty market.
    d. Developing managerial skill.
        1. Putting more resources into development programs.
        2. Changing the strategy of management development programs.
    e. Raising money.
        1. Revising dividend program.
        2. Arranging equity financing.
    f. Enhancing reputation.
        1. Improving quality of product.
        2. Improving after-sale service.

These are only a few illustrations of marketing-related strategic planning activities. Of course, all of the other aspects of strategic planning impinge directly or indirectly on the marketing focus of the firm.

To a very considerable extent strategic planning involves those things which have a long-term effect on the organization. Also, it is characterized primarily by an analytical approach to the environments and is more oriented toward the discovery process than toward the solution process. In addition, it is directed more toward "what to do" than "how to do it," although by saying this we once more are in the gray area between strategic planning and management control. Whether the territory of the latter is entered depends upon the approach taken and how far down the hierarchical line planning goes.

For example, it is clear that a decision to enter a new market is strategic. Also, it is a "what to do" decision. Then, the decision to enter a new market by means of an acquisition is also strategic, but this becomes part of a "how to do it" program. Also, the decision to acquire by means of a cash payment or exchange of stock is a "how to do it" approach. These illustrations are offered to emphasize that strategic planning does not stop with "what to do," but continues with analyses of broad alternatives until the planning decision is reasonably refined. As we showed in Figure 8–3 of Chapter 8, a given strategy yields certain tactics for one event. Those tactics may dictate a strategy for a following event. The decision to enter a new market may have been the result of appraisals of ways of reaching a specified earnings growth objective. Other alternatives, such as to modify price or distribution policies, broaden product lines, or intensify marketing effort in present market areas, may have been analyzed and rejected.

Considerations for strategic planning.   There are almost as many "key factors" underlying strategic planning as there are people making those plans. These are the planning premises referred to in Chapter 4. One set of these premises was the basis for a paper presented by a prominent American business executive to an international conference in Sweden. The conference was designed to "address some of the most perplexing and least understood of the new issues that are likely to affect the corporation and its environment in the seventies and eighties."[4]

In a presentation to that conference, the chairman of the board and chief executive officer of Westinghouse discussed four essential ingredients of long-range strategic planning. He said that those considerations must be a part of that planning if we are to enter the 1980s in better condition than we are now. He added that slighting them will guarantee failure for almost any business enterprise.[5] Because of their relevance to both marketing and planning we use them as the foundation of this section of the chapter.

The first consideration in strategic planning is the need to plan for continual improvement in productivity. Such improvement is necessary because people will continue to demand more and better satisfaction of their wants and needs in all areas: social, cultural, and material. To meet these demands business has to plan for new facilities, procedures and concepts to improve productivity. The second consideration lies in excellence of product design, service, and management to bring about increased productivity and satisfaction. The third point made was that planning should recognize that the upcoming decade will be a consumer-

---

[4] Herman Kahn, ed., *The Future of the Corporation* (New York: Mason & Lipscomb Publishers, 1974), p. 3.

[5] Donald C. Burnham, "Corporate Planning and Social Problems," in Kahn, *The Future of the Corporation*, pp. 73–81.

oriented decade. This too will require reliability and quality of both product and service. Finally, strategic planning must recognize that business will need to become more involved in society and its problems of people living together.

Management control

We earlier defined management as the analysis and rationalization of environments for the dual purposes of establishing aims, plans, and policies, and for the effective use of resources. Further, we stated that this definition sorted out two separate activities of management: the decision to do something and the act of doing whatever was decided on. Strategic planning is the first activity, the decision to do something; it is based upon all sorts of analyses and ideally is done with the full participation of all of the managers of functional and other relevant divisions acting as a group (Level 1). Management control is the second level of the planning hierarchy. It is the art and science of accomplishing effectively and efficiently whatever was decided at the first level. The managers who participated in the strategic planning process put on their other hats and begin to implement the decisions. This is the rationalization process, the application of modern methods of efficiency, and is handled in the appropriate group of executives and their subordinates at Level 2.

The analyses required of the marketing manager are decision-oriented and/or problem-solving-oriented. The goal of the analyses and problem-solving approach has two dimensions: (1) effectiveness in accomplishing the objective set forth and (2) efficiency in the use of resources in attaining the objective. We turn again to Anthony's definition:

> *Management control* is the process by which managers assure that resources are obtained and used effectively and efficiently in the accomplishment of the organization's objectives.[6]

The objectives of the firm may guarantee that certain functions will be operated inefficiently in terms of the optimum use of resources. For example, an objective may be established to provide a given level of customer service in after-sale repair service—say, two-day repairs. A companion policy may require that the company's own repair facilities be used. The turnaround time of two days may require more personnel, equipment, and space than can be used efficiently. So the policy may dictate that those repair facilities *not* be used as efficiently as possible. Thus the proper interpretation of efficiency is being as efficient as possible *given the constraints of the entire organization,* rather than being

---

[6] Anthony, *Planning and Control Systems,* p. 27.

as efficient as possible without considering other elements of the organization.

The management control activities related to marketing and envisioned by the definition include such things as:

Deciding on minor product improvements.

Formulating promotion programs.

Realigning channels of distribution.

Developing delivery service schedules.

Selecting advertising agencies.

Adjusting price and discount practices.

For example, the decisions relating to product *improvements* require the manager to make a series of analyses, but with a different approach and goal than when analysis is made for the development of new products. The improvement may be along the line of quality improvement; so analyses of the nature of the improvement and alternative methods of bringing it about must be made. In this respect, the analyses are heavily oriented toward developing information concerning market needs and wants and the level of competition. Of course, the cost of proposed improvements must be considered. After the nature of the improvements has been decided, the most efficient way of handling them must be determined.

The choices in developing promotion programs also illustrate management control activities. What are the costs and potential returns from one set of promotional mixes compared with those of other sets? Should more reliance be placed on personal promotion by salesmen; on promotion through distributors; or on point of sale promotion? What role should price, discounts, coupons, contests, and gimmicks play in the promotional program? What portions of the budget should be spent on these types of promotional schemes compared with advertising? What mix among the advertising media is most effective?

Overlap with strategic planning. Planning at this level for the most effective and efficient methods of doing something often has overtones of strategic planning. This is because management control planning must also embrace (1) the development of marketing objectives, (2) the acquisition of resources required to attain the objectives, and (3) the development of policies and guidelines to attain the objectives. While the broad marketing objectives may be specified in the corporate plan, the specific ones may have to be developed at Level 2 in the managerial hierarchy.

The corporate objective may be to reduce reliance on sales to the defense industries. To accomplish this objective the marketing manager has several fairly obvious alternatives. First, he may bring about the desired result by relative neglect of defense industries and increase effort in another market. Or, without neglecting the one market, he may concentrate on another. A third strategy to be analyzed may be a selective dropping of some defense customers. The alternatives are almost endless.

The marketing manager also will have to develop a strategy to pursue objectives concerning acquisition of resources within the overall framework, again with almost endless alternatives. If the corporate objective is, for example, to improve management development, several possibilities arise. Arrangements may be made for internal seminars for marketing people, released time for attending college, encouragement of a self-imposed study program, fostering of attendance at professional meetings, and so on.

Still within the framework established by corporate strategic planning, the marketing strategic planning may require the development of policies and guidelines to attain the marketing objective. If the corporate objective is to increase sales by entering a new territory and by acquiring another company already operating in that geographic area, the marketing manager has a strategic problem of integrating the marketing program with that of the acquired company. Once more, many alternative strategies may be considered.

After defining a program through strategic marketing planning, the marketing manager is then at the point of implementing what has been designed. The managerial function entails the implementation of a strategic program which the managerial group at Level 2 has developed and which is designed to implement the strategic program developed at Level 1. Thus, the marketing manager is a "planner" at two levels and a "doer" at one.

In implementing marketing strategy, the primary goal of the marketing manager is efficiency. Modern methods of information gathering, data processing, and tools of analysis are used to aid in the rationalization process of performing the job efficiently. These techniques may help determine consumer preferences for product design, the most effective promotion mix, the most efficient channels of distibution, and the most profitable price system.

Operational control

In the planning hierarchy, management control overlaps with strategic planning on one side and operational control on the other. At times, in the blurred zones, management control and operational control become indistinguishable from one another. The focus of operational control is on task performance within the framework of decisions made, policies and guidelines established, and rules laid down in the management control process. Anthony's definition states:

Operational control is the process of assuring that specific tasks are carried out effectively and efficiently.[7]

The management of inventory as an element of attention to customer service serves as an excellent point of departure to show not only the integrated relationship of the three elements in the hierarchy of planning, but also to make a specific differentiation between management control and operational control. Strategic planning may have set the objective that customers will be able to be served from stock 85 percent of the time. Management control will design the inventory system and establish the reorder point at an appropriate level. Operational control devises a system to assure that the proper steps are taken when inventory reaches that predetermined level. The system may be as simple as an instruction manual that tells the new clerk, "Call the supplier and he'll know what to do." On the other hand, it may be as complex as a completely automated production line or oil refinery.

Many of the tasks that need to be performed are subject to this form of programmed control: telephone order-taking by either tape recorder or human clerk; order processing; planning salesmen's calls; routing delivery trucks; direct-mail advertising; bill paying, and others. One control characteristic is that little or no judgment is required; observance of rules and following of directions is the major responsibility of the person or machine.

A final point concerning the planning hierarchy

We have avoided any implication whatsoever that strategic planning, management control, and operational control are discrete activities. Management control is a process which involves both planning and management and is carried on within guidelines established by strategic planning. The major, and almost exclusive, thrust of strategic planning is analysis. Twin thrusts of analysis and rationalization occupy those in managerial control. The final stage of the continuum is at the operational control level where the almost exclusive goal of management is rationalization. This is graphically illustrated in Figure 9–1.

Not all will agree with the label of strategic planning attached to the planning at the functional level. We are not concerned with the label, only with the concept; so there has been no prior attempt made to explain why we did not call it something else such as "tactical" or "implementation" planning. There is one fundamental reason for it, and several minor ones. The fundamental reason first: the overall marketing objectives are clearly the result of strategic planning. Within this framework the marketing manager and the staff hope to develop a series

---

[7] Ibid., p. 69.

FIGURE 9–1
Overlap of Types of Planning

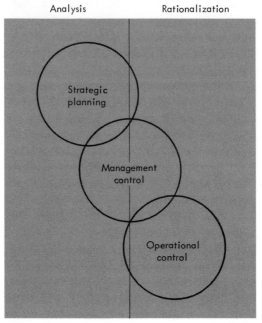

of subobjectives, a series of subguidelines, a series of subdecisions to acquire and use resources. This process requires the same types of analyses as does the overall process of strategic planning. The breadth and depth of the analyses are not as great as for the "parent" analyses, and they are more constrained in other ways, but the same types of thinking are required. There are trade-offs internal to marketing which may result in different arrangements of resources and/or different mixes.

Figure 9–2 traces the process through an example. Note that items 4*a*, 4*b*, and 4*c* follow the definitions and patterns of our definitions and patterns of strategic planning, management control, and operational control. The types of analyses and actions at each level of the planning hierarchy are different, whether the planning is at the corporate level or the functional level.

If the selection of the alternatives in 4*a* of Figure 9–2 were done at the corporate level, there would be little quarrel about whether they were strategic. Guidelines should be established at the corporate level, since this would allow other functional area executives to be involved in some of the key decisions.

In summary, the point is that some decisions which normally would be considered functional area decisions (1) have an impact on several areas of the firm; (2) have a long-term impact; (3) involve the setting

FIGURE 9–2
An Example of the Planning Hierarchy

Corporate level

1. Analyses: Opportunities, resources, and so on.
2. Objective: Test-market a new product.
3. Guideline: Have report and recommended action within one year.
4. Resources: A given number of dollars.

Functional level

1. Constraints: Guidelines and resources
2. Resources used: Dollars; test-market; experts in research design, consumer behavior, promotion, and so on.
3. Problems:
   a. Decide to do *something*.
   b. Do it.
4. Planning approach:
   a. For deciding what to do:
      1. Establish planning premises.
      2. State subobjectives for the market test.
      3. Determine the kinds of resources required.
      4. Develop guidelines for implementation.
   b. For planning for doing it:
      1. Set up guidelines for obtaining resources.
      2. Design a system for using resources effectively and efficiently.
      3. Write up the procedures or rules to be followed.
   c. For doing it:
      1. All subsequent steps specified by rules.
      2. Report.

of objectives and guidelines; (4) deal with acquisition of resources; and (5) have to do with strategic matters. Thus, they are strategic decisions, whether they are made by Level 1 or Level 2 people, or by the foreman of the shipping room. They require a substantially different set of analyses and lines of communication. They even require different methods of communication than do the typical nonstrategic decisions. Furthermore, they require different types of information. For these reasons we have called them strategic and have said that our reason for doing so is to emphasize the different management skills needed. If managers consider them to be tactical rather than strategic, the implications for other areas of the firm are likely to be ignored.

The pattern of discussion and analyses of almost every managerial activity in this book has three elements. First, we have taken a normative approach: what *should* the managers do? Second we have looked at what many managers do that is inconsistent with what they should do. Third, we have examined situations in which managers actually do what they should do. Our discussion of planning in prior chapters, this chapter, and in those to come follows this pattern. Two articles appearing in the summer of 1975 help us continue this approach.

Henry Mintzberg reported the results of his study of managers. He said that a part of the folklore about managerial work is that "the manager is a reflective, systematic planner."[8] He added that none of the evidence supports that statement. As a fact to offset the folklore, he said that many studies have shown that "managers work at an unrelenting pace, that their activities are characterized by brevity, variety, and discontinuity, and that they are strongly oriented to action and dislike reflective activities."[9] He cited his study, which included five chief executives, and another study of 160 British middle and top managers to show that managers work only a few minutes at a time on any one activity.

It was not clear from the article whether managers were (1) moving from one activity to another and making decisions on the run without a planned base for them or (2) whether these decisions were made within the framework of a planning program.

The other segment of our format showing that managers actually do what they should do in planning was reported the same week. *Business Week* said that "Raytheon Co. is a company that has become so confident about corporate planning that it even makes public its long-term goals."[10] In the 1960s the company decided to deemphasize defense contracts which accounted for 85 percent of its business. The objectives of doubling sales to $1 billion and reducing government contracts to 50 percent of the product mix by 1970 were met. In that year new objectives were announced to be reached by 1975: $1.8 billion in sales with 55 percent of them commercial sales, and an increase in earnings per share of 50 percent. All of these were accomplished a year ahead of schedule.[11] This implies a very significant amount of reflective thinking and organized planning by managers.

OBJECTIVES

Hierarchical interaction: Setting objectives

Need for objectives. The development of objectives is an orderly way of moving into the future; so an objective refers to a desired future state of affairs for the firm. To prevent organizational drift, a great network of objectives in a number of different areas is needed to assure effectiveness in satisfying the consumer and efficiency in managing the business. Peter Drucker has identified eight areas for which objectives

[8] Henry Mintzberg, "The Manager's Job: Folklore and Fact," *Harvard Business Review*, July–August 1975, p. 50.

[9] Ibid.

[10] "Raytheon's Five Year Plans That Work," *Business Week*, July 14, 1975, p. 113.

[11] Ibid.

are needed.[12] They are: market standing, innovation, productivity, physical and financial resources, profitability, manager performance and development, worker performance and attitude, and public responsibility. George Steiner covers essentially the same subjects, but is more specific in certain areas when he identifies nine aspects of a structure for the network of objectives. His areas are: profitability, sales and markets, products, finance, stability, personnel, organization, flexibility, and research and development.[13]

A convenient way of grouping these areas into broad categories is on the basis of the external and internal environments, despite the fact that the fit may not be perfect. Customers, competitors, and the public in general are three elements of the external environment for which objectives are needed. Those aspects of the internal environment for which objectives are needed pertain to the overall effectiveness and efficiency of the firm: the organization itself, the resources of the firm, and performance as reflected in financial statements.

A regrouping of Drucker's eight suggested areas into environmental areas is shown in Figure 9–3.

FIGURE 9–3
Areas of Objectives

External environment

Customers:	1.	Innovation, including research and development.
Competitors:	2.	Market standing.
Public:	3.	Public responsibility.

Internal environment

Organization:	4.	Manager performance and development.
	5.	Worker performance and development.
Resources:	6.	Physical, financial, intangible.
Performance:	7.	Profits.
	8.	Productivity.

Characteristics of objectives. Objectives should have certain characteristics if they are to be useful for planning:

Interaction. Probably the most pervasive characteristic of a network of objectives is the interaction of the various people involved in developing and refining the objectives. Some examples are:

1. Interaction among various levels of management and staff to identify opportunities and problems

[12] Peter Drucker, *The Practice of Management* (New York: Harper and Row, 1968), p. 63.
[13] George A. Steiner, *Top Management Planning* (London: The Macmillan Company, 1969), pp. 150–53.

2. Interaction among and within functional areas to give meaning to otherwise meaningless statements—for example, "good service at low cost"
3. Interaction to make apparently conflicting objectives compatible with one another—for example, "reduce frequency of being out of stock" and "reduce investment in inventory."

Flexibility. Considering all environments, objectives are presumably the best possible at the time they are stated. However, the objectives must be capable of being modified as needed—a requisite that certainly implies constant review of the network. The organization also should have the flexibility to respond quickly to sudden changes in the environments.

Specificity. Objectives generally must be specific in order to be workable. Abstract or philosophical statements are generally acceptable only as a point of departure for more refined objectives. It is operationally meaningless, for example, to establish an objective of "good service at low cost." Such terms can be made more concrete by quantifying the cost of providing different qualities of service and choosing one of them, anointing it, and identifying that level as being good service at low cost. (A technique for giving more concrete meaning to the term "good service at low cost" is discussed in Chapter 15.)

On the other hand, some objectives probably have to be stated abstractly. A promotion objective may be stated: "Design an advertising program which will improve the corporate image." Or a sales personnel objective may be stated: "Develop a program to improve sales personnel morale and loyalty to the company." Specific dollar expenditures could be identified, but that only puts a price on the objective; it does not reduce the abstraction. Perhaps the words "by 15 percent" could be added to these objectives to give a feeling of concreteness to the statement. Programs can be designed to improve the image and morale. Attitudes of the public and sales personnel can be measured before and after and the programs are implemented.

Reasonableness. The objective must be reasonably attainable, yet it should not be so easily attainable that no particular ingenuity or extra effort is required. Of course, this statement implies a certain set of philosophies of management. Objectives should be barely reachable so that managers have to strain to attain them. Naturally, if such a program is followed, appraisal of the managers who fail to reach their objectives must take into account the reasonableness of the objectives.

Interrelatedness. Not only should objectives be interrelated among functional areas, but they should be interrelated with shorter-term goals and targets as well as budgets. Sometimes objectives do not mesh well with one another because of conflicts or oversight, or bad planning.

Sometimes unexpected environmental forces cause the development of an imbalance of objectives.

Several years ago one of our former students returned to do graduate work in two succeeding fall semesters. The sales force in which he had been employed exceeded its annual quota by August in both years. Rather than deluge the factory with more orders than could be filled, the sales force was put on leave with full salary for the remainder of the year. We were never able to determine the causes for this, but several possibilities come to mind: no planning at all, bad planning which failed to anticipate a growth in demand, very high and unrecognized motivation of sales representatives, severe production problems, or extraordinary failure of coordination between marketing and production objectives.

Types of objectives. Apart from personal and philosophical attitudes and approaches, information is probably the single most important ingredient in setting marketing objectives. However, it develops that objectives are frequently set in something resembling an information desert. Accordingly, the "art of the possible" is often practiced in setting objectives. Let us now examine some types of objectives, keeping in mind that customer satisfaction is the end to be reached.

Innovation. These objectives are discussed first because of our prior emphasis on the inevitability of change, crises of major or minor proportions which accompany change, and the need for planning for that change. Again, this is the process of discovery of opportunities and problems. Innovations may take several forms, and, depending upon the orientation of the firm, objectives may be related to some of the following examples:

1. Modification of existing products (an automatic tuning button for color television sets).
2. Introduction of a brand new product (a microscope of such power that previously unseen viruses become visible).
3. Development of products in anticipation of technological change (parts and related linkages to accommodate a new rotary engine).
4. Design of products known to be needed because of visible trends (pollution control systems).
5. Change in processes required by overall market goals (miniaturization to make devices more portable, such as radios).
6. Development of new concepts as distinct from products (replacing salesmen with computerized linkages between suppliers and customers).

We have already seen some of the characteristics of innovation and reaction to it: time lag between perfection and acceptance, unwillingness to adopt new things, and so on. One of the important functions of marketing in relation to innovation, and one of its most difficult tasks, is to market the concept of innovation.

Market standing. The president of a small industrial firm told the authors that he could obtain 100 percent of the market for a particular product in a very large geographic region, and eventually 100 percent of the national market. The product is a staple item comprising a small proportion of the total sales in an industry with very rapid growth. Based upon observation, knowledge of other producers, and analysis, his conclusion is that other producers that serve almost the entire market want to drop the product. These producers continue to make the product at a small profit, but they do so only as a service to long-time customers of other products. They feel that their resources could be turned to other products yielding a higher profit.

This company president has market-standing goals to capture 100 percent of the market in one region after another. Because of environmental circumstances, he just might do it! As companion objectives in reaching the market, he has tentatively decided upon a method of distribution as well as the quality of service to be provided. Other companies are not so fortunate in their knowledge of market standing. This illustration was introduced because it impinges upon several of the following objectives related to market standing:

1. The desired future share of the target market now served.
2. The desired future share of an enlarged target market.
3. New products needed in present target market.
4. Old products abandoned in present target market.
5. The new markets for new products.
6. Method of distribution.
7. The quality of service to be offered.

Other types of objectives. In one way or another the objectives set in some areas impinge upon the marketing program simply because they affect the organization as a whole. *Public responsibility* is one of those areas. It is external to the firm, but it can have a major effect upon the marketing function. For decades business firms have recognized their responsibility to the public in one way or another, such as mobilizing employees for charitable contributions, granting scholarships for education, or establishing plants in poverty areas. Arguments have raged as to whether business even has any right (in relationship to stockholders) to do these things, much less whether it has a responsibility. There is now some reason to believe "that a new concept of social responsibility of business has begun to emerge—a concept that is much less a matter of charity and much more a matter of practical business sense."[14]

Manager and worker performance and development are areas which need objectives in such areas as recruitment and retention, training and education, expectations, and aspirations. *Physical and financial* resources are what make the marketing effort possible. The objectives should be directed to the provision of those resources required to attain the innovation and market-standing objectives. *Profits and productivity* both relate to many facets of the firm, including market areas and the improvement of efficiency of marketing performance. The objectives set in these areas will be directly related to the marketing program of a firm.

A final point concerning objectives and plans

In Chapter 4 we observed that sometimes objectives are "discussed" during the course of the planning process and that sometimes plans were based upon objectives already held. In the final analysis, two aspects of objectives are significant in this respect. First, objectives are involved in creating plans. Second, they are involved in carrying out missions and plans.

One reason we made so much of the notion of a statement of mission of the organization in Chapter 4 is that it provides an excellent starting point for setting *specific* objectives. If the start is made very low in the hierarchy, the options are limited because attention is focused on the immediate problem. One has to force attention to broader things to avoid suffering from "marketing myopia." For example, if the objective is developed at the lower level to improve efficiency of sales personnel in the Eastern Territory, several alternatives come to mind immediately:

1. Have them travel by plane.
2. Give them dictaphones.
3. Require fewer reports.
4. Provide better promotional support.
5. Revise the incentive program.

After a little reflection and perhaps a bit of analysis, others may come to mind:

1. Reduce the size of the territory of each person.
2. Have salespeople concentrate on certain customers.
3. Replace the territory manager.
4. Hire a manufacturer's representative.
5. Improve service to the customer.

---

[14] Emmanuel Mesthene and Herbert Holloman, "The New Meaning of Social Responsibility," *Innovation*, February 1972, p. 2.

The alternatives continue to broaden:

1. Give them an additional product line.
2. Remove some elements of the present product line.

Yet, there are other alternatives which should be considered seriously:

1. Close down that territory completely.
2. Sell the division involved.
3. Sell the entire company.
4. Acquire another company.
5. Merge with another company.

If the statement of mission does not generate creativity as a useful starting point, then perhaps it is at fault. Just as starting low in the hierarchy of objectives may be limiting, starting high may have a similar limiting effect—the forest getting in the way of the trees.

One can move up and down the hierarchy of objectives if the one general statement is made: improve earnings.[15] This immediately opens doors to different types of objectives to be reached in different ways. First, earnings can be increased by doing more of what is now being done and doing it the same way it is now being done. The firm can expand to a new market and not change procedures. Second, earnings may be increased by doing what is now being done, but doing it more efficiently. Third, earnings can be increased by doing less than what is now being done, and doing it the same way or more efficiently. In this approach unprofitable products may be dropped without a change in methods. Or unprofitable products may be dropped and productivity increased. Fourth, earnings may be increased by doing more of what is now being done and doing it more efficiently, as by entering a new territory and at the same time increasing productivity.

A whole range of alternatives is opened up by that one general objective which requires analyses of both external and internal environments. It opens the door to the discovery process to search for opportunities and to ferret out problems. It encourages the problem-solvers to find better ways of doing things. It encourages planners to identify mistakes of the past and correct them. It encourages planners to think through what they want to have happen. And so on. The list of possibilities growing from this one objective is almost endless and ranges from the mundane to the daring. For example, to improve earnings the following alternatives come to mind:

1. Improve efficiency of sales personnel.
2. Sell the division.

---

[15] For comment on this subject see Charles H. Granger, "The Hierarchy of Objectives," *Harvard Business Review*, May–June 1964, p. 71.

3. Sell the company and put the proceeds in Treasury bonds.
4. Integrate vertically and horizontally.
5. Try to get the law changed.
6. Set up an international division.
7. Convert short-term debt to long-term.
8. Raise equity capital.
9. Develop a management training program.
10. Automate the production line.

If the statement of mission does not stimulate creativity and serve as a useful starting point, then starting in the middle of the hierarchy is better than at the top or at the bottom. If the start is made at the top—for example, by creating an international division—the analyst may never see many of the other alternatives.

Of course, setting objectives without taking action is an exercise in futility. Two questions are significant. How does a firm go about setting marketing objectives and making marketing plans for the organization? And how does it translate this planning process into action? The chapters in Part III are concerned with the development of marketing strategies based upon marketing objectives. Those chapters translate marketing objectives into marketing strategies in the five major areas with which marketing effort is concerned: product, channels, logistics, promotion, and price. A chapter to translate these strategies into marketing action follows each of the strategy chapters.

PART THREE

Strategic and managerial functions of marketing management

chapter 10 | # Product strategies and policies

The product and the future
    Marketing, the firm, and the product
    Product planning and corporate planning
    Interdepartmental coordination
    New organizations for new products
    Shortened product life cycles
Product planning
    Management concern
    Planning and organization
    Features of product policy
        Flow of new products
        Improvement of present products
Product life cycles and marketing strategy
    The nature of product life cycles
    Life cycles and profit objectives
        Product mix and quality of product
        Product introduction to meet sales objectives
    Life cycles and the marketing mix
        Introduction
        Growth
        Maturity
        Saturation
        Decline
    A different perspective
Other product strategies
    The product line and the product mix
    Product elimination
        Strategic implications
        Organization for elimination
    Product diversification
        Vertical diversificaton
        Horizontal diversification
        Lateral diversification
Kinds of products
    Consumers' goods
    Industrial goods
Summary and Conclusions

THE PRODUCT AND THE FUTURE

Marketing, the firm, and the product

The product or service marketed is the major focus of marketing. If the marketing concept and, consequently, the notions of the marketing-oriented company are accepted, practically every act of the company revolves around the product. It is the vehicle for exercising the art and science of management in setting objectives, planning, and implementation of plans.

In this sense, the word "product" signifies more than the superficial aspects of its physical features, or what is ordinarily labeled form utility. A collection of parts and materials may be referred to as a stereo set, but this tangible object is an incomplete product without guarantees, postsale service, aesthetic as well as functional appeal, and the tangible and intangible benefits the customer anticipates from using it. In short, product and, as we use it, form utility refer to a complete satisfaction-producing bundle. In addition to tangible items, the bundle consists of less tangible services and guarantees and the intangible but very real benefits to be derived. The less tangible benefits from purchasing a particular stereo set may be the comforting knowledge that if something goes wrong soon after purchase, the maker will make it good. An intangible benefit may be derived from pride of ownership of what others consider a prestige product.

Whenever the word "product" is used in this chapter or elsewhere in this book, it is used in this broad context. Moreover, the word "service" can and should be considered a perfectly acceptable substitute.

We have said that the firm is created and maintained to bring satisfaction to its owners and managers. The marketing concept embraces satisfaction of consumers. Profit is the element of the marketing concept which bridges the gap between what might otherwise be polar positions of satisfaction for producer and consumer. All of the elements of the marketing mix and the activities of management are directed to identifying the zone of satisfaction in which the wants and needs of consumers and producers are more or less in balance.

In an analysis of interdepartmental conflict which arise from directing the efforts of all departments toward the marketing concept, Philip Kotler made two significant points.[1] First, as long as a department is judged on the basis of the efficiency with which it performs its own tasks, it is going to fight to maintain its standards. Second, marketing should show more restraint in interrupting production schedules and multiplying product design and material costs. His conclusion was that top manage-

---

[1] Philip Kotler, "Diagnosing the Marketing Takeover," *Harvard Business Review,* November–December 1965, pp. 70–72.

ment should reduce its emphasis on a narrowly conceived concept of departmental efficiency and increase its emphasis on interdepartmental policies designed to advance the interests of the company as a whole. In short, as we have put it, sometimes the various departments act as if they do not all work for the same firm.

Our emphasis has been on the firm as a whole and on an organizational approach designed to coordinate actions and resolve conflicts in the objective-setting and planning stages. Product development and planning are not solely functions of marketing, production, or research and development. They are functions of the firm. The development of products and strategies and policies to market them is future oriented and necessarily affects the future of the firm.

Product planning and corporate planning

New-product development—and the improvement of old products—is destined to become increasingly important. Enormous resources of time, talent, and money are required for the discovery of product opportunities and the development of products. While Du Pont may be typical of nothing but Du Pont, a look at some of their figures provides a clue to the enormity of the investments in and costs of product development. It was reported a few years ago that it cost Du Pont about $70,000 per year to maintain one scientist at its central research department. This does not include $88,000 per person in capital investment. Both figures were double the 1952 levels. According to this report, "Du Pont wistfully figures that it takes the lifetimes of two highly paid researchers to yield a single major commercial development. However, a single process or product can be worth lifetimes of work by whole batteries of Ph.D.'s."[2]

The marketing-oriented company is becoming more commonplace, and the marketing concept is becoming the usual one in company policy. Further, more companies are developing strategic marketing plans. Research and development already captures the attention of top managers, and the strategic aspects of product planning promise to increase its influence in the development of corporate plans.

Coordination with research and development

The importance of interdepartmental coordination was pointed out in a study which found that the companies "which have had the most successful new-product programs during recent years were those that were able to maintain an effective balance between fundamental research

[2] *The Innovators* (Princeton, N.J.: Dow Jones Books, 1968), p. 28. This is a collection of articles written by the staff of *The Wall Street Journal*.

and applied product development."[3] This study made two other relevant points. First, management has recognized that long-range planning and management by objectives can be applied to research and new-product development. Second, top management is likely to play a more aggressive role in developing these product-related goals and in maintaining control of the entire product program.

Thus, better product planning improves corporate plans, and interdepartmental coordination is encouraged through more careful control. This means more marketing inputs into R&D, and vice versa.

New organizations for new products

Many companies have recognized the problems of coordinating activities among several departments of the same firm. Further, under many existing reward systems, department managers are often reluctant to take over a new product until it has been proved a success. Such companies as 3-M, Du Pont, and General Mills recognized this problem years ago and created separate organizational units to handle the transition of a product from research to the market.

This *venture management concept* has gained momentum in the past few years to the point that it is becoming commonplace. Authority for success of a new product is assigned to one person who assembles a team of experts from different departments of the firm and coordinates all events in the process. Marketing, production, and R&D people are all involved in the project, often before research has even begun. In addition to smoothing the development and marketing of the product, the team provides an outlet for the entreprenuerially inclined manager and a training ground for managers in general. Such a group is often called a venture team. This concept is similar to the *project management concept* which is widely used by companies engaged in defense work and is coming into use in other types of business.

A third concept commonly used is *brand management*. A brand manager manages the entire marketing effort for a particular product. Such an organization is common in industries where product differences make it very difficult for one individual to manage them all effectively. Brand managers, sometimes called product managers, have existed for some time, but the concept is in a state of flux (see Chapter 11).

All three of these concepts are related and share the advantages of better coordination of resources, faster decisions at the several stages of development, marketing, and manufacturing, and minimum interruption of activities in the major departments. Together with the improved tools of analysis, they should result in improved decision making.

---

[3] Paul E. Holden, Carlton A. Pederson, and Gayton E. Germane, *Top Management* (New York: McGraw-Hill Book Company, 1968), p. 115.

Shortened product life cycles

The product life cycle will be described more fully and discussed from a strategic point of view later in this chapter and in a managerial context in Chapter 11. However, the cycle necessarily affects the future role of the product in organization planning, the subject of this section.

Product life cycles are becoming shorter, which brings increased pressure for new-product development. Also, as the number of new products and new brands grows, there is increased need for improved product planning and management. For example, the life expectancy of health and beauty aids, household products, and food products has fallen from about three years to about 18 months. The number of new brands introduced in 1965 was double the 1961 figure.[4]

Among the reasons for the shortened life cycle is the proliferation of new brands and new products coming on the market. The failure rate of new products is variously estimated at 60 to 90 percent. The exact numbers are not so important as is the fact that many new products fail.

If cumulative knowledge leads to innovations, increasing numbers of new products can be expected; 91 percent of those who have ever received doctorates in the physical sciences are alive today.[5] The circle grows larger: more knowledge, more innovations, more new products, more failures, shorter life cycles, more expense, more need for better product planning.

PRODUCT PLANNING

The concerns that marketing managers have about the product are directly related to the purpose of the organization and form the bases on which objectives are stated. In turn, product evaluation is at the heart of much corporate thinking and effort regarding planning and the organizational structure.

Management concerns

Management's concerns with the product are related to corporate purpose, analysis of environments, and objectives. The purpose of the organization reflects its basic interest in the product: What business does the firm want to be in? The product is also a focal point in environmental analysis leading to the development of objectives. Where do its special strengths and weaknesses lie? Are these strengths compatible with the

---

[4] *The Nielsen Researcher* (Chicago: A. C. Nielsen Company, 1968), pp. 10–11.
[5] Robert H. Myers, "Profiles of the Future: Marketing Opportunities," *Business Horizons*, February 1972, p. 6.

areas of greatest opportunity? What is required for success in the industry in terms of serving the market and maintaining a competitive existence? How well has the firm performed in such areas as market share, profitability, quality, price, and service?

The continuing managerial concern is reflected in the firm's objectives. Should the firm try to be a technological leader or should it be a follower—or both? The answers to this question will determine whether the company is going to pioneer in developing and marketing products which will be copied or is going to be the copier. Growth objectives are also product oriented: should growth take place by acquisition, merger, or internal development, or a combination of these methods? The answer to how fast the firm wants to grow is also product related.

Planning and organization

The managerial concerns with product, expressed above in the framework of corporate purpose, analysis of environments, and objectives, are related to both the development of new products and the evaluation of present offerings. Planning and organization are the methods management uses to cope with their concerns.

Planning. Certain decision areas enter into the planning process in terms of the development of objectives, strategies, and policies directly related to the product. First, *acquisition of the resources* required for long- and short-term development projects must be planned. This not only requires a planned rate of return on the resources but a planned allocation to assure the development of a backlog of usable products. Closely related to acquisition is the *effective use* of resources allocated to product research and development in discovering opportunities and in terms of meeting company objectives.

Third, plans should assure that the company will have a *balanced product program* to meet not only present needs but potential future needs. Fourth, plans must be made to meet the ever-changing wants and needs of the customer in terms of *satisfying prices and values*. This requires not only considerable analysis but also a substantial amount of guessing. Fifth, the type of desired *organization structure* must be planned to meet the needs of the company as it moves into the future.

Organization. The hierarchical relationships in the organization structure should have certain characteristics to assure that the firm's product receives the proper attention. One such characteristic is the involvement of top management in *planning the product program*. This involves the attainment of a good mix in development projects. It also calls for provision of channels through which product ideas can move from their source to some level at which they will be seriously considered.

A second organizational characteristic pertains to *product elimination*.

There must be some means by which products can be dropped. A third characteristic relates to *product design and acceptance,* often handled by committees. We have seen how conflicts may develop between manufacturing, marketing, R&D, and finance over cost and design features. Fourth, the organization should be designed to cope with *product failure* so that those in charge of products that do fail are not automatically "punished." In fact, a system should be devised to encourage innovation, even though some innovations fail. Most products that are introduced do fail, and most that are worked on are never introduced. If only successes are rewarded, risk-taking tends to be discouraged. To encourage risk-taking, there should be some method of "rewarding failure." Fifth, a system for *control of planning* and control of the organization must be developed.

Features of product policy

There are two broad features or requirements of product policy: There should be a program for the continuous flow of new products, and a positive plan for present-product improvement.

Flow of new products. The importance of maintaining the flow of new products was suggested in discussion of the shortened life cycles of many products. There are several ways to do this, and they are all expensive. First, of course, is research and development of products from the laboratory. One company president said that one of his greatest worries was keeping a balance in the "technological bank": "We have spent approximately $19 million of assets from our 'technological bank.' This bank needs constant replenishing or we are in real trouble so far as our long-range plans are concerned."[6]

Planned R&D expenditures are strategic decisions. The question of how much should be spent does not seem to have a single answer. Some companies use a rule of thumb for R&D somewhat similar to that used in advertising expenditures, allotting it a given percentage of sales. One company allocated 3 percent of sales to R&D. When management was asked how it knew this was right, the response was, "How do you know it's wrong?"[7]

A second method of maintaining this flow is by continuous research in the market to determine consumer needs and wants. This too is an expensive undertaking, and it may be more fruitless. Consumers cannot always perceive a want, simply because they have never really thought of certain things. They can sometimes answer if asked specifically whether they want a particular thing, however.

[6] Holden, Pederson, and Germane, *Top Management,* p. 102.

[7] Robert H. Deming, *Characteristics of an Effective Management Control System* (Boston: Division of Research, Harvard University, 1968), p. 159.

A third method of maintaining a new-product flow is by imitation of others. Years ago, one company developed the stainless steel razor blade and spent many dollars promoting it, only to have it copied in short order. When another company more recently developed a two-headed blade, the same thing happened. The adoption and adaptation of processes or products of one industry by another was discussed in Chapters 3 and 7. If imitation is the most sincere form of flattery, there certainly are a lot of flatterers in business. Theodore Levitt makes a case for a firm supporting an organized strategy of imitation in his article "Innovative Imitation."[8] Since companies will end up imitating others anyway, he suggests that if they do it on a systematic basis they can get into the act sooner.

Improvement of present products. When a product has about run its course, management has several alternatives: (1) drop it and cut losses; (2) keep it, with its losses, because it is important to some customers who are important to the firm; (3) change it, by improving it or just by altering it; and (4) find new uses for it.

A change made to prolong the life of the product is sometimes called recycling. The changes made may range from basic product improvements to new packaging, flavors, sizes, or even new premiums. Packaging changes may be from bottles to cans, tubes to bottles, glass to plastic, red to blue. Recycling extends the economic lives of many products.

There are many examples of finding new uses for old products. Probably the most widely used example is nylon. The synthetic was used first for women's hosiery, parachutes, rope, and thread, and then in broadwoven fabrics such as taffeta and twill. Soon it found use in tire cord, textured yarns for sweaters and men's hose, and, eventually, carpet yarns. Jell-O and Scotch brand tape are other examples. The lives of such products are extended by four techniques: (1) promoting more frequent uses by current users, (2) suggesting more varied uses by current users, (3) locating new users, and (4) creating new uses for basic materials.[9]

PRODUCT LIFE CYCLES AND MARKETING STRATEGY

The nature of product life cycles

Products, like people, start out as a vague hope, a gleam in someone's eye. When something clicks, the embryo of an idea is formed; it goes through a gestation period, and a working model is developed. The product passes through a series of developmental stages during which

---

[8] In *Harvard Business Review*, September–October 1966.

[9] Theodore Levitt, "Exploit the Product Life Cycle," *Harvard Business Review*, November–December 1965, pp. 90–91.

it is nurtured and prepared for growth. Eventually it reaches maturity, where the growth rate begins to ease off. After it reaches "middle age" and market saturation, the product slides into old age, and obsolescence sets in. At some point, when its usefulness as a profit generator begins to wane and it perhaps becomes a burden, product euthanasia is performed and it is withdrawn from the market. Somewhere along the line, however, new life may be injected into the aging product.

Figure 10–1 shows the five stages in the life cycle: introduction, growth

FIGURE 10–1
Life Cycle of a Product

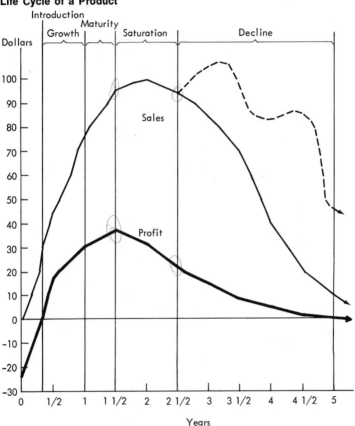

maturity, saturation, and decline. In most illustrations of the cycle it is depicted as looking rather like a bell with the right third cut off, and each of the five stages is assumed to cover the same period of time. Figure 10–1 illustrates our concept of the cycle, with a relatively short time in the introductory period and varying lengths of time in each of the other periods. The solid line shows sales throughout the five-year period, and we have also plotted profit.

The product whose life cycle is illustrated in the figure is a tablet to relieve the discomforts of indigestion. For the first year and a half nothing unusual happened. The product was introduced and given a big promotional send-off, and normal promotional efforts were continued. At year 1½ competitor A launched an imitative product—perhaps after reading Levitt's article on "Innovative Imitation." The product growth rate slowed down.

At this point the four ways of extending product life suggested above were used as strategic elements in managing the product cycle. When brand CA (Competitor A) was introduced at the start of the second year, it was no surprise; a plan had been prepared to cope with it. The promotion program designed to encourage current users to use the product more frequently was stepped up. Users were told that recent research by an independent testing agency showed that if two units per day were used, the results would be three times greater. Alternating ads showed varied uses for the product.

The dotted line in Figure 10–1 shows what happened to sales for several months after the introduction of brand CA and before competitor B came in. Then the firm went after new users by offering a special deal, and at the same time other *tactics* were applied to implement its basic strategies. The package was redesigned and the size of the container was changed, among other things. Although it was declining, there was a profit. At year 4½, however, six other competitors entered the market, and the firm decided to abandon the product.

While no tactics were developed for the fourth strategic move (find new uses for the basic materials) that too had been planned for. While the R&D laboratories were working on these materials, the marketing department had been watching the rapidly rising sales of a competitor's product. The lab discovered that by making a minor change to the indigestion pill and liquifying it, the perfect innovatively imitative product was introduced, so the firm started interrupting some other product's life cycle.

At times rather wierd alternative uses for products just seem to develop. In the summer of 1975 sales of Preparation H—a hemorrhoid ointment—boomed as a facial cream. "The closet cosmetic's virtues, according to devotees: smoothing away wrinkles, tightening pores and giving the complexion a luminous glow." The manufacturer declined comment.[10]

Thus Figure 10–1 shows what happens in the typical product life cycle. The product is introduced and promoted, grows in market accep-

---

[10] "Closet Cosmetic," *Newsweek*, July 14, 1975, p. 56.

tance, and rather rapidly reaches maturity. A competitor intro〔
imitation which begins to play havoc with sales. The power of 〔
keeps the firm from being caught off guard by innovative i〔
Strategies that had been designed and planned for are dusted off and
several elements of the marketing mix are used to implement them:
product design (new flavor), promotion (new package, new advertising
program), and price ("cents-off" deal). When sales and profits get to
a predetermined level or competition gets too intense, the product is
abandoned. Hopefully, a product will be ready to take the place of
the abandoned one.

Life cycles and profit objectives

One of the several uses of the concept of the life cycle is to help
determine the length of the profit stream, the magnitude of profit and
cash flow in the several stages, and the length of the cash flow stream.
Sam Goodman refers to the *quality* of profit, to distinguish it from *quantity* of profit.[11] The concept of the life cycle can be helpful to the marketing manager-planner in developing strategies concerning the mix of products in the several stages of the cycle.

Certainly, the life cycle of a product is not known in advance, nor
do marketing people know what the effect on sales and profits will
be if they try to extend that cycle. But that is nothing new to businessmen. They generally know nothing about the future anyway; uncertainty
is something they live with. Accordingly, estimating the length of time
a product will be in a certain stage is not a new venture. What may
be new, however, is the next step: estimating the probability of the
product having a given total life. In addition it is also possible to make
probability estimates of the length of time the product will be in any
one stage.

Product mix and quality of profit. One of the concerns of management
is with steadiness of earnings. This applies with equal force to small
and large companies. None wants a feast for a year or two, followed
by famine; all prefer stable growth toward a given objective. For example, say that a company's five-year objective is to earn 1,000 units of
money. One pattern of relatively steady growth may be to earn in successive years 25, 75, 150, 300, and 450 units, to total 1,000 for the five-year
period. A pattern of unsteady growth may be 300, 600, −800, −400,
1,300.

The earnings results are the same. But with the second pattern, a
manager who is head of a large business is likely to have some explaining
to do to the stockholders and financial analysts. If it is a small business,

---

[11] Sam R. Goodman, *Techniques of Profitability Analysis* (New York: Wiley Interscience, 1970), p. 70.

the erratic earnings record may upset the bank. Further, the proprietor may have withdrawn earnings, believing that the first years were the beginnings of great things, and thus impaired the cash flow position.

The second situation could happen easily. Say that in years one and two a firm had a disproportionately large number of products in the later stages of maturity or saturation and few in the introductory stage. Conversely, in years three and four it had too many in the introductory stage. Those contributing so handsomely in the first two years may now be in the decline stage. The business must earn a large number of units in the fifth year if it is to reach its five-year objective.

The life cycle concept, therefore, is a significant element in the development of strategy for growth. The strategy may be based upon several factors.

1. The length of time the profit stream will last.
2. The amount of profit generated by each product in the product mix.
3. The contribution—or loss—from products in each stage.
4. The risk involved in each stage of the cycle for each product.
5. The weight to be assigned for the quality of profit based upon the risk involved.

All of this is easy when you say it; if you say it faster, it sounds easier! There are complexities involved, however.

Product introduction to meet sales objectives. To give the reader a feeling for the complexity of the process of product introduction, we will use an example involving the introduction of 14 products over a 10-year period in order to meet an objective of increasing sales 5 percent per year for 10 years. For convenience it is assumed that all growth will come from new products. Changing the older products would make the arithmetic a bit more complicated. We also simplify the arithmetic by our life cycle assumptions:

1. The product is introduced the first day of the first year of its life and is dropped the last day of the fifth year.
2. Profits are "satisfactory" in all five years.
3. Sales of each product are identical in comparable years of each product's life: 75, 100, 85, 40, and 10 units in years 1 through 5.

The sales objective for each of the ten years is shown on Table 10–1, line 1. The objective is to increase sales 5 percent per year. Line 2 shows the sales of older, staple products of 1,000 units each year. Line 3 shows the introduction of Product A in year 1. This introduction meets the objective. Check lines 17 and 18, which show sales and the variance between actual sales and the sales objectives, and line 19, which shows the cumulative variance.

TABLE 10–1

Product Introduction to Meet Sales Objectives (14 products introduced over a ten-year period to yield 5 percent sales growth per year)

Line		1	2	3	4	5	6	7	8	9	10
							Year				
1.	Sales objective (units)	1,050	1,103	1,158	1,216	1,277	1,341	1,408	1,478	1,552	1,630
2.	Sales of staple products (units)	1,000	1,000	1,000	1,000	1,000	1,000	1,000	1,000	1,000	1,000
3.	New product A	75	100	85	40	10	—	—	—	—	—
4.	New product B			75	100	85	40	10	—	—	—
5.	New product C				75	100	85	40	10	—	—
6.	New product D					75	100	85	40	10	—
7.	New product E						75	100	85	40	10
8.	New product F							75	100	85	40
9.	New product G							75	100	85	40
10.	New product H								75	100	85
11.	New product I								75	100	85
12.	New product J									75	100
13.	New product K									75	100
14.	New product L										75
15.	New product M										75
16.	New product N										75
17.	Total sales (units)	1,075	1,100	1,160	1,215	1,270	1,300	1,385	1,485	1,570	1,685
18.	Variance (line 17 minus line 1)	+25	−3	+2	−1	−7	−41	−23	+7	+18	+55
19.	Cumulative variance	+25	+22	+24	+23	+16	−25	−48	−41	−23	+32

Notice that the next introduction is in year 3, after which there is one each year until year 7, when two introductions become necessary. Figure 10–2 shows what these life cycles look like when plotted against sales objectives.

FIGURE 10–2
Product Introduction to Meet Sales Objectives (14 products introduced over 10-year period to yield 5 percent sales growth per year

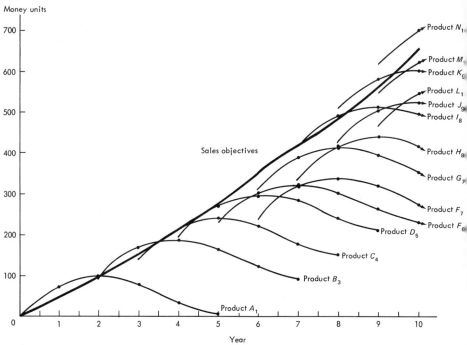

Note: F_7 for example, means Product F was introduced in year 7. The full five-year cycles is no shown for Products F–N.

The example above deals with only 14 products over a 10-year period, and none of them were failures. Imagine the planning that must go into product strategy development and management in such companies as General Foods, 3-M, or Procter & Gamble, which may have several hundred products on the shelves at one time. Such firms bring in dozens of new products every year, and half or more of them will fail.

Certain assumptions were made in the example regarding (1) the number of product ideas that never got to the product evaluation committee (about 75 percent) and (2) the proportion of new product ideas which were rejected (about 50 percent). To get 40 products to the introduction stage would require 320 products or product ideas at the start for a survival rate of 12.5 percent. About half of these could be expected to fail.

Life cycles and the marketing mix

Two broad dimensions of product life cycles—their nature and their relation to profit objectives—have been discussed. A third dimension is the development of strategies for marketing products in the several stages. The elements of the marketing mix are the basic tools the manager uses in developing marketing strategy. The effectiveness of each of these elements in the various stages of the product cycle underlies strategy development.

There is no all-purpose marketing mix strategy to fit all kinds of products. To provide an insight to the problem and to illustrate the application of the concept, we will use the results of a study concerned with the elasticity of the marketing devices in various cycle stages which was made by a Finnish economist.[12] The elements considered were product quality, advertising, service, and price. Channels of distribution were not included, and presumably there was some sort of equation of advertising with promotion. Figure 10–3 illustrates the concept as applied to the five stages of the product life cycle.

Introduction. At the beginning of a product's life the public knows nothing about it, and an obvious requirement is to tell the public about the "better mousetrap." But who will try it first? Fortunately for marketers, there is a large group of people who will try anything once. However, for that group to be satisfied and pass the word, the quality of the product must be satisfactory. The relative impact of each of the elements of the mix in the introductory stage is shown in Figure 10–3.

As would be expected, the quality of the product has the greatest impact in this stage and advertising is second. Compared to these elements, price is apparently not very important to first-users. This is one of the reasons that many newly introduced products carry a high price to skim the market. When market forces call for it, the price is ultimately lowered. (The skimming policy is discussed in Chapter 18.) The novelty value of the product is apparently significant, but first-users must be told about it, and this accounts for the tremendous promotion expenditures which almost invariably accompany the introduction of any new product.

---

[12] We have tried to locate a more modern study, but have been unsuccessful. We *suspect* that the conclusions would be the same but do not know this. Even so, we think the concept is important for marketers to know. The only source readily available to us is in Sam R. Goodman, *Techniques of Profitability Analysis* (New York: Wiley-Interscience, 1970), pp. 77–78, citing G. Mickwitz, *Marketing and Competition* (Helsinki: Central-tryckeriet, 1959). We have applied index numbers to Mickwitz's concept to portray it graphically.

FIGURE 10–3

The Significance of the Marketing Mix In the Stages of the Life Cycle

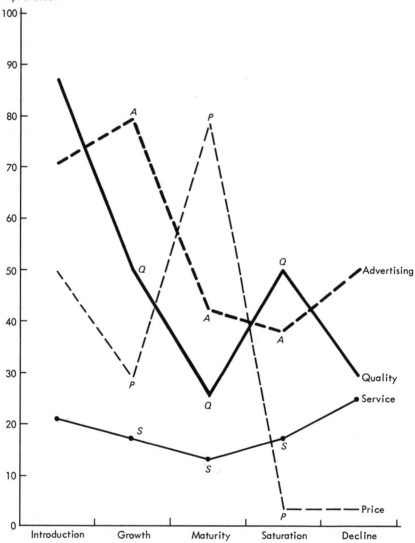

Source: Data calculated from Exhibit 15. Sam R. Goodman, *Techniques of Profitability Analysis* (New York: Wiley-Interscience, 1970), p. 77. See footnote 12 for original source.

Growth. In the growth stage advertising has an even greater impact than in the introductory stage. The impact of quality and price falls. The product has been accepted by those who know of it, so the appropriate strategy is to let more people know about it. It should not be inferred that quality—or any other of the elements—is unimportant. Figure 10–3 shows the relative *impact* of these elements in the various product life stages. Consumers are very much concerned with quality at this stage. They are more suspicious than the first-users, or perhaps merely less daring. At any rate, advertising has the most impact in this stage.

A significant question of strategy may be raised at this point. The skimming price policy is so widely used in the early stages that it is almost a commonplace. The diagram based on the study shows the impact of price to be a poor third in the first two stages. What if instead of a skimming policy a strategy of penetration was used? Penetration implies a low price from the outset in order to penetrate the market deeply. Would a lower price at the outset have a greater impact on sales in these two stages?

Maturity. Price has a greater impact in the maturity stage. The obvious reason price impact moves from a very poor third to a runaway first is related to what happens in the stages of the life cycle. So is the reason advertising and quality go so low on the impact scale at this stage.

Total advertising expenditures are more than likely higher at this point than they were in either of the other two stages. If not, they almost certainly have not fallen significantly. As for quality, it probably has risen; bugs in earlier production runs may have been eliminated, feedback from the market may have led to minor improvements and so on.

Price assumes a new importance in this stage because competitors have come into the market with their innovative imitations. Now the consumer has a choice. Each of the producers has a "better" product than any of the others, each has spent a good deal on advertising to tell about it, and each provides the "best" service. Price therefore becomes a differentiating factor.

What has probably happened to price to give it such an impact? The innovative company, since it has been a creative copier many times in the past, knows that it is going to be imitated. Accordingly, in its original marketing strategy a price strategy to accommodate competitors is developed. About the time—or just before—the competition hits the market, it again lowers price.

Saturation. The impact of price hits a new low in the saturation period. Quality is again the primary factor, with advertising second. At this stage prices are competitive with one another, so their impact is relatively light—almost to the point of having no impact at all. All of the competitors are advertising at about the same rate. Therefore the way in which consumers perceive the quality of the product once again has a great impact.

Service has had such a low and declining profile in the first three stages that its level of impact was more or less obvious. In this stage it becomes more important, and in the next stage almost as important as quality. In the saturation stage little is left for product differentiation. Price is about the same, and all competitors are advertising about the same amount. Thus the quality of the product and the service available for it are important ways of differentiating among competing products.

Decline. In the declining stage the advertising program apparently has the greatest impact. This may be because people now recognize quality, price, and service and need to be reminded or persuaded to buy. This stage can be a very profitable one for firms that have not yet withdrawn from the market. Product development costs have been recovered, investments in machinery and channel development have paid off, and competition has declined.

A different perspective

While this section will not tell you anything new, it will provide a different perspective on the impact of elements of the marketing mix. Figure 10–4 indicates more clearly the level of impact for each element in each stage. It also shows the pattern of the first, second, third, and fourth levels of impact throughout the five stages of the product life cycle. This pattern was developed by connecting the points on Figure 10–3 which showed the highest impact in each stage, then the second highest, and so on.

From this perspective two points emerge. First, during the first three stages the elements of the marketing mix have a fairly high impact on the life cycle. In the next two stages, the impact drops dramatically. The heavy solid line traces the impact of the most important elements.

Second, the impact of these elements is not very strong at the end of the cycle. This suggests that the momentum of the marketing effort expended in the early stages carries the product on into the saturation and decline stages. Also, it suggests that without the marketing effort in the later stages, particularly in the declining stage, the product might experience its death throes earlier.

OTHER PRODUCT STRATEGIES

In addition to the role of the product life cycle in marketing strategy, the product is the center of other aspects of strategic planning for the

FIGURE 10–4
Relative Degree of Impact of Elements of the Marketing Mix in Various Stages of the Life Cycle

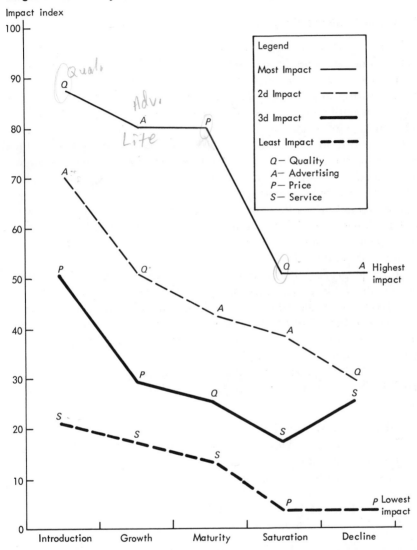

Source: Data calculated from Exhibit 15, Sam R. Goodman, *Techniques of Profitability Analysis* (New York: Wiley-Interscience, 1970), p. 77. See text footnote 12 for original source.

ɔme other product-related strategies have to do with the product
oduct elimination, and product diversification.

The product line and the product mix

A *product line* consists of a group of products that perform roughly
similar functions and have similar uses and physical characteristics.

Costume jewelry is a product line. The similarity in the function and
use of earrings, necklaces, bracelets, and anklets is clear—attraction and
adornment—although in this case there is not much physical similarity
between some of them.

The context in which the term is used may have to be identified
in order for the meaning to be clear. One company may have a product
line consisting of "recorded music," while others may specialize in classi-
cal, country-western, pop, or jazz.

The *product mix* is the entire output of the firm. It may be characterized by breadth, which refers to the number of product lines, and by
depth, which embraces the alternatives of size, color, price, and so on
within each product line.

Both the product line and the product mix, as well as the breadth
and depth of the project mix, are probably originally planned to meet
the objectives of the company. Later the breadth and depth may be
the result of the firm's (1) reacting to competitors, (2) seeing an opportunity to expand, or (3) seeing an opportunity to add to profits by
paring the unprofitable items.

A number of forces may influence the development of strategy for
the breadth and depth of a product line. The strategy may be varied
to:

1. Offset seasonal or cyclical variations.
2. Balance the line with high and low profit margin products.
3. Balance old and new products.
4. Meet competitors' offerings (innovative imitation).
5. Use excess marketing capacity.
6. Satisfy distributors' wants and needs.
7. Satisfy other customer demands.

Product elimination

Materials shortages which first surfaced in 1973 have caused many
companies to reappraise their product mixes. In a 1974 cover story,
Business Week said:

> It's a new way of life for everyone. Because of worsening raw-material
> scarcities, price controls, and the fear of an energy crunch, companies of

every size, shape, and business are reexamining their product lines and shifting the whole thrust to their product mix and marketing strategy. Their object is to maximize profit and to make the most efficient use of the materials. . . . Lower-margin products are being dropped or deemphasized in favor of those that offer higher margins.[13]

It is typical for 20 to 30 percent of a company's products to account for about 70 percent of its profits. The majority of products, which account for most of the losses or a small proportion of profits, are being looked at very carefully. As a result, in recent months:

GE has dropped many of its smaller appliances.

Shell is dropping some of its rubber and fertilizer production.

Philco-Ford has cut 50 percent of its color-TV screen sizes and 40 percent of its refrigerator models.

Some papermakers have cut their lines by up to 60 percent.

Auto makers cut from 375 models in 1970 to 300 in 1974.

Strategic implications. Dropping products may be as important a strategy for the firm as adding them. The dropping of a product can have an impact upon many other segments of the firm and the market, and the decision cannot be taken lightly. A number of questions arise, one of which concerns the impact that dropping the product would have on profit.

Whether the product is profitable depends upon the costing system used and what is meant by profit. If the accounting system requires each product to bear a portion of overhead, a given product may show a loss. However, if a direct product costing system is used, that loser may be making a comfortable contribution to overhead. Dropping it may actually reduce profit because other products will have to pick up its share of overhead. Accordingly it may be more profitable to the firm to keep the product, as long as it makes a contribution.

This contribution-margin concept is a two-edged sword, however. Too great a reliance on it may cause the firm to end up with a variety of products, each one of which makes a contribution to overhead but which collectively do not cover all overhead. This concept, familiar to readers who have taken a basic accounting course, is discussed in Chapter 20.

Another question pertains to the effects on both production and marketing costs of a decision to drop a product. If the product is dropped, the resources of the firm may become underused, which would cause

---

[13] "The Squeeze on Product Mix," *Business Week*, January 5, 1974, pp. 50–55. The examples used in this section are also taken from this article.

an increase in marketing and production unit costs. If it is *not* dropped, it may use scarce executive and other resources to the point that other potentially more profitable products will not be produced, or additional resources may have to be acquired for the new products. This is the opportunity-cost concept.

A third question concerns the impact on customers and distributors if the product is dropped. While the product may be unprofitable, it may be such an integral part of the attraction of the product line that other products will suffer from its omission. For example, if a customer has to go somewhere else to buy the dropped product, he may also go elsewhere for his other needs.

A fourth question concerns the general competitive posture of the company, which might suffer if it is not able to offer a particular product. All these questions emphasize the significance of product elimination as a matter of strategic concern.

Organization for elimination. The strategic implications of the dropping of products indicate that the process requires careful managerial attention and must be planned for. A set of alternative policies which take into account the implications of dropping must be established, and procedures for dropping which will assure that these implications are considered must be developed.

Organization for elimination often takes the form of an elimination review committee which evaluates appropriate economic and marketing factors. Once the strategy and policies of dropping products are developed and the mechanism for implementation is set up, the dropping procedures become a tactical matter for action by the product manager. Chapter 11, Product Management, discusses some factors for evaluation of product addition factors. Approximately the same matters are considered when the product reaches the end of the cycle, and these also are discussed in Chapter 11.

Product diversification

Diversification is a major strategic concern which has a more profound effect on the firm than merely adding or dropping products. Companies diversify for many reasons: survival and growth, stability, to meet changing market conditions, and so on. In the summer of 1975, one major oil company was discussing merger with a major manufacturer. The objective of the oil company was to diversify into a non-petroleum-related business. Still another oil company announced it had no intentions of going that route.

Diversification objectives are basically derived from the broader long-range sales and other objectives. These objectives can be identified as the alternative directions diversification can take.

Vertical diversification. Most companies buy some of the components that go into their products. The lawnmower maker probably buys his motors, the auto maker buys wheels, the aircraft maker buys engines, and so on. If the company decides to diversify vertically, it may start to manufacture some of these components itself.

This type of diversification does not make much sense if the industry sales trend is down. However, it may be a good direction to take if the objective is to strengthen the firm's position in the industry. Vertical integration or diversification may mean that a manufacturing company enters the distribution channels and becomes a wholesaler or retailer, or a retailer acts as a wholesaler.

Horizontal diversification. Sometimes companies diversify into a new line of products to serve approximately the market already served. A company currently manufacturing snow skis and other winter sports equipment may diversify into summer sports items. This strategy may be desirable to strengthen the position of the company in an industry in which it already has expertise.

Lateral diversification. In the lateral approach, a company enters an industry completely "foreign" to its basic business. This often happens when conglomerates are formed. The approach is useful if the reason for diversification is to provide stability. It also should be noted that lateral diversification often occurs for strictly financial reasons. One company may need money to continue successful operation or a company may be acquired solely because it is profitable.

KINDS OF PRODUCTS

In line with one of the stated objectives of this book, we have cast the foregoing discussions of product strategy in a conceptual framework. Our concern has been to discuss the concept without regard for the nature of the product. The ideas explored and the concepts analyzed are as applicable to one product as they are to another. For example, the relation between product planning and corporate planning is as relevant for an airplane maker as for a cosmetics producer. Most of the differences that exist are in degree rather than in kind. The foundations of strategies for a high fashion item are similar to those for a staple. Life cycles may be different in magnitude but not in concept, and so on.

In this section, however, we will differentiate among various types of products. We do this for two reasons: the reader needs to know some of the jargon, and different strategies are required for marketing some types of goods. Even though the strategies stem from the same concepts, different ones may be required for marketing consumers' goods and for marketing industrial goods. There also may be different strategies for marketing each of the three types of consumers' goods: convenience, shopping, and specialty.

With convenience goods, however, the same marketing strategy may be useful for one as for the other, and the same is true for shopping goods and various classes of industrial goods. Therefore we can repeat that the concepts discussed in this chapter are appropriate foundations for most types of strategies, even though specific strategies differ.

The definitions used in this section are those of the American Marketing Association.[14] These terms help define many issues on a stratified basis and permit analyses of and generalizations about groups of products.

Consumers' goods

Consumers' goods are destined for use by ultimate consumers or households and are in such form that they can be used without commercial processing. Certain articles (for example, typewriters) may be either consumers' or industrial goods, depending upon whether they are destined for use by the ultimate consumer or household or by an industrial, business, or institutional user.

The *ultimate consumer* is one who buys or uses goods or services to satisfy personal or household wants rather than for resale or for use in business, institutional, or industrial operations. The definition distinguishes sharply between industrial users and ultimate consumers. A firm buying and using an office machine, a drum of lubricating oil, or a carload of steel billets is an industrial user of those products, not an ultimate consumer of them. A vital difference exists between the purposes motivating the two types of purchases. This in turn results in highly significant differences in buying methods, marketing organization, and selling practices.

Consumers' goods are typically classified into convenience, shopping, and specialty goods.

Convenience goods are those the customer usually purchases frequently, immediately, and with the minimum of effort in comparison and buying. Examples of merchandise customarily bought as convenience goods are tobacco products, soap, newspapers, magazines, chewing gum, small packaged confections, and many food products. These articles are usually of small unit value and are bought in small quantities at any one time, although when a number of them are bought together, as in a supermarket, the combined purchase may assume sizable proportions in both bulk and value.

The convenience involved may be in terms of nearness to the buyer's home, easy accessibility to some means of transport, or close proximity

---

[14] *Marketing Definitions* (Chicago: The American Marketing Association), 1960.

to places where people go during the day or evening—for example, downtown to work.

Shopping goods are those the customer, in the process of selection and purchase, characteristically compares on such bases as suitability, quality, price, and style. Examples of goods that most consumers probably buy as shopping goods are: millinery, furniture, dress goods, women's ready-to-wear clothes and shoes, used automobiles, and major appliances.

It should be emphasized that a given article may be bought by one customer as a shopping good and by another as a specialty or convenience good. The general classification depends upon the way in which the average or typical buyer purchases the item.

Specialty goods are those with unique characteristics or brand identifications for which a significant group of buyers are habitually willing to make a special purchasing effort. Examples of articles that are usually bought as specialty goods are specific brands and types of fancy foods, hi-fi components, certain types of sporting equipment, photographic equipment, and men's suits.

Price is not usually the primary factor in consumer choice of specialty goods, although their prices are often higher than those of other articles serving the same basic want but without their special characteristics. A retail store that makes its appeal on the basis of a restricted class of shopping goods is known as a specialty store. The distinction between shopping and specialty goods is not always clear.

Industrial goods

Industrial goods are goods which are destined to be sold primarily for use in producing other goods or rendering services, as contrasted with goods to be sold primarily to the ultimate consumer. They include equipment (installed and accessory), component parts, maintenance, repair, and operating supplies, raw materials, and fabricating materials.

The distinguishing characteristic of these goods is that they are primarily destined to be used in carrying on business or industrial activities, rather than for consumption by individual ultimate consumers or resale to them. The category also includes merchandise destined for use in various types of institutional enterprises.

Relatively few goods are exclusively industrial goods. The same article may be an industrial good under one set of circumstances and a consumers' good under other conditions.

Equipment consists of industrial goods that do not become part of the physical product and are exhausted only after repeated use, such as machinery, installed equipment and accessories, or auxiliary equipment. Installed equipment includes such items as boilers, linotype machines, power lathes, and bank vaults. Accessories include such items as gauges, meters, and control devices. Auxiliary equipment includes such items as trucks, typewriters, filing cases, and industrial hoists.

Fabricating materials are industrial goods that become a part of the finished product and have undergone processing beyond that required for raw materials, but not as much as for finished parts. Examples are plastic moulding compounds.

SUMMARY AND CONCLUSIONS

This chapter, the first of two on the product, has been concerned with product strategies and policies, things with which the top management of the firm should deal. When the marketing manager, along with other top managers, is dealing with product strategies and policies, he is functioning in his role of manager of the firm. He is concerned with management *and* the marketing function.

The product is the first element of the marketing mix to be considered in the design of a marketing plan and program. As functional managers, marketing managers are more concerned with the future than any of their counterparts in the firm, with the possible exception of financial managers. Product lives are notoriously short; if the marketing manager looks only to the end of the next fiscal year, he may be out of business.

This chapter, therefore, began with discussion of the product in the context of the future because planning is the vehicle for taking the firm into the future. It then considered the way management looks at the product—or the way it should do so. The significance of life cycles of products was recognized in use of that concept to round out the discussion of product strategies and policies.

Finally, classes of products were identified in a rather perfunctory manner. While we emphasized the universality of the concepts discussed as foundations for marketing strategy, we recognize that specific strategies stemming from these foundations may differ. Accordingly, products were classified into consumers' goods and industrial goods and further into more or less homogeneous groups for which common strategies could be developed.

chapter 11 | Product management

Definitions
    Product management
    Product line
    Product mix
The product manager's job
    Hierarchical relationships
    The position of product manager
    The reporting hierarchy
    Standards of performance
Functions of the product manager
    The discovery and filtering of new products
    Preventing product failures
Managing the marketing mix
Conclusion

DEFINITIONS

We concluded Chapter 10, Product Strategies and Policies, with definitions of types of products. We begin this chapter with definitions because they fairly accurately show what we are going to do. The definitions are those prepared under the auspices of the American Marketing Association.[1]

The product as the focal point of *top managers,* including the marketing manager, was discussed in Chapter 10. That chapter analyzed the product objectives, strategic planning, and policy considerations which give direction to the firm. Also, the marketing manager was identified with our concept of management *and* the marketing function in the context of the product as an element of the marketing mix.

In this chapter we identify the marketing manager with our concept of management *of* the marketing function in the same context—the prod-

---

[1] *Marketing definitions* (Chicago: The American Marketing Association), 1960.

uct as an element of the marketing mix. Specifically what follows is concerned with product management in the context of product strategies developed earlier.

Product management is the planning, direction, and control of all phases of the life cycle of products including *the creation or discovery of ideas for new products, the screening of such ideas, the coordination of the work of research and physical development of products, their packaging and branding, their introduction on the market, their market development, their modification, the discovery of new uses for them, their repair and servicing, and their deletion.*

Product management does not necessarily equate to the work of the executive known as the product manager, because the dimensions of that job vary widely from company to company, sometimes embracing all the activities listed in the definition and sometimes being limited to the sales promotion of the products in the manager's care. The work of the product manager is done within the framework established by the strategies, plans, and policies of Level 1 management. Within that framework, the manager in turn will develop objectives, strategies, plans, and policies for implementation of the corporate program.

The *product line* is a group of products that are closely related either because they satisfy a class of need, are used together, are sold to the same customer groups, are marketed through the same type of outlets, or fall within given price ranges. Example: carpenters' tools. Sublines of products may be distinguished, such as hammers or saws, within a product line.

The *product mix* is the composite of products offered for sale by a firm or a business unit. Toothpaste is a product. The five-ounce tube of Breath Kleen toothpaste is an item. Toothpastes and powders, mouthwashes, and other allied items compose an oral hygiene product line. Soaps, cosmetics, dentifrices, drug items, cake mixes, shortenings, and other items may comprise a product mix if marketed by the same company.

Note that for convenience in discussing product management we consider that all of the functions and activities devised are performed by one executive, the *product manager*. The reader's attention is called again to the statement that this work is often divided among several people. Notable exceptions exist not only in ordinary organizational structures but also in those systems variously referred to as venture management, project management, and matrix management. The fact that the work of product management is often performed by several people underscores the importance of well-defined objectives, plans, and strategies. It also emphasizes the need for excellent control systems to provide coordination at the top instead of having coordination "just develop."

THE PRODUCT MANAGER'S JOB

Hierarchical relationships

There is no one best organization structure; so we must discuss the product manager's position in the organization in general terms. We do, however, assume a marketing organization. That organization may be the marketing-oriented company or it may be the marketing department of the firm. While the product manager's job is not restricted to marketing alone, it is essentially a marketing-oriented activity. Accordingly it should be and usually is a primary responsibility of marketing management.

Even so, the product manager has to cross organization lines to deal with manufacturing, finance, and other company departments. This requirement influences the authority granted the product manager as well as reporting relationships with other managers and with the top management group. A typical organization chart of a company with many products will show that the structure begins at the top with the president. Either directly or indirectly through an executive vice president, the marketing manager—presumably a vice president—reports to the president. The marketing manager is responsible for one or more product group managers. A group manager may be in charge of food products such as dog foods, cereals, and soup. The product manager is then under the immediate jurisdiction of the group manager. One product manager may be in charge of dog food, another in charge of cereals, and a third in charge of soup.

A large company has been used to delineate the narrowing of responsibility so as to emphasize the concept of the areas of responsibility. One person in a large organization may be responsible for one product or one brand of a product. In a small organization one person may be responsible for several or all products and/or brands.

The position of product manager

To perform properly and to make the appropriate decisions, the product manager must have an understanding with top management concerning expectations, the extent of authority, responsibilities, and the way in which he or she is to be evaluated as a manager. The profile of the position should spell out those things.[2]

---

[2] For a more complete discussion of these subjects see Phillip Marvin, *Product Planning Simplified* (New York: American Management Association, 1972), Chapters 19 and 20.

Function. A general description of the function provides a foundation for other facets of the position profile. Phillip Marvin suggests that the description might read:

> Under the direction of _____ and within the framework of established company policy, the new product manager is responsible for the successful development and initial operation of new ventures in terms of achieving profit objectives in accordance with approved plans.[3]

Note what this simple statement does other than identify the manager's immediate boss. It assumes a framework of predetermined objectives, plans, and policies, and establishes the responsibility of the manager to attain those objectives. Even though Marvin cast the statement in terms of new products, it is equally applicable to old ones.

Duties and responsibilities. The product manager, in theory, often acts just as the general manager of another small business might act. As suggested earlier, this means that the manager may have to cross departmental lines to reach sales, advertising, manufacturing, finance, personnel, and others. This is an especially significant point in the undertaking of new ventures under the corporate umbrella. In such instances the new venture manager may have his or her own R&D, purchasing, pilot production, and other groups. In practice, however, the product manager does not have the authority of a general manager. The manager's "authority" is often limited by his persuasive abilities.

The concept of the product or brand manager is in a state of flux, and many companies are either switching from brand management or are working structural changes. Such companies as PepsiCo., Purex, Eastman Kodak, and Levi Strauss are abandoning the system.[4] Others such as General Mills, Pillsbury, and Heinz are making certain structural changes. Several fundamental forces are influencing these changes in companies oriented toward consumer goods markets. One factor is the proliferation of new products and a corresponding shortening of product life cycles which require a different kind of attention to the product and its market than has been the case in the past. With fewer products, a principal concern was keeping market share. With shorter life cycles, future demand and social changes become more important.

Increased attention to market segmentation by age, income, lifestyle, benefits expected to be derived from the product, and other factors is a second factor. The reward system for product managers has been oriented more toward volume and market share in the short run; so market segmentation as a longer-run phenomenon has tended to be neg-

---

[3] Ibid., p. 205.

[4] "The brand manager: No longer king," *Business Week*, June 9, 1973, pp. 58–66. This article is the source of facts mentioned in this section.

lected, which leads to a third factor. Many of the decisions brand managers supposedly had authority to make are now becoming major policy decisions to be made by the Level 1 managers for the company. A fourth factor, related to the third, centers on the increased role of strategic planning, the recognition of interdepartmental relationships, and the increasing importance of market research.

What is being done? No one structure has emerged, so generalizations are probably out of order. Specifically, PepsiCo. is moving to a functional approach which the product manager concept largely replaced when Proctor & Gamble introduced it in 1927. Brand decisions are being made at the top level of management. Separate specialists in advertising, promotion, planning, and other marketing activities work for all brands. A manager of market planning does the coordinating product managers used to do in some companies.

In Pillsbury, a team approach is used with the product manager acting more like a team leader. Heinz combines product management and market management. For example, a single product manager once handled bottled ketchup for both the grocery division and the food service division. In the institutional market, one product manager handles ketchup, bottled sauces, mustard, and other table condiments. Similarly, one manager for Heublein supervises all vodka brands. Formerly there were three product groups, each with a vodka brand and each product group headed by a product manager. Kodak reorganized toward markets and channels of distribution. It has separate divisions for international, consumer products, and business systems.[5]

Even the product manager's job, mode of operation, authority and responsibility may vary widely from company to company. The following are areas for which a product manager may be responsible:

The discovery and screening of new opportunities and the products to exploit them.

Launching new products.

Developing the marketing mix.

Auditing product and market strengths.

Evaluating the competition.

Arranging for service systems.

Dropping unprofitable products.

These responsibilities and functions are discussed later in this chapter.

Authority. One of the key points in management is that a manager must have authority to carry out his responsibilities. Accordingly, a manager who has the responsibility for achieving a profit objective and for

---

[5] Ibid.

dropping unprofitable products must also have the authority to drop them. This means *full* authority for final decisions where they control the objectives the manager is responsible for achieving.

What does this imply? It says simply that the manager does not have to get approval from anyone else, but it implies that like any other good manager he will seek counsel from other departments that may be affected. For example, both the act of dropping and the timing of the dropping will affect production and marketing and other activities. Production will be affected because of the effect on production costs. Timing is important because of raw materials on hand. Marketing may be affected because of the impact on product lines and customer relations. Timing is also important because of inventory in the channels.

We make this brief excursion into "it-could-be-land" for a purpose. The reader knows by now that we strongly oppose the sort of independence in which separate departments behave as if they weren't working for the same firm. If product managers are given profit objectives, along with full authority to drop products, they are in effect told that they are *not* a part of a system of corporate, marketing, manufacturing, financial, and other resources and objectives.

Our point is to emphasize the importance of identification of duties, responsibilities, and authority. Having responsibility for profit objectives is fine. Having responsibility for dropping products after consultation with others affected is fine also, provided there is no substantial adverse impact on others. If conflict should arise because of a substantial adverse impact, the product manager's responsibility should be to use an established mechanism to resolve the conflict. That mechanism should enable the top management to coordinate these types of things. If the product is retained for the corporate good, the product manager's profit objectives should be modified. We are not proposing management by committee; rather, we are proposing management by system. The mechanism may consist of one person whose responsibility is to resolve interdepartmental conflicts.

As mentioned in the preceding section, the product manager often does not have authority commensurate with responsibility. In some companies, when persuasion fails, the product manager may have to appeal to a higher authority for support.

The reporting hierarchy

A good generalization here is that the product manager should report to an authority who in turn has authority to act or approve actions. But, that generalization has a tendency to fail at times in the case of product management. Obviously the product manager cannot give instructions to manufacturing to start producing! The manager's responsibilities may cover so many areas that at times the reporting hierarchy becomes confused.

The authors of one study wrote of a reporting hierarchy which had product managers reporting to a given authority but which allowed out-of-channel-communication. It apparently works smoothly according to all concerned. The president reserved the right to call anyone, including line management, at any time and gave product managers the right to call him. Program managers and group vice presidents were asked if this practice of communicating outside established lines caused any organization problems. Reportedly they seemed unconcerned and even thought the approach was necessary.[6]

Standards of performance

It is important to the product manager and the manager's evaluators that everyone involved know the criteria used for evaluation. Because of the qualitative factors surrounding a product manager's work, these criteria may be hard to develop. Also some philosophical problems arise in developing criteria because of the very large number of product failures.

If half the products fail, should the product manager be fired every time one fails? In Chapter 10 we said that the company needed to develop a system of rewarding failure. Obviously, a company can't go around handing out bonuses every time a manager has a failure! Nor can it punish all failures. The criterion of performance should be so designed that management looks behind failures and successes to determine their causes.

Who is the best manager, A or B? A did *everything* right—market research, product design, promotion, pricing—yet the product failed. People said they would like it, but didn't. Conversely, B did everything wrong, in retrospect, but events occurred that nobody could have anticipated, and consequently the product was a success.

Marvin suggests some criteria that may be used to judge performance.[7]

Are the phases of the project completed according to plan?

Are deviations from the plan justified?

How effectively were deviations dealt with?

Are the various phases of the program structured to maintain objectives?

Is the future properly attended to?

[6] Paul E. Holden, Carlton A. Pederson, Gayton E. Germane, *Top Management* (New York: McGraw-Hill Book Company, 1968), p. 110.

[7] Marvin, *Product Planning Simplified*, p. 208.

This is a general list, to be sure. But it offers guidance for the appropriate evaluation of product managers. In particular companies one can expect to find these performance measures varying from very precise to very general. Also one may expect to find considerable variation in the range of functions be to evaluated.

FUNCTIONS OF THE PRODUCT MANAGER

The discovery and filtering of new products

The discovery of new products. In Chapter 6 we pointed out that about three quarters of the product or process innovations reported on were demand-induced by the market or by production. Since this study cut across five manufacturing industries perhaps we can be reasonably comfortable in generalizing to the extent of saying that a "big bundle" of the innovations are stimulated by demand.

Of the 75 percent of innovations noted above, 45 percent were stimulated by a perceived market demand or need; we can safely say that external environmental analyses are important sources. And about one third were developed as a result of a production need. About one fifth were knowledge induced.

Perceived market demand. "Why don't they?" can be one of the fruitful sources of new product ideas. Many "why don't they" ideas filter back to the company through the sales force or through members of the channel of distribution. Because such a large number of ideas are generated this way, more companies are formalizing an information system which will insure that these ideas are collected at a level at which they can be systematically evaluated.

Complaints are a variation of the "why don't they" source of ideas. One of the things that is new about a new product is its improved characteristics which will provide the customer with greater satisfaction. The complaint department, instead of being considered a necessary evil, is often turned into a valuable source of new ideas.

A program of *customer research* to give customers a formal opportunity to comment upon product and/or service is another fruitful way of developing ideas. One of the banks in our town ran a formal market research program to try to discover what people wanted in the way of banking services. There was a follow-up program in the newspaper ads. Another bank enclosed a service questionaire in customer statements. There were at least two purposes to these studies. One was product improvement (service in this case) by better performance of the existing product; a second was to discover new wants and needs of customers, presumably so the banks could design new products to meet those wants.

Another type of customer research can have the effect of creating a new product merely by finding new uses for an old one. A company can find out the many ways its products are used other than the originally intended way. If feasible, it can then market the old product to a new market. There are also many miscellaneous sources of new product ideas. For example, in another context we mentioned the GE program of technology transfer in which it regularly publishes a list of "technology" available. GE laboratories develop things that may not fit GE objectives; so they license others to use the patents. The space agency NASA also has a formal program of transferring technology from its files to public uses. Similarly the list of patents is another source of new ideas.

Somewhere we read of a company which placed an advertisement for product ideas and got several thousand responses. Then there is the company suggestion box. There is no shortage of good ideas; programs need to be developed to harvest them.

Production need. Many new products arise from within a company's own offices and factory. As employees—secretaries, accountants, janitors, craftsmen, and others—do their work they often find short cuts and other means of improving the processes they deal with.

Knowledge-induced. Sometimes—20 percent of the time in the study mentioned above—somebody discovers something in doing pure research or in tinkering around. New markets are then created around the discovery.

The breakdown used above is merely a vehicle for stratifying sources of ideas. We would hate to be responsible for putting all new product ideas in one or the other category! In fact, it really wouldn't be a very useful exercise. Was the isotope a knowledge-induced product? On the one hand, yes, because until we progressed in nuclear energy research to a given point, it was not possible. Yet, medical professionals have long wanted improved diagnostic methods. Was miniaturization of various things—calculators, radios, eavesdropping equipment, hearing aids—the aftermath of discovery? or was it done because we needed or wanted smaller devices? It really isn't important. The point is that every company should develop a conscious program of new product ideas, or product improvement ideas, or ideas for alternative uses of existing products. This should be done systematically. We have outlined one systematic approach:

1. Find ideas from the wants and needs of the public.
2. Find them internally in the firm.
3. Find uses for new knowledge developed internally.

Within each of these three categories a formalized program may be established. For example, under point 1, a complaint department will not only hold the customer's hand but also to serve as a formal channel for product improvement.

In short, to provide a steady flow of new ideas on a structured basis, an environment and channel through which they can flow is helpful. Perhaps we should mention an advertising program built around this very notion: Ford's "better idea" series. Its underlying theme was that Ford had better ideas and got them from consumers; if you have a better idea, write "Better Ideas", Box . . . .

The Department of Commerce published a booklet on the subject of developing new products.[8] It listed a number of those products and their sources. Those below were selected to show the diversity of sources of ideas.

Source	Product	Company
Executive's wife	Onion soup	Meat packer
Customer inquiry	Foot warmer	Appliance maker
Mechanic (in company survey)	Hoist	Garage equipment maker
Advertising agency	Deodorant for garbage	Chemical company
Inventor	Film viewer	Plastic product company
Patent office	Kitchen gadget	Gadget maker
Sales report	Washer	Plumbing equipment
Museum exhibit	New vase	Pottery manufacturer
List of needed inventions	Film slide viewer	Plastic company
Food broker	Apple juice	Canner

Filtering new product ideas. Someone, of course, has to check out ideas and suggestions as they flow in. There are several filters through which new product ideas should pass.

Company objectives. The first filter consists of the *mission and objectives* of the firm. If a product candidate is not consistent with them, one of two things should happen. First, the candidate should be rejected. Second, the objectives should be reexamined. Incompatibility between product and objectives is one of the reasons for the GE program; in the course of its research it develops technology and/or products which do not fit into its program. This can be a critical point in the future of the company. We have said repeatedly that to reject a product because it is incompatible with objectives may be doing the right thing for the wrong reasons. Perhaps changes in objectives would make the product acceptable. Of course, even with changed objectives, the product might fail to pass for other reasons. The fact that some companies become conglomerates illustrates this point.

Product concept. The second step in the filtering process is to identify the *product concept* of the product in terms of what the idea would mean if transformed into a product. In short what is the function of the new product? Is it an improvement on an old product? The concept

---

[8] Gustav E. Larson, "Locating Ideas for New Products," reprinted in Thomas L. Berg and Abe Schuchman, eds., *Product Strategy and Management* (New York: Holt, Rinehart and Winston, Inc., 1963), pp. 420–22.

statement, accompanied by drawings if necessary for clarity of presentation, is used as a basis for further evaluation. The information included should be limited at this point to whatever is required to provide an understanding of the concept of the product.

The resource posture. The third filter is the *resource posture* of the company. The technical and economic requirements of the product are compared with the resources of the company. If the required resources are not available, one of two alternatives exists. Reject the product immediately; or review the companys' desire and ability to acquire the necessary resources, and then make the decision. This too can be a critical point in the future of the company. Just because resources are not available to fit the requirements of a particular idea is not adequate reason to reject it. To do so may close the door to a potentially great opportunity for the company. Ordinarily this step in the filtering process will reject many, perhaps most ideas. However, once in a while a product concept may come along that will cause a review of objectives (the first filter) and a decision to acquire resources. The product manager must be discerning enough to be able to identify at least some of the potentially good ideas that do not fit present objectives and refer them to higher authority. A part of the folklore of business is that several large companies are still looking for the people who rejected the Xerography idea from which Xerox Corporation grew.

We don't really know how or where two sets of ideas originated. We only know that their adoption caused significant review of objectives and resources. Or perhaps it was the other way around: the review of objectives and resources caused the end result. We refer to (1) former oil companies which acquired coal mines, and (2) aircraft companies that built rail passenger cars.

These comments are not made to negate our generalization that resource posture is a filter. Our emphasis is that availability of resources is an excellent guideline and policy for rejection, and that *guidelines and policies should not be used as absolute and invariable standards.* Look at one or two guidelines to see what the implications of this statement are. It is a perfectly good policy to prohibit setting forests on fire. As a standard, this policy would prohibit setting back-fires to help control a forest fire. More to the point of marketing: it may be policy to ship on Monday those orders received after noon on Friday, and all customers know about it. Would you open your warehouse at 2:00 a.m. Sunday to make an emergency shipment to a good customer to help combat a serious and potentially costly or dangerous emergency?

Technical feasibility. The first subject to be considered is whether the product idea can be made technically feasible. Notice our choice of words. We did not ask if the product idea *was* or *is* technically feasible. We asked if *it could be made* technically feasible. There is a world of difference between the two. Look around you for the difference. Start with the printing of this book and the light you are reading it by, neither of which was technically feasible at one time. We do not make this distinction to build a straw man for the purpose of pushing it over. Most people have run into the incredibly stupid people who say "It won't work." If you haven't met the type yet, you will. Fortunately, another look around you will show that those who insist that it can be made technically feasible eventually call the shots. Of course the next question—and closely related—is, can it be made technically feasible economically? You can be reasonably certain that the technical difficulties can be ironed out, but you can't be sure that the cost of doing so will be economically worthwhile to the company.

Marketing feasibility. Naturally, the question of economic feasibility is related to the ability to market the product. If the idea has progressed this far through the filtering process, it is time to identify the potential market for the product in terms of magnitude, geographic location, potential for growth, and the like. Also it is time to resolve such questions as compatibility with the product line and suitability of channels of distribution.

In addition to marketing research, one key approach to defining market feasibility is test marketing. This is exactly what it sounds like: getting information about the product from the market. Test marketing provides information about the total marketing program that the company should anticipate using when the product is in complete production and marketing. Thus it is important that the test be entered into systematically and with adequate time to formulate a reasonable marketing program.

There are three major reasons for test marketing. First, many resources are required to prepare a product idea for production and wide area marketing. It may be necessary to construct a plant to produce the product, new sales personnel may be needed, new advertising efforts may have to be expended, and new service facilities may be necessary, just for starters. Without market data, it will be very difficult to determine what size of plant or how many sales people will be needed. Furthermore, if the product does not achieve market acceptance, many of these expenditures will be wasted. Appropriate test marketing costs a small fraction of full-scale production and marketing expenses, and helps prevent large losses. Second, the company has the opportunity to observe actual consumer reaction to the product and accumulate data on such things as frequency of purchase. Third, the company has the opportunity to test under experimental conditions a variety of marketing programs and to vary certain marketing tactics, such as price and advertising media, to determine their effects on purchase patterns.

The type of testing procedure can vary widely. Some kinds of data can be collected by using laboratory conditions for taste and appearance testing; others seem to require the actual market environment. Another division of types of tests is the normal as against the controlled. In the normal test, marketing effort is directed through the channels of distribution in a way that closely parallels the way the product would move under nontest conditions. Regular wholesalers and retailers are exposed to the product through the company's regular sales force. Controlled tests bypass normal channel promotional efforts and are largely designed to determine the final consumer's reaction. Companies may choose the controlled test because it requires less time to conduct.[9]

For consumer products particularly, the selection of the test market areas is critical. Normal areas are often small-to-medium-size metropolitan areas which have, at minimum, the following characteristics:

1. They are representative of larger areas in population characteristics, income and expenditure patterns, available advertising media, available wholesalers and retailers, competitive conditions, and other factors.

2. They are small enough to be manageable. The city needs to be treated as a total entity. It is difficult, if not impossible, to test only in a part of a city. Clearly the economics of testing would be significantly diminished if it were done in a city the size of New York.

3. Related to 2 above, the city should be relatively isolated to avoid having purchases made by consumers living in other cities.

Of course, even successful test marketing does not insure the success of the product on a broader marketing scale. There are occasions when test marketing is not appropriate. Some of the occasions are:

1. When the new product is highly specialized and even in national distribution would have a small volume of sales. The expense of test marketing in the range of $50,000–$500,000 may preclude its use.[10]
2. When test markets reveal new products to potential competitors. If such revelations would produce competing products quickly, it is possible that the risk of losing the total market to competition exceeds the risk of not testing.
3. When the product can be expected to have a short life cycle, as toys often do. Then test marketing is inappropriate largely because of competitive reaction.

Successful test marketing is not always indicative of success. In one study, however, a majority of companies said that the results enabled them to predict ultimate market performance.[11] But there have been ob-

---

[9] For a brief but excellent discussion of this and other test marketing issues, see Jack J. Honomickl, "Test Marketing Practices Are Documented in Private Survey," *Advertising Age*, April 10, 1972, p. 30.

[10] "New Products: The Push is on in Marketing," *Business Week*, March 4, 1972, p. 72–77.

[11] Honomickl, "Test Marketing Practices."

vious failures, such as that of Post cereals with freeze-dried fruit, and Campbell with Red Kettle Soups.

Figure 11–1 offers a rundown of product evaluation methods. It is much more complete than our relatively brief discussion. We present this figure for two related reasons. First, it shows how complex the process of product evaluation is. Second, it has the perspective of real life. In another context, we said that if you read one of our statements

FIGURE 11–1
New Product Evaluation Check List

FINANCIAL		MARKET	
Return on investment	____	Size and growth trend	____
Industry profit trends	____	Utilizes management skills	____
Discount–cash flow history	____	Uses marketing organization	____
Cash or stock requirement	____	Research cost	____
Time to profitability	____	Repeat possibilities	____
Dollar volume potential	____	Complements long–range planning	____
Complements long–range planning	____	Territory restrictions	____
Price competition	____	Seasonal aspects	____
Risk ratio versus return on investment	____	Product design and packaging	____
Cost of marketing	____	Advertising–public relation costs	____

COMPETITION		PRODUCTION	
Number and size	____	Low tool cost	____
Strength of brand loyalty	____	Uses present facilities	____
Quality	____	Uses present labor relations	____
Product advantages	____	Effect on labor relations	____
Price advantages	____	Manufacturing	____
Personnel advantages	____	Raw materials availability	____
Marketing advantages	____	Inventory requirements	____
Ease of entry	____	Caliber of competitive products	____
Opportunity for improvement	____	Outside purchase ratio in–plant production	____
Historical trends	____		

SALES AND DISTRIBUTION		RESEARCH AND DEVELOPMENT	
Cost of sales	____	Low development cost	____
Physical distribution	____	Materials feasibility	____
Discount factors	____	Technology rating	____
Utilizes personnel skills	____	Success history—similar products	____
Sales service requirements	____	Development time	____
Sales appeal	____	Personnel limits	____
Freight factors	____	Facilities adequate	____
Caliber of competitive sales	____	Experience factors	____
Cost of new sales organization	____	Output warrants investment	____
Price factors	____	Within risk criteria complements long–range planning	____

LEGAL			
		Project no. _____ Date: _____	
Patent or acquisition feasibility	____		
Disclaimer form accepted	____	Product, process or business	
Copywrite trademark validity	____		
Infringement liability	____		
Option —royalty terms	____	(signature) (dept. or division)	
Patent application feasibility	____		

Source: From Bruce Payne, *Planning For Company Growth* (New York: McGraw-Hill Book Company, 1963), p. 142. Used with permission of McGraw-Hill Book Company.

fast, it makes everything seem easy. The same holds for our discussion of filtering new products.

But if the reader spends a bit of time with Figure 11–1, several points should become apparent. First, one may be able to read Bruce Payne's list fast, but one certainly can't check out all its points fast. There are seven major factors to evaluate, with 60 or 70 subareas. Second, many of these items are interrelated with each other; some are dependent upon others. Third, notice how he has tied long-range planning to the whole concept of new product evaluation in the Financial, Market, and Research and Development sections.

After developing information on each of the components of "Financial," for example, the evaluator will develop an opinion about the major subject. Figure 11–2 suggests an approach to evaluation. After each evaluation factor has been rated, a score is developed for the product. The company may have a minimum score as a cut-off point.

The approach shown in Figure 11–2 assumes that each of the evaluation

FIGURE 11–2
New Product Evaluation Chart—Preliminary

Evaluation Factors	Poor 1 2 3 4 5	Fair 6 7	Good 8 9	Excellent 10	Reasons for Evaluation	Total Score
Financial						
Market						
Competition						
Research and Development						
Production						
Sales and Distribution						
Legal						

Project#_____ Date: _____   Total _____

(Name of patentee, product or company)   (Signature)

(Summary recommendation)   (Department or division)

Source: From Bruce Payne, *Planning For Company Growth* (New York: McGraw-Hill Book Company, 1963), p. 143. Used with permission of McGraw-Hill Book Company.

factors is equally important. This may not be the case. Barry Richman suggests that they be weighted.[12] For example, the company may have such a good name among consumers that anything it produces will have an advantage over competing products. Call this goodwill, image, market posture, or whatever, it has some value. Should this factor be weighted more heavily in the analysis?

Other factors may also give the company a competitive edge, such as its channels of distribution, its distributors, its outlets, and its sales people. Moreover, the part performance of research and development may be so good that products entering the market have fewer bugs than is typical in the industry. The quality of managerial and staff people may also provide an edge. They may do their homework more thoroughly than others. These factors perhaps ought to be weighted more heavily in the evaluation process than some of the others.

Figure 11–3 is a revised version of 11–2. It reflects some additional

FIGURE 11–3
New Product Evaluation Chart—An Alternative

Evaluation Factors	A Weight Factors	B Product Compatibility Values*										C Scores
		Poor					Fair		Good			
		0	.1 .2	.3 .4	.5	.6 .7		.8	.9 1.0			A x B
The company	.20											
Marketing	.20											
R&D	.20											
Management	.15											
Financial	.05											
The market	.10											
Production	.05											
Location	.05											
Other (specify)	–											
Total	1.00											

Source: Modification of Figure 11–2 (page 243).
* Check appropriate value in section B.

---

[12] Barry M. Richman, "A Rating Scale for Product Innovation," in Berg and Schuchman, *Product Strategy and Management* pp. 437–39.

factors of importance and deletes some of those shown in 11–2. The difference is that the evaluation factors are weighted as suggested by Richman. Also, the scores, or "Product Compatibility Values" as Richman calls them, are changed to decimals so that the perfect score is 1.0.

Naturally, the complicated analyses underlying the evaluations are not made until some decision has been reached on the first three steps in the filtering process related to company objectives, the concept of the product, and the resource posture of the company. At that time our fourth filter, technical feasibility, becomes important. The R&D evaluation factor in Figure 11–1 is then relevant. Next our final step, checking marketing feasibility including economic feasibility, is taken.

Figure 11–4 is a visual representation of the steps taken in moving from an idea to a market-ready product. So far, our discussion has reached the halfway point: the decision to develop.

Preventing product failures (why products fail)

There are a number of functions for the product manager other than the discovery and filtering of new products. They include such things as auditing product strengths, determining market strengths, evaluating competitive moves, providing for product service, developing a marketing plan for the several stages of the life cycle, and many others.

In the final analysis, the manager's function is to keep products alive and successful, and the functions mentioned above are functions to keep products alive. But there is an opposite side of the coin—product failure. Let us look at selected reasons for product failure and learn from them.

This approach has logic to it. We know that half or more of new product introductions fail. The first objective is to turn potential failures into success, and then optimize success. A marginally successful product is better for the firm than a resounding failure would be—at least for a while. One might call this a positive approach to the negative side of product success.

The successes and rewards of failure. Many years ago one of the authors heard a banker bragging about his very low credit loss ratio, something less than one percent. A colleague of the author responded to the effect that if the banker would raise his loss rate, he would raise his profits. The banker nearly had a stroke, for to bankers in those days having a credit loss was almost a capital offense. Yet today the new breed of banker fully understands what is meant by increasing the loss ratio. We don't want to eliminate product failures completely— that's easily done merely by not introducing any. We only want to do our homework better so that the failures we do have won't be for the wrong reasons. Then we can increase the number of failures and also the total profits!

FIGURE 11–4
Flow Chart for New Product Planning

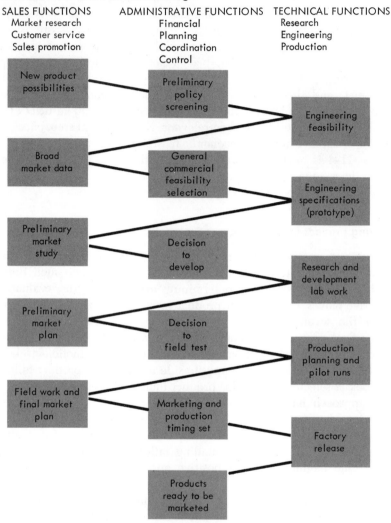

Source: From Bruce Payne, *Planning For Company Growth* (New York: McGraw-Hill Book Company, 1963), p. 145. Used with permission of McGraw-Hill Book Company.

Reasons for failure. Marvin has identified the 12 reasons for failure listed below.[13] We have discussed some of them in other contexts; others are fairly clear anyway; so we can be brief.

Timing off.

Impractical product.

---

[13] Marvin, *Product Planning Simplified,* pp. 104–16.

Changed customer needs.

Basic assumptions forgotten.

Unclear goals.

Product competed with customers' sales.

Failure to see opportunity.

Bad market analysis.

Poor information on competitors.

Overselling product proposals.

Incompatibility with line.

Disparity in supply and demand.

Timing. There are several aspects of timing which may influence success or failure. We have quoted before the saying that there is no force more powerful than that exerted by an idea whose time has come. Introducing a product before the market is ready for it is a hazard of innovation. In some cases, market analysis would raise a question about current acceptance of a product. Losses could be minimized either by market testing or by limiting the initial production facility. In addition, better analyses of the risks involved, including probability analyses of the several variables affecting success or failure, will improve the effectiveness of decisions.

Chrysler had this problem in the 1930s when it introduced a radically new styling which was years ahead of its time. The fact of failure is not bad in itself, but the company used that styling on two of its lines. There is another side to timing. The product may have been timely when conceived, but by the time it is marketed its time may have passed. Chrysler again had this trouble in the period after World War II. It designed a car based upon expressed consumer preferences, but when it was ready for market those preferences had changed. A more current market analysis would have sent up some signals warning of possible change. The Edsel is said to have had similar difficulties.

The second aspect of timing is something that can be better controlled: the introduction of a product to meet a seasonal demand. By properly planning the entire program, and by carefully monitoring the stages, the product manager can reasonably expect to complete things on time.

Even here, however, the fates may conspire. The manager may have the finest PERT chart imaginable. That won't help if the key engineer has a heart attack or if a supplier's plant burns down. Can such events be anticipated and protections built in? It is possible, of course, to have a "backup" for everything: suppliers, engineers, and facilities; but this would not be economical. However, planning for contingencies of this type may prevent the effects from being as serious as they otherwise might.

A third aspect of timing is the result of either bad management or poor guessing. When a cycle is virtually certain to change or is in process of changing, the product manager who is caught unaware deserves the failures he allows to fall in his lap. For example, there is probably many a new hospital supply product manager who wishes he had read the signs that the number of hospital beds was catching up with the effective demand for them. We are in the midst of a changing cycle of ages. One effect? School enrollment in the lower grades is falling, and the march of that decline will continue right into the high schools, colleges, bridal salons, obstetrical wards, production lines, and marketing programs. Marketing managers and other managers are very well aware of these signs and are actively taking them into account in their planning programs. The lesson for timing lies where most of the answers to failure have their roots: in environmental analysis and attention to the future.

The impractical product. Some products are brought to the market with inadequate testing, either in production or marketing. Or the market testing may have been properly structured but the test was distorted by competitors' actions. A product may be a resounding success in the test market but fail miserably in a national market. The cause of this kind of failure lies in applying generalizations from one market to the total market. The fact is that there are differences in regional markets. Product managers should be sensitive to these differences and accommodate them in their overall analyses. At times product managers become too committed to an idea and will rationalize away any negative aspect. Objectivity is important.

Incompatibility with product line. This cause of failure is clearly one that can be avoided. It is bad management when a product fails because it doesn't fit the line; the key to success here lies in planning. Many times a product line is not a thing that just evolves. It is a carefully planned concept with the parts of the product mix carefully thought out, the marketing mix well structured, and the total marketing plan working well. In short, the product line is well managed by people who understand it. When an "outsider" is introduced that is incompatible with the other products and has a substantially different product concept, the managers involved may not have the expertise to deal with it. They may not be able to adjust their thinking to a different level, and this may reduce their effectiveness.

Another type of incompatibility may be traced to bad planning in two or more dimensions. The company may have two or more products in different price brackets. Potential buyers who were expected to buy the higher priced product may not perceive a difference in value between it and the lower priced one. The economy product may have been priced low with the expectation that the higher priced one would bear a very large share of overhead. When volume does not materialize, disaster strikes both products. Why the failure? Perhaps the marketing plan

FIGURE 11–5
The Marketing Mix in Life Cycle Stages

Element	Introduction	Growth	Maturity	Saturation	Decline
Objective	To get trial	Establish strong brand position with distributors and end users	Maintain and strengthen loyalty	Defend market position, strengthen distribution relations	Get the last of the profit
Competitive situation	None	Rapid growth, aggressive	Intense. Declining unit profits, competitor dropouts	Stable. Increase in market share unlikely to be worth the cost	Everybody squeezed, fewer competitors
Product	Few models, high quality	Modular, flexible, more models for developing segments	Tighten lines not serving good markets. Product improvement and differentation	Lower production costs remove negative aspects	Reduce line to major profit producers
Price	Good value. Consider use positioning and rest of cycle. High trade discounts	Long price line from low to premium customary discounts	Attention to broadening market. Promotional pricing to extend brand coverage	Defensive to keep market position. Watch for incremental price opportunities	Maintain profit levels without regard to market share
Distribution	Exclusive or selective	Intensive and extensive. Quick service to dealers. High dealer inventory	Intensive and extensive. Quick service to dealers. Low dealer inventory	No change	Phase out marginal outlets
Promotion objective and media	Create awareness, get eary trial. Personal sales samples, fairly heavy advertising	Create strong brand awareness and preference. Maximum use of mass media	Maintain and strengthen consumer-dealer relations. Continue mass media, contests, training courses, sales promotion	Increase frequency of use. Mass advertising, dealer promotions	Rapid phase-out, sustain enough to sell a profitable volume
Marketing intelligence focus	Discover weaknesses. Identify developing user	Market position, market gaps. Product gaps. Opportunity segment	More attention to product improvement. Search for broader market and new promotion themes.	Alert for improvement opportunities, watch for signs of decline	Determine point of product elimination

Source: Developed from verbal description in Chester R. Wasson, *Product Management: Product Life Cycles and Competitive Marketing Strategy* (St. Charles, Illinois: Challenge Books, 1971), pp. 168–86.

was faulty in some element of the marketing mix. Perhaps it was the product design that was at fault in not making an adequate differentiation between the two similar products. Perhaps the failure was in the channels, in that inappropriate outlets were chosen for each product. Perhaps there was too great—or too small—a price differential.

The fault may not have been with the operational marketing plan at all. Perhaps the strategic marketing plan called for one product at two prices where the market would only accept one price. Again, this comes back to environmental analysis and the ability of the product manager to: (1) develop information that reflects the market as it is and as it is likely to be; (2) to interpret the information properly; and (3) to design plans reflecting an objective analysis of the environmental conditions.

As stated earlier, we will not cover all 12 of the causes of failure. Having discussed the functions of the product manager and a few of the causes of product failure, let us look at some of the types of key decisions product managers make.

MANAGING THE MARKETING MIX

The major group of decisions of the product manager involves management of the product mix. For the sake of brevity, we have summarized the things the product manager has to manage and the concepts for managing them, over the course of the product life cycle, in Figure 11–5. The reader will already be familiar with most of the concepts, but it provides a useful summary.

CONCLUSION

Product management is a complicated job. Its primary concern is implementing a strategy worked out at another managerial level. As we examine the nature of product management and its functions, two things should be clear: first, why the role of marketing in the organization is emphasized; and second, the importance of a systematic approach to marketing. Turning that coin over, the many areas of business which must be coordinated show us the importance of a systematic approach to business in general. While this chapter has been mainly concerned with implementation and management of the product, this has been discussed in relation to objectives, planning, and strategy.

chapter 12	# Distribution channel strategies and policies

Marketing and the channels of distribution
    Environmental conditions
    The external system
The function of channels of distribution
The traditional view of channels
    An illustration
    The traditional concept
The channel as a support system for the marketing effort
    Support of marketing or performance of tasks?
    An illustration
    One channel component's record: Some insights
    How a channel component supports the marketing system
    How to effect coordination to support the marketing system
The strategy of channel design
    Make or buy strategies
    Channel length and width
Marketing management and channel strategy
Conclusion

MARKETING AND THE CHANNELS OF DISTRIBUTION

Environmental conditions

The second element of the marketing mix is the channel of distribution. Remember, the first element is the product. The channel is the means by which the product is placed in the hands of the user. When we refer to a channel we refer collectively to all of those institutions and agencies which provide place utility and time utility.

In Chapter 2 we referred to the first-order environmental conditions as those uncontrollable forces existing outside the firm. However, we also said that the enterprising marketing manager will consider all of those external elements to be variable and use them to design the environment he wants.[1] If undesirable elements are considered to be constants, the manager's options are limited to two: (1) accept things as they are and live within an externally imposed framework; (2) adapt the firm to the situation. On the other hand, if he considers all of the elements of the environment as variable, he has a third option: he may adapt the environment to the needs of the firm.

There is a long list of companies whose managers considered the so-called uncontrollable and constant elements of the environment to be variable and took action to redesign them. In short, while those segments of the environment cannot be controlled, they can be influenced, and channel environments have undergone many changes as members sought out new opportunities or searched for solutions to old problems or both. A few instances of redesigning the environment are listed below. While we state a channel-oriented, service-oriented reason for the developments, note that there were mixed motives unrelated to channels which were behind the movement: profit, power, growth.

1.   Manufacturers such as tire makers have opened retail stores to give better control over the producer-user relationship.

2.   Retailers such as grocery chains have integrated backward in the channel to perform wholesaling and warehousing functions in order to gain greater control over both effectiveness and efficiency in the creation of time and place utility.

3.   Wholesalers such as food wholesalers have created voluntary chains of retailers to preserve their own existence, as chains of retailers began their own wholesaling function.

4.   As for the facilitating agencies, because lending institutions were not providing the type of services manufacturers felt were needed, manufacturers such as auto companies created their own financing agencies. Also, many channel members of all types have built their own warehouses and bought their own trucks because their service and economic requirements were not adequately met by transport companies and warehousemen.

Channels of distribution are external to the firm which uses them except in cases such as those mentioned above where the firm has integrated the channel functions. They are typically what we have referred to as the first-order environmental conditions. However, in dealing with those first-order conditions which relate to the channels, the marketing manager must also consider the second-, third-, and fourth-order environmental conditions which are internal to the firm. For example, one of those second-order conditions related to the channel may involve a logis-

---

[1] See William R. Davidson, "Distribution Breakthrough," in Lee Adler, ed., *Plotting Marketing Strategy: A New Orientation* (New York: Simon & Schuster, 1967), p. 260.

tics-related decision to reduce the number of distribution warehouses used. If logistics matters are not under the jurisdiction of the marketing manager, the decision is external to marketing but has an impact upon the marketing manager. He will have to react to thāt decision; so he should have a part in making it. The management of goods in the channel will be affected.

The channel program may be changed drastically if the marketing manager seeks a more extensive distribution program for his goods by getting new wholesalers or retailers to handle his product. This type of action falls in the category of third-order environmental conditions. The impact may be felt in the credit department (new customers), finance department (additional inventory), and the production department (new schedules). Because they have an impact on or require a reaction from some other departments, these marketing-related decisions should be considered as decisions of the firm. Thus, they are Level 1 decisions.

The fourth-order environmental conditions are those existing when the decisions are internal to marketing and have little or no impact on other departments. An illustration of this set of conditions as applied to channels is a change in the pattern of calls on retailers made by salesman of a wholesaler. For example instead of calling on all retailers, the salespeople may begin to make telephone calls to some retailers, weekly visits to others, and no calls at all to others.

As we have related the environmental conditions to the channels of distribution we have done three things. First, we have emphasized that all of the environmental elements should be considered variables and thus adjustable. Second, we have identified indirectly some of the elements of the channels (manufacturers, wholesalers, retailers, transportation companies, and warehousing companies). Third, we have related the channels to the environmental conditions first discussed in Chapter 2.

Now, we will shift emphasis slightly and establish the relationship between the channels of distribution and the marketing-oriented company. Remember, there are two very fundamental marketing ideas tied up in the concept of the marketing-oriented company. The first is the marketing concept itself which ties together the consumer-producer satisfactions discussed in Chapters 6 and 8 and illustrated in Figures 6–1, 6–2, 8–2, and 8–3. The second is that consumer-producer satisfaction should permeate the entire organization—not just marketing but production, finance, accounting, and all other departments.

The external system

Once more we refer to an earlier discussion to put our present discussion of the channels in perspective. We pointed out in Chapter 2 that each firm deals with suppliers, intermediaries, and customers, all of which relate to and become the channels of distribution. Each firm is (1) a customer of some supplier, (2) is linked to that supplier by intermediate agencies (wholesaler, transportation company), (3) is a supplier to customers of its own, and (4) is linked to its customers, again by intermediate agencies. Because of these linkages, the concept of the channel needs to be examined in a systems framework as a sequence of functions rather than as institutions performing certain tasks.[2]

Let's look at each of these four roles starting with the producer of raw materials. Remember that the producer has got to have some measure of satisfaction too, so note the two-way street of satisfaction between the producer and the customer. Also, note that our use of the word "producer" refers to a producer of services (wholesaler) as well as to a producer of goods.

1. Raw material producer
    a. Is a customer of and has to be satisfied by:
        1. Machinery, parts, and supplies producers.
        2. Transportation, warehousing companies.
    b. As a customer, has to satisfy:
        1. Suppliers.
        2. Transportation and distribution companies.
    c. Performs function: harvests or mines.
    d. Has a customer to be satisfied.
    e. Uses middlemen, transportation, distribution, other companies.
        1. Has to satisfy them.
        2. Has to be satisfied by them.
2. Transportation, distribution, other companies
    a. Have two customers:
        1. Shipper.
        2. Receiver.
    b. Have to provide satisfaction.
    c. Have to receive satisfaction.
3. Manufacturer
    a. Is a customer to be satisfied by:
        1. Raw material producers.
        2. Transportation, distribution, other companies.
        3. Middlemen.
    b. Has a customer to satisfy.
    c. Has middlemen, transportation, etc. to satisfy.

---

[2] For a full development of this theme see William P. Dommermuth and R. Clifton Andersen, "Distribution Systems: Firms, Functions, and Efficiencies," in R. Clifton Andersen and William P. Dommermuth, eds., *Distribution Systems: Firms, Functions and Efficiencies* (New York: Appleton-Century-Crofts, 1972), pp. 32–41.

4. Middleman (wholesaler, retailer, broker, etc.)
   a. Is a customer to be satisfied by:
      1. Manufacturers.
      2. Other middlemen.
      3. Transportation, etc.
   b. Has a customer to be satisfied:
      1. Another middleman.
      2. Transportation, etc.
      3. Ultimate user.
5. Ultimate user
   a. Is a customer to be satisfied by all of above.
   b. Has to provide satisfaction to all of the above.
   c. Has to provide satisfaction to disposal agency.
6. Disposal agency (solid, gas, liquid waste disposal)
   a. Has to satisfy:
      1. Ultimate user.
      2. The public.

This outline should emphasize what an incredibly complex job it is to manage the firm in relation to its channels of distribution. The marketing manager has a multifaceted balancing act to perform. The manager must not only help balance the satisfactions of the firm with those of its customers, but also help balance the satisfactions of all of the intermediary agencies in the channels. Or, for the moment equating the interests of the firm and its customers, we can say that the firm has two major systems to bring into balance: the firm and its channels of distribution. Of course, we recognize that the channels have the three subsystems discussed: suppliers, intermediaries, and customers. To those we have added the disposal agency which somehow must handle the debris of our civilization.

In the first course in economics the concepts of form, time, and place utility are introduced. In Chapter 10, we discussed form utility in a broad sense when we analyzed several aspects of the satisfaction-giving nature of the product. There we said that if marketing is what the firm is all about, the product or service is what marketing is all about. The channels of distribution create time and place utility for the product. This means that one objective of distribution strategy is to make it as easy as possible for the buyer to acquire the product and to do so as efficiently as possible for the manufacturer or other channel member.[3] The marketing-oriented company, as we have seen, has two characteristics. First, it seeks to satisfy the consumer at a profit to itself. Second, the entire organization is oriented toward this joint satisfaction process.

---

[3] John M. Rathwell, *Managing the Marketing Function: Concepts, Analysis and Applications* (New York: John Wiley and Sons, Inc., 1969), p. 469.

The consumer-producer satisfaction objective is attained through the creation of form, time, and place utility: the manufacture of a product or service designed to provide the desired satisfaction and making it available when and where it is wanted. As we bring the channels of distribution into focus and relate them to the creation of time and place utility, we can see that the whole process of creating these utilities is actually a continuum. Some refer to manufacturing and wholesaling and transportation and retailing as if each were a discrete step in the process because each is often performed by different companies.

When companies, for example manufacturing companies, integrate the several steps through ownership of the segments of the channel, they recognize the unity of the process of distribution. Through these *vertical marketing systems* they are able to create form, time, and place utility on a continuum.

Certainly not the same, but a similar, effect can be attained if each of the components of the channel system (1) adopts the marketing concept and (2) recognizes that it is a means to an end. In short, the discrete steps of the distribution process can become more like parts of the continuum if managers of each of the elements recognize not only their true function but also the true function of the channels of distribution.

THE FUNCTION OF CHANNELS OF DISTRIBUTION

The function of channels of distribution is to support the marketing effort of the firm.

THE TRADITIONAL VIEW OF CHANNELS

To emphasize that the several elements of the channel exist as means to an end—not as ends themselves—we gave a major topic head to a one-sentence statement of the channel function. We will see in this section that not only strategic but also managerial and operational problems arise in the channel because channel members too often act in an almost completely independent manner rather than as part of a system. When each member attempts to operate at his most efficient level to meet his own objectives, the effectiveness and the efficiency of the entire system and each of its parts is diminished.

An illustration

To illustrate this extremely significant point, we give an exaggerated example of goods moving through a channel where each channel member acts in his best short-term interest to have an efficient operation.

Fact 1. A manufacturer has 20,000 pounds of goods ready to ship to a warehouse to arrive on the 14th of the month. That particular shipment will leave the warehouse on the 2d of the following month.

Consideration 1a. Transportation. Let us say that the 20,000-pound shipment only partially fills the rail car or semitrailer, either of which could hold 40,000 pounds. This is the typical shipment of the manufacturer. What type of discussion do you think would have been carried on between the production, marketing, and transportation division if the company owned its own trucks? Surely, a study would have been made to see if 40,000-pound shipments would benefit the system because it would benefit the transportation division.

But what if the carrier is a for-hire carrier? The shipper and the carrier as separate entities should be thinking along the lines described above. The shipper's approach should be: If I reduce the carrier's cost, or increase its revenue per trip, I can get a lower unit rate. The carrier's approach should be the same: How can I help the shipper attain its marketing objectives at a lower cost? It is a well established fact that many shippers and many carriers do exactly this. It is also a fact that while it is not an unusual practice, it is far from being a typical practice. The shipper and carrier both should act as if the carrier were a part of the firm.

Now, a note of caution: sometimes a shipper makes demands on its own private carrier system that a common carrier should not meet and still reap its own satisfaction. There are bound to be conflicts in the channel; middle men are both buyers and sellers, and each has its own objectives. Conflict is both pervasive and inherent in channel systems characterized by behavioral independence for mutual ends.[4] Yet, the conflicts must be resolved, and obviously each member will resolve it to his satisfaction.

Consideration 1b. Warehouseman. The "Standard Contract Terms and Conditions For Merchandise Warehousemen" now works against our shipper. That contract provides that a full month's storage will apply on goods received between the first and 15th of the month and a full month's storage charge will apply to all goods in store on the first day of the next and succeeding calendar months. Therefore, since the goods were received on the 14th, one month's charge is levied. A second month's storage is charged because they were in store on the first of the following month even though the goods were out on the second. Therefore, a charge for two months—60 days—is levied for 20 days storage.

This is clearly in the interest of efficiency for the warehouseman and the user in that bookkeeping chores are reduced. But, what other effects

---

[4] Larry J. Rosenberg and Louis W. Stern, "Toward the Analysis of Conflict in Distribution Channels: A Descriptive Model," *Journal of Marketing*, October 1970, p. 40.

are felt? First, if the shipper had delayed the shipment two days, it would have arrived on the 16th when only one half month's storage would apply. Second, if he had shipped less, the shipment would have left the warehouse before the first. The effect is to discourage large shipments which may have many economies for shipper, carrier, and warehouseman. In general, the rigidity imposed by such a pricing mechanism reduces the options of all concerned. A simple change to a daily or even weekly charge would do wonders. Also, eliminating the one month's charge for goods in store on the first would encourage larger shipments and more frequent inventory turnover. On the other hand the authors know of one public warehouse which provides the daily price option. Some users have chosen the standard approach even though they pay about 8 percent more for the service. Their trade-off is lower bookkeeping costs.

Fact 2. The manufacturer has an exceptionally broad line—let us say six models or sizes of product. The wholesaler prefers frequent shipments of smaller amounts to reduce his inventory costs. Furthermore, three of the models move very slowly.

Consideration 2. Inventory. The conflicts here are evident. Depending upon which is the dominant factor—or "channel captain"—either the wholesaler or the manufacturer may have its feet held to the fire. If the wholesaler is dominant and the manufacturer pays the freight, the wholesaler may demand in its self interest smaller shipments than are economical from a transportation point of view. Furthermore, the probability of stock-out is increased. In addition, it may refuse to handle the entire line.

Our point is not that the dominant force is wrong—in this case the wholesaler. Our negative point is that it is acting unilaterally in its short-term interest as if it were a discrete step in the marketing process; as if its ends were the only ends to be served. Our positive point is that it is a means to an end; that it occupies a position on a continuum in the marketing process; and that it and the manufacturer should integrate their activities to smooth the process. They should be working together to attain more or less common objectives. The wholesaler should recognize that its function is to support the total marketing effort.

Again, conflicts of interest may arise. Again, it is likely that these conflicts will be resolved on the basis of long-run self interest. The logical starting point in conflict resolution is to ask, how would the marketing flow be enhanced if the manufacturer and wholesaler were under the same corporate roof?

The traditional view of channels is one of independence of the components instead of mutual interdependence. We have looked at several aspects of this by real-to-life illustrations of actions of some of the elements: manufacturer; transportation; warehousman; and wholesaler. No particular useful function would be served by doing the same for the retailer, so we will leave the illustration of the operational aspects of the traditional view and their strategic implications.

Another aspect of the problem is that some of the middlemen are both purchasing and selling institutions. Manufacturers, wholesalers, and retailers as marketing institutions are still examined primarily in their roles as sellers rather than buyers.[5] Philip McVey pointed out a long time ago that each link in the system considers itself as a purchasing agent for the link closer to the consumer before viewing itself as a selling agent for the link closer to production.[6] We have emphasized in an earlier section of this chapter that they should be examined *first in their roles as strategic supports for the marketing effort, and second as sellers and buyers seeking their own satisfactions.*

The traditional channel concept

The concept. The typical view is that the course taken by the title to the goods is the course of the channel; the title holder is the channel member. This view, however, does recognize that the broker, agent, and manufacturer's retail stores are members because they either play a significant part in the entire exchange process or title passes indirectly through them. Under this traditional approach, transportation companies, banks, advertising agencies, and others who participate in the flow are referred to as facilitating agencies and are not considered members of the channel.

Limitations. The difficulty with this view is that, because each owns the goods, channel members tend to think that their role starts when they get them and ends when they sell them. It is hard for them to think of themselves as links in a marketing chain. Paradoxically, if the title does not pass at each phase because a vertical marketing system under the control of the owner has been established, the problem all but disappears.

Take, for instance, a company which has a fully integrated vertical marketing system and sells groceries to the public. Let's look at the steps.

1. For some reason it wants a private brand of vegetables; so it builds a cannery and contracts with farmers to grow vegetables—perhaps on its land. Or it may contract with a cannery to do all this.
2. It sends trucks to the cannery and delivers its own goods to its own warehouse.

---

[5] Philip Kotler and Sidney J. Levy, "Buying Is Marketing Too!" *Journal of Marketing,* January 1973, p. 54.

[6] Philip McVey, "Are the Channels of Distribution What the Textbooks Say?" *Journal of Marketing,* January 1960, pp. 61–65.

3. From the warehouse, it delivers its own goods on its truck to its own retail stores, located where it wanted them and built by its own construction company.
4. It has arranged with the corporate treasurer for funds to support the activities all along the way.
5. It has had the in-house advertising agency work with the marketing manager to develop the marketing program, including package and label design.

Despite all of this, title has never passed from the time seed was put in the ground (or the can was taken from the cannery) until the can passed through the checkout counter. However we have had the services of a manufacturer, a transportation division, a warehouse division—acting as both warehouseman and wholesaler—retail division, an advertising function, and a financing function. Each stage in the continuum is designed to support the overall marketing effort. The important thing about a channel is not the institutions that make it up, but the functions they perform.[7] In this illustration, the middlemen were eliminated but their functions continued. That channel consisted of several functions in a continuum between producer and checkout stand. The elements all acted to support the marketing effort of the firm.

The independent channel members must function in the absence of a vertical marketing system. We have repeatedly recognized that independent channel members cannot act the same way as a vertical system. However, they can have the same objective: to support the marketing effort. This broad limitation can be subdivided into several component parts which we will discuss next.

Incomplete marketing structure. The marketing structure links the producer and consumer. (We do not ignore those segments which supply the producer and handle the consumer's cast-offs; we just don't talk about them here.) The linkage is through a continuum. Thus, one of the limitations of the traditional view is its implication of discreteness in the system. In the same connection, but on a conceptual basis, the structure is incomplete when it ignores or plays down the role of the channel members as both buyers and sellers rather than just sellers. That is, each channel component not only has a customer but also is a customer.

Components excluded. A second limitation is that the vital role played by the so-called facilitating agencies is ignored. There are too many illustrations of the role played by those who perform the ancillary

---

[7] Philip Kotler, *Marketing Decision Making: A Model Building Approach* (New York: Holt, Rinehart and Winston, 1971), p. 288.

functions in the success and failures of marketing programs for them to be ignored. Let's look at a few.

At one time new trucks purchased by carriers could be financed only over a three-year maximum term. This delayed expansion, for a truck could not earn enough to pay for itself in three years. A huge market opened when five-year terms were granted.

A mobile home factory in Canada was on the verge of failure despite great demand. That demand could not be translated into sales because reasonable financing terms were not available. Also in this country a tremendous market opened up when easy terms were established.

General Motors Acceptance Corporation enlarged their market for GM cars by making more liberal financing terms available. Other producers did the same.

A good portion of the textile industry depends upon the "factoring" of its accounts receivable. (A factoring firm buys the accounts receivable.)

Oil companies expanded their sales of accessories by granting extended terms on credit card purchases.

Thus to exclude those who perform the ancillary functions from consideration as parts of the channel is flying in the face of reality. They are all critical elements in helping market a product.

Form-place-time satisfactions. The typical buyer or possessor of the goods along the channel does not buy or care to possess, finance, advertise, or consume a can of peas because it is a can of peas. The person concerned wants to buy, possess, finance, advertise, or consume a bundle of satisfactions represented by that can of peas. Other things being equal, wholesalers would as soon handle a can of cat litter as a can of peas—or a can full of nothing. The same along the line. Even the user is after the satisfaction the peas bring—not just the peas. True, maybe only a can of peas can provide the specific satisfaction wanted. Moving from the symbolic can of peas to specific situations, many people go into a particular business because they get satisfaction from a particular product. They open a pet store because they like pets, or a fashion clothing store because they like clothes.

Included in satisfaction each step of the way are form, place, and time satisfaction. Consumers don't buy wheels, fenders, engines and the like. They buy automobiles to get not only transportation but also an exhibition delivered wherever and whenever they wish. In other words, consumers buy satisfaction through a marketing program which combines form and place and time utility in the mixture desired. The role of the channel system in supporting the marketing effort will now be examined.

THE CHANNEL AS A SUPPORT SYSTEM FOR THE MARKETING EFFORT

Support of marketing or performance of tasks?

In the discussion of the traditional view of channels we have indicated what the systems view of the channel is. To summarize: (1) its function is to support the marketing effort; (2) its activities work toward that common goal, with each element of the channel being a part of the continuum stretching from the mine to the garbage dump by way of the miner, manufacturer, wholesaler, retailer, and consumer.

Before leaving completely the traditional view to analyze the implications of the strategic view, we present a brief comparison of the two views which will serve as both a bridge to and a foundation for further discussion of channel strategy. The distinctions between the two concepts can be illustrated very clearly by using the public warehouse and the distribution center as vehicles for comparison.

It would perhaps be preferable to use another component of the channel system for this comparison, but "hard" data on retailers and wholesalers to illustrate certain of our points is unavailable. It is available for warehousing. But there is an advantage to using warehousing to illustrate our points because that is a non-owning function which must clearly satisfy the customer and the customer's customer. The points we make concerning the role of each of the components of the channel in the channel system are important. Basically, we refer to one element in the entire system; one link in a chain. However, other points are embedded in this one. For example: the marketing concept; the need of the company to know what both its customers and its customers' customers require in the way of satisfaction; and the need for the company to think beyond the tasks it performs as a wholesaler, a retailer, a carrier, or a warehouseman—these are all implied in the term "the marketing-oriented company."

In short, managers need to recognize the dual roles ascribed to all top-level managers. First the manager of one of the elements of the channel system needs to recognize the role to be played in creating and operating an effective channel *component* to create an effective channel *system*. In this role the manager is concerned with the strategic role of that type of business in the channel system and its relationship with other channel components. Second, the manager of one of the *components* must be concerned with the efficiency of operating the firm to create an efficient channel *system*. Cast in terms you have become accustomed to in this book, the component managers must be concerned with management *and* the channels as well as management *of* the channels. So, even though warehousing and distribution center are used as bases for comparison, the concepts are transferrable to each of the other elements of the channel.

An illustration

Note that the distinctions between the public warehouse and distribution center concepts depend to a considerable extent on attitudes or frames of mind and performance *objectives* as well as actual performance. The distinction does not depend on whether a company is called a warehouse or distribution center. Because of those attitudes, the activities of the two are sometimes different, and, as we shall see, they are distinct from one another. The processes of handling, storing, etc. are the same, but what goes on before the goods arrive and after they leave constitutes the difference.

Except in those instances where storage adds to the product—aging, for example—storage is wasteful. Wasteful, but necessary. The shorter the period goods spend in a warehouse, the less wasteful the process is. Accordingly, the ideal situation is to have goods flow through the warehouse with only a minimum stop-off period. Leaders in the warehouse industry have been preaching this doctrine for at least 30 years. Unfortunately, they have not been heard, or if heard they have been largely ignored.

Now look at Part A of Figure 12–1. The warehouse, shown in the center, typically thinks of itself as just that—a warehouse. The arrows show the flow of goods and imply that the goods are the focal point. The closed boxes symbolize two things. First, they symbolize the popular, traditional view that each is a discrete step in the process. Second, they symbolize the lack of "mutual interest" except as "necessary evils" and the lack of communication among the several elements. In effect, they say that the manufacturer calls the carrier and then loses interest in the goods, provided they get where they are going on time and in good shape. The carrier develops an interest in them only when it picks them up, and loses interest when it delivers them to the warehouse. At that point, the warehouse develops an interest: receives, handles them in, stores, reports stocks to owner, handles them out, documents them, and then loses interest. The same "show of interest" prevails on the outbound side. It calls the carrier, and that's all. The warehouse portrayed in Part A is concerned with performing warehouse tasks and not with the distribution system.

Now look at Part B of Figure 12–1. An entirely different framework has been established. The distribution center is in a quite different posi-

FIGURE 12–1
Public Warehouse and Distribution Center Concepts Compared

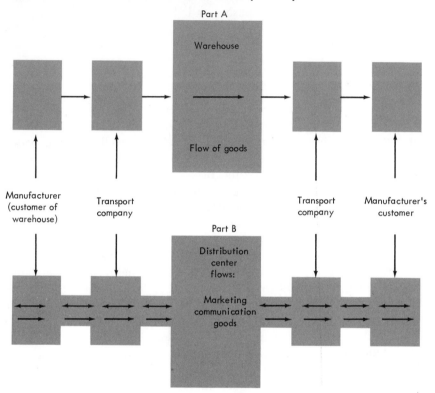

tion from that of the warehouse in Part A. What is done differently? First, the manager of the distribution center determines what the marketing objectives of the manufacturer (the customer) are. Second, the manager operates the facilities to help attain those objectives. In this connection the manager may work with the carrier on the customer's behalf for rate and service adjustments. But working with the carrier is a two-way street also, for the carrier too has to make a profit. By working with the carrier and the shipper, the shipping patterns may be adjusted—quantity shipped, method of packing, delays in loading, frequency of payment of bills. Also, the distribution center manager may work with the carrier to reduce carrier costs in delivering to the warehouse. These are some of the elements of the environment which are external to the distribution center; the ones we said earlier were constants and uncontrollable. These are the ones we said should be considered variables in order to design the environment the manager wants.

Internally, there are things the distribution center manager can do.

For one, the manager can change the pricing system from the method which discourages the flow-through concept to one which encourages it. For another, as an understanding of the customer's shipping patterns is developed, internal handling systems can be adjusted to accommodate the customer's program at reduced cost to shipper, carrier, and customer.

Third, the manager can work with the customer's customer who may be a retailer, wholesaler, or broker as well as with the outbound carrier. If the manufacturer's customer is not satisfied with service from the distribution center, the manufacturer can be very hostile. Just as the center manager worked with the center's customer to relate distribution operations to marketing objectives, the manager should also work with the customer's customer. For example, the customer's customer—say, a retailer—may be encouraged to make changes which will result in cost and service improvements to both. Or the center manager may make changes resulting in cost and service improvements to the retailer.

In short, the arrows in Part B of Figure 12–1 relate to the flow of marketing communications as well as to the flow of goods. The activities of the distribution center are strategic in nature, not just process-oriented to accomplish tasks related to storage. It not only performs the tasks and goes through the several processes of handling, storage, and the like, but also relates those tasks to the distribution system. It supports the marketeing effort of the firm; it is in reality a marketing support system.

One channel component's record: Some insights

A study of the decision process in selecting warehousemen strongly supports the discussions of Figure 12–1.[8] The statements and responses by both users and warehousemen are shown in Figure 12–2. Note that only about 12 percent of the users agreed that warehousemen are creative in suggesting ways to reduce costs. Some 44 percent of the users apparently felt that warehousemen do not even understand what their role is—and 19 percent had no opinion on the statement. Considering users' attitudes toward the first two statements, it should be no surprise that 55 percent think warehousemen sell space rather than service.

These user attitudes support the statements that the typical warehouseman is oriented toward the performance of warehouse tasks as distinct from the marketing effort of the firm. This study by Professor B. J. LaLonde and his associates makes possible an inference that warehouse-

---

[8] The data on attitudes of the users were taken from Bernard J. LaLonde and others, "The Public Warehouse Decision: An Interim Report" (Columbus: The Ohio State University College of Administrative Science, 1973), reprinted from *Warehousing Review*, January/February 1973. The data on attitudes of the public warehousemen are from data supplied by the authors of the study.

FIGURE 12–2
Attitude of Users and Public Warehousemen toward Warehouse Services (in percentages of those questioned)

Statement*	Agree	No opinion	Disagree
Most warehousemen are creative in suggesting ways to reduce total distribution costs.			
Users	11.6	14.5	73.9
Warehousemen	53.8	11.5	34.7
Most warehousemen do not understand how they fit into shippers' distribution systems.			
Users	43.5	18.8	37.7
Warehousemen	30.8	7.7	61.5
Most warehouse salesmen try to sell space rather than provide distribution service to shippers.			
Users	55.1	8.7	36.2
Warehousemen	34.7	7.7	57.6

* Slightly modified to save space.
Source: See text footnotes 8 and 9.

men do not consider the same things to be important that the users consider important. Tie this to the marketing concept! How can you satisfy your customers if you don't know what they consider important in a product?

The variation in responses by public warehousemen and users to 24 key factors in three broad categories is astounding.[9] All three categories are intimately related to marketing communication between a firm and its customers. One of the categories consisted of seven reasons for using public warehousing. The researchers asked public warehousemen and users to rank each of the seven factors on a five-point scale ranging from "Important" to "Not Important." The percentage of warehousemen checking the first two levels of importance of each factor was not even close to the percentage of users checking those items. The disagreements ranged from 15 percentage points to 46 percentage points. For example, 25 percent of the warehousemen and 40 percent of the users thought that changes in transportation rate structures were an important factor—a difference of 15 percentage points. At the other extreme, 72 percent of the warehousemen considered important "Personal Sales Calls from Warehouses as Source of Information." Only 26 percent of the users considered that factor important—a difference of 46 percentage points.

A second category was "Facility and Equipment Characteristics" with 11 factors. The differences in what was considered important here were not so great. They ranged from 15 to 25 percentage points. The third category, "Rates and Service Characteristics," had six factors. The differ-

[9] The data referred to in this discussion are from Bernard J. LaLonde and others, "The Public Warehouse Selection Decision and New Marketing Strategies," Tables 18, 19, 20.

ences in the user-warehouseman perspective of the importance of these factors ranged from 9 to 26 percentage points.

How a channel component supports the marketing system

We have indicated the apparent dissatisfaction of users of public warehouses with the way in which this component of the channel system performs its role. The apparent cause is the preoccupation with warehousing *tasks* instead of warehousing *functions* and the failure to apply the marketing concept either to the warehouse-customer relationship or to the warehouse-channel continuum. We have shown in this section by specific reference to one component of the channel what we mean when we say that the function of the channel system and each of its components is to support the marketing effort of the firm.

In recapitulation, we can say that a component of the channel system—or the channel system as a whole—in functioning as a marketing support system does several things.

1. It helps identify a channel of distribution for the customer.
2. It helps develop means of going through the channel.
3. It helps the customer attain his marketing objectives.
4. It, in effect, becomes a part of the customer's managerial staff—an extension of the arms of the firm.
   a. It provides the customer information on distribution.
   b. It recommends means of carrying out the customer's policies.
5. It differentiates between the channel *system* and channel component *processes* or *tasks.*
   a. The channel system facilitates the working of the several processes of each component.
   b. Concern with the system is effectiveness.
   c. Concern with the processes is efficiency.

We now turn our attention to other strategic aspects of the channels of distribution.

How to effect coordination to support the marketing system

Philip McVey pointed out that integrated channel action of the type suggested above is a rare luxury in marketing.[10] His reasons were much the same as ours. He made several specific points:

1. The businessman is concerned with suppliers and customers instead of with a channel.

---

[10] McVey, "Are the Channels of Distribution What the Textbooks Say?" p. 63.

2. He deals with those adjacent to him and not with other links.
3. When his sale is paid for, he can turn his attention to his on-going problems.

Bert McCammon writes,

> Marketing channels have been traditionally viewed as fragmented, potentially unstable, networks in which vertically aligned firms bargain with each other at arm's length, terminate relationships with impunity and otherwise behave autonomously.[11]

McCammon visualizes three types of centrally coordinated systems: corporate, administered, and contractual.[12] We have already mentioned the corporate system in our discussion of vertical channel systems. Also we have alluded to the administered system which arises from a channel captain exerting leadership over adjacent components and bringing some of the economies of a system to the channels. The third method of achieving coordination is through contractual agreements such as the voluntary buying groups and shipper's associations we have mentioned. We will discuss these more fully in Chapter 13.

THE STRATEGY OF CHANNEL DESIGN[13]

The functions and activities of channel members can be performed in many different ways. The decision-making process in channel design is the conversion process between inputs and outputs. Any distribution channel is a particular configuration of components for performing the channel functions. Each channel configuration operates at a certain level of costs with a certain generation of sales.

Too often the decisions that affect the marketing channel system result in a patchwork affair. One reason for this is the lack of environmental analysis. In developing a marketing channel framework, the typical firm faces three kinds of situations. Either a new product is being introduced to a new market, the market for an old product is being broadened by the addition of new marketing channels, or a going concern is adding a new product for sale to its traditional market. In the process of resolving these alternatives the channel selection process involves determining what marketing functions the firm is able and willing to perform for itself, the degree of control it wishes, the amount of manufacturing

---

[11] Bert C. McCammon, Jr., "The Emergence and Growth of Contractually Integrated Channels in the American Economy," in Andersen and Dommermuth, *Distribution Systems*, p. 451.

[12] Ibid., p. 452.

[13] This section was adapted from a paper prepared by Professor Roger E. Jerman.

specialization or integration desired, the availability of various kinds of middlemen, and the alternative use of its funds and resources.[14]

Make or buy strategies

Each channel alternative has a unique cost, and this cost problem is primarily an economic integration problem. The manufacturer may decide to perform some or all of the functions discussed in the previous section. Many channel decisions are of the "make or buy" type. It is a question of whether the firm should perform some part of the distribution process or whether the task should be farmed out to independent agents.[15] The two alternatives of the decision-making process are depicted in Figure 12–3. When the manufacturer elects to perform some

FIGURE 12–3
Make or Buy Strategy

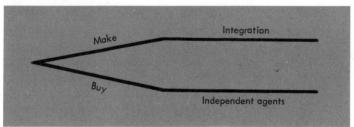

or all of the functions of the marketing channel, it is referred to as vertical integration.

The make or buy decision is not an all or nothing situation. A policy of vertical integration in a marketing channel can be a modest step or the manufacturer can become a fully integrated firm. There are segments of the marketing channel that represent opportunities for vertical integration; in many situations the decision calls for only partial integration at any particular level.

At present, manufacturers seem to be assuming more of the functions through forward integration. This is partly because of their size and capability. As they integrate they achieve greater degrees of channel control and are better able to project their total marketing plan through the channel. It is important to recognize that the use of vertical integration by a manufacturer has its counterpart among the marketing channel institutions.

---
[14] William Lazer, *Marketing Management: A Systems Perspective* (New York: John Wiley & Sons, Inc., 1971), p. 305.
[15] For a discussion of factors to consider see Wroe Alderson and Paul E. Green, *Planning and Problem Solving in Marketing* (Homewood, Ill.: Richard D. Irwin, Inc., 1964), p. 311.

All this integration, with the ultimate aim often being control, is inviting the attention of government agencies. Business firms are not allowed to make trade-channel arrangements which lessen competition, act as an unreasonable restraint on trade, or tend to create a monopoly. The federal government appears to be broadening its attack on channel decisions, both on the independent agent agreements and, especially, on the ownership involved in integration.[16]

The result is that the channel decision-making process is moving from a two-part model involving buying and selling systems to a three part model involving the government regulatory process. The strategic point is that both the buying and selling system start working through the regulatory process of government to get what they formerly would have negotiated on a one-to-one basis via a direct interface. This additional variable significantly changes the channel selection process. It may even slow down, stop, or reverse the development of vertical systems which are all parts of one corporate umbrella or which are constituted by contract.

Channel length and width

If the integration branch is chosen, the decision-making process involves the degree of integration and then the subsequent internal administration of the desired degree of ownership. This administration is at the level of the management *of* channels of distribution and will be discussed in Chapter 13.

If middlemen are to be used, the key strategic and managerial decisions have to do with (*a*) length of the channel and (*b*) width of the channel. The decision involving the length of the marketing channel means deciding the number of institutions through which, or to which, the product is sold on its way to the final buyer. The basic choices in consumer goods distribution are shown in Figure 12–4. Control is generally the key issue here. The longer the channel, the more difficult it is to keep performance on target. Once the intermediaries are established, the supporting facilitating agencies are partially predetermined for that particular structure.

Once the length is determined, decisions must be made with regard to the width of the marketing channel for a particular product. This means deciding through how many different classes of middlemen at a particular level the product will be sold. For example, if retailers are used, should distribution be through hardware, food, drug, or other kinds of stores. Because of the relatively long-term commitment, both length and width of the channel become strategic and high-level mana-

---

[16] See the 1962 Supreme Court decision forcing the Brown Shoe Company to divest itself of G. R. Kinney, Inc., and also S. Powell Bridges, "The Schwinn Case: A Landmark Decision," *Business Horizons*, August 1968, pp. 77–85.

FIGURE 12–4
Consumer Goods Distribution Alternatives

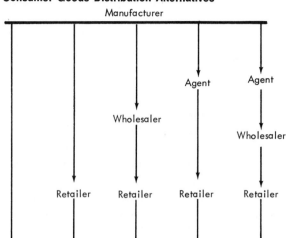

gerial decisions, and therefore are part of management *and* channels of distribution.

MARKETING MANAGEMENT AND CHANNEL STRATEGY

The underlying theme of channel strategy can be expressed by the following formula: Want + Recognition + Need + Availability = Opportunity. This formula is based on the management of change. In selecting marketing channels, one must understand that they are not static behavior systems. They are dynamic, ever-changing ones, and are in a state of constant evolution. Change leads to opportunity.

Compatible with the marketing concept, the firm must begin the channel selection process by analyzing the consumer and then working backward through various channels. The selection of channels depends largely on the buying patterns or habits of both the end consumer and the middlemen, with the decision-making process of the end consumer ultimately influencing the channel. This is the want-need part of the above formula.

The role of channels of distribution in a market-oriented firm is to provide the availability to match and complement the need, thus providing strategic opportunities for the firm. Therefore, distribution strategy is concerned with availability, or time and place utility. Products and services have to be available to buying systems when and where they are desired. The objective of distribution strategy is to make it as easy as possible for the ultimate consumer or industrial user to physically acquire the product and to do so as efficiently as possible for the manufacturer.

The marketing channel is one part of the distribution component of a firm. The marketing channel provides the structure within which the rest of the marketing plan is carried out. It is the means of physically placing the product in a location convenient to buying systems. Channel of distribution strategy is critical in product-augmented type competition because of the substitutability aspects of the decision-making process of the buying system relative to availability. Unless the product is available when and where the buyer wishes it to be, then a competing product will be bought, or at best there will be some erosion in the buyer-seller relationship. To understand the role of channels of distribution in a marketing-oriented firm, one needs a framework of analysis. Marketing management can be viewed as the task of optimizing the relationship between controllable variables in a firm's marketing mix and the noncontrollable or environmental variable.

A primary objective of the marketing system is the effective and efficient distribution of products from point of production to point of consumption and disposition. Management *and* the channels of distribution is concerned with the effectiveness of these objectives. Management *of* channels of distribution is concerned with the efficiency of these objectives, the subject of Chapter 13. There is a hierarchy of policies related to marketing channels as shown in Figure 12–5.

FIGURE 12–5
Hierarchy of Marketing Channel Policies

Decision type	Hierarchy of marketing channel policies	Nature of trade-off	Channel management
Strategic planning	Marketing channel policies of top management: president, marketing, other executives	Interfirm and interdepart-mental	Management and channels of distribution
Managerial control	Marketing channel policies of marketing executive within above guidelines	Interdepartmental and intradepart-mental	
Operational control	Performance of channel tasks	Intradepartmental	Management of channels of distribution

Conceptually, management *and* the channels of distribution includes all of strategic planning and the top part of managerial control. Management *of* channels of distribution includes the bottom part of managerial control and all of operational control.

Management *and* the channels of distribution is more concerned with the philosophical role of channels of distribution in a market-oriented firm, particularly as it relates to the broader system of the total firm. Management *of* channels of distribution is primarily concerned with the role of channels of distribution in the marketing mix decision, and with its subsequent administration.[17]

CONCLUSION

To comprehend management *and* channels of distribution it is necessary to view the marketing channel as a system. The institutional parts of the channel such as retailers and wholesalers have received considerable attention in the literature, particularly in the institutional approach to the study of marketing. This approach visualized channels of distribution as a sequence of institutions (producer-wholesaler-retailer-consumer). The approach tended to degenerate into a description of various marketing channels prevalent in specific industries. We have viewed the channels of distribution as a sequence of functions, rather than institutions, in a systems framework. This approach is of greater value in generating new ideas about the dynamics of channel structure, efficiency, and profitability. By considering the channel as a marketing support system and its function as supporting the marketing effort of the firm, many opportunities for improvement are opened. For example when this view is taken, concern can shift from just wholesaling and just retailing to concern for improving the linkages between the two. This added dimension forces managers to concern themselves with the system as well as with its parts. The results are more complete service to the consumer, more effectiveness in attaining objectives of all involved, and more efficiency in operation.

---

[17] For an analysis of implications for marketing, manufacturing, and finance of comprehensive systems of shared facilities and services in the channel see Walter F. Friedman, "Physical Distribution: the Concept of Shared Services," *Harvard Business Review*, March–April 1975, pp. 24 et seq.

| # Distribution channel management

Objectives of channel management derived from channel theory
Improve efficiency of marketing program
Improve effectiveness of channel
Control inventory for customer service, corporate cost
Improve service to middlemen
Maximize efficiency
Other Objectives
Channel management and marketing satisfactions
Product and patronage satisfaction
Variables in the satisfaction process
Retail and wholesale systems
Retail operations
The wholesaling system
Size and efficiency: Channel implications
Types of channel decisions
Sell direct or use a middleman
Selection of channel components
Selective or intensive channels
Multiple channels
Other decision areas
Conclusion

Because of our emphasis on the function of channel components in Chapter 12, we dealt with operations and types of middlemen only incidentally. This approach, of course, is consistent with the format of the book; we discuss primarily the strategic aspects of elements of the marketing mix in one chapter and the operational aspects in another. This chapter has four major parts. The first, objectives of channel management, is concerned with the operational aspects of what channels are supposed to do. The second part relates these objectives to satisfaction of wants and needs of consumers and channel members. The third part examines the environment of the system and the operational aspects of attaining channel objectives. In this part, while we focus attention on the retail segment, we also examine the wholesale segment. Accordingly, when we turn to wholesaling, we resort to an outline which identifies the types, characteristics, and activities of wholesalers whose function and role have already been discussed. Finally, we look at some of the types of channel decisions managers have to make. Thus, while Chapter 12 was concerned with management *and* the channels of distribution in looking at strategic aspects of channels, this chapter is concerned with management *of* the channels and with decision making, operations, and implementation of strategies.

OBJECTIVES OF CHANNEL MANAGEMENT DERIVED FROM CHANNEL THEORY

There are several theoretical explanations of channels which can be helpful in identifying objectives of channel management.[1] In the sections which follow, we identify a potential objective of the channel manager and then relate it to one of the theoretical explanations of trade channel.

Objective: Improve efficiency of marketing program

The transvection concept was originally conceived by Wroe Alderson. He believed that consideration should be given to the entire sequence of transactions from raw material stage through the final sale of the finished product. Apparently Alderson's major concern was with cost reduction by finding the optimal number of steps in the channel. This type of approach will disclose the total cost of the distribution process for it matches an original producer of raw material and an ultimate consumer through all of the transformations the material goes through, and the sorting processes performed by manufacturer, wholesaler, and retailer.[2]

Objective: Improve effectiveness of the channel

The marketing flow concept is useful in analyzing how effectively the marketing job is done and is concerned with the entire marketing channel system. It differs from the transvection concept in a rather subtle

[1] The theories of trade channels discussed here are more fully analyzed in Edwin H. Lewis, *Marketing Channels: Structure and Strategy* (New York: McGraw-Hill Book Company, 1968), pp. 138–48. Full citations to the individual theories and authors are provided by Professor Lewis.

[2] Wroe Alderson, *Dynamic Marketing Behavior* (Homewood, Ill: Richard D. Irwin, Inc. 1965), p. 22. See also Chapter 3, especially pp. 86–97, in Alderson.

manner. If low cost is what is wanted, the transvection concept will provide it. If effectiveness is wanted, the flow or systems concept will provide that. In our discussion of this concept in Chapter 12, we assumed a combination of efficiency and effectiveness.

Objective: Control inventory for customer service, corporate cost

The depot theory of distribution developed by Leo V. Aspinwall states that the ultimate consumer determines the rate at which goods move to the point of final consumption. As we point out in Chapter 12, storage is wasteful. However, we use it because business is incapable of (1) scheduling production to exactly meet consumer buying schedules and (2) accurately projecting consumer demand at all times. Accordingly, we must have an inventory policy that is related to consumer demand. This, in turn, implies that the goods must move at a controlled rate toward ultimate use. Further, the presence of a "depot" or warehouse facilitates the sorting process.

Objective: Improve service to middlemen

The *sorting concept* was also enunciated by Wroe Alderson and is an application of the transvection concept. He said that the basic function of marketing is sorting.[3] It includes four processes:

1. *Sorting out* involves grading or inspection of a heterogeneous supply into separate lots.
2. *Accumulation* or *concentration* is the bringing together of large stocks of similar products.
3. *Allocation* or breaking bulk breaks down the large stocks into smaller ones.
4. *Assorting* is the building of assortments and is the final step in taking products off the market. The other three aspects are signifiant because of their contribution in the final building of assortments.

In the late 1950s, General Foods revamped its distribution pattern using a program parallel to this one. One of the program developers, John Crossen, had this to say:

> The new market-centered distribution system . . . has come about because of a realization that the entire process of moving foods from farm to table is not a series of separate and distinct segments called growing, processing, selling and shipping, but a tightly-integrated effort. . . . ·

✿ ✿ ✿ ✿ ✿

---

[3] Ibid., p. 34.

We would not recommend this system if it made for economy but impaired service; we would still recommend it if our estimates indicated increased costs—within reasonable limits—accompanied by the improved service implied in the model as it stands.[4]

Objective: Maximize efficiency

Postponement is an operational approach to the theory of sorting. Alderson felt that costs could be reduced by postponing changes in form, identity, and location of inventory to the last possible moment. His reasoning was that sorting in large lots is the most efficient way; the closer the product moves to the user, the more differentiated it becomes; and the greater the differentiation, the higher the risks of buying and stocking.

Louis Bucklin gave an explanation of why, in many cases, the changes Alderson spoke of being postponed to the latest point were actually made at the earliest time. Of course, this is the reverse of postponement. Bucklin's thinking is that costs are reduced by making changes while quantities are still large.

Other objectives

The above objectives have theories and operational objectives. These may be refined even further. Crossen identified some of these refinements in the context of the General Foods pilot program. His company saw one set of objectives for its customers and another set for the company. The objectives for the customers were:

Individualized service.

Improved order taking and delivery procedures.

Better information on order status, shipments, and sales.

Lower inventory investment with greater turn and reduced warehouse space.

The objectives for the company were:

Improved customer goodwill.

Better communication among sales, warehousing, accounting, and order processing.

Better inventory management

---

[4] John E. Crossen, "Scientific Approach to Physical Distribution—A Market-Centered Service System" in, R. Clifton Anderson and William P. Dommermuth, eds., *Distribution Systems—Firms, Functions, and Efficiencies* (New York: Appleton-Century-Crofts, 1972), pp. 204 and 207.

Reduced costs of transportation, handling, and sales.

A revised price structure recognizing the now-known costs.[5]

Now, moving from the objective foundation in the channel, we examine the relationships between channel management and marketing satisfactions. The reader should review (1) the discussion of the hierarchy of satisfactions in Chapter 3; (2) the satisfaction process and the concept of consumer and corporate satisfaction in Chapter 6; and (3) Chapter 8 which relates consumer behavior and the marketing function. In reviewing and reflecting on these things, remember that while the focus of the discussion is on the ultimate consumer, each middleman, as a customer of someone else, is also a consumer.

Having looked at some objectives of channel management, we now come to the second part of this chapter; to relate these objectives to the satisfaction process.

CHANNEL MANAGEMENT AND MARKETING SATISFACTIONS

Product and patronage satisfactions

Remember, we are not concerning ourselves with the management of retail and wholesale institutions directly; we are concerned with them as institutions which are elements of the channels of distribution. Another fact to remember is that, up to a point, the middleman and the manufacturer have one thing in common: they both are interested in customer satisfaction. However, there is a difference. Customer satisfaction to the manufacturer means satisfaction with the product and service before and after the sale. The retailer, on the other hand, is probably more concerned with seeing that the customer as a customer *of the store* is satisfied than in seeing the customer satisfied as a customer *of the product.* To the retailer, store satisfaction (or patronage satisfaction) is more important than product satisfaction. If the product fails, the store may replace it and retain a satisfied customer of the store while the manufacturer loses a customer of the product. The retailer may be in position to switch brands. The same things apply to the wholesaler in his relations with the retailer.

Patronage satisfaction is very important to the producer also, and it enters into his consideration in setting up channels. Regardless of how diligent the producer may be in looking to before-and-after sales service, the retailer is the immediate contact with the user of the product, and the wholesaler is the immediate contact with the retailer. Accordingly, a customer who cannot get satisfaction from a retailer (or a retailer

---

[5] Ibid., pp. 207–8.

from a wholesaler) is likely to be dissatisfied with the product. To this extent, there is a "loose connection" in the channel, and "patronage satisfaction" may point the way toward a better linkage of the processes.

Variables in the satisfaction process

In selecting the retailing and wholesaling components of the channel the manufacturer must keep in mind that there are now three customers to satisfy: the ultimate user, the retailer, and the wholesaler. Since the manufacturer must also be satisfied, there are four groups in the channel—which makes for an extremely complex program of satisfaction. The consumer's satisfaction may be considered a variable which is dependent upon *six* independent variables. The concepts of (1) form, (2) time, and (3) place utility make up three of the variables, while the institutions of (4) retailing, (5) wholesaling, and (6) manufacturing make up the others. The retailer, wholesaler, and manufacturer each have a similar satisfaction network. Thus, the total channel satisfaction network consists of four dependent variables and 28 independent variables.

The dependent variables are:
1. Customer satisfaction.
2. Retailer satisfaction.
3. Wholesaler satisfaction.
4. Manufacturer satisfaction.

The independent variables for each of the dependent variables are:
Concepts:
1. Form utility
2. Time utility
3. Place utility

Institutions:
4. The customer
5. The retailer
6. The wholesaler
7. The manufacturer

Figure 13–1 is a diagram of the network of channel satisfactions showing the dependent and independent variables. We do not include transportation and warehousing companies. In addition, we consider form utility to be everything associated with the product: usefulness, design, service, and so on. Let us now examine these independent variables from the standpoint of the responsible party for delivering satisfaction. Remember one outstanding fact of human behavior: if we think

FIGURE 13–1
A Network of Channel Satisfactions (manufacturer, wholesaler, retailer, customer)

Dependent variable	Independent variables	Responsibility for delivering satisfaction

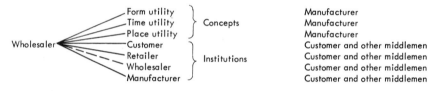

1. Customer will be satisfied if all other things satisfy him.

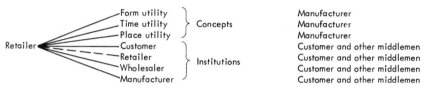

2. Retailer will be satisfied if all other things satisfy him.

3. Wholesaler will be satisfied if all other things satisfy him.

4. Manufacturer will be satisfied if all other things satisfy him.

* Form utility is used here to include everything associated with the product as an element of the marketing mix.

something is true, it may as well be true so far as we as holders of the opinion are concerned.

Form utility is the responsibility of the manufacturer. We show it as a joint responsibility of the middlemen and the manufacturer for two reasons. If a consumer tries to buy clothing of a given size, color, or fabric, and it is not available, the purchaser's question to the retailer is likely to be, "Why don't you make clothes like that?" To this extent the middleman bears a burden that does not belong to it, because it cannot *control* what the manufacturer makes. However, it can *influence* the manufacturer's decision. Also, it can switch suppliers. Second, for various reasons the middleman may not stock the item for reasons of its own or because the manufacturer may not be willing.

The consumer, who is only vaguely aware of the wholesaler, holds both retailer and manufacturer responsible for form utility (the nature of the product). The retailer holds the manufacturer responsible, a responsibility the manufacturer accepts. However, one of the functions of the retailer and wholesaler is to assist the manufacture in this process. Some large middlemen may even specify the characteristics of the product. Again, the customer holds the retailer responsible for time and place utilities. The fact that the canner didn't ship the peas or that the warehouse they were in burned, or the truck delivering them overturned, is irrelevant. They were not there when and where the buyer wanted them; so the retailer is held responsible. The retailer often with a similar perspective, turns to the wholesaler.

In a rather complicated way, the middlemen and the manufacturer hold the manufacturer responsible. Here we get into some special situations. A retailer who runs out today and has not placed an order can hardly hold the manufacturer responsible, but may try to do so. When we show the manufacturer as the responsible party, we imply that a timely order has been placed but not properly filled. Also, we have implicitly placed the burden of holding inventory and inventory management on the manufacturer. Perhaps that is partially where it belongs. If the manufacturer has been working with channel members properly, it has *tried* to help them develop economic inventory management programs.

The *customer, retailer, wholesaler,* and *manufacturer* are also independent variables. Remember the relationships that exist among these four:

1. The *customer* is served by three suppliers: the retailer directly and the wholesaler and manufacturer because they serve the retailer. Thus (1) to get satisfaction from the retailer, the customer looks to both retailer and manufacturer, and (2) to get satisfaction from the manufacturer, looks to both. Mostly, the customer has no real knowledge of the existence of the wholesaler.
2. The *retailer* serves a customer and is a customer. Thus, the retailer wears two hats. Accordingly, the customer, wholesaler, and manufacturer are responsible for delivery of satisfaction to the retailer as they buy from and sell to the retailer.
3. The *wholesaler* also serves one customer (the retailer) and is a customer of the manufacturer. Accordingly, all institutions are re-

sponsible for the wholesaler's satisfaction; the customer less so than the others.

4. The *manufacturer* depends upon three customers for satisfaction: the ultimate customer (user), the retailer, and the wholesaler.

While there are 28 dependent variables upon which the three dependent variables depend, there are actually only 24 which have to be considered. In Figure 13–1 we have shown certain relationships with a dash line. For example, the Customer-Customer, Retailer-Retailer, Wholesaler-Wholesaler, and Manufacturer-Manufacturer relationships will each be satisfied as the other six relationships fall into place. This complex maze or network of relationships is incomplete, as stated at the outset. Had we put the facilitating agencies in the network the relationships would have become more complex.

We can now turn in the third part of the chapter to examine some operational aspects of the retailing and wholesaling components of the channels.

THE RETAILING SYSTEM

In this brief introduction we call the reader's attention to two things. First, as a result of our focus on retailing and wholesaling as institutions we do not analyze their operations to any appreciable extent. For the most part, we merely identify the types and methods of retail operations to help the reader develop a feeling for the types of institutions in the channel.

Second, even though the topic heading of this section is "The Retailing System" we show the role of the wholesaling system in serving retailers. For this reason, when we move to the topic headed "The Wholesaling System" we will already have discussed its role. Accordingly, except for a brief introduction which relates wholesaling to the system, that section consists of an outline of the characteristics and types of wholesalers. We offer this preview so that in studying the retailer, the reader will relate the wholesaler's role to it.

Retail operations

One of the objectives we discussed earlier in this chapter was to improve service to middlemen. The sorting concept and one of its aspects, *assorting*, was discussed. Remember, assorting is the bringing together of different products for wholesalers and retailers. Recall any retail store you have been in recently, and you will see the implications of the process and what it means. The retailer is able to handle a few of several hundred—or several thousand—items for sale to the ultimate consumer. These are two factors which set retailing apart from other channel segments: (1) an assortment of goods (2) for their ultimate consumers.

Types of retail operations. Door-to-door. To the total marketing structure this type of operation is not very important. Almost everyone has had some experience with this type of marketing—if not with the Avon representative, then with the Fuller brush distributor, or the magazine seller.

How can they exist? For one reason, there is enough of an apparent gap in the channel structure that a large market segment is not being served by other institutions. For another reason, while the total cost to all participants in the process may appear to be very high, the actual cost is kept within bounds by the method of operation. The actual salespeople are paid a commission on what they sell; they generally have no inventory; they operate from their homes. In other words the costs to the firm are variable for there is little or no selling overhead. The salespeople's earnings are directly related to the time worked. Whether the compensation is sufficient reward for effort is a question for them to resolve; their hourly compensation may be so low that they are underemployed. If they do indeed represent an underuse of labor resources, then the cost to society may be high.

Single-line stores. These are stores that specialize: groceries, sporting goods, motorcycles, clothing, and the like. Within this group, there are the limited-line stores which may handle a limited assortment of the goods. For example, the grocery store may limit itself as the neighborhood convenience store has; the golfers' supplies at the pro shop at the golf course may be very incomplete when compared with those at the sporting goods store. Single-line stores have an advantage over others in that they can adjust to specific markets by their marketing mix. They may become drop-in types of stores open all the time for certain food lines. Or they may become specialty stores by virtue of wide and/or deep product assortments. Of course, the latter situation may be a handicap in that they may have to handle a large number of slow-moving items at a high inventory cost. On the other hand, some, such as convenience food stores, make no attempt to handle everything. If an item is a slow mover, they may drop it.

Specialty shops. These are usually small shops that cater to a fairly select segment of the market. They ordinarily handle special types of shopping goods: king-size clothes, high-fashion dresses, high quality clothing, and the like. Usually, they have relatively few customers whose tastes are known to the owners and sales people; so buying mistakes are limited.

Department stores. The department store is a collection of limited line and specialty shops housed in one building and under one ownership, although it may have leased departments. Departments may range from artists' works to zoological supplies. Typically they include home furnishings, household gadgets, clothing, fabrics, and hardware. Their market is typically people seeking shopping goods. Some departments, such as jewelry, furs, and shoes, are leased to outside firms when the management lacks expertise in buying or selling, or when it doesn't want managerial headaches associated with the department.

Vending machines. There are millions of vending machines, handling practically everything that can be put in a slot.

Catalogue sales. The most widely known stores of this kind are Sears, and Wards, although there are many others. One can now order from a catalogue available in the seat-pocket of an airliner. Catalogue stores sell many things, including cheeses; soaps; smoked meats; and household thing-a-ma-jigs. Many large mail order houses have assortments comparable to any department stores. Others are highly specialized. To be able to exist, these stores must put customer satisfaction at the highest level in their objectives. Since a customer may order from a picture or description, the merchandise must be returnable.

Variety stores. These are the outgrowth of the old "dime store." Even today many refer to them as "dime" or five-and-ten-cent stores. They typically handle a wide variety of relatively inexpensive goods and provide a minimum amount of service. The lines have outgrown those of their predecessor ten-cent store forebears for they now handle such things as automotive supplies, garden tools and supplies, clothing, and fabric lines.

Methods of operation. *Full-service operations.* Retailers offer a wide variety of services. A customer may be waited on by counter salespeople, have the purchases charged and delivered, or arrange for special orders or special showings of merchandise. Naturally these extra services are costly, and of course the cost finds its way into price. Several things have contributed to the decline of the full-service retailer including the rise of the discount house. Chains in the grocery field have had their impact. In addition, increased cost consciousness (leading to the use of effort analysis to detect uneconomic operations) and the continuing cost-price squeeze have contributed to the decline of many of these services.

Supermarkets. These large grocery retailing stores really began in the 1930s. Their basic marketing appeal is a large assortment of goods at a low price. Self-service is an operating characteristic. Most food sales today are made by supermarkets. Other retailers have taken cues from the grocery field and opened their own supermarkets. Some are found in the home-care centers which deal in lumber, hardware, tools, and the like. Also there are supermarket-type drug stores. The contemporary variety store is a supermarket version of the old dime store and is sometimes called a junior department store.

Discount houses. This type of institution emerged after World War II, and is probably one of the most profound developments in retailing. While discount houses of sorts have always existed, they were smaller. It is difficult to say whether the present discount house is a new type of institution or an old institution with a new marketing approach. The latter is the more likely alternative. The founders discovered marketing opportunities that existed because the marketing services other retailers offered were either not wanted or not needed by a large segment of the market: personal salesmanship in the stores, credit, delivery, and so on. A second explanation is related to the first. The new discounters could be satisfied with a lower markup than the traditional ones. By combining low markups with few services, a new breed of retailer was able to fill a very large marketing gap.

Franchise arrangements. The major things the franchiser provides are an idea, an approach to its exploitation, management expertise, and a marketing program. The franchiser may also provide equipment and/or products. The franchisee usually gets a market territory and agrees to follow the operating and marketing practices of the franchiser. There are two main types of franchising systems. One is a voluntary association of retailers and/or wholesalers, known as a voluntary chain. The other is a retailer network sponsored by a manufacturer.

The *voluntary food chain* was the answer of independent retailers and wholesalers to the threat of chain stores. Wholesalers, to assure their own continued existence, wanted to assure the continued existence of their customers. By voluntarily banding together, each helped preserve the other. The buying power of each independent is concentrated through the wholesaler. Thus, independents can act like chains with huge buying power and management expertise in operations and marketing provided by the wholesaler. A second type of voluntary chain is a *retailer cooperative chain.* In this case, the retailers form a wholesale organization to serve them. The second type of franchising system is the *manufacturer-sponsored group,* such as Holiday Inns, Colonel Sanders Fried Chicken, McDonald's.

These franchising systems are attempts to coordinate channel components or create vertical marketing systems. This is done on a *contractual* basis as distinct from (1) the coordination on an administered basis by one member of the channel or (2) on a planned basis by corporate ownership. McCammon reports that the most comprehensive forms of contractual systems account for 35 to 40 percent of total retail sales.[6] He adds that this is an incomplete figure since it does not include sales of retailers "belonging to other programmed groups, procuring

---

[6] Bert C. McCammon, Jr., "Perspectives for Distribution Programming," in Louis P. Bucklin, ed., *Vertical Marketing Systems* (Glenview, Ill.: Scott, Foresman and Company, 1970), p. 46.

merchandise on a contractual basis or participating in programs sponsored by resident buying offices."[7]

Location of retail operations. Retail stores have traditionally located in relation to their markets. The downtown locations were established because they were considered to be central to customer locations. Neighborhood locations were used by those entrepreneurs who were seeking to tap the relatively small neighborhood market. Sometimes as one store after another located in a neighborhood, a small shopping district would develop, usually as a "strip" of stores. Since the 1950s, however, new "downtowns" have been created by real estate developers and others. These planned shopping centers have typically been built around a large department store which serves as a magnet for shoppers. Like almost everything else, shopping centers have been classified.

Regional shopping centers are the largest of the three categories. They are really new "downtowns" and are so large that they must draw on a population concentration of a minimum of 150,000 people located in a radius of a half dozen miles or so.[8] Such a center will include at least one large department store—sometimes more—and perhaps dozens of smaller stores. In one center built in the early 1950s—Northgate in Seattle—a person could be born in the hospital at Northgate, visit the doctor there, arrange for the future with the mortician, and trade with the usual types of stores, including those that sold only nuts and those that sold only candy.

Community shopping centers are somewhat smaller than the regional centers but still comparable to many downtowns of smaller cities. To survive, the experts say that these centers must have a population of 40,000 to 150,000 within a three- to four-mile radius of the center. These usually have department, variety, and grocery stores among many other types.

Neighborhood shopping centers serve the population within a few minutes' driving time. These usually have a grocery store, drug store, variety store, and miscellaneous "service type" stores such as barber and beauty shops, laundry facilities, and the like.

The wholesaling system

Introduction. We stated previously that the role of the wholesaler in the retail system would be discussed along with the retail system. We also said that this section would be presented mostly in outline form.

---

[7] Ibid.

[8] E. Jerome McCarthy, *Basic Marketing*, 5th ed. (Homewood, Ill.: Richard D. Irwin, Inc., 1975), p. 328. McCarthy is our source for population concentrations required for other types of shopping centers.

We analyzed one of the objectives of the channel system—to improve service to middlemen—in light of Wroe Alderson's sorting concept and the modifications of that concept by Bucklin and others. Our discussion of retailing centered on the fourth feature of that concept: assorting, or the bringing together of different products for the wholesaler or retailer. The retailer, in our discussion was the recipient of the assortment. The wholesaling system, which is outlined below, also performs the other three functions leading to assorting. Those functions are:

1. *Sorting* out a heterogeneous supply into separate lots
2. *Accumulating* or concentrating large stocks of different products
3. *Allocating* (breaking bulk) large stocks to smaller ones.

Agent middlemen

Characteristics:
1. Do not take title; often do not take possession.
2. Serve in lieu of sales force.
3. Sell to other middlemen.
4. Serve small manufacturers mostly; may serve large ones in peripheral areas or until a sales force is economically justified.
5. Help find markets.

Types of agent middlemen:
1. Brokers
    a. May represent buyer or seller.
    b. Serve many principals but may not have a continuous relationship with any.
    c. Find buyer, send order to be delivered direct.
    d. Serve on commission basis.
2. Manufacturers' Agents
    a. Usually represent principals on a continuing basis.
    b. Do not handle competing lines.
    c. Several may represent the same firm in different areas.
    d. Serve on commission basis.
3. Sales Agents
    a. Often perform entire marketing function of the firm.
    b. Differ from manufacturers' agents:
        1. May specify products to be made.
        2. Sell all of the output.
        3. Have considerable latitude in pricing.

Wholesalers

Characteristics:
1. Ordinarily take title to goods.
2. Buy in large quantities, sell in small.

Types:
1. Full Service
    a. Offer complete line in areas of specialty.
    b. May provide financing, market information, marketing advice.
2. Limited Service
    a. Handle limited line.
    b. Cash and carry.

Size and efficiency: Channel implications

Effectiveness and efficiency. Effectiveness and efficiency are not the same thing. We have emphasized this point many times in this book, and will do so several more times. Nor does the size of an organization necessarily have anything to do with whether it is effective and efficient. A small retailer may be just as effective in his operation as a large one because of the framework of objectives each has. Effectiveness is the degree to which objectives are attained.

Efficiency is a measure of how well resources are used to yield a certain result. We recognize that the way in which we use the word "efficient" has certain overtones of effectiveness implied. With that in mind we can say that the large retailers have certain competitive advantages over the small ones and that they are capable of being more efficient. The competitive advantages and potential for greater efficiency stem from their greater command of financial resources, on the one hand, and their size on the other. In the final analysis, both generally boil down to the same thing. Why do they have a competitive advantage?

Management. The manager of a small company may have to buy merchandise for the entire operation, negotiate with a number of manufacturers, wholesalers, or retailers, and develop the advertising program—in addition to manning the cash register, supervising employees, and so on. The manager of the middlesized company may have a few executives to share these managerial burdens, one in charge of buying, another in charge of selling, and so on.

The division of labor may be complete in the very large operation with a buyer in charge of each major product group, someone in charge of negotiations with others in the channel, and someone in charge of real estate management. Each of these executives may become expert in a particular field, including market analysis and product selection. The small company manager must be content with being a jack-of-all-trades.

Purchasing. Clearly, there is an advantage in buying for a very large operation or for dozens of branches.

Other elements of the marketing mix. The large middleman may design its own *product* and either manufacture it or have it manufactured. The large middleman may integrate the *channels of distribution* by performing the wholesaling, warehousing, transportation, and retailing functions to reduce costs and/or to increase control of service. Also, it may have an advantage in *promotion* over smaller competitors. Since the company may have several outlets in the area served by radio, television, and newspapers, it can afford to use large-area methods of promotion more easily than the small or one-outlet manager. In addition, many manufacturers have promotion allowances or cooperative advertising programs that the large retailer or wholesaler can use more effectively. Finally, all of these economies make it possible for the large company to have lower *prices*. However, its prices are not always lower than those of the small company. The latter may sacrifice some profit to be competitive.

Financial resources. It does not necessarily follow that a large company is fiancially stronger relative to its needs than a small one, but it seems to work out that way often. With a stronger financial base—and certainly a larger one—the large company has more flexibility to experiment with new lines or new marketing programs. With strong financial backup, a failure in a given line that would be a disaster for a small retail company may be only a nuisance for a large one. In fact, the large company may even budget funds for experimentation and possible loss.

Channel implications. All in all it appears that the large middleman generally has advantages over the small one. At the same time, its overhead costs are typically higher because of the specialization of management. It may very well be that small stores are more efficient in terms of revenue per man-hour or in terms of profit as a percent of sales. The large outlet can make a smaller net profit per sales dollar than the small one and still bring in substantial amounts or dollars for its owners.

We have discussed the implications of size on channels elsewhere; a simple listing of some will suffice here.

1. Large stores may be able to control channels.
2. They may integrate backward to the product to increase efficiency.
3. They may make better buys because they are better customers.
4. Their size and control over channels may cause them to misuse their power.
5. By being so powerful in the channel, they may inhibit innovations of newcomers by keeping newcomers out.

Having looked at some aspects of retail and wholesale operations we now turn, in the fourth and final part of this chapter, to examine some of the types of channel decisions managers must make.

TYPES OF CHANNEL DECISIONS

One series of channel decisions to be made has a certain amount of obvious logic. These decisions involve channel selection and are fairly sequential in nature. First, should the company sell direct to customers, indirectly through a middleman, or both? Second, when that problem is resolved, the selection of the appropriate channel components must be made. Third, the number of components to be used must be determined. Fourth, the possibility of using multiple channels should be considered.

Sell direct or use a middleman

The decision to use a middleman or bypass him completely is a typical "Make or Buy" decision. About the only generalization that can be made on this subject is that the manager does what is most rewarding for the company and its customers. We can stratify the problem, however, and look at some situations from which generalizations may be made.

First, we should recognize that the decision is not really a one-or-the-other decision; it is a matter of fitting the decision to the environment, and there may be several environments surrounding one product. Second, we should recognize that the decision may not even be planned as a permanent one. Let us look at the functions of the channels and the environments. Remember that one of the functions of the wholesaler is to buy in large quantities and sell in smaller ones. Also, remember that there are several segments of a market for the same product. One of these segments may buy the commodity in units of one while another may buy in quantities larger than those most wholesalers purchase. One of these markets may be served indirectly through middlemen; the other directly from the manufacturer.

This problem has another dimension, however: conflict with middlemen. The large customer is the least costly to serve, so the wholesaler may rightly complain if the manufacturer handles the best and leaves only the high-cost customers to it. This conflict is sometimes resolved by paying the distributor a commission on all sales in the territory even though some customers are handled as "house accounts." Another environmental situation calling for use of both approaches may be identified. One market area may justify the use of company salesmen and the direct marketing approach. Another area may be so small that it is uneconomic to market except through middlemen. Timing is the second decision factor mentioned. A manufacturer may use middlemen until sales in the area—or of the product line—justify the use of its own sales force.

The above comments are made from the manufacturer's point of view.

We should not forget that the retailer too is a customer and is served by the channel. If it has the power in the channel to be able to choose, it may decide to buy some of its products directly from the manufacturer and some indirectly through brokers or wholesalers. Again, the factors upon which the decision turns are the self-interest of the retailer and the willingness to absorb some of the functions of middlemen.

The retailer may want to buy certain types of hand tools through a hardware wholesaler because it wants the assortment function performed for it. Yet, it may prefer to buy other tools direct. Or, the retailer may not be willing to buy, put the merchandise on the shelves, replenish stock, or do anything but make shelf or floor space available and run the product through the checkout stand. In this case a rack jobber takes care of all the other activities, and the retailer is paid the equivalent of a commission. Resolving the question of whether to buy directly or indirectly does not require an either-or decision. Rather, the decision turns on when and under what conditions to use the direct approach and when and under what conditions to use the indirect approach. Also, it is not a problem exclusive to the manufacturer; the wholesaler and retailer have similar decisions to make.

Selection of channel components

Let us return to the manufacturer's point of view. Remember, if the maker doesn't give total satisfaction to the consumer, a customer may be lost. Yet, unless the maker markets direct to the ultimate user, the only thing it has *complete* control over is the product itself. Who would you turn to first if your hair dryer stopped working the week after you bought it? Or if your coat came apart at the seams on the second wearing? The retailer is the obvious first stop. Unless you are persistent you may not go to the manufacturer at all—just cuss the product and switch brands, or even stop trading with a particular store.

In this sense, the selection of a reliable channel component is almost as important as the selection of the product itself. But this is only one aspect of the selection decision. So far we have implied that "a retailer is a retailer." This is not so. Let's take a commodity and look at where it is sold. Think of places you have seen water skis or tennis racquets sold: your drug stores, discount houses, department stores, hardware stores, sporting goods stores, bait shops, marinas, boat dealerships, variety stores, auto supply stores—is one of these retailers the same as any other? The selection decision has many facets to be taken into account.

The foundation of the selection process is to determine what objective the manufacturer has in mind: the target market which will best serve his ends. The obvious starting point is to look to the ultimate user's buying preferences. The usual questions of size of market and its geographic location, where customers like to buy, and their buying habits, need to be answered. Once this is determined for the product, the types of retailers to be used may be identified.

These several types of retailers as purchasers may have their own buying habits and preferences. By matching the buying characteristics and preferences of consumers and retailers with the marketing aspirations of the manufacturer, the selection variables are narrowed. An example will clarify this point. Suppose an auto supply store is a likely candidate for handling skis or tennis racquets. Also suppose that the store's wholesalers are not interested in handling the items, while those who do handle them are not interested in serving an auto supply store. This failure to match eliminates auto supply stores, or it calls for a different kind of channel decision. Perhaps direct marketing is the answer. Another facet of the component selection decision is the need to define the necessary return to the manufacturer. Or, what does the manufacturer want from a channel component? Service? Promotion? Exposure?

In recapitulation, the channel selection decision will have several elements, all built on the manufacturer's objectives: (1) Determine who the user is, where he buys, and what his wants are. (2) Do the same thing for middlemen who buy for resale. (3) Match up these characteristics with the manufacturer's desires.

Selective or intensive channels

This is not a particularly hard decision to make once the company objectives and marketing plan are worked out. There are two basic factors to consider. Does the company want *selective* distribution, or does it want *intensive* distribution? If it wants selective distribution, it has two decision alternatives: will it establish exclusive dealerships *or* few dealerships? If it wants intensive distribution, the problem is easily handled by letting any responsible dealer handle it if the manufacturer can make a profit. These channel decisions almost fall into place after other marketing questions are answered outside the channel decision framework.

Multiple channels

We have already dealt with this question in part. In our discussion of direct or indirect channels we referred to large and small purchasers. The situation discussed there was that involving competitive multiple channels. There are also complementary multiple channels where channel competition does not enter into the situation. Complementary channel decisions arise when a company produces multiple products to unrelated market segments. Such a complementary multiple channel exists when a salt company markets table salt through one channel and salt for ice removal on roads through another. These complementary multiple channels pose no real problems. The competitive multiple channel system, however, is a headache producer. Formerly one went to the grocery store to buy certain things and to the drug store to buy others. Now almost everything the druggist sells—other than prescriptions—is also handled by the grocer and/or the discount house. Some grocery stores even have prescription pharmacies in-house. Drug stores in turn have begun to stock other things: children's toys, hardware items, decorator objects for homes, and in some cases, major appliances.

This is one of the characterisitcs of *scrambled merchandising*, which is increasingly prevalent. Shoppers formerly went to the fish market for fish, the department store for hose, the hardware store for tools, the electrician's shop for an extension cord, the ice house for ice. Now they go to the grocery store for all of them. Or to the ten-cent store, drug store, or electrician's shop for everything but fish. Or maybe even for that!

Other decision areas

Other decision areas involved in channel management we will only list. They relate to managerial factors, such as:

1. Management of channel components.
2. Investment in channel developments.
3. Internal organization of the company to manage the channel system.

CONCLUSION

The product or service purchased by the ultimate consumer is superficially the thing from which the consumer derives satisfaction. We say "superficially" because we are dealing with only one part of the satisfaction delivery system: form utility. The other elements of that delivery system, time and place utility, are provided by the channels. Since the function of the channel system is to support the marketing effort of the firm, it is easy to see why our emphasis has been on channel functions. However, without appropriate relationships among the channel components, the channel function cannot be effectively performed. So again it is easy to see why our focus has been on structure of the channel system.

Note that the first part of this chapter was devoted to objectives designed to improve the functioning of the system. Also, note that the last part was devoted to types of decisions related to the use of the structure. One of the bridges we built between function and the use of the structure was the relation to satisfaction of all the institutions in the channel—including the consumer. The other was the environment of the middlemen, the structure itself.

We saw how some companies have resorted to corporate or contractual vertical marketing systems to try to improve the function by changing the structure. The third approach to improving functioning is through administrative systems whereby independent companies continue to exist, but more or less act in unison—or act as if they were a system instead of a collection of parts.

We think the latter approach is a very desirable objective. If for no other reason, it will preserve the independence of independents. However, for this structure to prevail, all of the would-be survivors will have to adopt the marketing concept, adapt to the realities of the interrelationships of the network of satisfactions portrayed in Figure 13–1, and accept the fact of life that the components are means to the end—not ends—of supporting the marketing system.

In short, the present structure of the channel system as represented by the nonaffiliated independents precludes performing the function effectively and efficiently. Therefore, structure will have to change if independents are to survive, for the function is unlikely to change. But, the function will be fulfilled by corporate or contractual changes in the structure.

chapter 14 | # Logistics strategies and policies

Environmental conditions affecting logistics management
    First-order conditions
    Second- and third-order conditions
    Fourth-order conditions
    Other strategic considerations
Relation of logistics to marketing
    Some aspects of customer service
    Small firms
Some problem-causing characteristics
    Nature of logistics problems
    "Natural" problems
    Conceptual problems
        Introduction
        The traffic management concept
        The transportation concept
        The total logistics concept
        The profit maximization concept
        Customer service
        Physical and temporal proximity
        Economic proximity
        Relations with carriers
        Summary of conceptual problems
    Organizational Problems
Conclusion

Among the terms used to describe the concept and function of logistics are physical supply and distribution management, business logistics, and materials management. Since all are generally accepted and used almost interchangeably, we use logistics both because of the inclusiveness of the term and because of the length of time it has been around. The dictionary defines the word as the branch of military science having to do with the moving, supplying, and quartering of troops. Using that definition as a point of departure, we can say that business logistics is the branch of management having to do with moving, supplying, and warehousing goods, and serving customers. We consider that logistics begins with the raw materials and ends with the final disposition of the junked product.

Some of the major components of logistics are transportation, warehousing, management of inventory, and the location of production and distribution points. Other components include such things as order processing, materials handling, packaging, and market forecasting. Also, some writers include production planning as a component of logistics.

A simple definition of logistics management is that it is the management of the logistics function. Even though that is a nice definition, it does not tell us a great deal about what logistics managers do or should do. In Chapter 3, we expressed the same thought about management in general and set forth a definition for that broad concept. We have a parallel definition of logistics management, which provides a framework useful in differentiating among the activities of distribution managers.

> Logistics management is both the analysis and rationalization of all functions, components, and activities of materials and information management for the dual purpose of (1) strategic planning, including setting of objectives, and (2) for the efficient management of physical distribution resources to achieve those objectives effectively.[1]

This definition separates the activities of the logistics manager into two substantially different categories: planning at both the corporate and functional level, and implementation at the functional level. The development of logistics strategies and policies within the framework of corporate and marketing strategies and policies is the subject of this chapter.

In Chapters 12 and 13 we stated that the function of the channels of distribution is to support the marketing effort of the firm. As one of the components of the channel system, logistics has the same marketing support function. We make this point again in a logistics context because too often managers of transportation and warehousing elements of the logistics system do not have this view. Too many manage their companies as if transportation and warehousing were ends unto themselves. Our view is that they are means to an end, and that end is to support the marketing effort of the firm.

ENVIRONMENTAL CONDITIONS AFFECTING LOGISTICS MANAGEMENT

Each of the functional managers examines and analyzes the environment of the firm from a different point of view. The marketing manager

---

[1] James A. Constantin, "Traffic and Distribution Management in the Hierarchical Structure," *International Journal of Physical Distribution Management,* June 1971, p. 122.

searches it for problems and opportunities from a marketing point of view, and is to be forgiven if he, in effect, draws *tentative* inferences from his analysis, makes *tentative* plans, and reaches *tentative* conclusions—"other things remaining the same." For example, he may see an apparent opportunity to capture a large share of the present market by adding a new item to the product line and improving delivery time to customers. A great deal of analysis and some "other things remaining the same" assumptions must be made to determine if the opportunity is more apparent than real. He will start by assuming that funds for product development will be available, that production resources are available, that delivery schedules can be met, and that marketing efforts will be successful. As the analytical process unfolds, each of the appropriate functional areas examines those "other things" and provides the results which are fed into the tentative analyses resulting in revised tentative inferences, plans, and conclusions. The process is repeated until some firm decision is made.

In the early 1970s Union Carbide began implementing a program[2] which illustrates several things with which we are concerned:

The value of planning to discover potential problems and opportunities

The development of programs either to adapt the external (first-order) environment or to adapt to it

The development of programs affecting the internal (second-order) environment

The trade-offs between logistics and marketing

The development of programs affecting the environment of the logistics system (fourth-order conditions).

First-order conditions

These are conditions which are completely external to the firm and in the logistics context refer to such aspects of the environment as transportation rates and services, warehousing policies, work rules, and government policies.

To illustrate some of these first-order conditions we refer again to Union Carbide. Prices had been barely holding their own or falling for several years, while costs were rising. Transport rates were up 56 percent since 1963 with most of the increase coming in 1970 and 1971. The company logistics analysts expected national transport rates to rise at the rate of 10 percent per year, at least through the mid-1970s. Transportation costs alone accounted for 13 percent of the sales dollar. In five years they expected the figure to be 20 percent of expanded

---

[2] "The Basic Problem: Skyrocketing Rates," *Purchasing Week*, October 25, 1971, pp. 17, 18.

revenue. Other logistics costs, such as warehousing and order filling, were rising at almost the same rate.

Second- and third-order conditions

We identified these as conditions internal to the firm where action taken in one area would have an impact on another functional area. Continuing with our illustration, Union Carbide logistics, marketing, and other managers studied and changed some logistics policies which affected the other departments. One of the changes involved customer service and therefore had an impact upon the marketing program. In order to improve efficiency in use of tank trucks, the volume of product required for a price discount was raised to 40,000 pounds. The potential effect on customers was noted, and even though it was anticipated that some customers would be lost, the program was implemented.

This is the type of thing we refer to as cost management, as distinct from cost reduction. The effect of such a decision may reduce sales, but company profits are increased. In our illustration the company lost about $125,000 in sales, but transport savings were estimated to be about $500,000. (We add parenthetically to provide a good ending to this part of the story that the marketing department later regained most of the lost customers.)

Another logistics policy was established after discussions with the marketing manager because of its impact on customer service. It involved the requirement that customers release company trucks and rail cars more quickly than formerly. Some companies could not adapt to this change, which was external to them. The first quarter after the detention policy was inaugurated, the company lost $140,000 in sales. Annual savings to Union Carbide were estimated to be about $1,000,000.

Fourth-order conditions

These are the environmental conditions existing almost wholly within one functional area. Adaptations of them or to them will have little effect upon operations of other departments except that things may go more smoothly. In dealing with them the functional area is concerned with improving its efficiency and effectiveness. The planning underlying the decisions may be strategic. On the other hand, management control or operational control may be involved.

As a strategic measure, to again apply the illustration to our concept, the company decided to establish a series of regional traffic groups. While the objective was to improve logistics efficiency, it involved additional manpower resources. Also, its impact on other departments is designed to make things work better. Nevertheless, the company anticipated savings of $2 to 3 million per year. Presumably, customer service will be improved in this case, as distinct from the negative effects previously cited. Since we are more concerned here with development of logistics strategies and policies, we need not discuss other matters related to logistics management as such—improved routing of trucks, improved vehicle selection policies, and so on.

Other strategic considerations

The analysis of the environments may disclose a number of strategic alternatives. For example, Union Carbide had a number of other things in mind, some of which fit neatly into one of the categories, some of which do not.

For example, the company had in mind, and in some stage of development, plans for

Improvement of a systems and logistics capability

Strengthening its organization

Capital planning

Support of a research and development program within distribution

Other

One of the company cost management studies was directed toward the economics of on-time delivery. It must be noted here that any logistics department can provide *any* quality of service the company is willing to pay for: one-day delivery to all customers, all of the time, or, for that matter, one-hour service! Of course, the company will soon be a *former* company. The cost of perfection comes high! In order to arrive at a customer service policy that is economic, the costs of providing different qualities of service were studied. It was found that up to a point of about 95 percent on-time delivery the cost did not change appreciably, but from that point on it skyrocketed. Figure 14–1 shows this situation graphically.

An official of the company summed up the company attitude toward environmental analysis in general, and logistics analysis in particular. While cost-cutting in the logistics area was the focus of attention, the impact on marketing was a prime consideration. Thus cost management with marketing-logistics "trade-offs" was the objective to be attained.

> Distribution is now one of our prime cost-cutting targets. This problem is considered so critical that task forces currently are reviewing all phases of distribution operations, and additional changes may be implemented— even at the risk of sacrificing market share in some areas.[3]

---

[3] Ibid., p. 18.

FIGURE 14–1
The Cost-Performance Trade-off

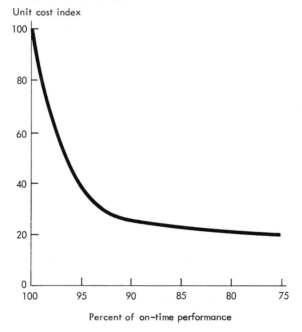

Source: *Purchasing Week,* now *Purchasing World;* October 25, 1971, p. 18.

RELATION OF LOGISTICS TO MARKETING

Some aspects of customer service

Environmental analysis is necessary to reduce the probability that change will catch the firm by surprise. We cannot think of a single significant development in the logistics area in recent years that had not sent its "feelers" out well in advance to be noticed by an alert observer who could read the signs well. Of course, we often see the signs but don't recognize them for what they are until later. The detective work of environmental analysis is not enough. The follow-through planning and development of appropriate alternatives "to make happen what you want to have happen" is necessary, and this is not the job of just the logistics department or of the marketing department. As we have seen, customer service may mean one thing to logistics people, another to marketing, and still a third to the firm; so on fundamental strategies affecting the firm as a whole, the Level 1 executives whose functions are affected should all be in on the decision. In the Union

Carbide illustrations and in Figure 14–1 we can see two possible extremes of thought.

Acting on its own, in a vacuum, there is a motive for the logistics department to require heavier truck loading, quicker turn-around time on equipment, and reduced on-time delivery schedules. The motive is cost reduction. In its own vacuum, the marketing department has a motive to do just the opposite: require lighter loading, slower turn-around time, and increased on-time performance. The motive is to increase sales by improving customer service.

As we have seen in prior discussions and will show in future ones, the types of situations mentioned above are not at all unusual. The strategic planning process is designed to help prevent them. When policies on those things which affect the firm as a whole are set by the affected Level 1 executives, implications of alternatives can be identified and appropriate trade-offs can be arranged. In short, the above situations do not call for "marketing" policies or "logistics" policies. They call for *corporate* policies and should be made at the corporate level. logistics people are not immune to the cost reduction syndrome. Nor are marketing people immune to the volume syndrome. The group therapy provided by Level 1 planning is helpful in suppressing the syndromes.

We used Union Carbide's experience to provide a concrete representation of some fundamental aspects of planning, which results in a systems approach to corporate management. Every one of the adjustments made reflected four major concepts: first, an approach of a marketing-oriented company to strategic planning; second, the attention to customer service as a central goal of the marketing-oriented company; third, the function of logistics in customer service; and fourth, the idea of cost management as it impinges upon the firm as a whole and as reflected in the several trade-offs between customer service and logistics costs. With respect to cost management, two other points emerged. First, the elusive, abstract notion of "good service at low cost" can be given a reasonably concrete meaning. Second, these types of policies cannot be developed soundly without information on the nature of both markets and costs.

Small firms

While we used Union Carbide, a company with sales of hundreds of millions of dollars, to illustrate the concepts, it should not be inferred that they are applicable only to the large firm. They are equally applicable to firms with sales of six or seven figures. While they are important to the large firm, they may be vital to the small one. To the large firm higher costs which are not offset by higher prices may mean only lower executive bonuses and dividends. To the small firm, they may mean failure.

The only conceptual differences in the application of strategic planning and the development of policies between large and small firms is that the process may be more informal, because only a few people are involved, compared with a greater number for large firms. Also, the manager may wear several hats. The marketing manager may also function as the logistics manager. If he is wise, he will have talks with himself, acting in both roles. When Level 1 meets, each of those wearing more than one hat has an opportunity to be concerned with trade-offs. Because of the informality and the more rapid and frequent communication among the managers, these types of trade-offs are not as difficult to arrange in the small company as in the large one. Simply because the marketing manager is involved in logistics decisions—and vice versa—the two points of view may be more or less automatically considered in almost any decision.

Our experience in these matters with small companies has led us to believe that there is little, if any, problem of jurisdictional disputes: marketing versus logistics. The problem appears to be that the marketing man who also makes logistics decisions is not aware of the many logistics alternatives open to him. The obverse side of that coin is that the person in charge of logistics may not be aware of the marketing implications of logistics decisions unless he is also in charge of marketing.

In our discussion of environments we have alluded to some logistics problems for which policy statements are desirable. We turn now to examine some of these things in another context.

SOME PROBLEM-CAUSING CHARACTERISTICS

Nature of logistics problems

The frequent small-quantity orders of customers may pose a problem for the logistics manager. Because of more frequent deliveries, there is more exposure to failure in inventory management, warehouse replenishment, order processing, on-time delivery, and so on. A series of questions arise. Is this a problem arising from a series of *internal* decisions, such as one caused by price discount policy? By a compensation policy for sales personnel? By a promotion policy designed to provide frequent service as a competitive measure? By the practice of individual salespersons exercising initiative (as distinct from acting under a specific company policy)?

On the other hand, does the problem stem from external forces, such as a logistics policy internally generated by the customer? A third pos-

sibility is that it is an external problem generated by the internal practices of third parties, such as transportation companies, whose rate
structures do not discourage small shipments. A fourth possibility is
that it is an external problem caused by the low quality of service
and the high cost to the carrier of providing that service relative to
the revenue received from it.

At this point, analysis and solution of the problem become incredibly
complex because in seeking to solve its own internal problem, the shipper
("our" company) must seek the roots of the problem in the internal
structure of an external agency, the carrier. Also, a number of potential
sources of the problem exist, such as: (1) a rate level that is too low,
considering the cost of service; (2) a rate structure improperly conceived; (3) operating practices that are inconsistent with the state of
the technological art.

A fourth cause of the logistics problem may be external to the external
agency. The problem may have its roots in a problem of the carriers,
which, in turn, may have its roots in policies of the Interstate Commerce
Commission.

A fifth cause of the logistics problem is very closely related to the
fourth, in that it may be (1) external to the firm; and (2) external
to the carrier as well, and may stem from "natural" causes. What makes
this type of problem so complex is that it has two facets. If the company
did not have the problem of dealing with small shipments to certain
low-density demand areas, the carrier would not have the problem of
serving these areas. That they exist and must be served by some producer
and by some carrier is a fact of life, but it being a fact in no way
reduces the magnitude of the problem.

How do we go about dealing with an environment that is so complex
and which is characterized by such close, yet distant interrelationships?
We are tempted to suggest to the manager that he turn it over to a
subordinate, and when no solution is forthcoming, complain about the
quality of college people these days. But that isn't much help; so we
suggest that these problems be categorized and the several categories
systematically analyzed for causes of the problems.

We suggest three broad categories of problems: "natural"; conceptual; and organizational—categories that have been useful to us. Even
as we suggest these categories we warn that some of the problems do
not fit neatly into any one of them; so we "force" them. We also warn
that they overlap one another. With these notes of caution, we turn
to our discussion of them.

Certain natural, conceptual, and organizational problems are resistances to the effectiveness of the logistics function in performing its
basic role. That role, as we have seen, is to serve as a means to establish

the most favorable balance between distribution cost and customer service to support the marketing effort of the company.

"Natural" problems

One of the characteristics of almost any kind of social or economic activity is an unbalanced relationship between a given result and the forces which cause that result—sort of a law of inverse proportions. For example, a relatively small effort will produce disproportionately large results or, vice-versa, a relatively large effort produces relatively small results. A few of these inverse relationships which affect distribution cost and customer service are listed below. Note that some of the points mentioned influence the shipper directly through the several logistics components, while some influence him indirectly through the carrier; so a double balancing act between distribution cost and customer service is necessary.

The Company:
A relatively small number of customers account for a large proportion of sales and a large proportion of profits
A relatively large number of products account for a small proportion of sales and a large proportion of costs.

Inventory:
A relatively small number of items account for a large proportion of investment
A relatively large number of items account for a small proportion of shipments.

The Carrier:
A relatively small number of shipments account for a large proportion of revenue and a small proportion of cost
A relatively large number of towns account for a small proportion of shipment destinations and a small proportion of revenue.

How to cope with these "natural" imbalances is one of the problems of the logistics manager in maintaining the desired balance between distribution cost and customer service. If the imbalances in one area could be paired with imbalances in another the solution would be much easier. In the listing of imbalances, for example, if the large number of products which accounted for a large proportion of costs were bought by the large proportion of customers who accounted for a disproportionately large share of costs, the tentative and apparent solution would be easy. Drop the products and drop the customers. Even that tentative and apparent solution may not be the permanent and evident solution, however, because of the implications of such a logistics-marketing decision on production cost and overall profitability of the firm in the short run, and perhaps even in the long run. Dropping the products may have two effects which may be interrelated or independent of one another. Lower production rates may raise the average cost of producing the remaining products to an unacceptably high level. Also, the dropped product may have been making a contribution to overhead which the company cannot afford to lose. Furthermore, the dropping of the unprofitable items may seriously impair the total marketing effort by breaking up the product line. In addition, it may very easily turn out that the products are unprofitable simply because of the methods of accounting for costs.

As for the carrier imbalances, we can't just say, "That is their problem, not ours." In one very real way it is more the problem of the shipper than of the carrier. While passing no judgment on adequacy of carrier profits, it is a fact that they do make a profit and that they are in business. For convenience, we use the motor carrier of general commodities to illustrate our point.

These carriers say that on a very large proportion of their shipments they do not cover even direct cost, which has an adverse effect on total profits as well as on other shipments which must subsidize the unprofitable ones. Service is often not good on some of these shipments and the price is high. For both of these reasons—poor service and high cost—the shipper can't ignore the problem. When the shipper gets poor service at high cost as a customer of the carrier, it is very difficult for it to give good service at low cost to its own customer.

Thus, we see that a policy concerning the problem of imbalances caused by the "law" of inverse proportions is not confined to the logistics manager. He must coordinate activities and policy decisions with a number of others:

The marketing manager, in identifying acceptable customer service levels and customers and products which may be candidates for dropping

The production manager, in determining the effect on production cost of dropping products

The controller, to determine not only what the actual *relevant* costs are but also the effect of dropping customers on overall profits

The carriers, to devise means of reducing carrier problems arising from imbalances.

The fact that one significant action by the logistics manager has such far-reaching effects again points up the significance of the strategic planning process and the value and necessity of the trade-offs being made at a high policy level. There are at least two means of making the logistics area more effective and efficient in either adapting to its environment or adapting its environment to the system. One way is to apply some of the concepts of planning to help create a system from the parts of the firm. Another is to make adjustments to mechanisms internal to the logistics field and to create a system of interworking parts out of a collection of independently operating parts. We will now look at some of these concepts and internal adjustments to the logistics machinery by examining some of the conceptual problems with which the logistics manager must cope.

Conceptual problems

To retain perspective, we restate that the overall problem we are concerned with is the maintenance of a favorable balance between customer service and distribution cost. We have just examined some of the imbalances which create logistics problems, so now we can look at some problems of a conceptual nature which arise in trying to cope.

To follow our basic pattern we will first deal with the internal environment and look at concepts related internally to the logistics concept, and then broaden our scope to the internal environment of the firm. Then we will move externally to deal with customer service on the one hand and carriers on the other. The two aspects of the internal environment are interrelated as are the two facets of the external environment, and the internal and external environments are also interrelated. Accordingly, we do not attempt to keep the tentacles of one discussion from reaching out toward another, for to do so would create an artificial situation. Our approach is to analyze the nature of the overall problem from the perspective of each of the four conceptual areas. The objective of the discussion is to focus attention upon environmental problems in the development of logistics strategies and policies, at both the corporate level and the functional level.

The logistics concept does nothing more than view all of the separate logistics activities as interdependent parts of a whole logistics system, which, in turn, is nothing more than one of several interdependent parts of the marketing system of the firm. Perhaps aspiring managers and managers who read this will allow us to share in their consternation that this subject has to be mentioned as a problem. We cannot point to any reasons satisfactory to us which explain why such a large segment of business ignored the logistics concept for so many years. Of course, some firms have used the logistics concept for years, but only in the past decade or so have many moved in the direction of systematically viewing the firm as interdependent parts instead of independent parts. To say that the computer made it possible is comforting, but it is patent nonsense. The computer improved efficiency and effectiveness by (1) making possible *some* analyses not otherwise feasible and (2) by speeding up processing of data.

The traffic management concept. Let us look at the alternatives to the logistics concept. First, there is the *traffic management* concept where the primary emphasis is on selection of rates and routes, usually by one mode of transportation. The primary concern is with the reduction of *transportation* cost through rate negotiation and the routing of freight. A study of 26 large and profitable companies showed that about a third traditionally confined themselves to a single means of transportation. The study illustrated the result by referring to the case of a large container company. The traffic department, dominated by people with long railroad experience, did a great job of negotiating rates.

> But no one gave much thought to identifying and costing out other transportation alternatives, much less to analyzing the economics of redistribution points or achieving the best possible product mix at each manufacturing location. At the time of the survey, top management had become aware of some of these missed opportunities, and was beginning to move out of its traditional narrow mold toward more aggressive handling of its distribution function.[4]

The transportation concept. This concept is broader, for it is concerned primarily with minimizing transportation costs. Transportation departments oriented in this direction are typically very skilled in devising a *transportation* mix which will reduce transportation cost both in negotiating rates and in managing the transport operation as a whole. This group, in effect, views transportation as an end in itself and the specific objective is *cost reduction*. In the study referred to above, about half of the companies fell in this category. After commenting on the successful results of the efforts of one company, the author said:

> Yet for all its aggressiveness in the transportation area, many of the company's marketing and service policies go unchallenged by top management. No one is really concerned with analyzing the functional interfaces or making imaginative cost-versus-value appraisals.[5]

The total logistics concept. As stated, this concept views all of the parts of the logistics system as interdependent and views the logistics system as a subsystem of the firm. Again referring to the above study, only 5 of the 26 companies really managed the distribution function with consistent attention to the balance between distribution costs and cus-

[4] Robert P. Neuschel, "Physical Distribution: Forgotten Profit Frontier," in Roland Mann, ed., *The Arts of Top Management* (New York: McGraw-Hill Book Company, 1971), p. 272.
[5] Ibid., p. 273.

tomer service. The author said that there were three ways in which the common feature of their approach manifested itself:[6]

1. The executives heading the major functions viewed distribution from the corporate rather than the functional point of view, and were committed to the trade-off between costs and service when the action resulted in the corporate good. This approach to *cost management* is in direct contrast to a narrow approach to *cost reduction.*

2. The transportation personnel were "free from the parochialism found in many of the traffic departments studied,"[7] and understood well the interactions among marketing, logistics, manufacturing, and operations in general.

3. All of the companies stressed the importance of adequate and timely cost information as one basis for analyzing alternatives and trade-offs.

The profit maximization concept. When we identified the logistics concept as envisioning the logistics function as one of a group of subsystems dedicated to the marketing objectives, by implication we covered this topic. At one stage in the evolutionary process of the logistics concept a number of people looked upon it as a systematic way of reducing costs. That stage did not last very long, however, because the mere application of a systems analysis to logistics made the next step almost inevitable. Today, we do not hear of any firms who have adopted the logistics concept who have not begun to view it in a profit-making sense rather than a cost-reduction sense. For a short period, it was referred to as the "total cost approach." Even then (late 1950s, early 1960s) many who referred to it in that manner practiced it in a profit maximization context.

Customer service. Since providing an economic level of satisfactory customer service is what marketing is all about, and since logistics is a major feature of the customer service mix, and since balancing distribution cost with customer service is central to what logistics is all about, perhaps we can be forgiven for allowing the subject to pop up so frequently. So far, we have not said much about cost in the cost-service balancing act the logistics people are supposed to be so adept at. We now look at it from the perspective of the role of cost in customer service from the point of view of a company and of the customer.

We have implied that it costs a bundle. What is a bundle? We saw that for Union Carbide, *transportation* costs equalled about 13 percent of sales. Heskett estimated that *physical distribution* costs account for about 24 percent of GNP, excluding services.[8] One study showed the

---

[6] Ibid., pp. 273, 274.

[7] Ibid.

[8] J. L. Heskett, Robert M. Ivie, and Nicholas A. Glaskowsky, Jr., *Business Logistics* (New York: The Ronald Press Company, 1964), p. 17.

percent physical distribution costs were of net sales for several industry groups.[9] The data:

Food and food products . . . . 34.4 percent
Primary and fabricated metals. 33.1
Chemicals, petroleum, rubber 26.0
Paper 19.9
Wood products 16.8
Textiles 16.2
Electrical and nonelectrical machinery 11.4

If the major functions of a business were ranked according to dollar costs, in a large number of industries physical distribution costs would rank near the top. These costs may be looked at in several ways in connection with balancing cost and service. The greater proportion distribution costs are of sales, the greater the *tendency* should be to seek cost reduction without forgetting for a moment the significance of cost management. A moderate percentage cost reduction can mean a great deal to the shipper whose total physical distribution costs are 20 to 30 percent of sales, especially if profit on sales is very low. Using the foregoing data showing the percent distribution costs are of sales, we have prepared an illustration showing the effects of a cost reduction program and those of a cost management program.

First, look at Table 14–1, which shows that a 10 percent cost reduction would mean for profits in a given industry. But let us look at the alternative method of increasing profits, namely, increasing sales. Column 4 of Table 14–1 shows how much sales would have to increase in order to yield the same profit increase as would follow from the cost reduction, in logistics.

Two questions arise. First, can logistics costs be decreased so easily? Second, how much would it cost to increase sales the amount shown? To the first question, our answer is resoundingly positive in most firms, based upon our personal experiences and those of others. We don't know the answer to the second question, but common sense tells us that most businesses are trying constantly to do just that. Besides, it is not an either/or proposition. We make the comparison as a dramatic means of showing the value of a moderate cost reduction. For example, in the machinery industry, to increase profits by 1.1 percentage points ($11 per $1,000 of sales) two paths may be followed: (1) decrease logistics costs 10 percent, or (2) increase sales 27.5 percent ($275 per $1,000 of sales).

Now, let us look at cost management to show trade-off implications.

---

[9] Richard E. Snyder, "Physical Distribution Costs," *Distribution Age,* January 1962. To our knowledge there is not a similar study available which shows more recent data. We use these numbers with confidence, because even if they were twice overstated in relation to today's costs, the magnitude would still be so great that not a word of discussion would need to be changed.

TABLE 14–1
Increase in Profit from Logistics Cost Reduction or Increase in Sales

(1) *Industry*	*(2)* *Logistics cost per* *$1,000 sales* *(dollars)*	*(3)* *Profit from cost* *reduction of 10* *percent (dollars)*	*(4)* *Increased sales to* *earn same profit* *(dollars)*
Food and food products* 350		35	2,333
Primary and fabricated metals. 330		33	825
Chemicals, petroleum, rubber 260		26	650
Paper 200		20	500
Wood products 170		17	425
Textiles 160		16	400
Electrical and nonelectrical machinery 114		11	275

Note: Assume profits equal 4 percent of sales except in food and food products.
* Profit is approximately 1 to 1½ percent on sales in grocery stores. We use this figure to show the tremendous leverage if distribution cost savings could be passed through the channels to the grocery store.

After having reduced cost by 10 percent, a firm in the machinery industry may find that by improving customer service it can increase sales 5 percent. But this improved service may increase warehousing costs by 10 percent. We continue the assumption that profits are 4 percent of sales. The average logistics costs in that industry per $1,000 of sales are as follows:[10]

> Transportation . . . . $ 93.70
> Warehousing. 8.00
> Other 12.30
> Total. $114.00

With these facts in mind, let us go through several steps. At 4 percent, profit on $1,000 of sales is $40; a reduction of 10 percent in transportation cost ($9.37) increases profit to $49.37, or 4.94 percent of sales. To earn $9.37 more profit through increased sales alone, sales would have to rise $234.25, or 23.4 percent. Now assume the firm can improve customer service and increase sales 5 percent, or $50, by increasing warehouse cost 10 percent.

Distribution costs now look like this:

> Transportation $93.70
> Less 10 percent 9.37
>   ‾‾‾‾‾
> $ 84.33
> Warehousing. 8.00
> Plus 10 percent 80
>   ‾‾‾‾
>   8.80
> Other (unchanged) 12.30
>   ‾‾‾‾‾‾‾
>   Total. $105.43

---
[10] Ibid.

The net effect of these changes is shown below:

	Before	After	Dollar change	Percent change
Sales	$1,000	$1,050	$50	+5.0
Distribution cost	114	105	9	−7.9
Profit.	40	49	9	+22.5
Profitability (percent)	4	4.7	−	+17.5

At a profitability rate of 4.7 percent, the profit on sales is now $47 per thousand instead of $40, an increase of 17.5 percent. We have shown the effect of both cost reduction and cost management in this illustration. Also, we have shown the importance of coordinating marketing effort and logistics effort. If transportation, warehousing, and marketing were managed by three different people, as is very often the case, this total view involving trade-offs would be hard to develop at the functional level. Disregarding the question of who manages what, the coordination involving trade-offs could be arranged if it took place at Level 1 of the organization.

Even if transportation and warehousing were managed by one person, that manager would be reluctant to increase warehousing costs to improve customer service—given the way in which many managerial reward systems work. He would be delighted to reduce transportation costs.

Our machinery illustration was chosen at random, and warehousing costs were a small proportion of the total. Look at Table 14–2 for a

TABLE 14–2
Percent Distribution Costs Are of Net Sales

	Food	Metals	Chem- icals	Paper	Wood	Textiles	Machin- ery
Transportation	17.68	11.38	14.83	8.95	11.97	5.62	9.37
Warehousing	8.07	11.30	5.46	5.29	0.30	6.74	0.80
Other	8.67	10.46	5.66	5.69	4.50	3.79	1.23
Total	34.42	33.14	25.95	19.93	16.77	16.15	11.40

Source: Richard E. Snyder, "Physical Distribution Costs," *Distribution Worldwide*, January 1962.

breakdown of the logistics costs. Then go through the same arithmetic exercise for other industries and see how they come out. In fact, change our assumptions. For example, in the case of machinery, would it have been worthwhile to increase warehousing costs 2, 3, 4 times instead of just 10 percent to get a 5 percent increase in sales? Or look at food and food products where transportation cost is a much larger proportion of sales than it is in the machinery industry and where warehousing is an even larger proportion.

We have looked at cost management with emphasis on cost reduction—despite the fact that we did increase warehousing costs in our illustration. Even so, we were looking at this as an offensive step to increase sales. With the same figures, look at the effect of increasing these costs to improve customer service to prevent sales declines. At the same time, think of the process as one of increasing total costs to increase total profits. Our illustration was a neat one in that it came out by increasing profits and increasing the profitability rate from 4 percent of sales to 4.7 percent. Maybe we would be happier with a 3.5 percent return on a $1,200 sale ($42) than we would be with a 4 percent return on $1,000. The 20 percent increase in sales would be earned by increasing distribution costs. But is this good? Profits are up from $40 to $42, but we paid a high price for that 20 percent increase in sales by increasing distribution costs. What would happen if sales fell and distribution costs didn't change?

The logistics contribution to customer service mainly has to do with timeliness and economy of providing goods to the customer; so proximity to the customer is an important matter. We distinguish three types of proximity: physical, temporal, and economic.

Physical and temporal proximity. Physical proximity to the market refers to the distance separating seller and customer. Temporal proximity refers to the relative amount of time required to deliver the goods, while economic proximity means the relative expense of providing service. It does not necessarily follow that the three are identical. In fact, the logistics concept in general and the logistics practices of a number of companies have been built upon the differences among them. Furthermore, pricing and other marketing strategies of some companies have been designed around these differences to enable them to enter distant markets.

We use a simple but very realistic situation to illustrate our point. Let us locate a customer at Norman, Oklahoma, who has suppliers as follows: Oklahoma City—20 miles; Dallas—200 miles; St. Louis—500 miles; New York—1,500 miles. Which is the closest supplier? In a physical sense it is obvious. In an economic sense not enough information is provided. In a temporal sense, for most practical purposes, they are equally close; the customer is overnight away in all cases. To be sure, either the customer or the supplier can jump in his car or truck and have what he needs from Oklahoma City in his store in an hour or so. Or, because of excellent service by Mistletoe Express, a carrier can be used. This is recognized, but most deliveries are not made on this basis.

While air freight must be used to make New York overnight away, Dallas and St. Louis are that far away by motor truck. But what about the cost? To start with, we were only concerned about time, but since cost is a significant factor we now bring it into the analysis. If the price policies of suppliers include payment of transportation charges and base prices at the factory are the same, cost to the customer doesn't enter the picture at all. Again, it is timeliness of delivery, and in both cases timeliness means overnight.

How about New York and its overnight delivery? Isn't it more expensive? It might be, but a very substantial portion of the marketing strategy of the airlines is based upon the fact that in many cases the total cost is less when shipments move by air, even though transport costs may be greater. Also, the marketing strategy and the logistics strategy of at least two companies we know of is based upon the same premise.

In the 1950s the airlines began pushing the total cost concept of physical distribution. This concept merely recognizes that the transportation rate is only one element of the total logistics cost. Others include interest, spoilage, and pilferage; cost of inventory; opportunity cost of money invested in inventory; differential packaging cost by air and by surface; warehousing; and other costs. In many cases, the total cost by air is less than the total cost by surface transport. Not only do the airlines emphasize cost, but also they emphasize the customer service element of shortening the lead time between placing and receiving the orders. Also, one company announced, in the early-to-mid-1960s, that henceforth all of its overseas shipments would leave this country by air. In addition, in the mid-1950s, another company closed all of its distribution points and began making delivery by air.

Economic proximity. We have tied economic and temporal proximity together by citing price policies of some companies which result in freight absorption by the shipper. But what is the situation for the customer who pays the freight bill? In this respect, we cited the total cost approach which indicated that the shipper may find, after total cost analysis, that air freight is cheaper. But what if it is more expensive? Two things: (1) New York is economically farther away, so it is not considered a source of supply because cost is paramount in the customer's mind; (2) the customer uses New York suppliers for other reasons. The same holds true from the Dallas and St. Louis suppliers.

But this does not end the alternatives. Our emphasis has been on actual transit time, which, in a very real sense, is irrelevant. The important aspect of the time factor pertains to whether the goods are available when the customer wants them, not how long the trip takes. By carefully scheduling shipments for a specific arrival date, water transportation, with its lower rates, may be used. Inland water carriers have not shown the same enthusiasm for attempting to capture a potential market for their slow transportation that the air carriers did for their fast transportation.

The potential market for inland water carriers refers to shipments of 15–20 tons of relatively high-value freight. At least one coastwise water carrier (Sea-Land) does aim at that market. Its profitable results have shown that it is both ignorant and stupid to make *universal* application of a very good generalization: "You can't ship high-value goods by water; the inventory costs will eat you up." The air carriers faced up to the counterpart of that statement: "You can't use air transportation except in emergencies and for certain very high-value goods; the high rates will eat you up."

Both of these are good generalizations, "other things remaining the same." When the airlines looked at those other things, enough of them did not remain the same to prevent them from building a still rapidly growing business around them. The same holds true for Sea-Land and slow water transportation.

There is yet another facet of economic proximity. The rail rate structure may make one production point either as close as a given market or closer to it than another production point located physically closer to the market in question. Sometimes, extensive geographic areas of the country are grouped together and rates are made from group to group and not from point to point. The result is that the same rate will apply to one pair of points a given distance apart as applies to another pair a greater or lesser distance apart.

In addition, it is not at all unusual to find a rate lower for a greater distance between A and C than the one between B and C. For that matter, it is not unusual to find a rate lower for a movement from A to C through B than the one from B to C. These will be discussed more in Chapter 15 devoted to managing logistics decisions.

In this portion of the analysis of the contribution of the logistics concept to customer service, we have added the proximity to the customer as another dimension of service. We showed how this dimension may enter the strategic planning of the firm in several ways. Under varying conditions of marketing strategy, physical, temporal, and economic proximity to the customer are ingredients in the strategic planning for the firm and for the logistics department. This dimension of customer service again underscores the necessity of information on both customer needs and wants as well as cost information for analysis and control.

In summary, there are at least three approaches to balancing customer service and distribution cost: (1) cut off the customer whose costs are too high; (2) by better planning and managing of the logistics function, reduce the company costs so it can afford to retain the customer; (3) through the same processes reduce the costs and pass part of the savings to the customer as an element of marketing pricing policy for competitive pricing. Putting the case slightly differently, the approach of the firm may be to improve productivity and profitability for its own profit goals or to provide it more flexibility in its pricing strategy. Once more we emphasize that none of this is possible without information.

Relations with carriers. This facet of the logistics conceptual problems related to the external environment is a two-edged sword. Traditionally, marketing people, including professors in their classrooms and in their textbooks, refer to transportation and warehousing companies as "facilitating agencies." We have no quarrel with calling them that, and have done so ourselves in other chapters.

However, transportation and warehousing companies must be considered as extensions of the arms of the firm in the channels of distribution. Too often marketing people have considered them in a detached sort of way as a means of moving goods along the channel of distribution. Typically, in discussing channels of distribution and drawing diagrams to express the flow in the channels, a series of closed boxes is used, as shown in Figure 2–2, Part A, of Chapter 2. Goods are at one point in the channel at a point in time. At another point in time they need to be elsewhere; so a "facilitating agency" takes care of the situation. One conjures up a vision of a series of stops and starts; a series of discrete steps in the process of distribution.

Not only have marketing people viewed the process this way, but the typical "traffic management" and "transportation" department approaches discussed above did the same thing. In one way, however, the traffic and transportation approach recognized the flow concept in part by arranging for special rates for goods stopping over in transit.[11]

Part B of Figure 2–2 is also symbolic. It recognizes the supply function of logistics in getting goods to the manufacturer. The openness of the boxes depicts the necessity of two-way communication links among the channel members, including the warehousing and transportation companies. They become extensions of the arm of the firm in the channels and may perform a strategic function.

Perhaps one of the oldest illustrations of this concept in action is the decades-old approach of the automobile companies, which at least figuratively, if not literally, view the freight car and the semitrailer as an integral part of their assembly lines. Some of the railroads report frequently to the assembly plant on car locations. Truckers schedule arrivals of parts with a very narrow time tolerance for deviation.

Other illustrations of companies similarly using the carriers as extensions of their own arms abound. A firm in the Southwest working with an airline, for example, arranged for East Coast shipments to be sent air freight to the East for delivery direct to customers, and to the post office, truckers, and local cartage companies for delivery to customers.

---

[11] It is ironic to note, however, that the transit privileges were set up primarily to enable some railroads to participate in certain traffic and for some areas to participate in the processing or storage; not primarily for customer convenience.

This system was devised in response to a marketing need to improve delivery times for competitive reasons.

Another feature of the relationship with carriers centers on the logistics department helping the carrier do its job more effectively and efficiently in providing good service at low cost. There are a number of ways of accomplishing this: clearly marking shipments, consolidating them for ease in handling and identification, having them ready when the carrier calls, and using loading and unloading equipment to shorten turnaround time.

The carriers who have adopted the marketing concept—notably air and rail—have recognized the importance of insinuating themselves into the channels of distribution as extensions of the arms of the firm. The air freight divisions of the airlines have done much to further the development of the logistics concept in business as a part of their own marketing program. They have worked diligently to become effective as arms of the firm in the channel system.

One of the best rail illustrations of this approach is the rapid development of the unit train since the mid- and late 1960s. Basically, the unit train shuttles back and forth between two points serving one shipper and one consignee in trainload lots. Most of these trains handle bulk commodities, such as coal, grain, minerals, and the like. They operate on a schedule and are active participants in the flow of goods through the channels of distribution.

Summary of conceptual problems. In looking at the problems of logistics arising from more or less natural causes, we pointed out that a number of imbalances existed which made it difficult to attain the favorable cost-service balance with which both marketing and logistics managers are concerned. We also pointed out that there were some problems of a conceptual nature which arise when the firm attempts to cope with imbalances between cost and service.

We grouped these conceptual problems into internal and external groups, and subdivided each. The internal group included problems in developing (1) the logistics concept, and (2) the concept of profit maximization. In the external environment we returned to the familiar customer service, but looked at it from a different perspective—mainly that of the firm in light of cost rather than from the market-oriented approach. The other dimension of the external environment was concerned with the facilitating agencies as parts of the channels of distribution and functioning as extensions of the arms of the firm in those channels. We looked at both sides of this coin: as a shipper seeking an extension of its arms, and to a lesser extent as a carrier seeking to become an extension of the arms of the firm. We now turn to our final set of problems, those related to the organization.

Organizational problems

So much has now been said which impinges upon the organization that only a few comments are necessary to round out the discussion. We have discussed the fact that logistics costs are a very large proportion of total costs. In commenting on some logistics practices of very large firms, we expressed our amazement that top managers would allow such situations to exist. One author expressed it this way:

> If the half dozen major functions vital to the operation of any industrial business were to be ranked in order of the time and attention they receive from top management, it is safe to say that physical distribution would come somewhere near the bottom of the list.[12]

We do not know why some top managers began to recognize potential profit for improvement in the late 1950s. We can suggest several reasons. One of them is that this is about the time that the marketing concept began to be recognized, and this recognition probably had some spillover into the role of logistics in marketing planning. Second, it was about the time that strategic planning became a more significant managerial function, and the environmental analysis and discipline required for that effort uncovered the need for looking at logistics costs and functions. A third possible explanation is that the cost-price crunch got so severe that all facets of the firm came under scrutiny. A fourth possibility lies in a statement quoted elsewhere: there is no force more powerful than that exerted by an idea whose time has come. More likely, it was all of these together; that the total environment was such that very successful applications of the logistics concepts over a long number of years by some companies were adopted by others.

Thus management recognition of the importance of logistics is an essential first step in the solving of organizational problems. Other problems which arise involve the placement of the logistics function in the *functional* hierarchy. The planning aspects of the *function* should rank at least equally with the marketing, production, and other functions in the *planning* process at Level 1.

This juxtaposition of *functions* at the planning level is necessary if the executives in the strategic planning process are to have the benefit of full information presented and evaluated on an unbiased basis. Also, functional independence and functional status is necessary to provide sufficient clout for the functionary to command attention to his requests for information prepared in a format useful to him.

We speak of the "function" and "functionary" because this is not the place to analyze factors influencing where the function should be

---

[12] Neuschel, "Physical Distribution: Forgotten Profit Frontier," p. 263.

placed in the organization chart. In another context we made some remarks along this line, with particular reference to smaller businesses, but provided little analytical support. There are several places where the planning aspects of the logistics function may be housed:

1. In a staff planning position divorced from operations.
2. At the vice presidential level.
3. At a lower level but reporting to a vice president other than marketing or production.

Once the organizational problem of status for the logistics planning function is resolved, there are several other problems of lesser magnitude. One of them pertains to the location of the logistics operating function. As a matter of convenience to the Level 1 planners and policy makers, it is desirable to have all of the operating departments of logistics housed in one place. Logistics planning is often made a staff function in the planning or controller's department. Sometimes it is placed in an operations research department or under an executive vice president.[13] If planning is separated, then operations can be placed in the most convenient department, preferably marketing.

Other organizational problems center on information for control and analysis and personnel. As with any other function, specialized expertise is necessary because of the many specialized things logistics people do. Traffic managers are necessary to select the best rates and routes, negotiate with carriers, and select the best transportation mix. Other skills are necessary in selection and use of equipment, supervising drivers, and dealing with customers on distribution matters. Still others are useful with skills in operations research to insure efficient task performance.

Logistics functions in the firm have lagged behind other functional areas such as marketing, production, and finance in both the application of known concepts and in the use of known tools of analysis. Also, the function has been a stepchild from an organizational point of view in that for top management it was a little-understood and little-appreciated function. From all appearances management is beginning to appreciate the usefulness of logistics management in development of strategy for the marketing oriented firm.

One of several concepts known to logistics people for decades is in process of "coming into its own." We refer here to pool distribution. This concept is simple. A shipper may have a number of shipments going to different consignees in a given area. The consignees can be served in three ways. First, the shipper can maintain inventory in a

[13] Jack W. Farrell, "Is Distribution Planning a Growing Function?", *Traffic Management*, August 1974, pp. 30–35.

warehouse in the area and serve all shippers from that inventory. Second, the shipper can consign a trailer or rail car to a warehouseman with instructions for local delivery to the several consignees. Third, if the shipper does not have enough freight to the area to justify a trailer or car, it can pool freight with others who have the same problem and consign the vehicle to the warehouseman for delivery. The latter two are variations on the same theme.

The advantage of this approach over the first one is that costs of warehousing are eliminated. The near-term future, five years or so, is likely to see shippers adopt this distribution strategy to such an extent that the method of distribution will grow at a very rapid rate. It is a significant element in logistics strategy because of the potential for reduction in costs of warehousing. Walter F. Friedman has analyzed other future developments in logistics which will have an impact upon marketing and manufacturing practices in the future.[14]

CONCLUSION

Strategic planning for the marketing-oriented company obviously is concerned with customer service and profit. Customer service has many dimensions because of the many levels of customers who must be pleased. The company not only has to satisfy the resellers but also the ultimate consumer. The several customers in the chain have different needs to be satisfied and toward which customer service is oriented. Service to these groups may range from market information to advertising assistance. The element of customer service we have been concerned with involves supplying the customer with goods. With certain exceptions, such as mail order houses, the major emphasis on delivery by extractors, manufacturers, processors, and wholesalers, is on delivery to resellers.

We have grouped all of those activities related to putting goods into the hands of the customers and called them, collectively, the logistics function. Further, we have said that the purpose of the logistics function is to balance customer service and cost in order to attain the objectives of the firm. In identifying this purpose, by implication we say several things that logistics managers do not do. They *do not* tell the marketing people what the best decision is regarding customer service. Instead, they identify logistics-related costs of providing different levels of customer service. This gave rise to the statement that the logistics department could respond to any level of service the company was willing and able to finance.

---

[14] Walter F. Friedman, "Physical Distribution: The Concept of Shared Services," *Harvard Business Review*, March–April 1975, p. 24 et seq.

Logistics managers *do not* tell marketing what customers to drop, or what territories to try to build up. They do tell them what the logistics-related cost of serving certain customers is and the overall effect on costs resulting from the build-up of a territory. They *do not* tell marketing people what prices to charge. They do tell them that if price discounts could be established to encourage customers to buy in larger quantities and less frequently, costs would go down. Logistics managers *do not* tell marketing and production people how to design their product. They do tell them that a changed design could lower (or would increase) transportation cost.

Logistics costs are significant costs of converting a raw material into a satisfied customer. While the logistics people presumably do not know what is necessary to satisfy customers, that being a marketing job, they do know the total cost of physically delivering the source of satisfaction and they know that timely delivery is one aspect of satisfaction. Consequently, decisions which affect the choice of concepts underlying methods of delivery of satisfaction and the degree of satisfaction delivered are as strategic as the choice of methods and intensity of delivering were.

Accordingly, good strategic planning for the firm requires the full consideration of the logistics function. The almost endless number and variety of trade-offs involving marketing-logistics-production-finance decisions imply an orientation of the firm toward recognizing the importance of treating each part as a part of the system with the system being oriented toward satisfying the consumer at a profit. For these trade-offs to be made effectively, the notion of cost reduction as a path to profit should be replaced by the more realistic concept of cost management. These words apply with equal force—probably with greater force—in belt-tightening situations.

For cost management to be possible, to say nothing of effective, information useful for managers needs to be available. The problems affecting logistics which arise from our "law" of inverse proportions probably can't be solved, but they can be made less repressive. Perhaps we can't even solve the conceptual and organizational problems of the environment, but we can also cut them down to size.

What can management do?

1. Top managers can recognize the importance of logistics in the individual situation and give it the place in the hierarchy that it deserves. The relative importance will vary from firm to firm and industry to industry.

2. Top managers can endow the function with sufficient stature and resources to enable it to work.

3. Logistics managers can understand the economics of distribution in order to appraise different logistics strategies.

4. Logistics managers can assure themselves of the supply of information necessary for appraising alternative distribution configurations and strategies.

5. Logistics managers can know the right techniques of analysis and see that there is someone around to apply them.

6. Logistics managers can upgrade their knowledge and skills and those of their staff.

chapter 15 | # Logistics management and operations

Logistics decisions
  Customer service and environmental conditions
The transportation environment
  Types of carriers
  Transportation rate structures
  Other transportation rates and services
Managerial decisions on carriers and rates
  Carrier decisions
  Decisions pertaining to rates
The warehousing environment
  Types of warehouses
  Storage and warehousing
  Functions of warehouses
Managerial Decisions on Warehousing
  Direct service
  Indirect service
    Selection of distribution points
    Division of territories
  Good service at low cost
  Changes in managerial policies
Summary and Conclusions

LOGISTICS DECISIONS

The thrust of logistics decisions is in balancing customer service and cost while attaining the objectives of the firm. Several significant factors underlie these decisions. First, the magnitude of logistics costs makes logistics decisions important to the profit goals of the firm. Second, they have a significant impact upon marketing strategy as it pertains to customer service. Third, they may sometimes be residual decisions, in that an action taken to exploit a marketing opportunity may predetermine their nature. Similarly, decisions made for logistics reasons such as to improve efficiency or reduce costs may predetermine the nature of decisions in marketing, production, and finance.

Logistics personnel or departments include under their jurisdiction the activities of transportation, warehousing, and management of inventory. Some also include the functions of purchasing, order processing, and production planning, among others. The logistics activities may be under the jurisdiction of such functional managers as the marketing manager, the production manager, the controller, or the purchasing manager. Sometimes they are separated from other functions, under the jurisdiction of a physical distribution manager. These functional managers are responsible for the Level 2 decisions concerning logistics.

Customer service and environmental conditions

We have noted that when the organization has developed a strategic planning program which involves all appropriate Level 1 executives, the setting of objectives for the firm becomes possible. The consideration of possible trade-offs in the results of decisions and the interrelationship of Level 1 and Level 2 decisions, which is important in all managerial objective setting, also affects logistics decisions. Before establishing such a corporate objective as serving 90 percent of the customers two days after orders are received and meeting this objective 90 percent of the time, the effects of such a policy on not only logistics but many interrelated aspects of the environment must be considered. The effects on the organization of customer service decisions, for example, are far-reaching.

The customer service level has a direct effect on logistics activities. Such decisions have an impact on:

1. Logistics costs.
2. Decisions affecting type and mix of transportation to be used: rail, motor, other for-hire transportation companies, and the possible use of private transportation.
3. Type and location of warehousing facilities required and use of public or company-owned warehouses.
4. Type of order-receiving and order-processing methods and inventory management systems to be used.

A customer service objective could also affect the elements of the marketing mix in a variety of ways. For example, the following possible results would have to be considered:

1. The projected impact on sales of a revised customer service level.
2. The impact on promotion policy and methods to establish a competitive edge if the change is an improvement in service—or to retain a competitive position if the change is to a lower customer service level.

3. The impact on price policy if an adjustment is desirable or necessary to reflect different customer service levels.
4. The impact on the distribution channels. The mix among middlemen may be changed by using more or fewer wholesalers and more or fewer direct sales to retailers and ultimate users.

The financial manager of the firm has to react to and accommodate the impact of customer service decisions on:

1. Working capital as a result of changed inventory requirements or changing employee needs.
2. Financial requirements of need for more or fewer private vehicles and warehouses in response to a logistics decision made in response to a changed customer service level.
3. Capacity of data processing equipment as more or less information is required to control a changed customer service level.

The production or manufacturing department is also affected. It feels the impact on:

1. Production costs (space, machines, and workers) as production runs are changed to meet a changed inventory policy.
2. Effects on space, machines, and workers as a result of changed production runs.
3. Overtime requirements.
4. Supervision requirements as frequency of set-ups and length of production runs change.

In addition, the shock wave of a customer service level decision sets off a series of miscellaneous tremors, such as:

1. Change in the demands made on the personnel and accounting departments for people and types of information.
2. Jurisdictional problems with unions.
3. Organizational and personnel problems arising from requiring one department—marketing—to "share" its jurisdiction over customer service with other departments.
4. Similar problems arising from a future blurring of orthodox line-staff relations by requiring a "line" manager to engage in the "staff" work of planning.

In addition to these purely internal matters, external environmental conditions must be analyzed as they pertain to the customer, transportation and warehousing companies, financial institutions and stockholders (who may be asked to provide additional funds), unions, competitors, and government. All of these would, of course, be considered as the several impacts discussed above are appraised.

We will assume that these interrelationships of decisions have been or will be taken into account in our analyses of the environment of the major components of logistics, transportation and warehousing, and of logistics decisions relating to the environmental conditions.

THE TRANSPORTATION ENVIRONMENT

We have referred to those conditions existing outside the firm and therefore uncontrollable by it as first-order environment conditions. Except in cases where the company controls and operates its own vehicles, the transportation system is subject to these conditions. There are some widely held misconceptions concerning the transportation environment which have been reflected in the views of many people regarding the transportation function.

One such misconception is that rates are set by the Interstate Commerce Commission (or state regulatory commissions). The fact is that rates are set by the carriers, the approval of the ICC is necessary. Most people only know of ICC action in those cases where general increases have been requested. The carriers set the rates requested, and, after hearings are held, the ICC approves, modifies, or rejects the request.

A second misconception is that because rates are supposedly set by regulatory authority, they cannot be changed and therefore bargaining with carriers over rates is impossible. The fact is the carriers and shippers are constantly negotiating with one another for rate changes. Carriers initiate some of these bargaining sessions in furthering their marketing effort, and shippers initiate others for their own marketing reasons. The resulting rate is submitted to the regulatory authority for approval. Every year the ICC alone approves thousands of rate changes. Approval may be granted without hearings when there are no protests, or hearings may be required. The ICC plays a passive role and in effect approves many unprotested rates by taking no action at all.

A third misconception is that because of an ICC and court decision of the 1940s all rail rates are uniform throughout the country. But that decision applied only to one segment of the rate structure, under which a very small percentage of the goods moves. The rates on which practically all goods move are far from being uniform. In fact, such inconsistent relationships exist that generalizations regarding the rate structure are virtually impossible. About the only possible generalization on transportation rates is that there is no safe generalization that can be made.

Types of carriers

Many companies, for a number of reasons, acquire their own vehicles and handle their own transportation. These operations are referred to as private carriage and the company is a *private carrier,* as distinct from a *for-hire carrier.*

There are many types of for-hire carriers. *Common carriers* make themselves available to the public to perform certain types of transportation. For example, a common carrier of household goods holds itself out to the general public to handle household goods. The ICC recognizes a number of types of common carriers by motor vehicle: general commodities, bulk commodities, frozen food, and a dozen or so more. Common carriers must have approval of a regulatory body to operate, must publish their rates, must offer certain types and qualities of service, and so on. Railroads, airlines, and bus companies are examples of common carriers of both people and goods.

Contract carriers offer a very specialized service and limit themselves to serving relatively few customers, as distinct from the public at large. They too must have authority to operate and must not discriminate unduly among customers. Some automobile haulers and some freight airlines are examples of contract carriers, as are some oil field haulers.

Freight forwarders are another specialized type of carrier. Their main function is to consolidate shipments from many shippers or to many consignees and forward them to destination. They may use their own trucks or may buy transportation from other common carriers. They too must have authority to operate.

Shippers' associations are set up on a cooperative basis to perform the same functions as the freight forwarder.

Exempt carriers are those that are exempt from economic regulation, although they are subject to safety regulation. One type of exempt carrier hauls only commodities exempt from regulation, mainly certain kinds of agricultural products such as grain, cattle, eggs, and fish. Regulated carriers sometimes haul exempt commodities. For example, some common carriers by water (barge lines) often move loads that are exempt from economic regulation. Motor common carriers may do the same thing. Some farm co-ops have set up truck lines to handle agricultural products, and within broad limits they may also handle certain government freight. Also, carriers that operate only in urban areas called commercial zones are exempt from regulation.

In addition, there are express companies and small parcel delivery companies. Among the latter are the United Parcel Service and the U.S. Postal Service.

The logistics manager may use any or all of these types of carriers and forms of transportation. The mix chosen will depend upon the service available and the objectives of the company. It is not unusual for a shipper to own a steamship (or perhaps a steamship line), use barges, belong to a shippers' association, own its own trucks, and also use all other forms, down to parcel post. The mix is determined by the firm's need to keep in balance customer service, logistics cost, and objectives of the firm. Some of carrier selection decisions may be strategic and some may be managerial. For strategic reasons a steel company may own a steamship company, a barge line, and a railroad, among other forms of transportation. From a managerial viewpoint a company may develop a transport mix consisting of several types of carriers because it is the most efficient mix (the rationalization process).

Transportation rate structures

Most of the comments in the sections that follow are applicable to rail, motor, air, and water transportation companies, although for our example we have drawn heavily on rail classifications, rates, and situations. For example, we use weights applicable to railroads in discussing incentive rates or exceptions to the classification or to class and commodity rates. Slight changes in numbers and a few words would make the same statements applicable to other carriers.

Class rates and classification of freight. A two-step process is involved in quoting a rate for a shipment by common carrier. The first step is to find the *class* into which a commodity has been placed. Classes are found in a book called a *classification.* The second step is to turn to a *tariff,* which is nothing more than a price list. The charges levied for a shipment for given distances are shown in the tariff for each of the major classes of goods. Rates quoted in this fashion are *class rates.*

The classification is a book which contains descriptions and ratings of all commodities, as well as rules of the carrier regarding packing and handling the shipment. The ratings of the commodities or the classes into which they are placed are typically made by a classification committee composed of representatives from carriers in the industry concerned. There are several pieces of information regarding each commodity. For example, if the shipper is interested in moving antenna kits for television, he will find the following under the heading of "antennae or antenna kits, television receiving set":

Description	Less than carload rating	Carload minimum (pounds)	Carload rating
SU, in boxes (set up)	150	10,000R*	100
KD, or folded, in boxes (knocked down)	100	30,000	55

* R indicates minimum weight in a standard car.

The basic class for freight is Class 100; other classes are expressed in relation to this class. In the above example, if the antennae were shipped knocked down in less than carload lots (lcl), they would be rated as Class 100, which would bring forth a given rate, depending on distance shipped. The rating of 150 for each set-up antenna in boxes means that the rate would be 150 percent of that charged when the rating is 100. The rating of 55 results in a rate which is 55 percent of the Class 100 rate.

To qualify for the carload (cl) rating, the shipment must weigh at least the amount shown in the carload minimum column, or the shipper must pay for that much weight. If a shipment weighs 25,000 pounds, the shipper can do one of two things. First, it can make an lcl shipment. If the Class 100 rate were $4.50 per 100 pounds between two points, lcl shipment would cost $1,125 (25,000 pounds @ $4.50 per 100). Second, the shipper could ship 25,000 pounds as a carload of 30,000 pounds and pay $2.48 per hundred (55 percent of $4.50), or a total of $744. By paying for more weight than is shipped, the shipper saves $381.

The "R" in the carload minimum column warns the shipper that the minimum weight is 10,000 pounds in a standard car, but higher in larger cars. There is a table in the classification which shows the minimum weight changes by size of car.

Classification factors: Cost and demand. We have noted that the pricing of freight movements under class rates is a two-stage process: the commodities are rated for general purposes, and then charges are levied by class for different distances. The same general factors of supply (cost) and demand (market conditions) considered in any other pricing process are considered in the classification process. However, the classification process is almost infinitely more complex than the pricing process in other industries.

Cost factors typically relate to the nature of the product and may affect the cost of providing service. Cost factors include the following:

1. Density. A light bulky product such as television antennae (SU) weighs relatively little but takes up a lot of space. Accordingly, it is charged more per 100 pounds than if it were knocked down.

2. Characteristics regarding damage. Because the carrier is responsible for loss and damage, the susceptibility of the product to spoilage, damage, pilferage, and so on is considered in classifying it. If the commodity is one which might damage other commodities or carrier equipment, that fact is considered. For example, certain acids or a stud horse (seriously!) will typically bear higher ratings than like weights of inert liquids or a mare.

3. Loading characteristics. This is not as important in rail as in motor, for railroads handle relatively few lcl shipments. Carload shipments are loaded by the shipper, so carrier costs are not involved.

4. Other. Such additional factors as volume of goods offered at one time, direction of flow of traffic, regularity of movement, and so on are significant in determining the classification.

Demand factors are sometimes known as value-of-service factors. These factors include such things as the following:

1. The degree and extent of competition among carriers for the product.

2. The value of the product. A high-value product can usually justify a higher rate than a low-value one, but competitive forces among carriers may keep the rate low.

3. Competition among commodities or among producers. This aspect of competition may also influence the actual rate that can be charged.

In summary, the classification factors are those that are concerned with the cost to the carrier of rendering the service and the value of that service to the shipper.

Exceptions to the classification. A second type of rate is the exception rate. This type is similar to the class rate. It involves a modification of the classification governing the movement of a commodity between certain points or in a certain area. The modification may be a change in (1) description of the article, (2) rules governing packaging, (3) the minimum weight, (4) the rating, or (5) any combination of these. The exceptions may be initiated by the carrier for its own marketing reasons or by the shipper. Exception rates are lower than class rates.

Commodity rates. The third major type of rate is the commodity rate. Unlike class and exception rates, commodity rates are quoted directly in a tariff instead of through a classification. These rates are typically lower than the corresponding class and exception rates. (If they are not, it is because somebody goofed.)

Some commodity rates are related to class rates in that they are expressed as a given percentage of Class 100. A second type is scaled with some relationship to distance but with no necessary relationship to the class rate scale. A third type has no relation to any transportation factor. It is published in response to the need of somebody—carrier, shipper, region.

When class and exception rates will not meet the needs of those involved in transportation, a commodity rate is published. The rate may be applicable only between two points or among a limited number of points. It is significant that such a rate may have no relationship to a rate on the same commodity in another part of the country. On the other hand, some commodity rates, for example those on grain, have a very close relationship to one another. For example, rates between Omaha and Houston bear a close relationship to those between Kansas City and New York.

Other transportation rates and services

Class, exception, and commodity rates are the foundation of the rate system. Variations on these basic rates also can play a significant role in the marketing programs of both carriers and shippers.

One type of incentive rate was discussed in consideration of multiple minimum weights. Another is used by railroads to encourage volume movements by offering *multiple-car* rates and *trainload* rates when many cars are tendered at one time. Other carriers also offer incentive rates on smaller shipments.

A *proportional* rate is a part of a through rate. In order for a proportional rate to apply by rail carrier, the shipment must have had a prior movement or be destined to have a subsequent one. The proportional rate is designed to be lower than the regular rate between two points. It is used in transit privileges, a service widely available by rail.

Transportation companies offer a variety of services to serve their own needs as well as those of shippers. The transit privilege is designed to make it possible for a shipper to stop its goods off at some point prior to destination and later resume the shipment without losing the benefits of a through rate. For example, a rate from A to B is 100 and from B to C may also be 100. However, a through rate from A to C may be only 150. Without the transit privilege , if goods are stopped off at B and later reshipped, the rate is 200. With a proportional rate of 50 from B to C, which applies on shipments having prior transportation, the shipper pays 100 from A to B and 50 from B to C. It retains the benefit of the through rate, although there may be a small charge levied for the service.

There are many kinds of transit privileges. Grain may be stored in transit; metal may be fabricated in transit; cattle may be fed in transit. A variation is the stop-off privilege. Under this program, a shipper may have a car stopped in transit to partially unload or load, and it still will retain the through rate. Also, it may be allowed a carload rate, even though neither the original loading nor that added at a stop-off point met the carload minimum—as long as together they do meet it. This service is also a valuable one in the marketing effort, for it broadens shippers' options while keeping transport costs down.

Piggyback, fishyback (water), and birdyback (air) are also valuable services which make possible the shipment of sealed containers of goods. There are many other services offered by carriers. With the current attitudes of many carriers toward their customers and toward marketing their services, almost any type of service a shipper asks for will at least be considered. If it can be done at a profit, the carrier will probably introduce the service. In order to prevent discrimination among persons, places, and commodities, a special service has to be published in a tariff and made available to everyone on the same terms. Carriers may or may not charge for these services.

These services, like all aspects of the carriers and their rates, are parts of the transportation environment that logistics managers seek to adapt to their purposes or to which they adapt. All possibilities must be weighed in their decisions on rates and carriers.

MANAGERIAL DECISIONS ON CARRIERS AND RATES

The types of decisions discussed in this section are those concerned with management of the logistics function. They are made within the framework established by strategic planning and policy making, and as such they are concerned with the rationalization process designed to improve efficiency. To be sure, some of the situations described and opportunities referred to have strategic overtones, which illustrates a point made in the opening chapters: there is an overlap between strategic decisions concerned with effectiveness in attaining objectives and managerial control decisions concerned with efficiency of operations.

In discussing specific logistics decisions, we will define a situation, suggest specific alternative actions, and consider some of the effects of these alternatives. We believe the reader will be capable of making the connection between these elements, drawing inferences, and seeing implications, so we will only set the stage.

The discussion of managerial decisions pertaining to logistics is in terms of five phases. The first phase is a brief description of the situation. We make the assumption that the situation describes the *real* problem, not just an apparent one. The second phase is to identify opportunities. Note that in this phase a problem is converted to an opportunity. We have identified the opportunity in broad terms and have used the word "other" to encourage the reader to think about the situation and try to name some additional opportunities. The word "other" also keeps options open and is a symbol of the probable incompleteness of a list.

The third phase of the format for logistics decision making is to consider a series of alternative approaches to capitalize on each opportunity discovered, including "other." The fourth phase is to identify the nature of the internal effects of dealing with the external environment, including "other." In the fifth phase, those effects are traced to specific departments, again including "other."

The process should continue within each affected department to provide feedback to the logistics decision maker as well as to other decision makers. In this manner the logistics manager becomes concerned not only with management *and* the logistics function but with management *of* the logistics function. Thus, the perspective of the firm as a whole is preserved without losing sight of departmental needs.

Carrier decisions

Two hypothetical situations illustrate the types of carrier decisions faced by logistics managers.

Situation 1. Small shipments are delayed excessively by general commodity carriers.

Opportunities:
1. Improve service.
2. Other.

Alternative 1: Switch to freight forwarder; join shippers' association.
   Internal effects:
   1. Improves efficiency and profit. (How?)
   2. Other.
   Departments affected:
   1. Marketing: Service is improved. (How?)
   2. Logistics: Routines are changed.
   3. Company: Profits improve. (To what extent? Why?)
   4. Other.
   External and internal departments affected: (?)

Alternative 2: Switch to air freight, bus express, small parcel company.
   Internal effects:
   1. Improve service.
   2. Increase costs.
   3. Other.
   Departments affected:
   1. Marketing: service.
   2. Finance: working capital.
   3. Other.
   External effects: (Think of some. How about carriers, customers?)
   External and internal departments affected: (?)

Situation 2. The company private fleet moves some goods outbound to customer and returns empty. This is costly.
Opportunities:
1. Improve efficiency.
2. Other.

Alternative 1: Sell fleet.
   Internal effects:
   1. Release drivers and maintenance men.
   2. Dispose of unused shops and parking areas.
   3. Other.
   Departments affected by release of drivers and others:
   1. Personnel: Retrain or relocate employees; other.
   2. Finance: working capital, workmen's compensation; social security contribution; other.
   3. Logistics: fewer people to supervise; other.
   4. Other.
   Departments affected by disposition of facilities:
   1. Logistics: use as warehouse.

2. Production: use as factory.
3. Finance: new capital available from sale; needed for re-modeling.
4. Other.

Alternative 2: Find suppliers near present destinations.
   Internal effects:
   1. Change in routine.
   2. Other.
   Departments affected:
   1. Purchasing: finding suppliers.
   2. Production: quality of supplies.
   3. Logistics: developing new controls.
   4. Other.

Alternative 3: Acquire company at other end with complementary transport movements.
   Internal effects: (Name some.)

[*Turn to page 334 to finish this unit before studying Figure 15–1*]

IGURE 15–1:   A Format for Analyses Underlying Managerial Decisions

Situation	Opportunities	Alternatives	Internal adjustments or effects	Departments affected
			1. Release personnel	1. Personnel: Retrain, relocate 2. Finance: Working capital 3. Logistics: Supervisor 4. Other
		1. Sell fleet	2. Dispose of building and parking lot 3. Other	1. Production: Factory space 2. Logistics: Warehouses 3. Finance: Capital 4. Other
		2. Find suppliers near destination	1. Change in routine 2. Other	1. Purchasing: New suppliers 2. Production: Materials 3. Other
	1. Improve efficiency	3. Acquire company at other end	1. Every department 2. Other	1. Finance: Funds, taxes, severance pay 2. Personnel: Seniority, unions, severance policy 3. Other
Private fleet has one-way movement	2. Other	4. Exempt commodities for return load	1. Buyer of exempt items 2. Reduce cost 3. Other	1. Purchasing: Buy and sell 2. Logistics: Scheduling trips 3. Other
		5. Other	1. ? 2. ?	?

Departments affected: (Name the ways they may be affected.)
1. Finance.
2. Personnel.
3. Logistics.
4. Other.

Alternative 4: Other. (Think back on some of the types of carriers and commodities previously discussed.)

Figure 15–1 visualizes *Situation 2* as a whole and makes it possible to trace the paths of different actions.

Decisions pertaining to rates

As a setting for these decisions, say that a company now ships a certain commodity in 30,000-pound lots and the commodity moves on class rates at Class 100. The rate the firm seeks to get adjusted is $1 per 100 pounds between the points it is interested in, points O (origin) and M_1 (one of its market areas; and M_2, M_3, . . . M_n (its other market areas) all of which are the same distance from O. The carload minimum is 30,000 pounds. The lcl class is 130, which brings forth a rate of $1.30 from origin to each market area.

The firm's customers buy in lots of all sizes, ranging from 10,000 to 100,000 pounds. Some of them are eyeing other suppliers which are so located that their rates are lower. All customers are facing a cost-price squeeze and are under pressure to reduce costs.

After the situation is analyzed, the following alternatives are developed. The firm can:

1. Ask the carrier to reclassify the commodity to Class 85, which would reduce the rate from $1 per hundred pounds to 85 cents.
2. Get an exception to the classification to apply between points O and M_1.
3. Accept a proffered commodity rate to apply to one of the other market areas.
4. Acquire its own vehicles to improve the quality of service.
5. Other.

Alternative 1: The carrier analyzes its situation and finds that since the commodity is a class-rated item, any change in classification would apply all over the country. Because the firm's competitive situation is unique, similar reductions for all shippers of the commodity are not called for. The carrier refuses to unnecessarily reduce its price for all shippers merely to keep the firm's business but suggests Alternative 2 between O and M_1.

Alternative 2: The firm asks for an exception to the classification to apply between O and M_1. It asks for Class 85, which would have the following effect:

Now: 30,000, Class 100 @ $1.00 = $300
Change: 30,000, Class 85 @ $ .85 = $255
Effect: Savings to the firm of 15 cents per hundred pounds; loss to carrier of $45 per car.

The carrier, which has its own profit squeeze, cannot stand a loss in revenue per car but suggests a change in minimum weight to 40,000 for Class 85. The firm's savings would still be 15 cents per hundred, but the carrier revenue per car would rise to $340 per car, or a gain of $40.

This looks like a good deal from a logistics point of view. But how would it affect other divisions of the firm? In marketing, customers will have to be persuaded to buy in 40,000-pound lots instead of 30,000. Some will do it. Some cannot or will not, so volume of sales will drop. Will price policies have to be changed regarding volume discounts? In production, these questions must be considered: What is the effect of the loss in volume on unit production costs? What other production costs will change as a result of lower demand? What about the length of the production run and frequency of set-up costs? In finance, how will the loss of customers affect the cash flow of the firm? Many other questions will relate to effects of this decision on other departments, workers, employees, bankers, stockholders, and customers.

The company, after considering all the implications of the carrier proposal, accepts it, but, after full internal consideration, also asks for a multiple minimum rate. The classification of the first 40,000 pounds will be Class 85. On all commodities shipped in excess of 40,000 pounds, up to a total of 100,000 pounds, it asks for Class 75. The marketing department may have generated this request in order to retain a large customer or acquire one. The charges are now:

40,000 @ 85 = $340 on a 40,000-pound shipment
+60,000 @ 75 = $450 on a 60,000-pound shipment
100,000   = $790 on a 100,000-pound shipment

compared with a previous Class 100 charge of $1,000 for 100,000 pounds. Compare the per car charge of $790, with the multiple minimum described, with a Class 85 charge with a single minimum of $850.

Thus in this alternative the total transportation charge has been reduced to further the marketing effort of the firm and to meet its cost reduction goals. The exception to the classification has been made.

Alternative 3: One of the points made in Chapter 14 concerning strategic aspects of logistics pertained to the carriers' role in the channels of distribution. We stated that they should be considered as "extensions of arms of the firm," and they should consider themselves in that light in looking to their own marketing programs. The carrier approaches the marketing department to encourage it to ship to Market M_3. In checking with logistics, it is found that competition is so fierce the firm cannot enter that market without a freight rate of 50. The present class rate is 100; an exception rate of 85 also applies. To further its own marketing program—to insinuate itself into the firm's channels of distribution as an extension of the arm of the firm—the carrier introduces a commodity rate of 50 to apply from O to M_3, with minimum weight of 75,000 pounds.

Alternative 4: The firm has still another alternative to substitute for or supplement these rate adjustments based on exceptions to the classification and commodity rates. It can acquire its own vehicles as a private carrier.

To avoid complicating a simple situation, let us suppose that on 40,000-pound shipments and above, private transportation is no longer feasible because highway load limits will be exceeded. However, it is necessary to analyze customers receiving smaller lots to determine how far the firm can go to serve them. The firm may find, for example, that it cannot accept orders for less than 20,000 pounds and will handle all orders between 20,000 and 40,000 pounds in its own vehicles. While it does not want to lose the volume contributed by the smaller customers, taking all other factors into account—production, finance, personnel, and so on—it is losing money on them. It can do two things here: try to discover a way of making them profitable, or drop them. Others are served by private vehicle at high cost, but to drop them would adversely affect production costs and cash flow.

This section on the transportation environment has emphasized several points. The impact of logistics decisions on the total environment, internal and external, has been considered, with emphasis on the discovery of problems and opportunities for the logistics department. The discussion emphasized that logistics decisions are made in a framework of the organization as a whole, not just logistics or any other department. As with all managerial functions, we are concerned not only with management *of* the logistics function but with management *and* logistics function.

THE WAREHOUSING ENVIRONMENT

As with transportation, warehousing is a means to the end of supporting the marketing effort of a firm. Specifically, the logistics manager uses it as a tool to accomplish his objectives. This section will discuss the types of warehouses and the differences between warehousing and storage. Then the functional role of warehousing in the marketing process will be analyzed through an examination of some relevant decisions to be made by the logistics manager.

Types of warehouses

Warehouses can be classified as public or private and as general merchandise or special. A *private warehouse,* like a private carrier, is for the use of its owner and is not open to the public. A *public warehouse* holds itself open to service for the public at large. The fundamental reason a company would operate its own warehouse is that this affords better control over both service and cost.

As the name implies, a *general merchandise warehouse* handles almost anything that does not need special facilities or special care. But many such warehouses are a mixture, often providing some special care, such as refrigeration. *Specialized warehouses* are equipped for special purposes: grain elevators, bulk vegetable oil tanks, household goods, cotton compresses, frozen food, and so on.

Storage and warehousing

The words "storage" and "warehousing" are often used interchangeably, but a special meaning may also be applied to each. Seasonally produced goods and others for which there is no immediate need must come to rest for an indefinite period. *Storage* implies a resting place for goods that can just sit there until someone decides how they will be used. They are stored because there is nothing else to do with them.

Warehousing connotes a dynamic relationship among goods, their housing, and their demand. It implies that the goods are on their way somewhere else but have paused and may have something done to them. The warehouse is used as a strategic or tactical marketing tool to accomplish some objective. It not only regulates the flow of goods through the distribution channels, it regulates the mix of that flow. It may receive large quantities of mustard from one producer, flour from another, and canned tomatoes from a third. It interrupts their flow through the channel long enough to break these shipments, mix them, and forward them to many other members of the channel. Note that the canned tomatoes may have been in storage for several months, since the last harvest, before they are warehoused.

The basic distinction between storage and warehousing is that some goods come to rest in a storage facility and some flow through a warehouse as a distribution center. These latter terms are often used to identify a concept and a facility: the *flow through* concept is practiced by a *distribution center.*

Functions of warehouses

The basic function of warehousing is to serve as a strategic and tactical tool of the organization in furthering its marketing program. It does this in part by providing the goods with physical, economic, and temporal proximity to the market and by providing certain services to the user.

One of the principal concerns of logistics is the economic and timely movement of goods through space. The use of warehousing makes it possible for the manager to manage these economic and temporal problems and the costs associated with them. In Chapter 14 it was noted that transportation costs for one company were equal to 13 percent of sales. Several studies have shown that all logistics costs account for about 20 percent of sales.[1] Warehousing costs may be 6 to 8 percent of sales. Logistics costs of individual industries and individual firms will vary widely from the average.

This chapter considers transportation and warehousing as the principal components of logistics. The latter can play a powerful role in reducing costs of the former. In general, the two work in tandem in establishing physical, economic, and temporal proximity of seller and buyer. Since these concepts were discussed in Chapter 14, we only mention them briefly here to place them in context.

Physical proximity. Physical proximity refers to the actual distance separating a buyer and seller. The fact that distance is considered by many to be a significant factor in marketing is traceable to a misconception about transportation rates and their relationshp to distance. Class rates do progress with distance, and commodity rates may have a relationship to it. However, it is not at all unusual for a rate for 250 miles to be much higher than one for a greater distance, with ICC approval.

Economic proximity. Economic proximity can have either relation to physical proximity. Regardless of what the Rand-McNally Atlas says, Columbus is economically closer to San Francisco than Denver is if a shipper pays a rate of 100 from Columbus to San Francisco and 125 from Denver to San Francisco. The rail rate structure has many such provisions. This refers not to the cost of providing transportation but to the price paid for it.

Temporal proximity. Temporal proximity can have little relation to higher economic or physical proximity. Again, regardless of the Rand-McNally Atlas, Paris is closer to New York than Chicago is if a shipper uses a seven-hour air freight schedule from Paris instead of a three-day surface movement from Chicago.

---

[1] James A. Constantin, *Principles of Logistics Management* (New York: Appleton-Century-Crofts, 1966), Chapter 6.

Warehouse services. In addition to being a factor in putting a producer nearer his market physically, economically, and temporally, warehousing performs many other functions. One is to aid in financing. Lending institutions have come to accept a warehouse receipt for goods in storage as collateral for loans. This applies not only to goods actually on a warehouseman's premises but also to those under the warehouseman's control, even though they may be on the owner's premises, a concept called field warehousing. Goods on the owner's premises under the control of a warehouseman may be segregated by a painted line, a wire fence, or a sign, or they may be placed in a separate building. The warehouseman will then issue a receipt which can be used as collateral for financing. Since he is responsible to the lending agency, the supervision he exercises over the goods is a matter of judgment based upon experience. The owner may not remove the goods without approval of the warehouseman, who must have the approval of the lender.

Other warehousing functions involve serving as a kind of field office, order taker, disbursing agent, or inventory reporter. Some warehouses have rooms with desk space for salespeople or in which the storer can set up displays of merchandise. They take orders from customers, see to delivery, and report on inventory levels, as required.

Another set of warehousing functions includes such activities as receiving inbound shipments, breaking bulk, consolidating outbound shipments, and arranging for transportation. There are two facets of the break-bulk function. One involves receiving a large shipment of packaged goods and breaking them into smaller units for shipments. The other involves receiving goods literally in bulk and packaging them in containers more suitable to the customer's needs.

Warehouse pricing. There are many different approaches to pricing. Most quotations by warehousemen consist of several elements: (1) so many cents per square foot for storage (sometimes cubic feet are used), (2) charges for handling in and handling out, (3) clerical costs for activities such as processing reports and freight bills, and (4) miscellaneous charges for such services as stenciling packages, repairing broken crates, and breaking bulk.

MANAGERIAL DECISIONS ON WAREHOUSING

Managerial decisions on warehousing, like all decisions which have an impact on other parts of the firm, should be made within a framework considering their effects on all departments concerned. Three major types of decisions are considered in this section:

1. Whether service should be direct from factory to customer.
2. Whether it should be indirect through distribution centers. If indirect service is decided on, other decisions are required.

    a. The selection of distribution points (number and location).
    b. The determination of territorial boundaries of the several distribution points.
3. What constitutes good service at low cost. This involves analyses of the following costs at different levels of service.
    a. Transportation.
    b. Inventory.
    c. Warehousing.
    d. Information.
    e. All of these combined.

The discussion of these managerial decisions will be based on a customer service objective of providing delivery to 90 percent of the customers two days after orders have been received.

Direct service

In accomplishing the stated customer service objective, no real problem arises for customers located two days away when present transportation policies are followed. However, if the building of other factories is ruled out, in order to fulfill the objective with direct service all customers will have to be brought to within two days' distance. One method of doing this is to serve them by air freight at a higher transportation cost. Another method is to work out an arrangement with the customer under which he receives periodic shipments to arrive on a certain day, with unanticipated needs being filled by air freight. This would probably require more inventory in the pipeline and thus more working capital. These two approaches require additional working capital or adjustments in the procurement policies of customers. Accordingly, both have an impact on other divisions of the firm such as finance and marketing, and strategic decisions are required.

A third approach was used by an Oklahoma City company. It was purely a managerial decision with no additional resources required and no adverse impact on any other department. The problem was handed by the marketing department to the late C. D. Forbes, vice president, traffic, of the Macklanburg-Duncan Company. Basically, the problem was one of temporal proximity. Customers on the East Coast were one or two days away from eastern suppliers and several days away from M-D. Company policies excluded certain obvious alternatives: an eastern branch plant or warehouse location, use of wholesalers. Forbes had the option of continuing present service levels and serving what customers could be retained, or finding some other approach.

Forbes chose the latter; after analysis of external and internal environments, he discovered an alternative solution. An airline which considered itself an extension of the arms of the firm analyzed its internal environment and found plenty of space on late evening and night flights from Oklahoma City. A special rate *and* service were worked out. M-D also made certain internal adjustments. The airline took the shipments to eastern airports and delivered them according to instructions from M-D to the appropriate ground carrier: trucking companies; REA express; the post office; local delivery companies; and United Parcel Service. M-D prepared all ground-shipping documents.

The result was that at no increase in cost to M-D, improved customer service resulted in retention of eastern customers who were brought to within two days of Oklahoma City; some in the airport cities got overnight service. This accomplishment was due to (1) a close working relation between marketing and logistics in a marketing-oriented company, (2) recognition by the firm that carriers are extensions of the arms of the firm in the channels, (3) a similar recognition by a marketing-oriented airline, and (4) imaginative managers.

Indirect service

The decision to provide indirect service raises many strategic decisions requiring allocation of resources. In this chapter on management of the logistics function, it is assumed that those strategic decisions have been made and policies to implement them have been set. Because they are strategic decisions, no attention is given in this chapter to such matters as whether distribution centers and transportation used should be public or private. Further, it is assumed that the selection of the number of distribution centers and inventory requirements will be made within policy guidelines.

Selection of distribution points. The very large organization with several plants, dozens of products, and hundreds of customer locations may need a number of distribution points. For such companies, determining the most effective number and location of distribution points is such a complex problem that computer-based programs are required for systematic analysis.[2]

Reasonably simple methods are available for the smaller company with less complex requirements. These methods are also useful to the very large company in distribution from its major distribution centers to outlying cities. These large companies may serve their total market from a dozen or two distribution points selected with the help of a computer program. The authors have used the techniques discussed in this chapter many times in helping major companies design distribu-

---

[2] See A. A. Kuehn and M. J. Hamburger, "A Heuristic Program for Locating Warehouses," *Management Science,* July 1963.

tion patterns from those major distribution points to other large and small cities.

These methods of analysis provide good results, perhaps even the best results. The "typical" company (whatever that may be) which distributes nationally will have a distribution pattern that can be easily predicted:

1. Most of the sales or customers will be in and around large cities.
2. The volume of sales will decrease as distance from the central city increases.
3. The number of customers may increase as distance from the central cities increase, and the size of the order may decrease.

This probable pattern follows the law of inverse proportions discussed in Chapter 14 as one of the "natural" problems of the logistics manager.

Plotting the location of customers as well as their volume of purchases should reveal obvious territories and distribution locations in each territory. In the event such locations are not obvious, a simple set of calculations can be made to identify the most economic point of distribution for each territory. The format for such an analysis is shown in Table 15–1.

TABLE 15–1
Format for Determining the Least Cost Distribution Point for a Territory

		Possible distribution points			
		A		*B*	
(1) *Customer location point*	*(2)* *Weight of shipment (100 lbs.)*	*(3)* *Rate (cents per 100 lbs.)*	*(4)* *Charge (dollars) (col. 2 × col. 3)*	*(5)* *Rate (cents per 100 lbs.)*	*(6)* *Charge (dollar (col. 2 × col. .*
A	200,000	50*	100,000	250	500,000
B	150,000	300	450,000	50*	75,000
C	50,000	200	100,000	220	110,000
D	75,000	200	150,000	180	135,000
E	25,000	400	100,000	460	115,000
Totals.	500,000		900,000		935,000
		$1.80 (Col. 4 ÷ Col. 2)		$1.87 (Col. 6 ÷ Col. 2)	

* Local delivery charge from warehouse.

Column 1 lists the cities in which customers are located, and column 2 shows the number of pounds (in hundreds) received in each city during a period. Columns 3 and 5 show the rate per hundred pounds from potential distribution points, while columns 2, 4, and 6 are summed to show the total weight received by all cities and the total charges which would have to be paid if the distribution point is located at point A or B. Then the total charges which would have been incurred from each of A and B (columns 4 and 6) is divided by the total weight. The result is that if the customers had been served from point A, the weighted average transportation rate would have been $1.80 per 100 pounds. From point B, it would have been $1.87.

Under the conditions described, therefore, point A is the lowest cost point. This example uses a static situation, but the fact that a distribution point is set up in a territory will have implications for better service which may change the totals considerably. Changes in sales patterns may make it desirable to relocate distribution points at some later date. Of course, if a private distribution center is used, the company is locked in to using that point.

This "rough and ready" approach is not adequate for large distribution systems requiring analyses of many points and those that require consideration of marketing service variables. Computer-based models are available to accommodate analyses of complex systems, as we have noted.

Once the location of the distribution centers has been determined, the territorial boundary lines to separate the sales territories must be drawn. This, too, can be a very complex situation for large companies, but in many cases it can be done almost by inspection. There is also a simple exercise in arithmetic to help draw the boundaries. Assume that distribution centers will be located at both A and X. The problem is to determine which cities will be served by A and which will be served by X. Figure 15–2 shows the dividing points into two typical territories. The critical factors are:

1. Transportation from factory to warehouse. In this case you should assume large volume shipments.
2. Warehouse charges. Assume they are the same at points A and X, the distribution points for Territories I and II.
3. Transportation from warehouse to customer, by less than truckload (ltl) motor shipment. None of the assumptions is critical to the concept.

Because in many cases rail rates have a tendency to taper with distance, inbound costs are represented by a curved line. The perpendicular rising from the rate line represents warehouse charges. Transportation costs outbound are shown from A toward 0 and X, and from X toward A and the next distribution point. The point of equilibrium which marks the division point between Territories I and II is established by the intersection of the lines for outbound costs from distribution points A and X.

FIGURE 15–2
Division of Territories of Distribution Points

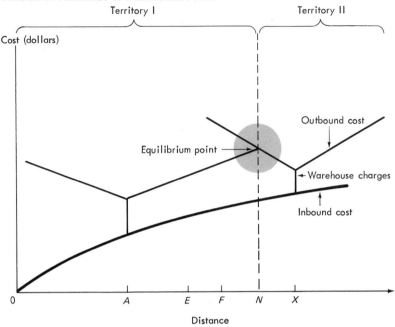

In Figure 15–2, point N is the point of indifference and therefore the territorial dividing line, other things remaining the same. If all forces did not remain the same, which ones would cause a shift in the boundary line? We assumed outbound movements by common carrier. If instead the company used its own trucks outbound, there might be a situation in which, point X would serve point F, which is now not in Territory II. Suppose that customers are fairly evenly distributed between A and E and that their demand fairly well fills up the truck making deliveries from A. Also, suppose that from point X back toward A, there is truck capacity to handle freight destined for F. Under these conditions, the alternative of serving F from N appears to be better than dispatching a second truck from A to deliver to F. (There are several other reasons why F might be served from A. Think of some.)

There are other situations which could call for alternative logistics decisions or could involve other departments, such as marketing. Assume, for example, that the trucks from A to E and from X to N are both full. This leaves F on a plateau. Our emphasis on using a mix of transportation should make one alternative obvious: use a for-hire carrier for point F.

The situation described is typical, whether the outbound trucks are owned by the company or by a warehouseman who must make the decision concerning F. As a matter of practice, company trucks (or those of the warehouseman) will serve only selected, large customers in the cities along the way, and common carriers will be used to reach others that are costly to serve. In other words, the common carriers may be given the traffic to low-volume, high-cost customers, even though the private trucks pass the doors of these customers. This sound like dirty pool, but it is the carriers, by their rate structure, that make this practice possible. They have set the rules of the game, and good cost analyses by the warehouseman and the company lead them to take advantage of it.

Another alternative for dealing with F required consultation with marketing people. Perhaps the firm would be better off not serving F and letting competitors have it. Or perhaps a lower quality of service at a lower cost would be called for.

Having completed our discussion on two of the major decision areas, whether to offer direct or indirect service, and having discussed some methods of analysis of indirect service, we turn now to the third major decision area.

Good service at low cost

Quality of service is an important factor in attracting and retaining satisfied and profitable customers. A significant trade-off is possible between high-quality service and the cost of providing it. Good service at low cost is an abstract term, but it can be given concrete meaning by comparing the cost of different levels of customer service. As we have seen, one way service can be improved is by creating distribution points near the sources of demand. It can be inferred intuitively that the more distribution points used, the higher the cost. The critical problem is to relate the cost of distribution points to the service they can provide.

Several steps are involved in the process of developing information for this decision. One approach was described by a distribution consultant, W. Clayton Hill, in the 1960s, and the following discussion is based on his work.[3] This discussion will shed light on:

1. The reconciliation of conflicting objectives of good service at low cost.
2. The acceptance of increased costs in one area in order to reduce costs in another.
3. The reasons for the apparent enigma of distribution cost increasing as distribution gets closer to the customer.

---

[3] W. Clayton Hill, "Reorganizing Distribution for Higher Profits," *Industrial Marketing*, vol. 48, no. 2, February 1963, pp. 77–84.

4. The relative importance of individual items in the cost mix consisting of transportation, inventory investment and maintenance, warehousing, information, and the importance of analyzing them all together.

Together these factors emphasize two major points: a reasonable and simple approach to quantifying good service at low cost, and the significance of cost management.

The first step in the process of quantifying the term "good service at low cost" is to determine the number of locations required in order to offer different qualities of service. The critical factors in determining the time required to serve customers are their number and location and the time required to reach them from different locations. Hill's determination of the relationships between the number of distribution points and the percentage of the U.S. market which could be served in one day and two days is as follows:

	Percent of market served in	
Number of points	*One day*	*Two days*
5	33	86
17	81	97
25	90	100
50	96	100
100	99	100

Figure 15–3 shows this graphically.

The second step is to identify how the cost of the major logistics elements will vary with the number of distribution points. These elements are transportation, inventory, warehousing, and information. Figure 15–4 shows how the cost of each of these elements varies.

Transportation. As the number of distribution points increases, transportation costs will decline. If there are only a few distribution points, compared with many, each will serve a larger territory, and outbound ltl shipments will move longer distances by higher ltl rates. A transportation cost index is shown below and is graphed in Figure 15–4A. (Five distribution points equals 100 in the various cost indexes.)

Number of points	*Transportation cost index*
5	100
17	84
25	79
50	74
100	70

Inventory. Inventory investment rises as the number of distribution points increases, because of the cumulative effect of larger safety stocks required to prevent stock-outs. Inventory maintenance costs are estimated to be 22 percent of investment. Figure 15–4B shows the impact of the

FIGURE 15–3
Relation of Number of Distribution Points to Percentage of U.S. Market Served

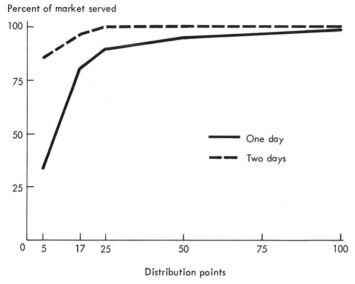

Percent of market served

Source: W. Clayton Hill, "Reorganizing Distribution for Higher Profits," *Industrial Marketing*, vol. 48 (February 1963), pp. 77–84.

number of distribution points on cost of maintaining inventory. The table below shows the relationship between number of distribution points and inventory investment and maintenance.

	Inventory indexes	
Number of points	*Investment*	*Maintenance*
5	100	100
17	146	146
25	166	166
50	209	209
100	273	273

Warehousing. Warehouse handling costs also increase with larger numbers of distribution points. These changes are shown below and are graphed in Figure 15–4C. Note the proportionate increase in cost in this case.

Number of points	*Warehousing cost index*
5	100
17	124
25	139
50	194
100	271

FIGURE 15–4
Variation of Cost Elements with Number of Distribution Points

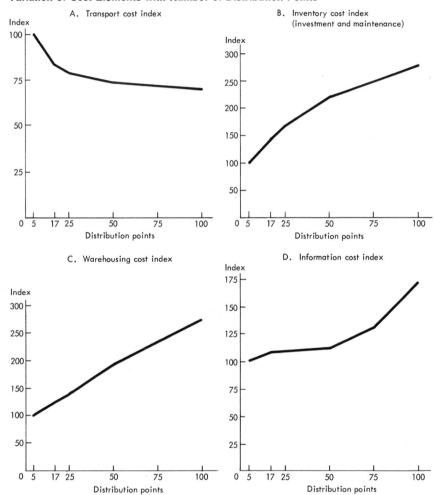

A. Transport cost index

B. Inventory cost index
(investment and maintenance)

C. Warehousing cost index

D. Information cost index

Source: Indexes and drawings by the authors from basic data in W. Clayton Hill, "Reorganizing Distribution for Higher Profits," *Industrial Marketing,* vol. 48 (February 1963), pp. 77–84.

Information.   Information costs concerning inventory shipped and on hand will also increase with the number of distribution points in the system. The relation is shown below and graphed in Figure 15–4D.

Number of points	Information cost index
5	100
17	108
25	111
50	131
100	173

Total costs. Since the cost of three of the four logistics elements considered above rises as the number of distribution points increases, total costs also can be expected to rise. The figures reflecting this change are shown below.

Number of points	Total cost index
5	100
17	105
25	108
50	121
100	141

This relationship is shown in Figure 15–5.

FIGURE 15–5
Variation of Total Cost with Number of Distribution Points

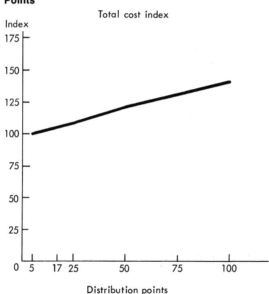

Source: Indexes and drawings by the authors for basic data in W. Clayton Hill, "Reorganizing Distribution for Higher Profits," *Industrial Marketing*, vol. 48, February 1963, pp. 77–84.

Although the index numbers used above obscure the relative importance of each of the cost components, Table 15–2 indicates this relationship. The table clearly shows that transportation and inventory maintenance costs are the two most important cost components. Dollar expenditures for these elements accompanying a change in the number of distribution points from 5 to 100 are shown in Table 15–3.

TABLE 15–2
Cost and Percentage of Total Cost for Each Logistics Cost Component Related to Number of Distribution Points

| Number of points | Total cost | | Percentage of total cost | | | |
	Dollars (000)	Percent	Trans- portation	Inventory maintenance	Ware- housing	Infor- mation
5.........	$4,475	100	59%	27%	4%	10%
17........	4,693	100	47	38	5	10
25........	4,840	100	43	42	5	10
50........	5,400	100	36	46	7	11
100.......	6,310	100	29	51	8	12

These relationships suggest some interesting opportunities for significant managerial decisions which could improve efficiency and reduce cost. They also provide a reason for reviewing a particular customer service level. Within the present framework of analysis, if the company moves from 5 points to 100 points, transportation costs fall 30 percent (30 points on the index in Table 15–3) and change from 59 percent

TABLE 15–3
Variation in Cost of Transportation and Maintenance of Inventory with Number of Distribution Points

| Number of points | Transportation | | Inventory maintenance | |
	Dollars (000)	Index	Dollars (000)	Index
5............	$2,632	100	$1,205	100
17...........	2,211	84	1,761	146
25...........	2,082	79	1,997	166
50...........	1,934	73	2,513	209
100..........	1,847	70	3,172	263

of total cost to 29 percent (Table 15–2). Inventory costs in the same situation rise 163 percent to become 51 percent of total costs instead of 27 percent.

Changes in managerial policies

The previous discussions were based upon some assumed or implied policies within a given policy framework. What happens if we change that framework? Managerial decisions concerning each of the logistics cost elements can give rise to additional problems and opportunities in the goal of providing good customer service at low cost. What would happen to transportation, warehousing, and inventory costs if certain policies were changed?

Take for example a liquid (or granular) detergent now shipped from the factory, packaged to go on the grocer's shelf. It is shipped in 20,000-pound lots to meet carload minimum weights, inventory, replacement schedules, economic production runs, and so on. An alternative is to ship the detergent in tank cars or tank trucks to get a lower rate, and have the warehouse receive the shipment, acquire cartons, packages, or plastic bottles locally, and package it for the grocer's shelf. What impact would this have on inbound transportation costs and on packaging materials, production schedules and costs, inventory investment, and so on? What effect would it have on warehousing costs if inventory were stored in bulk and packaged by the warehouseman in minimum economic production runs, for flow through the warehouse as packaged items?

As for inventory costs, what would happen if different customer service levels were set for different customers, products, and territories? For example, using the familiar ABC system (from basic accounting courses, among other sources), Group A commodities could be stored in all distribution centers in the system; Group B in perhaps 20 percent of the centers; and Group C in perhaps 5 percent of the centers. The relative cost of providing selected customer service levels attained by

TABLE 15–4
Cost of Providing Levels of Customer Service Related to Number of Distribution Points

Number of points	Market service				Total cost index
	In one day		In two days		
	Percent of market service	Index	Percent of market service	Index	
5............	33	100	86	100	100
17...........	81	245	97	113	105
25...........	90	273	100	116	108
50...........	96	291	100	116	121
100..........	99	300	100	116	145

using different numbers of distribution points is indicated in Table 15–4 and Figure 15–6.

These data give concrete meaning to the otherwise vague concept of "good service at low cost," and may temper the enthusiasm of the marketing manager for one-day service. They also provide Level 1

FIGURE 15–6

Cost of Providing Levels of Customer Service Related to Number of Distribution Points

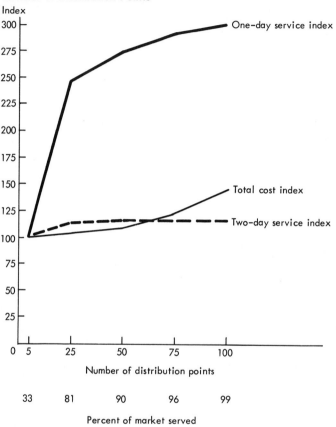

executives with a basis for setting customer service levels. (Because the immediate focus here is on logistics costs and customer service, we assume the effects on other departments such as production will be taken into account in reaching such decisions.)

The data presented so far use five distribution points as the base of 100. Comparison of 17, 25, 50, and 100 points with 5 points shows how cost and percent of market served change from one number of distribution points to the next. This is indicated in Table 15–5.

To simplify the discussion, we will establish a policy constraint: Service to only 81 percent of the market in one day after the order is received is not acceptable. Since 17 distribution points would deliver this service, more than 17—or at least 25 in the illustration—will be

TABLE 15–5
Improvement of Service and Increase in Cost with Increase in Number of Distribution Points

Changes in number of points		Changes in percent of market served				Service improvement		Cost increase
From	To	One day		Two days		One day	Two days	
		From	To	From	To			
5	17	33%	81%	86%	97%	145%	13%	5%
17	25	81	90	97	100	11	3	3
25	50	90	96	100	100	7	0	12
25	100	90	99	100	100	10	0	34
50	100	96	99	100	100	3	0	20

required. Consideration of the data in Table 15–5 suggests the types of questions to be evaluated:

1. Is a 7 percent increase in the market served in one day worth a 12 percent increase in cost (from 25 to 50 points)?
2. Is a 10 percent increase in the market served in one day worth a 34 percent increase in cost (from 25 to 100 points)?
3. Is a 3 percent increase in the market served in one day worth a 20 percent increase in cost (from 50 to 100 points)?

One of our definitions of customer service relates to the number of days required to serve the market after the order has been received. Could customer service be increased by speeding up the order-receiving process? Chapter 14 noted the practice of one company in which salesmen wrote up daily orders each night and mailed them in. These orders were received one to several days later. After a WATS service, coupled with an all-hours receiving service was inaugurated, orders were received the night they were sent, and paperwork on them was started the next day. A faster system became possible with the development of a portable computer terminal that is held to the customer's telephone. With this device an order can be transmitted to the company computer at the moment the customer gives it, confirmed instantaneously, and started being processed all within moments. For technical reasons the company referred to stopped using that system.

The time required to serve customers involved some important variables: transportation, warehouse handling, and order and transmission processing, both of which can be either fast or slow. To simplify the discussion we will make an assumption that is realistic but does not necessarily hold true: The faster the process, the more expensive it is. Also, we shift away from the earlier one- and two-day delivery schedules.

There are a number of alternativies when these variables are combined in certain ways. Different customer service levels can be attained. Or the same service level can be attained in different ways.

A decision tree such as that shown in Figure 15–7 is a helpful means of analyzing this problem. To make the analysis simple we assume that there are two speeds for each of the four variables shown at the top of Figure 15–7: fast and slow. Also, for the sake of simplicity we use one-day and one-half-day increments in speed (even for order transmission, which can take only a few seconds by phone or by the portable computer terminal we spoke of!)

Note that for transportation there are two options, fast and slow. For Option 1, take the fast route requiring 1.0 days. There is another choice at the "junction" of warehouse handling where again you can go fast or slow. Keep on the fast route which takes 0.5 days. At order processing and order transmission, the same fast-slow alternatives are present. The fast route for each of those two tasks requires 0.5 days. Thus, if Option 1 is to take the fast route at each branch, the time lapse is 2.5 days (1.0 + 0.5 + 0.5 + 0.5).

Table 15–6 shows the 16 possible combinations with time required ranging from 2.5 days for Option 1 to 7.0 days for Option 9 where the slow route was taken at each junction. Another way of using the decision tree is to use dollar figures when money costs are more important than time costs. Part B of Table 15–6 shows another aspect of the decision tree analysis which was referred to earlier. There are several ways of attaining the same quality of service. The 16 different options result in 10 possible time lapses. To illustrate the types of decisions possible several possible combinations will be examined. First, options 8 and 14 provide for six-day delivery after the salesman takes the order. Even though the results are the same, the components differ significantly. Option 8 calls for one-day (fast) transportation service and slow order transmission, processing, and warehouse handling. Option 14 calls for two-day (slow) transportation and order transmission, but fast order processing and warehouse handling.

Option 8 would be more costly because transportation is the most costly of the several components. There is little need for the premium service when it is wasted. By decreasing expenditures on transportation and increasing them for order processing and transmission, the same six-day service could be attained.

Note what can be done with another mix. Since Option 8 involves fast transportation, it can be retained as a requirement and Option 7, which, in addition to fast transportation calls for fast order transmission and slow physical handling and order processing, can be considered. Note that this is the opposite of the program in Option 14. Option 7 reduces the time lapse to 3.5 days from the 6.0 days contemplated

FIGURE 15–7
A Decision Tree: Logistics Activities

Days required	Transportation	Warehouse handling	Order processing	Order transmission
Fast	1	0.5	0.5	0.5
Slow	2	1.0	1.0	3.0

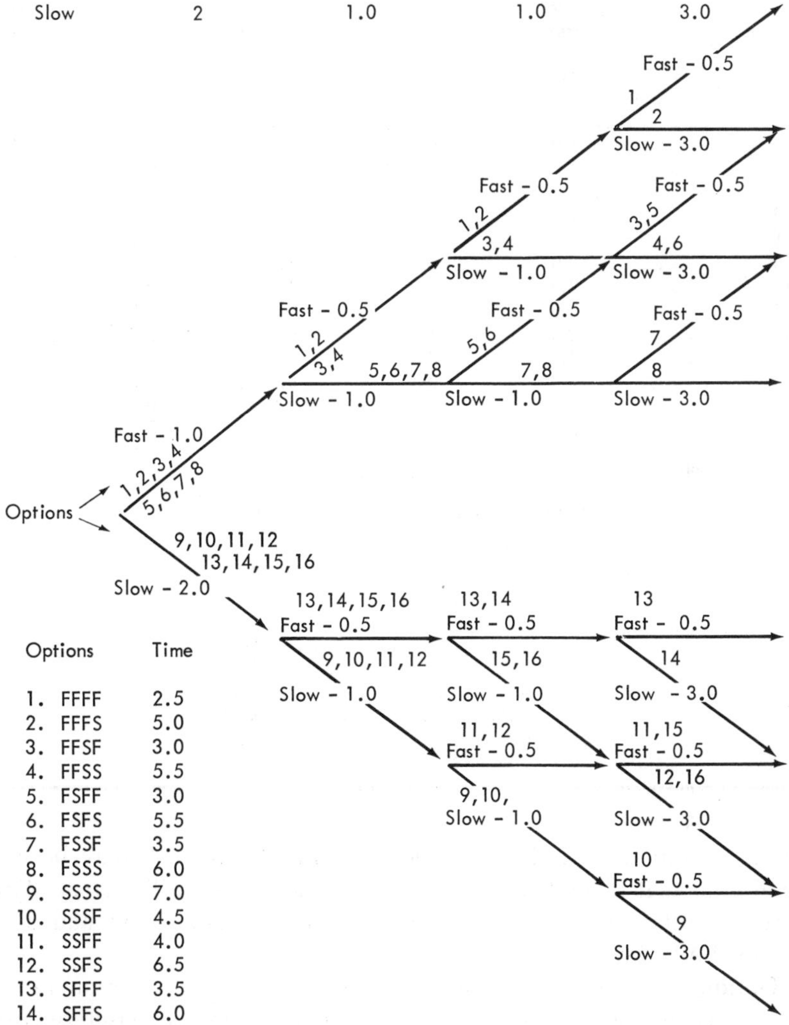

Options	Time
1. FFFF	2.5
2. FFFS	5.0
3. FFSF	3.0
4. FFSS	5.5
5. FSFF	3.0
6. FSFS	5.5
7. FSSF	3.5
8. FSSS	6.0
9. SSSS	7.0
10. SSSF	4.5
11. SSFF	4.0
12. SSFS	6.5
13. SFFF	3.5
14. SFFS	6.0
15. SFSF	4.0
16. SFSS	6.5

* Times are for illustrative purposes; only half and whole days are used which results in some distortions. For example, order transmission as described in the text may be instantaneous, but we have used 0.5 days.

TABLE 15–6
Time Required for Delivery under Different Options

A. Days Required

Option	Transpor- tation	Warehouse handling	Order processing	Order transmission	Total time
1	1.0	0.5	0.5	0.5	2.5
2	1.0	0.5	0.5	3.0	5.0
3	1.0	0.5	1.0	0.5	3.0
4	1.0	0.5	1.0	3.0	5.5
5	1.0	1.0	0.5	0.5	3.0
6	1.0	1.0	0.5	3.0	5.5
7	1.0	1.0	1.0	0.5	3.5
8	1.0	1.0	1.0	3.0	6.0
9	2.0	1.0	1.0	3.0	7.0
10	2.0	1.0	1.0	0.5	4.5
11	2.0	1.0	0.5	0.5	4.0
12	2.0	1.0	0.5	3.0	6.5
13	2.0	0.5	0.5	0.5	3.5
14	2.0	0.5	0.5	3.0	6.0
15	2.0	0.5	1.0	0.5	4.0
16	2.0	0.5	1.0	3.0	6.5

B. Recapitulation

Number of days	Options
2.5	1
3.0	3,5
3.5	7,13
4.0	11,15
4.5	10
5.0	2
5.5	4,6
6.0	8,14
6.5	12,16
7.0	9

by both Options 8 and 14. While the cost of Option 7 may be a bit more than that of Option 8, the service is also better. The small difference in cost is the difference between an air mail stamp and a call on the WATS line.

Option 7 may cost more than just "a bit more" than Option 14. The cost of using fast transportation will probably not be offset by using the slower processing and handling methods of Option 7. However, if the low-cost transport of Option 14 is desirable, time savings can be significant by adopting Option 10. The cost of Option 19 is apparently less than that of 14 because the cheapest versions of the three high-cost elements of the cost mix are used. Again, a call on the WATS line replaces a postage stamp, and the result is 4.5-day service instead of 6.0. Not only is Option 10 a lower-cost option than 14, it also provides better service.

The techniques described above for analyzing service to customers in general have been applied by James Arbury and others to individual customers.[4]

SUMMARY AND CONCLUSIONS

This chapter began with a discussion of customer service and the environmental conditions with which the logistics manager must cope. The emphasis was on the impact of customer service levels on logistics decisions and their effect on other activities of the firm such as marketing and finance.

In order to analyze some of the logistics decisions affecting transportation, the transportation environment was analyzed. The types of carriers and rate structures were discussed as were the various types of transportation rates and services. These analyses provided a foundation for the discussion of the types of decisions affecting transportation which logistics managers must make.

Warehousing is another component of the set of logistics activities. A foundation was laid for the discussion of managerial decisions affecting warehousing by an analysis of the warehousing environment. Here, the types and functions of warehouses were discussed. With this foundation several key managerial issues affecting the use of warehouses were discussed.

One of the most important logistics decisions is whether service to customers should be direct from the factory or indirect through either a public or private warehouse. These two were separated, and the first analysis was of those decisions affecting direct service. The decisions affecting indirect service are more complex, so that subject was subdivided. The first subdivision dealt with the selection of distribution points, and a technique for selection was presented. The second subdivision was concerned with the division of territories between two distribution centers. In this discussion, a number of alternatives and implications were discussed.

The third major decision area was concerned with good service at low cost. It applied with equal force to situations involving direct and indirect service. In this discussion trade-off between quality and cost of service were analyzed to help give concrete meaning to the abstract concept of good service at low cost.

These decision areas were analyzed and discussed within a given policy framework. We then raised a series of "what if" types of questions and explored their implications for the logistics manager. For example

---

[4] James Arbury, et al., *A New Approach to Physical Distribution* (New York: American Management Association, Inc., 1967), pp. 50–69.

we asked what would happen if different customer service levels were set for different customers, products, or territories.

Finally, as a device to show the complex interrelationships of the several components, a decision tree was constructed. Only four variables were used: time required for transportation, warehouse handling, order processing, and order transmission. Even so, the analysis resulted in 16 options. We analyzed the implications of some of these options.

One thread ran through the entire chapter: the one major function of logistics activities is to support the marketing effort of the firm. One conscious omission—not an oversight—was that we did not deal with decisions on day-to-day operations of either transportation systems or warehouse facilities. Since this is a marketing book, such discussions would be out of place.

| # Promotion strategies and policies

The communication process
Communication strategy decision process
The components of promotion
    Personal selling
    Advertising
    Sales promotion
    Other forms of promotion
Organization and institutions of promotion
    The sales force
    Sales agents
    Advertising and sales promotion
    The advertising agency
Role variation
    Planning promotion strategy
    Corporate-level planning and decision areas
    Positioning of product
    Dimensions of promotion strategy
    Specific target audiences
    Messages and communication tasks
    Assignment of tasks to promotion instruments
    Magnitude of the promotion effort
    Promotion budget allocation
Summary

Promotion is one of the major communication variables in the marketing mix. Promotion presents to the market the company's entire offer including the company itself, its products, services, and prices, and its distributors. It is the key pipeline for information flowing from the firm to the customer either directly or through the channel of distribution. In its original Latin form, the term promotion meant to "move forward." As applied in the marketing situation, it simply means persuasive communication. The firm must communicate with numerous individuals and groups in order to carry on its marketing functions. Much of this communication must be persuasive in nature since certain ideas, concepts, and philosophies of the firm must be accepted by the market if the marketing process is to function smoothly. The methods used to communicate necessarily vary with the audience, situations, and resources available. The general objective, however, is to persuade others to respond favorably.

In this chapter we will examine the strategic role of promotion in marketing. This will involve first a brief look at the communication process, some of the various instruments and institutions used in promotion, and how promotion strategy may vary among different environments. Then we will develop some of the strategic decision processes in developing promotion objectives and budgets. Your study of this chapter and Chapter 17, Promotion Management, will be helped substantially if you will check the stages in the consumer satisfaction process discussed in Chapters 6 and 8. Note especially Figure 8–3 (page 178).

THE COMMUNICATION PROCESS

An understanding of the communication process is essential to effective promotional strategy. In this section you will find two different but related depictions of the process: the theoretical and the adapted.

The theoretical communication process

Communication is the transmission of an idea from a source to a receiver. It may occur between a large number of different organisms but our basic concern is that which occurs between human beings. And it is important to remember that marketing communication is communication among people, no matter whether the company originating the message is large or small or the intended receiver is one person or one million. Communication theorists offer a useful model of the communication process, and it is shown in Figure 16–1.

The basic model is shown in the bold-outlined boxes in the middle

FIGURE 16–1
The Theoretical Communication Process

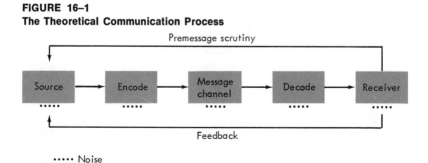

Premessage scrutiny

Source → Encode → Message channel → Decode → Receiver

Feedback

····· Noise

of the figure. The *source* is the one which originates the idea to be communicated. This idea is *encoded* into some kind of transmittable symbols. Common symbols that we all use to communicate with are words, nonword sounds, and pictures. It is, however, reasonable and proper to consider any of the senses as possible vehicles for communication. In this context we might well encode our message using smell, taste, or feel as well as sight and hearing. This encoding step is normally automatic when we engage in everyday communication, but even then we sometimes find ourselves saying, "How shall I say it?" which simply means we are searching for the appropriate symbols to communicate our message.

Once encoded, the idea is then transmitted through some medium or *message channel*. Advertising, for example, flows through television, radio, newspapers, and numerous other message channels. An idea or message so transmitted does not automatically and directly go to the receiver. It must first be *decoded* by the receiver. This means that each intended receiver must receive the symbols sent by the source and derive the idea the source intended. Then the process is complete.

If an idea could be transmitted in the manner described above without distortion or misunderstanding, the communication process would be very efficient indeed. But unfortunately there are many distractions in the environment within which we communicate and these are classified as *noise*. Noise can be further classified as: internal noise, external noise, and competitive noise.

Internal noise is that which is internal to the communication process itself. If, for example, the source were to encode a message using words that were not in the vocabulary of the receiver, some portion of the idea would be lost. Radio static, or a rolling television picture would have a similar effect. Marketing communicators have some control over internal noise insofar as they can study the receiver's language capability or attempt to eliminate technical message channel problems. Complete elimination is probably not possible, however.

External noise, as the name implies, is that which distorts or obscures the message but is outside the communication process. For example, while you are reading this section, you will be exposed to many other stimuli such as the normal sounds of other people moving about you or a flickering reading light. None of these may get your complete attention, but each may cause temporary inattention to these paragraphs. Marketing communications are particularly sensitive to problems of external noise because they often cannot control it nor be held responsible for its distortive effects. But they make sincere attempts to minimize its effect. For example, salespeople will often try to make their presentations to clients in a place or at a time when interruptions, by coworkers or telephone calls, will not distract the client receiver.

Competitive noise is the same as external noise except that it is intentionally introduced from another source, and serves as a distraction to the receiver. Advertisers sometimes have the effect of introducing competitive noise when they present competing messages to prospective consumers.

The marketing communicator has two kinds of actions available to him to increase the efficiency of the communication process. These are the premessage scrutiny and feedback shown in Figure 16–1. *Premessage scrutiny* is an activity which should occur *before* the communication process begins. It is a recognition that effective and efficient communication is receiver-oriented rather than source-oriented. Hence the source expands some effort to identify the receiver and those aspects about the receiver, such as his or her vocabulary, which will enhance the chance of communication taking place. Second, *after* the message has been transmitted, the source seeks some *feedback* about the idea received by the receiver. The source, in effect, uses feedback from the receiver to compare the idea originally sent with the idea received. If there is a great difference, the source may decide to repeat the message, or to change symbols, or, perhaps, to change the message channel.

The fundamental objective of communication is the transmission of an idea from a source to a receiver. *Whether the communication is successful is largely the responsibility of the source.* Hence the source must be aware of the potential pitfalls and take steps to minimize their effects.

The adapted communication process

An adapted communication process is shown in Figure 16–2. This process recognizes that the source of the idea and the actual communi-

FIGURE 16–2
The Adapted Communication Process

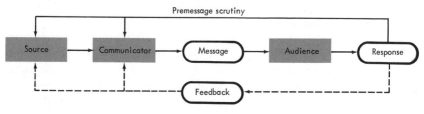

cator may be different entities. For example the message a sales representative presents as communicator may have originated with someone else. Or an advertisement as a communicator is clearly not the source of the order. Further the diagram of the adapted process shows clearly that the marketing communicator is looking for a response to his communication, not just consumption of his message.

Examples of the communication process applied to marketing are shown in Figure 16–3, where a salesperson is used as the channel of communication between a selling and a buying firm, and in Figure 16–4 where advertising is the channel between the seller and the prospect.

FIGURE 16–3
An Application of the Communication Process Using a Salesperson as the Communicator

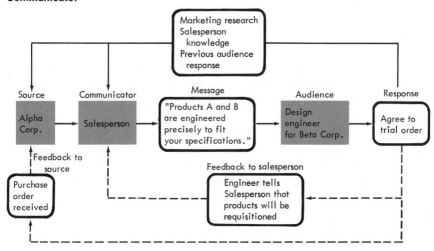

FIGURE 16–4
An Application of the Communication Process Using an Advertising Medium as the Communicator

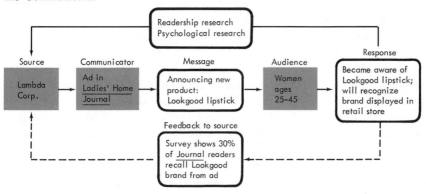

COMMUNICATION STRATEGY DECISION PROCESS

The communication process, when reversed, can represent a step-by-step decision process for developing a communication strategy. By beginning at the end with audience response and working backward through source and feedback, a logical order of decision appears.

The first step in the process is that of setting communication objectives—that is, what responses does the firm desire to evoke from its audiences? The firm may intend that its audience be motivated to purchase its product or it may only intend that the audience record in their memory the name of the store where the product is available. The objectives may be many and varied, but it is essential to good communication planning that the objectives be clearly defined.

Next, the communication targets should be selected. The audience for the communication may or may not be prospective purchasers. In fact, it is not uncommon for firms to direct many of their messages at those who influence purchases rather than those who are actually involved in the final transactions. Dry cereal manufacturers, for example, aim much of their advertising at children who, in turn, communicate their desires for a particular brand of cereal to their mothers. The importance of defining the communication targets cannot be overemphasized. Not only is it important to know who these targets are, but also to have enough knowledge about them to predict how they may respond to various messages. This means that the marketing communicator must have a great deal of socioeconomic and psychological information about his prospective audiences.

The third step is to create messages that will evoke the desired responses from the audiences. Appropriate appeals, cues, themes, and other message elements are developed in order to inform and influence the audience. Fourth, the channels of communication that will carry the messages to the various target audiences are selected. This decision normally involves a combination of advertising, salesmen, sales promotion, and other devices. The object, of course, is to choose the combination that will most effectively deliver the messages for the least cost to the communicator.

Although there are no decisions to make in regard to the selection of the source (the business organization originating the communication), there frequently are problems regarding the audience's perception of the source. For example, if a firm is relatively unknown to a prospective buyer, a salesperson from the firm may find it difficult to get an interview. The salesperson may also find that the client questions much of the information in the sales presentation because of a lack of confidence in the source. Most firms, therefore, spend considerable effort to develop their credibility in the market place. Much of this can be done by promotion, but it also entails having a reputation for good products and service. Finally, there should be specific plans for gathering and interpreting feedback. If marketing communicators are unable to measure the effectiveness of their effort, they run the risk of compounding their mistakes in the future and performing less effectively and less efficiently than is desired.

THE COMPONENTS OF PROMOTION

Marketing managers have several methods or instruments of promotion available to them. The most basic of these are personal selling, advertising, sales promotion, and publicity. Many companies use predominantly personal selling—or advertising—to the exclusion or near exclusion of the other promotional instruments. Most firms, however, seek to find a strategic balance of all available instruments to fit the particular circumstances of their industry and markets. The key is to assign the communication tasks in proper apportionment to the various promotional instruments.

Personal selling

The most common method of promotion is personal selling. The U.S. Department of Labor reported over 5.4 million sales representatives in April 1973.[1] This figure included retail sales clerks, brokers, sellers of insurance, manufacturers' representatives, and even newsboys—anyone at least 16 years old who made a living predominantly in a selling capacity. It would be a rare and cloistered individual today who does not have substantial contact with sales people of various types.

The salesperson is unique among the promotional instruments in having the ability to perceive a direct response (feedback) throughout the communication and make adjustments accordingly. Good salespersons can tell immediately whether their communication with their audience is effective or not. They can be very flexible in changing their presentation to fit the circumstances, thus increasing both their effectiveness and their efficiency. Also, with specific knowledge of a client's need for information, the sales presentation can be geared precisely to those needs.

Sales representatives have a variety of resources available to them: they can physically demonstrate the product, show films or still pictures of the product in the demonstration, and communicate through the use of all the senses rather than just the sight or sight and sound typical of mass communication.

Personal selling is normally the most expensive form of promotion. Studies indicate that the cost of an individual sales call to an industrial account averaged $57.71 in 1971.[2] These figures have increased sub-

---

[1] *Statistical Abstract of the U.S.* (Washington: U.S. Government Printing Office, 1973), p. 233.

[2] "How Your Competitors Put the Lid on Sales Call Costs," *Sales Management*, June 26, 1972, p. 21.

stantially over the years as salaries, travel expenses, and supervisory and organizational overhead have increased. The figure also includes a wide variation of sales costs from one company to another. The McGraw-Hill studies in 1967 showed ranges from $3.75 to $450 per call.[3]

Advertising

Advertising has been defined in many ways through the years, and these definitions have left some confusion as to what areas are included in the field. The key elements shared in most definitions are the terms "paid" and "nonpersonal." For example, the American Marketing Association defines advertising as "any paid form of nonpersonal presentation in promotion of ideas, goods, or services by an identified sponsor."[4] Albert W. Frey and Jean C. Halterman note that it consists of nonpersonal visual and oral messages disseminated through paid media for the purpose of achieving one or more objectives.[5] Although the defining of advertising appears academic, there are practical benefits to the company that establishes exact boundaries for its advertising activities. Certainly the organization and control of the advertising function of a company can be better executed if everyone concerned is aware of the exact activities included.

The dollar volume of advertising has increased steadily since World War II to an estimated $28.3 billion in 1975.[6] This amount is divided among various media including newspapers, magazines, television, radio, billboards, transit, and others. Although television continues to show substantial annual increases, newspapers still control the largest share of the total advertising dollar volume. This is because of the substantial amount of local advertising carried by newspapers. Well over 80 percent of newspapers' annual advertising income is from local advertising.

Sales promotion

Sales promotion includes the activities that supplement and reinforce personal selling and advertising. It is generally considered a motivating activity, aimed at salesmen, middlemen, and consumers. Most sales

[3] "McGraw-Hill Survey Shows Sales Costs Average $42," *Advertising Age,* May 6, 1968, p. 114.

[4] *Marketing Definitions: A Glossary of Marketing Terms,* compiled by the Committee on Definitions of the American Marketing Association, Ralph S. Alexander, Chairman (Chicago: American Marketing Association: 1960).

[5] Albert W. Frey and Jean C. Halterman, *Advertising,* 4th ed. (New York: The Ronald Press Co., 1970), p. 3.

[6] *Advertising Age,* December 29, 1975, p. 34.

promotion activities are short-term in length, and noncontinuous. A firm may employ various sales promotion activities throughout the year, but each of these activities has a specific objective and operates over a limited time period.

Personal selling is reinforced frequently by sales promotional activities in the form of contests, prizes, and awards geared to increase the efficiency and output of the sales force.[7] Similar programs may be designed for the salesmen of wholesalers and retailers. In certain industries it is not uncommon for a manufacturer to offer commissions (referred to as "spiffs" or "PM's"—push money) to retail sales clerks for each unit of the manufacturer's products sold. Also, temporary case allowances, display material, travel incentives for reseller-management, and other techniques are frequently used to encourage the middlemen to exert extraordinary selling effort.

A large share of the more than 15 billion dollars per year spent on sales promotion is in the area of consumer-directed promotions.[8] While most national advertising attempts to develop favorable consumer attitudes toward the advertised brand, sales pomotion is designed generally to cause some type of immediate action. John F. Luick and William L. Ziegler place these activities in two classifications. First, there are those activities such as samples, price-off coupons, and refund offers that attempt to get nonusers to try a product—typically a new product. Second, price-off promotions, premiums, and contests and sweepstakes are better suited to increase the use of a product.[9] The first classification is sometimes referred to as samping, the latter as loading.

Other forms of promotion

In addition to the above, such forms of promotion as public relations, publicity, and even educational seminars are often used as means of promotion.

Public relations combines various techniques to create favorable attitudes toward the firm. While other forms of promotion are generally concerned with the distribution and sale of products, public relations frequently communicates ideas not related to the company's products. The goal of public relations may be to develop a particular image of the company within the minds of various publics and minimize the

---

[7] See Albert Haring and Malcolm Morris, *Contests, Prizes, Awards for Sales Motivation* (New York: Sales and Marketing Executives International, 1968).

[8] Martin Everett, "From Brass to Class," *Sales Management,* November 1, 1971, p. 20. See also E. S. Mahany, "Promotion is a Marketing Bridge," *Advertising and Sales Promotion,* January 1965, pp. 57–58.

[9] John F. Luick and William Lee Ziegler, *Sales Promotion and Modern Merchandising* (New York: McGraw-Hill Book Co., 1968), p. 36.

potential for adverse activities (such as strikes, pickets, unfavorable legislation, and law suits) toward the company.[10]

Publicity is information placed in media because of its newsworthiness. It is distinguished from advertising in that no payment is made to the media nor is the company generally identified as the source of the information. The company may run an ad in the same media, but the company pays the media for the ad, and it generally is identified as the sponsor.

One last area to be identified as a means of promotion is the company-sponsored *educational seminar.* Some firms, because of the nature of their product and industry, conduct seminars for potential customers. In these seminars new products are introduced along with new technology and new product uses. These are more common in industrial marketing than in consumer goods industries.

ORGANIZATION AND INSTITUTIONS OF PROMOTION

In the foregoing paragraphs we have discussed briefly several methods of promotion. It is most important in any firm that these tools of promotion be coordinated toward achieving common goals. The organizations for such coordination takes varied forms, depending on the size of the firm, the nature of its business and markets, the number of products and product lines, and the resources available to the firm. Because a large share of the promotional effort is conducted through outside agencies, there is a problem of organizing for maximum efficiency and coordinating the efforts of the several agencies. Our purpose here is to examine some of these agencies and their relationship to their counterparts within the firm.

The sales force

The organization of a sales force takes many shapes. The basis for the organization may be geographic where the representatives are responsible for all sales of all products within a geographic area. This would be the case particularly for a firm that had one limited but closely related line of products, and essentially had no other complicating factors. If the product line became too large for one person to handle effectively in a territory, the organization might be divided on a product basis.

Another common practice is to organize by customers. For example, a large industrial food catering firm might have one group of people calling on industrial plants, another group calling on schools, and yet another calling on hospitals and other health care institutions.

---

[10] The oil companies during the energy crisis of 1974 used public relations to explain their substantial profits to the public.

Sales agents

Although most firms employ their own sales force, many use manufacturers' representatives or similar agents either totally or in combination with their own sales force. A manufacturers' rep, as he is commonly called, is an independent businessman who represents a number of sellers in a particular geographic market area. The manufacturers' representative may consist of one person or many to cover a geographic region. It specializes in a group of customers (for example, hardware stores in the state of Georgia) and by representing several manufacturers, puts together a variety of products that comprises a product line that will appeal to these customers. The major advantages of using a manufacturers' rep are (1) it provides immediate entry into a particular market, and (2) is a variable cost in that payment is by commission only on those products which are sold. The major disadvantages are that (1) it is frequently difficult to find good reps who are not already carrying a competing line of products, and (2) since they are not totally dependent upon the sale of your product, it is often difficult to motivate them to maintain the sales performance standards you have set. Even companies that have existing sales forces occasionally use manufacturers' reps for the introduction of products that are unrelated to the line handled by the existing sales force. The company may continue using manufacturers' reps until such time as a full line of products have been developed and it becomes economic to develop a sales force to handle these products.

Advertising and sales promotion

On a U.S. Navy combat ship the deck department is subordinate to the gunnery department, while the opposite is true on a cargo ship. A similar situation arises with advertising and sales promotion. In most manufacturing firms, advertising is clearly dominant over sales promotion; therefore, the sales promotion activities will be organized generally within the advertising department. On the other hand, the functions of a department store call for a large amount of display and other sales promotion activities. The department store organization will, therefore, usually have advertising as a subfunction within the sales promotion department.

The size of the advertising department varies greatly from one firm to another. It depends, of course, upon the use of advertising by the firm as well as the use of advertising agencies. If the agency does most of the planning and production of advertising, the firm is likely to have a relatively small group of people responsible for coordinating the activities between the agency and the firm.

The advertising agency

Although it started many years ago as a seller of media space, the typical advertising agency today is a large, integrated firm which is a specialist in all facets of advertising and many other marketing functions. It is capable of conducting marketing research to provide it and its clients with information on which most advertising decisions are made. The agency employs media specialists, creative writers and artists, and other personnel who specialize in the planning and production of advertising campaigns. An account executive is generally assigned to each client and acts as the agency's representative in coordinating the efforts and arrangements between the client and the agency.

Advertising agencies are used by many companies, not only because of their expertise but also because of the traditional fee arrangement. For a number of years agencies have been compensated by a standard 15 percent of media costs. This fee was a discount given by the media to the agencies. For example, suppose an advertising agency placed a series of ads for a company in *Time* magazine, for which Time charged $100,000. The agency would be billed for $100,000 less a 15 percent discount, or a net of $85,000. The agency in turn would bill the company for the full $100,000. This fee arrangement has come under fire in recent years, and a number of agencies have dropped the system in favor of a negotiated fee.

ROLE VARIATION

The basic role of promotion in the marketing mix varies greatly among industries, companies, products, and markets. This wide variety of promotion programs adds to the complication of designing a promotional strategy. It also increases the importance of identifying concepts that will assist the marketing manager in his planning.

Generally, promotion plays a less important role in the marketing of industrial goods than in the marketing of consumer goods. The unit of sale is usually much larger and the buying procedure more formalized. Products may be customized according to buyer specification. Purchase contracts are not uncommon, meaning that the negotiations and actual purchase may tend to be infrequent. The buyers are generally professionals, easily identified, small in number, and usually trained to search and negotiate for the "best" purchase (that is, the highest quality at lowest price). These factors point to a greater emphasis on product quality, price, and service rather than promotion. On the other hand, most consumer goods are purchased frequently in small units of sale at a large number of retail outlets. The buyers are relatively untrained and seek information and assurance. The buying process is informal and brand loyalty low. Promotion becomes a more important variable in the marketing of consumer goods because of these factors.

One way of considering the role of promotion is in its use to facilitate the movement of goods through the channels of distribution. The basic promotion strategy may change by varying the targets of promotion activity among the various points within the channel. This is generally referred to as *push* vs. *pull* promotion strategy. A push strategy is shown in Figure 16–5. The product is *pushed* through the channel by applying

FIGURE 16–5
Push and Pull Promotional Strategies

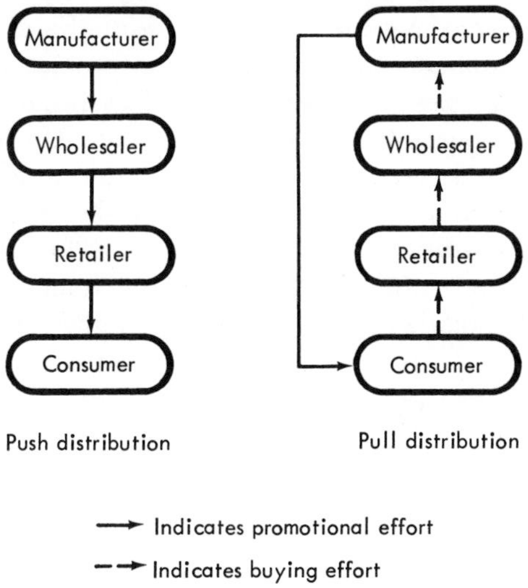
Manufacturer
Wholesaler
Retailer
Consumer
Push distribution
Manufacturer
Wholesaler
Retailer
Consumer
Pull distribution
Indicates promotional effort
Indicates buying effort

promotional activity at each point from top to bottom. A typical situation would involve personal selling by each intermediary in the channel. That is, the manufacturer persuades the wholesaler to purchase and resell the product. The wholesaler convinces the retailer to handle the product, and the retailer's salespeople sell the product to consumers. This process is not uncommon in industrial marketing where personal selling is the primary promotional tool used in the transfer of goods.

Pull strategy differs in that the primary promotion activity is targeted at the *end* of the distribution channel—that is, at the consumer or ultimate purchaser. This is also illustrated in Figure 16–5. Here the consumer is "presold" (typically by advertising) and seeks the product without additional promotional assistance from the retailer, who in turn purchases without persuasion from the wholesaler, and so forth up the entire ladder of distribution.

In reality, most strategies involve a combination of push and pull, since most manufacturers and intermediaries find it prudent to apply promotional activities at various points in the distribution channel. Also, there are strong implications for pricing policy, since wide margins (for push) or low prices (for pull) may be necessary to implement a strategy. A manufacturer's advertising plus a retailer's displays combined with well-informed retail sales personnel may be essential to effect the sale of large volumes of some products. Certainly the effective marketing of most products today requires the cooperative promotional efforts of manufacturers, wholesalers, and retailers.

The importance of promotion also varies throughout the life cycle of the product, as we have shown in Chapter 10. Competitive conditions and buying behavior change from one phase of the cycle to the next, causing different emphases to be placed upon promotion. In the introductory phase where only a select market of early adopters is sought, promotion is less important than product quality. However, as Figure 10–4 in Chapter 10 shows, as the product is introduced to the mass market in the growth phase, advertising has the greatest impact. In the maturity and saturation phases, it is second to price and quality of product, respectively. In the decline phase, it once more becomes the element of the marketing mix with the highest impact. As Hans Thorelli says:

> . . . now you have the shake-out phase, when everyone is engaged in a life-and-death kind of embrace and you have to slug it out with your competitors. That is when attention typically turns to advertising and sales promotion, to emphasizing style versus function, and to service.[11]

The amount and type of promotional activity is also related to the buyers' purchase process. Although this process will vary from person to person and from product to product, we can generalize about the process, the decision stages through which a buyer goes, and the relative importance of promotion in assisting the buyer through the various stages. Robert J. Lavidge and Gary A. Steiner have proposed six stages in the process: (1) awareness, (2) knowledge, (3) liking, (4) preference, (5) conviction, and (6) purchase.[12] There has been similar ordering and identifying of buying stages by other sources, but all are conceptually similar.[13] The essential point is that there is a process and that the amount and type of promotion necessary to help a buyer through the process varies with the circumstances.

The notion of the buying process discounts the idea that promotion's

---

[11] Hans B. Thorelli, "Market Strategy over the Market Life Cycle," *Bulletin of the Bureau of Market Research*, no. 26, September 1967, p. 18.

[12] Robert J. Lavidge and Gary A. Steiner, "A Model for Predictive Measurements of Advertising Effectiveness," *Journal of Marketing*, October 1961, pp. 59–62.

[13] Cf., Everett M. Rogers, *Diffusion of Innovations* (New York: Free Press of Glencoe, Inc., 1962), pp. 76–120.

only role is to sell products. In fact, it eventually does assist greatly in the sale of products, but only by helping to move the buyer through the essential stages of the buying process. The role may be to create awareness of the product, provide information about the product, to stimulate comparison or trial, to develop a more positive attitude toward the brand (reduce perceived risk), to convince a customer that the product is the best available, to persuade a customer to actually purchase the product, or even to "remind" current users and purchasers who are already convinced of the product's superiority. Certainly the decision as to which types of promotion to use will be highly dependent upon the strategic role or roles assigned.

PLANNING PROMOTION STRATEGY

Corporate-level planning and decision areas

In the foregoing paragraphs we have discussed general roles of promotion. We can now shift from the general to the specific features of planning promotion strategy and to the assignment of specific tasks and objectives to the various promotional instruments. Figure 16–6 presents a suggested flow of the major activities and decisions involved in the development of a promotion strategy. Since that strategy must be developed within the framework of both corporate and marketing objectives, the strategic decisions in the first phase are Level 1 decisions to be made by top management.

Perhaps the single most important decision is the selection and definition of target markets. This is where management studies all available information relating to markets, competition, and its own resources, and selects the marketing areas in which its opportunities are the greatest and where its competitive advantage is the strongest.

Frederick E. Webster, Jr., dicusses three factors to be considered in the selection of what he refers to as a segmentation strategy. First is a consideration of the resource constraints of the firm. Markets should be selected in which the firm will obtain maximum advantage from its strength while minimizing its weaknesses. The second factor is the existence of market opportunities. In examining the total market, management should be able to identify areas that are inadequately served by existing suppliers. If these areas fit the resources of a particular firm, they automatically become opportunities for that firm. If these areas *can be made to fit* the resources of the firm or if the resources of the firm *can be adjusted to fit* those areas, they also are opportunities. The third factor to be considered is whether the firm can obtain a unique competitive advantage. This is the distinction that sets the company apart from its competition, and avoids the "head-on" or "me-too" type of strategy so prevalent where firms have no competitive differen-

FIGURE 16–6
The Flow of Decisions and Processes in Planning a Promotion Strategy

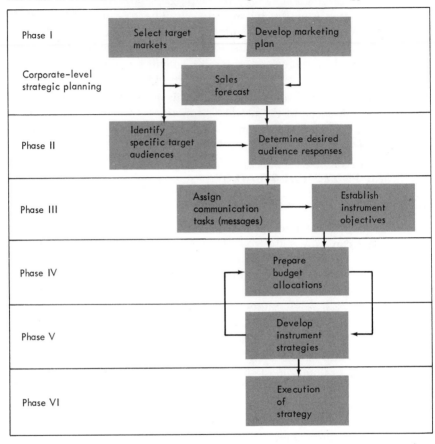

tials. Many small firms ably compete with large firms in the same industry by narrowing their market targets to distinct segments.[14]

Positioning of product

A related approach is the development of a product's "position" in the mind of the buyer. The concept of positioning considers the strengths and weaknesses not only of the product but of competitive products as well.[15] The central idea is for the company to determine a unique

---

[14] Frederick E. Webster, Jr., *Marketing Communication* (New York: The Ronald Press, 1971), p. 32.

[15] For a full discussion of the positioning concept, see Jack Trout and Al Ries, "The Positioning Era Cometh," *Advertising Age,* April 24, 1972, pp. 35–38; "Positioning Cuts Through Chaos in Marketplace," *Advertising Age,* May 1, 1972, pp. 51–53; and "How to Position Your Product," *Advertising Age,* May 8, 1972, pp. 114–15.

position in the market place for its product in relation to competitive products. Once determined, this position is then communicated to the market through various promotional techniques. Consider, for example, the apparent positioning of Era (a non-phosphate liquid detergent) by Procter and Gamble in a late 1972 test market. If Era had been positioned as a liquid detergent (which physically it was), it could only have hoped to gain a small share of the total detergent market. As a nonphosphate detergent (which physically it was), there was the problem of overcoming the housewives' dissatisfaction with the cleaning power of other nonphosphates on the market. Therefore, Era was positioned with powdered detergents, with television commercials emphasizing Era's cleaning power and low cost (compared directly with powdered detergents). The sales force sought shelf-space with the leading powdered detergents, distinctly apart from other liquid nonphosphate detergents. You might also watch baby products manufacturers carefully as they attempt to reposition their products to adjust to a declining baby market. We have seen in Chapter 10 how Johnson & Johnson adopted this strategy in marketing its baby shampoo.

Positioning as a concept is most helpful when combined with market segmentation. In fact, it is more accurate to say that the concept is workable *only* in conjunction with market segmentation.[16] The Schaefer beer company, for example, determined that a large portion of the beer consumed in the U.S. was consumed by a small percentage of the population. This group was defined as the 25-to-49-year-old, middle-income male, who typically drank several beers each evening. Schaefer, therefore positioned its product as "the one beer to have when having more." The result of this strategy was to increase its market share substantially to become one of the two leading beers in the eastern U.S.[17]

Dimensions of promotion strategy

Promotion strategy may be altered by changing any one or a combination of four dimensions of promotion: (1) audience, (2) message, (3) instrument, and (4) magnitude. The target audience may vary among various consumer or industrial buying segments, levels of distribution, or among individuals with varying degrees of influence upon the final purchase. The message to be communicated will obviously vary among types of audiences and will, therefore, greatly affect the total strategy. It is also evident that there are a number of instruments of promotion available, and that a strategy emphasizing mass com-

---

[16] See Jack Springer, "Put People in Positioning, New Product Expert Says," *Advertising Age*, September 4, 1972, pp. 31–32.

[17] Jonathan Kwitny. "Positioning Ads: Why Is Schaefer Beer the One Beer to Have when Having More . . . ?" *The Wall Street Journal*, December 13, 1972, p. 1.

munications is vastly different from one using predominantly personal selling. Finally, the magnitude of promotion—the amount of money available to spend on promotion and the intensity of the promotion over a given time—can greatly alter the strategy. Over the next few pages each of these four dimensions will be discussed in more detail and in relation to the phases shown in Figure 16–6.

Specific target audiences

Once the overall marketing and sales goals have been established, the planning of the promotion strategy can begin. Following the diagram in Figure 16–6, the first step is to specifically identify those individuals and groups with whom the company desires to communicate.[18] If the company is a manufacturer of consumer goods, it is likely that both middlemen and ultimate consumers will be among the selected audiences. But the question becomes who among the individuals in the employ of certain middlemen should be the recipients of the company's communication? That is, which individuals should be called upon by the company salesmen or receive literature or brochures lauding the advantages of the company's products? Or who among the family and friends of the ultimate consumers are the appropriate audiences for TV commercials, or readers of magazine ads, or receivers of price-off coupons from the company?

At the middleman level, the audiences can be logically divided into two categories: purchasers and influentials. The initial decision by a wholesaler or a retailer to stock a certain item typically is made either by a buying committee or an individual specializing in the merchandising of certain items. These purchasing groups or individuals make their decisions based upon their experience, their knowledge of their customers, and the information supplied by their suppliers and other sources—the influentials. The influentials are those people generally known to good company salespeople who can and do influence purchasing decisions. It might be a shelver in a supermarket, a secretary in a buying office, a warehouse foreman in a wholesaling establishment, or any number of individuals whose opinions and attitudes toward the company and its products are important to the ultimate achievement of the company goals.

Consumers also may be divided into several target audiences. Frederick E. Webster, Jr., identifies these as roles in a buying group as they relate to the determination of the need to purchase a product or service, the acquisition and processing of information to make the

---

[18] This step is shown as the second phase of the promotion strategy planning process, since it follows the corporate level planning accomplished in the first phase of the process.

buying decision, the actual purchase behavior, and the consumption of the product or service. These four roles can be called influencers, deciders, purchasers, and users.[19] Children are frequently the influencers in purchases of particular food items in the home, especially dry cereals. However, they are almost never the deciders or purchasers, and occasionally are not even the users. Upon the instructions from his wife (the decider), a husband may purchase a tree at the local nursery. The children may have heavily influenced the decision to purchase the tree, and the ultimate user may eventually be the family dog.

These same four roles may be assumed by individuals in an industrial purchasing situation. As stated earlier, the industrial purchase is generally made by a purchasing agent. The decision to purchase could have been made by a design engineer who was influenced in the decision by some of his professional colleagues. The user of the product could be someone on the assembly line. Similarly, an office typewriter purchase may be made by a purchasing agent, upon a decision of the office manager, after the secretary (user) suggested that efficiency would be improved with a new typewriter (influencer).

If the company in fact elects to communicate with these audiences, it should also determine the response desired from each of them. This is the beginning of the establishment of communication objectives as opposed to sales objectives. Even though the ultimate objective of promotion may be to increase the company's sales, this can only be achieved through a series of many communication stimuli—each intended (directly or indirectly) to help the buyer move through the buying process.

Messages and communications tasks

At this stage in the planning process (third phase), the company will need to determine the nature of the message to be communicated to the target audiences. The messages will necessarily vary according to the communication objectives established for the varying market segments. Certain audiences may be totally unaware of the product's existence; others may be aware of the product but have preference for a competing product; and still others may be prime prospects for purchase of the product, but have little knowledge of its quality or functional advantages. There may be numerous other market situations which will call for other messages. It is obvious that the message should not be designed to be all-encompassing, but should be designed to fit the informational needs of specific audiences.

When a company makes decisions concerning messages, in reality it is establishing communication tasks and objectives. This becomes

---

[19] Webster, *Marketing Communication*, pp. 88–92.

phase three in the promotional strategy decision process. It is virtually impossible to list all of the promotional objectives that might be used. These objectives by their nature are tailored to fit specific circumstances. We can, however, present a framework that is useful in developing promotional objectives.

For a promotion objective to be workable, it must: (1) state what is to be accomplished, (2) define the target of the promotion effort, (3) express in quantifiable terms the degree of success to be attained to satisfy the firm, and (4) state the time period for applying these efforts.[20]

This format is shown in Figure 16–7 and illustrated with several pos-

FIGURE 16–7
Hypothetical Examples of Promotion Objectives

Promotion objective	Target audience	Quantifiable goal	Time period	Task
1. To make target audience aware of new product X	Housewives, ages 25–50	60% of target audience	March 1 to Sept. 1	Heavy advertising
2. To cause initial trial of product X	Same	20% of target audience	March 1 to Sept. 1	Coupon distribution
3. Gain distribution in retail outlets (shelf space)	Drugstores, super-markets, discount department stores	80% of key accounts }	Feb. 1 to April 1	Sales force coverage
		100% of key accounts and 50% of secondary accounts }	April 1 to June 1	
4. To obtain dealer displays and local advertising tie-ins	Same, and key accounts	One display per five accounts; One ad tie-in per ten accounts	Feb. 1 to April 1	Sales force coverage

sible promotional objectives for a hypothetical company. In this case the company is introducing a new product through drugstores, super-markets, and discount department stores to housewives in the age bracket of 25 to 50 years of age. Each objective has the target audience noted, states what is to be accomplished, notes the degree of success that is established as a goal, gives the time period for accomplishment of this goal, and broadly specifies what tasks have to be accomplished in order to achieve the promotional objective. It is important to note that this format includes specific, quantifiable, reachable goals. In that way it is possible to determine the degree of success or failure of a

---

[20] This is developed from similar enumerations for advertising objectives in Russell H. Colley, ed., *Defining Advertising Goals* (New York: Association of National Advertisers, 1961), and James F. Engle, Hugh G. Wales, and Martin R. Warshaw, *Promotional Strategy*, 3d ed. (Homewood, Ill.: Richard D. Irwin, Inc., 1975), pp. 176–9.

promotional program. Without quantifying the goals, it becomes impossible to measure the effectiveness of promotion.

Assignment of tasks to promotion instruments

The promotion manager is aware of the personal selling, advertising and sales promotion resources available for use. In developing promotional objectives, under most circumstances there will be no difficulty in assigning the various promotional tasks to the instruments available. Most of the decisions will involve specific media, techniques, or personnel. For example, the second objective in Figure 16–7 is to cause initial trial of Product X. This could be accomplished with numerous techniques, including distribution of a small sample of the product, distribution of coupons redeemable for one regular size of the product, distribution of coupons with a designated price-off, and so on.

It is possible for a company to develop a unique promotion strategy by the particular assortment of promotion instruments used. A classic example is shown in the contrast between Avon and Revlon, where Avon relies heavily upon personal selling and Revlon upon advertising. Hershey for many years used no media advertising while its major competitors advertised heavily. While there is no set formula for a proper balance among promotion instruments, the emphasis or lack of emphasis on one or another instrument can be strategically effective.

The selection of a promotion instrument for a specific task generally depends upon three criteria. The first is the ability of the instrument to perform the task in question. For example, a point-of-purchase display may be far more effective in inducing impulse purchases than any other form of promotion. Purchase of life insurance is generally accepted as a complicated process for which the expertise and persuasion of a salesman is needed. In recent years, however, several companies have successfully informed and persuaded their clientele by direct mail advertising.

Another factor to consider is the ability of the various promotion instruments to reach the desired target audiences. In the mid 1960s, a major steel producing firm recognized that numerous packaging material decisions were being influenced by people unknown to their sales force. Primarily, plastics and aluminum were being substituted for tinplate. In order to reach these unknown influentials, television commercials were prepared and shown during the early evening news-time periods. Although there was a great deal of waste (the commercials reached millions of viewers who were in no way involved in packaging material decisions), it was thought that this particular method would have the best chance to reach the particular influential individuals. Finally, the cost factors must be considered. We discussed the relative costs of the various promotional instruments earlier in this chapter. It is necessary here only to point out that cost is a major factor in determining the promotion mix. Most firms are very cautious in their functional expenditures.

Magnitude of promotion effort

The final dimension of promotion strategy is magnitude—the volume of persuasive communication over a given period of time. This can be accomplished in many ways, such as a large buildup of the sales force and an intensified selling effort, or a massive advertising and/or sales promotion campaign. Accurate promotion expenditure estimates are available only for advertising, but an examination of those figures are very revealing. For example in 1969, Coors Beer was the leading brand in 9 of the 11 states in which it was distributed.[21] Yet it had the lowest advertising cost per barrel of any of the major brewers in the U.S. every year from 1963 through 1971.[22]

In the study of the 1968–69 advertising expenditures of over 1.5 million corporations taken from internal revenue service sources, *Advertising Age* reported that the average expenditure for all industrial groups was approximately stable at 1.16 percent of sales. The industry groups with the highest ratio of advertising to sales were soap, cleaners, and toilet goods with 10.06 percent, and drugs with 9.25 percent.[23] Seven of the top 11 national advertisers of 1971 were either soap or drug producing firms.[24]

The magnitude of a single campaign can be substantial. This is illustrated by the change in corporate design initiated by the Coca-Cola Company in October of 1969. The change was to the "dynamic contour" on 40 million wooden case shells, on point-of-purchase material at 2 million retail outlets, on 25,000 vehicles, on 40,000 vending machines, and on numerous other miscellaneous items. The cost estimates have ranged from 15 to 60 million dollars. The parent company shared this expense with local bottlers and dealers over the five years needed to complete the change.[25]

A large amount of promotion can also be achieved on a limited budget by strategic scheduling. In advertising, this concept is called flighting, and refers to the bunching of advertising messages in a given media

---

[21] The Brewery That Breaks All The Rules," *Business Week*, August 22, 1970, p. 60.

[22] "Advertising Costs for Beer, Ale, and Malt Liquor," *Advertising Age*, October 30, 1972, pp. 145–46.

[23] "Percentage of Sales Invested in Advertising in 1968–69," *Advertising Age*, April 10, 1972, p. 48.

[24] "The Top 100 National Advertisers of 1971," *Advertising Age*, July 24, 1972, p. 55.

[25] "Coke Swings in 1970 with New Packaging," *Advertising and Sales Promotion*, November 1969, pp. 33–36.

over a short period of time. This practice gives greater visibility and allows the advertiser to surmount a threshold of awareness that would not otherwise be possible if the same number of messages were spread over a long time period.

Promotion budget allocation

The magnitude of promotion is basically controlled through the budgeting process. This is where top management decisions are made concerning the overall level of promotion effort and the allocation of effort among the various promotion instruments. Through the budgeting process, the marketing manager can coordinate personal selling and advertising and assign specific tasks and budgets to organizational units. He can also view the various budget requests as part of the firm's capital budgeting problem. In that way the same financial criteria can be used for allocating various parts of the promotion budget as are used in determining the wisdom of other investments.

Theoretically, the allocation process simply follows the fundamentals of marginal analysis. Phillip Kotler states that "the total promotional budget should be established at a level where the marginal profit from the marginal promotional dollar just equals the marginal profit from using the dollar in the best nonpromotional alternative. . . . The total promotional budget itself should be divided among advertising, personal selling, sales promotion, and publicity in a way that gives the same marginal profit on the marginal dollar spent in each of these directions." He concludes that the problem is largely lack of data on the probable marginal effects of investments in promotion versus other activities, or of expanding the alternative instruments of promotion.[26]

Traditional approaches to promotional budgeting all but ignore the theoretical foundations. The objective and task method most nearly approaches the marginal analysis concepts. Other methods include percentage of sales, arbitrary allocation, competitive parity, all-you-can-afford, and return on investment. Each of these will be discussed briefly in the following paragraphs.

Percentage of sales. Probably the most commonly used method of determining the promotion budget is to budget a percentage of sales. It is simple to develop and use, but difficult to defend. The main criticism of this method is that it puts the cart before the horse—expected sales are assumed to cause promotional expenditures. Its primary advantages are simplicity and comparability. It is not only easy to compare one year's budget with another, but one company's budget with another. This is particularly useful as an after-the-fact control technique and aid for planning.

---

[26] Phillip Kotler, *Marketing Management*, 1st ed. (Englewood Cliffs, N.J.: Prentice-Hall, Inc., 1967), p. 452.

Arbitrary allocation. This is another commonly used method of determining the promotion budget. It too is a simple approach in that an arbitrary amount is determined which may or may not relate to the funds needed to accomplish the promotional objectives.

Competitive parity. This method of budget allocation establishes a company's promotion budget in direct relation to competitive activity. Salesmen are added to compensate for additional competitive salesmen in the field. Advertising is geared to a "share of the mind" concept, where the number of advertising messages should somehow relate to the company's share of the market. This method does have the advantage of recognizing and adapting to the competitive environment. However, it implicitly assumes that competitors have perfect knowledge and decision-making abilities and, therefore, develop optimal promotion budgets.

All you can afford. This method has been used with some degree of success in introducing new products where aggressive promotion is necessary. However, this technique works better as a philosophy than as a budget allocation method. It is quite possible that the amount allocated will not be related to promotional objectives, and very well may be much more or much less than is necessary.

Objective and task. Of all the methods discussed, this is the most scientific and most nearly approaches the ideal. In fact, this is the approach recommended to fit the promotion strategy planning process as discussed in this chapter. First, the promotion objectives are clearly specified, followed by a detailed enumeration of the tasks necessary to accomplish these objectives. An estimate is then made of the cost of these efforts, and these total costs become a promotion budget.

The relationships between Phases IV and V of Figure 16–6 are established by the objective and task method. By using this process, the allocation of the budget is directly tied into the strategic selection of the promotional mix. Here key discussions must be made relating to the cost-effectiveness of various combinations of advertising, personal selling, sales promotion, and publicity.

SUMMARY

This chapter has dealt with the strategic planning and decision areas of the promotion variable. The implementation, execution, and management of promotion will be discussed next in Chapter 17.

Of all criticisms leveled against the functions of marketing, perhaps the most valid concerns the wastefulness and lack of productivity involved in promotion. Far too frequently the promotion budget is developed by assuming the continuation of past practices rather than *strategically* setting and measuring objectives that must be accomplished in order to achieve effective and efficient marketing.

chapter 17 | Promotion management

Personal selling
Selling functions
Selling tasks
Sales organizations
Sales force size
Sales territories
Developing a sales force
Motivation and supervision
Evaluation and control
Advertising
Advertising objectives
The advertising message
Advertising media decisions
Measurement and evaluation
Summary

The purpose of this chapter is to examine some of the managerial and operating problems and opportunities in the area of promotion. Since the typical company separates the promotion function into two organizational units—personal selling and advertising—we will follow that pattern. In the first section we deal with various conceptual aspects of the selling function. The advertising section will include the operational aspects of sales promotion as well as advertising. Many major strategic decisions will have been made by top management before the promotion strategy is developed which in turn will have been designed to set the stage for promotion operations. It will have been determined, for example, that there will or will not be a sales force, the channels of distribution and the types of customers will have been selected, budgets developed, advertising strategy mapped out and overall promotional plans laid. Our concern now is to identify approaches to implementing these plans.

PERSONAL SELLING

For most companies salespeople are of critical importance. They are the key link between the company and its markets. The company communicates with its markets through them, and they are the prime carriers of feedback information from the markets. Since they are typically the only representatives of the company known directly to customers, in their territories they are the company.

The sales force has particular importance in industrial marketing where predominantly push strategies are commonly used. It is often the only communication link with the markets, is responsible for most if not all of the persuasion necessary to sell the products, and handles all the negotiations needed to complete the sale. It may also be charged with providing technical assistance to clients which, presumably, will lead to additional product sales.

The role of the sales force in consumer products should not be underestimated. Even when a predominately pull strategy is used, it may play a very important role. In such a case, sales responsibilities will most likely be in the channels of distribution. The representative will apprise retailers and wholesalers of the advertising and sales promotion campaigns and seek their assistance by building product displays, gaining appropriate shelf space, tie-in advertising in local media, displaying point-of-purchase material, and related activities.

Selling functions

The job of selling will vary widely depending upon the product or service being sold, the type of buyer, and the strategy being used by the selling firm. The selling environment is important in deciding the particular role for a sales representative. In any case the functions to be performed remain basically the same: (1) locating customers, (2) evaluating customers' needs, (3) recommending a purchase to fulfill needs, (4) persuading customers to make the purchase recommended, (5) negotiating and closing sales, and (6) following up to ensure satisfaction. A given sales job will emphasize certain of these functions over others. But no single function should ever be totally ignored if the salesperson is truly a person who helps the customer buy. All too frequently, however, we encounter salespeople who assume away the importance of all functions except those of recommendation and persuasion.

Selling tasks

Sales jobs also can be classified according to their relative emphasis on certain tasks, which can be categorized as: (1) account development, (2) account maintenance, and (3) program support. Account development involves finding new customers, aggressively and creatively persuading customers to buy, getting the initial orders, and convincing customers of the advantages of continual purchases of the company's products. Account maintenance involves keeping the customers happy with the company's products and service, promoting a continuing and closer relationship between the company and its customers, trouble-shooting for problems, and generally keeping the orders flowing into the company. Program support is similar to account maintenance, except that it is primarily involved with tasks not directly involving orders for the company's products—such as posting point-of-purchase material, building displays, developing cooperative advertising ideas and lay-outs, giving technical management and product assistance, or assisting with field research projects. Note how these sales tasks relate to the stages of the consumer satisfaction process developed in Chapters 6 and 8. It is not unusual for a salesperson to be assigned all three of these tasks. However, each task requires different abilities and even different emotions for outstanding performance. James A. Belasco noted that at any one time a salesperson may occupy the role of "persuader, service-man, information-gatherer, problem-definer, advocate, information reporter, expediter, coordinator, travelor, scheduler, display-arranger, and customer ego-builder."[1]

The increasing complexity of markets, vertical integration of buyers, systems buying, and other recent developments are causing sales managers to evaluate their selling organizations and divide the tasks accordingly.[2] The increasing complication of the sales job and the mental, physical, and emotional demands made upon the individual lend support to a separation of selling tasks among different salespeople.

Sales organizations

The marketing manager is faced with the problem of organizing the sales force in such a manner that the sales personnel effectively and efficiently perform those selling tasks necessary to achieve the company's long- and short-range goals. Traditionally, this is accomplished by organizing on a geographic, product line, or type of customer basis, or some combination of these bases. As mentioned earlier, complicating environmental factors (primarily market structures and competitive forces) have caused some innovative and unique organizational structures to be developed.

The sales organization should be designed to handle any special problems of the selling situation. This means that, first of all, it should be

---

[1] James A. Belasco, "The Salesman's Role Revisited," *Journal of Marketing*, April 1966, p. 7.

[2] See George H. Kahn and Abraham Schuhman, "Specialize Your Salesman," *Harvard Business Review* (January–February 1961) pp. 90–98 and Alton F. Doody and William G. Nickels, "Structuring Organizations for Strategic Selling," *MSU Business Topics*, Autumn 1972, pp. 27–34.

flexible enough to accommodate changes in the market, company resources, competitive actions, products and innovations, distribution channels, or any other area that may dictate prudent alterations in the sales organization. Since many of the situational changes often come quickly and unexpectedly, the flexibility of the organization should be such that structural change can be accomplished without undue delay.

Certain problems are unique to the sales organization, but must be considered thoroughly prior to structuring it. One problem that is always present in field sales organizations is the physical distance between the representative and the sales manager. This complicates the ability to motivate and supervise the sales force on a continuing basis, and even to give technical assistance in some situations. It is sometimes possible to mitigate this problem by reduction in the span of control at the supervisory level, extensive use of the telephone, and through prudent territorial design and routing patterns.

Another problem is the question of how many products one person can effectively handle. This is closely related to the problem of determining how many customers should be assigned to each person, and how frequently they should be called upon. Some pharmaceutical companies, for example, consider a six-week territory coverage as the minimum length of time between calls upon doctors. A more frequent interval is considered undesirable by the doctors. In addition, sales calls are made at breaks in the doctor's schedule, and the length of each call is, as one pharmaceutical detailman once said, "about as long as it takes the doctor to smoke a cigarette or drink a cup of coffee."[3] The psychologically (if not actually) fixed length and frequency of sales calls undoubtedly limits the number of products a salesman can effectively handle. These factors were dominant in a decision of one pharmaceutical company to establish a separate sales organization to handle new products. General Foods has different sales divisions for coffee, gelatin, dog food, and frozen food—all products sold in supermarkets. It is possible for a supermarket manager to have as many as six separate Procter & Gamble salesmen calling on the same day selling detergents, bar soaps, cake mixes, toothpaste, paper products, and coffee.

Sales force size

All of the factors mentioned above and many more enter into the decision of setting the size of the sales force. The overall corporate and marketing strategy, the long-range promotion strategy, the company resources, the selected distribution channels, the competitive environment, and the availability of manpower should be considered. Two major approaches to setting sales force size have been proposed. Walter J.

---

[3] This same salesman, with tongue in check, lauded the success of the 100mm cigarettes as a direct factor in increasing his productivity.

Semlow used marginal analysis in relation to return on investment; the logic is excellent, but the required assumptions restrict the actual use of the techniques.[4] Walter J. Talley, Jr., assumes that one territory equals one person, and uses incremental costs along with customer classes and call frequencies to compute present and potential call loads for the assignment of salespeople.[5]

The workload method presented in Figure 17–1 is similar to that

FIGURE 17–1
The Workload Method of Computing Sales Force Size

I. Computation of total sales effort (hours) required per year:

Customer classifi- cation	Number of customers ×	Frequency (calls per year)	Total calls = per year ×	Effort (hours per call) =	Annual sales effort required (hours)
A.	45	50	2,250	2.0	4,500
B.	1,040	50	52,000	.75	39,000
C.	670	25	16,750	.50	8,375
D.	820	12	9,840	.50	4,920
E.	1,280	4	5,120	.25	1,280
Total.	3,855		85,960		58,075

II. Computation of effort available (hours) per person per year:

(Workweeks × hours worked per week) . . . . (50 × 40) = 2,000
Less nonselling (travel, training, records, etc.)
time (8 hours per week) . . . . (50 × 8) = ___400
  Net hours available per person per year.   1,600

III. Computation of number of salespersons needed.

$$\frac{\text{Total annual sales effort required (hours)}}{\text{Hours available per person per year}} = \frac{58,075}{1,600} = 36.3 \text{ or } 37 \text{ maximum*}$$

* Less than maximum may be needed as certain accounts are eliminated because of geographic location and/or extraordinary costs of servicing. If calculations are made for each customer classification instead of all of them together as shown, the number required rises to 39.

proposed by Talley, and is one commonly used, with variations to suit particular circumstances. The first step is to classify customers in the market area on the basis of frequency and length of call needed to accomplish the company's objectives with these customers. In a sense, this is very similar to the objective-task method of determining the promotional budget, in that the *task* necessary to accomplish a set objective

[4] Walter J. Semlow, "How Many Salesmen Do You Need?" *Harvard Business Review*, May–June 1959, pp. 126–32. See also Henry C. Lucas, Jr., Charles B. Weinberg, and Kenneth W. Clowes, "Sales Response as a Function of Territorial Potential and Sales Representative Workload," *Journal of Marketing Research*, August, 1975, pp. 298–305.

[5] Walter J. Talley, Jr., "How to Design Sales Territories," *Journal of Marketing*, January 1961, pp. 7–13.

is computed in frequency of call, effort (time) per call, and total effort (hours) required. Each representative is presumed to have an equal amount of time available to devote to customer calls (in our illustration—1,600 hours per year). This figure is divided into the annual sales effort required to properly cover the entire market area, the quotient being the number of sales personnel needed.

Sales territories

This same logic can be developed further to design territorial assignments and routing patterns.[6] A sales territory should be a group of present and potential *customers*, logically and geographically located in such a manner as to achieve efficient coverage and managerial control. The word *customers* is emphasized to distinguish this from the common conception of a territory as a mere geographic area with arbitrary or political boundaries. It is quite possible and in fact common for territories to overlap geographically in order to gain effective and efficient call patterns.

Other than the basic factor of the total workload required of the salesperson, the sales manager should also consider such factors as market potential, topography and its influence on travel requirements, differences among customers, customer concentration, marketing channels, level of competitive activity, and the individual salesperson's ability.[7] Each of these factors will have differing degrees of influence on territorial design.

Routing patterns should minimize wasted travel and waiting time, and expenses of travel and overnight accommodations. At the same time, appropriate coverage and frequency of calls should be maintained while fitting into buyers' time schedules as closely as possible. Routing patterns to meet these criteria are very simple to design. There are several techniques available which may be applied by hand methods where few routes are involved. The computer is useful for larger problems.[8]

Developing a sales force

One of the primary roles of the sales manager is to develop effective sales personnel for the organization. Managerial proficiency in recruiting,

---

[6] See particularly the methodology of the "build-up" method of establishing territories in William J. Stanton and Richard H. Buskirk, *Management of the Sales Force*, 4th ed. (Homewood, Ill.: Richard D. Irwin, Inc., 1974), pp. 602–6.

[7] Kenneth R. Davis and Frederick E. Webster, Jr., *Sales Force Management* (New York: The Ronald Press Company, 1968) pp. 347–50.

[8] See, for example, Richard B. Maffei, "Modern Methods for Local Delivery Route Design," *Journal of Marketing*, July 1965, pp. 13–18. Also see Brian F. O'Neil and D. Clay Whybark, "Vehicle Routing From Central Facilities," *International Journal of Physical Distribution*, February 1972, pp. 92–93.

selecting, and training the sales force will greatly reduce other managerial problems. It is simple logic that a person with all the most appropriate background characteristics and best sales training will likely produce the most sales while requiring the least amount of managerial supervision.

Recruiting. Although staff personnel assistance may be needed, the field sales manager is generally responsible for recruiting prospective sales personnel. This process should begin with the development of a job description and specification of the personal attributes and background characteristics necessary or desirable for the position. These specifications may include age, previous selling experience, education, appearance, health, personality, integrity, and other criteria.

Once these are determined, recruitment commences, utilizing any source where qualified applicants may be found. These sources may include any or all of the following company personnel: friends of company salespeople; students nearing graduation at (or alumni of) colleges, high schools, and vo-tech or trade schools; employees of customers or suppliers; current salesmen of related products (including competitors); general public (via advertising or "walk-ins"); professional clubs and associations; and government or private employment agencies. Each of these sources will produce varying calibers and types of candidates. Therefore the choice sources should be considered in light of the job specifications.

Selection. It is possible for the recruiting process to bring in a large number of possible candidates, who must be processed in such a manner that the best possible prospect is hired. The selection process actually begins with the selection of recruitment sources and the qualifying information made available to prospective candidates at that time. For example, using only college placement offices eliminates all but college-educated prospects.

George D. Downing lists nine steps in the selection process, emphasizing that selection is a process aimed at screening the candidates, matching each with the job specifications, and selecting the individual who matches best. His process includes (1) the initial application form (with basic qualifications only), (2) a preliminary interview, (3) a personal credibility check, (4) a longer application form (with full information including personal references), (5) an interview in more depth, (6) testing (intelligence, aptitude, dexterity, personality and interest, and achievement), (7) a physical examination, (8) the final interview, and (9) decision and placement.[9]

Psychological testing has been used in the selection process for many

---

[9] George D. Downing, *Sales Management* (New York: John Wiley & Sons, Inc., 1969), pp. 252–56.

years, yet it still remains a very controversial topic. Many people have condemned this type of testing as unreliable and invalid; some have even criticized it as being discriminatory. At the other extreme, there are those who blindly trust the technique and even allow the selection decision to be made automatically by the results of a psychological test. This type of controversy makes it imperative that the sales manager be knowledgeable about testing techniques used in the selection process, and understand fully the limitations on use of such techniques. Psychological tests can be—and frequently are—excellent *predictive* tools. But they should never be used blindly without proper validation, nor should they be used singularly as the *only* tool in the selection process.[10]

Training. The first step for the newly hired salesperson is the training program. This may consist of on-the-job training, formal training sessions, or a combination of both. Many programs start with formalized training and end on the job. Even experienced salespeople who are new to the company need a training program, since much of the material to be covered relates to that company and its products, markets, policies, and accepted methods of selling.

The goals of the sales training program should be to:

1. Impact knowledge concerning:
   a. Company products.
   b. Company policies and operations.
   c. Markets.
   d. Competition.
2. Develop selling skills—the ability to handle a selling situation in a manner totally acceptable to the company.
3. Influence attitudes toward the company and its products, the market, and the job itself.
4. Develop good work habits that will help the individual use time more efficiently.

The specific content of the training program will vary, of course, from one company to another. But the emphasis placed upon various parts of the program will vary even within a company, depending upon the individuals to be trained. As mentioned above, the new sales representative with previous selling experience will have a greater need for knowledge of the company's products, markets, and policies than for training in the skill of selling. A new representative who comes from within the company will require less orientation to the firm and its

---

[10] For an excellent discussion on the controversy and use of psychological testing of sales applicants. See Davis and Webster, *Sales Force Management*, pp. 403–17; also Richard S. Barrett, "Guide to Using Psychological Tests," *Harvard Business Review*, September–October 1963, pp. 138–46.

general policies than to other matters. One of the most important areas of training involves retraining of the present sales force. It is generally accepted that the training program should be continuous throughout the career of an individual, with periodic sessions to update product knowledge, correct possible bad work habits, review basic selling techniques, and provide other substantive training to improve sales proficiency.

Motivation and supervision

The fact that the field salesperson works alone poses some problems for the sales manager. Somehow ways must be found (1) to motivate the salesforce to perform as intended, and (2) supervise sales efforts in order to give direction and suggestions that will improve performance. These are two of the most important and time consuming functions of the sales manager.

No matter how well a person is trained, performance will be only mediocre if the person is poorly motivated. The sales manager must develop a program of appropriate incentives as rewards for specific effort. This task is not a simple one, since it is attempting to provide similar incentives for a variety of complex human beings with different needs, wants, and desires.

Salesforce compensation. The primary incentive for the salesforce is, of course, the compensation plan. It is generally intended to (1) stimulate a high level of performance by a continuous reward system for specific achievements, (2) provide adequate incentive to cause the individual to perform all the tasks and details of the job, and (3) at the same time be fair to the individual and competitive with the compensation of other firms with comparable positions. In addition, the plan may attempt to encourage specific achievements, such as keeping expenses in line, getting new accounts, performing certain nonselling tasks, surpassing sales objectives on certain product lines, and similar achievements. Occasionally, part of the compensation will be tied to team effort where it is desirable for groups of salespeople to work together toward common goals.

It is important that the compensation plan be clearly understood by all participants. Many plans become complicated in an attempt to provide incentives for as many activities as possible. This is acceptable as long as the representatives can comprehend the plan and be able to at least roughly approximate their earnings at any time. They should also be able to know the effect upon their earnings of any action (or lack of action) they may take.

The plan also should be based as much as possible upon factors controlled by the individual. For example, if sales decrease because of regional economic cutbacks (e.g., the aircraft industry shutdowns in Seattle in the early 1970s), compensation should not be severely reduced. This factor has been a prime argument against compensation based upon territorial profitability, since the individual cannot possibly control all of the many factors that affect profits.

There is a wide variety of types of compensation plans, but they are generally categorized as (1) straight salary, (2) straight commission, (3) base salary plus commission, and (4) any of the first three types plus bonus and/or profit sharing.

A straight salary plan is generally considered to provide more management control of sales activities, while a straight commission allows the least management control. If income is tied directly to sales produced, the sales representative will not be inclined to perform activities other than selling. However, if compensation does not depend solely upon sales, the representative will be more willing to perform nonselling or other tasks as directed. For that reason, a straight salary plan is frequently used where technical assistance or other services are required, or where there is little direct relationship (either actual or apparent) between the individual salesman's activities and level of sales..

Straight commission plans have the advantage of making selling costs a variable expense but, as mentioned above, reduce managerial control. They are typically used where there is a direct relationship between sales efforts and sales produced, little training or supervision is desired by management, nonselling activities are unimportant, seasonal sales are common, or where part-time people may be used. Some of the disadvantages of the straight commission plan can be overcome by use of a base salary or drawing account.

By using some combination of salary, commission, bonus, and profit sharing, the compensation plan can become "all things to all people." The plan can cover numerous objectives of management, and can be flexible enough to meet most contingencies. In summary, the salary offers security, the commission offers incentive, the bonus rewards special achievement, and profit sharing develops team spirit and attitudes.

Other incentives. The sales manager may use other means to motivate the sales force.[11] Competitive performance contests, premium programs, and special awards are used frequently as added incentives to achieve specific objectives. Sales meetings can provide a forum for inspirational activities that promote *esprit de corps* and sales motivation.

---

[11] Special sales incentive programs are discussed in Albert Haring and Malcolm Morris, *Contests, Prizes, Awards for Sales Motivation* (New York: Sales and Marketing Executives International, 1968). See also Henry O. Pruden, William H. Cunningham, and Wilke D. English, "Nonfinancial Incentives for Salesmen," *Journal of Marketing*, October 1972, pp. 55–59.

Often the best incentives are the irreplaceable pat on the back and the words, "Well done," from the sales manager. One word of caution: no compensation plan nor special incentive program can fully replace the sales manager. Properly planned and executed programs can reduce problems substantially, but cannot substitute for good recruiting, training, supervision, and other functions of the sales manager.

Evaluation and control

The performance of the sales force—individually, by units, and as a whole—should be evaluated against a prearranged set of standards known both to the sales force and to the sales managers. The sales force is thus controlled by the setting of objectives and standards, evaluating performance against these standards, and taking corrective action where needed.

The standard most used in evaluation is the *sales quota*—that is, the assigned volume and assortment (generally by product or product lines) of sales for each person for the time period of the evaluation. Sales quotas are also assigned to units (districts, divisions, and so forth) on the same bases as individual quotas. In both cases the quotas are sales goals and should be accurate, realistic, and acceptable.

A sales quota should be an accurate measure of the market potential tempered by two other factors: work load and experience.[12] Work load is a measure of the amount of physical effort and time required to cover a particular territory. The differences among territories can be dramatic, based upon the density of the market (customers for office supplies in downtown New York City on the one hand, or in several northwestern states on the other). Experience refers to both the experience of the individual salesperson and the company's experience in a given market area. Higher sales are expected from the more experienced personnel. Also, once a company is established in a particular market area, sales will be easier, even for the new, inexperienced salesperson.

Evaluation is frequently made against other standards than sales volume. Quotas based on gross margin or net profit are often used as a reflection of the importance placed upon profit rather than volume. This type of quota system directs the sales units to emphasize the more profitable products, but gives them discretion in the assortment of sales that will achieve the quota. This is particularly desirable where purchase patterns vary greatly from one market area to another. Generally, however, profit goals may be achieved by assigning sales volume quotas

---

[12] Davis and Webster, *Sales Force Management,* p. 291.

by product groups, with each group representing a separate profit category.

Also, quotas are frequently established on a combination of factors, including sales volume, expenses, and certain related activities such as full-line distribution, merchandising efforts, or other activities that can be realistically assigned and measured. In any case, however, it must be remembered that a quota of any type should meet the same three criteria—accuracy, realism, and acceptability.

Salespeople are generally evaluated on other standards that may explain their successes and failures in performing their jobs. These may include call rate (calls per day), sales per call (usually called "batting average" denoting the percentage of total calls resulting in a sale), market penetration (market share by sales volume and by number of customers), days worked, field expenses, routing efficiency, and any number of other items which may pertain directly to an individual's selling job.

Electronic data processing has substantially altered the patterns of evaluation. Information derived from past records, customer orders received, and salespeople's activity reports can be fed into the computer for special and very rapid analysis. Because of the computer, it is now possible for the sales manager to spot flaws in performance and to apply corrective action much more rapidly than before. It is also possible to be more accurate in the development of market potential and individual quotas. Technology is available for the development and use of total sales management information systems. The high costs of installing and operating such systems, however, will likely keep them scarce for several years to come.

ADVERTISING

Advertising, like all other marketing variables, requires efficient and effective management. All too often advertising practitioners are so enmeshed in its creative and persuasive aspects that they lose sight of the fact that advertising is an alternative choice among possible business activities and that its final evaluation must ultimately rest upon how well it achieves the firm's goals.[13] The overall, long-range goals of advertising are to enhance the sales and/or the reputation of the company. This is accomplished through *product* and *institutional* advertising. Most advertising is concerned with the promotion of products or specific brands of products, while institutional advertising promotes the good name and reputation of the firm. Institutional or corporate advertising may be intended to establish the firm as a good stock investment or

---

[13] Dorothy Cohen, *Advertising* (New York: John Wiley & Sons, Inc., 1972), p. 3.

a good place to work. Generally, however, its long-range goals are to assist in the increase of sales. This may be done by promoting the firm as a reputable organization, the manufacturer (or seller) of fine quality merchandise, dependable service, and, in general, a fine place with which the reader would enjoy doing business.

Advertising objectives

An individual advertisement or group of advertisements should have more immediate, specific, and measurable objectives—such as changing awareness levels, influencing or altering attitudes, or even causing specific action towards a purchase. The setting of promotion goals was discussed earlier, but should be reviewed again in relation with the management of the advertising function. The setting of advertising objectives should follow a similar pattern to that established in Chapter 16. The objectives should be stated in such a way that the "doers"—the people who write the copy, prepare the layouts, buy the media, etc.—have no problem in carrying out the plans that will accomplish the objectives.

First, there should be detailed statements as to exactly what is to be accomplished by the advertising and during what time period. If at all possible these statements should include quantitative benchmarks so that the degree of success or failure can be measured. For example, if a company expects its advertising campaign to increase awareness of its products, it should state this in measurable terms—such as "increase awareness from the present level of 40 percent to at least 65 percent by the end of the year." This type of statement (1) expresses the current level of awareness as a percentage of the implied target market, (2) designates the goal to be achieved by stating the desired level of awareness, and (3) states a definite date by which the objective is to be accomplished.

It is better to state the degree of accomplishment in terms of "from-to" rather than just a specified amount of increase.[14] Although this requires management to know the current level of awareness, attitudes, opinions, usage rate or whatever it is that advertising is to affect, it is necessary in order to measure changes. Also, a change from 10 percent to 35 percent poses a substantially different problem than a change from 60 percent to 85 percent although the increment of change in percentage points is the same in both cases.

Second, it should be stated precisely to whom the advertising is to be directed. The description of the target audiences should include

---

[14] David T. Kollat, Roger D. Blackwell, and James F. Robeson, *Strategic Marketing* (New York: Holt, Rinehart and Winston, Inc., 1972), p. 344.

demographics (age, sex, income, and so forth), psychological factors, buying patterns, and other analytic or descriptive information that could be used in the development of the detailed advertising plans. Such information is essential to the creative staff in developing appropriate advertising themes, copy, and layout. The media selection and schedule also will depend greatly upon detailed knowledge of the target audience. The development of the message and the media plans will be discussed in more detail later in this chapter.

Finally, the creative platform or theme should be clearly developed. This usually consists of a generalized statement of the message to be communicated, expressed in such a manner that the writers and artists can develop detailed copy and illustrations which will communicate the basic message ideas to particular target audiences and through the various media. For many years Zippo lighters successfully used the same basic them: "Zippo lighters work; if any Zippo ever fails to work, we'll fix it free." This theme was then translated into specific ads (frequently using testimonials) which have been credited with much of the continued success of the lighter.[15]

An example of advertising objectives.[16]   Ethan Allen, a popularly priced line of American Traditional furniture, is sold through franchised stores and Ethan Allen gallaries within major department and furniture stores. With a marketing objective to achieve sales equal to production capacity, the following research material was used to establish advertising objectives:

> The furniture industry was (late 1960s) a four-billion-dollar industry (wholesale) composed of more than 5,000 manufacturers. The largest share of the market held by a manufacturer was not more than 3 percent. Market shares were roughly equal to distribution shares.
> Little or no brand awareness existed. Consumers, on the average, are not aware of more than one brand.
> Half of the furniture sales were accounted for by eight states; fifty metropolitan areas accounted for over half the total sales.
> The primary purchaser is a woman, 25–54 years old, with a family annual income of $5,000–$15,000. However, the male is an important factor in the purchase decision.
> Style and quality rank as the two most important criteria when a furniture purchase is considered.
> Consumers generally approach the retail store with uncertainty; they rely on the store's image.
> Consumers are very concerned about the appearance of the furniture in the home. Emotional involvement varies by room.

---

[15] "The Zippo Lighter Campaign," in *Advertising Service for Students: Outstanding Advertising Case Histories* (Southport, Conn.: Thomas E. Maytham, 1969), p. 11.

[16] The details of this case are from "The Ethan Allen Furniture Campaign," ibid., p. 63.

The following advertising objectives were developed:

1. Build traffic in retail outlets.
2. Increase awareness of Ethan Allen as a manufacturer of an extensive line of quality home furnishings.
3. Increase awareness of Ethan Allen's unique service concept.
4. Obtain requests for 250,000 "Treasuries" (a home decorating book).

In addition, the following *specific* objectives were developed:

Creative:	1.	Achieve brand name familiarity with potential customers.
	2.	Establish a quality image.
	3.	Achieve high awareness of the unique service concept with potential consumers.
Media:	1.	Reach the mass family market with the best frequency possible.
	2.	Select women 25–54 years of age in middle-income homes as the primary target.
	3.	Concentrate additional advertising support in major metropolitan markets where the greatest sales opportunities exist.
Creative platform:		To position Ethan Allen as the home furnishings manufacturer who "Cares about your home almost as much as you do."

The campaign, then, featured a series of full-page magazine ads featuring a variety of decorating problems and their solutions as an example of Ethan Allen's unique decorating service. These ads were illustrated with four-color photographs of room settings presenting a quality image of Ethan Allen furniture and accessories.

National women's service and shelter magazines were chosen as the primary media, some with regional split runs so that dealer listings could accompany the basic ads. A newspaper mat program and some television commercials were made available for dealers to use in their local advertising.

Although sales continued to increase, it was necessary for Ethan Allen to develop a research program to ascertain the success of the advertising campaign. Special market research was needed to measure consumer awareness of the unique service concept and the image of Ethan Allen as a manufacturer of high-quality merchandise.

The advertising message

The logic of advertising planning places the development of the advertising message before selection of the media which will carry the message. In this way media may be selected that fit the requirements of the message (need for product demonstration, background mood or tone, fragrances, etc.) as well as the reading, listening, and viewing habits of the target audiences. The development of the message content and presentation is generally referred to as the creative function of advertising.[17] The creative platform specifies the message content and gives a general theme for the advertising campaign. Then the specialists in copy, art, and film prepare the actual advertisements as they are to appear in the various media. Both what the advertiser says and how he says it are important in the development of the advertising message, because both content and form affect the total impression perceived by the audience.[18]

Message content. The decision as to what will be said should come from a thorough analysis of the product's attributes, the consumers' purchasing patterns and attitudes toward the product, and the current competitive position of the product. This is a significant part of the marketing program where the assistance of good marketing research is essential. The development of the message content could mean disastrous results if based upon false notions or poor information.[19] Management is generally more concerned with the content of the message than with the form the advertisements take as they are developed by the creative specialists. The advertising agency generally works closely with the company to develop a theme that stresses the benefit that will accrue to the purchaser of the product and, if possible, attempts to differentiate the product from competitive products. Product benefits are commonly featured in advertisements, but product differentiation is generally more difficult to achieve and is, therefore, a greater challenge to the creative specialists. Comparison with competitive products is often invited or implied in the advertising copy. One recent and very noticeable trend, however, has been the distinct increase of direct product comparison as the primary theme of advertisements.[20]

Message form and presentation. An advertising message, in order to be effective communication, must (1) attract attention, (2) develop interest, and (3) achieve the response desired. Much of the form a given advertisement takes is aimed at accomplishing these three goals in a step-by-step process with its target audience. An advertisement in a magazine, for example, must first attract the reader's attention before it can communicate a message. This may not be a simple task, since

[17] Albert W. Frey and Jean C. Halterman, *Advertising*, 4th ed. (New York: The Ronald Press Company, 1970), pp. 225–26.

[18] Ibid., pp. 249–50.

[19] A *special* plea for the use of accurate market information is made at this point primarily because of the authors' general observations of a multitude of "off-target" advertisements, probably based upon the advertisers' personal opinions and perceptions of how the market views their products.

[20] This trend can be at least partially attributable to the consumer movement and the consumers' growing awareness and demand for factual product information.

the magazine will have many advertisements. Also, the reader may be skimming through the magazine and, unless something very unusual or attractive to him catches his eye, he probably will not even notice a particular advertisement. For that reason, creative specialists are very concerned with such things as the size of the ad, use or misuse of color in the ad, boldness of print, unusual headlines, motion, contrast, illustrations, and other attention-getting techniques. In fact, it is very easy for the attention goal to gain so much prominence in the mind of the advertiser that all too frequently the attention-getting value of the ad is overemphasized and fails to achieve any real informative or persuasive goal.

The attention of the audience must be held long enough so that an interest in "completing" the ad is developed. This means that a radio or television commercial must be so interesting to the intended audiences that they will stay mentally and physically "tuned in" throughout the commercial—that is, they will *receive* the message as the advertiser intended it to be received. A print ad generally attempts to be so intriguing in its headline, illustration, and layout design that the reader is compelled to read the copy. Some advertisements are able to relate their story primarily through the illustration with little or no copy. Outdoor posters and billboards typically fit in this category.

The true success of any advertisement, however, is in its ability to accomplish its communication objective—to cause the target audience to *respond as intended*. Does a series of television commercials for coffee cause the middle-income housewife to change her attitude toward that particular brand of coffee? Does the chemical company advertisement on the back cover of *Business Week* cause the businessman to have more confidence in the company, and perhaps even be a bit more receptive to its sales people? Does the newspaper advertisement of a local clothing store cause potential customers to visit the store?

Whatever the objective or whoever the target audience of the advertisement may be, the real question is: Did the right people respond to the advertisement as the advertiser intended? For example, the coffee advertiser should not be overly concerned if his television commercials did not affect the brand attitude of the male viewing audience, if the commercial was designed specifically for female audiences. However, the advertiser should be concerned if tests show that the commercials have had little or no effect on the housewives' attitudes toward the brand—if, in fact, that was the goal intended for the commercials.

Advertising media decisions

It is obvious that the advertising message cannot achieve its objective if it is not seen nor heard by the target audience. The message must be delivered and exposed to as many of the target audience as possible, perhaps several times in order that the message be received and responded to as intended. The advertising manager, then, has two important media decisions to make: selection and scheduling. Each of these will be discussed after a brief survey of the major types of advertising media available.

Types of media. The relative importance of the various media is illustrated in Table 17–1 which shows the dollar amount of advertising carried by these media in 1973 and 1974. The importance of each medium to a particular advertiser will depend upon a number of variables

TABLE 17–1
Advertising Volume by Media, 1973 and 1974

	1973		1974		
Medium	*Millions*	*Percent of total*	*Millions*	*Percent of total*	*Percent change 1974/1973*
Newspapers					
Total	$ 7,595	30.2%	$ 8,001	29.9%	+ 5.3%
National	1,111	4.4	1,194	4.5	+ 7.5
Local.	6,484	25.8	6,807	25.4	+ 5.0
Magazines					
Total	1,448	5.7	1,504	5.6	+ 3.8
Weeklies	583	2.3	630	2.3	+ 8.0
Women's.	362	1.4	372	1.4	+ 2.8
Monthlies	503	2.0	502	1.9	– 0.2
Farm publications. . . .	65	0.3	72	0.3	+10.5
Television					
Total	4,460	17.7	4,851*	18.1	+ 8.8
Network	1,968	7.8	2,145*	8.0	+ 9.0
Spot	1,377	5.5	1,495*	5.6	+ 8.6
Local.	1,115	4.4	1,211*	4.5	+ 8.6
Radio					
Total	1,723	6.9	1,835	6.9	+ 6.5
Network	68	0.3	72	0.3	+ 6.0
Spot	400	1.6	408	1.5	+ 2.0
Local.	1,255	5.0	1,355	5.1	+ 8.0
Direct mail.	3,698	14.7	3,986*	14.9	+ 7.8
Business papers	865	3.4	900	3.4	+ 4.0
Outdoor					
Total	308	1.2	345	1.3	+12.0
National	200	0.8	225	0.8	+12.5
Local.	108	0.4	120	0.5	+11.0
Miscellaneous					
Total	4,958	19.8	5,286*	19.7	+ 6.6
National	2,575	10.3	2,759*	10.3	+ 7.1
Local.	2,383	9.5	2,527*	9.4	+ 6.0
Total					
National	13,775	54.8	14,760*	55.1	+ 7.2
Local.	11,345	45.2	12,020*	44.9	+ 6.0
Grand Total	$25,120	100.0%	$26,780*	100.0%	+ 6.6%

* Revised.
Source: *Advertising Age,* September 15, 1975, p. 51.

related to the particular needs and resources of the advertiser. Each class of media has certain characteristics which should be considered by the advertiser prior to the development of a media plan. Those characteristics that are of primary interest concern the medium's cost, its ability to reach the target audience, and its special capabilities in message presentation.

Newspapers can provide a large degree of audience selectivity, particularly on a geographic basis, for a reasonable cost. Intensive coverage of a geographic area can be achieved with newspapers. Flexibility and precision in programming and timing is possible because of the large number of newspapers and their frequent printing schedules. An advertising manager may change the emphasis in the advertising program on short notice from one market area to another, with confidence that the newspapers carrying the advertisements will be delivered to the market during certain hours on a certain day. Since newspapers generally are discarded after a few days, the life span of a newspaper advertisement is relatively short. This feature also provides some flexibility in that the advertiser may change the message frequently. If the strategy calls for constant or prolonged impressions upon the market, this short life span could make newspaper advertising rather expensive. Advertising rates are usually quoted on a line basis, with many newspapers having a rate differential between local and national advertisers.

Magazines have greater ability to give high quality printing and effective color reproduction than newspapers. They can also be highly selective in reaching desired market segments because of their specialized editorial appeal. Most magazines give national coverage, but many have regional or even metropolitan editions. The life span of a magazine is considerably longer than that of a newspaper. There is also a secondary circulation of readers other than the original purchaser or subscriber. Advertising rates are generally based upon circulation and audience selectivity. They are quoted on a page or part-of-page basis, with higher costs for the use of color and placement on one of the covers.

Television, the newest of the major media, has the advantage of combining sight, sound, and motion in a commercial message, allowing the advertiser to approximate a person-to-person relationship with the viewing audience. Products and services can be demonstrated, sometimes more effectively than in real life. The A. C. Nielsen Company estimated that 96 percent of all U.S. households owned at least one television set in 1972.[21] This near saturation provides a cumulative reach of approximately 95 percent of both the adult market and the children's market.[22] Although certain programs and times attract a select audience (daytime serials for adult women, Saturday morning cartoons for children, pro-

---

[21] *Nielsen Newscast*, vol. 21, no. 4 (Fall 1972), p. 11.

[22] *BBDO Audience Coverage and Cost Guide*, 14th ed., 1975, p. 8.

fessional football for adult males, etc.) television is generally not efficient in reaching selective audiences. For example, it is difficult to reach certain age and income groups precisely via television without also reaching many other viewers not in the target market.

Radio offers the advertiser a wide selection in almost any geographic area. There are over 6,000 AM and FM stations in the U.S. today, reaching three fourths of the adult market daily. Either spot or network programming is available. The primary advantage of radio is its flexibility in time, audience, and geographic coverage. By using local radio spots an advertiser can be highly selective in reaching a fairly specific target audience and at a reasonable cost. Of course, each message must be carefully prepared and delivered, since it utilizes sound only and its exposure life ends with a single broadcast.

Outdoor advertising is frequently purchased city by city in mass lots called "showing." A "100 showing" places the advertising posters in the most important areas of a given market to assure full coverage and repetition. Whether the posters are seen or the message read depends heavily upon the audience itself as well as the creativity developed in the advertisement and the actual placement of the posters. Smaller posters, painted bulletins, and electric spectaculars are usually sold individually, so the advertiser picks the exact location. Outdoor advertising offers much flexibility in geographical coverage, but is limited to short copy and very little target audience selectivity.

Besides the major media mentioned above, the advertiser has numerous other types of media available for transmitting messages. These include car cards and transit advertising, catalogues and directories, direct mail, advertising specialties (matchbooks, ball-point pens, etc.), and other miscellaneous media of varying degrees of importance.

The media selection process. The basic purpose of the media plan is to reach as many of the intended target audience as possible and effectively communicate the message at the most economical cost. Therefore, the selection of media is an involved process which takes a number of factors into consideration. Some of these factors are discussed below.[23]

Nature of the market. This is perhaps the most important and obvious consideration, since the advertising message must be carried by media that are seen, heard, or read by the target audience. It would be foolish, for example, to attempt to reach children under 12 by advertising on late-night television.

The product or service. The advertising message for certain products or services may require the uniqueness of particular media. For example, the color available in some print media may be advantageous for the advertising of food products. Action toys frequently need the demonstra-

---

[23] Adopted from Frederick E. Webster, Jr. *Marketing Communication* (New York: The Ronald Press, 1971), pp. 491–93.

tion ability of television. Also, legal or ethical restrictions may influence media choice, such as the broadcast ban on cigarettes imposed in 1971.

Distribution channels.   The geographic area in which the product is distributed affects media choice. Using media whose coverage extends beyond the distribution boundaries of the product would result in a great deal of waste. The reseller support involved in the campaign is another consideration. Frequently local media will be used to satisfy these requirements.

Characteristics and availability of media.   Each medium has certain characteristics which should be considered in the selection process. One of the most important characteristics is the "reach" of the medium. Reach is defined as the net unduplicated audience delivered by a medium or a media schedule. The choice of a medium would include that quantitative aspect as well as numerous qualitative factors. For example, a product may develop prestige by being advertised in certain magazines or on certain television programs. Special editions of print media or special programming by radio and television lend themselves to advantageous tie-ins for certain products. Endorsement by certain magazines such as *Good Housekeeping* or *Parent's Magazine* also may be very desirable. In addition, availability of media can be very important to the flexibility of a media schedule. Some advertising must be scheduled months in advance, while others can be virtually last-minute insertions. The closing dates of media become an important consideration in media selection.

Nature of competition.   The competitive activity associated with a product can have an important bearing on the selection of advertising media. Advertisers may elect to meet competition head on, by advertising in the same media as those chosen by the competition. Or they may elect to dissociate from competitive advertising by using separate and distinct media. The former is the more usual practice, as is evident by the numerous advertisements for similar products in magazines, newspapers, and other media.

In summary, the selection of media involves a number of factors, the principal one being the quantitative distribution of the advertising message to as many members of the target audience as possible, for the lowest possible cost. The media plan involves the selection of a number of specific media combined to be as efficient and effective as possible in the delivery of the advertising message.

Media scheduling.   The media plan not only includes selection of media but also its scheduling. This involves the frequency, repetition, and continuity of exposure of the advertising message to the target audience. Frequency is a measure of the number of times each person in the audience is exposed to the advertising message in a given period of time. The repetition of an advertising message is certainly not uncommon and not without reason. It may be necessary to repeat the message several times in order to bring about changes in attitudes that are prerequisites to the purchase of a product. Also, repetition of an advertising message keeps a particular brand foremost in the mind of the audience. This is particularly important for frequently purchased consumer products with low brand loyalty.

Another part of media scheduling is continuity of advertising message. This refers to the regularity of messages using certain media over a period of time. It is generally accepted that advertising messages must be scheduled in a sequence close enough together so that advertisements are not totally forgotten and that they may in fact build upon one another. The learning process will erode over a period of time if the advertising message is not repeated.

The cost of advertising has to enter into the scheduling process. For example, it may not be possible for an advertiser to maintain a level of continuity throughout a long period of time because of the costs involved. He may, however, revert to flighting—a concept referring to the bunching of advertising for a short period of time. This would give great visibility and awareness at somewhat lesser cost than an evenly spaced schedule over a longer period of time.

Cost comparisons are made of various media in the scheduling process. A commonly used measure is cost per thousand (CPM), a concept that shows the cost of reaching 1,000 audience members. Although the dollar cost of advertising on a prime time television show is more than that of a Saturday morning cartoon, the CPM for an audience of males between 18 and 30 may be much lower. The concept is used in measuring the cost of reaching a specific target audience of interest to the advertiser.

In recent years computer models have become more important in the media selection and scheduling processes. Since there are literally hundreds of different media available, each with its own unique characteristics, the amount of information available for media selection and scheduling is almost infinite. Therefore, the computer is ideal for approaching these decisions on a scientific basis. Advertising agencies in particular have been active in developing media programming and models.

Measurement and evaluation

Measuring the results of an advertising campaign is, to say the least, difficult. The advertiser would like to know if the money invested in an advertising campaign was a worthwhile investment. Too frequently, advertising is judged by the sales patterns which developed during the life of the campaign. As has been discussed earlier, however, advertising infrequently causes sales directly; at best it changes the attitudes and predispositions of potential consumers and gives them information needed to make the purchase.

The effectiveness of advertising can be measured only if appropriate communication objectives are established. Even then, the cost of evaluation may at times exceed the benefits to be derived. Therefore, subobjectives or even proxy objectives may be used in order to expedite the measurement process. Once the advertising campaign is underway, the host of variables which may effect its success is so large that accurate measurement may be seriously impaired. Also, measurement may be so expensive and time consuming that the results would hardly be worth the expenditure of resources.

Pretesting advertisements. For the reasons outlined above, pretesting may be the wisest investment in the evaluation process. Pretesting refers to testing the effects of advertisements before they appear on a national scale, in limited market areas and usually under controlled conditions.[24] By using checklists, consumer jury tests, surveys, limited inquiry and split-run tests, controlled market tests, and other techniques, it is possible to predict with varying accuracy the performance of specific advertisements. Such tests frequently allow the advertiser to rework an ad and improve the probability of its success in the market place. One major drawback of pretesting, however, is that only single ads or very modified segments of a campaign can be tested. As has been previously discussed, a total campaign can have a synergistic effect on its subparts. The effectiveness or lack of effectiveness of a single advertisement would be expected to be different from the degree of effectiveness of the entire campaign. Nonetheless, pretesting can be a valuable technique.

Measuring effectiveness. Most techniques that seek to measure advertising effectiveness in actuality measure consumer response. Many of the techniques are those used in pretesting but are done after the advertisements have been run on a wide scale. Other techniques attempt to measure the effects of the entire campaign rather than specific advertisements. Advertising evaluation can be divided into three areas: media exposure, individual advertisement effect, and overall effect of the advertising campaign. The reader will probably be familiar with some of the techniques used to measure media exposure—for example, the diary approach used by A. C. Nielsen in gathering data regarding television audiences. The purpose of all such techniques is to determine the degree of exposure of advertisements to audiences. No attempt is made to ascertain any audience response.

The measurement of the effects of individual advertisements is accomplished most frequently in print media. The Starch Advertisement

---

[24] Frey and Halterman, *Advertising*, p. 448.

Readership Service prepared by Daniel Starch and Staff reports percentages of respondents who recall particular advertisements in magazines. Their technique involves a national sample whereby interviewers ask respondents if they recall seeing or reading any part of particular advertisements. These tests are conducted shortly after publication of the magazine. From this type of report, advertisers can learn whether their advertisement was noted by the magazine readership and to what degree the message was read and remembered.

Beyond these and similar techniques, the measurement of advertisement effectiveness becomes very difficult. The overall evaluation of the advertising campaign should measure the effect of the campaign on product sales. As the saying goes, the proof of the pudding is in the eating. But the many marketing and competitive variables encountered during an advertising campaign render difficult any precise measurement of the relationship between advertising and sales. The communicative aspects of an advertising campaign, however, can and should be measured frequently. Changes in the degree or level or awareness can be measured by simple recall methods. Attitude measurement is more difficult but more important to the advertiser. Attitude measurement has two distinct tasks to perform: to measure the extent to which the campaign has succeeded in convincing potential buyers that the benefits offered by the product are in fact important, and second, to measure the effectiveness of the campaign in associating the product with that particular benefit. A successful campaign for Crest toothpaste convinces consumers that the reduction of dental cavities is desirable *and* that Crest is effective in reducing cavities.[25]

SUMMARY

This chapter has examined some of the managerial and operating problems, opportunities, and techniques in the area of promotion. The management of personal selling and advertising were discussed to the exclusion of sales promotion and publicity. Although each topic was discussed only briefly, the reader should now have a basic understanding of the type of promotion operating decisions taking place in an organization.

The similarity between personal selling and advertising management is not as strong as the similarities noted in promotion strategy. However, similarities do exist. The primary difference is that personal selling decisions typically center on people.

---

[25] Webster, *Marketing Communication,* p. 671.

| # Price strategies and policies

Theoretical aspects of price determination
    Elasticity of demand
    Pure competition
    Monopoly
    Oligopoly
Factors affecting price strategy
    Objectives
    The internal environment
    The external environment
Some representative price strategies
    Skimming pricing
    Penetration pricing
Methods of price determination
    Cost-oriented approaches
    Market test approaches
    Break-even analysis
    Modified break-even
    In practice
    Transfer pricing
Conclusion

Price is important to both consumers and producers. While it is an important source of information upon which consumers make purchase decisions, it is not the only one.[1] The quantity of goods consumers are willing to buy at a given price determines the size of the market for goods at that price. For example, if consumers are willing to pay up to $1.00 for an item, and at that price they are willing to buy 100 million items, a market is clearly identified. But what about producers? If the lowest cost at which the item can be produced by any producer is $3.00, there is no effective supply for the item. The demand is there but it is

---

[1] For another perspective see Jan G. Udell, "How Important Is Pricing in Competitive Strategy?" *Journal of Marketing*, January 1964, pp. 44–48.

not sufficiently strong to make consumers want to pay a high enough price to cover the cost of producing it, including a profit. So what happens? Consumers cannot pay more than $1.00; producers cannot sell for less than $3.00.

In a production-oriented industry, the answer is simple. A myopic industry will say in effect that there is no effective demand and close the books on that problem. In a marketing-oriented industry or firm, there will be a different response, or there should be a different response. That response should center on what we refer to in this book as the discovery process: Here is an opportunity to serve a huge market; here is a problem of high-cost production and a low-price market; let us find a way to serve that market by reducing cost or by adjusting the consumer's willingness to pay only $1.00.

The product is the most obvious starting point. This has been the case for product after product in industry after industry where this problem existed. The demand for automobiles was great in the early part of this century, but the *effective* demand was low. The mass of the market could pay only a few hundred dollars. Henry Ford redesigned not only the automobile, but also the production process to accommodate the demand. Until the 1950s the power boat was mostly for the rich because of high prices. Until the 1930s home ownership was difficult because of the unavailability of credit to the mass market. Other products and industries with the same opportunities of mass markets but low effective demand because of high price have included the private airplane market, high fidelity record players, motorcycles, college educations, hospital services, and retirement benefits.

In all of these cases, price was too high for a big market to be an effective market because cost was too high. When costs were lowered to make possible lower prices, a problem of price strategy developed. Every time costs were lowered, a group of producers was willing and able to produce at a lower price. Some auto makers could produce at $10.00 per car, and some consumers could buy at that level. Ford could produce at several hundred dollars per car, and many consumers could buy at that price. Others produced at different cost levels between the two extremes, and consumers bought at those levels.

Thus, we have a different level of effective demand at each of a series of prices. In effect we have a schedule of demand at a series of prices which we call a demand curve. On the other side, we have a supply schedule reflecting willingness of producers to produce at a series of prices. This creates a supply curve. Now, we have the familiar demand and supply curves which reflect the willingness of consumers to buy and producers to sell at each of a series of prices. We also have a series of price strategy problems for each firm of the industry. There are some theoretical aspects of price determination which are helpful in developing price strategy for the firm. Even though these are covered in the first courses in economics, we will review some of them in this chapter.

Before doing that, however, since this discussion concerns marketing management, we remind the reader of the role of marketing in this process. Above we discussed the product as one element of the marketing mix useful in converting plain demand into effective demand. We remind you of the role of channels of distribution in creation of effective demand. If the commodity is not readily available to the potential consumer, it will not be bought. Remember how the mail order empires were built on this situation? An opportunity to serve rural America was discovered and a new effective demand was created by those institutions.

We also remind the reader of the role of logistics in the creation of effective demand. Perishable fruits, vegetables, and flowers serve to illustrate this point as do high-fashion clothing, advertising mats, and the ability to restock empty shelves quickly. If people do not know of the availability of goods, they cannot be effective demanders. Further, by the use of persuasion and information on how certain of the consumers' problems can be solved, promotion may encourage people to pay a higher price for an item than they otherwise would. This element also can create an effective demand where only a latent demand existed before.

This brings us to price as the final element of the marketing mix which we handle as we did other elements. This chapter is concerned with price as an element of marketing strategy. It covers first some theoretical aspects of price. Then it deals with factors affecting price strategy, some types of strategies, and finally some methods of price determination. Chapter 19 covers the problems of managing pricing decisions.

THEORETICAL ASPECTS OF PRICE DETERMINATION

Since we have discussed effective demand already, and since marketing people are consumer oriented, let us first examine some aspects of demand. Remember, this is a review; we are not going into great detail. In looking at demand elasticity, we examine the usual price and income elasticity of demand. We add a dimension to the elasticity concepts the reader may not have been exposed to before: the behavior elasticity of demand.

Elasticity of demand

Price elasticity. Elasticity is one of the more important notions of economic theory which marketing people are concerned with. You will remember from your study of economics that there are at least two types of elasticity of demand: price elasticity and income elasticity of demand. In Chapter 8 we discussed a third type: behavior elasticity of demand. Marketing people are interested in all three types. Remember that demand is said to be price elastic if there is an appreciable change in the dollar quantity of goods taken from the market following a small change in price. On the other hand, if a change in price does not materially affect the amount demanded, demand is said to be price inelastic.[2] What does this mean to managers who are trying to develop a price strategy?

If they have some reason to believe that their sales will go up substantially if price is reduced—a little price elastic—there may be strong incentive to lower price. Of course, the company may not dare lower price for fear of setting off a price war. Or, conversely, suppose demand for a particular commodity is price inelastic. There would be relatively little reason for marketing strategists to consider lowering price, for the only effect would be to lower revenue in the short run. In the long run, however, the company may attract additional customers from competitors. Or a lowered price may be considered to offset other disadvantages a firm has in the market place.

Income elasticity.   Income elasticity is the same as price elasticity except that it pertains to changes in people's income rather than changes in price. Why mention income elasticity of demand in a discussion of price strategy? Price elasticity and income elasticity may either complement or offset one another. Suppose the demand for a commodity is income elastic. This means that as their incomes rise, people will spend proportionately more on the commodity. Furniture, entertainment, vacations, and "luxury" items or "postponable" items in general seem to fit this category. On the other hand, price increases in these items would normally cause people to spend less on them. Hence we call them price elastic. Marketing people designing a price strategy would certainly want to know the relative power of each type of elasticity. For example, suppose the company has a cost-price squeeze. It knows that a rise in prices may cause people to reduce purchases because of price elasticity. It also knows that because of income elasticity, higher incomes mean that people will buy more. The price strategists may then decide to raise prices and lose some customers, hoping to gain enough additional customers eventually because of rising incomes to offset the losses.

Behavior elasticity.   The third type of elasticity mentioned, behavior elasticity, is a broader concept than the price and income elasticity

---

[2] Technically the definitions of elasticity are more precise; i.e. where the ratio of the relative change in quantity demanded to the relative change in price is greater than one, demand is said to be elastic. When the ratio is between zero and one, demand is said to be inelastic.

concepts. In fact, it really is the factor underlying both of these concepts. When we speak in economic terms of consumers responding to price change in one way or another, or when we describe the shape of a demand curve at a series of prices, or when we speak of a change in demand, we are in effect taking into consideration the behavioral aspects of demand. It is not all economic; a substantial portion is behavioral.

The pricing strategists will take into account the behavioral pattern of consumers as they view price or income elasticity factors. Let's suppose a company has developed a beautiful and extremely useful item very easily manufactured at a very low cost—say, for a dime. It would make a perfect Christmas gift, a don't-be-mad-anymore gift, a Valentine gift, and so on. Now let's assume that gifts are income elastic and that incomes are rising. At $1.49 the company can make a fortune if it sells the number expected. What price should it set? Why? Such situations arise. The company strategists priced the gift item at $1.49 and tried to market it as a birthday and anniversary gift. It bombed. They raised the price "moderately" to $14.95 and made a fortune. Such actions are common in cosmetics and perfumes.

This is a chapter on price strategy, but we cannot separate it from marketing strategy. In the case cited the price strategy was inconsistent with the rest of the marketing strategy developed. As a part of another kind of marketing strategy, that price strategy may have been very good. Suppose the company had marketed it not as a "significant date" type of gift, but just as a casual gift. "I saw it, thought of you, and bought it." Then, the $1.49 might have been in order.

These concepts are important in the consideration of marketing problems, because they give us a frame of reference in which to consider the importance of price in the decision-making process of the consumer. Elasticity helps the marketing manager analyze the position when considering price strategy and when considering overall marketing strategy.

No discussion of pricing would be complete without a consideration of the efforts of economists over a great number of years.[3] Much has been written about various economic views on the relationship of price to both buyers and sellers. It is not our intention to review the intricacies of what economists have written on the subject, but their views do provide a sound and meaningful foundation for the study of price.

The economist deals largely with what may be called market structures. These structures describe the character of the industry whose products are for sale and the character of the relationship between this industry and its customers and its prospective customers.

---

[3] Modern price theory is descended fundamentally from Alfred Marshall, *Principles of Economics* (London: Macmillan & Company, 1890).

Pure competition

The most common starting point in discussions of this type is the theoretical model of pure competition. The purely competitive market is characterized by a large number of buyers and sellers, no one of whom can influence the price of goods or have any appreciable effect upon the quantity available. Also, a characteristic of the purely competitive industry is that entry to and exit from the industry is easy. With this market structure there is no need for advertising or other special efforts to differentiate one product from another, since the producer can sell all the goods that he can produce at the market price. Even though there is probably no industry that meets these requirements of pure competition, there are a number of situations in which the marketing manager has to accept the going price. And of course, that price is where the amount demanded and amount offered are in equilibrium. This situation is shown in Figure 18–1. Part A shows the quantities that the market will demand at a series of prices, line *DD*. Line SS shows the quantities producers are willing to sell at that series of prices. Demand and supply are in equilibrium at a price of $1.00.

For the individual producer the demand curve shown in Part B of Figure 18–1 is flat. No one would pay more than the market price, and the producer presumably would not sell for less. Accordingly, since the price decision is out of his hands the only decision to be made is how much to produce for sale at the going price. The producer will produce the quantity that yields the greatest profit. That point is where the marginal cost of production equals the marginal revenue from sales. This will be discussed in the next section.

It is difficult if not impossible to find a structure such as this anywhere in our economy. It is sometimes suggested that agriculture fits the economist's definition of a purely competitive industry. However, farmers through their marketing agencies combine and cooperate with one another, and are thus able to gain certain advantages in the market place. Government restrictions on planting, price floors, and the like also affect price and production policies. Further, for many kinds of agricultural commodities it is clear that the customer perceives differences in what appear to be the same products. Also, as a part of their marketing programs, producers brand their products: Dole pineapples, Chiquita bananas, Sunkist oranges, and so on. Notice the different prices at which commodities such as fruits and vegetables are sold. Some of these are graded according to government standards but many others bring different prices for the same variety, unit, and size. These differences are often caused by differences in consumer perceptions of the product. Producer marketing programs are geared to create as many differences in consumer perceptions as they can. You will remember that the product

FIGURE 18-1
The Firm under Conditions of Pure
Competition

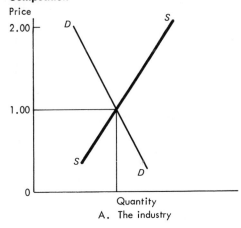

A. The industry

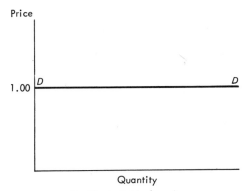

B. The individual producer

continues to be a bundle of physical and psychological values almost
without consideration of what particular product is involved. If we think
that a Chiquita label or a Sunkist stamp makes a banana better or
an orange outstanding, they might as well be better.

Monopoly

At the other extreme is the economist's model of monopoly, based
upon the notion of a single seller of a product for which there is no
reasonable substitute. Because the monopolist can control price by the
production policy pursued, there is a tendency to restrict output in
order to increase profit. We pointed out that there are competitive situa-

tions in which the seller has to take the market price or the buyer has to pay the market price even though pure competition does not really exist. Monopoly situations are similar. Even though there is no pure monopoly, individual sellers can sometimes influence price by withholding production. So, there are situations in which price and production relationships are similar to those which exist in a monopoly situation.

Figure 18–2 illustrates the use of marginal analysis by a monopo-

FIGURE 18–2
The Firm under Conditions of Monopoly

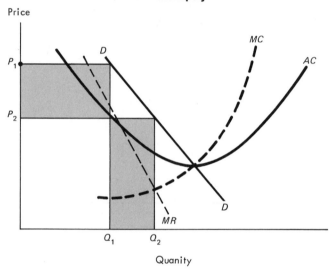

list—or by some firm which can control price and/or production. Let's construct a situation in which the reader is the marketing manager of a firm that has a demand schedule as shown by line DD. Since this is a review of basic economics, we do not develop all the supporting tables. In Chapter 19, for other reasons, we do develop supporting tables for a similar analysis. Notice the line drawn from price P_1 to the demand curve. From there it drops to Q_1 to the amount produced. Since you know that high prices do not always mean high profits, calculate the costs of producing and marketing your product at different levels of production. The first figure you will get will be the total cost of producing several different quantities. Those total costs are divided by the number produced to determine average cost. As you can see, price is well above average cost, so your firm is making money producing Q_1 output.

But you are not through. You have to calculate what it costs to pro-

duce one more unit at each level of output. Incidentally remember that
one unit may mean 100,000 cases of tomatoes or 250,000 kilowatt hours
of electricity, or one motorcycle. Also remember that if it costs $100
to produce one unit and $175 to produce two units, the marginal cost
is $75. In other words, marginal cost is what it costs to produce one
more unit. Now plot the marginal cost curve. Notice how it intersects
the average cost curve at the lowest point of the latter.

You need still more information: the marginal revenue curve. If the
price for one unit is $200, and falls to $180 each for two units, the
total revenue from both is $360 compared with $200 for the first unit.
The difference is the marginal revenue of $160—that is, the amount
added to total revenue by the last unit sold. After calculating and plotting the marginal revenue curve, you are ready for analysis.

The point at which marginal revenue equals marginal cost is the
most profitable point of production, given the price shown for demand
at that level. To show this relationship, start at the intersection of MR
and MC and draw a line down to Q_2 to find out how much to produce.
To find price, extend the line from the intersection of MR and MC
to intersect the demand curve. From that point draw a line to the price
axis to associate price with demand at that level, and get P_2. What
are the results?

1. Price falls from P_1 to P_2.
2. Output rises from Q_1 to Q_2.
3. Profit rises to its maximum amount given the cost and price relationships shown. Why? If you produce one more unit, the cost rises
more than revenue; if you produce one less unit, revenue falls more
than cost does.

Two industries sometimes described as being monopolistic are public
utilities and telephone companies. It is interesting to note, however,
that while these firms appear to be monopolies, many of their actions
related to price are restricted by agencies of both state and federal
governments. This represents an attempt to foster efficiency in providing
these kinds of services while prohibiting the "excess" profits which would
presumably accrue to such a monopolist. In a sense the regulatory
agencies are substitutes for competition. So except in very unusual circumstances actual nonmarket-created monopoly is a market structure
that, like pure competition, is not found in the actual market place.
But the individual firm strives to become something like a monopolist
to the particular segment of the market it serves.

Oligopoly

On the other hand, there is a structure known as oligopoly which
does appear in the market place and is much more important to our

study of pricing. In an oligopoly there are few sellers; their products are often perceived by the consumer as very different from one another, but these products all tend in a technical sense to be substitutes. You should keep in mind that a firm in an oligopolistic industry may differentiate its product from another's in the same industry by pricing it differently. But more importantly it may also differentiate its product on a number of other bases, such as product design, quality, attendant services, or warranties. Among the industries characterized as oligopolies are steel, automobiles, and chemicals. You can see that if one were interested only in transporting oneself from point A to point B when one purchased an automobile, that the product of any of the four major domestic automobile producers would be satisfactory. Yet purchasers' loyalty to the products of one manufacturer over another demonstrates that the companies have been able through a variety of efforts to differentiate their products from one another.

The demand curve faced by an oligopolistic firm has been called the "kinked demand curve" and is shown in Figure 18–3.

FIGURE 18–3
The Firm under Condition of Oligopoly

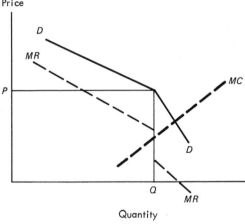

The price *P* and the quantity *Q* are the levels generating maximum profits. Unlike other demand curves shown in this chapter, the kinked demand curve is largely a subjective evaluation by the individual firm and is based on a perception of what rival firms would do if the firm changed its price. If one firm raised its price, for example, the belief is that other firms in the industry would not follow suit. When this situation occurs, the higher-priced product is at a competitive disadvantage and its producer faces a loss of revenue and profits. If, on the other hand, this same firm were to lower its price, it would expect its rivals would follow suit. The result of this would be reduced revenue for the firm and for the entire industry. The shape of the demand curve below the kink shows a condition of inelastic demand. Not enough new sales would be generated to offset revenue loss from the lower price.

Such a situation is often used to explain why prices seem to be rigid in those industries composed of relatively few firms. It is said that the most efficient (often the largest) firm keeps a close eye on costs and market conditions. Price actions by this firm are followed closely by others in the industry. This is described as price leadership. There is evidence that some price leadership does take place, but it is probably not as widespread or faultless as was once believed.

In all three of these structures, as defined by economic theory, we find useful notions. We know, for example, that there is a demand for products. This demand may not be exactly as it has been characterized in the theory but it nonetheless exists and is useful for you as a concept. We also know that there is a market price. It seems often to be a price that is determined by the interaction of the forces of supply and demand. Unfortunately, it is not always easy for us to define exactly what supply curves and demand curves look like, and, therefore, it is not easy for us to draw a graph and obtain the market price. There are other problems, but at this point the value of the concepts of supply and demand is that we know that they exist in some form. They help us get a perspective on the problems of price.

FACTORS AFFECTING PRICE STRATEGY

The formulation of the strategy for any marketing tool is influenced by three broad categories of factors. First, every organization that is well managed will have a set of objectives to govern the actions and coordinate the decisions of the several executives so that they contribute to the well-being of the organization as a whole.

In addition to the objectives of the firm, the pricing decision is affected by two classes of environmental factors: those in the internal environment and those in the external environment. These environmental factors are separated here for discussion purposes only; in practice they are constantly interactive, changing and adapting to differences in one another. The view presented here shows the magnitude and number of influences on the initial price decision. We now discuss these categories in turn.

Objectives

There are many possible objectives which pricing strategy may be designed to achieve. The following is one list.

1. Survival.
2. Short-run profitability.
3. Long-run profitability.
4. Minimizing the risk of a large loss.
5. Having the firm's behavior regarded as acceptable, and preferably meritorious, by the community.
6. Exposing the firm to no more than tolerable risk of legal prosecution.
7. Limiting indebtedness to a "safe" amount.
8. Gaining prestige for the firm by becoming the biggest firm in the industry, dealing with the "best" customers, and so on.
9. Making the latest discoveries and improvements in the product available promptly to customers.[4]

As can be seen, this list includes both financial and nonfinancial objectives, and so brings up two important issues in pricing decisions. First, pricing decisions are so fundamental to the overall performance of the firm that the pricing objectives often look like the objectives of the firm. This is in contrast to objectives used in making other functional decisions which are directly related to overall goals. This is not surprising since the organization itself is made up of a series of specialists, each of which focuses on his own functional area of responsibility. But they must be part of a coordinated effort and emphasize the organization. Second, because the price decision is so important, normally one finds more participants in the decision than just the marketing manager. Inputs are offered by the marketing manager because of his knowledge of market, distribution, and competitive conditions. Financial executives provide guidance in the areas of money needs to achieve objectives. Accountants provide historical and future costs. Top management contributes in nonfinancial areas. So the pricing decision is and should be a decision of the organization.

Among some of the pricing objectives which are finance- or market-oriented are the following: return on invested capital, a particular return on sales volume, and the attainment of a certain share of the market. Notice that the above list of objectives of pricing strategy combines these profit-oriented types of objectives with those having other qualities. These latter types reflect not only the personal perspectives and desires of owners and managers (prestige, forward thinking), but also the protective instincts (against large losses, against prosecution). But one set is no good without the other, since both affect the ability of the firm to perform in the market place and hence affect its survival.

---

[4] Alfred R. Oxenfeldt, *Pricing for Marketing Executives* (San Francisco: Wadsworth Publishing Co., 1961), p. 58.

The internal environment

Just as objectives do, the internal environment of the firm permeates the entire price determination process. The aspects of the internal environment which have the greatest influence are frequently the result of past and present management decisions in other operating areas. But they can be best characterized as those parts of the environmental picture which are controllable by the individual firm.

Product. Remember that a product is something more than a bundle of raw materials put together in some unique way. If the product is a new product, we do not know precisely what additional values the consumer will impute to it, but we can safely assume that such values will ultimately be a part of the product. If the product is an old one and the firm is anticipating entering a market against existing competition, then we have a better idea of the consumer's total view of the product. The total view helps measure the value that the consumer places on the product when it is compared with other products and services for which he exchanges his dollars.

There are technical aspects of the product which influence its initial price. Among these are perishability, variety of use, uniqueness which might allow patent protection, seasonality of production, and post-purchase service requirements. It is clear that while these aspects deal directly with the product and its inherent nature, the influences are far less easily identified. Perishability may influence costs by increasing transportation and storage costs and by increasing the risk to manufacturers (or growers) and to the channel member through which the product flows. Many produce commodities fall in this category as does fashion merchandise, particularly clothing. It is also important to realize that sales of one product in a line may have a definite effect on sales of another. Conceptually, these two products can be either substitutes for one another, complementary (increases in sales of one resulting in increases in sales of another), or not related. For example, if the sales of staplers rise, the demand for staples is likely to follow suit. On the other hand, it has been suggested that increased emphasis by U.S. auto manufacturers on sales of compact cars has, in addition to cutting into foreign car sales, also taken sales from other domestic lines. A strategy based on these conditions has been called "product line pricing."[5]

Variety of use is dependent upon the nature of the consumer because it is the customer who frequently finds new uses for old products. Have you seen, for example, spoked wagon wheels that used to adorn the

---

[5] Alfred R. Oxenfeldt, "Product Line Pricing," *Harvard Business Review*, July–August, 1966, pp. 137–44.

driveway entrance to a home? And then there is the consumer-motivated use of a hemorrhoid ointment as a facial cream—mentioned in Chapter 10. On the other hand, there are many products with narrow usage but which are sufficiently unique to be accorded the protection of a patent, providing near-monopoly protection to the producer for many years.

Seasonality of production also affects costs. It is difficult to operate a business for only a portion of the year because the producer must recover sufficient revenues from the sales of his seasonal production to cover costs incurred while he waits for the next production period. The product also has characteristics which influence the amount of fixed and variable costs associated with its production. Some products require large investments in equipment and machinery to make them marketable. For example, if all automobiles were made with a minimum of heavy machinery and automated equipment, the market price would undoubtedly be several times the current prices. In the discussion of the nature of a product, we said that the product includes such things as guarantees, warranties, and post-purchase services. While these may be required by the market, they also affect costs.

Company size and financial resources. Company size influences the initial price level by restricting the degree of risk the individual firm can take. Clearly, for many small firms, the short-run profit considerations are more critical to survival than they are for larger firms which can absorb short-run losses in anticipation of long-run returns. Further, the larger company usually has more resources that can be committed to the acquisition of environmental information. If the small firm enters a market that is populated by larger firms, the small firm faces competitors with entrenched market positions. These, coupled with risk and cost factors, encourage it to "follow the leader" or "go with the market price." Further, without assuming that large size necessarily assumes more available financial resources, the firm which has the freedom of action allowed by financial strength can consider sacrificing early profits for larger future market shares. The firm can also develop funds for product research and development which would permit additional competitive tools to be used in the market.

Industry position. The firm's position in its industry affects the pricing latitude it has. This is not the same as company size. A leader in a particular industry may be large or small in terms of dollar sales. The authors are familiar with a firm having annual sales of $6 million which dominates an industry in which much larger companies have a smaller stake. This kind of situation creates some conflicting opportunities for the smaller firm. It is the leader, but its competitors are companies which can afford more expenditures for marketing programs as well as for product research and development. The strength of the market position of the smaller firm is one of the factors holding the larger firms back.

Costs. Costs receive more attention from writers on pricing than any other factor, a perfectly understandable situation. Costs must be covered in order for the firm to remain in business. Costs are customarily classified as fixed and variable. Fixed costs tend to go on regardless of the number of units sold. Transportation companies, for example, provide us with an observable situation of high fixed costs. An airline requires little additional expense to operate a 747 aircraft completely full than to operate with no paying passengers at all. Depreciation on the plane, crew salaries, ground crew and equipment costs, and landing and storage fees remain constant. On the other hand, the furniture industry is characterized by comparatively low fixed costs and high variable costs. Most of its costs vary with the level of output. In essence, then, fixed costs are those which continue with little regard to the level of output of a firm while variable costs change substantially with substantial changes in output.

These cost relationships can be changed in the long run. The airline can sell its aircraft and equipment and release its employees, but to do so would make it unable to respond to increased market requirements. More realistically, a firm may stop producing a component of its product and buy it from an outside supplier, thus increasing variable costs but reducing fixed costs. Or it may disband its advertising department and use an agency. Clearly, a high ratio of variable costs to fixed costs makes life somewhat more relaxed for executives charged with pricing responsibility because variable costs can be changed more rapidly; but, as shown in Figure 18–4, the characteristics of costs and volume alter profit opportunities substantially.

Notice that below the break-even volume the high-fixed-cost industry incurs losses at a much greater rate than the high-variable-cost industry. But profits at quantities above break-even volume are also greater. The airlines again provide good examples. During the years 1969–1970 many prominent domestic airlines had large losses on operations because of a reduction in the number of passenger miles flown. Subsequent rises in passenger numbers and cancellations of new airplane orders produced greater numbers of passengers on each scheduled trip. This led to a dramatic turnaround in airline profits.

Given these differing cost structures, some pricing guidance emerges:

1. High-fixed-cost firms need to view their profitability in longer terms than those with low fixed costs.

2. Changes in prices are more difficult to justify in terms of covering costs in high-fixed-cost industries.

3. The use of marginal cost and marginal revenue concepts is particularly helpful to the high-fixed-cost industry when it considers alterations in its initial price. The cost of "one more unit" is very low.

Whatever the character of costs, the firm must carefully include them in pricing decisions. In Chapter 20 we explore in greater detail the

FIGURE 18–4
Break-Even Points and Profit Opportunities for Two Different Cost Structures

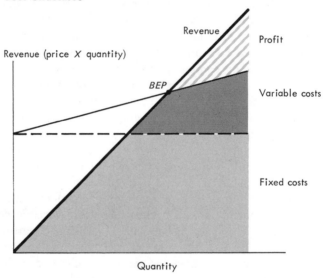

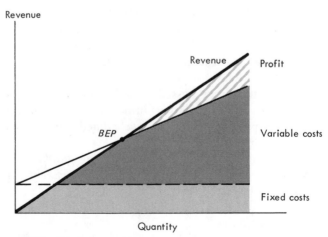

BEP = Break-even point.

relationships of cost-price-volume from the point of view of control of the total marketing effort.

Ease of entry into the market. Ease of entry into the market is a determinant of possible future competition; so it is a particularly important factor in the pricing of a new product. Several of the previous paragraphs allude to this issue. If a potential competitor can produce a product with a minimum of investment and little risk of market failure, then the pricing decision would undoubtedly be different than if the potential competitor would need large amounts of capital, skilled labor, equipment, and money to enter. High-fixed-cost industries would be more difficult to enter than those in which costs are mostly variable. The strength of a company's market position also creates differences. Among the other factors which impede market entry are patent protection, the strength of the total product line of current competitors, consumer buying customs, and distribution channels. A more detailed discussion of these external environmental factors is presented in the next section.

The external environment

Marketing is basically an externally-oriented activity of the firm. It deals with external environment within the constraints of the firm's objectives and its internal environment. But it is important to note that even these constraints may be modified by external factors. For example, when external conditions demonstrate that the objectives are not achievable in their present form, the objectives should be changed. In this section some of the fundamental factors which affect pricing as well as other marketing decisions are discussed. Considerations included here are the impact on pricing and marketing of the consumer, industry structure and competition, economic conditions, distribution channels, public policy, and values and ethics. As you study the material you will discover that the impact of these factors varies widely.

The consumer. The consumer's influence on price is as pervasive as it is on the construction of distribution channels, the design of the product, and the development of promotional strategy. It is important whether the firm is concerned with the pricing of new or old products. Moreover, the consumer affects not only the level of price but also many of the intermediate actions which take place between manufacture and final sale. For example, as we shall soon see, the willingness (or ability) of the consumer to fabricate his own product, e.g., waffles eliminates the need to bake, package, freeze, and store frozen waffles in the supermarket's display case. But if the consumer prefers a different approach to preparation of meals, the manufacturer must somehow identify this preference as an opportunity and design the whole product package to satisfy both the consumer and the firm. By "product package" we mean, of course, not just the physical product but its price, availability, and all other satisfaction-bringing elements of the marketing mix. Obviously, the transfer of the cooking responsibility from the consumer to the manufacturer affects the materials and labor involved in production and distribution. Equally obviously, price will be affected.

We have examined the concepts of price and income elasticity of demand as one of the basic economic measures of the consumer's influence on price. We also showed that elasticity is based upon the consumer's concept of product value. Remember, value is relative for each consumer, and it is measured each time a purchase is made.[6] In effect, the consumer must say, "Since my resources are limited and I cannot have everything, will Good A give me more or less satisfaction than Good B?" And when that consumer looks at each of the available goods, it is seen as a whole bundle of satisfactions. Thus the consumer's concept of the product will also affect the decision to purchase, and that concept of the product may change from time to time. This, coupled with the complexities of need-satisfactions provided by most products, presents the marketer with some of the most challenging and perplexing problems, and, of course, opportunities!

In our developed economy, such problems arise with nearly every product. The influence on price results both from the effect on the basic costs incurred when physical product variations must be made to satisfy consumer requirements and from the margins which may be available because of the value the consumer places on the product. It is useful to observe that the consumer must receive value from purchases at least equivalent to the value placed on labor (or the money derived from that labor) or else some other product would be chosen or there would be no purchase.

One of the difficulties here is that we do not all see products in the same way, and therefore do not always get the same satisfaction. You can think of many examples of instances when two of your friends, each with the same resources, chose to exchange those resources for totally different products. One might satisfy a need for food, while the other was willing to forego food in favor of socializing with friends at a local pub.

We have been using the term "product" in the foregoing discussion as a generic term. We have talked about automobiles, not about General Motors automobiles of about the Chevrolet brand. But the strength of

---

[6] Indeed, the customer uses price levels to help him assess the quality of the product. See Zarrel V. Lambert, "Price and Choice Behavior," *Journal of Marketing Research*, February 1972, pp. 35–40, and an earlier report by the same author, "Product Perception: An Important Variable in Price Strategy," *Journal of Marketing*, October 1970, pp. 68–76.

the image a consumer or prospective consumer has of the company or its brand influences the value he places on the product and thus influences its price. In sum, then, the consumer's perceptions of the product, its manufacturer, its brand, and of the relationship the product has with all other available products are key determinants in the pricing process. But there are other somewhat more visible and measurable consumer influences on price.

The location of production facilities with respect to the consumer influences pricing decisions. Wide separations of the consumer and manufacturer increase costs of transportation and levels of inventory and therefore increase the risks to producer. Demographic characteristics, such as age, income, marital status, number of children, and sex are factors which can be used to differentiate groups of consumers from one another. Further, these differences affect the resources consumers are willing to exchange for certain products. Levels of consumer knowledge about the product, its features, and its operation affect the amount and kinds of information the consumer requires before buying. This is, of course, the reason why we rarely find computers sold by mail. And, at the other extreme, most chewing gum is not sold by sales clerks in retail stores. In the first case, the prospective buyer requires considerable information before he can make his decision. In the latter, what little is required is available on the product package.

Usage characteristics are derived from a combination of product characteristics and consumer preferences. We know that the largest amount of lawn fertilizer is sold during the time of year when the grass needs it. We also know that frequency of purchase varies for some kinds of goods—while we may buy bread on a weekly basis we may buy the fertilizer only once every 45–60 days. These differences affect costs and therefore the prices of the various goods.

Industry structure and competition. The effect of industry structure on price was discussed in a different context in an earlier section of this chapter; we now look at it from another perspective. If the industry is characterized by a small number of producers and the products are very similar, it may be difficult for an individual producer to raise prices without losing customers or to lower them without fear of retaliation. Thus it is difficult to change prices without major detrimental effects. This is the type of industry which has often been criticized for prolonged price rigidity and for having "administered prices."

Administered prices are said to exist when prices of individual firms are very close to one another and seem to vary together. Critics claim that these prices are not related to market conditions and are, in fact, arbitrary. In effect, this amounts to price leadership, since individual firms become accustomed to following one firm's price actions. This single firm is known as a price leader and is typically accorded its position because it is either the largest or most managerially efficient or both.

Aside from this example, the whole impact of competition is very important to the pricing decision. Competition in this case refers to both existing and prospective competitors. At the broadest level of generalization, all firms compete with all other firms for a portion of the consumer's dollar. We can, as consumers, choose to buy textbooks rather than medical care, to buy food rather than pay the electric bill. But we normally do not define competition thus broadly, partly because the obvious complexity of relationships makes meaningful analysis extremely difficult. We do expect those firms marketing products which satisfy essentially the same consumer needs to see themselves as competitors. For example, manufacturers of sheet glass compete not only with other manufacturers of sheet glass but also with those producing structural and decorative aluminum and steel, as well as plywood and concrete; an involved competitive environment, to be sure! In the pricing decision, the marketer must consider the importance of price to the consumer and the response of his competitors to his price decisions.

Again, these factors apply to pricing decisions for either new or old products. If marketers of a new product expect no direct competition, no matter what initial price they set,[7] then their concern is mainly with indirect competitors who have other kinds of products. And surely their pricing decision would be different under those circumstances than if they expected nearly immediate direct competition.

Economic conditions. A traditional input in any business forecasting is the overall condition of the economy at the time pricing decisions emerge in the marketplace. Our measures of economic conditions are a prelude to more detailed consumer analysis. An ebullient economy characterized by optimism reacts differently to price decisions than does an economy in recession. Further, general economic conditions affect the internal decision-making environment within the firm. Optimism and caution are alternatively influential on our own personal decisions as well as our business decisions. And present and forecast economic conditions influence our optimism and caution.

Distribution channels. Again we intertwine the strategic aspects of pricing with strategic decisions made in other marketing functions. Further, we cannot even now remove the consumer from direct influence, for he has much to say about how products and services are distributed. Alternative channels of distribution perform different kinds and amounts of services for manufacturers. Services offered by channel members must be paid for. And since the initial price we are setting includes this

---

[7] This is possible when patents have been issued or when the producer controls all available raw materials, or in some other similar situation.

compensation, the set price must be adequate to provide returns and incentives to the channel. For example, if you expect a retailer to buy and pay for a stock of your product, to display it, and to service it if need be, his compensation needs are greater than if you simply want him to have a catalogue from which his customer may order. If you intend to sell through vending machines, the channel compensation must somehow cover the costs of stocking and paying for the machine itself. And so on. You know that many of the same products are sold through different channels of distribution. Each type of channel requires special consideration during the pricing decision making. Further, it is important to consider all the different channels through which a product flows to assure that compensation for the same services is approximately equal. The best way of determining the required amount of channel compensation is through consultation with the channel members themselves. The levels of channel compensation may appear to be set by manufacturers and simply offered to wholesaler and retailer organizations on a "take it or leave it" basis. However, these organizations may just "leave it." So there is, in fact, considerable negotiation surrounding both the levels of service offered by channel members and their respective compensations. This is especially true when one of the channel members is more powerful than the manufacturer. In fact, the channel member may be powerful enough to dictate pricing terms.

Public policy. The impact of public policy on pricing decisions cannot be ignored. Various governmental units have enacted laws and created administrative procedures which affect pricing strategy. Antitrust legislation, fair trade laws, and unfair sales acts (see Chapters 7 and 19) all restrict certain pricing practices. Further, the federal government has in the recent past restricted price decisions, particularly with respect to new prices for existing products, by requiring approval of such price decisions by an administrative board which applied measures of profit/sales ratios to requests. It is clear that the initial price determination process must take these restraints into consideration.

Ethics. Finally, there are the underlying societal and individual values and ethics. These values and ethics permeate the basic fabric of our society, and while standards are not always applied equally it is essential that decision makers consider them when developing a pricing strategy.

It has been suggested that ethical pricing strategies can and should be developed. Among the examples cited is the case of the pharmaceutical house which, having developed a treatment for a rare disease, finds that the disease is so rare that economical production of the drug is not possible. Still, production is continued, and the price determined is below cost of production.

As you can see, a multitude of factors influence the formulation of price strategy. The challenge of dealing with these factors is not so much that of identifying each individual factor as it is one of defining the interactions and resolving the conflicts among them. One thing can be said: it is manifestly unreliable and unrealistic to expect price strategy to be developed on the foundation of only one of these factors. The more factors considered during the strategic process, the more orderly the managerial process can be. Pricing is a complex and demanding process and should be accorded importance consistent with this fact.

SOME REPRESENTATIVE PRICE STRATEGIES

Establishment of price strategies involves both new and old products. Two possible extremes are available for pricing new products: skimming and penetration pricing. In practice, we find strategies developed along the continuum between these two extremes. If we consider the extremes, the influencing factors become clearer. For existing or imitative products, other strategies are available.

Skimming pricing

Essentially, a skimming price is a high introductory price. Among the conditions under which a skimming price strategy might be desirable are the following.

1. The firm has some advantageous positions which serve as barriers to others and thus limit the opportunity for competitors to enter the market. Such barriers include a particular marketing skill, such as that possessed by O. M. Scott & Sons in lawn care products; patent protection; or control over raw materials.

2. There is a segment of the market willing to pay a high price for something new; so the producer is not particularly price-sensitive.

3. The length of the product life cycle is anticipated to be short; so the product is "dead" before competitors can begin production.

4. The firm needs to generate cash either to cover research and development expense or to finance additional marketing effort. One variation of a skimming price strategy is to set a high beginning price with the express purpose of reducing price as the market demand expands. This is about the same as trying to follow the demand curve.

Penetration pricing

As opposed to skimming pricing, penetration pricing contemplates a low introductory price. Some conditions under which this may be appropriate are listed below. (Notice that many of these conditions are the opposite of those listed under skimming pricing.)

1.   There are low barriers to entry in the industry. Potential competitors seeing comparatively low margins may be reluctant to commit their resources for little return.

2.   The market appears to be price-sensitive and there is an absence of a large enough group of potential customers willing to pay high prices for the product.

3.   The product looks as though it may have a long life in the market, and so there will be a definite advantage to moving quickly into as many market segments as possible.

4.   The firm is willing to support a lower earnings record in the initial stages, preferring to wait for longer-run gains.

5.   There are other available products which may be substitutes for the new product.

6.   There are substantial economies of scale in production, thus encouraging long production runs and requiring larger markets early in the product life cycle.

It is unlikely that a firm would adopt either of these new product-pricing strategies as a permanent policy for use with all new products developed. Each new product is considered on its own merits. This need not necessarily be so with imitative products which are just new to a particular firm.

METHODS OF PRICE DETERMINATION

This chapter has thus far been concerned with certain theoretical aspects of price determination and with those forces which influence the initial price set by the firm. There are three basic approaches to pricing, and all of them accommodate the several factors we have discussed which influence price.

Cost-oriented approaches

One of the ways to set a price appears simple: start with the costs of production; add some percentage of general and administrative expense and marketing cost; then add a fixed percentage of this total for profit. And there you have it! In modified form this takes place but it is not as easy as it sounds. Several problems quickly arise. First, in its simplest form, cost-plus-pricing ignores some critical external factors influencing price, not the least of which is the consumer. Second, cost is not always easy to define. Of course we can calculate the amount of raw materials in our product, but how do we handle the purchasing agent's salary, among other overhead costs? Easy, you say? "We'll just prorate it based on the percentage of all raw materials used in the one product." But it is no harder nor does it take more effort to order two carloads of steel than to order one carload. Well in that case we don't need to allocate any of the purchasing agent's salary to the product under consideration. Right? Obviously not, but what to do with it is a problem. This is particularly a problem for manufacturers. Sometimes channel members find the process a little easier since they have an invoice with unit costs on it. However, they too have overhead costs to contend with.

The retailer may simply take the invoice price and mark it up 50 percent, or may choose to use the manufacturer's suggested retail price (on which the margin has often been calculated). Either way the retailer does not take into consideration variations in many objectives, and internal or external constraints. While simple, this rule-of-thumb markup policy on known costs suffers from the same deficiencies that a manufacturer's markup on unknown costs suffers from. It considers neither market demand nor the retailer's overhead. Cost-plus or fixed-gross-margin pricing is widespread. The reader should be aware of its weaknesses and know that "it's easier said than done."

Market test approaches

Market test approaches which often accompany a skimming price strategy are useful for new products—but not essential. One way to test market prices is to place products in limited geographic areas at different prices. The variety of prices can be determined by analysis of market, competitive, product, and other influencing factors. One advantage of this method is that an opportunity exists to test a variety of marketing tools in concert with one another. A disadvantage is that market testing is time consuming, alerts potential competitors, and sometimes has results that are difficult to measure. Nonetheless, in spite of its shortcomings, it is superior to a strictly cost-oriented approach if conditions permit effective use.

Break-even analysis

Break-even analysis is useful as a price determination tool both conceptually and mechanically. Conceptually it recognizes that there is some volume point below which losses will be incurred. But more importantly it recognizes the different effects which result when costs are fixed than when they are variable. Notice in Figure 18–5 that variable costs are depicted as the sloping line. This is the graphical representation of traditional break-even analysis.

FIGURE 18–5
Linear Break-Even Analysis

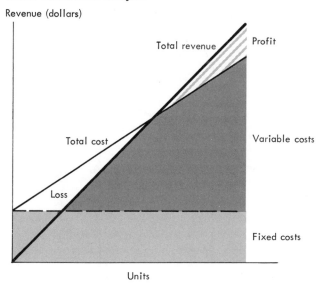

Revenue (dollars)

Total revenue

Profit

Total cost

Variable costs

Loss

Fixed costs

Units

Figure 18–5 appears to assume that price has already been set, since we have a total revenue (units × price per unit) line. In fact several such diagrams could be drawn with different total revenue lines. Such a diagram might look like Figure 18–6. In this figure you will undoubtedly see that there is an assumption of a relationship between price and units sold: that fewer units will be sold at higher prices. While this is not always true, it is not so unrealistic as to warrant changing the assumption. Notice that if we can hold the higher price and can sell beyond the break-even point, profits will rise at a higher rate than at lower prices and higher volume. The reader should redraw the diagram to see if changing some of the fixed costs to variable cost would produce the opposite effect around the break-even point. Unfortunately, cost and revenue lines are rarely so nice and straight. A somewhat more realistic representation is shown in Figure 18–7.

Modified break-even

These representations are based on the assumption that the firm is searching for dollar profits. Some firms search for opportunities to earn a target rate of return on their investment. This is another way of

FIGURE 18–6
A Family of Break-Even Points

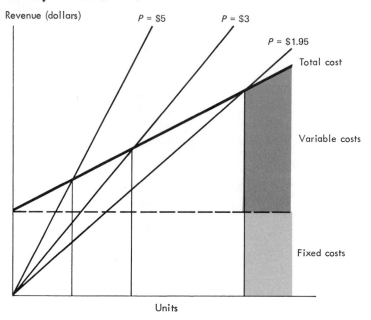

FIGURE 18–7
Curvilinear Break-Even Analysis

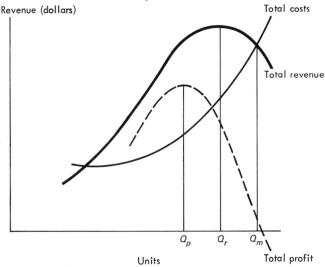

Q_p = Maximum profit.
Q_r = Maximum revenues.
Q_m = Maximum market penetration without a loss.

measuring profit, and indeed, the target rate of return becomes about like the break-even point.

In practice

Companies which are systematic and orderly in determining pricing strategy take into consideration in some way the various factors we have discussed as influencing price determination. In effect we are saying that the list of factors is realistic. A company can reasonably be expected to consider its objectives (which may well be oriented toward return on investment); its internal environment (costs, resources, products, company strengths and weaknesses); and its external environments (competition, economic and legal factors); its anticipated channels of distribution; and, most importantly, the market the company wishes to serve.

Transfer pricing

In an economy characterized by a high degree of horizontal and vertical integration, one of the most interesting pricing problems arises when one unit sells some or all of its output to another unit in the same company. This situation arises chiefly when the units are nearly autonomous operating divisions with individual profit goals. Each unit is known as a "profit center."

For example, a major automobile manufacturer is supplied with automatic transmissions by a wholly-owned subsidiary. The subsidiary also supplies transmissions to other manufacturers. The revenue received by the transmission subsidiary is the sum of that received by actual sale to the others plus an intracompany transfer of funds to pay for those transmissions used in the company's own products. Clearly the price to outsiders is governed by the same factors discussed throughout this chapter. The intracompany transfer price, or the price to insiders, is often viewed as a totally different pricing problem. Purchasing agents may feel that they should get a better price from one of the company's divisions than from an independent supplier. But the transmission-making unit has profit goals of its own; therefore it needs to be able to view its customers, both inside and outside, in approximately the same way. It must try to serve each well enough to get the business.

The key to effective transfer pricing is to so construct the transfer pricing system that the pricing decision requires the consideration of the same factors as do any other pricing decisions. Joel Dean once pointed out that an integrated firm functions best if it is a miniature, competitive, free-enterprise system.[8]

[8] Joel Dean, "Decentralization and Intracompany Pricing," *Harvard Business Review*, July–August 1955, p. 67.

CONCLUSION

This is the final chapter on the development of strategies for the various elements of the marketing mix. Accordingly, these concluding remarks are designed to sharpen and "set" the reader's perspective of the roles of strategy and implementation in the organization.

First, we remind the reader of a part of our definition of management as being the analysis of environments for the purpose of developing objectives and plans and for devising strategies and policies for the effective attainment of the objectives. In this chapter, among other things, we emphasized the analyses underlying the development of price strategies. We did this by first reviewing some of the things taught in first economics courses about competition, monopoly, and elasticity. However, we related these specifically to the pricing aspects of the marketing effort.

Second, we discussed some of the environmental factors which need to be analyzed because they affect the strategy of price. These environmental factors had already been discussed in another context in Chapter 7. In that chapter we discussed such things as the financial resources of the company, production costs, and the like. This leads us to our next point.

Third, early in the book we emphasized that the marketing manager had to act in two capacities: as a manager of the firm and as a manager of the marketing function. The development of price strategy has such an influence upon the way in which the objectives of the organization are attained that pricing should be a strategic factor for all the top executives to consider—not just the marketing manager. Also, price strategies affect so many other departments—production, finance, accounting—that they should have a say in their development. In short, this is management *and* the marketing function, for the emphasis is on the organization.

Fourth, we looked at some representative price strategies. Once again, our emphasis was upon the organization, its objectives, and resources as partial keys to what type of price strategy to develop.

Fifth, we looked at some methods of analysis to help devise price strategies. These are important because a firm which adopts a cost-plus strategy is a different type of firm than one which develops a strict market-oriented price strategy. For one reason, the former may become a price leader, while the latter may be a me-too price setter. On the other hand, the former may not even enter a market if its cost-plus approach results in a price higher than current market price. Its profit policy may preclude selling at less than a given percent markup on cost.

Again, these are strategies. Now, as a preview for the next chapter on managing pricing decisions we look at the other side of our definition of management. First, we said that in addition to the analysis, management was the rationalization of the environments for the purpose of efficiently executing strategies. Second, the next chapter takes as given that corporate strategy affecting the pricing element of the marketing mix has been devised. So we will be concerned with the strategy and tactics of implementing corporate strategy. Third, we now view the marketing manager as a person who is responsible for that function. Accordingly, we don't worry much about the effects of implementing pricing strategy on—say—production. That has already been resolved; coordination has already been achieved. Fourth, we will be looking at methods of implementation. Again, we will focus on efficiency. Fifth, we will be looking at methods of analysis for implementing strategies.

chapter 19 | # Managing pricing decisions

General price policies
Single-price policy
Semivariable-price policy
Variable-price policy
Methods of pricing
Complete pricing methods
Other pricing methods
Multistage pricing
Selection of target markets
Selection of a brand image
Composition of the marketing mix
Selection of a specific price policy
Choice of price strategies
Selection of a specific price
Managed price adjustments
Discounts
Functional discounts
Quantity discounts
Cash discounts
Seasonal discounts
Geographic adjustments
F.O.B. origin
Uniform delivered prices
Zone pricing
Basing point systems
Freight absorption
Freight equalization
Other trade adjustments
Promotional allowances
Trade-ins
Premiums
Trading stamps
Legal issues in price management
Robinson-Patman Act
Resale price maintenance
Historical development
The case for and against resale price maintenance
Sales below cost
Price versus non-price competition
Conclusion

Pricing decisions range from the extremely simple to the incredibly complex. If a farmer is selling cotton, corn, or cattle, deciding is simple. A bid price is quoted on a public market, so he can take it or leave it. If he leaves it, the product can be held off the market for a higher price—which may not materialize. On the other hand if a contractor is pricing a product in response to an invitation to bid, the *process* of pricing may be very complex. The result of the process may depend upon any number of factors. Suppose, for example, a contractor is asked to bid on building a suspension bridge or a supertanker. The process is complex because of the many components and services which must be bought from other suppliers—who have their own pricing problems. The result will depend upon the seller's circumstances. If the contractor has much work, he may place a very high price on his product, or he may not even choose to bid.

Between the extremes mentioned, the process may range from reasonably simple to reasonably complex. If you're selling wigs or women's wear to a particular market, the process may be as simple as finding out what your competitors are doing and then doing the same. But if you sell a line of bicycles in several different models, you have a more complex set of problems.

This chapter introduces the reader to four things the manager has to be concerned with in making and managing pricing decisions. First, some general price policies are identified. Second, some of the widely used methods of pricing are analyzed. Third, an approach to pricing which is sequential in nature and is based upon environmental analyses and other marketing decisions is introduced. Finally, some managed price adjustments are examined.

GENERAL PRICE POLICIES

Throughout this book, emphasis has been placed on the need to set objectives for the operation of the firm. Objectives which are clear, concise, and communicated to all managers in the firm tell those managers what direction they should be going. Most managers of different parts of the firm, in order to maintain orderly progress toward these objectives, will set policies to guide their overall decision making. In pricing, these policies take three general forms: single price, semivariable price, and variable price.

Single-price policy

The seller who follows a single-price policy has decided that all customers will pay exactly the same price regardless of quantity purchased, anticipated use, location, or anything else. This policy has the advantage of minimizing the price management decisions which would otherwise have to be made. But it disregards not only the economics of mass production, distribution, and selling, but also the expectations of consumers. Still, the single-price policy is practiced widely by retail stores. The price of a man's shirt will normally be $8.98 for one or a dozen.

Semivariable-price policy

This widely used policy permits some price adjustments in the market place, but usually the adjustments are at previously specified points. A common example of pricing under this policy is seen in quantity discounts.

Variable-price policy

Under this policy, the selling price is completely negotiated at the point of sale. It provides maximum flexibility when dealing with consumers but is fraught with potential legal problems since price discrimination can easily arise. A variable-price policy often appears in construction and professional services business where bids are offered on particular jobs. Also, it may be found in the retail sale of automobiles and other "big-ticket" items. Sometimes the trade-in allowance is used to vary the actual selling price. Where each sale is a unique combination of products and/or services tailor-made for individual customers, this type of policy provides a certain flexibility not found in alternative policies.

In general, the material in this chapter deals with those adjustments to prices set under a semivariable-price policy. This is the area in which most pricing decisions fall. But the extremes of single-price or variable-price policies, should not be ignored nor thought to be unimportant.

METHODS OF PRICING

Some of these methods of pricing were mentioned in Chapter 18 in discussions of price strategies. We examine them here in the context of our discussion of actually setting price. Alfred R. Oxenfeldt identifies three broad types of pricing methods: complete; partial; and price-line pricing. For convenience we discuss these in two categories: complete and other methods of pricing.[1]

Complete pricing methods

Cost-plus pricing. In Chapter 18 we introduced the subject of cost-plus pricing as one approach to price strategy. Since cost will depend

---

[1] Alfred R. Oxenfeldt, *Pricing for Marketing Executives* (San Francisco: Wadsworth Publishing Company, Inc., 1961), pp. 70–72.

upon both the economies of scale and the rate of output, we discuss cost in that context. In this method, the manager starts with the basic cost of the product and adds a margin for profit to reach the profit objectives of the firm. On the surface this appears to be a very simple and straightforward procedure. It isn't. In the first place we must ask what costs are to be considered basic costs. Second, we must ask what the margin is supposed to cover. Let's look at some of the complicating factors concerning costs and their use as bases for pricing. To make the discussion as simple as possible we will illustrate these points by using a start-up situation: a plant is to be built to manufacture a new product. Also, we will assume that whatever price evolves, it is "right" so far as the market is concerned. We make this assumption to avoid complicating the discussion of a pricing concept with market situations which we will discuss later.

Some very fundamental factors influence what cost figure will be used as the base for the price decision. First, whether there are economies of scale in production is an influential factor. Second, the capacity of the initial plant will have an influence on cost. Third, the rate of output of the plant chosen will also have an effect. When all three of these matters are considered, then a decision has to be made concerning a "standard" cost.

Figure 19–1 shows cost curves reflecting economies of scale, in which production costs decrease as the plant gets larger. If a plant of size A is built, the lowest cost of production is reached at 200,000 units, while the comparable figure for size B is 600,000 units. The figure shows that economies of scale are present: unit cost for A is $3.00 at the most efficient rate of output while for B it is $2.40. Ordinarily these curves are shown on the same chart, but for simplicity's sake we have put them on different charts. To show how they fit together, we have drawn the curves for the plant of size A with a light line on the second chart.

Later we will examine some of the assumptions underlying the costs at various levels of production in the two sizes of plants. For now, however, let us accept them as sound estimates made in a realistic setting. In one way cost determination is a relatively straightforward exercise. We estimate both the fixed costs of resources required for the two sizes of plants and the variable costs of operations. Total cost is then divided by the number of units produced at various rates of output to arrive at the unit cost at that level of production. For example, look at Figure 19–1 and compare the cost of producing 150,000 units in both of the plants A and B. At that rate of output in plant A, 75 percent of capacity is used, and the cost is $3.20 per unit ($Q3$ and $C3$ on the diagram). However, the capacity of plant B is used only 25 percent; so the cost is $5.60 ($Q5$ and $C5$). Once this basic information

FIGURE 19–1
Unit Costs in Two Plant Sizes at Various Rates of Output

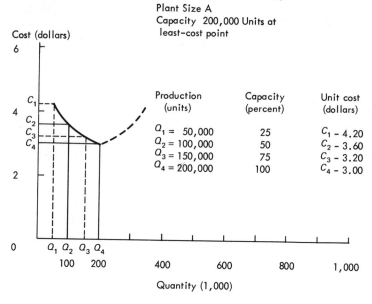

Plant Size A
Capacity 200,000 Units at least-cost point

Production (units)	Capacity (percent)	Unit cost (dollars)
$Q_1 = 50,000$	25	$C_1 - 4.20$
$Q_2 = 100,000$	50	$C_2 - 3.60$
$Q_3 = 150,000$	75	$C_3 - 3.20$
$Q_4 = 200,000$	100	$C_4 - 3.00$

Quantity (1,000)

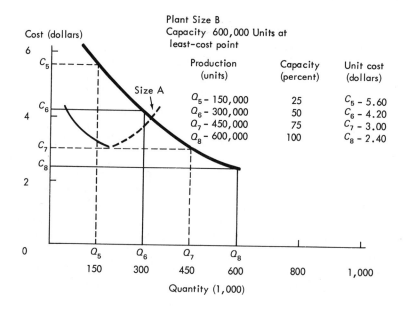

Plant Size B
Capacity 600,000 Units at least-cost point

Production (units)	Capacity (percent)	Unit cost (dollars)
$Q_5 - 150,000$	25	$C_5 - 5.60$
$Q_6 - 300,000$	50	$C_6 - 4.20$
$Q_7 - 450,000$	75	$C_7 - 3.00$
$Q_8 - 600,000$	100	$C_8 - 2.40$

Quantity (1,000)

is developed the really tough price decisions have to be made. There are at least three sets of decisions:

1. What size plant to use as the base. As we have just seen, this makes a very great difference.
2. What rate of output to use as the base. Using Figure 19–1, compare the cost at 50 percent and 75 percent of capacity for either plant size. Note the difference.
3. Whether to add a flat sum to cost to arrive at price or add a percentage of cost.

The approach we are going to use is to determine the expected value of the several alternatives. This involves two steps. First, we estimate the probability of being able to sell different amounts of the product. Second, we multiply the profit to be derived from those different amounts by the probability of each amount being sold. The result of this exercise is a table showing the *expected value* of each level of sales. This very simple concept will be illustrated in a moment.

Where do the probability figures come from? Because we want to illustrate another point, we assume they come from two very reputable sources using very acceptable and widely used techniques. First, the market research department using one set of research and forecasting techniques has developed a set of probabilities. Second, the sales force in its own research developed another set of probabilities by having sales people talk to their customers. The point we illustrate later is a simple one: What does the manager of pricing do when faced with different sales forecasts made by two different groups, each of which has a good track record?

Size of plant. Table 19–1 illustrates this decision. Lines 1 and 2, columns 6 and 8, show that there is only a 20 percent chance that sales will be 150,000 or less. (Probability, 0.2.) The sales force is more optimistic than is the market research group. The latter puts a probability of .05 that sales will be less than 150,000. The sales force analysis says that the probability of that event occurring is zero. It may already have orders for 150,000 units! A look at other probabilities shows why the Plant B size would be chosen. The cumulative probability of selling at least 300,000 units is 0.6 (.05 + .15 + .40), and the capacity of A is only 200,000 units.

Rate of output. Plant size B has been chosen. Now, we have to determine the rate of output which best suits the needs. In Table 19–1 we assume that we are going to use a flat figure of $2.00 per unit to add to cost in order to arrive at price. First, note again the different opinions of market research (Column 6) and sales (Column 8). They are reasonably close together. Which do we use? Here is where the expected value concept comes in.

TABLE 19–1
Expected Value Approach to Pricing Decisions (profit = cost plus $2.00 per unit)

	(1)	(2)	(3)	(4)	(5)	(6)	(7)	(8)	(9)
						Probability estimates by			
						Market research		Sales force	
Line	Percent capacity	Sales (units)	Unit cost (estimate)	Unit profit (col. 3 × 50%)	Total profit ($2.00 × col. 2)	Probability (estimate)	Expected value (col. 6 × col. 5)	Probability (estimate)	Expected value (col. 8 × col. 5)
1........	0–25	<150,000*	n.a.†	–*	–*	.05	–*	.0	$ 0
2........	25	150,000	n.a.	n.a.	$ 300,000	.15	$ 45,000	.2	60,000
3........	50	300,000	n.a.	n.a.	600,000	.4	240,000	.4	240,000
4........	75	450,000	n.a.	n.a.	900,000	.3	270,000	.25	225,000
5........	100	600,000	n.a.	n.a.	1,200,000	.1	120,000	.15	180,000

* The probability of selling less than 150,000 units is so small that calculations are not made.
† n.a. = not available.

Look at line 3. Sales are 300,000 units, and at a profit of $2.00 per unit, the total profit is $600,000 (Column 5). Both market research and sales assign a probability of .4 that sales will be 300,000 units. Again, that means there is a 40 percent chance that sales will be 300,000. $600,000 times .4 is $240,000, the expected value of that choice. Now look at Column 8. Obviously $240,000 is the highest expected value. So, if only the sales force forecast were used, the highest expected value is obvious. Now look at Column 7 for the research department's opinion on probability and the resulting expected value.

The market and cost plus. We made the assumptions that whatever price we used would be a "good" market price. This was to look at the mechanics of one tool to aid the price manager. Above, we looked also at the implications of these decisions on profit, "other things remaining the same." One "other thing" we want to look at is price and the market; another is cost and the competition.

Alternative A: If we take the highest expected value from Table 19–1, price will be $5.00. (Figure 19–1 shows cost at 75 percent output is $3.00 plus $2.00 profit.)

Alternative B: If we used only the sales department estimates of probability and the highest expected value, price will be $6.20. Cost at 50 percent output is $4.20 plus $2.00 profit. Remember, we are going to use A or B above as the price regardless of how much we sell. Let's tabulate that over the range of sales to look at profit—again ignoring the market. See Table 19–2. Note that we are not departing from the

TABLE 19–2
Effect on Profit of Alternative Price Methods

Alter- native	Price	Type of profit	Sales 150,000, unit cost $5.60	Sales 300,000, unit cost $4.20	Sales 450,000, unit cost $3.00	Sales 600,000, unit cost $2.40
A	5.00	Unit	(0.60)	0.80	2.00	2.60
		Total	(90,000)	240,000	900,000	1,560,000
B	6.20	Unit	0.60	2.00	3.20	3.80
		Total	90,000	600,000	1,440,000	2,280,000

conclusions above relative to the expected value. We are looking at implications of the two alternatives when we use the price and profit derived from each. Solely from the point of view of profit, Alternative B is clearly the best.

But we have ignored the market long enough. Price B is 24 percent greater than Price A. The price manager cannot assume that everything will be sold at any one of the two prices mentioned. He must have some idea of what quantities will be sold at what prices. It may very well be that he will have to assume a demand schedule. If such a schedule of demand is developed as a result of research or educated guesses, the price manager then has a basis for applying economic theory. We have constructed such a demand curve for Figure 19–2.

FIGURE 19–2
Demand, Revenue, and Cost Data for Price Analysis

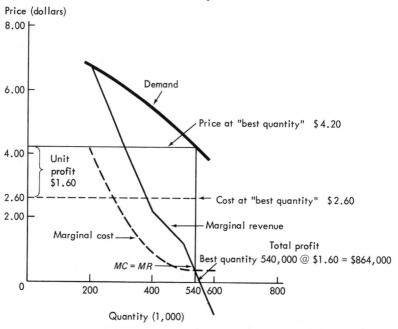

(1) Quantity (units)	(2) Unit price*	(3) Total revenue	(4) Marginal revenue	(5) Unit cost†	(6) Total cost	(7) Marginal cost	(8) Total profit
100,000	$7.50	$ 750,000	—	$6.20	$ 620,000	—	$130,000
200,000	7.10	1,420,000	$670,000	5.20	1,040,000	$420,000	380,000
300,000	6.20	1,860,000	440,000	4.20	1,260,000	220,000	600,000
400,000	5.20	2,080,000	220,000	3.40	1,360,000	100,000	720,000
500,000	4.40	2,200,000	120,000	2.80	1,400,000	40,000	800,000
600,000	3.50	2,100,000	100,000	2.40	1,440,000	40,000	660,000

* Demand curve was assumed. Prices read from it.
† Unit costs from Figure 19–1.

We "sort of" based it on the prices and costs previously discussed. Once we have a demand curve, we can read the schedule of prices from it—or vice versa—and then get total revenue (Column 3). Marginal revenue (Column 4) is then computed and plotted. Each increment of 100,000 units (Column 1) is divided into the corresponding decrement of marginal revenue and the results plotted as the marginal revenue curve. Unit costs are derived from Figure 19–1; total and marginal costs are then computed (Columns 6 and 7). The latter is plotted, and the point where it intersects with marginal revenue is the point of maximum profit. It is the maximum because if you add another unit of production, you add more to costs than you do to revenue. Also it means that if you drop back a unit of production, you reduce revenue more than you reduce costs. That intersection takes place at a point above 540,000 units on the scale. We drew a line from that quantity of production vertically to meet the demand curve—since that is the amount demanded. To find the best price, we drew a line from the demand curve to horizontally the price axis, intersecting it at $4.20. Thus, considering the shape of the demand curve and the costs of production, the most profitable price and production decision is to sell 540,000 units at $4.20 to yield a unit profit of $1.60 or a total profit of $864,000.

We have previously discussed the difficulty of measuring price elasticity in a real-world situation and have pointed out several efforts to measure it. Sidney Bennett and J. B. Wilkinson[2] have recently studied this phenomenon. With the cooperation of a discount store they selected several commodities for study—motor oil, candy, aspirin, flashcubes, and a household cleaner. They changed the prices every week for six weeks on the control items and left the competitive product alone. The experiment produced some rather inconsistent results. We are accustomed to the concept of a negatively sloping demand curve: as price falls, more goods are sold. Few argue with this as a generalization. Note that in this case, however, the generalization did not always hold. The sales responses to successive price drops on Bayer aspirin over the six weeks were as follows:

Week	Units sold
1	7.4
2	12.0
3	5.2
4	7.0
5	17.0
6	10.5

Week 2 followed the expected pattern: more sales at a lower price. In week 3, however, there were fewer sales at a lower price: the demand curve doubled back on itself. It did the same thing in week 6. The only product in the experiment which did not show a fall in demand at some point when price was reduced was the flashcube. It is seldom that a firm can afford to experiment in this manner, but companies often experiment in different markets with different prices.

[2] Sidney Bennett and J. B. Wilkinson, "Price Quantity Relationships and Price Elasticity under In-Store Experimentation," *Journal of Business Research*, January 1974, pp. 27–38.

Competitors and cost plus. Let us return to the point where we ignored the market by saying that whatever price we came up with would be a good price acceptable to the market. Look back at those alternatives on Table 19–2. In a vacuum, Alternative B obviously is the best because it results in the highest unit profit. Nevertheless, even though the market will accept the price—because we said it would—we may want to adopt a much lower price in order to discourage those lurking competitors. Or, bringing the market back into consideration, we may want to adopt any of the other strategies discussed in Chapter 18 on price strategy. We may set an initial high price to skim the cream; then lower it, or slide down the demand curve, as it becomes necessary. Or we may want to follow a market penetration policy and put price very low to get as much of the market as soon as possible.

In this section on cost-plus pricing we have gone beyond just the basic notion of cost-plus. In fact, when we brought in market considerations we switched from cost-plus to a theoretical foundation which ignored the markup methods. Our discussions of other methods of pricing can be much more brief since we have already alluded to them.

Flexible markup pricing. This method is a variation on the cost-plus method in that the markup will vary with circumstances. The market situation at one time or place may call for a different markup than is usual. Also, competitive considerations may call for a local change in markup policies.

Experimental pricing. Few people other than college students and professors know the shape of a demand curve. In an attempt to learn something about their curves some companies will experiment with different prices in different areas. In Chapter 18 on price strategies we mentioned the many attempts airlines have made to find the shape of their demand curves and to segment their markets.

Other pricing methods

The *research method* involves surveys of consumer actions, opinions, and intentions to determine what appears to be an effective price. A variant of it is just a "gut feeling" about a particular price on the part of the pricing manager. Sometimes pricing is done by *following the leader*. This is in principle just as complex a decision to make as if the manager were setting his own price irrespective of what others do. Of course, the decision may be a cavalier one with only one thought behind it: others charge that figure and so will we.

Price maintenance is simply sticking with a price that has been charged for years. There may be several reasons for this. The company may want to continue a reputation for an unchanging price. Or the public may be accustomed to a given price, and the inconvenience of a change may cause consumption to drop. Companies which market through vending machines have had to face up to this problem many times as costs go up. Years ago some would package pennies in cigarette packages to make change. Candy companies and soft drink bottlers have found it difficult to change prices when vending machines are used except in increments of five cents. Sometimes "price changes" are made by lowering either the quality or the quantity of the product. Or the quality or quantity may be increased to compensate for a partial increase in cost and to justify a higher price. Chewing gum and candy companies have both done this. A couple of decades or so ago there was a renewed effort to have two-cent coins minted to help solve this problem.

Inverted pricing is another method. The user of this method starts with a retail price objective, works back through the several channel members' discounts, the maker's costs and profit margin, and then designs a product to meet those general specifications. For example, a manufacturer may think that an opportunity exists to tap a market in the $75–$80 range for his whatzits. The next lowest price is $49.95; the next highest, $99.95. Thus the whole process starts with the price instead of ending with it.

Multistage pricing

In Chapter 2, and elsewhere in contexts other than pricing, we have alluded to some aspects of multistage pricing. Alfred Oxenfeldt first wrote about this approach, but he said that it probably resembles the thinking that has guided some managements for many years.[3] This approach consists of several steps. As each step is taken, the price range narrows until a decision is finally reached.

Selection of target markets. Generally speaking, the first step often establishes a narrow price range out of an almost infinite range. What price ranges would be present in the following target markets (low, medium, high, in-between)?

1. An automobile for the teen-age market.
2. A sound reproduction system for "finicky" and expert music lovers.
3. A spring vacation package trip for college students. For doctors.
4. A snack-type food item.
5. A dry cleaning and storage service for fur coats.
6. A new wonder drug.

The point, of course, is that a "perfect" sound reproduction system will be almost certain to contain high-cost items. A sound reproduction system for a child's toy will almost certainly be cheap.

---

[3] Oxenfeldt, *Pricing for Marketing Executives*, pp. 72–76.

Selection of a brand image. In a way, this is related to the first step. If a company's objective is to be known as a producer of very high quality items, its price range will have to be near the top of the line. Right or wrong, many equate price with quality. Would you pay $14.95 for a $20.00 bill? How about $25 for a $20 gold piece? The desired image may be good quality for a low price or good quality at a high price. Timex and Omega watches cultivate different images as do Rolls-Royce and Pinto, Sears and Nieman-Marcus. Perhaps the desired image is strictly one of low prices. In some industries, such as utilities, the desired image is quality of service. Currently, in the energy shortage, the energy companies are projecting an image of service and are encouraging conservation. In some cases the image desired has little to do with price directly, but in others the image is strongly price-oriented and price-based. Thus, the image the company desires further defines the price range.

Composition of the marketing mix. The third stage in this multistage approach to pricing relates to elements of the marketing mix other than product and price. The philosophy of the promotion program as well as the selection of media impinges upon them. If the firm decides to make its appeal for patronage on some basis other than price, it will have to be concerned with such things as convenience, quality, and special characteristics of the product. Notice the difference in the advertising of grocery stores, on the one hand, and cigarettes on the other. Also, notice the difference in the advertising of car manufacturers and car dealers with respect to price. In the case of convenience grocery stores such as the 7-11 chain, price is not mentioned. A recurrent theme is convenience: "It's about time." The emphasis is on time saved—that is, on service rather than on price.

Selection of a specific price policy. At this point in the multistage pricing process, the role of price in the marketing program will have been established. Now the task is to determine a set of policies to enable price to perform its assigned functions. We have already looked at several policies: a single-price policy; a semivariable-price policy; and a variable-price policy.

When the first three stages have been completed, some of the policies to be developed are already indicated. For example, one set of policies relates to the brand aspects of management of prices and to such things as price stability, resale price maintenance, and price uniformity. If a low and highly competitive price has been assigned a major role in the marketing mix as a means of attracting customers, it almost follows that stability will not be an important factor. Changes may be made frequently. In addition, there will probably be no attempt toward resale price maintenance. Furthermore, prices are not likely to be uniform over a large region; local variations will probably be widespread. On the other hand, in those instances involving other target markets, images, and marketing mixes, a different set of policies may be developed. For some of the fast-food drive-ins, price is only one element of the marketing mix, and not necessarily a dominant one. Service, convenience, and quality are all wrapped up together. As a result, prices are likely to be stable and uniform.

A second set of policies relates to the role of price in the promotional program. Products aimed at a high-income target market may carry no list price at all. Others may advertise a price for prestige purposes. Steuben glass, for example, will often have an ad displaying an item with the price apparently quoted almost as an afterthought—$2250. Or a firm may use price to indicate the target market it is aiming for: the firm name, a drawing of a man's jacket, and a simple statement, "Sport coats from $250." On the other hand, everybody's mail box is full of coupons offering a few cents off on this or that; newspapers are loaded with "carload sale" ads; and TV ads scream that "we will not be undersold." Then there are stores which, in addition to back-to-school and post-Christmas sales, have quarterly "we're overloaded with inventory" sales; semiannual fire sales; and annual going-out-of business sales.

Two additional sets of policies have to do with competitors and the product line. Again, the prior stages have indicated the direction of these policies. With regard to competitors, price policy depends on whether the firm follows the leader, meets competition, or makes competition with prices about average, above those of its competitors, or below them. Likewise, when strategy as an element of the marketing mix has been determined, certain questions regarding price are more or less simultaneously determined. If the completeness of the line is to be emphasized, prices of the elements of that line will reflect the "product team" concept. If a company markets four different stereos, each must be priced in relation to the others so that the price range on one model flows into the price range of the next.

Choice of price strategies.   When the time comes to devise a price strategy, it has almost been predetermined by the decisions made in the prior stages of pricing and in the design of other elements of the marketing mix. Also, the overall objectives of the firm will have further narrowed the range of choices. Price, like a saw, is a tool to be used as a means to an end. Like the saw, price may be used in many ways. The saw may be used to rough-cut a giant mahogany log, or used with the skill of the craftsman to make delicate components for a desk, or used with the finesse of a surgeon entering the skull.

One strategy of price may be compared to a buzz saw: let everybody around know about it—"Never before such low prices." Another strategy borrows the skill of a craftsman, as in the series of "Coke" ads that ran in the winter of 1974. The theme was that the quality was unchanged—the same as it had been back in the 1930s. Then, almost as if he were talking to himself, with a faraway sound in his voice, the announcer noted that in some sizes of bottles the price was still the same as in the 30s. The surgeon's-saw approach may be seen when perfume is advertised at "fifty dollars the ounce"—not "$50 an ounce." The ultimate in finesse is reached when prices are not even mentioned; that strategy says, in effect, "If you've got to ask the price, you can't afford it."

Price strategy is much like other kinds of strategy—the managers think through the alternatives, try to guess what their competitors' reactions to each alternative will be, relate the alternatives to the objectives of the firm, and select the appropriate one. The strategy may be to minimize the possibility of loss or to maximize the chance of gain.

Selection of a specific price. While all of these steps in multistage pricing successively reduce the range of prices, there comes a time when the specific price must be set. Now the price manager has to quit talking about doing something and actually do it. As a part of the decision whether to punt, pass, or feint, the manager will want to review several factors and take into consideration several groups of people.

Among the factors to be considered are:

1. The firm and its objectives. What is price supposed to do?
2. The market and its reaction. How good are the manager's guesses about demand elasticity?

Among the groups to be considered are:

1. Other members of the firm—cost accountants, financial staff, and manufacturing officers.
2. Customers, including resellers.
3. Competitors
4. Governments

One method of selecting the specific price from a range is to go through the process of equating marginal cost to marginal revenue and relating that to the demand curve. Of course, this method may be impossible to use, for as pointed out earlier chances are very good that the company does not know the shape of its demand curve. A second method is to charge the highest price within some acceptable range. By doing this, the price manager has not closed out all options. The price can later be reduced to other levels in the acceptable range, and much more easily than it can be increased. A third method is what Oxenfeldt has referred to as the differential method. The price is set at a level that maintains a historic differential among competitors. This has been common in the retail gasoline business, where independent retailers have maintained prices one or two cents below major oil company prices. Of course, if the firm is the price leader in the industry, this can't be done so easily. But, it can set its price at such a level that, if competitors change their prices, they can maintain the historic differential. For example, if a price decrease is called for and the leader's price has been traditionally higher than that of its competitors, it must leave them room to operate. As price leader, the firm in effect sets prices for its competitors. Accordingly, it must estimate their costs and leave them the option to maintain the differential and still show a profit. If that option is not open, a price war may result. If an increase is necessary because of increased costs, the firm must make the increase sufficiently high to enable competitors to cover their increased costs and still maintain the differential. Why would a price manager be so concerned with maintaining a differential? Is this not contrary to a competitive system? The answers to these questions are tied up with the role of price in competition as viewed by many businessmen. First, it must be recognized that this differential method is more applicable to those industries where very large companies are dominant. Do not infer from this statement that it is confined to them, for the mon-and-pop stores face similar situations.

Second, price is one of the most powerful tools in the competitive tool kit and one of the most explosive. Third, price leadership is one of the tribal customs of business. Fourth, practically all of nature as well as man's institutions strive for balance or the maintenance of an equilibrium. Sometimes, some element of nature or an institution seeks to upset that balance in order to create a new equilibrium. Mostly, however, we try to bring about a new equilibrium in evolutionary rather than revolutionary stages. The setting of price by maintaining a differential reflects all of these things. The large companies are fairly sure that they couldn't force one another out of business if they wanted to. And they don't want to for fear of governmental reaction. Second, if they use price as a weapon, they may set off a price war detrimental to all participants—even though it may be good for consumers. Third, since price leadership is fairly well accepted as a way of maintaining competitive balances, the leader must act "responsibly." That is, all concerned in the industry must be given the option of maintaining their place in the pecking order. Good, bad, or indifferent—whatever we may think of it—price leadership exists. So the differential approach is one method of setting price.

Now we turn from methods of pricing to discuss some methods of making adjustments in the prices once they are set.

MANAGED PRICE ADJUSTMENTS

Discounts

Some of the most common adjustments in price fall into the classification of discounts. They are given for a variety of reasons, most of which the reader will recognize.

Functional discounts. When a producer uses intermediaries in the distribution of his product, obviously they must be compensated for their services. This compensation comes in the form of a discount from the base price. Thus when you purchase a textbook from a book store, you will pay more for the book than the retailer did. The discount may be 20 percent. From this 20 percent, the retailer pays the cost of shipping the books from the publisher as well as the wages and salaries of employees who unpack, shelve, and sell the books; the light bill; rent on the store; payments on the furniture and fixtures; instance, and so on. The publisher finds that this method of distribution is more efficient in getting his product to the customer. Think of the time and effort that would be required if one were to deal directly with the manufacturer (publisher) of every book one buys. But textbooks have a more limited market than, say, chewing gum. For chewing gum the distribution is so intensive that another intermediary is utilized: a wholesaler or distributor. This intermediary is also compensated for its services by being able to resell the product for slightly more than it paid. Wholesaler margins are often a smaller percentage than those of the retailer. This is another way of saying that the service the wholesaler performs *per unit* requires less compensation.

Keep in mind that functional discounts are typically stated in terms of percent off the base price. In this way the dollar amounts are not emphasized. Further, barring certain legal restrictions to be considered later in the chapter, this arrangement permits wholesalers or retailers to vary the price at which they resell the product. The early discount store made its impact by reducing its selling prices and its effective gross margin. Of course, at the same time it also reduced its expenses by reducing services, and hoped to turn its inventory faster and thus make greater dollar profits.

Functional discounts are reductions in price given to particular buyers in return for services. However, this practice has sufficient history to suggest that many functional discounts accrue to buyers who do not fulfill entirely their service promises. Still, such discounts continue to be available and are perhaps of substantial benefit to manufacturers. The marketing manager should continually scrutinize this practice with the same vigor that the purchasing agent searches for alternative sources of raw materials. Tradition by itself is an insufficient reason to compensate an intermediary for services which it does not render.

Quantity discounts. Another price adjustment common at all levels in the distribution channel is the quantity discount. A carload of steel will be priced at less per ton than a single sheet. A case of catsup will cost the grocer less per bottle than if the bottles were bought one at a time. And you will see the meat market selling packaged lunch meat at $1.19 each or three for $3.25. All of these efforts are designed to increase the size of each order by individual consumers. In such a case the seller may have realized savings in administrative, production, transportation, and selling costs which in effect are passed on to the buyer. Quantity discounts, to the extent that they successfully increase average order size, are also useful to production planners. They may be better able to schedule economic production runs. Finally, quantity discounts satisfy the demands of large buyers who insist on lower prices and eliminate the need to classify them as wholesalers or retailers if they are to qualify for discounts. The quantity is often the deciding factor in putting large retailers in as advantageous a buying position as smaller wholesalers.

Cash discounts. Everyone is familiar with cash discounts. A common notation on an invoice is 2/10 net 30. This offers the buyer a 2 percent discount if payment is made within 10 days or, put another way, shows the buyer that the period of time between the 11th and 30th day costs 2 percent of the invoice total. There is some question as to whether cash discounts actually are worth their cost, especially when they are particularly difficult to administer.

Seasonal discounts. One of the authors at one time managed a firm selling irrigation equipment. The demand for this equipment was quite seasonal, with fall and early winter being slow months. To encourage purchases during this slow period prospective customers were offered a discount. Similar discounts can be used to assist in clearing out an abundant seasonal production. Another example of seasonal discounts is the reduction in price often available to tourists when they travel during the off-season. Summer resort areas often offer reduced prices to those who visit during the winter months. The converse is often true in ski resort areas.

Discounts are an important part of price management, and so are premiums. A seller may require a premium when extraordinary services are demanded, as in the steel industry where "extras" include special coatings and other-than-stock sizes. The clothing tailor operates in much the same way. In addition, it should now be clear that a single transaction between one seller and buyer could contain all of the types of discounts discussed. A retailer may buy seasonal merchandise ahead of time in order to earn seasonal as well as functional discounts. The retailer may also buy larger than minimum quantities and pay the bill quickly, thus earning both quantity and cash discounts. In each case the retailer performs a service or a series of services for the seller in return for this compensation. Every seller needs to watch discounting practices carefully to insure that the services received are commensurate with the discounts and to examine available alternatives if they are not.

Geographic adjustments

The geographic separation of producer and consumer has made the physical movement of goods so important that it is very difficult to conceive of the system working without attention to transportation expense. But, as was earlier noted, producers of the same products are rarely positioned in the same spatial relationship with all prospective consumers. Put another way, some producers have a location advantage in serving prospective consumers. To compensate for this advantage numerous geographic price management approaches have been created.

F.O.B. origin. The alternative to adjusting to freight expense variation is to transfer the freight cost and the risk to the buyer at the seller's shipping dock. This is called free-on-board (F.O.B.) origin pricing. Every buyer directly pays the costs of transporting goods from the production or distribution point. While treating all buyers alike, this method of pricing clearly increases the costs of distant buyers relative to those nearby.

Uniform delivered prices. At the other extreme from F.O.B. origin pricing are uniform delivered prices. A seller may decide to pay the transportation costs from seller to buyer because (1) transportation costs are very small per unit, or (2) he has a strong desire to compete in a wider geographic market. This is sometimes called F.O.B. destination pricing, and sometimes total freight absorption. The net result is that the more distant a buyer, the better the price he gets. Note that the seller using first-, second-, or third-class U.S. mail for delivery is in effect using a uniform delivered price. Magazine and book publishers are among the first to come to mind. But in those situations in which the transportation costs vary, the seller is clearly adjusting his net price to individual buyers according to their locations. It is this adjustment which has caused the Federal Trade Commission to view uniform delivered prices with some disfavor since it involves price discrimination. However, no law specifically prohibits such practices.

The seller who can sell a product to all potential buyers at the same price has an obvious advantage. The advantage is competitive, and permits the seller to place more weight on other factors in locating production and distribution facilities. The disadvantage, of course, arises in that the seller may be unable to control the transportation portion of the costs and may, consequently, have to deduct it from profits. But there is a whole continuum of price adjustments between the F.O.B. shipping dock price at one extreme and uniform delivered prices at the other. Between these are a number of variations which contain elements of both. We note in passing that F.O.B. carrier's terminal or job site pricing is different from F.O.B. shipper's dock or consignee's dock pricing. In the former case, the shipper pays drayage, if any; in the latter, the consignee pays it.

Zone pricing. A variation of uniform delivered prices is zone pricing. In this case the seller divides the area he wishes to serve into a series of geographic zones. Within each zone, each buyer pays the same transportation cost. In Figure 19–3, an Oklahoma City seller offers all custom-

FIGURE 19–3
Uniform Delivered Price Zones

Source: Authors' computations.

ers in Zone III his product delivered for the same price. This permits him to compete favorably on a price basis with a producer of the same product located in St. Louis, for customers in St. Louis (A). But very likely the Oklahoma City producer would have a price disadvantage in East St. Louis (B), just across the river in Illinois. One of the best-known zone pricing systems is that used by the U.S. Postal Service for parcel post. Similar transportation rate structures are used by other agencies.

Basing-point systems. A major type of price adjustment that has been widely used is basing-point pricing. Under a *single-basing-point* system, the seller designates a particular location as the point from which freight charges to destination are computed. This single basing point may be the shipping dock of the producer's factory, in which case the pricing system is identical to F.O.B. origin pricing. Ordinarily, however, the single basing point chosen is some city other than the actual shipping point. The basing point may be the city where the largest competitor's plant is located.[4] In oligopolistic industries having a "price leader," the price leader's plant will often be the basing point for small producers.

Figure 19–4 shows the single-basing-point arrangement established

FIGURE 19–4
The Corn Products Basing-Point System

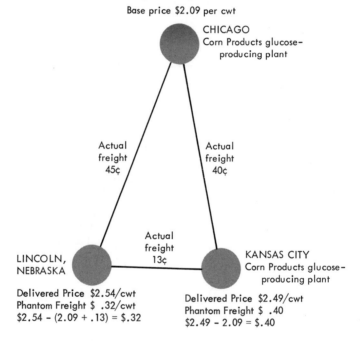

Base price $2.09 per cwt

CHICAGO
Corn Products glucose-
producing plant

Actual
freight
45¢

Actual
freight
40¢

Actual
freight
13¢

LINCOLN,
NEBRASKA

Delivered Price $2.54/cwt
Phantom Freight $ .32/cwt
$2.54 − (2.09 + .13) = $.32

KANSAS CITY
Corn Products glucose-
producing plant

Delivered Price $2.49/cwt
Phantom Freight $ .40
$2.49 − 2.09 = $.40

by the Corn Products Refining Company. This system was challenged by the Federal Trade Commission as systematic price discrimination and the challenge was upheld by the United States Supreme Court.[5] The Corn Products Refining Company had producing plants in both Chicago and Kansas City, and its pricing policy was to sell glucose at $2.09 per hundredweight plus freight from Chicago, its single basing

---

[4] Earl W. Kintner, A *Robinson-Patman Primer* (New York: The Macmillan Company, 1970), p. 61.

[5] *Corn Products Refining Co.* v. *FTC* 324 US 726 (1945).

point. This policy resulted in Kansas City buyers who were supplied from the Kansas City producing plant paying freight charges from Chicago of $.40 per hundredweight which they did not incur. Such charges are known as "phantom freight." Buyers in Lincoln, Nebraska, had to pay phantom freight charges of $.32 per hundredweight on shipments from Kansas City.

There have been several similar landmark cases dealing with single-basing-point systems. Probably the most famous is the Pittsburgh-plus case, which after 20 years of litigation ended in a consent decree between the FTC and the U.S. Steel Corporation in 1948.[6] A variation of the single-basing-point pricing system is the use of *multiple basing points*. There is no fundamental difference between single- and multiple-basing-point pricing systems other than the number of locations assigned the title "basing point." Following the consent decree in 1948 involving the Pittsburgh-plus case, the U.S. Steel Corporation adopted the practice of offering its steel products for sale F.O.B. its mills, but at the same time permitting a mill to meet the base price plus freight of a distant customer if this combination was lower than the mill's F.O.B. price.[7] In effect, this made both the company's own mills and those of its competitors basing points. Figure 19–5 diagrams what happens. No matter that Figure 19–5 is in terms of producer A; producer B undoubtedly would have a similar practice.

FIGURE 19–5
An Example of a Multiple Basing Point System

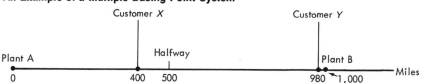

Assume that the base price is the same for both plants (not unrealistic in an industry such as steel). Producer A sells to Buyer X at the base price, and the buyer pays the freight for 400 miles. Producer A sells to Buyer Y at the base price, and the buyer pays the freight amount equivalent to a 20-mile trip. Producer A then absorbs the difference between the actual freight and that which the buyer pays.

Freight absorption. As can be seen in Figure 19–5, freight absorption is an integral part of a multiple-basing-point system. The seller absorbs as a reduction in his return from the sale a portion of the actual freight costs. This is a competitive tool. A slight modification of this pricing system is found among many catalogue and mail order houses across

---

[6] Vernon A. Mund, *Government and Business*, 4th ed. (New York: Harper and Row, 1965), p. 245.
[7] Ibid.

the country. Their practice is essentially to ignore the actual shipping and handling fees in favor of letting the customer add a fixed amount to the total dollar amount of his order. The exact amount added is determined by the amount of the order. This, of course, is an easier calculation for the customer. As inspection of some of these catalogues seems to suggest, the amount added to small orders is more than sufficient to pay for the costs incurred. The very large order, on the other hand, may not make much of a dent in the actual costs. For example:

Up to $2.00	add 39¢
$2.01 to $3.00	add 59¢
$3.01 to $4.00	add 69¢
$4.01 to $6.00	add 79¢
$6.01 to $9.00	add 89¢
Over $9.00	add 99¢

Clearly, such a schedule could also be thought of as a variation of a quantity discount, or even as a promotional tool. The net result is to adjust the actual market price of the products involved.

Freight equalization. Another variation of the multiple-basing-point pricing system is freight equalization. In this case, the seller offers his products for sale at his F.O.B. origin price and adds an amount for freight charges equal to what the customer would pay if he bought from the nearest supplier.

All of the preceding geographic price adjustments have the effect of recognizing the variations in the market. We know that producers of the same products are not located in the same city nor do all customers for a particular product normally live in the same city. Furthermore we also know that many companies seek to expand the market for their products and that consumers often seek to expand the range of products available to them. Consequently, producers must be attentive to the real differences in the market and adjust to them. In geographic price adjustments, there is room for discriminatory practices which are fundamental violations of antitrust statutes. Many of the practices noted here have been legally challenged and have been modified as a result of these challenges. The courts, however, continue to use as their basic measuring stick (1) whether collective action (collusion or conspiracy) was present[8] or (2) whether competition was injured by the practice. When neither of these can be shown, all of the geographic pricing adjustments noted are legal.

Other trade adjustments

In addition to the discount and geographic price adjustments discussed, sellers often find innovative and useful ways of effectively adjust-

---

[8] Collusion on price is specifically prohibited by Section 1 of the Sherman Act.

ing prices to intermediaries while accomplishing other objectives. Even though some of the following points were discussed in Chapters 16 and 17 on promotion, we mention them here because of their impact on price.

Promotional allowances. It is common for manufacturers to engage in cooperative promotional programs and to provide promotional materials at no charge to both wholesalers and retailers. Among the former are allowances for cooperative advertising, while point-of-purchase display pieces are among the latter. The distribution channel members are all elements of the marketing system, and it is essential to the effectiveness of the system that all elements work together. Thus the effect of cooperative advertising programs is often system-wide. Many small intermediaries find promotional programs difficult to finance without the assistance of their suppliers. The cooperative expenditure contributes materially to the intermediary's success by permitting it to do things it could not normally do.

The same analysis may be applied to other kinds of promotional allowances. These allowances often serve the dual purpose of providing information to the consumer and offering a real price break to the channel member. Generally such allowances are efficient because of this dual purpose. It is perhaps easier to see the price issue if we consider a common practice in the consumer soft goods business. Suppose you are the manufacturer of salad dressing and the following events are going to occur: (1) you are planning to enter a new market; (2) you intend to back your entry with a promotional campaign directed at the ultimate consumer; (3) you intend to develop substantial support for your product at the retail level, hopefully getting favorable in-store treatment (aisle-end or eye-level shelf space). Under these circumstances you want to insure adequate retailer stocks but you do not want to establish a lowered base price because such a price would be difficult to raise and would offer lower percentage discounts. What can you do?

There are a number of alternative courses of action. You could promote heavily to the consumer, trying to *pull* the product through the channel. Or you could stick by your base price and increase your selling effort to the retailer. Or you could, as often happens, say to your retailer prospects: "If you buy 10 cases of my salad dressing, then I will give you a case free." The retailer takes the 11 cases for which he paid the price of 10 and sells them at the base price or perhaps uses the additional 10 percent plus margin to offer your product at a decreased price. In the former case the retailer gains the standard margin on the first 10 cases and the total price on the 11th, which is an increase in margin or a decrease in cost however you wish to consider it. In the latter case, the retailer probably maintains his standard margin on salad dressing but, because the retail selling price is decreased, your product may suddenly have a price advantage over other salad dressings. If the customer thinks this price decrease is a bargain, he may buy increased quantities so the retailer orders an additional 50 cases. Everyone is a winner—you, the retailer, and the consumer. And it happens all the time.

Trade-ins. Many retailers use trade-in allowances to reduce the actual selling price of the product. It is common knowledge that for some of these trade-ins there is an established secondary market. Probably the best known is in automobiles. In this market the used car is such an integral part of the automobile retail structure that average wholesale and retail values are published in so-called "blue" and "red" books. If you trade your present car in, you can determine independently something of the value. Still, the trade-in is used to reduce the price of a new car. In other products, however, the secondary market is not nearly as well established. Moreover, many retailers make little or no effort to resell trade-ins. An example is the trade-in of $1.00 for an old tie on a new one. Such an effort is clearly a net reduction in price to the consumer.

Premiums. When a manufacturer packs a towel in its detergent or a plastic drinking cup with its fabric softener, or a retailer offers a free shirt and matching tie with the purchase of a two-pants suit, this is, in effect, offering a reduction in price in the amount of the value to consumers of the attached premium. To the extent that the premium has no value to consumers, the price reduction will be nonexistent. In addition, premiums have promotional value in that they often change the appearance of the product in the eyes of the consumer.

Trading stamps.[9] Sometimes viewed solely as a sales promotion tool by retailers, trading stamps also have the effect of adjusting the actual retail price paid by the consumer for a product. The nature of the trading stamp is such, however, that the price reduction is normally far less visible at the time of purchase than other price adjustments. Depending on the issuing company's policy, a book of trading stamps will require customer purchases of between $120 and $150. So it may be some time before the purchaser collects enough stamps to redeem them for merchandise. Occasionally large quantities of stamps are offered, in which case the price adjustment is easier to see. For example, an Oklahoma City automobile dealer once offered 100,000 stamps with the purchase of a new car. Trading stamps are another example of

---

[9] For an interesting story on one of the country's leading trading stamp companies, see Stanley H. Brown, "Sperry & Hutchinson's Very Successful Stagnation," *Fortune,* November 1964, pp. 157 ff. See also Gilbert A. Churchill, Jr., Neil M. Ford, and Urban B. Ozanne, "The Trading Stamp—Price Relationship," *Journal of Marketing Research,* vol. 8, February 1971, pp. 130–6.

a dual purpose tool: they have both promotional and price-adjusting value.

Credit. Credit can be successfully used to adjust price by permitting the consumer to take delivery of a product while paying for it over an extended period of time, sometimes at low interest rates and sometimes with no interest.

Deals. There are those times when sellers see an advantage to temporary price reductions as an incentive to consumers to purchase new or improved products. Charles L. Hinkle suggests that price deals:

1. Are more effective when used during off-season or low-volume periods.
2. Induce consumers to be extremely price-conscious if used very frequently.
3. Are progressively less successful the closer together they are.
4. Are more effective for newer brands than established ones.
5. Are not particularly useful in countering a new product coming into the market.
6. Are not a substitute for other marketing efforts.[10]

LEGAL ISSUES IN PRICE MANAGEMENT

Although we have already considered in some detail the legal environment within which marketing managers must operate, there is one law which has special importance because it is the foundation of federal price regulation. There are also two classes of laws which are solely directed at price management and deserve careful scrutiny at this time.

The Robinson-Patman Act

Perhaps the keystone of price legislation is the Robinson-Patman Act of 1936 which amends Section 2 of the Clayton Act. The act is divided into six parts. Section 2(*a*) is the first and most important of these parts and contains the following statement:

> . . . it shall be unlawful for any person engaged in commerce . . . to discriminate in price between different purchasers of commodities of like grade and quality . . . where the effect of such discrimination may be substantially to lessen competition or tend to create a monopoly in any line of commerce or to injure, destroy or prevent competition . . . .

Section 2(*a*), however, provides that differences in cost of manufcturing, sales, or delivery may justify differences in price. Also changes in market conditions or the marketability of goods, such as perishable or seasonal products, or a firm's going out of business may justify differences.

---

[10] Charles L. Hinkle, "The Strategy of Price Deals," *Harvard Business Review,* July–August 1965, pp. 75–85.

Section 2(b) allows sellers to engage in price discrimination if the purpose is to meet competition. Section 2(c) prohibits sellers from paying brokerage fees or commissions to agents of a buyer and prohibits the buyer from accepting them when no actual services are performed. Sections 2(d) and 2(e) require that any services, allowances, facilities, or other benefits must be offered on "proportionally equal terms" to all competing customers. Section 2(f) makes buyers subject to prosecution for accepting a discriminatory price.

There are volumes of materials in case law dealing with the Robinson-Patman Act. But the net effect is to insist that every buyer must have an equal opportunity to purchase products under optimum conditions. For the marketing manager, the law places constraints not only on the actual dollar prices which can be charged, but also on a number of other practices. For example, a common marketing practice is to have manufacturers or wholesalers share retail advertising cost with the retailer. This is called cooperative advertising in that the parties cooperate to present advertising to the customer with each paying part of the bill. The effect of such cooperation is to multiply the promotional effort of both parties. But the marketing manager who is considering a cooperative program must be sure that competing customers all get a proportionate opportunity to participate in it whether they buy one dollars worth of product or one million dollars worth. As a practical matter, any inducement offered to prospective purchasers must be carefully considered.

The Robinson-Patman Act also gives the Federal Trade Commission the authority to specify the maximum quantity discount a seller can offer. In this way a large buyer may have no price advantage over medium-sized buyers.

Resale price maintenance

Resale price maintenance laws, sometimes called "fair trade" laws, are state laws originally designed to regulate products in *intrastate* commerce. Today such laws are used to regulate products in *interstate* commerce, but such regulation has become possible, as we shall see, only because Congress has excluded parties to resale price maintenance agreements from prosecution under antitrust statutes.

Resale price maintenance laws make it possible for "a manufacturer or distributor of a product bearing the 'trademark, brand, or name of the producer' to fix by contract the minimum or actual wholesale and retail prices of such products as they move on to the final consumers."[11] Note that a trademark, brand, or other means of identifying a particular

---

[11] Mund, *Government and Business*, p. 292.

producer's product is essential for the producer to invoke these laws. Otherwise the product would be impossible to identify in the market.

Historical development. The first resale price maintenance law was passed by the California legislature in 1931 under the impetus of independent retail druggists. The original law required that the producer make a contract with each seller of his product to sell at a specified price. You can see how cumbersome this must have been for a producer whose goods were widely distributed in many outlets, and, further, the disadvantage to intrastate producers who faced competition from products produced in another state and to those retailers who were competing with other retailers who refused to sign resale price maintenance agreements. In response to this situation, in 1933, the California legislature amended its original law to legalize the "non-signers clause" which required all sellers duly notified of an executed agreement with *one* seller in the state to conform to the provisions of the agreement. In effect now the law made horizontal price-fixing a relatively easy task.

Since many goods were in interstate commerce, however, and not subject to these state laws for control of resale prices, it was necessary for Congress to exempt such resale price maintenance agreements from Sherman Act and Federal Trade Commission Act provisions. The Miller-Tydings Act of 1937 did this. As time passed, state price maintenance laws were upheld by the U.S. Supreme Court, but in 1951 the Court ruled that the Miller-Tydings Act did not apply to non-signers and therefore struck a serious blow to resale price programs.[12] In 1952 Congress responded with the McGuire Act, which makes the use of the non-signers clause legal.

The case for and against resale price maintenance. Mund summarizes the arguments of proponents and opponents of this legislation as follows:[13]

For	*Against*
Maintains competition by permitting small retailers to compete with large independents and chains.	Promotes inefficiency and even rewards it by prohibiting lower-cost retailers from passing savings on to the consumer.
Fair-trade prices are tested by the market	Ignores varying needs of consumers: discount stores with minimum service must sell at the same price as full-service retailers
Protects established brand names by not confusing the public on what constitutes a "fair" price	There is no reason why branded goods should have special protection from price competition
Provides a fair return to the merchant	Increases prices to consumers

---

[12] Ibid, p. 296.
[13] Ibid, pp. 299–301.

This is but a brief overview of the alternative positions. Historically the proponents for resale price maintenance have included certain manufacturers, high-cost large retailers, and small retailers. The opponents have been low-margin retailers, labor and consumer groups, and antitrust agencies. Some manufacturers have supported this legislation in the past, but since the laws customarily do not provide for state enforcement, the policing of agreements—particularly in the light of the non-signers clause—has become an arduous and costly process. These costs have given impetus to abandoning support of these laws. Further, some state courts have declared that resale price maintenance agreements are an illegal extension of state police powers. Such decisions have weakened the system.

It should be noted that resale price maintenance agreements have been made by manufacturers of cosmetics, liquors, drugs, and electrical appliances. These tend to be products for which demand is not highly perishable or seasonal, where few trade-ins or other retailer-controlled price adjustments are possible, or where the products are not affected by many style changes. Resale price maintenance has not had widespread acceptance across many product lines. Interest in using them has waned substantially as a number of state supreme courts have declared the non-signers clause unconstitutional.

On balance, the arguments for these laws seem to suggest that resale price maintenance agreements protect competitors rather than competition. Clearly there is substance to the argument that inefficiency is sanctioned by fixing retailer margins at a level at which small retailers can operate at a profit. In doing so, the consumer likely pays more for these products than he would if such agreements were not in force. We shall have a word to say about non-price competition at the end of this chapter. Suffice it to say at this point that it would be quite impossible to require every merchant selling a particular product to have the same location, public image, objectives, costs, complementary products, and physical facilities. So long as a particular merchant uniquely satisfies a segment of the market, then that market will patronize his establishment. If he cannot or will not serve a market, then he will, and should, fail.

Sales below cost

During the same time period that resale price maintenance laws were gathering strength, another class of legislation also arose. These laws were called variously Unfair Trade Practices Acts, Unfair Practices Acts, or Unfair Sales Acts. These acts, which are state statutes, prohibit sales of products at prices below the seller's cost. Some states have a more complicated method of calculation than others. In California for instance, cost is the seller's invoice cost plus overhead. Other states simply provide for a percentage of the invoice cost to be added as cost of doing business. The California statute, adopted in 1935, has been a model statute for many other states.[14] The California law required that proof be presented that the seller intended to injure competition or destroy competitors. This provision has since been modified so that if a seller sells below cost it is presumed that he intended to injure competition or destroy competitors. The Oklahoma law, which has been tested through the U.S. Supreme Court, specifies that the minimum price at which a wholesaler may sell a product to a retailer is cost plus inbound freight. Other states apply an additional 2 percent to this figure as the cost of doing business. The retailer in turn must charge cost plus inbound freight plus 6 percent.

Unfair Trade Practices Acts are designed to prevent predatory pricing on the part of a seller whose objective is to drive competition out. At the extreme, presumably one merchant who was willing to incur losses for an extended period of time could ultimately drive all competitors out and subsequently raise prices above previous competitive levels, recovering not only previous losses but extracting undue profits in the future. More realistically, these laws are designed to prohibit so-called "loss leaders," those sales of products below cost used to attract customers to a particular store. This practice is freely admitted by those who use it. Their objective is clearly to draw in customers who will then purchase enough other products to increase sales and profits for the entire store. The U.S. Supreme Court argued that this was "a destructive means of competition" and that it played "on the gullibility of customers."[15] It should be noted that meeting competition is not a sound defense for selling below cost.

The intent of these laws seem laudable at first glance. The weaknesses of fair trade laws do not prevail here. Efficient businesses may price lower than those that are inefficient. But we tend to forget that Section 3 of the Robinson-Patman Act offers fundamental protection by prohibiting sales at unreasonably low prices for the purpose of destroying competition or eliminating a competitor. Among the other difficulties with such laws are that enforcement is again left to the parties in the market. While state authorities have the responsibility for enforcement, priorities often do not permit much effort in this area. Consequently it is common to find trade associations performing the watch-dog role.

PRICE VERSUS NON-PRICE COMPETITION

There is a tendency to overemphasize the power of price as a marketing tool. We believe that if everything else were equal, price would be the deciding factor, but everything else is seldom if ever equal. Con-

---

[14] Ibid, pp. 304–5.

[15] Ibid, p. 307.

sequently, even in the industrial market where buyers are commonly described as more rational, such things as delivery time, minimum order size, technical assistance, and supplier reputation cause orders to go to higher priced suppliers. If gasoline were purchased completely on the basis of price, then, in many communities, major oil companies would sell no gasoline at retail since the independent retailers are often two cents a gallon under the majors' price.

CONCLUSION

This chapter has emphasized the management of strategic price policies and the management of price decisions as powerful elements of the marketing mix. It has been demonstrated that the seller can adjust its base price through discounts, give consideration to geographic and promotional factors, and be attentive to the legal parameters around price management activity. Such adjustments must be kept in perspective. Marketing managers must know why they are taking a particular action, basing it on a systematic consideration of relevent alternatives.

Note that resale price maintenance agreements are no longer exempt from antitrust legislation. Congress, in late 1975, repealed the Miller-Tydings Act. Thus for the time being, at least, only those goods in intrastate commerce in states with effective laws are now subject to these restrictions.

PART FOUR

Management of the marketing system

chapter 20

Control of marketing
strategy and management

The nature and purpose of control
The purpose of controls
Control systems
Control of marketing operations
Steps in the control of operations
Cost-price-volume relationships
Control of productivity and profitability
Other aspects of control systems
Conclusion

Marketing management has been discussed in this book in terms of planning and action. Much emphasis was placed in the beginning chapters on constructing an orderly framework within which marketing managers could operate efficiently and effectively. We discussed in some detail the application of planning principles, the environmental influences on this planning process, and the basic information requirements for taking the planning perspective into the arena of management action. From there we went on to the areas of marketing in which decisions must be made. These areas—product, channel, logistics, promotion, and price—have two distinct facets to them. We have suggested that the strategic and managerial or operational facets of each functional area can and should be separated for analytical and study purposes and, further, that this separation should continue throughout the marketing management process.

The word management implies three essential components: (1) what the firm wants to do or where it wants to go: planning; (2) a series of actions taken to get it there: decision making; and (3) a check to (a) see whether it is getting where it wants to go, and (b) to see if it has got there: evaluation or control. The marketing manager must systematize the evelution or control process. In one sense control is the measurement of results. Management must act on the discrepancies between what was expected (objectives) and what was achieved (results). Of course, control is the action based upon information.

THE NATURE AND PURPOSE OF CONTROL

The purpose of controls

The purpose of marketing control is to serve as a measurement process designed to evaluate the functioning of the marketing system. Because it deals with relationships, marketing control procedures can and should be set up to evaluate the operations of the total enterprise, including the nonhuman or systems relationships, those who manage and those who are managed, and the results of the total management process. In this context control can be defined as a mechanism for the systematic detection and correction of deviations from planned occurrences. There are three aspects of the central system to consider. First, control is an active process. It is not something that is thought of after a marketing system has been constructed and put into operation. Control data is essential for further planning activity; thus, at the outset the marketing manager must be as concerned with his measurement-of-results techniques as he is with the development of objectives. Second, it is all too easy to consider the control process as a kind of cross-sectional activity; that is, as a photograph of the marketing system at an instant of time. You can readily see the pitfalls of such a conception. The sales manager who sets, as one criterion for measuring the performance of sales personnel the making of 1,000 sales calls a year and then waits for the entire year to pass before starting the measurement process, is inviting disaster. The manager may have waited too long. The fact that a salesperson will not meet the objective will become clear before the year has ended if a good control system exists.

Third, the great benefits of the control process for those whose responsibility it is to control should not be overlooked. Marketing managers gain insight into their own abilities and techniques during the process of evaluating others.

Control systems

We have suggested that control is an ongoing process, much like planning, and that the results of control become some of the inputs to the next planning cycle. Ideally, we would expect a control system set up in conjunction with a plan of action and operated continuously to respond automatically to deviations from the norm. It is doubtful if this ideal can be made completely operational. Thomas A. Staudt and

Donald A. Taylor handle this point very well.[1] They say, "It is doubtful, however, whether it is possible to design a managerial system that will operate as smoothly as a temperature control system." They give several reasons for their position.

1.   There are many objectives in the total system which call for several subsystems. Conflicts in objectives and thus in subsystems may prevent an animate system from functioning as smoothly as an inanimate system.

2.   The forces which call for change or stimulate it are too varied and dynamic to devise control systems capable of reacting to all environment changes.

3.   The need for change is not always evident.

4.   Managerial systems function through people, and people are prone to make mistakes, or not visualize all possible alternatives.

Despite these flaws, a control system is essential. Even the temperature control system has its difficulties in coping with change. If the sensor fails, the system fails; if a sender fails, the system fails; if the power fails, the system fails. Inanimate control systems have their flaws, too.

CONTROL OF MARKETING OPERATIONS

Almost every time we have had anything to say about the marketing function we have reemphasized that the firm as a whole had to be considered. Also, we have discussed the importance of having adequate information as a basis for decision as well as for a basis for control. Many firms do not have their information in a form suitable for the several different types of analyses which underlie some rather significant decisions affecting the firm and the marketing effort.

One of the problems of control is a very simple one: managers often are unable to trace conveniently and accurately the various steps leading to a given result. They may be able to find one explanation, but the right explanation may elude them, because information is not available in suitable form. For example, the profit for a given product may have varied enough from expectations to cause a manager to look into the situation. The manager may trace the change down to (1) a particular territory, (2) a particular salesperson in that territory, (3) a particular product, and finally (4) to a particular customer. This may be the answer, but is it? The answer *appears* to be that the volume of sales of a particular product or salesperson has increased or decreased. The *real* answer rather than the *apparent* answer may lie buried in the relationships among cost, volume, and price. We will come back to this.

[1] Thomas A. Staudt and Donald A. Taylor, A *Managerial Introduction to Marketing*, 2d ed. (New York: Prentice-Hall, 1970), pp. 553–54.

Or the answer may lie almost anywhere else in the organization. We will come back to this too.

Our concern is with the economic performance of marketing operations. To be able to measure and control marketing profitability and productivity, managers must have information on costs and performance. So our first discussion centers on the nature of information required for managerial control purposes. The second discussion will be concerned with the performance itself. We hope the reader will watch for two things. First, note that the discussion of information centers on production costs and accounting methods. Second, note that volume of sales is not the only criterion of performance; cost, price, and volume are interrelated criteria.

Steps in the control of operations

Chapter 5 was devoted to the general subject of information; so we can be relatively brief in our present discussion. An information system designed to aid management in measuring and controlling performance should have certain characteristics:[2]

1. The system should have a plan and a design.
2. Reporting should be integrated.
3. Data should be gathered at the lowest level.
4. Information should be reported on an exceptions basis and by key areas.
5. Reporting should be compared with a standard.
6. Cost-price-volume relationship should be clarified.

Plan and design the system. This is probably the most important step to be taken because all of the other desired characteristics of an information system flow from it. Managers will have an information system of some sort—however good or bad, complete or incomplete, accurate or inaccurate. Some of these systems just develop over time because occasionally a need was perceived by someone in authority who asked for a report. Systems which develop in this manner may provide all of the information required, but in a form which limits its usefulness.

Information systems for control should be designed and not allowed to just grow. One underlying criterion for the design should be the objectives and plans of the organization. A second should be the needs of the managers for information to enable them to direct the organization toward the execution of those plans. A third criterion should be that

---

[2] These criteria were suggested by Robert H. Deming, *Characteristics of an Effective Management Control System* (Boston: Harvard Business School, Division of Research, 1968). Those who seek a thorough and interesting discussion of concepts of control of both planning and operations should study this book.

only necessary information should be provided. An avalanche of unnecessary information can often paralyze a manager. A fourth criterion is that it should raise proper and timely questions.

Integrate reports. A second characteristic for a control system is that each of the relevant elements should be integrated to enable the decision maker to determine cause-and-effect relationships. Just knowing that orders are up is not sufficient for the control-minded manager. He must know why they are up and the effect of the rise. There are cause-effect relationships which managers need to be aware of, which require integrated reporting. For example, sales may be up during a given period, but profits down. The manager needs to be able to trace this relationship to its roots without ordering a special study. An integrated reporting system has a hierarchical structure which is shaped like a triangle. The base of the triangle contains large masses of data showing all appropriate detail. This, in effect, is the reference library. It is distilled for each successive layer of management. When the top of the triangle is reached, only an integrated summary is presented to top management.

Gather the data. As implied above, the data which will eventually rise to the top should be captured at the lowest possible level. If not captured there, it is lost for future reporting and analysis. Of course, the basic sources of information still remain and can eventually be tapped for special studies. It is at this point that the plan and design of the control information system is important. There is often a tendency to develop all data which the basic sources provide. Today, in the large firm with suitable electronic storage and retrieval systems, this may not be bad. In the smaller firm, it may be too costly to extract and store information for which there is no apparent need. We will not generalize on the extraction of data. In some cases the extra cost of getting all the data from basic documents, as distinct from getting just that currently needed may be relatively low.

However, we will generalize on the reporting of that data. With all those nice numbers readily at hand, there is a tendency to tell managers more than they want to know—and more than they need to know. Care should be taken to avoid smothering them with information. Again, here is where the plan and design of the system come into play. Only information needed, asked for, and used should be provided. What are some of the sources of information for control? Since we can't—or won't—try to identify all of them, we will use the elements of the marketing mix to show how raw data for control purposes may be generated.

Product. The purchase order is a valuable primary source document for many aspects of control. Information on sales by product, customer, territory, and salesman can be generated from it. When these data are related to and integrated with appropriate cost information sources, managers are in a position to determine profitability of each of these four key elements.

Promotion.   One special source of promotion control information is the coupon return. These may be coupons offering cents-off-the-regular-price which are mailed to "box holder" or selected mailing lists. Or they may be coupons offering further information. If the coupon is returned, the promotion people can tell which mailing, magazine, or newspaper it came from. Thus they have a clue as to the effectiveness of a given medium of promotion.

Channels of distribution: Institutions.   We have already mentioned the purchase order as a document showing who the customers are, their location, and their usage of the product. However. reports from middlemen may be helpful in identifying characteristics of end users of the product. These reports are not likely to be automatic. For that matter, they may not even be available, for the middleman may either (1) not have that information itself, or (2) may not be willing to part with it. However, for some items the manufacturer of certain types of goods may cause the information to be generated. Many durable goods, such as electric drills, hair dryers, and the like, are warrantied. When the purchaser completes the warranty card, he is often asked to tell where he bought the item and what he is going to use it for.

Channels of distribution: Logistics.   A bill of lading, waybill, or freight bill is prepared for every shipment made by a for-hire carrier. These documents show the name and location of the consignee, the size of the shipment, the type of carrier used, and the rate charged, among other things. While much of the data are also available from the purchase order and shipping order, these are the basic sources of information for logistics cost and service control. Periodic and routine reports from warehouses provide data for management of inventory.

Price.   The purchase order is again a basic source document for price information. It should show the actual price charged. This may be compared with the basic price structure to show the number, amount, and recipients of price discounts. However, this information may be incomplete for overall managerial purposes. It will show the price paid by the reseller, but it does not give insights into what the customer paid.

General.   Salespeople's reports have been mentioned as sources of information. These are a mixed bag. Sometimes they may be quite specific. For example, they may report on their calls, productivity, and expenses. Or the reports may be qualitative: competitors seem to be making inroads; customers are happy; and so on. Other general sources include the accounting department for appropriate cost information; the purchasing department for data on sources of supply; and research and development for new product development.

So far we have discussed *how* reporting should take place by emphasizing that control information should be integrated when passed on, and that it should be captured at the lowest level possible. We have also looked at some of the sources. Now we turn to a slightly different approach to see what *concepts* should be considered in developing reports for control purposes. There are at least three: information should be reported on an exceptions basis; it should focus on critical areas; and it should be presented with reference to standards.

Report exceptions. Once more we state a basic premise: management should get only that information for control that it *needs*. By reporting deviations from the norm, things which may need managerial attention are emphasized. The expectation is that these deviations from the standard indicate that a problem is developing. What should be reported? The safe hedging answer obviously is that "it depends." Practically everything needs to be reported to someone. A reasonably safe rule is that critical area reporting be combined with exceptions reporting to top managers. The critical areas are those which influence the performance of the organization: (1) where improper decisions would have a major impact; and (2) where dollar concentrations are the greatest.

The above are critical areas from an economic point of view and for which economic data are readily available for control decisions. However, there are areas which are equally critical, but for which quantitative data are not available and where the ability to make factual analyses is limited. These include such areas as personnel relations involving matters of employee security, morale, and motivation; public relations in a very broad sense involving the posture of the firm in meeting its obligations to the public—or what has been come to be called social responsibility; and the unquantifiable aspects of research and development.

Reporting by exception may have several characteristics. First, as a part of the design of the control system some sort of guidelines should be established. If the performance is outside those guidelines, special attention should be called to that fact. This, of course, implies that a second characteristic is present: that the reports show only significant facts and situations with which the managers at a given level are concerned. Reporting and managing by exception is a sound philosophy. But there is an important danger in this concept of control. Sales, profits, costs, productivity—everything may be within the guidelines established. Costs may even be slightly lower than the guidelines, and sales and profits slightly higher. Yet the firm may be in trouble. Why? The guidelines are only norms; they are averages of performance. But averages may obscure serious deviations. Consider the following situations in a summary report:

1. Sales in the North Central Region appear to be slightly up, but

well within the guidelines. However, look behind total sales. The company may have lost a customer who accounts for 10 percent of sales in the region. Or perhaps sales to all costomers in the region are down 10 percent. The losses are offset by a one-time sale to someone else in the region. Or prices may have risen, and even though volume fell net sales were up. The people directly involved know the circumstances, but these do not appear in the averages sent up to top management.

2.   Return on investment appears to be normal in the South Central Region, according to the summary report. The actual situation may be that profits in the region have fallen, and the decline has been obscured by the sale of a company-owned warehouse which reduced the investment base so that the effect of lower profits on ROI was offset.

3.   The marketing profit center showed an overall gain with an increased volume of sales. However, the gain may have resulted from reduced delivery times and smaller shipments. The increased cost may be borne by another cost center.

4.   All sales quotas were met, and some slightly exceeded. However, the explanation may lie not in the good work of the sales department but in an increase of overall economic activity. Analysis may disclose that sales for the industry were up 10 percent, while ours were up only 3 percent and our share of the market fell.

5.   Sales in the Northwest Region are off 8 percent.
Superficially this looks bad, but the lost sales may have been of products or to customers which were unprofitable. So the decline in sales volume means a rise in profit. The reduced volume may even have been planned for by the regional manager.

Certainly, someone in the organization knows about all of these situations. Our point is that summary reports to top management may give the wrong impression unless the control guidelines establish a procedure for checking the "normal." Reporting by exception to top management implies that somewhere down the managerial hierarchy someone has raised and satisfactorily answered three questions:

1.   Why did the firm meet the standards and quotas budgeted for?
2.   Why did it fall short of them?
3.   Why were they exceeded?

Supplementary reports can be used to provide the necessary elaboration of the summary report that management receives. They can provide answers to these three questions and thus enhance the value of exceptions reporting.

Report against a standard.   Control cannot effectively take place in a vacuum. Simple figures showing volume of sales or magnitude of costs provide few, if any, bases for control. There are two basic standards against which performance may be measured and which provide bases for control: (1) the budget; and (2) performance in a previous period— last month, or quarter, or year.

The budget, as an integrated part of the profit plan, is a useful standard for comparison. Deviations from the budget become immediately apparent. They can be traced to the appropriate responsibility center for corrective action. Of course, such deviations are not necessarily either good or bad. Also, corrective action does not necessarily imply the reduction or increase of expenditures to conform to the budget. It may involve decreasing or increasing the budget to match the expenditures. Such action may be called for by situations which have changed since the budget was originally prepared. For control purposes, comparison of performance with the budget is probably significantly more valuable than comparison with last year's performance. Reason? The budget should be a forward-looking document, while last year's performance is history. As a control measure, the value of last year's performance as a standard for comparison leaves much to be desired. Even as an *information* device it may have little or no value. The objective of management is the attainment of a given profit plan. The profit plan may have relatively little comparability with that of the previous year.

In concluding this discussion, we point out two things for emphasis. First, since the profit plan is the prime objective, the budget should be the major standard for comparison of performance. Second, since the profit plan is developed for objective attainment in the uncharted future, information on past performance will help the manager develop insights into the nature and magnitude of the control problem the company faces.

Cost-price-volume relationships

The format of a control system for operations should facilitate decisions by showing interrelationships among the three key areas of cost, prices, and volume of sales. Throughout this book we have emphasized the importance of developing a way of thinking about functional area interrelationships which will make functional managers recognize the impact of their decisions on areas other than their own. Participation in objective setting and planning is one means of fostering this recognition of the interdependence of departments.

Establishing the proper kind of objectives at Level 1 and developing *policy* guidelines which provide for coordination of effort from the beginning rather than at the end is the second step in this process. The third step involves establishing a control system and reporting system for top management which reflects the appropriate interactions. The major economic elements of such a system are:

1. The budget and its characteristics.
2. Profit planning and improvement.
3. Profit, investment, and cost-center control.
4. Cost-price-volume relationships.

The first three elements are primarily concerned with the *control of planning*. The fourth is appropriate for this part of the chapter concerned with the *control of operations*.

In what follows, we present an example of an approach to control of the marketing effort. This is not a hypothetical case. With one exception, all the numbers are real, but the situations are designed. Also, some of the situations do not actually exist, but they could.

The exception in which the numbers are not real involves price. Here, for simplicity in discussion, we have used a weighted average price to calculate revenue. While we use four products (A, B, C, D), there is really only one product with what may be called "standard equipment"—Product A. Products B, C, and D have more or less equipment than the standard. Right, wrong, or indifferent, management has allocated fixed costs to each product equally.

In addition to discussing the very important step of classifying expenses into functional from natural accounts, two major points are illustrated: cost analysis and effort analysis.

Functional accounts. Typically, a company's accounting records classify expenditures in terms of what they buy: wages and salaries; freight; sales commissions; depreciation; and so on. For summary purposes these so-called natural accounts are all very well, but they are inadequate for decision making. The classification of costs by function—or what they are incurred for—is necessary to assure adequate control. The natural accounts mentioned above should be broken down into their functional components, as shown in Table 20–1. For convenience in this table, we use only Products A and B instead of all four products. Figures for Products C and D have been compressed into A and B. Also, some internal expenditures have similarly been compressed.

Line 3 of the table shows the president's salary. Since it is a cost which cannot be traced to either Product A or B, it is assigned to a "General" category. On the other hand, the salaries of the supervisors in line 4 can be traced directly to their products; so the "General" category is not used. If control is really going to mean anything, only those costs which can be traced directly to a product should be assigned to it. The functional system illustrated by Table 20–1 has two other characteristics. First, it is constructed in a modular form. Second, costs

TABLE 20–1
Classification of Cost on a Functional Basis (in dollars)

Line	Cost item	Total	Product A	Product B	General
1	Fixed costs				
2	Module 1a, salaries				
3	1. President	27,350	–	–	27,350
4	2. Supervisor..............	33,100	16,550	16,550	–
5	3. Clerical	10,600	5,300	5,300	–
6	4. Other administrative........	49,650	–	–	49,650
7	Total, Module 1a	120,700	21,850	21,850	77,000
8	Module 1b, supplies, equipment, etc.				
9	1. Equipment	3,000	1,000	1,000	1,000
10	2. Telephone..............	3,000	–	–	3,000
11	3. Advertising	2,800	2,000	800	–
12	4. Travel and entertainment	4,200	500	500	3,200
13	Total, Module 1b	13,000	3,500	2,300	7,200
14	Total, lines 7 and 13	133,700	25,350	24,150	84,200
15	Miscellaneous	6,686	–	–	6,686
16	Total, lines 14 and 15.	140,386	25,350	24,150	90,886
17	Module 2, process 3.	296,520	148,260	148,260	–
18	Total fixed costs (lines 16 and 17) ...	436,906	173,610	172,410	90,886
19	Variable costs				
20	Modules 3 and 4 production				
21	1. Process 1	81,378	40,689	40,689	–
22	2. Process 2	117,468	58,734	58,734	–
23	3. Miscellaneous............	9,942	–	–	9,942
24	4. Total, lines 21, 22, 23	208,788	99,423	99,423	9,942
25	Module 5, materials.	85,222	42,611	42,611	–
26	Module 6, misc. labor	89,526	44,763	44,763	–
27	Total variable costs (lines 24, 25 26).	383,536	186,797	186,797	9,942
28	Total costs (lines 18, 27).	820,422	360,407	359,207	100,828

are separated into their fixed and variable components. These matters will be discussed next. Now we reissue a warning before going on to the next step: Management can be strangled with information; so only that which is relevant should be developed. For example, it may be desirable to break down the costs even further to show sales commissions on Product A by territory.

Fixed and variable cost separation.   Control over operations cannot be effective unless the costs are broken down into their fixed and variable components. Two preliminary comments are desirable. First, as stated earlier, Products A, B, C, and D are essentially the same product. Products B, C, and D differ from A only in that certain "frills" are added or removed. Second, because the nature of the product lends itself to such treatment, management has developed certain cost modules.

Production consists of three processes. A cost module was developed for each of the three processes. For example, the cost module for Process 1 includes the wage and other operating expenses incurred to perform that process. The total cost of that module is adequately supported by a functional classification of the several costs underlying the total figure. For example, the functional classification shows (a) wages for the machine operator, (b) wages for helpers, (c) machine operating expenses, and (d) other. Also, data underlying these include regular, vacation and overtime pay, fringe benefits, Social Security, and unemployment compensation for people involved, and comparable data for the machinery and equipment used.

Table 20–2 shows the breakdown of unit costs into their fixed and variable components and by product.

TABLE 20–2
Unit Cost Modules: Fixed and Variable Costs By Product* (in dollars)

			Product			
Line	Line of costs	Source module†	A	B	C	D
1	Variable costs					
2	Process 1.	3	2.33	2.33	.97	.97
3	Process 2.	4	1.40	.64	1.40	.64
4	Supplies, etc.‡.	5, 6	.69	.69	.69	.69
5	Total variable cost		4.42	3.66	3.06	2.30
6	Fixed costs					
7	Process 3.	2	1.28	1.28	1.28	1.28
8	Salaries, other	1	.81	.81	.81	.81
9	Total fixed cost.		2.09	2.09	2.09	2.09
10	Total cost (lines 5 and 9).		6.51	5.75	5.15	4.39

* Remember: the cost modules are supported by data classified on a functional basis (see Table 20–1).

† This column refers to an internal record showing the breakdown of costs.

‡ These are truly variable costs which vary directly with the number of units produced, regardless of product.

The costs shown in Table 20–2 are unit costs derived in two ways. The variable costs are standard costs developed by observation and timing. The underlying data not shown here have reduced the costs of each process to costs per minute. The modules are so constructed that if a wage increase or any other cost change should develop, it is a very simple matter to have the change reflected in the unit cost module. The fixed costs were developed by module also, but were handled a bit differently. The salaries will not change if zero units are produced or if the plant is operated at capacity. Also, the salaries are of three types: president, plant supervisor, clerical. All three are fixed, but are spread over different levels of capacity. The president's salary was allocated on the basis of capacity expected to be attained in three years. The plant manager's salary was allocated on the basis of capacity in one year. Clerical and other salaries were allocated at the "start-up" level.

Process 3 costs were allocated on similar bases.

Having looked at the separation of costs between fixed and variable on a per-unit basis, let us look at the total costs at various rates of output. Our purpose here is to provide basic information on the cost-volume relationship.

Volume of output. The reader will recall from common sense and basic economics that within a plant of a given capacity costs will fall as the rate of output increases. In Table 20–3 we show the total costs

TABLE 20–3
Cost of Operations at Various Rates of Output

Line		A. 50 percent (23,058 units) $	%	B. 60 percent (27,670 units) $	%	C. 70 percent (32,281 units) $	%	D. 80 percent (36,892 units) $	%
1	Fixed costs								
2	Salaries.	60,700	27	60,700	25	60,700	23	60,700	21
3	Process 3.	58,800	27	58,800	24	58,800	23	58,800	21
4	Total.	119,500	54	119,500	49	119,500	46	119,500	42
5	Variable costs								
	$4.42 per unit. . . .	101,900	46	122,300	51	142,700	54	163,000	58
6	Total cost	221,400	100	241,800	100	262,200	100	282,500	100
7	Breakeven (line 6 ÷ no. of units).	9.60		8.74		8.12		7.66	
	Breakeven index. . . .	100		91		86		80	

of operation at various capacity use rates: 50, 60, 70, and 80 percent. The total costs have been broken down into their fixed and variable components.

To simplify matters for this discussion we have used the variable cost of producing Product A as shown on Table 20–2, line 5, to arrive at the total variable cost. Of course, this overstates cost materially because the variable cost of Product A is $4.42 per unit, compared with $3.66 for Product B, but it illustrates our concept. Had we used the variable cost of each of the products in proportion to their output, we would have accomplished only one thing. The table would have been more cluttered and complicated with no increase in its usefulness. As one would expect, variable cost becomes a larger percent of the total as the rate of output rises. Also, the break-even point per unit falls as the rate of output rises.

Income analysis. Now let us look at the relationship of cost-price-volume from the point of view of net income, as shown in Table 20–4. Again, we modify facts to simplify the presentation. To show the total revenue, we use a weighted average figure for price. As before, if we showed the detail on each of Products A, B, C, and D we would only clutter up the table. Costs are from Table 20–3. Revenue is the weighted average price of $8.95 multiplied by that number of units produced at each level of operations. Notice the effect on net income as the use rate of capacity rises. At the price of $8.95, the break-even point is reached when rate of output reaches nearly 60 percent of capacity. Of course, that is also apparent from Table 20–3, which shows break-even cost at 50 percent capacity use rate to be $9.60 and at 60 percent, $8.74. We have shown net income at each rate of output. Also, we have left lines to provide other deductions for control purposes. For example, this table is for operations of the firm as a whole. It can also be broken down by territory and/or by product. If a discount needs to be given to a particular customer—or all of them in one territory—that can be easily reflected in the control sheet (Table 20–4). (But watch

TABLE 20–4
Revenue and Cost of Operations at Various Rates of Output (capacity 46,116 units)

Line		A. 50 percent (23,058 units)	B. 60 percent (27,670 units)	C. 70 percent (32,281 units)	D. 80 percent (36,893 units)
1	Total revenue*.	$206,400	$247,600	$288,900	$330,200
2	Total cost	221,000	241,800	262,200	282,600
3	Net income	(15,000)	5,800	26,700	47,600
4	Less:	†	†	†	†
5	Other costs.	†	†	†	†
6	Other costs.	†	†	†	†
7	Revised net	†	†	†	†

* Total revenue is the weighted average price of $8.95 multiplied by the number of units produced at each level of operations.

† This table was set up to provide flexibility in analysis. Lines 4–7 will accommodate any costs incurred after the budget was set up. Or, they will show the effect of proposed expenditures which may be under consideration: price discounts, sales commissions, and so on.

the price discrimination laws.) Or, if more advertising becomes necessary to increase volume from 60 to 70 percent of capacity, that can also be reflected.

It may be a fruitful exercise to examine this from another direction. For example, how much money can be spent above that budgeted in order to increase sales from 27,670 units (60 percent capacity) to 32,281 units (70 percent capacity)? A clue can be developed by finding the difference between net income at both levels.

Revenue-cost-net income. The cost-volume-price relationship is shown in a different way in Table 20–5. We have not reproduced the dollar figures from the other tables; only index numbers are shown.

TABLE 20–5
Revenue, Cost, and Net Income at Various Rates of Output (60 percent = 100)

Percent capacity	Number of units	Revenue index	Cost index	Net income index	Break-even index
60	27,670	100.0	100.0	100.0	100.0
70	32,281	116.7	108.4	460.3	92.9
80	36,892	133.4	116.9	820.7	87.6

Starting at 60 percent capacity, just above the break-even point, each 10 percent increase in the capacity use rate brings about:

a. A 17% increase in revenue

b. An 8% increase in cost

c. A 360% increase in net income

For control purposes these same types of analyses may be made for product, territory, customer, salesperson, and so on. Now, having looked at various aspects of controlling costs by noting the cost-price-volume relationships, we turn to an examination of effort analysis to help judge performance.

Control of productivity and profitability

In many places in this book we have spoken rather caustically of what we referred to as the "volume syndrome." In no way do we fault the use of volume as *one* measure of productivity and profitability. However, when used by itself, it can be a misleading index of profitability although serving adequately as an index of sales productivity. We cited or alluded to a number of instances where increased sales were made by offering customers special services, the costs of which were borne by other departments. Also, we have called attention to the importance of relating cost, price, and volume to one another in order to develop a realistic understanding of the value to the firm of the volume of sales.

Earlier in this chapter we referred to summary reports to top management and more detailed reports to other levels of management. We will now illustrate the nature of two of those reports to top management: (1) the order report; and (2) the sales and profitability report. Also, we will comment on the same reports to other levels of management. Of course, the purpose of these reports is to inform; the reason for being informed is to exercise control. Finally, we will discuss the concept of the marketing audit. From the marketing point of view, there are four critical control areas: territory, salesperson, customer, and product. Both the order status report and the sales report should be based upon these four critical areas.

The order status report.   The order status report provides a preview of things to come at some point in the future. In that sense it can serve as a warning device to pinpoint potential troublesome areas or points of potential advantage. Of course, the warning lead time depends upon the time required to fill the orders, and this depends, to a considerable extent, upon the industry and its practices. For example, orders for such things as machine tools, power generating plants, freight cars, and the like typically take many weeks, months, or years to fill. Thus, a large—or small—backlog of orders can serve as a warning of things to come in the rather distant future. Materials purchases, production schedules, labor requirements, needs for capital, and so on can be planned for far in advance. Also, shifts in sales efforts, promotional programs, price structures, channels of distribution, and logistics matters—all elements of the marketing mix—can be planned for and made. But, these plans are subject to change. An order on the books to be filled in 18 months may be cancelled before work commences if environmental changes develop.

On the other hand, production schedules of some industries are made on the basis of a forecast of demand with delivery made from inventory and with very short lead times. For bicycles, home appliances, and the like, demand may change dramatically from one weekly, biweekly, or monthly reporting period to the other. Reaction time is much shorter. If orders are up substantially, one set of problems arises. Emergency orders must be placed for materials, overtime arranged for, new shifts trained, short-term capital acquired—or lead time lengthened. A different approach is called for if orders are down.

The basic information is readily available; so the question arises of how much to provide to what level of management. Before commenting on that, let us look at the type of information required. The reporting period may be daily, weekly, biweekly, or any other period. Of course, policy may require interim reports if something "outstanding" develops. For our purposes, we will assume a weekly reporting period. Thus, the order status report will show at least the orders received:

1. In the current week of this year, compared with quota.
2. In the same week of last year.
3. In the year to date of this year, compared with quota.
4. In the year to date of last year.

In addition, the report may show the same data for orders actually billed, compared with the quota. Third, it may show similar unfilled orders.

Notice that we have used the term orders received—a total figure. This *may* be all the data that top management wants to see, or needs to see—barring outstanding developments. On the other hand, the production manager needs to have information on status of orders by product in order to control production schedules. The marketing manager may need the information not only by product, but also by customer, territory, and salesperson. A regional sales manager may need the information only for that territory—or, on the other hand, for all territories to gain better insight into the relative productivity of the region. Even individual salespeople may need some of the information, especially on their own customers.

The sales analysis and profitability report. If the order status report is a preview of things to come, the profitability report is a historical record of events which have transpired. The former makes it possible to exercise some control over the future before events take place. The profitability report makes possible the analysis of the past to provide a base for correction of failures of the past or capitalization on its successes. We refer to this report as a sales and profitability report rather than just a sales report. One reason is that for it to be useful it should analyze not only the volume of sales, but their profitability as well. A second and related reason is that, if profitability is included there may be a tendency to get away from the volume syndrome. Once more we refer to the four critical control areas: territory, salesperson, customer, and product. In addition, we refer to the comments made above concerning what information to report to whom for control. Finally, we also refer to previous comments concerning the period to be covered by the report.

There are four basic elements to this report: profit, volume of sales, cost per unit, and net price per unit. This information should be provided on an aggregate basis and by product. For example, profit should be shown as a total figure and then by each of products A, B, C, and D. However, the single figures on profit, volume cost, and price do not provide a basis for control and comparison. The following information should be provided under each of profit, volume, cost, and price:

Comparable period, last year.
This period, budgeted (the quota).
This period, actual.
Actual to budgeted, percent.

The format of this profitability report may look like Table 20–6 with the subsidiary information under Profit also appearing under Volume, Cost, and Price.

This basic format showing performance of the company by product may be expanded, as we discussed, for the order status report. For example, the same format may be used for a report by territory, by salesman, and/or by customer.

This summary report will make it possible for the manager at any level to see the cause-and-effect relationships among cost, volume, and

TABLE 20–6
The Profitability Report

| | Total | Product | | | | Notes |
		A	B	C	D	
Profit						
Comparable period last year.						
This period, budgeted						
This period, actual						
Actual to budgeted, percent.						
Volume of sales						
Cost (per unit)						
Price (actual or average)						

price and their collective impact on profit. Because earlier tables (20–2 to 20–5) have information showing the effect of volume on costs at a given price, we see no point in putting a lot of numbers on the format of the profitability report. We can use the format-in-blank to point up specific things we have previously referred to. One of our earlier points was that the manager should be able to look at the profit figure on a summary report and trace reasons for it through volume, cost, and price. Let's do that, making two or three sets of assumptions.

First, let us assume that sales were projected to be up 16.7 percent from 27,670 units to 32,281 units as shown on Table 20–4. At the established price of $8.95, this would increase revenue (Line 1) from $247,600 to $288,900, also 16.7 percent. The normal effect on net income (Line 3) would be to raise it from $5,800 to $26,700, an increase of 360 percent. So we further assume that the profit objective was $26,700. The reason for this great increase in profit on such a moderate increase in sales is that the costs are lowered from $8.74 per unit to $8.12 per unit as 70 percent of plant capacity is used instead of 60 percent (Line 7).

Now, let us make a hypothetical case, but one which is realistic. Let us say that profits were lower than projected. Using the format shown, the manager could trace the decline in profits to either a decline in price or an increase in unit cost. The "notes" column of the format could refer the manager to an explanation which could also be recorded on Table 20–4 on lines 4, 5, or 6. The explanation may be that competition forced a reduced price. Or it may be that this marketing manager is the one we referred to earlier, who took unilateral action to increase the customer service level and increased logistics costs considerably. The point we wish to make is not simply that profits were down. The manager would know that. The point is that the report is so constructed that one can see at a glance why profits were down. The manager is able to relate cost, price, and volume to profits.

Also, what is probably an even more significant point is that, if the top management requires, this kind of report showing interrelationships, the supporting records are likely to be kept as suggested by the tables referred to.

Furthermore, we showed only the overall effect of these things. Supporting analyses by territory, customer, or salesman may disclose that *all* of the increased cost—and reduced profit—can be traced to a specific customer of a given salesperson, who may have been forced to make such concessions to that one customer that the company actually lost money on the sale while otherwise meeting profit goals with others in all other territories. This too would give the manager something to control.

The marketing audit. Marketing audits have received increasing attention in recent years because they have a strength not available in other tools. Since they have grown up with the systems approach, they are systems-oriented. By definition, marketing audits are comprehensive. Their function is similar to that of the accounting audit. Philip Kotler suggests that marketing audits may be characterized as:

1. Periodic, rather than used only during a crisis.
2. Concerned with evaluating the basic framework for marketing action, as well as the performance within the framework.
3. Interested in appraising all the elements of the marketing operation and not just the most problem-ridden ones.[3]

The system orientation of the marketing audit in which the company evaluates elements of both its strategic and managerial action is its most valued quality. The same reasons for adopting a system perspective toward marketing management are also applicable to the use of the marketing audits. The comprehensive strength of the marketing audit can only be maintained if during the auditing process:

1. Objectives are evaluated.
2. Environmental conditions and markets are defined.
3. Means selected to achieve those objectives are evaluated.
4. Control systems used to measure achievements are evaluated.

One of the evaluation tasks under (2) above would be to measure the effectiveness of the marketing manager's decision on the number of salespeople to employ. Another task in the area would be to evaluate the geographic deployment of these salespeople. The concept of a marketing audit requires that the auditor consider the market characteristics before proceeding. The auditor would quite naturally want to evaluate those sales force decisions not only against the financial condition of the firm but also against its markets' requirements.

Alfred Oxenfeldt defined the marketing audit as a systematic, critical,

---

[3] Philip Kotler, *Marketing Management*, 2d ed. (New York: Prentice-Hall, Inc., 1972), p. 774.

and unbiased review and appraisal of the basic objectives and policies of the marketing function and of the organization, methods, procedures, and personnel employed to implement the policies and achieve the objectives.[4] It is clear that the marketing manager cannot be the person to conduct this audit if it is struly going to be critical and unbiased, since the manager is going to be one of those judged, along with the staff.

Other aspects of control systems

So far we have examined the nature of control documents and their use by managers to know what is going on. The thrust of the discussion has been centered on the knowledge needed to keep the company on its course. In this connection we next discuss another concept of a control system and show applications of it. Then, we briefly discuss the notion of a marketing controller.

Contribution-margin. The typical accounting system makes provision for the allocaton of all fixed costs to each product or product class, territory, etc. For example, some portion of the home office expenses, including the president's salary, legal expenses, and depreciation on the presidential jet, will appear as a charge against Product N or be assigned to Territory A. This is in accord with generally accepted accounting principles. As a managerial tool, it accomplishes only one purpose that we can see: it obscures the manager's view of the real cost situation and reduces the probability of any decision being a good one.

Let us illustrate. Say that a given product has a basic direct cost of $40,000. It is allocated a portion of corporate overhead, factory overhead, and a share of common costs amounting to $10,000 for a total assigned cost of $50,000. The total revenue from sales amounts to $45,000. On this basis, the product is a loser and may be dropped from the product line.

What happens? The $40,000 in direct costs cease. The $10,000 allocation for overhead continues; so it is reallocated to the other products. A presumably money-losing product is dropped, along with the $5,000 it was contributing to overhead. Other products have to make that up; so, in reality the company may be worse off for having dropped the product than it was before. In other words, the overhead allocation obscured the fact that the product was contributing $5,000 to overhead. If the resources can be reallocated to other products which contribute more, the decision may have been a good one. On the other hand, if the plant was operating at, say, 70 percent capacity with unit costs of $8.12, the reduced production may cause unit costs to rise.

---

[4] Alfred R. Oxenfeldt, "The Marketing Audit As a Total Evaluation Program," in *Analyzing and Improving Marketing Performance* (New York: American Management Association, 1959), p. 26.

Let us look at this from a positive point of view. Table 20–3 shows the breakdown of fixed and variable costs. It shows that at 60 percent capacity unit costs are $8.74 for 27,670 units. Now, assume that some company or government invites bids on 4,611 units of our Product A which normally sell for $8.95. So far as the producer is concerned, this can be a one-time bid. If it sells the 4,611 units, this will raise production to the 70 percent level and reduce unit costs to $8.12 for 32,281 units.

What can the company do? When operations are at 60 percent of capacity, all overhead salaries are covered. Even all Process 3 costs are covered; so it is unnecessary for the 4,611 units to cover anything more than the variable costs of $4.42 per unit, plus some contribution to overhead. Thus the company could bid, say, $6.08 per unit on 4,611 units. If it got the job, the "profit" of $1.66 each would raise the net income by $7,654 from $5,800 (Table 20–4, column B, line 3).

This type of incremental pricing on a one-time basis can be very profitable. The same type of information can be helpful in making a longer-term decision, such as manufacturing one of the products as a private brand for a chain store. Many alternatives are available to the producer, including handling the situation as described for the one-time bid. We will illustrate only one possible action. Let us say that the chain wants 4,611 units per year, which will move the producer to a 70 percent use rate.

Note that in Table 20–3 unit costs at 70 percent of capacity are $8.12, again down from $8.95. The company may keep the $8.95 price for other sales. With unit costs of $8.12, this would make the profit per unit on each of the 27,670 units 83 cents instead of the former 21 cents ($8.95 — $8.74). This makes total profit on 27,670 units amount to $22,966 (27,670 units times 83 cents) instead of $5,811 (27,670 times 21 cents). In addition, the other 4,611 units may be priced at the exact break-even cost of $8.12 (column C, line 7), and still be very profitable to the producer. The new customer has shared the cost of overhead with other customers. As stated, there are many variations on this theme.

Now that we have looked at control systems, let us turn to look at a marketing controller.

The marketing controller. So far as we know, Dr. Sam R. Goodman, vice president for finance of the Nestlé Company, is the father of the concept of the marketing controller.[5] Goodman visualizes the function of the marketing controller as administering the broad corporate financial/marketing planning function and being in charge of preparation of relevant analyses involving marketing and finance, especially those

---

[5] Sam R. Goodman, *Techniques of Profitability Analysis* (New York: Wiley-Interscience, 1970). See especially pages 18–20 for an outline of duties. In a later book, *The Marketing Controller* (New York: Advanced Management Research, Inc., 1972), Dr. Goodman enlarges upon the concept.

pertaining to plans and budgets. The controller's specific activities in these areas would involve all those activities associated with planning and analysis, reports on operations and performance, and cost estimates and evaluations. Goodman visualizes the marketing controller as being under the direction of and accountable to the controller. In this capacity the marketing controller would prescribe the content and frequency of preparation of budget and performance information. He would also provide the controller with marketing related data.

The relationship with marketing, as suggested by Goodman, is far from a casual one. In fact, Goodman suggests periodic meetings with the vice president for marketing and other marketing people to identify needs and develop information for meeting those needs of the marketing and other departments. Also, the marketing controller would be in constant contact with the vice president for administration regarding corporate objectives for planning and for planning the operation of the marketing department. In addition, the marketing controller would be in contact with other members of top management, including manufacturing, and purchasing vice presidents, the treasurer, and the auditor—among others.

In short, the marketing controller would be the financial liaison man between marketing and all other segments of the firm. He would see to it that control systems such as those discussed in this chapter—and others—were developed.

CONCLUSION

Effective control rests upon at least two foundation stones. First, corporate objectives, plans, and policies serve to determine what is to be controlled and for what purpose. Second, the availability of information in usable form provides the ability to control. In addition, so far as the marketing manager is concerned, control has two broad dimensions. First, the control of planning, which is a function of the manager's role as a member of the organization, is one dimension. The second dimension is the control of operations, which is a function of the manager's role as the one responsible for the marketing function. We have previously characterized these dimensions as (1) the strategic, where the emphasis of the marketing manager is on management *and* the marketing function; and (2) the managerial or operation control, where the focus of the marketing manager is on management *of* the marketing function.

As stated at the outset, even though this book has stressed both, this chapter has been confined almost exclusively to control of operations. Space limitations prevented us from being complete even there; so we could not find space to even consider control of planning.

chapter 21 | # The components of marketing management: Linkage and change

Central features of marketing management
    Management defined
    Approach to marketing management
    Concern of marketing management
Functional integration of the marketing-oriented firm
    As things often are: Problems
    As things should be: A starting point
    Integration through objectives
Planning and the planning effort
    Establishing responsibility
    Dimensions of planning
    Planning philosophies
    Approaches to planning
    Types of planning
Developing planning premises
    Information
    Opportunities
    Environments
    Consumer behavior
    Premises
Developing strategies and policies:
    the discovery process
    Product
    Channels of distribution
    Logistics
    Promotion
    Pricing
Developing managerial and operational control:
    Problem solving and decision making
    Strategic-managerial gray areas
    Prior arrangements for integration
    Concepts of decision points
    Decision orientation
Controlling the planning effort

CENTRAL FEATURES OF MARKETING MANAGEMENT

As a first step in working toward accomplishing the objective of this chapter—giving perspective to the several components of the marketing manager's job—we will recall several notions which are central to both the practice and study of marketing management, and therefore central to this book.

Management defined

The first thing of importance is to understand the meaning of management. We develop our own definition to reflect what managers do or should do and to serve as a part of the framework of our book. Our motive is simple: the usual listings of the elements of the management job do not constitute an adequate framework for our approach. We have no quarrel with the elements as such: establishing a mission, setting objectives, planning, organizing, staffing, directing, and controlling. By implication, they are included in our definition, but alone they are unsuitable for our purposes because of vast conceptual differences in the managerial approach to the several elements. For example, there is hardly any similarity at all in the decisions relating to whether a new product line should be introduced and the decisions involved in marketing the new product line.

The reasons the decisions are made differ: in the one case they are strategic decisions made to attain some corporate objective; in the other they are implementation decisions. In making the strategic decisions, Level 1 managers determined why the product line should be introduced and gave broad guidelines as to how it should be done as well as how all affected divisions should integrate their efforts. At the second level, the decisions are how to do it efficiently within the broad guidelines. The analyses underlying the decisions differ: in the one case the availability of resources and the responsiveness of the environment were considered; in the other the best ways of doing the job are again considered. The same process permeates the entire range of marketing decisions—all of which involve planning, organizing, staffing, directing, and controlling. Yet many of the same people are or should be involved in both sets of decisions.

Our definition of management reflects the twofold division of management activities: (1) managers first make a strategic decision to do something, and (2) they then make implementation decisions to do it well. *Effectiveness* in attaining objectives is the purpose of strategy, and *efficiency* in doing so is the goal in implementation. Our definition: management is the analysis and rationalization of all environments for the dual purposes of establishing aims, plans, and policies at all levels and for the effective, efficient, and systematic use of resources. Of course, doing the job well implies a control system.

Approach to marketing management

The second notion central to the study and practice of marketing has to do with the approach to marketing management: marketing managers have two sets of responsibilities. One of them is to the effectiveness of the organization; the other is to the department they manage. Accordingly we emphasize the firm and focus on marketing. Two concepts make this a necessary approach. First, to improve effectiveness, the several parts of the firm must operate as a system. This cannot be done unless the effects of marketing decisions on other segments of the firm are considered, and vice versa. Second, a firm imbued with the marketing philosophy must have all of its parts so imbued. The marketing concept is mostly applied to the thought of satisfying the consumer at a profit. We think the concept should have another dimension, an internal dimension. The needs and wants of the employees, owners, and creditors also deserve attention. In short, the firm should market itself to its people as well as market its products to its customers. Then the marketing philosophy can be the philosophy of the firm, making the application of the systems approach more feasible.

We emphasize the firm as one with a marketing philosophy which has certain ends—objectives. We focus on marketing as a means to those ends.

Concern of marketing management

The third notion central to the study and practice of marketing and to our book is our concern for a distinction between management *and* the marketing function and management *of* the marketing function. The philosophy underlying this concern both flows from and helps create our definition of management. In addition, our emphasis on the firm and our focus on marketing is both the product and the parent of this third notion. Thus the three are inextricably linked.

These three notions together determine the two-pronged thrust of the branches of the managerial function of the marketing manager. One prong is concerned with strategic matters affecting the firm. The role of the marketing manager is to function as a manager of the firm in helping develop objectives and devise corporate plans to reach them. Through the planning process the marketing manager and managers of other segments of the firm coordinate the several segments by defining guidelines designed to improve the firm's effectiveness. Through this process the several parts of the firm are brought into a semblance of a system. This implies trade-offs, or suboptimization of parts, in order to assure the effectiveness of the firm. In this Level 1 executive role, the marketing manager represents the marketing function at the corporate level. Thus:

1. We emphasize analyses for the development of objectives and the making of strategic plans.
2. We emphasize the firm.
3. We emphasize management *and* the marketing function.

The other prong is concerned with the marketing function itself and the efficient management of that function within the appropriate guidelines. Thus:

1. We emphasize analyses of a different sort for the rationalization process designed to create efficiency in the use of resources.
2. We focus on the marketing function itself.
3. We concentrate on management *of* the marketing function.

Now we turn to the integration and application of these concepts into the management of the firm and management of the marketing function.

FUNCTIONAL INTEGRATION OF THE MARKETING-ORIENTED FIRM

As things often are: Problems

The three notions just discussed sound good. In fact they have sounded good for generations. As words and as concepts they are completely consonant with those activities of management that have been talked about all these decades: planning, organizing, staffing, directing, and controlling. However, as they have been typically applied, the unifying aspects of planning and the coordinating aspects of directing have been virtually lost in the typical business firm.

There are several results of these losses. First, in many firms planning has been mostly confused with budgeting for next year and five years hence. Second, in a vacuum a marketing area manager has established objectives which are in reality corporate objectives. Third, also in a vacuum the manager has made decisions as marketing decisions which are in reality strategic decisions affecting the organization as a whole. Fourth, coordination is typically a passive thing which just happens through some more or less self-adjusting and self-compensating mechanism within the organization: someone else picks up the pieces; one department reacts to actions taken by another. Or coordination takes place at the time of implementation rather than at the time of conception of a decision.

Let us illustrate by drawing from an objective frequently used in other chapters. Also, since the focus of this book is on marketing, we use that functional area. We start with an assumed objective of the organization to increase profits by 60 percent in five years, a compounded growth rate of about 10 percent per year.

The marketing manager sets an objective of an increase in sales via the customer service route—an objective of serving 96 percent of the customers in one day after receipt of the order instead of the present 90 percent. On its face, this is a laudable thing. But what happens? (The numbers are from tables in Chapter 15.) First, the total cost of serving present customers goes up 12 percent with this service improvement of 7 percent. Second, the amount of money invested in inventory rises 26 percent. Third, the amount of working capital required rises 8 percent. (Inventory investment averages 30 percent of working capital. The illustration in Chapter 15 assumed $9.1 million inventory and $30.3 million working capital to support $50,000,000 sales.)

So this "marketing" objective requires nearly $2.5 million in additional working capital to support improved service to present customers. What will it require to support 5 to 10 percent more sales per year? For simplicity, not necessarily reality, assume that inventory support is a constant percentage of sales. The $11.4 million to support $50 million in sales is about 23 percent of sales. To serve an additional five million in sales, the additional working capital required would be $1.2 million. The increase in delivery time required $2.5 million investment for present customers or a total of $3.7 million to increase sales about 5 percent.

We do not quarrel with the extra investment or with the decision. We merely point out that this "marketing" decision is a corporate decision and should be treated as such. Unfortunately in many firms this is a typical occurrence profusely illustrated in current literature. Marketing people establish such objectives and just let the "coordination" happen, as a number of real-life illustrations show. Note that our hypothetical illustration called for a $2.5 million investment initially and that it was just a marketing decision. Contrast this with the desire of some other branch of the firm to spend $2.5 million for machinery, plants, advertising, and so on.

What about functional decisions which are strategic decisions affecting the firm as a whole or some part of it? Again, we draw on only one type of decision typical of those reported in the literature. One of the reasons for volume discounts is to reflect lower costs to the seller. Yet, "marketing" decisions are often made allowing an order of sufficient volume to qualify for a discount to be delivered in two or more segments, thus negating savings and even creating a loss. Or volume levels will be set without regard to the quantities required for transportation rate reductions. Again, the coordination is residual; it is a passive thing.

But these issues do not plague all companies. In other chapters we showed how some companies have designed their managerial structures to avoid such pitfalls. We cited some by name and kept the identity of others hidden.

We will now take a brief look at the basic ingredients of a managerial program designed to overcome the deficiencies discussed, and which incorporate those things we labeled Central. Features of Marketing Management.

As things should be: A starting point

The starting point in bringing about a functionally integrated marketing oriented firm is with the *concept* of what the organization is supposed to do. In Chapter 3 we looked behind the profit motive and said that business is an organization of human and other resources managed to bring satisfaction to its owners and/or managers. We made this rather unorthodox definition because many things managers do cannot be explained in the usual narrow views of business. Furthermore, there is no other one motive that we can think of which explains a wide variety of actions and personal motives.

We are not attempting to avoid an issue by bundling all motives into one and calling it satisfaction, but only to make discussions simpler. In this context, we recognized that the only way the firm as a vehicle for satisfaction can survive and provide the desired managerial satisfactions is to create, retain, and satisfy the consumer for whatever period and to whatever extent is consistent with the satisfaction requirements of the owners-managers. In this sense, marketing is the function of business.

Another facet of the concept of the organization pertains to an understanding of what management is, what it does, what its functions and challenges are. In this chapter we have gone through our definitions and commented on the two roles of management *and* the organization and management *of* the marketing function. It is almost vital to the setting of objectives, to planning, and to management that this distinction be recognized in the concept of the organization.

Conceptually, the organization should be so structured that functional area managers function at two levels. At Level 1 they are objective setters, planners, and policy makers who provide coordination (or integration) at the point of beginning. As Charles St. Thomas said,

> Too often we attempt to achieve integration of work at the time of implementation, and it is seldom successful. Integration must begin at the

planning stage, when we are determining what work is to be accomplished. . . .[1]

Disagreeing only mildly, we think that objective setting generally precedes planning, and it is at this point that integration process begins. Elmore Petersen, E. G. Plowman, and Joseph M. Trickett hold a similar view:

> One of the greatest management opportunities is to help define and constantly reinforce this feeling of purpose or mission within the organization. This not only precedes planning but is over and above the other aspects of management work.[2]

Not only should the organizational concept be based upon participation of department executives in the objective setting and planning processes, but also the staffing policies should be so based. One of the qualifications of a marketing or other manager should be his ability to perform the function as a planner at Level 1 as well as the ability to manage the functional area at Level 2. Unfortunately, the functional ability is too often the only factor considered.

Integration through objectives

To further our emphasis on the importance of integration of the several departments of the firm, we discuss a network of hierarchies in Chapter 3. The hierarchies of aims and objectives, among others, are the ones immediately relevant. We have already commented in this chapter about the hierarchy of satisfactions beginning with those of the chief executive and including other managers, employees, customers, and owners.

The mission of the organization is at the top of the hierarchy of aims. The mission statement gives the basic direction that the firm is destined to work toward. It is, in effect, an expression of what it will take to meet the satisfaction criteria the managers and owners have in mind. In this sense, it describes an overall framework within which specific objectives will be identified. Underlying the mission and objectives is a set of beliefs or a creed which reflects management's attitudes.

Objectives are next in the hierarchical scheme of things, and they have a hierarchical arrangement of their own. We related the hierarchy of objectives to the Level 1 and Level 2 activities of managers. Objectives of the firm not only provide direction, but provide a basis for integrating

---

[1] Charles E. St. Thomas, *Practical Business Planning* (New York: The American Management Association, 1965), p. 23.

[2] Elmore Petersen, E. Grosvenor Plowman, and Joseph M. Trickett, *Business Organization and Management*, 5th ed. (Homewood, Illinois: Richard D. Irwin, Inc. 1962), p. 7.

the several departments into a system. Objectives of the department—functional objectives—are set at the functional level within the framework identified by the objectives of the firm. And the process continues down the managerial hierarchy.

Thus, our discussion of objectives emphasized the firm and the function of integration of managerial effort. In this context we indicated that effectiveness of management can be measured against the degree to which objectives are attained. Also, our discussion focused on marketing objectives and the efficiency with which they are attained.

It is not critical to the analysis to determine the original source of the objectives but we are vitally concerned when an executive sets objectives without the others knowing about them and their consequences. This is the result of at least two kinds of bad management. The first is in failure to integrate at the source. The second is the result of a system of rewards so managed as to motivate one manager to profit at the expense of another and at the expense of the firm. We have at best a group of federated departments operating under the lax direction of "central management," and at worst a group of feudal baronies each striving for advantage. The smooth functioning of a system and its synergistic effects are absent.

Seeing that appropriate executives participate in setting objectives is at least one step in assuring that all departments will work for the same firm. In addition, the objectives will almost certainly be better thought out and more oriented to the profit of the firm if cause and effect analyses are made by the executives involved in the process. Thus the proper place to begin the integration of the marketing area into the firm is (1) in the concept of the organization and in the nature of the duties of the department executives as both planners and doers and (2) in the objective-setting process.

PLANNING AND THE PLANNING EFFORT

In a very real sense, developing the proper organizational concept can be the first step in planning for planning. However, the proper conceptual view of the role of executives in planning is a significant prerequisite to the planning process.

Establishing responsibility

The hierarchy we referred to as Level 1 is the planning hierarchy. It includes the chief executive of the firm, the company planning staff (if there is one), and the functional managers.

The chief executive is the key to the planning process by virtue of the power of the office as well as by personal participation. It is through his probing, questioning, and initiative that objectives related to satisfactions are identified and marketing orientation is assured. He is far from being a passive member of the effort. In addition to originating and participating in considering objectives, he also acts as an executive by approving functional plans as they fit the corporate plan, helping resolve built-in conflicts such as good service at low cost, and appraising results.

The company planning staff does the "homework" for the Level 1 group. Also it may be the operating vehicle which carries the project through under the direction of the Level 1 group. And it may originate objectives. The functional managers help prepare the company plan as well as their functional area plans. They appraise the results of the functional area plans as well as any subfunctional plans. Not included in the above are the board of directors at the top and the subfunctional managers at the bottom. The former reviews and approves the plan and appraises results. The latter participate in developing the functional plan. As called for, they provide analyses as bases for consideration of the company plan. Depending upon need, they prepare subfunctional plans.

Dimensions of planning

In Chapter 4 we introduced several dimensions of planning. We labeled one of them *crisis creation* based upon three assumptions: (1) change is the only managerial constant we know; (2) one of the prime activities of management is the management of change; (3) change causes crises. Since change of whatever magnitude causes a crisis of some magnitude, plans should be made for these crises. By using the term *crisis creation,* we sought to impart the notion of an activist role in bringing about change as distinct from a passive role of reacting to it. When a change is created, a crisis is created.

The philosophy of the offensive players of a football team is to create crises so that the game is played on their terms so far as possible. So it is with planning for crisis creation: the firm develops plans to "play the business game" on its terms. This is planning to make happen those things you want to have happen.

A second dimension of planning, *crisis prevention,* was also introduced. Sometimes a look into the future suggests that certain events may come to pass. About the most the organization can do is to actively take a defensive position to minimize the effect of the coming crisis. Simply stated, this process involves taking a look at the future, making estimates of how the firm will be affected, and developing plans to accommodate what may happen. The philosophy of the defensive players in a football game is to prevent crises they can't avert. They have planned for various contingencies. Many firms have awaited the arrival of events and then set out to accommodate the firm to them. Any football fan can guess what would happen if 11 players went out on the field with no plans at all to stop an offensive by the other team. Yet this is exactly what many firms have done. Professor John F. Mee has put it this way,

> Past practices have allowed events to happen that resulted in having to react to unfolding environmental conditions, thereby always allowing the past and the present conditions to shape their future.[3]

Planning philosophies

A part of planning the planning effort is developing a philosophy of planning. The dimensions of planning will certainly influence the philosophy adopted. We isolated three broad philosophies. First, *satisficing planning* is based upon the notion of doing as well as possible without making too many waves. On the other hand *optimizing planning* involves just that: optimizing or doing as well as is possible. Third, *adaptivizing planning* is an approach which is designed to place the firm in a better position to cope with the future.

Approaches to planning

In Chapter 4 we identified two basic approaches to planning. The *outside-in* approach implies that the external environment is analyzed first to determine problems, resistances, and opportunities. Its other side is the *inside-out* approach in which resources of the firm are examined for strengths and weaknesses before looking to the external environment. We did not try to choose between them. Our conclusion was that good managers would do both. Our point was that if you look externally first, and internally second, you might miss a great opportunity to fit an internal resource to an undisclosed opportunity. For example, an external analysis might not disclose a potential market for squared circles; so we would let our expert on that phenomenon go on designing triangles when the deputy assistant is as good a triangle maker as his chief. If we looked internally and found this great resource, we might be able to corner the market for squared circles!

Types of planning

These were discussed in another context in the opening pages of this chapter. Accordingly, we shall only mention three points. First,

---

[3] John F. Mee, "Causative Thinking," in William G. Ryan, ed., *Manager's Handbook* (Bloomington: Graduate School of Business, Indiana University. 1970), p. 89.

in Chapter 9 the several aspects and implications of strategic planning, management control, and operational control were discussed. Second, the marketing manager should be involved in strategic planning for the firm as a part of the integrative process, and be the leader involved in strategic planning for the functional area of marketing. Third, in his Level 2 capacity his planning for managerial control and operational control are efficiency oriented while his strategic planning is effectiveness oriented.

DEVELOPING PLANNING PREMISES

In our definition of management we said that one of the things managers do is to decide to do something. Before a decision can be made as to what to do, analyses must be made of such things as what needs to be done and what the firm is capable of doing or becoming capable of doing. Analyses of all sorts of things are necessary for the decision to do something. The organization of our book reflects this aspect of the managerial activities. Part II "Analysis for Marketing Strategy and Management," is, as its title implies, concerned with analysis. The analyses serve two purposes: (1) the development of information about the possible future upon which planning premises can be based; and (2) to provide bases for developing strategies and programs.

Four of the chapters were written with planning premises as one of the factors in mind: Chapter 5 on information, Chapter 6 on opportunities, Chapter 7 on environments, and Chapter 8 on consumer behavior. In addition aspects of the internal environment were discussed in many of the chapters. While these subjects were not discussed precisely in terms of their use as bases for planning premises, by inference as well as by design that was one of their purposes.

Information

Information is discussed in Chapter 5 in such a way as to serve the needs of the marketing manager when acting as a Level 1 executive and setting objectives, developing premises concerning the future, and making plans. To this end we explore such subjects as what information is, some issues in the design of information systems, and the firm as an information system. Also, information is discussed in the context of the needs of the marketing manager in managing the marketing function as a Level 2 executive. Because of the importance to the management decision process, the subject is explored as an essential ingredient in risk and uncertainty, problem solving, the discovery of problems and opportunities, evaluation of decisions, and the like. Furthermore, attention is directed specifically to marketing decisions as well as those concerned with the marketing organization and consumers. Finally, market research as an important aspect of marketing management is discussed.

Opportunities

Chapter 6 on opportunities does not have much to do with planning premises. It is more a reflection of a premise: the firm will seek to discover opportunities consonant with its mission, appraise them, and exploit desirable ones. The major concern of the chapter is with their discovery and with certain managerial problems in handling them.

Environments

Chapter 7 on the external environment, and the many discussions on the internal environment, have the same two motives underlying them: to improve the marketing manager's ability to look to the future as a basis for the planning premises as well as the planning process and objective setting; and to improve the marketing manager's understanding and management of the marketing function.

To these ends we discuss the social, economic, and political aspects of the external environment and the influence of science and technology as they affect the work of the marketing manager. The several discussions of the internal environment deal with the actual and potential strengths and weaknesses of the resource structure of the firm. Also they deal with the interrelationship of the several departments and their integration to make the firm a system.

Consumer behavior

Understanding the consumer is vital to effective marketing management. In no way do we underrate the significance of consumer behavior in establishing planning premises. For that reason we center a good bit of attention on those forces which partially explain why consumers behave as they do. While this subject is a significant one for planning premises, it may be even more significant in planning strategy for the company. Probably its greatest value to the marketing manager is its usefulness to him in managing the marketing function: finding out the whys of consumer wanting, needing, buying, being satisfied or dissatisfied, and how to communicate with consumers.

Premises

In Chapter 9 we discussed the nature of planning premises. Also, earlier in this chapter we suggested that companies should (1) plan to make happen those things they want to have happen (crisis creation) and (2) plan to accommodate those things that appear likely or destined to happen (crisis prevention).

A planning premise is a statement or assertion that serves as the basis for planning: "Government expenditures for housing will rise at the rate of 10 percent per year for the next seven years." Premises should be developed for every significant force which can have a significant effect on the firm. What this means is that a series of analyses should be made of such diverse subjects as possible government, diplomatic, economic, military, and social policies; state of the economy; state of the competitors and consumers in markets the firm is interested in; potential technological developments; resource structure of the firm; potential changes in labor relations; and so on.

We pause here in relating our discussion in the book to the planning process to survey the points on the route we have taken. The following is a list of the steps in the planning process:

The preliminaries:

1. Establish the concept of the organization
2. Determine the mission of the organization.
3. Set objectives of the organization for the appropriate managerial levels.
4. Plan the planning effort.

The process:

5. Develop planning premises.
6. Develop plans, strategies, and policies to attain the objectives.
7. Develop implementation plans at the functional level.
8. Develop systems for evaluation, integration, and control.
9. Design a system for review and modernization of purpose, mission, objectives, plans, and policies.

So far in this chapter we have gone through point 4 above. We are now at the point where we start to deal with the actual elements of the marketing mix as the action elements of the marketing program. The product itself, the channels of distribution, the logistics function, the promotional program, and the price structure all require managerial consideration from two points of view. In the first place, they are the means to the desired ends or objectives of the organization. Accordingly, they play a strategic role in the organization; so we examine each from a strategic point of view with emphasis on the firm and the effective attainment of corporate objectives.

Second, these elements must be managed; so we approach each of them from a managerial point of view. Our focus here is on the decision-making role of the marketing manager in managing the marketing function.

DEVELOPING STRATEGIES AND POLICIES: THE DISCOVERY PROCESS

One of the major functions of the planning process is to give direction to the firm as it makes its way into its desired future. A second major function is to use the analyses necessary for planning as a basis for discovery of opportunities and problems which otherwise would have remained hidden. This discovery function is also properly one to be considered in setting objectives as well as in managing the marketing function.

The marketing manager and staff are the proper ones to translate the elements of the marketing mix into vehicles to attain a substantial portion of corporate objectives. There is a logical order in which these elements should be considered in the development of corporate strategy. As pointed out in Chapter 2, the marketing manager and his staff will have already worked out a program which integrates these elements of the mix. If they have done their work well, they will present more than one alternative for the Level 1 group to consider. There is a logical order in which these elements should be considered, first by the marketing staff and then by the Level 1 executives.

There are many ways in which decisions concerning the elements of the marketing mix influence the firm as a whole. Also, each of the elements can be used strategically to accomplish approximately the same objectives. The format adopted for this portion of the discussion is to identify several roles performed by the marketing mix in setting objectives and integrating functions, and apply a different role to each of the elements. For example, one reason for having Level 1 executives deal with those situations which affect the firm as a whole is to resolve conflicts and integrate programs before they are begun. They perform this function for each of the elements. However, we discuss the resolution of conflicts and related matters only in our comments on the product strategy.

A second reason for Level 1 executives to deal with these matters is to help determine direction of the firm. Again, even though this motive is a part of each of the elements, we discuss it only in the context of channels of distribution. A third reason is to assure that customer service is given consideration in light of cost management. This is treated extensively in the discussion of logistics.

Fourth, communication linkages within the firm and between the firm and its market are summarized only in our section on promotion. Finally, pricing strategy is important in determining the amount of revenue and the extent to which costs are covered. In this sense price is a device to meet certain objectives including communicating to the buyer the value the seller thinks the product has. These notions are discussed in Chapter 18. We match a particular role with a particular element of the marketing mix to avoid redundancy in our discussion. It is obvious that these and other reasons explain the importance of the Level 1 executives dealing with strategic matters of the types illustrated.

Product

First, the product or service is designed to meet the requirements of the market identified by prior analyses as the one most suitable for a given effort. A number of conflicts among various departments are immediately apparent. Each involved executive has a particular point of view. The production manager suggests a basic alteration in the design of the product or the composition of its components in order to simplify production processes. The logistics manager suggests a change in size to accommodate transportation and storage requirements. The financial manager suggests using less costly components.

These and other conflicts should be resolved at the top level. Sometimes changes required to resolve conflicts may be fundamental; or they may be of little consequence. We know of a producer of reproductions of paintings who had to live with a bad situation because transportation requirements were not considered in the design of the picture frame. The type of carrier best suited to the producer's needs had maximum size requirements of 100 inches. When measured top, sides, and bottom along the length and across its width, the package came to 104 inches.

By default, the manufacturer was legally excluded from using the best carrier. We do not make the point that the design should have been altered. Had this transport factor been considered at the time the product was designed the decision *might* have been exactly the same—104 inches. But it would have been a decision made consciously with the effects known in advance. Artistic factors involving proportions might have won out over purely transportation factors. Incidentally, the size of the picture and the frame did not materially affect production costs. We were told that artistic considerations had no bearing either. Accordingly, the accident of a fraction of an inch in length, width, and thickness made it legally necessary to use an inferior service.

Channels of distribution

There are several aspects of the channels of distribution which impinge upon the firm as a whole. The product decision itself may to a considerable extent determine the channel of distribution. For example if the product is one which needs servicing and the manufacturer does not have proper facilities, a given channel is indicated. Middlemen who can provide the service will be required. In this case, the selection of middlemen is not a strategic matter for the firm; it is a marketing decision, other things remaining the same.

However, as we repeatedly emphasize, the discovery process involves challenging those "other things" in an attempt to discover more effective or more efficient alternatives. One such alternative is to establish company-owned service facilities. Consideration of such an alternative is clearly a strategic matter requiring the attention of Level 1 executives. A second strategic aspect of channels involves the vertical integration of the firm and its channels. A decision on whether the firm should own its own wholesale, transportation, storage, retail, and service facilities affects the entire structure of the organization. Not only are financial and personnel matters significant elements of the decision, but also the legal aspects may be controlling. This type of strategic decision influences the direction the firm is to take, among other things.

A third strategic aspect of channel decisions relates to the degree of control or extent of influence that is to be exercised over other channel members. Or conversely: the degree of control or influence the firm will allow other channel members to exercise over it. More than a decade ago one company decided to break relations with a giant retail organization which bought 25 percent of the company's output. Today, many firms are finding that they can more efficiently serve their customers by assuming "command" of the channel. A retailer may do this by adjusting its own inventory policy and hence its policy regarding the frequency and size of orders it places. A manufacturer may do the same thing at the other end of the channel by policies it establishes regarding the size of order it places or sends. The wholesaler may use both techniques. All may assume control over the transportation system by their decisions to provide their own services.

Logistics

One of the measures of customer satisfaction is the time required to provide customer service. Also, as we show in our logistics chapters, logistics costs are a significant portion of total cost. Accordingly, the customer service and cost management functions of logistics influence the development of corporate strategy. These two functions give some meaning to the otherwise abstract concept of "good service at low cost" by showing what different levels of customer service will cost. With such information, the Level 1 executives can establish customer service objectives. In addition to customer service, logistics performs a function complementary to other departments of the firm. By relating inventory costs to the economics of the production run, production strategies may result in greater effectiveness, efficiency, or both.

Pricing and purchasing strategies can be more effective if they are related to transportation capabilities and economics. There is little to be gained if the purchasing department buys in 50,000-pound units to qualify for a discount when the savings are consumed by having to pay less than truckload or less than carload rates on 5,000 pounds because the truck or car will hold only 45,000 pounds. Of if warehousing and/or inventory costs eat up the savings. On the other hand, greater savings may result by purchasing in even larger quantities to qualify for lower transport rates.

Furthermore, by a judicious arrangement of the several transportation and warehousing variables, including rate negotiation, the firm may be able to enter or stay in markets otherwise closed to it. The logistics function is a significant variable in the development of overall strategy of the firm. It is the segment of the firm which places the goods in the hands of the reseller from whom the ultimate customer purchases.

Promotion

While logistics provides the customer with the goods, it is through the promotional effort that the demand has been created. For most consumer goods and many industrial goods, the promotional efforts of the firm are an indirect means of communicating with the ultimate customer for pursuasion purposes and to provide information. As we have seen in Chapter 16, communication is at the heart of promotion strategy.

In many companies, the promotion variable has been a significant, and perhaps even controlling, variable in developing the organization strategy and structure of the firm. In this sense, it is often difficult to know whether the structure is designed along product lines or along promotional lines. In order to communicate with customers better, some firms create separate organizations to deal with institutions and retailers or other large buyers—that is, separate organizations for different types of users of the same product.

Likewise, problems of a firm in communicating with different customers concerning different *products* may influence organization strategy. One company manufacturing different brands of the same type of product—for example, soap—may have separate organizations for promoting each. In addition, a company may have different organizations to market products of different types; aluminum products to the building industry; aluminum products to the fabrication industry.

In certain specialized cases, the strategic importance of promotion is overwhelmingly clear. In the cosmetics industry, for example, a huge proportion of revenue is spent on advertising alone. One company spent about $20,000,000 on advertising in 1972. Total sales for 1972 were about $83,000,000.[4] It must be a strategic matter when 24 percent of revenue is spent on advertising! The same company planned to spend about one fourth of that budget on introducing one new product in 1973.[5]

Pricing

The final element of the marketing mix and its strategic role is discussed in Chapter 18. Price is the strategic factor which determines the amount of revenue and the extent to which costs are covered. Of course we recognize in this statement that revenue is a function of sales, and costs are a function of efficiency.

The strategic role of price, and thus the interest of Level 1 executives, is established when we recognize that price is a variable used to attain certain objectives such as using resources more fully, establishing an image for the product or company, enlarging, protecting, or segmenting a market, or attaining profit objectives.

One of the now classic stories of price strategy is that of the first maker of ball point pens. The strategy of the firm, as the story goes, was to make a killing more than to stay in business over the long run. The pen was initially priced at $15.00. In a matter of months competitors' pens were selling at about $1.00. The maker cut prices and in a few years went out of business with a good-sized fortune to show for his efforts. In this case it is probably accurate to say that the objective of quick riches determined price strategy.

Sometimes manufacturers have difficulty getting resellers to handle their products. As a result, to accomplish their objective of entering a market they may have to give high discounts to resellers resulting in higher prices to consumers.

In one case price strategy created other aspects of strategy. A nationally known radio maker once saw a gap in the price range of table radios, so it decided to price a radio at a given level in that range. The engineering department then set out to make a radio to be sold at that price. This is a horror story because in trying to manufacture at that level, they redesigned an expensive component to make it cheaper, put the radio together, marketed it, and then had to withdraw it because the cheap component failed too often.

Our definition of management reflects the two broad activities managers engage in: analysis underlying and leading to a decision to do something; rationalization, the process of managing resources efficiently

---

[4] "Noxell Goes to Her Head," *Investor's Reader*, January 3, 1973, inside cover.
[5] Ibid.

in doing the "something" decided on. The participation of the marketing manager in the process of developing strategies and policies for the firm—analysis—is one aspect of what we have referred to as management *and* the marketing function. Emphasis in this part of the planning process is on the firm as a whole, and on the discovery of opportunities and problems to be found in the future. The plans and policies are directed toward reaching the objectives. The Level 1 executives are primarily concerned in this phase with the effectiveness of their plans in reaching the objectives.

After completing this phase of the planning process involving the decision to "do something," the marketing manager then "does it." The manager's concern shifts to the management *of* the marketing function, the rationalization process.

DEVELOPING MANAGERIAL AND OPERATIONAL CONTROL: PROBLEM SOLVING AND DECISION MAKING

Efficiency is the objective of the marketing manager in managing the marketing function. Effectiveness has presumably been built into his program in the earlier phase of his work. His first task is to develop plans and devise programs involving the several elements of the marketing mix to make the corporate plans operative.

We did not devise an all-purpose outline as a guide to writing each of the chapters (11, 13, 15, 17, and 19) on management of the elements of the marketing mix. However, we did have in mind several basic points which served as guidelines and which constituted a broad framework for all of these chapters.

Strategic-managerial gray areas

First, the distinction is not always clear between the process of strategic planning for the firm and management of the marketing function. There is a broad gray area where the two overlap. We make no attempt to force a particular discussion into one or the other. In some cases you may think that what we consider to be a managerial control decision is really a strategic decision, or vice versa. For example, in Chapter 15 on logistics management, we analyze at some length the economics of good customer service at low cost. In that analysis we look at the cost of serving customers in one day after receiving the order compared with the cost of two-day service. Yet, in the present chapter we treat the same concept as a strategic factor.

It seems appropriate to discuss a strategic factor in a managerial control chapter because of the overall direction of that chapter. To pull part of a discussion out of its context and force it into another chapter would weaken both. Furthermore, we would be in effect attributing to real-life situations a clear-cut dichotomy between strategic planning and managerial control, which just does not exist.

Another of the gray areas is related to the discovery of opportunities and problems. These chapters are primarily directed toward problem solving and decision making, but this is the point at which alternatives to present techniques and concepts can be discovered. The attempt to work out solutions to a problem is in itself an opportunity to discover its roots and find some way to "wire around" them.

Prior arrangements for integration

Second, implementation plans and specific actions are derived from objectives, strategic plans, and corporate policies. Accordingly, we take notice of the act of integrating actions with other departments affected. Sometimes that notice takes the form of an implied assumption that the production department will react the way we want it to because it is operating within the same set of guidelines as we are. We are safe in assuming this because integration policies and programs were worked out prior to the implementation stage; conflicts were resolved. At other times we specifically identify the possible adverse actions or reactions of these other departments, partly because the context of the discussion makes it desirable and partly in order to pursue and emphasize the importance of the departments functioning as a system.

Concepts of decision points

A third aspect of our generalized approach has to do with our explanation and description of concepts. We look upon these concepts as being a part of the environment in which decisions are made. Our objective throughout the book is to deal with concepts more than with details. In these chapters we try to explain concepts underlying managerial decisions in sufficient detail so that their use and application by managers can be understood; and so that the environment in which the decision is made can be understood. Sometimes this poses a problem of effort analysis. Will our efforts to provide a complete explanation of why something is as it is, and your effort in understanding it, produce results commensurate with our joint efforts?

The concepts we select for discussion are those underlying the major managerial decisions the marketing manager and his staff have to make. Our discussion is limited to providing sufficient data to enable you (1) to understand the concept, (2) to understand the reasons for a decision, and (3) to understand the implications of the decision.

Decision orientation

This leads us to the fourth feature of our generalized approach to Chapters 11, 13, 15, 17, and 19. They are decision oriented. This approach involves several steps and in general raises several questions to which we direct our discussion.

1. What types of decisions have to be made?
2. What factors should be considered in making the decisions?
3. What approaches to the decisions are possible?
4. What are the implications of the decisions?

In summary, these chapters are directed to the work of the marketing manager at Level 2 where he is concerned with efficiency in management of the marketing function. Also, in these chapters we focus our attention on the marketing function where in the strategic chapters we emphasize the firm. Also, our concern is with the processes of problem solving and decision making rather than with the process of discovery of opportunities and problems.

How effective are the plans going to be in attaining objectives? How efficient has the marketing manager been? The next step in the planning process is the design of a program for measuring the results against the plans.

CONTROLLING THE PLANNING EFFORT

Planning for and designing a system of programs to control the planning effort is the final step in the planning process. Of course, the constant surveillance and evaluation of the plans with the intention of modifying them when desirable is a part of the management function in general and of the management of planning in particular. Some show the review and evaluation as the first step in the planning process.

After the plans for the marketing function have been completed they should be reviewed by the Level 1 group for internal consistency and for consistency with the corporate plan. Also, that group may revise the corporate plan again in light of the marketing program. In addition, it should review its policies designed to integrate the several functional areas. When conformity among plans of the firm and those of the functional area is confirmed, the control system may be established.

These controls are often in the form of budgets for the departments. However, to rely only upon budgets as the control system is to live in a fool's paradise. Also, reliance upon the fact that planned-for growth rates are being attained is building an escalator to the fool's paradise. The return on investment may have exceeded the planned-for rate because of some unforeseen factor affecting one product while other products fell far short of expectations. The overall view can be misleading.

Information systems designed to provide the needed information on each of the relevant decision areas are important. While these subjects are treated in Chapter 5, in Chapter 20 we discuss some concepts related to control of the marketing effort. For example, we discuss such things as the marketing audit and sales audit as control systems. Further we discuss the importance of control of information on such key factors as profitability of product, customer, territory, and salesperson. The orientation of the chapter is more toward concepts of control than toward the establishment of the control system.

CONCLUSION

Marketing is an exciting subject to study and an exciting segment of business to practice. It should be even more exciting in the future as more companies become marketing oriented, because then more people in the firm will be involved in *thinking* marketing. A part of the excitement comes from using the concepts of marketing to satisfy wants and needs of the public. A part comes from using concepts and tools of business to satisfy these wants and needs efficiently. And a part comes from working with other disciplines to satisfy the wants and needs of the firm in an effective manner.

Index

Index

A

Ackoff, Russell L., 59, 63, 65, 68, 94 n
A. C. Nielson Company, 401, 405
Adaptivizing, 66–70
Adler, Lee, 252
Administered prices, 425
Advertising, 101, 366, 369–70, 394–406
  costs, 404
  flighting, 380, 404
  measurement of effectiveness, 404–6
  media decisions, 399–404
  message, 397–99
  objectives, 395–97
  pretesting, 405
  producer satisfaction, 118–19
  product life cycle, 219, 220
  retail, 101–2
Agriculture, 412–13
Agriculture, U.S. Department of, 96
Alcoa, 102
Alderson, Wroe, 269, 275–77, 287
Alexander, Ralph S., 25 n, 366
Alexander, Tom, 109 n
American Association of Collegiate Schools
  of Business, 90
American Marketing Association, 229
Analytical premises, 57
Anderson, R. Clifton, 254, 268, 277
Anthony, Robert N., 182, 183 n, 186–88
Antidissatisfaction inoculation, 115, 180
Antimerger Act of 1950, 156
Anti-Trust Division of the Department of
  Justice, 153
Antitrust legislation, 153–54
Arthur D. Little Company, 109
Aspinwall, Leo V., 276
Association of Consulting Management
  Engineers, 50
AT&T, 157

B

Barrett, Richard S., 390 n
Basing-point pricing systems, 456–57

Basing-point pricing systems—*Cont.*
  freight absorption, 457–58
  freight equalization, 458
  multiple, 457–58
  Pittsburgh-plus case, 457
  single, 456–57
Beckhard, Richard, 18 n
Behavior elasticity, 410–11
Belasco, James A., 385
Below-cost sales; *see* Sales below cost
Bennett, Sidney, 445
Berg, Thomas L., 238 n, 244 n
Blackwell, Roger D., 163 n, 167 n, 170 n,
  395 n
Boulding, Kenneth, 167 n
Brand loyalty, 114, 173
  image, selection of, 448
  switching, 113–14
Brand manager; *see* Product manager
Break-even analysis, 430–33
Bridges, S. Powell, 270 n
Brion, John M., 37
Broker, 287
Bross, Irwin D. J., 85 n
Brown, Stanley H., 460 n
Brown Shoe Company, 270 n
Bruce-Biggs, B., 131
Bucklin, Louis, 277, 287
Budget, 477
Burck, Gilbert, 140 n
Bureau of Corporations, 153
Burnham, Donald C., 185 n
Business firm, 17–33, 493
  customer satisfaction, 160, 173–76
  marketing function, 4, 5, 36–37
  marketing-oriented; *see* Marketing-
    oriented company
  nature of, 34–36
  organization, 80–82
  social responsibility, 146–47, 149
Business Week, 12, 54, 222
Buskirk, Richard H., 388 n

C

Carborundum Company, 73
Carriers
  air freight, 316
  common, 326
  contract, 326
  exempt, 326
  managerial decisions, 31–34
  private or for-hire, 326
  rate setting, 325, 334–36
  relations with, 315–16
  types of, 325–27
  water, 314
Catalogue sales, 284
Celler-Kefauver Amendment to Clayton
    Act, 156
Census, Bureau of the, 96
Chain stores, 154–55
Channels of distribution, 24–28, 39, 102,
    251–73, 505–6
  buyer-manufacturer relationship, 103–4
  consumer satisfaction, 117
  customer system, 24
  decisions, 290–93
  environmental conditions, 251–53
  government regulations, 270
  hierarchy of marketing policies, 272
  information, 103–4, 106
  integration, 269–70
  length and width of, 270
  management of, 271–73, 274–94
  multiple, 292–93
  producer satisfaction, 119
  relationship with individual firms, 149
  selection of components, 291–92
  shortage economy, 13
  size of middleman, 288–89
  strategy of design, 268–71
  supplier, 24
  transportation system, 24
Chase Manhattan Bank, 12
Chief executive, 47, 498–99
Chrysler Company, 247
Churchill, Gilbert A., Jr., 460 n
Clayton Act, 153, 155, 461–62
  Celler-Kefauver Amendment, 156
Clowes, Kenneth W., 387 n
Cohen, Dorothy, 394 n
Colley, Russell H., 378 n
Collusion, 458
Commerce, U.S. Department of, new
    products booklet, 238
Commerce clause of U.S. Constitution,
    151
Commitment planning, 66–67, 69
Communications, 359, 360–65
  adapted, 362

Communications—*Cont.*
  message, 377–80
  strategy, 363–65
  theoretical, 360–62
    feedback, 362
    premessage scrutiny, 362
Community-firm relationship, 146
Competition, 28, 147–48, 154, 156
  price, 426, 465
  pure, 412–13
Comprehensive planning, 183
Computers, 107–9
Congress, U.S., 150–52, 154
Congruence, 167–71
Constantin, James A., 131 n, 296 n, 338 n
Consumer, 142–46
  information, 101–2
  manufacturer, 105
  marketing orientation to, 6–7
  price influence, 423–25
  prospective, 145–46
  satisfaction; *see* Consumer satisfaction
  value, 144–45
Consumer behavior, 159–81, 502
  habitual, 163
  problem-solving; *see* Problem-solving
      behavior
  rational, 164–65
  strategic aspects of, 176–80
  subset of human behavior, 161–62
Consumer goods, 226–27
  promotion, 370
Consumer satisfaction, 113–20, 122, 144,
    255
  anticipated, 179
  business firm planning for, 165–67,
      173–80
  channel management, 278–82
  form-time-place utility, 256
  hierarchy, 48
  problem-solving, 167–80
  realized, 180
Contingency planning, 66–69
Contribution margin concept, 223
Control, 469–90, 511
  cost-price-volume relationship, 477–83
  information, 471–77
  marketing operations, 471–90
  purpose, 470
  systems, 470–71
Convenience goods, 226–27
Cook, Frederic, 74 n, 135
Cost management, 43, 298–301, 308–9,
    311–12, 320
Cost-plus pricing, 438–46
  competition, 446
Cost-price-volume relationship, 477–83

Cost reduction, 43, 298, 308–09, 311–12, 320

Costs
  control over operations, 477–83
  fixed, 421
  marginal, 422
  prices, 421
  variable, 421
Cox, Donald F., 107 n
Crapper, Thomas, 71
Creditors, 148–49
  satisfaction, 48
Crisis creation and prevention, 499–500
Cross, James S., 25 n
Crossen, John, 276–77
Cunningham, William H., 392 n
Curtailment of abuses, 150–53
Customer service
  cost-service balance, 308–14, 322–24, 351–57
  distribution points, 352–53
  satisfaction; *see* Consumer satisfaction

D

Dale, E. E., 130–31
Davidson, William R., 252 n
Davis, Kenneth R., 388 n, 390 n, 393 n
Dean, Joel, 433
Demand-pull, 132
Deming, Robert H., 472 n
Demography, 129–30
Department stores, 283–84
Depot theory of distribution, 276
Diebold, John, 108 n
Discount, 452–54
Discount houses, 285
Discovery process, 121, 136, 504–5
  analysis, 124
Disposal agency, 255
Distribution
  centers; *see* Distribution centers
  channels of; *see* Channels of distribution
  costs, 308–12, 348–50
  points, 341–45, 348, 350–51
  pool, 318
Distribution centers, 262–65, 337; *see also* Distribution points; Warehousing
  location, 343
Distribution points, 341–45; *see also* Distribution centers
Dommermuth, William P., 254, 268, 277
Doody, Alton F., 385 n
Door-to-door sales, 283
Downing, George D., 389
Drucker, Peter, 26, 37 n, 55, 112 n, 132, 192–93
Duesenberry, James S., 161 n

Dun's, 58 n, 61
Du Pont Company, 205

E

Eagle, James F., 378 n
Ecology, 128–29
Economic environment, 139–40
Educated incapacity, 131
Educational seminar, 368
Effective demand, 408–9
Effective marketing management, 5, 9–10, 492–93, 509
  channels of distribution, 288
  information, 79–80
  manager, 19
Efficiency of marketing management, 4, 10–11, 492–93, 509
  channels of distribution, 288
  information, 79–80
  manager, 19
Elasticity of demand, 409–11, 424
Emerson, Alfred, 167 n
Employee-firm relationship, 146–47
  satisfactions, 47
Engel, James F., 163 n, 167 n, 170 n
English, Wilke D., 392 n
Environment, 502
  analysis of, 20
  channels of distribution, 251–53
  conditions affecting marketing management, 21–23
  external; *see* External environment
  first-order, 21–22, 297–98, 325
  fourth-order, 23, 298–99
  internal; *see* Internal environment
  logistics, 296–99
  management adaptation to, 41–43
  managerial decision problems, 30–31
  redesigning, 251–54
  second-order, 22–23, 298
  third-order, 23, 298–99
Ethan Allen Furniture Company, 396–97
Everett, Martin, 367 n
Ewing, David, 53–54, 56, 59, 62–63, 71, 75
Experimental pricing, 446
External environment, 21–28, 60, 73, 137–42, 253
  channels of distribution, 251–53
  economic, 139–40
  logistics, 297–98
  management adaptation to, 41–42
  marketing, 137–58
  outside-in approach to planning, 70–71
  political-governmental, 140–41, 150–56
  price strategy, 417, 423–28
  social, 138–39, 146–47, 149

F

Facilitating agencies, 26, 259–61, 315
Fair-practices codes, 154
Fair trade laws, 154, 462–64
Farrell, Jack W., 318 n
Federal Trade Commission, 153–55
  basing-point system, 456
  Robinson-Patman Act, 462
  uniform delivered prices, 454
Federal Trade Commission Act, 153
  Wheeler-Lea Amendment, 155
Feedback, 362
Festinger, Leon, 169 n
Flexible markup price, 446
Flighting, 380
F.O.B. origin, 454–55
  freight equalization, 458
Ford, Henry, 8, 25
Ford, Neil M., 460 n
Ford Motor Company, 105
Fortune, 79, 135
Franchise arrangements, 285
Freeman, Gaylord A., Jr., 149
Freight forwarder, 326
Frey, Albert, 366 n, 398 n, 405 n
Friedman, Walter F., 273 n, 319
Full-service retail operations, 284

G

Gemmill, Gary R., 134
General Electric Company, 132
  technology transfer, 237
General Foods Company, 276–77
General Motors Company, 25–26
Geographic market, 125
Germane, Gayton E., 206 n, 209 n, 235 n
Glaskowsky, Nicholas A., Jr., 308 n
Good, Robert E., 107 n
Goodman, Sam, 213, 217 n, 221 n, 489–90
Government-business relations, 150–56
  channels of distribution, 270
  curtailment of abuses, 150–53
  preventing further concentration of
    economic power, 151
  promotional action, 150
  protection from abusive marketing
    practices, 150–51
  regulatory actions, 150, 270
Granger, Charles H., 45
Green, Paul E., 269 n
Guidelines, 156

H

Habitual behavior, 163, 173
Hall, Calvin S., 169 n

Halterman, Jean C., 366 n, 398 n, 405 n
Hamburger, M. J., 341 n
Hanan, Mark, 135
Haring Albert, 367n
Harris, Marvin, 151
Heider, Fritz, 168 n
Heinz Company, 233
Henderson, James, 164 n
Hertz, David B., 87 n, 133
Heskett, J. L., 308
Heublein Company, 233
High-impact premises, 57
Hill, Richard M., 25 n, 134
Hill, W. Clayton, 345–46, 348 n
Hillway, Tyrus, 91
Hinkle, Charles L., 461 n
Hise, Richard T., 79
Hlavacek, James D., 234 n
Holden, Paul E., 206 n, 209 n, 235 n
Hollander, E. P., 168 n
Holloman, Herbert, 197 n
Honomickl, Jack J., 241 n
Horizontal diversification, 225
Howard, J. A., 170 n
Hudson's Bay Company, 103
Human behavior, 161–62
Hunt, R. G., 168 n

I

Implied premises, 57
Income elasticity, 410
Independent companies, 285, 294
Industrial goods, 227–28
  equipment, 227
  fabricating materials, 228
Industrial Research Institute, 109
Information, 29–30, 86–110, 501–2
  accuracy, 83–84
  advertising, 102
  characteristics of, 83–85, 88
  compatibility, 84
  control of marketing operations, 471–77
  data, 82–83, 85–86
  definition, 82
  distribution channels, 103–4
  flows, 15, 98–107
  managing, 81–86
  market research, 86
  marketing strategy, 81
  organization of company, 80–81
  personal selling, 102
  planning, 80–81
  priorities, 359
  promotion, 357
  quality, 84
  relevance, 83–84
  risk, 87

Information—*Cont.*
  scientific methods of acquisition, 87–89
  simplicity, 83, 85
  volume, 83–84
Information systems, 107–9, 512
  marketing control, 472
Inland water carriers, 314
Innovations, 112, 123, 132–36
  managerial, 40
  product, 40
Innovative imitation, 210, 212–13, 219
Innovative planning, 66
Inside-out approach to planning, 63, 72–74, 500
  internal environment analysis, 72
Integration, 4, 6–7, 269–70
  marketing-oriented form, 494–98
  vertical, 105, 269
Internal environment, 28–30, 71–72
  inside-out approach to planning, 72
  logistics, 298, 306
  managerial adaptation to, 42–43
  price strategy, 417, 419–23
Interstate Commerce Act, 152
Interstate Commerce Commission, 153
  rate-setting, 325
Inventory, 258
  distribution points, 346
Inverted pricing, 447
Ivie, Robert M., 308 n

J

Jawboning, 156
Jerman, Roger E., 268 n
Johnson and Johnson Company, 120–21
Judelson, Norman, 55 n

K

Kahn, George H., 385 n
Kahn, Herman, 126–27, 131, 185 n
Kaiser, Henry, 73
Katona, George, 163 n
Keggerreis, Robert J., 109 n
Kinney, G. R., Inc., 270 n
Kintner, Earl W., 456
Kodak Company, 233
Kollat, David T., 163 n, 167 n, 170 n, 395 n
Kotler, Philip, 204, 259 n, 260 n, 487 n
Kotler, Phillip, 145 n, 381 n
Kuehn, A. A., 341 n
Kwitny, Jonathan, 375 n

L

Labor, U.S. Department of, 96
Laissez-faire doctrine, 152

LaLonde, B. J., 265, 266 n
Lambert, Zarrel V., 424 n
Larson, Gustav E., 238 n
Lateral diversification, 225
Lavidge, Robert J., 372
Lazer, William, 112, 269 n
L'Eggs, 41
Levinson, Harry, 146 n
Levitt, Theodore, 130–31, 210, 212
Levy, Sidney J., 145 n, 259 n
Lewis, Edwin H., 275 n
Location of markets, 125
Logistics, 506–7
  costs-service balance, 308–14, 322–24
  management, 296, 322–58
  problems, 302
    conceptual, 303, 306–16
    natural, 303–6
    organizational, 303, 317–19
  strategies and policies, 295–321
  transportation, 325–30
Low impact premises, 57
Lucas, Henry C., Jr., 387 n
Luick, John F., 367 n

M

McCammon, Bert, 268, 285
McCarthy, E. Jerome, 286 n
McConkey, Dale D., 50
McGuire Act, 464
Macklanburg-Duncan Company, 340–41
McVey, Philip, 259, 267
Maffei, Richard B., 388 n
Mahany, E. S., 367 n
Make or buy strategy, 269, 290
Management
  channels of distribution, 288
  definition, 37–39, 492–93
  environment, 39–43, 156–58
  function, 39–40
  hierarchy of activities, 37–39, 44–49
  information, 81–86
  marketing function, 9–10
  planning, 54–61
  research, 133–36
  systems approach, 44–45
Management of change, 50, 54, 60, 70, 72
  marketing opportunities, 112
Management control, 182–83, 186–88
"Management Myopia," 131
Manager
  line and staff, 58–60
  planning, 57–59
Managerial hierarchy, 37–39, 44–49
  objectives and goals, 46–47
  purpose or mission, 45–46
  satisfactions, 47

Managerial innovation, 40–41
Mann, Roland, 307
Manufacturer, 104–6
  information flow, 105–6
  satisfaction, 254, 279–82
Manufacturers' agent, 287
Manufacturers Hanover Corporation, 18
Market analysis, 31–33
Market segmentation
  opportunity, 125–28
  strategy, 373
Market test, 430
Marketing, 3
  concept, 6–14
  corporate objectives, 6–7
  definition, 5–6
  integrated activities in firm, 417
  mix; see Marketing mix
  opportunities; see Marketing oppor-
      tunities
  promotion, 360
  shortage economy, 11–14
Marketing audit, 487–88
Marketing controller, 489–90
Marketing flow concept, 275–76
Marketing manager, 9, 15, 87
  channels of distribution, 255
  planning and policy making, 10
  product planning, 9
  responsibilities, 17–21
  shortage economy, 12
Marketing mix, 4, 12, 40– 41, 119, 504
  channels of distribution, 288–89
  multistage pricing, 448
  product life cycles, 217–221, 249
  product manager decisions, 250
  promotion, 179
  shortage economy, 13
"Marketing Myopia," 131
Marketing opportunities, 112–13, 123–32
  analysis of demand, 123
  demand-pull, 132
  demography, 129–30
  discovery process, 121
  ecology, 128–29
  geographic aspects, 125
  human resistance to, 131
  segmentation, 125
  technology-push, 132
Marketing-oriented company, 253
  channels of distribution, 253, 271
  characteristics, 255
  integration, 494–98
  planning, 52–74
  prices, 408
Marketing program, 12
Marketing research, 86, 205–6, 209
  data collection, 95–98

Marketing research—*Cont.*
  manager, 87, 88
  problem definition, 95
  procedure, 95–98
  scientific method, 87–88
Marlboro cigarettes, 120
Marquis, Donald G., 123
Marshall, Alfred, 411 n
Marvin, Phillip, 231 n, 232, 246
Maslow, Abraham H., 47
Mass market, 130
Matrix management, 134–35
Media, 399–404
  advertising decisions, 399–403
  cost comparisons, 404
  magazines, 401
  newspapers, 401
  outdoor advertising, 402
  radio, 402
  scheduling, 403–4
  selection, 402–3
  television, 401–2
  volume of advertising, 400
Mee, John F., 500
Mesthene, Emmanuel, 197 n
Mickwitz, G., 217 n
Middleman, 255, 287
  channel decisions, 290
  size and efficiency, 288–89
Miller, Ernest C., 55 n
Miller-Tydings Act, 154, 463
Mintzberg, Henry, 192
Mission of organization, 45, 497
  statement of, 197–99
Mobile homes, 68, 122
Model T Ford, 144
Modular homes, 68
Monopoly, 413–15
Morris, Malcolm, 367 n
Motel industry, 122
Multistage pricing, 447–51
Mund, Vernon A., 152 n, 457 n, 462 n,
    463
Myers, Robert H., 207
Myers, Summer, 123

N

National Industrial Recovery Act, 154
National Industrial Recovery Administra-
    tion (NRA), 154
National Planning Association, 54
National Science Foundation, 112–13
Neuschel, Robert P., 307 n, 317 n
New product, 205–7, 209–10
  Commerce Department booklet, 338
  company resources, 239
  customer research, 236

New product—*Cont.*
  evaluation, 242–43, 245
  failures, 245
  filtering ideas, 238–45
  impracticality, 248
  incompatibility with product line, 248
  market demand, 236
  objectives of company, 239
  planning flow chart, 246
  production need, 237
  pure research, 237
  technical feasibility, 239–40, 245
  technology transfer, 237
  test marketing, 240–41
  timing of introduction, 247–48
Nickels, William G., 385 n
Nicosia, F., 170 n
Noise, 361–62

O

Objectives, corporate, 6–7, 497–98
  development of, 49, 192
  external and internal environment, 193
  flexibility, 194
  hierarchy of, 15, 46–49
  improved earnings, 198
  innovation, 195
  interaction, 193
  interrelatedness, 194–95
  market standing, 196
  public responsibility, 196–97
  reasonableness, 194
  specificity, 194
  statement of mission, 197–99
  types of, 195
Oligopoly, 415–17
O'Neil, Brian F., 388 n
Operational control, 182–83, 188–89
Opportunity in marketing; *see* Marketing
    opportunities
Optimizing, 64–66
Order status report, 484–85
Organizational hierarchy, 15
Outside-in approach to planning, 63,
    70–73, 500
  analysis of external environment, 70–71
  forecast, 71–72
Owners
  relationship with managers, 148
  satisfaction, 48
Oxenfeldt, Alfred R., 418 n, 438, 447,
    450, 487–88
Ozanne, Urban B., 460 n

P

Patronage satisfaction, 278–79
Payne, Bruce, 242 n, 243, 246

Peach, W. N., 131 n
Pederson, Carlton A., 206 n, 209 n, 235 n
Penetration pricing, 428–29
People market, 126
Pepsi Co., 233
Personal selling, 365–67, 383–94
  organization, 385–94
  sales force, 386–94
  territories, 388
Peterson, Elmore, 497
Phantom freight, 457
Phelps, Ernest D., 109 n, 113 n
Phillips Petroleum Company, 102
Pillsbury Company, 233
Pittsburgh-plus case, 457
Planning, 52, 182–99, 498–504
  approaches to, 70–74
  for change, 53
  commitment, 66–67, 69
  contingency, 66–69
  hierarchy, 15, 189–91, 498–99
  innovation, 53
  long range, 54, 60, 183
  management, 54–57
  managers, 57–59
  philosophy of, 63–70
  premises, 55–57
  process, 61–62, 74–75
  product, 207–10
  program, 74–75
  strategy, 182–88
  systems approach, 15
Planning department, 59–61
Planning premises, 55–57, 502–3
Plowman, E. G., 497
Political-governmental environment,
    140–41
Pollution, 68
Pool distribution, 318–19
Positioning of product, 374–75
Postponement, 277
Premessage scrutiny, 362
Price, 407–35, 437–66, 508
  adjustments, 452–61
  company size and financial resources,
    420
  consumer satisfaction, 117–18
  costs, 421–23
  distribution channels, 426–27
  economic conditions, 426
  elasticity of demand, 122, 409–10
  ethics, 427
  firm-consumer interaction, 145
  industry position, 420, 425
  methods of determination; *see* Price
    determination methods
  objectives, 417–28
  penetration, 428–29

Price—*Cont.*
  producer satisfaction, 119
  product life cycle, 217, 219–20
  public policy, 427
  semivariable, 438
  shortage economy, 13
  single, 437–38
  skimming, 219, 428
  theoretical determination of, 409
  variable, 438
Price determination methods, 429–33
  break-even analysis, 430–33
  cost-oriented, 429–30
  market test approach, 430
  transfer, 433
Price discrimination, 454, 456
Price leadership, 417, 425, 451
Pricing decisions, management of, 437–66
  adjustments, 452–61
  cost-plus method, 438–46
  geographical considerations, 454–58
  legal issues, 461–65
  multistage, 447–51
  price maintenance method, 446
  research method, 446
Problem-solving behavior, 162–63, 170, 173–76
  business firm influence, 175–76
  evaluation, 170–72
Procedural premises, 57
Producer satisfaction, 115–22, 254
Product, 4, 204–28, 505
  consumer satisfaction, 117
  distribution; *see* Channels of distribution
  elimination, 209, 222–24
  failure, 209
  introduction, 214–17
  kinds of, 225–28
  life cycle, 207, 210–21, 249
  management, 229–50
  new product development; *see* New product
  organization, 208–9
  planning, 8–9, 207–10
  policy, 209–10
  positioning, 374–75
  price, 408, 419–420
  producer satisfaction, 118
  value, 424–25
Product diversification, 224–25
Product innovation, 40
Product line, 222, 230
  pricing, 418
Product manager, 206, 230–50
  authority, 233–34
  duties and responsibilities, 233–34
  evaluation of, 235–36

Product manager—*Cont.*
  functions of, 236–50
  new products, 232–33, 236–46
  product mix, 249–50
Product mix, 222, 230, 249–50; *see also,* Marketing mix
Product satisfaction, 278
Profit
  managerial satisfaction, 35
  product elimination, 223
  product life cycle, 213–14
Profit maximization concept, 308
Profitability report, 485–87
Project management concept, 206
Promotion, 359–406, 507–8
  advertising, 366, 369–70
  budgeting, 381–82
  communication process, 360–65
  consumer satisfaction, 117
  creation of selective dissatisfaction, 179
  magnitude of effort, 380–82
  objectives, 377–79
  personal selling, 365, 367
  producer satisfaction, 117–19
  public relations, 367–68
  push vs. pull strategy, 371–72
  sales force, 368–69
  shortage economy, 13
  strategic planning, 373–82
Protection from abusive marketing practices, 153–56
Proximity to market, 312–14, 338
Pruden, Henry O., 392 n
Public satisfactions from corporations, 48
Publicity, 368
Pure Food and Drug Act, 153

Q–R

Quant, Richard, 164 n
Rathwell, John M., 255
Rational behavior, 164
Raytheon Company, 192
Recycling, 32, 210
Resale price maintenance laws, 154, 462–64
Research, 86–98
  basic and applied, 91–92
  definition, 89
  management commitment, 133–36
  marketing, 86
  objectives, 92
  theory, 93–94
Research and development (R & D), 205–6, 209; *see also* Market Research
Resource conversion system, 30
Resource management system, 29
Responsiveness planning, 66, 69

Retailing
  channel decisions, 291
  cooperatives, 285
  independents, 285, 294
  location, 286
  methods of operation, 284–86
  satisfaction, 279–82
  sorting concept, 282
  types of operations, 284–86
Richman, Barry, 244–45
Ries, Al, 374n
Risk, 87
Robeson, James F., 395n
Robinson–Patman Act, 155, 461–62, 465
Rogers, Everett, M., 372
Roosevelt, Theodore, 153
Rosenberg, Larry J., 257
Ryan, William G., 500

S

Safeway Stores, 105
St. Thomas, Charles, 496
Sales agent, 287
Sales below cost, 464–65
  California law, 464–65
  competition, 465
  loss leaders, 465
  Oklahoma law, 465
  Robinson-Patman Act, 465
  Unfair Trade Practices Acts, 465
  U.S. Supreme Court, 465
Sales force, 386–94
  compensation, 391–92
  development of, 388–91
  evaluation, 393–94
  motivation, 391–94
  psychological testing, 389–91
  recruiting, 389
  selection, 389–90
  size, 386–88
  territories, 388
  training, 390–91
Sales and profitability report, 485–87
Sales promotion, 366–67
Sales quotas, 393–94
Sampling, 90
Sanders, Donald H., 83n
Satisfaction, 113–22
  anticipated, 115
  antidissatisfaction inoculation, 115
  business firm, 34, 36, 49–50
  consumer, 113–20, 122
  hierarchy of, 47–48
  marketing-oriented firm, 496
  patronage, 278
  producer, 115–22
  product, 278

Satisfaction—*Cont.*
  realized, 115
Satisficing, 63–64, 70
Schlaifer, Robert, 87 n
Schoderbak, Peter P., 83 n
Schuchman, Abraham, 238 n, 244 n, 385 n
Sears Roebuck Company, 105
  customer satisfaction, 115
Segmentation of markets; *see* Market
    segmentation
Selective dissatisfaction, creation of, 113–
    14, 175, 177, 179
Semlow, Walter J., 386–87
Service; *see* Product
Sevin, Charles H., 69
Sherman Anti-Trust Act, 152–53, 463
Sheth, J., 170 n
Shippers' associations, 326
Shopping centers, 286
Shopping goods, 227
Shortage economy, 11–14
  marketing tactics, 12–14
Simon, Herbert A., 63
Single-line stores, 283
Skimming pricing, 219, 428
Smith, Adam, 152
Snyder, Richard E., 309
Social environment, 138–39
Social responsibility of business, 149
Sorenson, Ralph, 130
Sorting concept, 276
  postponement, 277
  retailer, 282
  wholesaler, 287
Specialty goods, 227
  shops, 283
Springer, Jack, 375n
Standard Contract Terms and Conditions
    For Merchandise Warehousemen, 257
Stanton, William J., 388n
Starch, Daniel, 406
Starch Advertisement Readership Service,
    405–6
Staudt, Thomas A., 471
Steiner, Gary A., 372
Steiner, George, 37n, 46, 57, 60, 62n, 72,
    127, 193
Stern, Louis W., 257
Stern, Mark E., 46n
Strategic planning, 182–90
  analysis, 189
Sugar Trust case, 152
Supermarkets, 284
Suppliers, 106
  information, 106
  marketing program, 148
Surveys, 96–97
  mail, 97

Surveys—*Cont.*
 personal interview, 97
 telephone, 97
Systems approach to management, 44–45

T

Talley, Walter J., Jr., 387
Target market, 3
 advertising, 399
 multistage pricing, 447
 promotion, 376–79
 shortage economy, 13
Tarpey, Lawrence X., 155 n
Taylor, Donald A., 471
Technology-push, 132
Technology transfer, 237
Thompson, Stewart, 62
Thorelli, Hans, 372
Total logistics concept, 307
Trade press, 104
Trading stamps, 460
Traffic management concept, 307
Transaction, 6
Transfer pricing, 433
Transportation, 254, 257, 315–16
 concept, 307
 cost reduction, 307
 environment, 325–30
 rate structure, 327–30
 services, 330
 types of carriers, 325–27
Transportation, Department of, 96
Transportation Act of 1920, 154
Transvection concept, 275–76
Trickett, Joseph M., 497
Trout, Jack, 374
Trust-busting, 153

U

Udell, Jan G., 407n
Uncertainty in business decisions, 87
Unfair Trade Practices Acts, 154–55
 California law, 464–65
 Oklahoma law, 465
Uniform delivered prices, 454–55
Union Carbide Company, 297–98, 300–301
Unit train, 316
U.S. Steel Company, 102, 106
Utility
 consumer satisfaction, 256, 261–62, 279–81
 form, time, and place, 144n

V

Vail, Theodore, 45, 157
Value of product or service, 144–45
Vancil, Richard F., 59
Variety stores, 284
Vending machines, 284
Venture management, 112–13, 134–36, 206
Vertical diversification, 225
Vertical integration, 105, 269
Vertical marketing systems, 256, 259–60
Voluntary food chain, 285

W–Z

Wales, Hugh G., 378
Walker, Donald E., 83n
Want identification, 113
Ward's Automotive Reports, 106
Warehousing, 257, 265–67; *see also* Distribution centers
 channels of distribution, 315
 compared to distribution center, 262, 265
 distribution points, 347–48
 environment, 336–40
 functions of, 338
 managerial decisions, 339–58
 pricing, 339
 services, 339
  direct, 340
  indirect, 341–45
 storage, 337
 types of, 337
Warshaw, Martin R., 378
Wasson, Chester, 249n
Water carrier, 314
Webster, Frederick E., Jr., 372, 374n, 376, 377n, 388n, 390n, 393n, 402n, 406n
Weinberg, Charles B., 387n
Wheeler-Lea Amendment to Federal Trade Commission Act, 155
Wholesaler, 258
 satisfaction, 279–82
 system, 286–88
Whybark, D. Clay, 388n
Wilemon, David L., 134
Wilkinson, J. B., 445
Ziegler, William Lee, 367n
Zimmerman, Erich W., 131
Zone pricing, 455
 U. S. Postal Service, 455